Latin American Politics and Development

Latin American Politics and Development

SEVENTH EDITION

Edited by

Howard J. Wiarda, *University of Georgia*
Harvey F. Kline, *University of Alabama*

WESTVIEW
PRESS

A Member of the Perseus Books Group

Designed by Trish Wilkinson
Set in 10.5-point Adobe Caslon.

Library of Congress Cataloging-in-Publication Data

Latin American politics and development / edited by Howard J. Wiarda, Harvey F.
   Kline.—7th ed.
      p.   cm.
   Includes bibliographical references and index.
   ISBN 978-0-8133-4459-1 (alk. paper)
1. Latin America—Politics and government. I. Wiarda, Howard J., 1939– II. Kline,
Harvey F.
                                                                    F1410.L39 2011

980—dc22
2010003136

10 9 8 7 6 5 4 3 2 1

Contents

Tables and Maps

Acronyms

AID	Agency for International Development
GATT	General Agreement on Tariffs and Trade
GDP	Gross Domestic Product
GNP	Gross National Product
ISI	import-substitution industrialization
IADB	Inter-American Development Bank
IAF	Inter-American Foundation
IMF	International Monetary Fund
ALASI	Latin American Integration Association
NAFTA	North American Free Trade Agreement
NGOs	nongovernmental organizations
OAS	Organization of American States

Preface to the Seventh Edition

The first edition of this book was published in 1979, the second in 1985, the third in 1990, the fourth in 1996, the fifth in 2000, the sixth in 2007, and now the seventh in 2010. The issues we have sought to examine in all seven editions include why Latin America is different from the United States, why it lagged behind economically and politically, how societies cast historically in a medieval and semifeudal mode have gone about achieving modernization and development, what paths of national development the distinct countries of the area have followed (evolutionary or revolutionary; authoritarian, Marxist, or democratic; capitalist, socialist, or statist), and what developments and difficulties of democracy have been encountered in the area. These are large, meaty issues; their importance goes beyond the geographic confines of Latin America.

Each of the seven editions of the book has reflected the major dynamic changes occurring in Latin America itself. The decade of the 1970s was a period of authoritarianism and repression in much of the region with widespread human rights abuses, all of which resulted in interpretation about the area—corporatism, dependency theory, and bureaucratic-authoritarianism—that reflected scholars' pessimism about Latin America's future. Following this, the 1980s were a period of democratization throughout Latin America, with greater optimism about the area's political future (even though the economic prospects continued to be poor) and newer interpretations that stressed transitions to democracy.

In the early 1990s there was considerable agreement on goals for the region (labeled the "Washington consensus") between the United States and Latin America: democracy, economic liberalism, and free trade. By this point most of the authoritarian regimes of the area had given way, and with the collapse of the Soviet Union, Marxism-Leninism had become less attractive; democracy and liberalism therefore seemed the only viable option. But by the end of the 1990s and continuing into the twenty-first century, although democracy, economic reform, and freer trade were still high on the agenda, a number of cracks had appeared in the prevailing consensus. Democracy was still limited and not working well in quite a few countries: Much of Latin

America had achieved electoral democracy but not liberal or participatory democracy. Economic reform continued, but the neoliberal agenda had resulted in widespread unemployment and privation in many countries. Trade barriers continued to fall in Latin America, but in the United States protectionist political pressures prevented new trade initiatives.

While Latin America has gone through its political and economic ups and downs over this more than forty-year period, its society has been massively transformed. These are no longer the "sleepy," "backward," "underdeveloped" countries of cartoon and movie stereotypes. Since 1960, Latin America as a whole has gone from 70 percent rural to 70 percent urban and a 70 percent illiteracy rate to 70 percent literacy. The old two-class society is giving way, a new middle class is emerging, and poverty is slowly being reduced. These figures reflect the massive social changes underway throughout the area as well as the transformation from a peasant-agricultural economy to a more modern, industrial, and diversified one.

In the mid-1970s seventeen of the twenty countries were authoritarian, but today nineteen of the twenty (all except Cuba, and even there changes are likely soon) are democratic—incomplete democracies, but certainly better than the human rights–abusing regimes of earlier decades. Economically, quite a number of the countries are booming, with miraculous or East Asian–level growth rates, but others are still mired in underdevelopment. At the same time a host of new issues—rising crime and insecurity, social inequality, and globalization—have come to the fore. So, as always, Latin America reflects a mixture of successes and failures, of traditional and modern features, of mixed and often crazy-quilt regimes in an always-changing, dynamic context.

No longer a group of backward, underdeveloped countries, Latin America is one of the most exciting regions of the globe for the comparative study of economic, social, and political change. In previous decades the choice of developmental models seemed wide open, representing diverse routes to modernization, but by now the democratic–mixed economy route seems the only one conceivable, although with great variation still among the countries of the region. In most countries the state plays a major role in the economy, and the private sector is weaker than in the United States. Virtually every social, economic, and political issue, process, and policy present in the world can be found in Latin America. It thus remains an exciting, innovative, ever-changing, and endlessly fascinating living laboratory for study, travel, and research.

Not only is Latin America an interesting area to study, but it has also become increasingly important to the United States. After Canada, Mexico is now the United States' second largest trading partner in the world. Hispanics have become the largest minority in the United States, and are voting in increasing numbers. On a host of new, hot issues—including drugs, trade, immigration, tourism, energy, pollution, investment, the environment, democracy, and human rights—the United States and Latin America have become increasingly intertwined and interdependent. Yet conflict persists in U.S. relations with Cuba, Venezuela, and other countries. At the same time both Europe and Asia are also increasing their trade with and interest in Latin America and as a result, are often competing with the United States for influence.

This book offers in its introduction a broad, regionwide overview of the patterns and processes of Latin American history, politics, society, and development. It then proceeds to a detailed country-by-country treatment of all twenty Latin American countries. (The smaller, former British and Dutch colonies of the region are not included, and of the former French colonies, only Haiti is considered.) Major countries like Argentina, Brazil, Chile, Colombia, Cuba, Mexico, Peru, and Venezuela receive extended coverage, and the smaller countries receive complete but somewhat briefer treatment. Each country chapter is written by a leading specialist in the field. To facilitate comparisons between countries we have asked each of our authors as far as it is feasible to use a common outline and approach. We emphasize throughout both the unique features of each country as well as the common patterns and processes that exist. Instructors thus have maximum flexibility in the selection of which countries to study and which themes or developmental models to emphasize.

Latin American Politics and Development has throughout its previous editions emerged as one of the most durable yet innovative texts in the field, and we hope that this seventh edition will intrigue new students of Latin America as it has stimulated two generations of earlier ones. Many of these students have now gone on to careers in business, academia, private agencies, or foreign policy; it is always rewarding to meet, hear from, or run into these former as well as current students. We hope that some of our enthusiasm for the subject continues to rub off on them.

The editors wish to thank their wives and families, for whom this book has over the years become almost another addition to the household. Dottie Kline receives special recognition for her work to update Table 1.1. Thanks also to our contributors, both new and old; in each edition we have tried to bring in new faces, new ideas, and more women and minority contributors. Finally, we wish to thank acquisitions editor Karl Yambert of Westview Press for encouraging this new edition and shepherding it through the publication process.

Howard J. Wiarda
Harvey F. Kline

PART I

The Latin American Tradition and Process of Development

Howard J. Wiarda
Harvey F. Kline

1

The Context of
Latin American Politics

Profound social, economic, cultural, and political transformations are sweeping through Latin America, affecting all institutions and areas of life. Accelerated economic and social change, democratization, and globalization are having an impact on all countries, often incompletely and unevenly. Latin America, however, still has abundant poverty, malnutrition, disease, poor housing, and the worst distribution of income in the world; its economic and political institutions often fail to work well or as intended; and social and political reforms are still strongly needed. However, at least some of the countries—generally the larger, more stable, and richer ones—are making what appears to be a definitive breakthrough to democracy and development, and many of the small nations are modernizing as well.

We speak of "Latin America" as if it were a single, homogeneous region, but in fact the area is exceedingly diverse. Because of this diversity, we need to understand each country individually as well as the common patterns. While the Latin American countries share a common basis in law, language, history, culture, sociology, colonial experience, and overall political patterns that enables us to discuss the region in general terms, we also recognize that each country is different and becoming increasingly more so. Unity amid diversity is a theme that runs throughout this book, so in Part 1 we survey the general patterns before moving on to the individual countries in Part 2.

Throughout Latin America's history its leaders and people have debated their heritage and future, particularly between Western or non-Western; feudal, capitalist, or socialist; First World (developed nations) or Third World (developing ones); and evolutionary or revolutionary change. Conflict over these issues has often delayed development.

Now at last a consensus seems to be emerging, namely democracy in the political sphere, a modern mixed economy, and greater integration with the rest of the world. Authoritarianism seems to be on the decrease in Latin America, although when the economy declines and instability results, the authoritarian temptation is still often present. Marxism-Leninism is similarly in decline, even while social democracy and populism are still attractive options for many political leaders. More and more of Latin America is becoming middle class and centrist. The old extremes are no longer attractive, and the range of political and economic options has narrowed.

Driving these changes are democratization and globalization. Democracy is overwhelmingly the preferred form of government of Latin America, even though democracy does not always work well or quickly enough; it takes forms that are often different from that of the United States; and it is still threatened by upheaval, corruption, and vast social problems. Globalization affects Latin America in all areas of life, such as culture (movies and television), society (behavioral norms), politics (democracy), and, above all, economics. Latin America is now part of a global market economy. It has little choice but to open its markets to global trade and investment. With the Cold War over and the war on terrorism concentrated elsewhere, there is little foreign aid, and Latin America can no longer play the superpowers against each other. Instead it must have private investment and become globally competitive or else it will sink. If a country deviates from the path of democracy or free markets, that all-important investment will simply go elsewhere. All political leaders and economic sectors in Latin America now recognize these hard facts, even though they may still rail against them in populist fashion or still disagree on the precise balance between authority and democracy, statism and open markets, and unfettered capitalism and social justice. The Latin American countries vary greatly in how they manage development policy, but they no longer have much choice about the basic model to follow.

As Latin America has become more democratic and its economies more open, it has, in its own way, balanced outside pressures and domestic, often traditional, ways of doing things. Modernity and tradition often exist side by side in Latin America—the most traditional agricultural methods alongside the most modern skyscrapers—thereby reflecting the mixed, often transitional nature of Latin American society. Patronage considerations often remain as important as merit and electoral choice. Moreover, as democracy has come to the area, it has often been a more centralized, executive-centered form of democracy rather than one of separate and equal legislative and judicial branches. At the same time, despite privatization and neoliberalism, the state has remained a strong force in the economic and social programs, which is closer to the European tradition than to the U.S. laissez-faire model. Thus modernization in Latin America has represented a fascinating blend of U.S., European, and historic Latin American ways of doing things.

A Quick Snapshot

For the purposes of this book, Latin America consists of eighteen Spanish-speaking countries, one Portuguese-speaking country (Brazil), and one French or patois-speaking country (Haiti). Including South America, Central America, Mexico, and the Caribbean islands, it encompasses 8 million square miles (21 million square kilometers), which is about one fifth of the world's total land area. Its population is about 550 million, almost twice that of the United States. The former Dutch and British colonies in the area are also interesting and worthy of study, and although they are part of the *geographic* region of Latin America, they are not culturally, socially, religiously, or politically "Latin" American. For this reason, they are not included in this book.

The social and racial composition of Latin America is exceedingly diverse and complicated. At the time of Columbus's "discovery" of America in 1492, some areas (Mexico, parts of Central America, the western area of South America) had large numbers of indigenous people, whereas other areas did not. Even today the assimilation and integration of indigenous people into national life remains one of the great unsolved problems of these countries. Where there were few Indians or they died out and when the climate was right for plantation agriculture (such as in the Caribbean islands, northeast Brazil, some coastal areas), large numbers of African slaves were brought in. White Europeans formed the upper class and Indians and blacks were slaves, peasants, and subsistence agriculturists. From this, once the Indians had died off or had been eliminated, social and race relations in the Caribbean islands and northeast Brazil would then be written in terms of the relations between whites and blacks; on the rest of the mainland the major socioracial components remained white and Indian. Because of the African influence, the cultures of the Spanish colonies in the Caribbean and the Portuguese in Brazil were often different from those in the other Spanish-speaking countries. In some countries all three major racial strains (Indian, black, white), as well as Asian and Middle Eastern, are now present.

In contrast to North America, where the colonists took their wives and families along with them to settle and farm, the conquest of Latin America was viewed as a military campaign (no women initially), and widespread miscegenation between whites and Indians, whites and blacks, blacks and Indians, and all of their offspring took place right from the beginning. Hence a mulatto (white and black) element in the Caribbean and Brazil and a *mestizo* (white and Indian) element in the mainland countries of the Spanish empire emerged, with endless gradations based on color, hair, and facial features. Although there is racial prejudice, because of these many variations and gradations, Latin Americans tend not to typecast people as "black," "white," or "Indian" based solely on color as North Americans do. Indeed, in many of the Central American and Andean countries of South America, one is an *indio* or *indígeno* only if he or she dresses like a native American and speaks a language other than Spanish. Moving to a city, wearing Western clothes, becoming educated and speaking Spanish probably means that the person would no longer be called an "Indian," regardless that there has of course been no change of ethnic background.

The racial situation in Latin America is generally more fluid and permeable than it is in the United States: Higher education, wealth, the clothes one wears, and comportment tend to make one "whiter." Because being viewed as whiter is pragmatically seen by most Latin Americans as being easier and/or better, it has long been hard to launch Indian or black rights or power movements, although this is changing as well. Endlessly fascinating, the racial/social relations in Latin America are very different from those in the United States.

Richard C. Williamson, in *Latin American Societies in Transition*, suggests that in broad ethnic terms the countries of Latin America could be classified into four major groups (although many countries had regional variations):

1. Countries in which a mestizo population dominates;
2. Countries overwhelmingly European in character;
3. Countries with conspicuous Indian groupings, generally inhabiting the highlands; and
4. Countries dominated by African admixtures.[1]

The first group of countries includes the South American countries of Venezuela and Colombia, as well as Nicaragua, El Salvador, Honduras, and Panama in Central America and Mexico. The predominantly European countries are Argentina, Chile, Uruguay, and Costa Rica, and the countries with large Indian groups are Guatemala, Ecuador, Peru, Bolivia, and Paraguay. Finally, the countries dominated by African admixtures are Brazil and the Caribbean countries of Cuba, the Dominican Republic, and Haiti.

The economies of the area are similarly diverse. A few countries—namely Argentina, Brazil, Uruguay, Venezuela—have vast, rich agricultural lands comparable to the American Midwest, while in most of the others subsistence agriculture has predominated. Because of climate, few countries can grow the kind of grains grown in more temperate climates; hence sugar, coffee, cacao beans, and fruits have predominated. Mexico and the larger South

American countries have considerable mineral wealth and some have oil, but others have few natural resources and are likely to remain poor, regardless of whether they call themselves capitalist or socialist. Based on their resources, some countries—generally the bigger ones with large internal markets, such as Argentina, Brazil, Chile, and Mexico—are "making it" in the global economy and becoming competitive with the most efficient countries. Another group of Latin American countries is doing moderately well economically and improving their condition. A handful of countries, however, such as Bolivia, Paraguay, Ecuador, Haiti, Honduras, Nicaragua, are not doing well at all and are mired at the lower end of the rankings with the world's poorest nations.

The Latin American countries differ not only in people and economics, but also in terms of geography. The continent contains the world's second highest mountain range (over 20,000 feet), the Andes, which runs like a vertical spine up and down the Pacific Coast. Latin America also has some of the world's largest river systems—Amazon, Orinoco, Plate—but few of these connect major cities with agricultural areas or provide the internal transportation networks formed by the rivers and Great Lakes of North America. In many countries mountains come right down to the sea, leaving little coastal land for settlement and agricultural development. Much of the interior land is similarly unsuitable for cash crops, and although some countries have iron ore, few have coal, thereby making it difficult to produce steel, one of the keys to early industrial development. Hence, although nature has been kind to Latin America in some resources, it has been stingy in others, and although a few countries are resource-rich, others are stunningly poor.

One of the most startling features of South America is the vast Amazon basin, stretching nearly two thousand miles in all directions. Largely uninhabited until recently, the Amazon rain forest produces upward of 40 percent of the world's oxygen supply. Environmentalists seek to preserve this area, but Brazil and other countries on its perimeter see the Amazon's resources as the keys to their future development. Note from the map in Part 2 that most of South America's great cities are located on the ocean coast; only in recent decades have efforts been made to populate, develop, and exploit the vast interior.

Geographically, Latin America is a land of extremes: high mountains that are virtually impassable, lowlands that are densely tropical and also difficult to penetrate, and such extremes of heat, rainfall, and climate that make living and working difficult. Latin America largely lacked the resources that the United States had during its great march to modernization in the nineteenth century, which is one of the key reasons it lagged behind. Furthermore, the mountainous, chopped-up terrain made internal communications and transportation difficult, dividing Latin America into *patrias chicas* (small, isolated villages) and making national integration extremely difficult. Only now, with the advent of modern communications and transportation, have the Latin American countries begun to become better integrated and develop their vast potential.

The Economies

The Latin American economies were founded on a colonial system that was rapacious and exploitative. Under the prevailing economic theory of mercantilism, colonies such as those of Spain and Portugal existed solely for the benefit of the mother countries. The considerable gold, silver, and other resources of the colonies were drained away by the colonial powers. Ironically, Latin America's precious metals benefited the mother countries not at all but flowed through Spain and Portugal to England and Holland, where they helped launch the Industrial Revolution. As in the Americas, the north of Europe then forged ahead while the south fell farther behind.

The most characteristic feature of colonial Latin America was the feudal or semifeudal estate, patterned after the European model, with Spaniards and Portuguese as the overlords and Indians and blacks as peasants and slaves. Even after independence, Latin America remained mainly feudal; only slowly did capitalism and an entrepreneurial ethic develop. Under feudalism, the land, wealth, and people were all exploited; there was almost no effort to plow back the wealth of the land into development or to raise living standards. In accord with the feudal ethic and then-prevailing values, the total social product was fixed, and people had a duty to accept their station in life. Land, cattle, and peasants, then as now, were to the wealthy elites symbols of status and not necessarily to be used for productive purposes. However, the economic situation of the colonies varied considerably: The Caribbean islands and northeast Brazil were areas of large-scale sugar plantations, and Mexico, Central America, Colombia, Peru, Bolivia, and other areas of Brazil were valued for their mineral wealth. Argentina, Uruguay, and other farm areas were settled later because at the time there were better ways than agriculture to get rich quick.

Once the readily available precious metals were exhausted, the vast territory of Latin America was divided up among the Spanish and Portuguese conquerors, mostly into huge estates that were the size of U.S. states or counties and resembled medieval fiefdoms. Along with the land came the right to exploit the Indian labor living on it. Each Spanish and Portuguese conquistador could live like the feudal nobility: haughty, authoritarian, exploitative, and avoiding manual labor. These large estates were mainly self-sufficient, with their own priests, political authority (the landowners themselves), and social and economic life. Few areas in Latin America (Costa Rica comes closest) were founded on the productive, family-farm basis that the New England colonies were.

It was only in the last half of the nineteenth century that these feudal estates began to be converted into more capitalistic enterprises producing more intensively for a world market as well as home consumption. Sugar and tobacco in the Caribbean; bananas and coffee in Central America and Colombia; rubber in Brazil; and beef, hides, and wool in Argentina and Uruguay were the new crops being produced for profit. The old feudal estates began to modernize and become export-oriented enterprises. Foreign investment further stimulated this conversion process. Thus Latin America went through the first stages of economic development, but in the process many Indians and peasants were exploited even more than in the past or pushed off their communal lands into the infertile hillsides. The result was class polarization and, in Mexico, a violent revolution in 1910.

While production for the export market resulted in an economic quickening throughout Latin America that led to further growth later on, it also brought Latin America into the world economy for the first time, with both positive and negative consequences. Greater affluence led to greater political stability and new economic opportunities, but it also made Latin America subject to global economic forces over which it had no control. Particularly in countries where 60 percent or higher of export earnings depended on one crop, if that crop (for instance, sugar, coffee, or bananas) suffered a price decrease on world markets, the entire national economy could go into a tailspin. This is precisely what happened in virtually every price fluctuation, especially during the 1929–1930 world market crash, when not only did the bottom drop out of all the Latin American economies, but their political systems collapsed as well. Almost every country of the area had a military coup d'état associated with the depression; only Colombia and Mexico were exceptions.

Industrialization began in Latin America in the 1930s precisely because the countries had no export earnings to purchase imported manufactured goods and therefore had to produce them on their own. Most of the heavy industry—steel, electricity, petroleum, and manufacturing—was established as state-owned industries, reflecting the weakness of entrepreneurialism and the history of mercantilism. This system was called state capitalism in order to distinguish it from the laissez-faire capitalism of the United States. It was the beginning of Latin America's large but often bloated, inefficient, and patronage-dominated state sector.

During World War II and the postwar period Latin America developed rapidly on the basis of this import-substitution-industrialization (ISI) model. However, growing demand for new social programs outstripped the countries' ability to pay for them—and then came the massive oil price increases of the 1970s and the debt crisis of the 1980s. Latin America was unable to pay its obligations, and many countries slipped into near bankruptcy. As it had in the 1930s, economic downturn again helped produce political instability in the 1960s and 1970s.

In the 1990s and continuing in the new millennium, the Latin American economies began to recover, but in many countries the growth was anemic and debt continued to be a burden. Nevertheless, there was recovery throughout the region and many countries began to reform their economies. In an effort to become competitive in the global economy, many countries sold off inefficient public enterprises, opened previously protected economic sectors to competition, emphasized exports, and sought to reduce or streamline inefficient bureaucratic regulation. They also tried to diversify their economies internally and sought a wider range of trading partners. However, their reform efforts often produced mixed results because, although it was economically rational to reduce the size of the state, doing so conflicted with social justice requirements and the political patronage demands of rewarding friends and supporters with cushy state jobs.

Chile, Brazil, and Mexico were the chief leaders and beneficiaries of the new, free-market economic policies. Several countries did moderately well as middle-income countries, but others remained poor and backward, as shown in Table 1.1. Then, the global economic crisis of 2009 brought renewed pressures for state-led growth.

Classes and Social Forces

During the colonial period Latin America was structured on a fundamentally two-class basis. There was a small, white Hispanic or Portuguese elite at the top and a huge mass of Indians, black slaves, and peasants at the bottom, with almost no one in between. The two-class system was a reflection of feudal Spain and of the medieval Christian conception of each person being fixed and situated in his or her station in life. This strict social hierarchy was assumed to be immutable and in accord with God's ordering of the universe, and in Latin America the rigid class structure was further reinforced by racial criteria. Over time, as miscegenation progressed, a considerable number of mulattos and mestizos emerged, often forming a small middle class.

The onset of economic growth in the late nineteenth century and industrialization in the twentieth century eventually gave rise to new social forces, although for a long time the basic two-class structure of society did not change. In the early stages of modernization in the nineteenth century a new business-commercial class began to emerge alongside the traditional landed elite, but this new class thought like the old elite, intermarried with it, and adopted the same aristocratic, haughty ethos. Similarly, as a large middle class of shop owners, small businesspeople, government workers, and professionals began

Table 1.1   Indices of Modernization in Latin America, 2008

Country	Population in millions	Population growth rate*	GNI per capita	GDP growth rate*	Inflation*	Life expectancy***	Infant mortality****
Argentina	39.88	1	7,200	7	20	75	16
Bolivia	9.68	2	1,460	6	10	66	57
Brazil	191.97	1	7,350	5	6	73**	22
Chile	16.76	1	9,400	3	0	78	9
Colombia	44.53	1	4,660	3	8	73	20
Costa Rica	4.53	1	6,060	3	12	79	11
Cuba	11.25	0	..	..	..	78	7
Dominican Republic	9.84	1	4,390	5	10	72	38
Ecuador	13.48	1	3,640	7	8	75	22
El Salvador	6.13	0	3,480	3	6	71**	24
Guatemala	13.68	2	2,680	4	9	70	39
Haiti	9.78	2	660	1	9	61	76
Honduras	7.24	2	1,800	4	10	70	24
Mexico	106.35	1	9,980	2	7	75	35
Nicaragua	5.68	1	1,080	4	17	73	35
Panama	3.39	2	6,180	9	9	76	23
Paraguay	6.23	2	2,180	6	7	72	29
Peru	28.84	1	3,990	10	1	73**	20
Uruguay	3.33	0	8,260	9	9	76	14
Venezuela	27.94	2	9,230	5	31	74	19
Latin America	**565.29**	**1**	**6,780**	**6**	**8**	**73**	**26**

Source: World Bank. World Development Indicators 2009. http://ddp-ext.worldbank
.org/ext/dd[re[prts/ViewSharedReport?REPORT ID=9147&REQUEST TYPE=VIEWAD
VANCED, December 15, 2009

*   Annual percentage.
**   2008 data.
***   Life expectancy at birth in years (2007).
****   Mortality rate, under five, per one thousand live births (2007).

to emerge in the 1930s and thereafter, it too acquired conservative attitudes, disdained manual labor, and often allied with a repressive military to prevent left-wing and lower-class movements from acquiring power. Emerging new social movements were co-opted by the elites, and the two-class society was generally preserved.

During the 1930s as industrialization began, a working class also developed in Latin America; by the 1950s and 1960s peasant groups were being mobilized; and in the 1970s and thereafter women, indigenous elements, community and neighborhood groups, and other social movements and civil society also organized. At first the elite groups (oligarchy, church, army) that had long dominated Latin America tried either to co-opt these groups as they had others in the past or to send the army out to repress, kill, and intimidate them. Initially, these co-optation/repression or carrot-and-stick strategies worked when these new groups were small, heading off revolution or even democracy and enabling the old power structure to survive. However, as the labor movement, peasant elements, and other civil society groups grew in power, the old techniques of co-optation/repression proved less successful. These processes then produced a variety of outcomes in Latin America: dictatorships in some countries, democracy in others, revolution in still others, and in most alternation or muddling along between rival alternatives.

Latin America today is consequently much more pluralistic than before. There is still an old, landed, oligarchic class in most countries, but it has been largely supplanted by business, banking, industrial (including agri-industrial), and commercial groups. There is now a larger middle class that, depending on the country, may comprise 20 to 50 percent of the population. In many countries the business and middle classes, rather than the old oligarchies, dominate. These groups tend to favor a stable democracy both because it serves their interests and because the global international community now demands it.

At lower-class levels important changes are also occurring. Labor is organizing; peasants are mobilizing and sometimes marching on private lands; new neighborhood and community groups are forming; Protestantism is growing, especially evangelical groups; and women's organizations, racial and ethnic groups, and many nongovernmental organizations (NGOs) are becoming more active. At grassroots levels many of these groups have organized to get things done, often bypassing the traditional political parties, bureaucratic agencies, and patronage systems. In many countries, however, there are rivalries between these newer, more pluralistic civil society groups and the traditional, patronage-dominated ones. We must also remember that Latin America's pluralism is still more limited than is the chaotic hurly-burly of U.S. interest group pluralism, and it is also still more state-controlled and therefore less participatory and democratic. The number of plural groups is small, the elites and/or the state still try to co-opt and control them, and interest group lobbying as seen in the U.S. system is often absent. Nevertheless, Latin America is sufficiently pluralist that it is harder now to govern dictatorially, and that means a stronger base for democracy's survival.

Changing Political Culture

Political culture—the basic values and ideas that dominate in a society—varies from country to country and from region to region. Political culture provides a composite view of a society's beliefs as represented by its religious orientation, historical experience, and standard operating procedures. Political culture can be determined and analyzed using literature, music, other variables that shape the general culture, and, most importantly, public opinion surveys. Although we want to avoid stereotyping in speaking of political culture, when carefully used, it can be an important explanatory tool. Remember also that political culture may change (usually slowly) over time, there may be two or more (elite versus mass, left versus right) political cultures within a given society, and the diverse views and orientations that compose political culture may be in conflict.

Whereas the political culture of the United States is mainly democratic, liberal (believing in the classic freedoms of the Bill of Rights), and committed to representative government, that of Latin America has historically been more elitist, authoritarian, hierarchical, corporatist, and patrimonial. Latin American elitism stems from the Iberian tradition of nobility, the feudal landholding system, and a powerful tradition in Spanish-Portuguese political theory that holds that society should be governed by its "natural" elites.

Authoritarianism in Latin America derived from the prevailing elitist power structure, biblical precepts and medieval Christianity's emphasis on top-down rule, and the chaotic and often anarchic conditions in Latin America that seemed to demand strong government.

The notion of a hierarchy among people thus derived from early Christian political ideas as well as the social/power structure of medieval Spain and Portugal that was carried over to Latin America. God was at the top of this hierarchy, then archangels, angels, and so on until we reach mankind. Rulers received their mandate from God; land, cattle, military prowess, and high social and political status were similarly believed to derive from the "Great Chain of Being," God's unchanging design for the universe. Proceeding down through society, one eventually reaches workers and peasants, who have some, though limited, rights. In the New World, Indians and Africans were thought to be barely human. After a long debate, the Roman Catholic Church decided that Indians had souls; as a result they were given to Spanish conquerors in *encomiendas*, through which they would work for the Spanish, who had the duty of "civilizing" and "Christianizing" the less-fortunate Indians. The Church fathers initially decided, on the other hand, that Africans did not have souls and could therefore be enslaved, having no rights at all. It is obvious that this hierarchical conception is profoundly inegalitarian and undemocratic.

Another feature of Latin American political culture and institutions is corporatism, or the organization of the nation's interest group life under state regulation and control rather than on the basis of freedom of association. The main corporate groups in Latin America have been the church; the armed forces; the landed and business elites; and, more recently, the trade union movement, peasants, women, and indigenous elements. Corporatism, which is largely unknown in U.S. politics, is a way of both organizing and controlling interest group activity. Corporatism is thus often associated with authoritarianism and an illiberal society, and it reinforces the other undemocratic traits previously mentioned.

One other feature of traditional—and continuing—Latin American society and politics is patronage. Historically in Latin America this has been based on a system of mutual obligation: a favor for a favor. This is also a quasi-feudal concept with its roots in Greek and Christian philosophy: If I give you a gift, then you owe me a gift in return. Patronage manifests itself in various ways, including votes in return for gifts or money, votes in return for a government job, friends or relatives rewarded with government contracts, special access to those with good connections, and sometimes whole programs or government offices are doled out in return for critical political support. Although at high levels patronage verges on and is corruption, at low levels it constitutes the "grease" that keeps the machinery of government working.

These features of historic Latin American political culture—elitism, authoritarianism, hierarchy, corporatism, and patrimonialism—remained largely intact over three centuries of colonial rule and became deeply embedded in the customs and political processes. However, when Latin America became independent in the nineteenth century, a new political culture based on representative institutions emerged, even while the old political culture remained strong. The result was two political cultures—one authoritarian, the other nascently liberal—existing side by side and vying for dominance throughout all of the nineteenth century and much of the twentieth. The two political cultures also had different social bases: The more traditional one centered in the church, the landed elite, the military, and the conservative peasantry, while the newer, liberal one concentrated in urban areas among intellectuals, students, the emerging middle class, and some business elements. With no one single political culture being dominant—unlike the situation in the United States after the Civil War when the liberal-democratic ethos definitively triumphed—Latin American politics was often unstable and torn by frequent civil war between the two ways of life.

A third tradition—socialist, Marxist, social-democratic—then emerged in the 1930s, particularly among students, trade unionists, and intellectuals. Some of these groups favored a full-scale Marxist-Leninist regime, others wanted a redistribution of wealth, and still others advocated greater social welfare. The common themes of these groups included a strong role for the state in directing change, a leftist ideology, and anti-American nationalism. Fidel Castro, the Nicaraguan Sandinista revolution, and recently Hugo Chávez galvanized these leftist groups, which in the past often looked to the Soviet Union and/or China for support. However, the collapse of the Soviet Union and of Marxist-Leninist movements and regimes worldwide led to a severe drop in support for Marxist solutions, although in an updated social-democratic or populist form it may be possible for the left to come back to power.

Meanwhile the historic political culture, or at least some of its aspects, is fading. No one believes anymore that one must stay poor and one's children must have bloated bellies because God or Saint Thomas has willed it that way and one must accept one's station in life. The older notions of authority, hierarchy, and elitism, although still often present, are no longer the dominant political culture. At the same time, the groups that were the strongest proponents of the traditional political culture (the church, the landed oligarchy, the army, the conservative peasantry) are either changing internally or are losing influence. However, patronage and patrimonialism seem as strong as ever.

Latin America has modernized, democratized, and become part of the global economy. It is no longer the same Latin America portrayed in earlier editions of this book. Rising literacy, urbanization, social change, immigration, globalization, and democratization are all changing the appearance and culture of Latin America. Polls tell us that 60, 70, and even 80 percent of the public in most countries support democratic rule, while none of the other alternatives (authoritarianism or Marxism-Leninism) have much support. It may be that the historic conflict over political culture in Latin America is finally ending and that the democratic option with a modern mixed economy has finally emerged as triumphant.

And yet these same polls show that Latin Americans want an effective government, one that delivers real social and economic reform. Democracy and economic liberalism (or neoliberalism) are still weak and unconsolidated in Latin America. This means they could still be upset in some of the weaker and poorly institutionalized countries. Moreover—and this is what makes Latin America so interesting—the form that democracy takes there is often quite different from democracy in the United States. It is more organic, centralized, and with still-powerful patronage and corporatism features. Latin America now has formal, electoral democracy—whether it has genuinely liberal democracy may be quite another thing. Although the changes have been vast, the continuities from Latin America's past are still powerful.

An Assessment

Latin America's geography, economic underdevelopment, socioracial conditions, and traditions of political culture have historically retarded national unity, democracy, and development. However, the great forces of twentieth-century change—urbanization, industrialization, modernization, democratization, and now globalization—are breaking down the historic barriers and altering the foundations of traditional Latin American society. Latin America is thus experiencing many of the same revolutionary transformations that the United States, Western Europe, and Japan went through in earlier times. Although Latin America has commenced the process, there the time period is much more telescoped and the outcome is still likely to be a great variety of political systems rather than some pale imitation of the United States. To us that is healthy, invigorating, challenging, and interesting.

Although the changes have been immense and often inspiring, many problems still remain. Poverty, malnutrition, and malnutrition-related disease are still endemic in many areas. Too many people are ill-housed, ill-fed, ill-educated, and just plain ill. Wages are too low, the economies and democracies are often fragile, and the gap between the rich and the poor is greater than in any other area in the world. The political systems are often corrupt and ineffective; the standards of living of the rural and urban poor are woefully inadequate; and crime, violence, drug activity, and general personal insecurity are increasing. Frequently, social and economic change occurs faster than political systems can handle them, and thus fragmentation, ungovernability, and collapse are still lurking.

Three recent changes also command special attention. The first is the dramatic shift to democracy in all but one country (Cuba) of the area. The second is the new consensus on economic policy emphasizing free markets, reform of the state, export-led growth, and integration. Some of these economic reforms are still weak and limited, and in some countries where democracy is fragile and has not been consolidated, they could still be reversed. Nevertheless, the degree of progress over the previous two decades is often breathtaking.

The third profound change is the impact of globalization on Latin America in all its dimensions (cultural, political, economic), which has broken down its traditional isolation and forced all countries to become integrated into the modern world. Although this has mostly been for good, it has been damaging to marginal groups such as small farmers.

There is, overall, strong economic, social, and political reform; a growing realization that Latin America must take charge of its own future; and a great eagerness to enter the modern global community of developed nations. Later chapters detail which countries have made this great leap forward; examine how they have done so; and consider the successes, failures, and future prospects of all the Latin American nations.

2

The Pattern of Historical Development

Whereas the United States was founded during the seventeenth and eighteenth centuries, when modernization was beginning (capitalism, liberalism, pluralism, the Enlightenment, the Industrial Revolution), Latin America was founded in an earlier time when feudal and medieval practices and institutions still held sway. If the United States was "born free," Latin America was "born feudal," and these basic differences still account for many of the contrasts between the two areas. To a degree unknown in the United States, Latin America has long been dominated by a political, social, and economic structure that had its roots not in modernity but in medievalism. As such, much of Latin America's recent history involves the efforts to overcome or ameliorate that feudal past. Because this feudal legacy remains so strong, because the heavy hand of ancient history hangs so oppressively over the area, we must therefore come to grips with Latin America's past to understand its present and future.

The Conquest

The conquest of the Americas by Spain and Portugal was the extension of a reconquest of the Iberian Peninsula that had been occurring in the mother countries for the preceding seven centuries. In the eighth century AD the armies of a dynamic, expansionist Islam had crossed the Strait of Gibraltar from North Africa and conquered most of present-day Spain and Portugal. In the following centuries the Christian forces of Spain and Portugal had gradually retaken these conquered lands, until the last of the Islamic Moors were driven out in 1492, the same year that Columbus discovered America. Because of the long military campaign against the Moors, which was also a religious crusade to drive out the Islamic "infidels," Spanish and Portuguese institutions tended to be authoritarian, intolerant, militaristic, and undemocratic. These same practices and institutions were then carried over to Latin America.

The conquest of the Americas was one of the great epic adventures of all time, and its impact was worldwide. The encounter with the New World vastly expanded humankind's knowledge, exploration, and frontiers; led to a period of prolonged European world dominance; and helped stimulate the Industrial Revolution. It also led to the brutalization, death, and isolation of much of the New World's indigenous population.

At the time of Columbus's landing in America there were only three million indigenous people in all of North America but some thirty million in Latin America. The Indians in Latin America were often organized into large civilizations—Aztec, Maya, Inca—of five to seven million persons each, as compared with the generally smaller tribal, nomadic basis of most North American Indians. Whereas in North America, the Indians were often eliminated, pushed farther west, or confined to reservations, in Latin America the large numbers and organization of indigenous groups called for a different strategy. The Spanish tactic was usually to capture or kill the Indian chiefs, replace them with Spanish overlords, and rule (and enslave) them by dominating their own power structure, all the while seeking to Christianize, Hispanicize, and assimilate them into European ways. That has been the strategy for over five hundred years, but recently Indian groups in such countries as Mexico, Guatemala, Colombia, Ecuador, and Bolivia have been raising the issue of indigenous rights and seeking new degrees of autonomy from the nation-states that Spain and Portugal left in their wake.

The degree of colonial influence varied from place to place. The first area to receive the impact of Spanish colonial rule was Hispaniola, an island in the Caribbean that later was divided between the two independent countries of Haiti and the Dominican Republic. Here Spain carried out its first experiments in colonial rule: a slave-plantation economy, a two-class and caste society, an authoritarian political structure, and a church that served as an arm of the conquest. But Hispaniola had little gold and silver and, as the Indian population was decimated, largely by disease, Spain moved on to more valuable conquests.

Next came Cuba and Puerto Rico, but when the scarce precious metals and Indian labor supply were exhausted there also, Spain moved on to conquer Mexico and explored Florida and the North American Southeast. The conquest of Mexico by Cortéz was fundamentally different from the earlier island conquests. First, Spain found a huge Indian civilization, the Aztecs, with immense quantities of gold and silver and a virtually unlimited labor supply. Second, Mexico's huge mainland territory finally convinced the Spaniards that they had found a new continent and not just scattered islands on the outskirts of Asia. Mexico therefore became a serious and valuable colony to be settled and colonized by Spain, not just some way station en route to somewhere else.

From Mexico Cortéz's lieutenants fanned out to conquer Central America and the American Southwest. In the meantime Balboa had crossed the Isthmus of Panama to gaze out on the Pacific, and other Spanish conquistadores had explored both the east and west coasts of South America. From Panama in the 1530s the Pizarro brothers, using the same methods Cortéz had used in Mexico, moved south to conquer the vast Inca empire that stretched from southern Colombia in the north, through Ecuador and Peru, to Chile in the south. Meanwhile Portugal had gained a foothold on the coast of Brazil that sticks out toward Africa. Other Spanish explorers spilled over the Andes from Peru to discover and subdue Bolivia and Paraguay and then sailed all the way downriver to present-day Buenos Aires, which had been explored in the 1530s but was not settled until the 1580s. Meanwhile Chile, where the Indian resistance was especially strong, was conquered in the 1570s, and other previously unconquered territories were then explored and subdued.

In less than a hundred years after the initial discovery, then, Mexico, the Caribbean, Central America, and all of South America, east to west and north to south, had been conquered. Spain had most of the territory, and Portugal had Brazil. It was a remarkable feat in a short period of time, especially when one considers that it took North American settlers almost three hundred years to cross the continent from the Atlantic to the Pacific.

Colonial Society: Principles and Institutions

The institutions that Spain and, less aggressively, Portugal brought to the New World reflected the institutions that had developed in the mother countries during their centuries-long struggles against the Moors and their efforts to form unified nation-states out of disparate social and regional forces. These institutions included a rigid, authoritarian political system, a similarly rigid and hierarchical class structure, a statist and mercantilist economy, an absolutist church, and a similarly closed and absolutist educational system.

In the New World the Spanish and Portuguese conquerors found abundant territory that they could claim as feudal estates; abundant wealth that enabled them to live like grandees; and a ready-made "peasantry," in the forms of the indigenous Indian population or imported African slaves, that they could exploit. The men who accompanied Columbus and other explorers to the New World were often the second and third sons of the Spanish and

Portuguese aristocracy. Under Spanish law these men were prohibited from inheriting their father's land, which went to the first son. In the New World, however, they could acquire vast territories and servants and live like feudal overlords. The oligarchies of Latin America, then as now, were haughty, aloof, authoritarian, and disdainful of manual labor and those forced to work with their hands. Even to this day, this aristocratic ethos and power structure has been a very powerful force in Latin America.

The institutions established by Spain and Portugal in Latin America reflected and reinforced the medieval system of the mother countries. At the top was the king, who claimed absolute power, his authority having come from God (divine-right monarchy) and was therefore unquestionable. Below the king was the viceroy (literally "vice king"), similarly with absolute power and serving as the king's agent in the colonies. Below the viceroy was the captain-general, also absolute within his sphere of influence, and next came the landowner or *hacendado*, who also enjoyed absolute power within his own estate.

The economy was feudal and exploitative; the wealth of the colonies, in accord with the prevailing mercantilism, was drained off to benefit the mother countries and not used for the betterment of the colonies themselves. Similarly, the social structure was basically feudal and two-class, with a small group of Spaniards and Portuguese at the top, a large mass of Indians and Africans at the bottom, and almost no one in between. Democracy cannot be based on such a strict two-class structure, and Latin America was divided not only socially and economically, but also racially.

The Roman Catholic Church reinforced royal authority and policy in the colonies and was similarly absolutist and authoritarian. Its role was to Christianize and pacify the indigenous population and thus serve the Crown's assimilationist policies. Although some individual clergy sought to defend the Indians against enslavement and maltreatment, the church was primarily an arm of the state. Intellectual life and learning, monopolized by the church, was scholastic, based on rote memorization, deductive reasoning, and unquestioned orthodoxy.

It is not surprising that Latin America was founded on this feudal-absolutist basis in the early sixteenth century: That was before the onset of modernization, and most countries were still organized on that basis. What is surprising is that this system lasted so long—through three centuries of colonial rule, only slightly modified by the Latin American independence movements, and on into the twentieth century. Most Latin American countries are still struggling to overcome this feudal past.

The founding principles and institutions of Latin America were essentially medieval, pre-1500. In contrast, by the time the North American colonies were established, the back of feudalism had been broken in England and

Table 2.1 Contrasting Foundations of Latin and North American Society

Institutions	Latin America, 1492–1570	North America, Seventeenth Century
Political	Authoritarian, absolutist, centralized, corporatist	More liberal, early steps toward representative and democratic rule
Religious	Catholic orthodoxy and absolutism	Protestantism and religious pluralism
Economic	Feudal, mercantilist, patrimonialist	Emerging capitalist, entrepreneurial
Social	Hierarchical, two-class, rigid	More mobile, multiclass
Educational and intellectual	Scholastic and deductive	Empirical

Holland, and hence the thirteen colonies that would later form the United States were organized on a more modern basis. By that time the idea of limited government rather than absolutism had emerged, the Protestant Reformation had destroyed the older religious orthodoxy and given rise to religious and political pluralism, the Industrial Revolution was occurring, mercantilism was giving way to commerce and entrepreneurship, the scientific revolution was breaking the hold of the old scholasticism, and a new multiclass society was beginning to emerge. Founded on these principles and changes, North American society was modern from the start, whereas Latin America continued to be plagued by feudalism. These differences also explain why, from the start, the United States was destined to forge ahead while Latin America lagged behind. Table 2.1 summarizes these contrasting foundations of U.S. and Latin American society.

Spanish and Portuguese colonial rule lasted for over three centuries, from the late fifteenth through the early nineteenth centuries. It was a remarkably stable period, with few revolts against the colonial system, which is a testimony to its efficiency even if it was unjust. In the late eighteenth century, however, the first serious cracks began to appear in this monolithic colonial structure. Under the impact of the eighteenth-century Enlightenment, ideas of liberty, freedom, and nationalism began to creep in, and the examples of the American (1776) and French (1789) revolutions caused tremors in Latin America. In addition, a rising Latin American commercial class sought to break the monopolistic barriers of Spanish mercantilism so as to trade freely with other countries. One of the main sources of independence sentiment was the growing rivalries between creoles (persons of Spanish background born in the colonies) and peninsulars (officials sent out by the Spanish crown to govern the colonies). The creoles had growing economic and social influence, but the peninsulars monopolized all administrative positions. Denied the political power to go along with their rising prominence, many creoles began to think of doing away with the inconvenience of Spanish colonialism and move toward independence.

The immediate causes of Latin American independence were precipitated by events in Europe. In 1807 to 1808 the forces of Napoleon Bonaparte invaded the Iberian Peninsula, occupied both Spain and Portugal, ousted the reigning monarchs, and placed Napoleon's brother Joseph on the Spanish throne. The Latin American creoles opposed this usurpation of royal authority by Napoleon's army and, operating under longtime medieval doctrine, moved to hold power until the legitimate king could be restored. This was, in effect, an early declaration of independence. A few years later Napoleon's forces were driven from the peninsula, and the Spanish and Portuguese monarchies were restored. However, when the Spanish king accepted the principle of limited monarchy and a liberal constitution, the conservative creoles in Latin America moved for independence.

The independence struggles in Latin America waxed and waned for nearly two decades before succeeding in the 1820s. The first revolt in Argentina in 1807 was quashed by Spanish authorities, but independence fervor was also growing in Colombia, Mexico, Venezuela, and other countries. Although independence sentiment had waned for a time after 1814 when the Spanish monarchy was restored, it resumed again in 1820 as a result of the king's shortsighted policies.

Simón Bolívar, the "George Washington of Latin America," led the struggle against Spanish forces in Venezuela, Colombia, and Ecuador. José San Martín liberated Argentina and then crossed the Andes to drive the Spanish forces from Chile. From there, the key to the independence of the rest of South America was Lima, Peru, one of the most important Spanish viceroyalties and home of a sizable Spanish garrison. Bolívar came south overland and San Martín north by ship, and in the key battle of Ayacucho they defeated the royalist forces, ending Spanish authority in South America. The other main viceroyalty was Mexico City, but by 1821 independence forces were in control there, also. Once Mexico was freed, Central America, as part of the same administration, was liberated without much actual fighting. By 1824 all Spanish forces and authority had been removed from mainland Latin America. The two exceptions were Cuba and Puerto Rico, which remained Spanish colonies until 1898. For all of the nineteenth century their nationalism was frustrated by the lack of independence, which would in turn shape twentieth-century politics on the two islands.

Haiti and Brazil were also special cases. In Haiti a successful slave revolt in 1795 drove out the French colonial ruling class, destroyed the plantations, and established Haiti as the world's first black republic, unloved and unwelcome by the rest of the world (including the United States, which still practiced slavery). Haiti's economy went into decline, and its political system since then has alternated between repressive dictatorships and chaotic upheaval.

Brazil was a different story. When Napoleon's troops occupied Portugal, the royal family fled to Rio de Janeiro, the first reigning monarchs to set foot in Latin America. In 1821 the king, Dom João, was called back to Lisbon, but he left his son Pedro in charge of the kingdom of Brazil. The following year Pedro was also called back to Portugal, but he refused to go and declared Brazil an independent monarchy. Thus Brazil gained independence without the upheaval and destruction of the other countries and was a monarchy for the first seventy years. Brazil escaped the tumult that soon enveloped its Spanish-speaking neighbors.

The independence movements in Latin America had almost all been conservative movements of separation from the mother countries rather than full-scale social or political revolutions. Led and directed by the white, aristocratic, creole elite, they were aimed at holding power for the disposed monarch and in defense of the old social hierarchy. After they later became movements for independence, these groups retained their elitist, conservative orientation. When social revolution raised its head, it was either isolated and despised as in Haiti or brutally repressed as in Mexico, where large-scale Indian protest had been part of the independence struggle.

The same conservative orientation was present in the laws, constitutions, and institutions established in the new republics. The franchise was extremely limited: Only literates and property owners (less than 1 percent of the population) could vote, if and when there were elections. Thus, the feudal landholding and class system was kept intact even after independence. Furthermore, the church was given a privileged position, and Catholicism in most countries remained the official religion. However, a new, similarly conservative power force was added: the army, which replaced the crown as the ultimate authority and became almost a fourth branch of government. Although Latin America adopted constitutions modeled after the United States, in reality, checks and balances, human rights, and separation of powers existed mostly in theory. The laws and constitutions of the new Latin American states enshrined the existing power structure and perpetuated paternalistic, top-down, elite rule.

During the three-hundred-plus years of colonial rule, Latin America had had no experience with self-government, lacked infrastructure, and had none of the "web of sociability" (neighborhood, community, religious, civic, social groups) that nineteenth-century theorist Alexis de Tocqueville identified with U.S. democracy. With independence the Latin American economies also went into decline, and the social structure was severely disrupted. It should not be surprising, therefore, that after independence Latin America fell into chaos and that the disintegrative forces set loose by independence continued. The former viceroyalty of New Granada split up into the separate nations of Colombia, Ecuador, and Venezuela; the viceroyalty of Rio de la Plata divided into the separate countries of Argentina, Paraguay, and Uruguay; and the Central American Confederation disintegrated into the small "city-states" (too small to be economically viable) of Guatemala, El Salvador, Honduras, Nicaragua, and Costa Rica. Within the new nations, further fragmentation and confusion occurred. Only Brazil under its monarchy and Chile under a stable oligarchy escaped these divisive, disruptive, and disintegrative early postindependence forces.

Deprived of their Spanish markets but still lacking new ones, many of the countries slipped back into a more primitive barter economy, and living standards plummeted. Similarly, the old Spanish/Portuguese social-racial categories were formally abolished in most countries but were resurrected informally; at the same time, the level of education, literacy, integration, and assimilation was so low (in many countries the majority of the population did not speak the national language, participate in the national economy, or even know that they were a part of a nation-state) that pluralist and participatory democracy seemed only a distant dream. In the absence of political parties, organized interest groups, civil society, or well-established institutions of any kind, the Latin American countries sank into either dictatorship or anarchy, usually alternating between the two. Internationally Latin America was isolated and cut off from the modern, Western world. Hence the immediate postindependence period, from the mid-1820s until the mid-1850s, was in most countries a time of turbulence and decline.

Early Stirrings of Modernization

By the 1850s a degree of stability had begun to emerge in many Latin American countries. Some of the more vexing questions of early independence—sovereignty and borders, federalism versus unitarianism, church-state relations—had been resolved. By this time also the first generation of postindependence dictators (Juan Manuel de Rosas in Argentina, Antonio López de Santa Anna in Mexico) had passed from the scene. Agriculture began to recover, and a degree of order returned.

With increased stability at midcentury came foreign investment and greater productivity. The first banks in the region were chartered. British capital invested in the area provided a major stimulus to growth. New lands were opened to cultivation and new exports (sugar, coffee, tobacco, beef, wool) began to restore national coffers. The first highways, railways, and port facilities were built to transport the exports to foreign markets. The telephone and telegraph were introduced. The opportunities available in Latin America began to attract immigrants from Europe, who often brought knowledge and entrepreneurial skills with them. They opened small shops and started farms and prospered; often this new wealth intermixed with older landed wealth.

As Latin America's prospects began to improve, the area attracted other investors: France, Germany, Italy, and, most important, the United States, which began to replace England as the largest investor in the area. These changes, beginning at midcentury but accelerating in the 1870s and 1880s, represented the first stirrings of modernization in Latin America after nearly four centuries of stagnation. While they brought prosperity for the landed and business elites and stimulated the growth of a middle class, often peasant and Indian elements were left behind or had their lands taken from them for the sake of greater production for global markets.

Economic growth also increased political stability, although not in all countries. Three patterns may be observed. The first, in Argentina, Brazil, Chile, Peru, and other countries, involved the consolidation of power by an export-oriented landed oligarchy whose leaders rotated in the presidential palace over a thirty- to forty-year period. The second, in Mexico, Venezuela, and the Dominican Republic, involved the seizure of power by strong authoritarian dictators—no longer the simple men on horseback of the past but leaders who provided both long-term stability and development. A third pattern emerged slightly later, in the first decades of the twentieth century, in the smaller, weaker, resource-poor countries of Central America and the Caribbean. It involved U.S. military intervention and occupation and the carrying out by the U.S. Marines of many of the same policies as the order-and-progress oligarchs and dictators: pacification, infrastructure development (roads, communication, port facilities), and overall nation-building.

Two subperiods are discernible here. The first, 1850 to 1890, established the preconditions for Latin America's takeoff: greater stability, banks, investment, population increase, and infrastructure development. The second, 1890 to 1930, was the economic takeoff itself, the most stable and prosperous period in Latin American history. Under more stable regimes and exporting for the first time for a world market, Latin America began its development process. It was not at the rapid rate of the United States and Europe during the same period, but rather slow and steady.

Although Latin America's development was often impressive, it came under nondemocratic leadership: oligarchs, order-and-progress dictators, and U.S. military occupations. Hence the potential for future problems was also present even amid the growing prosperity. Three applecarts were upset even before the 1930s market crash caused the entire edifice to come crumbling down. In 1910 the order-and-progress dictator Porfirio Díaz was overthrown in Mexico, precipitating a bloody ten-year social revolution out of which Mexico's present political system emerged. In 1912 in Argentina and in the early 1920s in Chile a rising middle class challenged and eventually wrested political power away from the old oligarchs. These changes in some of the more advanced countries of Latin America thus provided a foretaste of what would occur in the other countries in later decades.

Upheaval and Restructuring

When the stock market crashed in the United States in 1929 and in Europe the following year, the effects were global. The bottom dropped out of the market for Latin America's exports, sending the economics of the area into a tailspin and crashing their political systems as well. Between 1930 and 1935 there were governmental overthrows in fourteen of the twenty Latin American countries—not just the usual substitution of one colonel for another, but rather real, transforming revolutions. The immediate causes of this collapse were economic, but deep-rooted social and political issues were also involved. By this time Latin America did have a business class, a middle class, and a restless trade union movement, but power was still monopolized by the old landowning oligarchs and something had to give. The chasm between the traditional holders of power and the new social and political forces clamoring for change had grown wider, and the new forces were demanding change and democratization while the older elites clung to their privileges at all costs. The 1930s Depression was the catalyst that collapsed the prevailing political as well as economic structure.

Once Humpty Dumpty (the Latin American political systems) had fallen off the wall, the question was how to put him back together again. A variety of solutions were tried—an important turning point to remember because this is the time when most of our country-by-country analyses begin. Some countries, after a brief interruption in the early 1930s, reverted by restoring oligarchic rule. In others new, tough dictatorships (Fulgencio Batista in Cuba, Anastasio Somoza in Nicaragua, Rafael Trujillo in the Dominican Republic, Jorge Ubico in Guatemala) brought the new business and middle classes into power and stimulated development, but under authoritarian auspices. (It is getting ahead of the story only a little bit to note that all these countries that had brutal right-wing dictatorships produced left-wing revolutions later on.) Mexico replaced the old regime with a one-party authoritarian/corporatist one that monopolized power for the next seventy years.

In Argentina and Brazil the regimes of Juan Perón and Getúlio Vargas, respectively, borrowed some semifascist features from Mussolini's Italy in an effort to bring labor unions into the system even while imposing strict controls over them. Other countries borrowed selectively from European corporatism and fascism while maintaining a democratic facade. Populism was still another option, whereas other countries—Chile and Uruguay followed by Costa Rica, Colombia, and Venezuela—moved toward democracy. The revolutionary alternative (as in Cuba) came later.

The 1930s were thus, in David Colliers's and Ruth Berins Colliers's words, a "critical juncture" in Latin American history, a period in which a variety of alternative developmental models—authoritarian, quasi-fascist, populist, single party, democratic—were tried out and came to power in the various Latin American countries.[1]

Some countries rotated among several of these options or tried to combine them. Many countries are still strongly shaped by the choices made and the directions taken during this period. The Depression years of the 1930s and the later war and postwar years of the 1940s were thus a time of both uncertainty and upheaval. Although the old, stable, oligarchic order had come crashing down, what would replace it was not altogether clear and, eighty years later, is still not clear in quite a number of countries.

As the demand for their products rose again during World War II, the Latin American economies began to recover from the devastation of the Depression; they were also stimulated by industrialization. The postwar period continued this economic growth, enabling some countries to move toward greater prosperity and democracy while others continued under dictatorship. Although gradual economic growth was occurring throughout the region in the 1940s and 1950s and stimulating further social change, the political systems of Latin America remained divided, full of conflict, and often unstable.

A key turning point in the region and in U.S.–Latin American relations was the Cuban revolution of 1959. Cuba became the first openly socialist country in Latin America, the first to ally itself with the Soviet Union, and the first to openly turn its back on the United States. The revolution initiated improvements in health care, education, and other social programs, although over time its economic policies proved a failure and its political system was hardly democratic (see chapter 17 for details)—but here we are concerned with the broader, region-wide impact of Cuba. First, Cuba added a new "model," a new option to the Latin American landscape, one that stood for armed revolution and a Marxist-Leninist political structure. Second, the Cuban revolution divided and thus hurt the prospects for democratic development and social reform in Latin America by splitting the reform groups into pro- and anti-Castro factions. Third, although the Cuban revolution forced the United States to pay closer attention to Latin America (the Peace Corps, the Alliance for Progress), it skewed U.S. policy by making the prevention of "another Cuba" (Marxist-Leninist, allied with the Soviet Union, housing missiles aimed at the United States) virtually the only goal of U.S.

policy. This was the "lesser evil" doctrine: When faced with the choice between a usually wobbly Latin American democracy that believed in freedom even for leftists and a tough, anti-Communist military regime, the U.S. government almost always opted for the military regime. But that policy polarized Latin America even more and led in the 1960s and 1970s to a series of civil conflicts and wars that tore several countries apart.

After a brief democratic interlude in the late 1950s and early 1960s, by the late 1960s and throughout the 1970s Latin America had succumbed to a new wave of militarism. By the mid-1970s fourteen of the twenty countries were under military-authoritarian rule, and in three others the military was so close to the surface of power that authoritarianism ruled even if civilians were still technically in office. That left only Colombia, Costa Rica, and Venezuela as democracies, and even they were elite-directed regimes.

The causes of this throwback to military authoritarianism were basically two: economic and political. By the 1960s Latin America's economies had become less competitive in global markets, the strategy of import-substitution-industrialization (ISI) was not working, the terms of trade had turned unfavorable (it cost Latin America more exports of sugars, bananas, coffee, whatever to pay for its imports than before), and the economies of the area could not pay for all the programs its citizens were demanding. Politically, the 1960s was a period when workers, peasants, and left-wing guerrillas were all mobilizing; the traditional wielders of power (elites, military) felt threatened by the mass mobilization, and they thus turned to the army to keep the lower classes in check. This was called "bureaucratic-authoritarianism": rule by the institutional armed forces and their civilian supporters, as distinct from the man-on-horseback leaders of the past.

By the late 1970s the steam had gone out of most of these military regimes, and Latin America began to reverse course and return to democracy. The armed forces had often proved just as corrupt and inefficient at running governments as their civilian predecessors; they were notorious human rights abusers and thus despised by their own people, and the international community led by the United States put pressure on them to return to the barracks. This resulted in one of the most amazing transformations in all of Latin American history: By the turn of the millennium, nineteen of the twenty Latin American countries were ruled democratically, with Cuba as the lone holdout. Latin America was the main arena of the "third wave" of democratization that affected the entire world and surely constituted one of the most significant events of the late twentieth century.

Many of these new democracies are still weak and not very well institutionalized. Crime and drugs are tearing some countries apart. They lack strong and independent legislatures, judiciaries and court systems, bureaucracies, political parties, interest groups, and local government. They are often not very effective in carrying out public policies. They are referred to as "electoral democracies," which means formal elections are held, but not "liberal democracies" in the sense of being open, pluralistic, and egalitarian. Many regimes in the area are still partial or limited democracies, designations that indicate links to Latin America's past. Nevertheless, even partial democracies are better than no democracies at all, no one doubts that an important breakthrough has been made, and certainly the human rights situation in virtually every country is far better now than it was two or three decades ago.

A Framework for Thinking

The 1930s was a critical juncture, a key turning point—maybe *the* key turning point in Latin American history. In that period, give or take a decade or two depending on the country, Latin America's old oligarchic, feudal, and medieval social, economic, and political structures began to collapse. In some cases they collapsed altogether, while in others they hung on but in attenuated form. What replaced the old order was then uncertain, often unstable, and frequently alternating between one type of regime and another. Regardless, there could be no doubt that Latin America had begun a profound transformation leading to modernization. At present, after decades of confusion and upheaval, a system of democracy and a mixed economy finally appear to be emerging, but this process is still incomplete, shows many continuities with Latin America's past, and remains fragile.

As we begin to probe more deeply into Latin America's political institutions and processes and as we go through the county-by-country analyses, readers should keep in mind the following framework for assessing the changes occurring: How much has changed in each country, what are the emerging patterns, and what outcomes are likely? This approach will not only give us a deeper understanding, but it is also fundamental to the comparative analysis that is at the heart of this book.

Changes in Political Culture

Until the 1930s Latin America still had been often feudal and medieval in its thinking, but then education increased; literacy expanded; and radio, television, VCRs, and computers brought new ideas even to the most isolated areas. The old fatalism and passivity faded, people were mobilized, and new and challenging ideas (democracy, socialism) arose. The Catholic Church, long a supporter of the traditional political culture, began to change, and

Protestantism as well as secular ideas made strong inroads. The fundamental beliefs, ideas, and orientations by which people ordered their lives began changing. So in each country we will want to know among which groups these ideas are changing, how deep and extensive the changes are, and what impact a changing, more democratic and participatory political culture has had on institutions and policy.

Economic Change

Latin America's economies are now more diversified toward business, industry, services, manufacturing, tourism, mining, and agri-industry, and they are no longer the subsistence and plantation agriculture of the past. The economies are larger, more complex, and integrated into world markets. Most of them are now moving away somewhat from the statism and mercantilism of the past toward a system of open markets, freer trade, greater efficiency, less corruption, and neoliberalism. These changes are creating greater affluence (although the wealth is unevenly distributed), creating new jobs and opportunities, and giving new dynamism to the economies of the area. However, there are also lags, uneven development, and some groups and countries doing much better than others. In addition, all of these changes, the positive and the negative alike, carry important political and policy implications that vary from country to country.

Social Change

The economic changes just outlined have also accelerated social change. The old landed oligarchy is giving way to a more diverse panoply of business, industrial, commercial, banking, and other new elites. A sizable middle class has grown up in every country, ranging from 20 to 50 percent of the population, whose size and political orientation help determine whether democracy survives. Labor unions have organized, peasant groups are mobilizing, and urban unemployed slum dwellers are becoming politicized. In addition, there are new women's groups, community organizations, civil society, and indigenous movements. Some of the older groups, such as the church and the military, are also undergoing change (more middle class, less elitist), and Roman Catholicism is being challenged in many countries by Protestant evangelicalism, which often involves quite different values and attitudes toward work and the role of the family. In a forty-year period Latin America has gone from being mostly rural to two-thirds urban. All these social changes and the far greater social pluralism force us to ask if political pluralism (which usually means democracy) can be far behind.

Political Institutions

Along with the political, cultural, economic, and social transformations in Latin America, there have also come changes in political institutions. First, political parties in most countries tend to be better organized, with a substantial mass base and real programs and ideology, as compared with the small, personalist, and patronage-based parties of the past, which still exist in some countries. Second, and reflecting the greater societal pluralism, there are far more interest groups, NGOs, and civil societies than ever before, whose agendas need to be satisfied—although U.S.-style lobbying is still seldom practiced in Latin America. Third, government agencies and institutions are being forced to modernize, increase efficiency, reduce corruption, and deliver real goods and services. Elections have become more honest and are recognized as the only legitimate route to power; legislatures, court systems, the police, and local government are likewise all being modernized in various ways.

Public Policy

Not only are Latin American political processes and institutions modernizing, but so are public policy programs. In the past, governments in Latin America had few functions, but now government is being called on to provide a host of new public policy programs: agrarian reform, family planning, education, economic development, the environment, housing, health care, and dozens of others. Moreover, with an aroused population, these programs are demanded as a matter of course, and governments in this new era of democracy have to deliver or they will be voted out. Rather than jobs, patronage, and handouts, public institutions in Latin America are called on to provide real public goods and services. Regardless, patronage and special favoritism still operate.

The International Environment

For centuries Latin America was isolated from the world, but now it is becoming closely integrated into it—politically, culturally, and economically. Globalization has come to Latin America. Politically Latin America is becoming democratic, and if a country deviates from that course, the full weight of international sanctions comes down on it. Culturally Latin America is being swept up in the world political culture of jeans, rock music, Coca-Cola, and consumerism; values, especially of young people, are becoming like those everywhere else (democratic, less authoritarian, less religious, less traditional). Economically Latin America is now a part of the global economy, with mostly good consequences (increased trade, commerce, jobs, affluence), but sometimes negative ones (currency uncertainties, fluctuating market demands, capital flight). Latin America can no longer choose among other economic options because foreign aid is meager and no other country is about to bail it out. It must join the global economy, compete with everyone else, and adopt some degree of neoliberal economic policies. It must do so not just because outside pressures force it to, but also because its own businesspeople, middle classes, and governments also recognize that they have no other choice.

All of these long-term modernizing and globalizing changes have had a profound effect on Latin America, but they vary between countries, within institutions, and even individuals, and they continue to show complex mixes of traditional and modern attitudes and practices. As Latin America enters a new millennium, we will want to know in general for the region and for individual countries just how democratic they actually are. Have the societies modernized sufficiently to provide a firmer basis for pluralism and democracy? How successful are the new reforms in favor of free trade and open markets, and will they pay off in terms of improved living standards? How strong are political parties, interest groups, and government institutions? Now that the Cold War is over, can U.S.–Latin American relations be put on a normal, more mature basis, and what of Latin America's relations with the rest of the world? These are some of the crucial questions that this book tries to answer.

In the next three chapters we examine the nature and role of interest groups and political parties in Latin America, describe government institutions and public policy, and analyze the overall political process and how it is changing. We then examine individual countries to see how they conform to these overall patterns.

3

Interest Groups and
Political Parties

L atin American political parties and interest groups, as suggested in the
last chapter, are involved in the current conflict in the area between its
corporatist, historic past and a newer system based on pluralism and democracy. Since the beginning of the 1990s the conflict has been between two different views of what the political rules of the game should be. On the one side
are the new forces who desire majority rule, human rights, and freedom of association. On the other side are those who favor traditional ways of doing
things, where the emphasis was often on creating an administrative state
above party and interest-group politics, and in which such agencies as the
church, the army, the university, and perhaps even the trade unions were often
more than mere interest groups, forming a part of the state system and being
inseparable from it.

The degree of government control over interest groups is of particular importance. Although this traditionally ranged from almost complete control to
almost complete freedom, as under liberalism, the usual pattern involved considerably more state control over interest groups than in the United States,
and this helped put interest-group behavior in Latin America in a different
framework than was the case in the United States. At least until the 1980s,
Latin America, as Charles Anderson has suggested,[1] never experienced a definitive democratic revolution—that is, a struggle resulting in agreement that
elections would be the only legitimate way to obtain public power. In the absence of such a consensus, political groups did not necessarily work for political power by seeking votes, support of political parties, or contacts with
elected representatives. Instead, groups might seek power through any number

of other strategies including coercion, economic might, technical expertise, and controlled violence. Any group that could mobilize votes was likely to do so for electoral purposes, but because that was not the only legitimated route to power, the result of any election was tentative. Given the varying power of the competing groups and the incomplete legitimacy of the government itself, the duration of any government was uncertain. Without a definitive term of office for any government, political competition became a constant, virtually permanent struggle and preoccupation.

Further, group behavior in Latin America was conditioned by a set of unwritten rules, called by Anderson the "living museum" effect. Before a new group could participate in the political system, it had to demonstrate tacitly both that it had a power resource and that it would respect the rights of already existing groups. The result was the gradual addition of new groups under these two conditions but seldom the elimination of older ones. Thus the newest, most modern groups coexisted with the oldest, most traditionalist ones, often leading to gridlock and paralysis.

A related factor was the practice of co-optation or repression. As new groups emerged as potential politically relevant actors, already established actors (particularly political parties or strong national leaders) sometimes offered to assist them in their new political activities. The deal struck was one mutually beneficial to each: The new group gained acceptance, prestige, and some of its original goals, while the established group or leader gained new support and increased political resources. The co-opted group dropped some of its original goals, leading many observers to be critical of the system because it did not provide for enough change. Those leaders and observers who preferred stability to more fundamental change, however, saw co-optation as beneficial to the political system.

In some circumstances, new groups—often more radical—refused to be co-opted, rejecting the rules of the game. Instead, they took steps indicating to established groups and leaders that they might act in a revolutionary fashion against the interests of the established elites. In the case of a group that violated the ground rules by employing mass violence, for example, an effort was made by the established interests to repress the new group, either by refusing it legal standing or in some cases through the use of counterviolence. Most commonly, such repression proved successful, and the new group, at least for the time being, disappeared or atrophied, thereby accomplishing none of its goals. The general success of repression made co-optation seem more desirable to new groups because obtaining some of their goals through co-optation was preferable to being repressed.

In a few cases the result was quite different. The established political groups failed to repress the emergent groups, and the latter came to power through revolutionary means, and then proceeded to eliminate the traditional power contenders. These are known as the "true," genuine, or social revolutions in Latin America and include only the Mexican Revolution of 1910–1920, the Bolivian Revolution of 1952, the Cuban Revolution of 1959, and the Nicaraguan Revolution of 1979. Examples of the reverse process—utilization of violence and repression to eliminate the newer challenging groups and secure in power the more traditional system—were Brazil in 1964 and Chile in 1973. Both led to the elimination of independent political parties, student associations, and labor and peasant unions as power groups.

Before the late 1980s we viewed the politically relevant groups of Latin America in this context of a historically patrimonial, corporative, and co-optive tradition. Since then there has been movement toward liberal democracy, though this has been to a greater degree in some countries than in others. Because some individuals and groups favor the new regime while others prefer the historical one, throughout Latin America there is conflict between the new supporters of democracy and the supporters of the traditional system. The chapters on Peru and Guatemala hold special interest in this regard, as both are cases in which presidents tried to govern within the old, unwritten rules rather than the new, written ones incorporated in constitutional and democratic precepts.

The Traditional Oligarchy

After independence three groups, often referred to as the "nineteenth-century oligarchy," were predominant in Latin America: the military, the Roman Catholic Church, and the large landholders. Through the process of economic growth and change, new groups emerged: first commercial elites; later industrial elites, students, and middle-income sectors; then industrial labor unions and peasants; and most recently groups representing indigenous people, women, consumers, nongovernmental organizations, and many others. Throughout the process, political parties have existed. Particularly since the end of the nineteenth century, the United States has been a politically relevant force in the domestic politics of the Latin American countries. During the Cold War years of conflict with Communist countries (1945–1989) the U.S. government seemed most interested in keeping Latin America out of the enemy camp. Today, however, in the absence of international enemies, U.S. governmental concerns have more to do with free trade, drugs, democracy, and human rights.

The Armed Forces

During the wars for independence, the Spanish American countries developed armies led by a great variety of individuals, including well-born creoles, priests, and people of more humble background. The officers did not come from military academies but rather were self-selected or chosen by other leaders. Few of the officers had previous military training, and the armies were much less professional than the armies we know today.

Following independence, the military element continued as one of the first important power groups. The national army was supposed to be preeminent, and in some countries national military academies were founded in the first quarter century after independence. Yet the national military was challenged by other local or regional armies. The early nineteenth century was a period of limited national integration, with the *patrias chicas* or regional subdivisions of the countries often dominated by local landowners or *caudillos*, men on horseback who had their own private armies. One aspect of the development of Latin America was the struggle between the central government and its army on the one hand and the local caudillos on the other, with the former winning out in most cases. One of the unanswered questions about Latin American politics even at the beginning of the new millennium is the extent to which outlying areas of the countries, in the mountains or jungles, are effectively covered by the laws made in the national capitals.

The development of Brazil varied somewhat from the norm because of the different colonizing power (Portugal) and because of the lack of a struggle for independence. The military first gained prominence in the Paraguayan War (1864–1870). Until 1930 the Brazilian states had powerful militias, in some cases of comparable strength to the national army.

Although Latin American militaries varied in the nineteenth century, a study of them reveals two general themes. First, various militaries, including the national one, became active in politics. At given times they were regional or personal organizations; at others, they were parts of political parties that were the participants in the civil wars frequently waged between rival factions. Second, however, the national military often played the role of a moderating power, staying above factional struggles, preferring that civilians govern, but taking over power temporarily when the civilians could not effectively rule. Although this moderating power did not emerge in all countries, it was seen in most. This was especially the case in Brazil, where, with the abdication of the emperor in 1889, the military became the chief moderator in the system.

As early as the 1830s and 1840s in Argentina and Mexico, and later in the other Latin American countries, national military academies were established. Their goal was to introduce professionalism into the military by requiring graduation rather than elite family connections for officer status. These academies for the most part succeeded in making entry and promotion in the officer corps proceed in a routinized manner, and by the 1950s it was only after a career of some twenty years that a Latin American officer was named a general and would then have potential political power.

Through professionalization, the military career was designed to be a highly specialized one that taught the skills for warfare but eschewed interest in political matters. Being an officer would supposedly absorb all the energy of its members, and this functional expertise would be distinct from that of politicians. Civilians were theoretically to have complete control of the military, which would stay out of politics. This model of professionalism, however, imported from Western Europe and the United States, never took complete root in Latin America. Usually in the absence of strong civilian institutions, the military continued to play politics and to exercise its moderating power—and coups d'état continued.

By the late 1950s and early 1960s a change had occurred in the nature of the role of the military in Latin America. The success of guerrilla revolutions in China, Indochina, Algeria, and Cuba led to a new emphasis on the military's role in counterinsurgency and internal defense functions. In addition, Latin American militaries—encouraged by U.S. military aid—began to assume responsibility for civic-action programs, which assisted civilians in the construction of roads, schools, and other public projects. This led to the military assuming a broader responsibility for nation-building.

The new professionalism, with its emphasis on counterinsurgency, was a product of the Cold War and may have been more in keeping with the Latin American political culture than the old professionalism had been. Military skills—management, administration, nation-building—were no longer viewed as separate or different from civilian skills. The military was to acquire the ability to help solve those national problems that might lead to insurgency, which was, in its very essence, a political rather than an apolitical task. The implication of the new professionalism was that, besides combating active guerrilla factions, the military would take care that social and economic reforms necessary to prevent insurgency were adopted if the civilians proved incapable of doing so. Although the new professionalism was also seen in the developed Western world and in other parts of the Third World, it was particularly prevalent in Latin America. Thus professionalism in Latin America led to more military intervention in politics, not less.

The end result of this process was called "bureaucratic authoritarianism,"[2] the rule of the military institution on a long-term basis. Seen especially in Argentina, Brazil, Chile, Peru, and Uruguay, this new form of military government was of the institution as a whole—not an individual general—and was based on the idea that the military could govern better than civilians. However, the military often governed repressively and violated human rights. The bureaucratic-authoritarian period lasted from the mid-1960s through the late 1970s, when the military in many countries was replaced by elected civilian governments.

Since the 1980s the Latin American militaries have begun transitions to constitutionalism, subservience to civilian control, and support of democratically elected presidents. The transformation has had its difficulties, including supporting a president who dismissed congress and the courts (Peru), playing a key role in overthrowing a president who attempted the same maneuver (Guatemala), putting down coups d'état against chief executives (Venezuela), helping civilian groups to depose unpopular presidents (Ecuador), and failing to intervene although key elements of public opinion and the U.S. ambassador apparently favored getting rid of the elected president (Colombia). In general the Latin American militaries are now in the process of learning a new role, that of "democratic sustainment," or support for civilian democracy, something that the U.S. Army is trying to help them learn.

It has always been difficult to compare the Latin American militaries cross-nationally. Trying to distinguish "civilian" from "military" regimes was similarly a meaningless task at times, or at best a difficult one. Often military personnel temporarily resigned their commissions to take leadership positions in civilian bureaucracies or as government ministers, and frequently they held military and civilian positions at the same time. In some cases an officer resigned his commission, was elected president, and then governed with strong military backing. In almost all instances, coups d'état were not just simple military affairs but rather were supported by groups of civilians as well. It was not unheard of for civilians to take a significant part in the ensuing governments. In fact, sometimes civilians actually drew the military into playing a larger political role. In short, Latin American governments were often coalitions made between certain factions of the militaries and certain factions of civilians in an attempt to control the pinnacles of power of the system.

We suggest that several dimensions of military involvement in politics be considered in the chapters that follow about individual countries. The first is whether the military still forcefully removes chief executives, an activity that in the new millennium has become a thing of the past in most countries. The second is the extent to which the military leaders have a say in nonmilitary matters. Although in the past, generals have protected their large-landowner friends and relatives, that phenomenon might also be passing. The final question is to what extent the moderating power of the military still obligates it to step in and unseat an incompetent president or one who has violated the rules of the game.

Considering this very complicated question, in 2000 Peter Smith classified all Latin American countries into four types:

Table 3.1   Patterns of Civil-Military Relations in 2000

Military control	*Military tutelage*	*Conditional military subordination*	*Civilian control**
None as of 2000 (with the possible exception of Guatemala)	Ecuador	Bolivia	Costa Rica
	El Salvador	Brazil	Mexico
	Guatemala	Chile	Haiti
	Venezuela	Colombia	Panama
		Dominican Republic	Argentina
		Honduras	Uruguay
		Nicaragua	
		Paraguay	
		Peru	

Source: Peter H. Smith, *Democracy in Latin America: Political Change in Comparative Prospective* (New York: Oxford University Press, 2005), 103.

*Grouped in this way because of structural variations.

1. Military control;
2. Military tutelage: in the case of crisis of the civilian government the armed forces supervise civilian authorities and play key roles in decision-making;
3. Conditional military subordination: the armed forces keep careful watch over civilians, protecting military prerogatives; and
4. Civilian control.

How Smith classified the Latin American countries is shown in Table 3.1.[3]

Besides the degree of military influence in the political system, several other interrelated questions should be kept in mind during the reading of the country chapters. These include the reason for military involvement in politics, what the results of military rule were, and how the military was internally divided. The military was one of the traditional pillars of Latin American society, with rights (*fueros*), responsibilities, and legal standing that can be traced back to colonial times. This meant that the military played a different role than it did in the United States. Although this seems to be a matter of the past, the cases of Peru (1992) and Guatemala (1993) show that, in some countries, the generals still play very important roles in politics.

The Roman Catholic Church

All Latin American countries were nominally Catholic, although the form of that religion varied from country to country. The Spanish and Portuguese came to "Christianize the heathens" as well as to seek precious metals. In areas of large Amerindian concentrations, religion became a mixture of pre-Columbian and Roman Catholic beliefs. To a lesser degree, Catholicism later blended with African religions, which also existed on their own in certain areas, especially in Brazil and Cuba. In contrast, religion in the large cities of Latin America was similar to that in the urban centers of the United States and Western Europe. In the more isolated small towns, however, Roman Catholicism was still of fifteenth-century vintage.

The power of the church hierarchy in politics also varies. Traditionally the church was one of the main sectors of Spanish and Portuguese corporate society, with rights and responsibilities in such areas as care for orphans, education, and public morals. During the nineteenth century, the church was one of the three major groups in politics, along with the military and the landed interests. Yet during the same century some laypeople wanted to strip the church of all its temporal power, including its lands. Generally speaking, the conflict over the role of the church had ended in most countries by the first part of the twentieth century.

In the 1960s to the 1980s the church changed, especially if by "church" we mean the top levels of the hierarchy that control the religious and political fortunes of the institution. These transformations were occasioned by the new theologies of the previous hundred years, as expressed through various papal encyclicals, Vatican II, and the conferences of the Latin American bishops at Medellín, Colombia, in 1968 and Puebla, Mexico, in 1979. Significant numbers of bishops (and many more parish priests and members of the various orders) subscribed to what was commonly called liberation theology. This new theology stressed that the church was of and for this world and should take stands against repression and violence, including the "institutionalized violence"—the life-demeaning and -threatening violence—experienced by the poor of the area. Liberation theology also stressed the equality of all believers—laypeople as well as clerics and bishops—as opposed to the former stress on hierarchy. The end result, in some parts of the area, was new, popular-level People's Churches, with lay leadership and only minimal involvement of priests.

It would be a mistake, however, to assume that all, or even most, members of the Latin American clergy ever subscribed to liberation theology. Many believed that the new social doctrine had taken the church more into politics than it should be. Some were concerned with the loss of traditional authority that the erosion of hierarchy had brought. As the various countries of Latin

America differ substantially in church authority and adherence of the bishops to liberation theology, we raise this issue now.

The result of the changes is a clergy that is no longer uniformly conservative, but rather one whose members differ on the role that the church should play in socioeconomic reform and on the nature of hierarchical relations within the church. At one extreme of this conflict is the traditional church elite, usually with social origins in the upper class or aspirations to be accepted by it, still very conservative viewpoints, and close connections to other supporters of the status quo. At the other end of this intraclergy conflict are those priests, of various social backgrounds, who see the major objective of the church being to assist the masses to obtain social justice. In some cases these priests have been openly revolutionary, even fighting in guerrilla wars. Other priests fall between these two extremes of political ideology, and still others favor a relaxing of the rigid hierarchy, thereby giving more discretion to local parish priests.

Liberation theology had its critics outside of Latin America. The Congregation of the Doctrine of the Faith, headed by German Cardinal Ratzinger (now Pope Benedict XVI), strongly opposed certain elements of liberation theology. In both 1984 and 1986 the Vatican officially condemned liberation theology's acceptance of Marxism and armed violence. Leonardo Boff, a Brazilian leader of liberation theology, was suspended and others silenced.

Although some argue that liberation theology weakened as the Marxist world disappeared, it was still present. In mid-2007 the Vatican strongly criticized the work of Jesuit Father Jon Sobrino. Sobrino was born in Spain but had been working in El Salvador since the 1980s. The Congregation for the Doctrine of the Faith warned pastors and all Catholics that there were "erroneous or dangerous propositions" in Father Sobrino's work.[4]

The church still participates in politics to defend its interests, although in most cases its wealth is no longer in land. Certain church interests are still the traditional ones: giving religious instruction in schools and running parochial high schools and universities—the cost of which has traditionally made higher education possible only for people of middle income or higher—and occasionally attempting to prevent divorce legislation and to make purely civil marriage difficult. At times the church has been a major proponent of human rights, especially when military governments deny them. A touchier issue has been that of birth control, and in most cases the Latin American hierarchies have fought artificial methods. In the face of the population explosion, however, many church officials have assisted in family-planning clinics, turned their heads when governments have promoted artificial methods of birth control, and occasionally even assisted in those governmental efforts.

Some analysts feel the Roman Catholic Church in Latin America is no longer a major contender. They argue that on certain issues its sway is still considerable, but that the church is no longer as influential politically as the army, the wealthy elites, or the U.S. Embassy. Modernization, urbanization, and secularism have also taken their toll on church attendance and the political power of the church. On the contrary, other analysts, pointing to the liberation theology of People's Churches, argue that the church or individual clerics connected to it are powerful as never before.

One of the most interesting phenomena in Latin America in recent decades has been the explosive growth of Protestant religious groups. In some countries, Protestants number upward of 25 to 35 percent of the population, and in Guatemala a Protestant general even became dictator for a time. The fastest growing of these sects were the evangelical Christians, not the older mainline churches. Protestantism was associated with being in the middle class, thus making it socially attractive, and was identified with a strong work ethic, obliging its members to work hard and save. Until recently, however, the Protestant groups have generally not become politically active.

Large Landowners

In all the countries of Latin America, save Costa Rica and Paraguay, the colonial period led to the establishment of a group of large landowners who had received their lands as royal grants. With the coming of independence these *latifundistas* (owners of large land tracts called *latifundios*) were more powerful than before, developing into one of the three major power groups of nineteenth-century politics. This was not to say that they operated monolithically: In some cases they were divided against each other.

In recent times such rifts have remained among the large landowners, usually along the lines of crop production. They might disagree on a governmental policy favoring livestock-raising to the detriment of crop-planting. However, the major conflict has been between those who have large tracts of land and the many landless peasants. In those circumstances the various groups of large landowners tend to coalesce. In some cases there is an umbrella organization to bring all of the various producer organizations together formally, while in others the coalition is much more informal.

In the 1960s the pressures for land reform were considerable, both from landless peasants and from foreign and domestic groups who saw this type of reform as a way to achieve social justice and to avoid Castro-like revolutions. In some countries, such as Mexico, land reform had previously come by revolution, while in others, such as Venezuela, a good bit of land had been distributed by the government to the landless. In still others, the power of the landed, in coalition with other status quo groups, led to the mere appearance of land reform rather than the reality. In many of the Latin American countries, especially those in which the amount of arable land is limited and where the population explosion has led to higher person-land ratios, the issue of breaking up large estates will continue for the foreseeable future. Given the historic power of the landed elite, change is likely to be slow in the absence of something approaching a social revolution.

Since the 1960s, with Latin America rapidly urbanizing and in some cases even industrializing, the rural issue has become less important. The traditional landowners still dominate in some countries, but in others power has passed to newer commercial and industrial elites. Although with large percentages of the population moving to the cities, land reform may still be necessary in some areas, many of the main social issues have become urban rather than rural.

Other Major Interest Groups

Commercial and Industrial Elites

Although not part of the traditional oligarchy, commercial elites have existed in Latin America since independence. One of the early political conflicts was between those who wanted free trade (the commercial elites and allied landed interests producing crops for export) and those who wanted protection of nascent industry (industrial elites with allied landed groups not producing for export). In recent decades the strength of these commercial and industrial groups has steadily grown.

With the exception of Colombia, the real push for industrialization in Latin America did not come until the Great Depression and World War II, when Latin America was cut off from trade with the industrialized world. Before those crises, industrial goods from England and the United States were cheaper than locally produced goods, even with the transportation costs and import duties.

Between the mid-1930s and the mid-1980s, Latin American countries experienced industrialization of the import substitution type—that is, producing goods that formerly were imported from the industrialized countries. This was the case in light consumer goods; some consumer durables, including assembly of North American and European automobiles; and some other heavy industries such as cement and steel. Because import substitution necessitated increased foreign trade to import capital goods, there was no longer much conflict between commercial and industrial elites: Expanded trade and industrialization now go together.

Since the 1980s the push of neoliberal presidents in Latin America has been for more foreign commerce in a world with lowered or altogether nonexistent trade barriers. In this "internationalization" of the Latin American economies, foreign trade is of utmost importance. Hence so are the commercial elites. Mexico entered a free trade association with the United States and Canada in 1994 through the North American Free Trade Agreement (NAFTA), Central America and the Dominican Republic in 2005 through the Central American Free Trade Association (CAFTA), and the goal is to eventually have a free trade association covering all of the Americas, all the way from Alaska to Tierra del Fuego.

A complicating factor in the consideration of the industrial elite is their relationship with the landed elite. In some countries, such as Argentina, the early industrialists were linked to the landed groups; later, individuals who began as industrialists then invested in land. The result was two intertwined groups, a marriage of older landed and newer moneyed wealth, with only vague boundaries separating them and some families and individuals straddling the line. Further, all these groups were opposed to agrarian reform.

Industrialists and commercial elites are highly organized in various chambers of commerce, industrial associations, and the like; are strategically located in major cities of Latin America; and generally favor a status quo that profits them. Thus they are often the driving forces in Latin American economic development. For this reason and because they are frequently represented in high official circles, no matter what government is in control, they are very powerful. Neoliberalism and globalism have made these groups even more essential to the functioning of the economy, and hence also to the political system.

The Middle Sectors

Although the Latin American countries began independence with a basically two-class system, there have always been individuals who fell statistically into the middle ranges, being neither very rich nor abjectly poor. These few individuals during the nineteenth century were primarily artisans and shopkeepers and, later, doctors and lawyers. The emergence of a larger middle sector, then, was a twentieth-century phenomenon, associated with urbanization, technological advances, industrialization, and the expansion of public education and the role of the government.

All of these changes necessitated a large number of white-collar, managerial workers. New teachers and government bureaucrats constituted part of this sector, as did office workers in private businesses. In addition, small businesses grew, particularly in the service sector of the economy. Many of these new nonmanual professions have been organized: teachers' associations, small-business associations, lawyers' associations, organizations of governmental bureaucrats, and so forth. Military officers, university students, political party officials, and even union and peasant-group leaders are usually considered middle class.

The people who filled the new middle-sector jobs were the product of so-cial mobility, with some coming from the lower class and others as "fallen aristocrats" from the upper class. They lacked a prolonged, common historical experience. This, together with their numerous and heterogeneous occupa-tions, temporarily impeded the formation of a sense of common identity as members of a middle class. Indeed, in some of the countries of Latin America this identification has yet to emerge. In Latin America the middle-class ideal is still to be a part of "society"—preferably high society.

In those countries of Latin America in which a large middle-sector group has emerged, certain generalizations about its political behavior can be made. In the early stages of political activities, coalitions tended to be formed with groups from the lower classes against the more traditional and oligarchic groups in power. Major goals included expanded suffrage, the promotion of urban growth and economic development, a greater role for public education, increased industrialization, and social-welfare programs.

In the later political evolution of the middle sectors the tendency has been to side with the established order against rising mass or populist movements. In some cases the middle-class movements allied with landowners, industri-alists, and the church against their working-class partners of earlier years; in other cases, when the more numerous lower class seemed ready to take power on its own, the middle sectors were instrumental in fomenting a middle-class military coup to prevent "premature democratization"[5] (a democratic system that the middle sectors could not control). Over the years, then, middle-class movements changed dramatically.

Because the status of the middle class varies greatly in Latin America, a number of factors should be considered when reading the chapters about indi-vidual countries, including the size of the middle-income group, its cohesion and relationships with political parties, and the degree of self-identification as members of a "middle class." Only time will tell if the middle sectors will act differently because of the years of bureaucratic authoritarianism, serve as a new, invigorated social base for democracy, or continue to ape and imitate the upper class and thus perpetuate an essentially two-class and polarized social structure. While in the 1990s the middle class favored stability at all costs and saw democracy as the best way of achieving and continuing stability, in the new millennium many have become impatient with the failure of democracy to produce better economic conditions.

Labor Unions

From its inception, organized labor in Latin America has been highly political. Virtually all important trade union groups of the area have been closely asso-ciated with a political party, strong leader, or government. On some occasions labor unions have grown independently until they were co-opted or re-pressed. In other cases labor unions have owed their origins directly to the efforts of a party, leader, or government.

Three characteristics of the Latin American economies have favored partisan unionism. First, unions came relatively early in the economic development of the region—in most cases earlier than in the United States and Western Europe. Second, the labor pool of employables has been much larger than the number who can get the relatively well-paid jobs in industry. An employer in that situation could almost always find people to replace striking workers unless the workers were protected by a party or the government. Further, Latin American unionism was influenced by ideological currents that came from Southern Europe, including anarchist and Marxist orientations. Finally, inflation has been a problem in Latin America in recent decades, making it important for unions to win the support of other political groups in the continual renegotiation of contracts to obtain higher salaries, which often need governmental approval.

The Latin American legal tradition required that unions be officially recognized by the government before they could collectively bargain. If a group could not obtain or retain this legal standing, it had little power. In addition, labor legislation varied greatly, including codes making it mandatory that labor organizers be employed full time by the industry that they were organizing, thus limiting the power of unions lacking leaders who were paid full salaries to spend part of the working day in union activities. This was only one of the many governmental restrictions placed on labor unions. In general, there is now a movement away from corporate or state control of unions toward greater freedom of association, and often conflict arises between the state and the free unions.

Although some union organizations were co-opted by the state, others remained outside the system. Key questions to consider when reading the country chapters include the extent to which workers are organized, how the labor code is used to prevent or facilitate worker organization, the nature of the relationships between labor and the political parties or between labor and the government, and the extent to which unions have been co-opted or repressed. Are the unions a declining or growing interest in Latin America?

Peasants

The term "peasant" refers to many different kinds of people in Latin America. Some prefer the Spanish term *campesinos* (people who live in the *campo*, the countryside) rather than the English term with its European-based connotations. The major groups of campesinos, who vary in importance from country to country, include indigenous groups who speak only their native language or who are bilingual in that language and Spanish; workers on the traditional hacienda tilling the fields in return for wages or part of the crops, with the owner as a patrón to care for the family or, more frequently, a manager-patrón who represents the absentee owner; workers on modern plantations, receiving wages but remaining outside of the older patrón-client relationship; persons with a small landholding (*minifundio*), legally held, of such a size that a bare existence is possible; persons who cultivate small plots, with no legal claim, perhaps moving every few years after the slash-and-burn method and the lack of crop rotation deplete the soil; and persons who have been given a small plot of land to work by a landowner in exchange for work on the large estate.

What all of these campesinos have in common, in the context of the extremely inequitable distribution of arable lands in Latin America, is a marginal existence due to their small amount of land or income and a high degree of insecurity due to their uncertain claims to the lands they cultivate. It was estimated in 1961 that over five million very small farms (below thirty acres, or twelve hectares) occupied only 3.7 percent of the land, while at the other extreme 100,000 holdings of more than 1,500 acres (607 hectares) took up some 65 percent of the land. Three decades later, the situation had changed little. At least eighty million people still lived on small landholdings with insufficient land to earn a minimum subsistence, or they worked as agricultural laborers with no land at all. For many of these rural people their only real chance of breaking out of this circle of poverty was by moving to an urban area, where they faced another—in some ways even worse—culture of poverty. For those who remained on the land, unless there was a dramatic restructuring of ownership, the present subhuman existence was likely to continue. Moreover, as commercial agriculture for export increased in many countries, the campesinos were increasingly shoved off the fertile lands into the sterile hillsides, where their ability to subsist has become even more precarious.

Rural peasant elements have long been active in politics, but only recently as independent, organized interest groups. The traditional political structure of the countryside was one in which participation in national politics meant taking part in the patronage system. The local patrónes, besides expecting work on the estate from the campesino, expected certain political behavior. In some countries this meant that the campesino belonged to the same political party as the patrón, voted for that party on election day, and, if necessary, served as cannon fodder in its civil wars. In other countries the national party organizations never reached the local levels, and restrictive suffrage laws prevented the peasants from participation in elections. In both patterns, for the peasants there was no such thing as national politics, only local politics, which might or might not have national party labels attached to the local person or groups in power.

This traditional system still exists in many areas of Latin America. Since the 1950s, however, signs of agrarian unrest and political mobilization have been more and more evident. In many cases major agrarian movements were organized by urban interests, namely political parties, especially those of the Marxist left. Some of these peasant movements have been openly revolutionary, seeking to reform and improve the land tenure system and to significantly change the entire power structure of the nation. They have employed strategies that include the illegal seizure of land, the elimination of landowners, and armed defense of the gains thus achieved. We could call these movements ones of revolutionary agrarianism. Less radical were the movements that sought to reform the social order partially through the elimination of a few of the most oppressive effects of the existing power structure that weighs on the peasant subculture, but doing so without threatening the power structure as such.

Although the percentage of campesinos has declined in most Latin American countries, over the past twenty years peasant organizations have become stronger—playing central roles in changing governments, determining national agendas, and fighting against international trade agreements. While urban unions have weakened, peasant movements have become increasingly central in movements of social change.[6]

The United States

Another important power element in Latin American politics is the United States. This influence usually has been seen in at least three interrelated ways: U.S. governmental representatives, U.S.-based private business, and U.S.-dominated international agencies. At times these groups work in harmony, and at times they operate at cross-purposes. The U.S. government has been interested in the area since Latin America's independence. Its first concern, that the new nations not fall under the control of European powers, led to the Monroe Doctrine in 1823. Originally a defensive statement, the doctrine was later changed through various corollaries to a more aggressive one, telling the Latin Americans that they could not sell lands to nonhemispheric governments or businesses (if the locations were strategic) and that the United States would intervene in Latin America to collect debts owed to nonhemispheric powers (the Roosevelt Corollary).

At various times the U.S. government has set standards that must be met before full diplomatic recognition was accorded to a Latin American nation. This de jure recognition policy, most memorable in the Wilson, early Kennedy, and Carter administrations, favored elected democratic governments, exclusion of the military from government, and a vision of human rights to be applied in Latin America. At other times the United States has pursued a de facto recognition policy, according full diplomatic standing to any government with effective control of its nation's territory.

Whatever recognition policy was followed, the U.S. ambassador to a Latin American country usually has had impressive powers. One ambassador to pre-Castro Cuba testified that he was second only to the president in influence in the country. This ambassadorial power has typically been used to support or defeat governments, focus governmental policy of the Latin American countries in certain directions, and assist U.S.-based corporations in the various countries. In Central America during the 1980s a number of U.S. ambassadors played this strong proconsular role, as did the ambassador to Colombia during the government of Ernesto Samper (1994–1998) because of the president's suspected ties to drug groups.

From their early beginnings, particularly in agribusiness (especially sugar and bananas), U.S.-based corporations in Latin America have grown dramatically. In addition to agribusiness, corporations later entered the extractive field (petroleum, copper, coal, iron ore), retailing, the services industry (accounting firms, computer outfits), and communications (telephones, telegraphs, computers). The most recent kind of U.S. corporation introduced to Latin America was the export-platform variety. This is a company that takes advantage of the low wages in a country to produce mass-market products—such as pocket calculators in Mexico or baseballs in Haiti—mainly for export to the industrialized world.

Furthermore, U.S. corporations in Latin America often enter into the politics of their host countries. Some of the instances have been flagrant: bribing public officials to keep taxes low or threatening to cut off a country's products if certain policies were approved by its government. However, most political activities of U.S. corporations currently are much less dramatic. Almost always, Latin Americans in the host countries buy stock in the U.S. corporations and hold high managerial positions in them. In many cases, U.S. businesses purchase Latin American corporations, the leaders of which then work for the new owners. The result is that the U.S. corporation develops contacts, obligations, and political influence similar to those possessed by domestic interest groups. In the 1980s, however, there were some indications that the era of large U.S. corporate holdings and hence influence in Latin America might be in decline. Many U.S. corporations, as a result of the recession in Latin America and the debt crisis, pulled up stakes, withdrew their capital, and moved on to more profitable and stable areas. Yet by the end of the 1980s the business climate had improved: Latin American governments rescinded restrictions on maximum profits and repatriation. Once again U.S. capital began to flow into the area. In the 1990s, as Latin American economies recovered, massive U.S. capital again flowed into the area.

Most foreign-aid and international lending organizations have been dominated historically by the United States. These agencies, especially active during the 1960s, when aid to Latin America began in large quantities, include the U.S. Agency for International Development (AID), which administers most of U.S. foreign aid; the World Bank; the International Monetary Fund (IMF); the Inter-American Development Bank, and a variety of others. The World Bank and the IMF were international agencies, results of post–World War II agreements between the countries of the West. However, the representation of the United States on the governing boards of both has been so large, which is based on the amount of money donated to the agencies, and the convergence of interests of the two with those of the U.S. government has been so great, that they can be considered U.S.-oriented groups. So can the Inter-American Development Bank (IADB). Although urged to do so by Latin American leaders who wanted a lending agency less dominated by the United States, in effect the IADB cannot lend to countries if the U.S. government does not want it to. Because economic development has been a central goal of the Latin American states for the past fifty years, loans for that development have come predominantly from AID, the World Bank, and the IADB. Furthermore, those loans were contingent many times on a monetary policy judged healthy by the IMF, so the officials of these four groups have much influence in the day-to-day policies of the governments of the area.

This power of the lending agencies was probably greatest during the 1960s and then again during the debt crisis of the 1980s. AID had most leverage or "conditionality" during the Alliance for Progress. This foreign-aid program, initiated by the Kennedy administration, attempted to change Latin America dramatically in a decade. Even though it failed, it did lead to large loans from the U.S. government, substantial progress in some fields, and a great deal of influence for the local AID head in the domestic politics of some Latin American countries. Some AID representatives sat in on cabinet meetings and wrote speeches for and gave advice to the local officials with whom they worked, while others largely ran the agencies or even ministries of the host government to which they were assigned.

However, the Alliance for Progress was terminated by the Nixon administration. Further, the power of the World Bank waned in the wake of the crisis of the industrialized economies of the West following the Arab oil embargo of 1973–1974 and with the growing power of OPEC. It was then that the private banks, which were recycling petrodollars, filled many of the needs of the Latin American countries. However, with the debt crisis of the 1980s the IMF and its Bretton Woods partner, the World Bank, regained much of their lost power.

In the meantime the economies of Latin America were undergoing crisis while protectionist measures rose in the importing nations. The Latin American nations were clamoring for access to U.S. markets, and they were likely to be partially successful in that quest. The U.S. government also initiated a new massive assistance program for Central America and the Caribbean designed to restore solvency and preserve stability. More recently, foreign aid has dwindled while direct private investment has multiplied.

The influence of U.S.-directed and-oriented groups—diplomatic, business, foreign-assistance—in Latin America is considerable. This is not to say that the power has been equal in all the Latin American countries. When a Latin American country is strategically important to the United States and when U.S. private investors have established a large investment in the economy (e.g., Cuba before Castro), U.S. elements are extremely powerful in domestic Latin politics. This does not mean, however, that the United States cannot have considerable influence in domestic politics in distant countries with relatively little private investment by U.S. corporations, as the example of Allende's Chile demonstrates. Nonetheless, with the end of the Cold War, U.S. foreign policy interest in Latin America, with the exception of a few countries, has waned: Private transactions are more important than official ones.

New Groups

Many new groups have appeared in Latin America in recent decades. Three of particular importance are indigenous groups, women's groups, and nongovernmental organizations (NGOs).

Indigenous Groups

Indigenous peoples constitute about 8 percent of the total population of Latin America, or an estimated forty million people. In some four hundred distinct groups, they are concentrated in southern Mexico, parts of Central America, and the central Andes of South America. In these states they constitute between 10 to 70 percent of the population. Some individual language groups have more than one million members. A dozen groups have more than a quarter million members, comprising some 73 percent of the total indigenous population of the region. Finally, two groups have less than one thousand members.

In the 1970s Amerindian populations in Latin America began to mobilize politically in unprecedented ways in order to protect their lands and cultures from the increasing influence of multinational companies, colonists, the state, and other intruders. In the 1980s they placed a greater emphasis on the recuperation of ethnic identities and the construction of a pan-indigenous cultural identity. In ways that vary throughout the region, Latin American indigenous peoples share the common goal of ending ethnic discrimination and the assimilationist policies of Latin American governments.

Contemporary Latin American indigenous organizations seek equal and legitimate status for their cultures, forms of social organization, laws, as well as the means to facilitate and control their economic development. Their ultimate goal is the transformation of what they view to be a discriminatory, homogeneous state into a "plurinational state," one whose institutions reflect the cultural diversity of society. In the 1990s seven Latin American states—Bolivia, Colombia, Ecuador, Mexico, Nicaragua, Peru, and Paraguay—recognized a milder version of this claim, declaring their societies "pluricultural and multiethnic." At the same time many individuals of indigenous background continue to follow the traditional assimilationist strategy of seeking to integrate themselves into Hispanic (i.e., Catholic, Spanish- or Portuguese-speaking, Western) culture.

The main component of rising indigenous nationalism is the struggle for territorial, political, economic, and cultural autonomy. Until 1987 only the Kuna of Panama enjoyed what could be described as territorial and political autonomy. In 1987 the Nicaraguan government established two multiethnic autonomous regions to accommodate claims of the Miskitu and other smaller groups, who had joined the anti-Sandinista counterrevolutionary guerrilla movement supported by the United States. Although the autonomous regions were largely a failure in terms of indigenous peoples' aspirations, their establishment inspired indigenous organizations throughout Latin America to make similar claims.

Only Colombia's indigenous population has achieved politico-territorial autonomy. The 1991 Colombian constitution elevated indigenous reserves (*resguardos*) to the status of municipal governments; recognized indigenous traditional leaders as public authorities and, with some restrictions, indigenous customary law as public and binding; and provided guaranteed representation in the national senate. The governments of Bolivia, Ecuador, Guatemala, and Mexico considered some type of politico-territorial autonomy arrangements following constitutional reforms or peace agreements with armed groups, but this process petered out over time and concluded in the 1990s.[7]

The most notable cases of members of indigenous groups taking part in national politics were in Peru in 2001, where Alejandro Toledo was elected president, and in Bolivia in 2006, when Evo Morales was elected president. While the Toledo presidency was troubled (see chapter 10), it is too soon to predict how Morales will do (see chapter 14).

Women's Groups

There is little doubt that women in Latin America are making progress in ascending to leadership positions in government, politics, and civil society. A 1999 study concluded that, although their numbers remain low, the percentage of women in national congresses and cabinets in Latin America (15 and 11 percent, respectively) is second only to the Nordic countries of Europe (36 and 35 percent) and is higher in the congress but lower in cabinets than in the United States (12 and 21 percent).[8]

More politicized women's groups emerged in the 1970s and 1980s, playing a prominent role in the struggles against authoritarian rule, thereby raising hopes that the return to democracy would generate greater opportunities for women in the region. The consolidation of democracy was expected to promote greater participation of women in the formulation and execution of laws governing their lives. From 1994 to 2004 women's participation rose, on average, from 9 to 14 percent in the executive branch (in ministerial positions), 5 to 13 percent in the senate, and 8 to 15 percent in the lower house or unicameral parliaments.[9] In that decade women's presence in the public spheres of the economy and society also grew. Such growth is a reflection of social changes such as women's entry into the labor force, rising educational levels, and changing attitudes about the role of women. Most notably, four women were elected presidents in their countries: Violeta Barrios de Chamorro in Nicaragua in 1990, Mireya Moscoso de Gruber in Panama in 1999, Michelle Bachelet in Chile in 2006, and Cristina Fernández de Kirchner in Argentina in 2007.

Figures on women's representation in politics show that their opportunities to exercise leadership are greater outside the main centers of power, in the lower levels of organizational hierarchy, outside the capital city area, and in less powerful governmental agencies. For example, women's presence in the judicial branch of government shows that they comprise 45 percent of the trial judges but only 20 percent at the appellate court level, and virtually zero at the supreme court level.

One important consequence of women's organizing has been the adoption of quota laws, intended to increase women's representation in political office. After pressure from organized women's groups, Argentina, Bolivia, Brazil, Costa Rica, the Dominican Republic, Ecuador, Panama, and Peru have passed national laws requiring political parties to reserve 20 to 40 percent of candidacies for women. Of course, that women are nominated does not necessarily mean that they are elected. Colombia even enacted a law making it mandatory that mayors have women as one-third of their appointed officials, but it is a law that is not always followed.

Despite the growth of women's representation, the women's movement has appeared to some observers to be increasingly fragmented and to have lost its visibility and capacity for political intervention. One reason for this is the weakening of cross-class links between middle-class feminists and working-class women's groups. In an important sense this is a consequence of democracy: As the access of middle-class women to power has increased during democracy, their connections with the lower classes seems to have grown weaker. Another split is between more traditional, social service–oriented women's groups and their often more militant, younger, feminist sisters.

In conclusion, the obstacles to women's full participation in Latin American democracies and economies stem from women's weaker social position, traditional gender roles and cultural expectations and stereotypes built around these roles, and blatant sex discrimination. Few Latin American countries have made efforts to make motherhood and work compatible, and no Latin American country has a comprehensive child-care policy. Although most countries have laws that require businesses that employ twenty or more women to have on-site day-care facilities, these laws are rarely enforced. Pregnancy discrimination is widespread in the region, some companies requiring a pregnancy test or a sterilization certificate as a condition of employment. Some fire women once they become pregnant. Although both actions are against the law, once again the laws are seldom enforced. Although cultural changes coming from women's improving position will help erode such discriminatory barriers, this is likely to happen only in the very long run.

Nongovernmental Organizations

Another newer type of group is the nongovernmental organizations (NGOs), which are increasingly important actors in Latin American politics. Although some are specific for individual countries, others are based on a general theme and have offices in many Latin American countries. Some NGOs are transnational, with headquarters in one country and activities in many countries. For instance, Amnesty International, the Environmental Defense Fund, and the Red Cross are transnational NGOs that have influenced recent events in Latin America. Local NGOs are shaping contemporary politics, too. For example, NGOs are providing community services in Mexico, raising racial consciousness in Brazil, extending credit to poor people in Colombia, defending indigenous peoples in Bolivia, and asserting women's rights in Argentina. Unlike interest groups, NGOs do not focus their activities exclusively on governments. They also work to change the policies of international institutions such as the World Bank, the practices of both private businesses as well as entire industries, and the behavior of individuals and society as a whole.[10]

Political Parties

In Latin America, political parties have often been only one set of groups among several, probably no more—and perhaps less—important than the army or the economic oligarchy. Elections were not the only legitimate route to power, nor were the parties themselves particularly strong or well organized. They were important actors in the political process in some of the more democratic countries, representing the chief means to gain high office. But frequently in other countries the parties were peripheral to the main focal points of power and the electoral arena was considered only one among several. Many Latin Americans have viewed political parties as divisive elements, and hence they are not held in high esteem. This increasingly seems to be the case in recent years, which is evident as candidates use the mass media rather than parties to get elected.

Many of the groups described earlier in this chapter have often joined political parties in their pursuit of governmental power. As a result there have been a myriad of political parties in the history of Latin America. Indeed, someone once quipped that to form a political party all you needed was a president, vice president, secretary-treasurer, and rubber stamp—but if times were bad, you could do without the vice president and the secretary-treasurer! Peter Smith shows that during the period of democracy since 1978, there are more political parties in most Latin American countries than during the 1940–1977 period.[11] Nevertheless, there have been certain characteristics common to parties, although the country chapters that follow show great national variation.

The first parties were usually founded by elite groups in competition with other factions of the elite. Mass demands played only a small role, although campesinos were sometimes mobilized by the party leaders, often to vote as they were instructed or to serve as cannon fodder. In many cases the first cleavage was between individuals in favor of free trade, federalism, and anticlericalism (the Liberals) and those who favored protectionism for nascent industry, centralism, and clericalism (the Conservatives). In most countries these original party divisions have long since disappeared, replaced by other cleavages.

With accelerating social and economic change in most countries of Latin America, the emergence of new social strata in the 1920s and 1930s led to the founding of new political parties. Some of these attracted the growing middle sectors, who were quite reformist in the early years but later changed as they became part of the system. In other cases new parties were more radical, calling for a basic restructuring of society and including elements from the working classes. Some of these originally radical parties were of international inspiration, and most of the countries have had Communist and socialist parties of differing effectiveness and legality. Other radical parties were primarily national ones, albeit with ideological inspiration traceable to Marxism.

One such party, founded in 1923 by the Peruvian Víctor Raúl Haya de la Torre, was the American Popular Revolutionary Alliance (APRA). Although APRA purported to be the beginning of a new international association of likeminded, democratic-left individuals in Latin America, this goal was never fully reached. At the same time, inspired by Haya and APRA, a number of similar national parties were founded by young Latin Americans. The most successful APRA-like party was Democratic Action (AD) in Venezuela, but many of the same programs have been advocated by numerous other parties of this type, including the Party of National Liberation (PLN) in Costa Rica and the National Revolutionary Movement (MNR) in Bolivia, as well as parties in Paraguay, the Dominican Republic, Guatemala, Honduras, and Argentina. Only in Venezuela and Costa Rica did the APRA-like parties come to power more than temporarily, albeit in a much less radical form. They favored liberal democracy, rapid reform, and economic growth. In most cases the APRA-like parties were led by members of the middle sectors, and they received much of their electoral support from middle- and lower-class ranks. APRA did come to power in Peru in 1986, although founder Haya was no longer living.

A newer group of political parties was the Christian-Democratic ones, particularly successful in Chile, Venezuela, Costa Rica, Nicaragua, and El Salvador. These parties often call for fundamental reforms but are guided by church teachings and papal encyclicals rather than Marx or Engels, even though they are nondenominational and open to all. The nature of the ideology of these parties varies from country to country.

Other parties in Latin America have been based on the leadership of one or a few persons, and hence do not fit into the neat party spectrum just described. Quite often the "man on horseback" was more important than the program of a party. This tradition of the caudillo was seen in Brazil, where Getúlio Vargas founded not one but two official political parties; in Ecuador, where personalistic parties have been strong contenders for the presidency; and in Communist Cuba, where in the 1960s the party was more Castroist than Communist. In Venezuela former military coup leader Hugo Chávez personalized not only a presidency but also an entire change of government structure.

The system of co-optation further complicates the attempt at classification. How is one to classify a political party, traditional in origin, that includes both large landowners and the peasants tied to them, as well as trade union members organized by the party and with the assistance of parts of the clergy? How does one classify a party such as the Mexican Institutional Revolutionary party (PRI), which until the mid-1990s made a conscious effort to co-opt and include all politically relevant sectors of the society?

With the increasing number of popularly elected governments in Latin America in the 1990s, political parties generally became more important than before. Democracy only exists if there is real competition between candidates, and throughout the world political parties have been the organizations that have presented such rival candidates. However, in some Latin American countries (e.g., Peru and Venezuela) political parties are held in such low esteem that attempts have been made to have democracy without parties. In addition, as pointed out in Chapter 5, political parties have less importance when countries move to "delegative democracy."

In addition to the traditional questions posed about parties in Latin America—the number of major parties, their programs and policies, the nature of electoral laws, the relationships between parties and the military—we need to ask questions posed all over the world in democracies. How are parties funded? Do they come up with programs and follow them after the elections? Are voters well informed about political party activities by the mass media? Are those countries that are trying to have democracy without parties having any success?

Conclusions and Implications

The preceding discussion has indicated that there have been many politically relevant groups in Latin America and that they use various means to secure and retain political power. Yet at least two other themes should be introduced that tend to complicate the picture.

First, it should be noted that the urban poor—outside the labor unions—have not been included in the discussion. This shows one of the biases of the system. Traditionally, a necessary first step in attaining political relevance is being organized. This means that potential groups, especially poorly educated and geographically dispersed ones like the peasants and the urban poor, face difficulties becoming politically relevant because they have difficulty organizing themselves or being organized from the outside. Although they are often numerically the largest, then, these tend to be the weakest groups in politics.

Second, not all politically relevant groups fall into the neat categories of this chapter. Anthony Leeds's research in Brazil has shown (at least in small towns, probably larger cities, and even perhaps the whole nation) a politically more relevant series of groups to be the patronage and family-based *panelinhas* ("little saucepans").[12] The same kind of informal family-based networks exist in other countries. These groups are composed of individuals with common interests but different occupations—say, a doctor, a large landowner, surely a lawyer, and a governmental official. The panelinha at the local level controls and endeavors to establish contacts with the panelinha at the state level, which might have contacts with a national panelinha. Of course, at the local level there are rival panelinhas, with contacts with likeminded ones at the state level, with contacts in the national patronage system as well. As is generally the case with such patrimonial-type relations, all interactions (except those within the panelinhas themselves) are vertical, and one level of panelinha must take care to ally with the winning one at the next higher level if it wants to have political power.

Similar research in other countries has revealed a parallel pattern of informal, elitist, familial, patronage politics. Whether called the panelinha system as in Brazil or the camarilla system as in Mexico, the process and dynamics are the same. The aspiring politician connects himself with an aspiring politician at a higher level, who is connected with an aspiring . . . and so forth on up to an aspiring candidate for the presidency. If the person in question becomes president, the various levels of camarillas prosper. If he remains powerful without becoming president, the camarillas continue functioning in expectation of what will take place at the next presidential election. If, however, the aspiring candidate is disgraced, is dismissed from the official party, or dies, then the whole system of various levels of camarillas connected with him disintegrates. The camarilla system operates outside of but overlapping the formal structure of groups and parties described here.

This discussion of panelinhas and camarillas raises the question of whether U.S.-style interest groups and political parties are operating and are important in Latin America, or if they are operating in the same way. The answer is: They are and they aren't. In the larger and better-institutionalized systems, the parties and interest groups are often important and function not unlike their North American or European counterparts. However, in the less-institutionalized, personalistic countries of Ecuador, Paraguay, and Central America (and even behind the scenes in the larger ones), family groups, cliques, clan alliances, and patronage networks frequently are more important, often disguised behind the appearance of partisan or ideological dispute. One must be careful therefore not to minimize the importance of a functional, operational party and interest-group system in some countries, while also recognizing that in others it is often the less formal network through which politics is carried out.

4

Government Machinery, the Role of the State, and Public Policy

Neither the classic Marxian categories nor the theory of liberalism gave more than secondary importance to the role of the state. In the Marxian paradigm the state or governmental system was viewed as part of the super-structure that was shaped, if not determined, by the underlying structure of class relations. In the liberal model the state was generally conceived as a ref-eree, umpiring the competition among the interest groups while not itself participating in the game—a kind of "black box" intermediary into which the "inputs" of the system go in the form of competing interests and pressures and from which come "outputs" or public policies. Neither of these two clas-sic models, however, adequately explains the Latin American systems.

In Latin America the state historically held an importance that it lacks in these classic models. The state was viewed as a powerful and independent agency in its own right, above and frequently autonomous from the class and interest-group struggle. Whether in socialist regimes such as Cuba's or capi-talist ones like Brazil's, it was the state and its central leadership that largely determined the shape of the system and its developmental directions.

The state did not merely reflect the class structure but rather, through its control of economic and political resources, in fact shaped the class system. The state was viewed as the prime regulator, coordinator, and pacesetter of the en-tire national system, the apex of the Latin American pyramid from which pa-tronage, wealth, power, and programs flowed. The critical importance of the state in the Latin American nations helped explain why the competition for control of it was so intense and sometimes violent.

Related to this was the contrasting way citizens of North America and Latin America tended to view government. In North America, government has usually been considered something of a necessary evil requiring elaborate checks and balances. Political theory in Iberia and Latin America, in contrast, viewed government as good, natural, and necessary for the welfare of society. If government was good, there was little reason to limit or put checks and balances on it. Hence, before we fall into the trap of condemning Latin America for its powerful autocratic executives, subservient parliaments, and weak local government, we must remember the different assumptions on which the Latin American systems are based.

With the neoliberal changes of the 1990s and at present, there has likewise been a change in the procedures about which much of Latin American politics revolve. The fundamental issues are still who controls the state apparatus and the immense power, patronage, and funds at its disposal as well as the ongoing efforts of the state or strong presidents to expand their power. Now, however, there are also issues of how much of the old corporatist structure will be retained, if any; how neoliberal or civil society dominates the political and economic systems; and how the historically powerful role of the state can be harmonized with the new demands for limited government, privatization, and democracy.

The Theory of the State: Constitutions and Legal Systems

After achieving independence early in the nineteenth century, the Latin American nations faced a severe legitimacy crisis. Monarchy was a possibility (and some nations did consider or experiment briefly with monarchical rule), but Latin America had just struggled through years of independence wars to rid itself of the Spanish imperial yoke, during which monarchy had been discredited. Liberalism and republicanism were attractive and seemed the wave of the future, but Latin America had no prior experience with liberal or republican rule.

The solution was ingenious, though often woefully misunderstood. The new nations of Latin America moved to adopt liberal and democratic forms, while at the same time preserving many of the organic, elitist, and authoritarian principles of the colonial tradition. The liberal and democratic forms not only provided goals and aspirations toward which society could strive, but they also helped present a progressive picture to the outside world. But these principles were circumscribed by a series of measures, authoritarian in content, that were truer to the realities and history of the area and to its existing oligarchic power relationships.

Virtually all the Latin American constitutions have provided for the historical three-part division of powers among executive, legislative, and judicial branches. In practice, however, the three powers are not coequal and were not intended to be. The executive is constitutionally given extensive powers to bypass the legislature, and judicial review until recently has been largely outside the Latin American legal tradition. The same kinds of apparent contradictions exist in other areas. Although one part of the constitution may be devoted to civilian institutions and the traditional three branches of government, another may give the armed forces a higher-order role to protect the nation, preserve internal order, and prevent internal disruption. However, the legislative branch is now increasing in power in many countries.

The same is true of human rights. Even though all the Latin American constitutions contain long lists of human and political rights, these same constitutions also give the executive power to declare a state of siege or emergency, suspend human rights, and rule by decree. The same applies to privilege. Although one section of the constitution may proclaim democratic and egalitarian principles, other parts may give special privileges to the church, the army, or the landed elites, and even while representative and republican precepts are enshrined in one quarter, authoritarian and elitist ones are legitimated in another. Increasingly, however, human rights and democratic precepts are being incorporated into Latin American basic law.

None of this is meant to imply approval of human-rights violations or of overthrows of democratic governments. Rather, it is only to point out how these have often been perceived differently in Latin America than in the United States or Europe. Hence, the real questions may concern the degrees of military intervention or limits on legislative authority and how and why these actions are taken. It has not simply been a matter of the military usurping the constitution, because it was often the constitution itself that gave the military the right—even obligation—to intervene in the political process under certain circumstances. Similarly, when human-rights violations are reported, we must understand this within the Latin American constitutional and legal tradition as well as our own. Human rights have not been conceived as constitutional absolutes, and frequently there is a constitutional provision for their suspension. Recently, however, human rights as well as democracy in Latin America are being viewed more and more according to universal standards.

The most important issues of Latin American politics involve the dynamics of change and process from both the Latin American as well as a global perspective. We cannot understand the region if we look only at the liberal and republican side of the Latin American tradition while ignoring the rest, nor should we simply condemn some action from the point of view of the North American constitutional tradition without seeing it in the Latin

American context. If the civil and military spheres are not strictly segregated as in the U.S. tradition, then what are their dynamic relations in Latin America, and what are the causes of military intervention? If strict separation of powers is not seen in the same light in Latin America and if the branches are not equal, what are their respective powers and interrelations? If hierarchy, authority, and special privilege have long been legitimated principles along with democratic and egalitarian ones, then how are these reconciled, glossed over, or challenged—and why? And how are these relations all changing as Latin America enters a more democratic era?

The sheer number of Latin American constitutions is another way in which they are misunderstood. The number of constitutions (thirty or more in some countries) ignores the fact that in most of the countries a new constitution is generally promulgated whenever a new amendment is added or when a major new interpretation requires official legitimization. To understand Latin American constitutionality, two things must be kept in mind: First, the Latin American constitutional tradition has been far more stable than the number of constitutions implies. Second, in most countries of the area there are only two main constitutional traditions, the one more centralized and even authoritarian and the other liberal and democratic, with the trend now increasing toward the democratic side. The many constitutions, then, generally signify the repeated alternations between these two basic traditions, with some variations.

These perspectives on the constitutional tradition also provide hints as to the distinct legal tradition of Latin America. Whereas in the United States laws and constitutions are based on a history and practice derived from British common law, those of Latin America derive from a code-law tradition. This difference has several implications. Where the U.S. legal system is founded on precedent and reinterpretation, the Latin American codes are complete bodies of law allowing little room for precedent or judicial reinterpretation. The codes are fixed and absolute; they embody a comprehensive framework of operating principles; and unlike the common-law tradition with its inductive reasoning based on cases, enforcement of the codes implies deductive reasoning. One begins not with facts or cases, but with general truth (the codes or constitution) and then one deduces rules or applications for specific circumstances from this truth.

Although one should not overstress the point and although mixed forms exist throughout Latin America, an understanding of the code-law system and its philosophical underpinnings carries us a considerable distance toward understanding Latin American behavior. The truths embodied in the codes, constitutions, and the deductive method have their origins and reflection in the Roman, medieval, and Catholic-scholastic tradition. The authoritarian, absolutist nature of the codes also finds reflection in (and helps reinforce) an absolutist, historically authoritarian political culture. The effort to cover all contingencies with one code or to engage in almost constant constitutional engineering to obtain a "perfect" document tends to rule out the logrolling, compromise, informal understandings, and unwritten rules that lie at the heart of U.S. or British political culture. Because courts and judges—in their role as applicators and enforcers of the law rather than creative interpreters of it—are bureaucrats and bureaucratic agencies, they do not enjoy the respect their counterparts do in the United States, thus making judicial review and even an independent judiciary difficult at best. These precepts and practices are changing as Latin America becomes more democratic and as U.S. legal precepts are incorporated into Latin American law.

Executive-Legislative-Judicial Relations

Power in the Latin American systems has historically been concentrated in the executive branch, specifically the presidency. Terms like *continuismo* (prolonging one's term of office beyond its constitutional limits), *personalismo* (emphasis on the person of the president rather than on the office), and, particularly, *machismo* (strong, manly authority) are all now so familiar that they form part of our own political lexicon. The present-day Latin American executive is heir to an imperial and autocratic tradition stemming from the absolute, virtually unlimited authority of the Spanish and Portuguese crowns. Of course, modern authoritarianism has multiple explanations for its origin (a reaction against earlier mass mobilization by populist and leftist leaders, the result of stresses generated by modernization, and the strategies of civilian and military elites for accelerating development) as well as various forms (caudillistic and more institutionalized arrangements). In any case, the Latin American presidency has long been an imperial presidency in ways that no president of the United States ever conceived.

The formal authority of Latin American executives is extensive. It derives from a president's powers as chief executive, commander in chief, and head of state, as well as from the broad emergency powers to declare a state of siege or emergency, suspend constitutional guarantees, and rule by decree. The presidency has been a chief beneficiary of many twentieth-century changes, among them radio and television, concentrated war-making powers, and broad responsibility for the economy. In addition many Latin American chief executives serve simultaneously as heads of state and presidents of their party machines. If the potential leader's route to power was the army, the president also has the enormous weight of armed might for use against foreign enemies and domestic foes. Considerable wealth, often generated because the lines between private and public wealth are not so sharply drawn as in North American political society, may also become an effective instrument of rule.

Perhaps the main difference lies in the fact that the Latin American systems, by tradition and history, are more centralized and executive oriented than those in the United States. National life swirls around the person occupying the presidency. The president is responsible not only for governance but also for the well-being of society as a whole and is the symbol of the national society in ways that a U.S. president is not. Not only is politics concentrated in the office and person of the president, but it is by presidential favors and patronage that contracts are determined; different clientele are served; and wealth, privilege, and social position are parceled out. The president is the national patrón, replacing the local landowners and men on horseback of the past. With both broad appointive powers and wide latitude in favoring friends and those who show loyalty, the Latin American president is truly the hub of the national system. Hence, when a good, able executive is in power, the system works exceedingly well; when this is not the case, the whole system breaks down.

Various gimmicks have been used to try to limit executive authority, though few have worked well. These range from the disastrous results of the experiment with a plural (nine-person government-by-committee) executive in Uruguay to the varied unsuccessful efforts at parliamentary or semiparliamentary rule in Chile, Brazil, Cuba, and Costa Rica. Constitutional gimmickry has not worked in limiting executive rule because it has been an area-wide tradition and cultural pattern that is, in effect, not simply some legal article. However, spreading democracy in Latin America is now forcing most presidents to work within a constitutional framework.

The role of the congress in such a system has not historically been to initiate or veto laws, much less to serve as a separate and coequal branch of government. Congress's functions can be understood if we begin not with the assumption of an independent branch but with one of an agency that has historically been subservient to the president and, along with the executive, a part of the same organic, integrated state system. The congress's role was thus to give advice and consent to presidential acts (but not much dissent), serve as a sounding board for new programs, represent the varied interests of the nation, and modify laws in some particulars (but not usually to nullify them). The legislature was also a place to bring some new faces into government as well as to pension off old ones, reward political friends and cronies, and ensure the opposition a voice while guaranteeing that it remained a minority. In recent years, however, the congress in several Latin American countries has acquired newfound power and autonomy.

In some countries (Chile, Colombia, Costa Rica) the congress has long enjoyed considerable independence and strength. A few congresses have even gone so far as to defy the executive—and gotten away with it. In 1992–1993, congresses in both Brazil and Venezuela removed the president from office for fiscal improprieties. Additionally, the congress may serve as a forum that allows the opposition to embarrass or undermine the government, as a means of gauging who is rising and who is falling in official favor, or as a way of weighing the relative strength of the various factions within the regime.

Many of the same comments apply to the courts and court system. First, the court system has not historically been a separate and coequal branch, nor was it intended or generally expected to be. Many Latin American supreme courts would declare a law unconstitutional or defy a determined executive only at the risk of embarrassment and danger to themselves, something the courts have assiduously avoided. Second, within these limits the Latin American court systems have often functioned not entirely badly. Third, the courts, through such devices as the writ of *amparo* (Mexico and Argentina), popular action and *tutela* (Colombia), and *segurança* (Brazil), have played an increasingly important role in controlling and overseeing governmental action, protecting civil liberties, and restricting executive authority even under dictatorial regimes.

The Latin American court system had its origins in the Iberian tradition. The chief influences historically were Roman law; Christianity and the Thomistic hierarchy of laws; and the traditional legal concepts of Iberia, most notably the *Siete Partidas* of Alfonso the Wise. In Latin America's codes, through lists of human rights and the hierarchy of courts, the influence of the French Napoleonic Code has been pronounced. In the situation of a supreme court passing (in theory at least) on the constitutionality of executive or legislative acts, the U.S. inspiration is also clear. At present the courts in various countries are increasing in power and beginning to assert themselves, but they often face problems of incompetence, corruption, and lack of adequate training.

It should be remembered, however, that what has made the system work is not so much the legislature or judiciary, but the executive. The formally institutionalized limits on executive power in terms of the usual checks and balances are still not extensive and frequently can be bypassed. More significant has been the informal balance of power within the system and the set of generally agreed upon understandings and rules of the game, beyond which even the strongest of Latin American presidents goes only at severe risk to his regime's survival. Nevertheless, the growing importance of congress and courts in many countries is a subject for further study.

Local Government and Federalism

Federalism in Latin America emerged from exactly the reverse of the situation that existed in the United States. In the United States in 1789 a national government was reluctantly accepted by thirteen self-governing colonies that had never had a central administration. In Latin America, by contrast, a federal structure was adopted in some countries (Argentina, Venezuela, Mexico, Brazil) that had always been centrally administered.

Although these four nations were federal in principle, the central government reserved the right to "intervene" in the states. As the authority of the central government grew during the 1920s and 1930s, its inclination to intervene also increased, thereby often negating the federal principle. Over a long period these major countries were progressively centralized with virtually all power concentrated in the national capital. Nevertheless, the dynamics of relations and tensions between the central government and its component states and regions, who still have some independent autonomy, make for one of the most interesting political arenas. Although recently there have been pressures to decentralize, in all countries the central state remains dominant.

The Latin American countries are structured after the French system of local government, with virtually all power concentrated in the central government and its ministries and authority flowing from the top down. Local government is ordinarily administered through the ministry of interior, which is also responsible for the national police. Almost all local officials historically were appointed by the central government and served as its agents at the local level. Local governments, on the other hand, have almost no power to tax or to run local social programs. These activities are generally administered by the central government according to a national plan. This system of centralized rule is also a means of concentrating power in oftentimes weak and uninstitutionalized nations.

Yet even though the theory has been that of a centralized state, the reality in Latin America has always been somewhat different. The Spanish and Portuguese crowns had difficulty enforcing their authority in the interior, which was far away and virtually autonomous. With the withdrawal of the Crown early in the nineteenth century, centrifugal tendencies were accelerated. Power drained off into the hands of local landowners or regional men on horseback, who competed for control of the national palace. With a weak central state and powerful centrifugal tendencies a strong de facto system of local rule did emerge in Latin America—contrary to what the laws or constitutions proclaimed.

Thereafter, nation-building in Latin America often consisted of two major ideals: populating and thus "civilizing" the vast empty interior and extending the central government's authority over the national territory. Toward the end of the nineteenth century, national armies and bureaucracies were created to replace the unprofessional armed bands under the local *caudillos*, national police agencies were established to enforce the central government's authority at the local level, and the collection of customs duties was centralized. Authority became more concentrated in the central state, the regional isolation of the *pa-*

tria chica weakened as roads and communications grids were developed, and the economy was similarly centralized more under the direction of the state.

In most of Latin America the process of centralization, begun in the 1870s and 1880s, is still in progress. Indeed, that is how development is often defined throughout the area. A developed political system is one in which the central agencies of the state exercise control and regulation over the disparate and centrifugal forces that comprise the system. In many countries this process is still incomplete, so in the vast interior, in the highlands, in diverse Indian communities, and among some groups (such as landowners, large industrialists, the military, and big multinationals), the authority of the central state is still tenuous. Even today isolated areas, especially those in the rugged mountains or tropical jungles, often have little governmental presence. Local strongmen—sometimes guerrillas or drug traffickers—may be more powerful than the national government's representatives. Indeed, the efforts of the central government to extend its sway over the entire nation constitute one of the main arenas of Latin American politics. Conversely, the local units, be they regions, towns, parishes, or Indian communities, still attempt to maintain some degree of autonomy. Thus centralization and decentralization are often going forward at the same time.

Fourth Branch of Government: The Autonomous State Agencies

One of the primary tools in the struggle to centralize power in Latin America from the 1930s to the 1980s was the government corporation or the autonomous agency. The growth of these agencies in many ways parallels that of the "alphabet agencies" in the United States, thereby giving the central government a means to extend its control into new areas. In fact, these agencies became so large and so pervasive that they could be termed a separate branch of government, and some Latin American constitutions even recognized them as such.

The proliferation of these agencies was such that in some countries they numbered in the hundreds. Many were regulatory agencies, often with far broader powers than their North American counterparts, with the authority to set or regulate prices, wages, and production quotas. Others administered vast government corporations, including steel, mining, electricity, sugar, coffee, tobacco, railroads, utilities, and petrochemicals. Still others were involved in social programs: education, social security, housing, relief activities, and the like. Many more participated in the administration of new services that the state had been called on to perform, such as national planning, agrarian reform, water supplies, and family planning.

The purposes for which these agencies were set up were diverse. Some, such as the agrarian-reform or family-planning agencies, were established as much to please the U.S. government and to qualify a country for U.S. and World Bank loans as they were in fact to carry out agrarian reform or family planning. Others were created to bring a recalcitrant or rebellious economic sector (such as labor or the business community) under government control and direction. Some were used to stimulate economic growth and development, to increase government efficiency and hence its legitimacy, or to create a capitalist structure and officially sanctioned entrepreneurial class where none had existed before. In addition, they also enabled more job seekers to be put on the public payroll.

The common feature of these myriad agencies was that they tended to serve as agents of centralization in that historic quest to "civilize" and bring order to what was, in the past even more than now, a vast, often unruly, near-empty territory with strong centrifugal propensities. The growth of these agencies, specifically the government corporations, meant that the degree of central state control and even ownership of the means of production increased significantly as well. As a result it is a fundamental mistake to think of the Latin American economies as private enterprise-dominated systems. It is not only Cuba that had a large public sector; on the contrary, all the Latin American economies were heavily influenced by the state.

This phenomenon had important implications. It meant that the stakes involved in the issue of control of the central government, with the vast resources involved, were very high. It also implied that very rapid structural change was readily possible. In countries where between 40 and 60 percent of the GNP was generated by the public sector and so much power was concentrated in the central state, the transformation from a state-capitalist to a state-socialist system was relatively easy and could happen almost overnight (as in Cuba, Ecuador, or Venezuela). All that was required was for a left or socialist element to capture the pinnacles of these highly centralized systems.

The growth of all these centralized state agencies had another implication that deserves mention. Although established as autonomous and self-governing bodies, the state corporations had in fact become heavily political agencies. They provided a wealth of sinecures, a means to put nearly everyone on the public payroll. They were giant patronage agencies by which one rewarded friends and cronies and found places for (and hence the loyalty or at least neutrality of) the opposition. Depending on the country, 30 to 50 percent of the gainfully employed labor force worked for the government. Many of the agencies were woefully inefficient, and the immense funds involved provided nearly endless opportunities for private enrichment from the great public trough. In performing these patronage and spoils functions, the state agencies preserved the status quo because large numbers of people—indeed virtually the entire middle class—were dependent on them for their livelihood and op-portunities for advancement. It is not surprising then that a significant part of the debt problems faced by many Latin American countries came from state agencies—not the national governments—receiving foreign loans.

Today the Latin American countries are trying to solve the problems of corruption, inefficiency, and overcentralization. With the neoliberal reforms of the 1990s, governments reduced the number and role of decentralized agencies. Many that were in productive activities were privatized. In the pro-cess, the benefits for poorer people in the countries have been reduced, as well as the number of jobs available to be passed out to political supporters. In the recent economic downturn, however, these state agencies have again been in-creased in size.

Public Policy and the Policy Process

By public policy we mean the actions of groups and leaders in authority to implement their decisions. No political system is completely successful in ac-complishing what it wishes, and this is certainly the case in those societies that are underdeveloped politically and economically like the Latin American countries. Further, there are certain uniquely Latin American traits, over and above the area's underdeveloped character, that militate against effective pub-lic policies.

Major Issues of Public Policy

Most of the historic issues of the nineteenth century—the role of the church, centralism or federalism—have been resolved or at least placed on the back burner in post–World War II Latin America. Although from time to time these old issues reemerge in some countries, the newer issues of eco-nomic development, agrarian reform, urban reform, and population growth largely replaced them in the last third of the twentieth century. Since the 1990s the central issues have been the illicit narcotics trade, the "Washing-ton Consensus"—and the trade liberalization that goes along with it—and the problems of the cities. Two prominent issues of the twentieth century either refuse to disappear (agrarian reform) or have largely been resolved (population policy).

Economic Development and the "Washington Consensus."   One goal of almost all sectors in the Latin American political process is economic development, although the individual countries still sometimes disagree on its nature and the best way to obtain it. For some, economic development means no more than a growth in the national economy, with a resulting larger gross domestic product. In this conception the nature and structure of the economy would not change at all, only the size. The kinds of products would remain the same, and the nature of trade relations with the outside world would vary only slightly, albeit expanded in amount.

Other Latin Americans define economic development as the industrialization and diversification of their economies. Traditionally, Latin American countries produced agricultural or other primary goods that were traded with the more developed countries of the North for industrial goods. Many Latin American countries concentrated on only one such primary good. Although they might have comparative advantage in those primary products, the national economies suffered when there was a world oversupply of them and were also vulnerable to crop failures and to quotas fixed by the industrial nations.

By the early 1960s it became evident that there was a general decline in the relative value of all such primary goods. The long-term trend was for industrial articles to increase in price more rapidly than primary goods. Although a frost in Brazil might mean a short-term increase in the price of Colombian coffee, by the 1960s a tractor imported to Colombia from the United States cost more bags of coffee beans than it had twenty years before. Although this example did not pertain to Venezuelan oil between 1973 and 1982, almost all other Latin American countries lost income from the declining terms of trade.

The middle position on economic policy, then, would call for two major policies of an economic nature: industrialization and diversification. The former would be for the purpose of import substitution. Rather than importing industrial goods, the Latin American country imports capital goods and technology, which it then uses to produce the goods that formerly were imported. Further, to lessen the dependence on one crop, a government makes tax and credit decisions that will encourage production of goods other than the traditional one for export. This vision of a new, economically developed society is one in which more goods of greater variety are produced for export while fewer manufactured goods are imported. Increased trade is an important facet of this policy, because hard currency is needed for the purchase of these capital goods.

By the late 1980s the "Washington Consensus" policy emerged in many Latin American countries. Although the term is often seen as synonymous with "neoliberalism" and "globalization," economist John Williamson, who coined the term, meant much more:

1. Fiscal discipline
2. A redirection of public expenditure priorities toward fields offering both high economic returns and the potential to improve income

distribution, such as primary health care, primary education, and infrastructure
3. Tax reform (to lower marginal rates and broaden the tax base)
4. Interest rate liberalization
5. A competitive exchange rate
6. Trade liberalization
7. Liberalization of inflows of foreign direct investment
8. Privatization
9. Deregulation (to abolish barriers to entry and exit)
10. Secure property rights

Since its implementation, the phrase "Washington Consensus" has become a lightning rod for dissatisfaction amongst antiglobalization protestors, developing country politicians and officials, trade negotiators, and numerous others. It is often used interchangeably with the phrase "neoliberal policies."[1]

To a certain extent the neoliberal economic system is like the traditional one, emphasizing products in which a nation had a comparative advantage. However, it also included privatization of government-owned enterprises and ending subsidies for the poor through pricing products at international levels. In the short run, at least, these new policies led to more unemployment and a greater disparity of income. The neoliberal leaders urged patience, but some politicians paid more attention to the cries of large numbers of suffering people. Hence, in recent years the new conflict (but in some ways much like the struggle of the 1930s) was between the Neoliberals and the supporters of a government-controlled economy.

Economic policy is often more complex than the preceding discussion indicates. What about inflation? Latin American countries have experienced "stagflation" (the combination of a stagnant economy and high inflation) for at least three decades, being in its most acute form in the first half of the 1980s. Is this to be solved by monetary measures as the Neoliberals suggest (printing less money, balancing budgets, maintaining a balance of trade between imports and exports), or is the real cause for inflation a structural one, based on the declining terms of trade and the concentration of economic power in the small group at the top in most of the Latin American countries? If the reason is structural, then more dramatic public policies are needed.

Another key question is: Who is to develop industry? The supporters of a strong role of the government suggest that national enterprise do it, whereas Neoliberals encourage foreign investment and multinational corporations. How will the generally negative balances of payment be redressed? What kinds of laws, if any, are needed to encourage the importation of capital goods and infrastructure materials while also discouraging the purchase of consumer goods from foreign countries? If national industry is to be developed, how is capital to be generated? Is this to be done by stopping capital flight, by reducing consumption by the lower and middle classes through forced savings, or by some combination of techniques?

After October 1973 a new economic issue arose: the value of petroleum. For the oil-exporting countries (Venezuela, Mexico, Ecuador), the question became how best to use the new wealth while keeping inflationary pressures at a minimum and protecting national industry. For the petroleum importers, the questions revolved around how to keep economic growth going while using more of the scarce hard-currency export earnings and reserves to purchase needed oil. Later, when oil prices declined, these economies also went into a tailspin.

By the early 1980s, whether these policy issues were successfully resolved or not, the question changed to how the debt crisis could or would be resolved. This crisis was caused by the energy crisis in two ways. First, by the late 1970s, all Latin American countries found that private banks, recycling petrodollars invested by OPEC members, were willing to lend money at real interest rates (corrected for inflation) that were near or even below zero. The debts were impossible to repay, however, because recession in the industrial world in the early 1980s resulted in fewer Latin American exports being bought. Second, the oil-exporting countries (especially Mexico and Venezuela) contracted debts under the assumption that the price of petroleum would continue increasing. By 1982, however, the oil glut led to much lower prices for their exports.

By the late 1980s, then, the new agenda revolved around the Neoliberal proposals to open markets, free trade, cut budgets, and have less protectionism. As in the struggle between the traditional and democratic models of government (see Chapter 5), the economic contest became one between individuals and groups who had benefited from the old mercantilist system and those who thought they would benefit more from the Neoliberal one. While in the early years of the new millennium neoliberal leaders tended to win presidential elections, recently the exact opposite has been the case. In the "pink socialist" elections, presidential candidates critical of neoliberalism were elected in Venezuela (Hugo Chávez, 1998, 2000, and 2006), Brazil (Luiz Inácio da Silva, 2002 and 2006), Uruguay (Tabaré Vázquez, 2004), Chile (Michelle Bachelet, 2006), Ecuador (Rafael Correa, 2006), Nicaragua (Daniel Ortega, 2006), Bolivia (Evo Morales, 2006), Argentina (Cristina Fernández de Kirchner, 2007), and El Salvador (Mauricio Funes, 2009). The recent rise of pink socialist governments indicate that some people in Latin America are losing faith in these neoliberal policies, which have done little to increase wages or decrease poverty.[2]

The Drug Trade. By the end of the twentieth century the governments of all the Latin American countries were concerned with policies to deal with the effects of the illicit drug trade. While there were three producer countries in which the crops for the cocaine trade were grown (Colombia, Peru, and Bolivia), all the others were "transit countries," through which the trade passed. When direct routes between Colombia and consuming countries (the United States and Western Europe) were blocked, the profit margin from the drugs made it possible for the traffickers to reroute them through Chile.

In 1975, when the U.S. government urged Mexico to spray its marijuana crop with herbicides, Colombia became the center of marijuana production in the hemisphere. Drug dealers from Medellín controlled that trade and, when they realized that more money was to be made in cocaine, a new drug of choice in the United States, they diversified their illicit industry. Coca was brought to Colombia from Bolivia and Peru for the manufacture of cocaine.

At the beginning the method to get the cocaine to the consumer nations was through "mules" (individuals carrying small amounts of the drugs). This means was dramatically changed when two Medellín drug leaders, Carlos Lehder and Jorge Luis Ochoa, decided to use airplanes, flying at low altitudes to avoid radar detection. That way they were able to sell a higher volume of drugs at lower prices. It is estimated that by 1979 Colombia shipped some 37 metric tons of cocaine and 15,000 tons of marijuana.

In the 1980s two Colombian groups, the Medellín and Cali cartels, dominated the world cocaine trade. After those organizations were dismantled in the 1990s, smaller Colombian groups took over. Coca production shifted according to eradication efforts, but the cocaine production remained in Colombia. Heroin production (and poppy growing) gave increased diversification to the drug traffickers. In the first years of the new millennium, however, Mexican drug groups took over the marketing of the products, shifting the profits of the enterprise.

The drug trade raises three issues for Latin American governments. For producing countries, the first is how to reduce if not eliminate drug production. This issue is especially difficult since, while the U.S. government encourages elimination, small marijuana, coca, and poppy producers resist it because they can earn a great deal more money growing the illicit crops. If enough is not done to eradicate crops, however, the wrath of the U.S. government is possible. If too much is done, there is the danger of pushing small producers into the arms of Marxist guerrilla groups.

The second question, for both producer and transit countries, is how to contain the violence that accompanies the trade. The high-profit possibilities lead to rival groups who use violence to eliminate competitors. Innocent people are often caught in the crossfire of rival groups.

The final question is how national political leaders can plan the national economy when large sums of foreign exchange enter the country through the drug trade. It is especially difficult to predict its levels, and unlike legitimate businesses, the drug dealers do not report their profits to the governments of their countries.

Urban Reform.   With few jobs or little future in the rural areas, many people left the countryside to seek a better life in the cities. There are both push and pull factors accounting for this internal migration. Some campesinos are pushed off the land, either because there are more children than the land can support or because the large landowners have mechanized production. Others are pulled to the cities by the better life that they believe will be found there. The movement has been dramatic: It is estimated that every year from 1970 to 1985 a population of some 8.75 million persons was incorporated into the cities of Latin America, and in the 1985 to 2000 period this increased to between 11 and 12 million per year. This urban growth affects the major cities, many of which doubled or tripled in size during the 1990s and continue their accelerated growth today.

Cities in Latin America were not prepared for such rapid growth; this was likewise true of U.S. cities during similar growth periods at the end of the nineteenth century and the beginning of the twentieth. There are, however, important differences between the Latin American and U.S. urban growth periods. Unlike that of the United States and Western Europe, Latin American urbanization was not accompanied by a surge of industrial growth, which means that not many of these new urbanites received jobs in industry. Only the lucky ones did, with others settling for hand-labor construction work and many more under- or unemployed. Furthermore, given the greater centralization of the state, the political dimension was also different in Latin America. Policies to meet the new problems of the cities were more likely to come from national than from city governments.

The problems are numerous and difficult. One is housing. Although some of the urban migrants rent rooms in large old houses where certain public utilities already exist, even more build makeshift homes in the open areas in and around the cities. Most of these new slums are built illegally on private or state-owned land and are completely devoid of such urban services as water, sewage facilities, electricity, roads, and effective police and fire protection. Some studies have shown that the life expectancy is lower for the dwellers of these shantytowns than for the campesinos. At least six Latin American cities are "mega-cities" with more than eight million people, and they demonstrate many of the worst symptoms of the region's underdevelopment: vast areas of shanty towns, huge numbers of poor people, high concentrations of air and water pollution, and serious levels of traffic congestion.[3]

Urban reform has so far failed to occur, partly because the urban poor have not yet developed effective political movements. Explanations offered for this situation include:

1. The new urban poor are too busy in the day-to-day attempt to make enough money to feed themselves and their children that they do not have time for political activities.
2. People often develop a sense of community in the shantytowns that seems to provide considerable security.
3. Additional security is received from the extended family and from the ceremonial kinship relationship in which people slightly higher in the social structure are godparents of a person's children.
4. Close contact is maintained between the urban poor and the rural areas from which they came, allowing a possibility of returning if things get extremely bad economically.
5. A high percentage of the urban poor are engaged in service work and petty commercial activities such as street vending, thereby forming an atomized labor force that lacks association with others like themselves.
6. Many who do obtain factory jobs work in very small factories, often of the cottage variety, with the owner filling the traditional patrón function.
7. Business people, industrialists, and governments participate in strategic activities designed to give the urban poor a bit of what they want.
8. The same elite groups participate in sanctions against the urban poor, who often have jobs in which they can be easily replaced by the unemployed if they engage in political activities.
9. Whether they will live longer or not, the new urban poor perceive themselves to be better off—or at least their children to be better off—than they have been in the countryside.

Whatever the precise reasons for lack of political influence of these lower-class urban residents, the flow of people into the cities has continued unabated—as have the problems. In late 2007 a Chilean chemical engineer said, "There are many pending tasks in South America. We have problems with pollution in cities and [with the] availability of water resources, threatened and endangered species, overexploitation of marine resources and a rise in diseases—especially skin cancer—caused by the thinning of the ozone layer."[4]

Agrarian Reform. In the second half of the twentieth century a major issue is that of the ownership of land, which is very inequitably distributed, with a small number of very large landholders and a great number of landless, illegal squatters and owners of very small holdings. Only in a few countries are there substantial numbers of middle-class farmers. During the 1960s, in large part because of the influence of the United States and fear of an agrarian revolution (such as how the Cuban one was perceived), many countries of Latin America set up agencies to deal with the problems of land. Yet only in

Nicaragua, Venezuela, and Mexico were there significant land reforms, and even there very limited advances. Even though land reform is not the issue today that it was in the 1960s, the problem still exists: Land ownership is very unevenly distributed, and over eighty million Latin Americans live in the countryside under subhuman conditions. Guerrilla movements took root in many Latin American countries because of the land problem, and in one, Nicaragua, the agrarian problem was one of the reasons for the victory of the Sandinistas in July 1979. Since then, some Latin American governments, often supported by the AID, have continued to support land reform as a way to prevent revolutions.

One very important reason that more dramatic land reforms have not occurred is the power of the large landowners. In some countries, however, they have given up a little land—again the co-optation strategy—to avoid giving up a lot. Another reason for the failure of land reform is the lack of good technical information about who owns what land and what it is being used for. If the land were divided among peasants, would production go up or down? What would be the best crops? Which kinds of seeds and fertilizers would be best? What does the peasant need in addition to land?

The *latifundios* vary greatly in their use and economic output. If a sizable estate is not used or is used very inefficiently, any granting of the land to campesinos would lead to increased agricultural production for either national consumption or export. If, however, the estate is effectively utilized by the large landowner, the goals of land reform and increased agricultural production are, at least for the short run, in conflict. Moreover, there are certain agricultural products that have economies of scale, which means they cannot be successfully grown on a family-sized farm. In this case, agrarian reform means long-term lower production unless the land holdings are held collectively.

Meanwhile, the agrarian issue has faded in importance. Latin America is now more urban than rural, a reversal from the situation forty to fifty years ago when land reform was first offered as a solution. There are still immense social, economic, and political inequalities and inefficiencies in the Latin American countryside that need to be addressed, as the Brazilian Landless Movement illustrates. The appearance of the Zapatista National Liberation Army (*Ejército Zapatista de Liberación Nacional*, EZLN) in Chiapas, Mexico, in the mid-1990s demonstrated that there are still areas within Latin American countries in which the land issue still has major importance.

Population Policy.   In the last half of the twentieth century another issue of Latin American politics was population growth. The population of Latin America tripled between 1950 and 2000 as the area experienced the highest growth rate in the world. Although the birthrate was higher in certain parts of Asia and Africa, death rates were lower in Latin America. The result was a population growth rate for the area of roughly 3 percent per year, which of course varied from country to country. Argentina and Uruguay both increased in population at about 1.0 percent a year, roughly comparable to the United States. Other countries, such as Brazil and Mexico, grew at between 2 and 3 percent a year, which meant that the population doubled every twenty-four to thirty-six years.

One of the key reasons for population growth was increasing life expectancy coupled with lower infant mortality rates, which changed dramatically after World War II. These improved rates were the result of better health care, education, more doctors, better sanitary conditions, and the eradication of some diseases, such as smallpox and malaria, through public-health programs. In many places the birthrate did not decrease dramatically, and life expectancy kept rising. The way to slow this growth, therefore, has to be through some control of the high birthrate.

Some countries (even strongly Catholic Colombia) developed family-planning programs. Further, it has become evident that even in those countries that lack effective programs, the birthrate has begun to fall. This decline was related to increased urbanization, education, and knowledge concerning ways to limit family size, not necessarily to organized family-planning programs. After all, it may make some sense for a rural peasant to have lots of children, both to put to work in the fields and to take care of the parents in their old age (especially in nations that have few effective social-security programs). For the urban poor, however, the argument for more rather than fewer children makes less sense, and it is precisely in the urban areas that the population growth rate has begun to fall. As a result, by the beginning of the new millennium, population growth rates had decreased in almost all Latin American countries. Only Paraguay and Guatemala had growth rates above 2 percent a year. The rates in Chile, Uruguay, and Cuba are now below 1 percent.[5]

Constraints in Latin American Policymaking

In the previous section some of the major issues of Latin American public policy were considered. The aim of this section is to outline some of the constraints—the conditions that affect political decisions as well as those that impede effective transition from policy outputs to policy outcomes.

Underdevelopment. The key feature of economic underdevelopment is that even a government wishing to change many things seldom has the revenue to do so. All allocative policies have money costs. This means that even if the governing coalition of a Latin American country decides that economic development through agrarian reform, urban reform, and birth control are desirable, there might not be enough money adequately to fund all policies.

In some instances in Latin America, policymakers honestly cannot do all that they would like, while in others legislation creates programs that are never funded. Governmental policy in Latin America, therefore, should be analyzed not only by studying established law but also by looking at the actual expenditures of governmental revenues and results of the policies.

Yet another feature of underdevelopment, more political than economic, is the lack of bureaucratic expertise. Bureaucracies in Latin America have had one very important purpose: to provide white-collar, nonmanual employment for the members of the middle sectors, especially those who, in the absence of such employment, would be likely to join the political opposition. Because of this co-optive and patronage function, the bureaucracies of the area many times were not efficient in the day-to-day running of governmental programs. They contain people who have jobs only because of personal connections, who do not have the necessary educational background, and who hold multiple bureaucratic jobs, working only briefly or not at all in any one.

For this reason some governments of Latin America went the route of decentralized agencies set up for specific policies in an attempt to insulate them from the more corrupt regular bureaucracy. But in many countries even this has failed to produce an effective bureaucracy. Therefore, even in the case of a policy that is accepted by the ruling coalition and is adequately funded, the policy consequence might not be what was intended.

The Neoliberals have called for smaller, more efficient, less corrupt bureaucracies. To a certain extent that has happened in many Latin American countries, albeit with considerable difficulties. No politician wants to cut his supporters out of the state bureaucracy, nor do most want to increase unemployment by laying off large numbers of bureaucrats. This is especially dangerous because most are highly educated and fairly well paid. Hence, they could contribute to the opposition with both money and technical expertise.

The Political System.   The rules of the traditional Latin American political game were described in Chapter 3. Here it is sufficient to repeat that a new group entering into the accepted circle of power groups traditionally needed to demonstrate that it would not do anything to harm already existing groups. This meant that many alternatives were closed for public policy by the rules of the game. In most countries of Latin America there were two possible ways to solve this dilemma. First, governmental policy could work in such a political system if the economy was expanding and steadily increasing governmental income. In such a case new revenues could be allocated to public policies in a distributive fashion—that is, by dividing up the bigger pie. However, governments still had difficulties with such distributive policies because industrialists, for example, preferred that the new revenue used for urban reform, which benefited them little, be employed for infrastructure improvements (roads and railroads), which helped them economically.

Nevertheless, the controversy over distributive policies was much less than that over redistributive ones—that is, policies that would take something away from one group and give it to another. For this reason, land reform encountered many difficulties. It was not surprising that before the falling prices that accompanied the oil glut of the early 1980s, Venezuela had one of the most successful reformist governments in Latin America, made possible by governmental taxes on foreign oil producers (and after 1976 by profits made by the government oil enterprise) as well as one of the most successful agrarian reforms, using lands that the government already owned.

Yet not all the governments of Latin America had the luxury of participating in only distributive policies; many required redistributive policies as well. If the economy was stagnant or, even worse, shrinking, there could hardly be any governmental programs at all. So a second possibility was a case-by-case, eclectic policy situation in which one group won on one policy issue, another group on another, and so forth. Although politically this was good short-run strategy, the long-term result often had contradictory effects, with detrimental ramifications for the economy, the people, and even the political system. Venezuela in the 1990s discovered that low prices for petroleum meant that the government, which had long used distributive policies, had to shift to redistributive ones. As the chapter on Venezuela shows, the shift was accompanied by mass dissatisfaction, bloodshed, attempted military coups d'état, the end of the political parties that had successfully brought democracy to the country for the first time in its history, the election of a populist president who had led a military coup d'état, and a constituent assembly to reform its democracy.

This dilemma of policymaking in the Latin American context was most evident in those countries where almost all individuals had organized into groups that had accepted the rules of the game. This was the case in Mexico,[6] and Argentina was at worst a situation of almost complete governmental stalemate or at best one of very eclectic and contradictory policies. Because all groups were politically relevant and involved and had agreed not to harm the interests of others, practically no agreed upon policy was possible.

The movements to democracy in Latin America do not seem to have changed this dilemma of policymaking. Strong political parties have not developed, with the result that majority rule has not meant effective presidential-congressional collaboration with successful redistributive policies. On the other hand, democracy might lead to executive-legislative gridlock. To an extent this is what happened during the Vicente Fox government in Mexico because his party did not have majorities in the national congress. In the 1990s Argentina seemed to have solved the problem to a considerable extent, while other countries seem to alternate between sometimes effective policy-making and paralysis that leads to gridlock.

The United States and the International Political Economy.   A third set of constraints on Latin American public policymaking relates to the position of these countries in a hemisphere that is dominated politically and economically by the United States and to the Latin American position in the international political economy. Some of the constraints on policymaking are dramatic, appearing on the front pages of newspapers. Guatemala in 1954 demonstrated that a Central American government could not enact a dramatic land reform adversely affecting U.S. business interests or launch a general social revolution without prompting a CIA-sponsored overthrow of the government. Eleven years later, the case of the Dominican Republic showed that the U.S. government might intervene militarily even if a coalition about to come to power only appeared dangerous from a U.S. security ("another Cuba") point of view. Chile in the 1970s illustrated that no matter how geographically remote and economically unimportant a country might be to the United States, the "giant of the north" can intervene through both governmental and private business agencies. The obvious exception to these generalizations is Cuba, where U.S. opposition was foreseen and, through planning and the clear leadership of Fidel Castro, the revolution survived. Further, in Peru and Venezuela major U.S. properties were nationalized without provoking a Marine intervention. So far, however, these cases are the exceptions and not the rule. Nicaragua during the Sandinista regime (1979–1990) is another case of a country constrained in its policy options by U.S. intervention.

There are other, more subtle ways in which the United States manipulates Latin America. The Agency for International Development (AID) uses its leverage to push certain programs: land reform in the 1960s, birth control in the 1970s, and private-sector initiatives in the 1980s and 1990s. Within these areas and elsewhere, AID officials often assist the Latin American governments in operational plans, although AID influence is much less now than it was thirty years ago. Likewise, international agencies that are in part dominated by the United States, such as the World Bank, the International Monetary Fund (IMF), and the Inter-American Development Bank (IADB), traditionally encourage the Latin American governments to follow austerity-based economic and fiscal policy decisions. For example, the IMF might push a Latin American government to devalue its currency and tighten its belt. If the country refuses, World Bank and IADB loans become unlikely, AID will be hesitant to offer credit to the country, and even the private banks of the United States and Western Europe will be reluctant to extend credit.

During the 1970s and early 1980s many Latin Americans accepted the argument of "dependency," or that they were underdeveloped because the United States had exploited their resources and therefore they needed to break the hold of this dependency on the United States. Regardless of the arguments of the dependency theorists, however, most Latin American governments recognize pragmatically that they must deal realistically with the United States. For better or worse, the United States is the major political and economic power in the hemisphere. Latin America is stuck in a dependency position, but it also desperately needs U.S. and other capital if it is to develop. Hence, the real question is not whether Latin America can dispense with the United States but whether the Latin American countries can reap some advantages from this relationship. Can they get the necessary capital and help from the United States without losing their sovereignty? That is the trick. To try to achieve that goal, clever Latin American presidents manipulate the U.S. Embassy as adeptly as the Embassy does the politics of the Latin American countries, particularly if they have commodities or strategic assets that the United States must have.

Conclusions and Implications

In the previous pages, we have generalized about the issues and constraints of public policy in Latin America. Although there are great commonalities among the Latin American countries on these matters, there are also notable differences. We suggest that the following questions be considered when reading the chapters about individual countries:

1. What are the major issues of public policy in the individual Latin American countries?
2. Which of these issues lead to governmental policies and which do not, and why?
3. What kinds of policies—distributive or redistributive—are designed?
4. What does the nature of the governing coalition suggest about which issues become policies?
5. How effective is the bureaucracy in translating official policy outputs into policy outcomes?
6. What are the major constraints on policymaking?
7. Who benefits from public policy: elites or the public?
8. How have globalization, trade, and economic interdependence changed the operating procedures and rules of the game?

We should warn that definitive answers to these questions should not always be expected. The study of public policy in Latin America is primarily one of the last thirty years. The authors of the individual chapters have often been hindered by a lack of empirical studies on which to base their conclusions—a condition that, it is hoped, will soon be rectified as new and better studies become available.

5

The Struggle for Democracy
in Latin America

In the preceding chapters we have made reference to how Latin America became more democratic after the late 1970s. While we maintain that position, we also feel that it is important to draw attention to the characteristics of democracy—a term that is really quite complex—and to the difficulties that Latin American countries have had in achieving and maintaining constitutional governments. In this chapter we discuss the ongoing conflict between three models of government in the area: the traditional "living museum" form discussed in chapter 3, liberal democracy, and a combination of the two called "delegative democracy," which at its extreme might better be considered to be "semiauthoritarian" instead of democratic.

The Democratic Wave

There is no doubt that, both in the world in general and in Latin America, the 1980s brought remarkable change. Communism collapsed in the Soviet Union, which then had elections and disappeared as a political system, being replaced by a smaller Russia. In some countries of Asia and Africa dictatorships disintegrated and elections ensued. In Latin America the changes might have seemed less dramatic, regardless that in the 1980s military dictatorships ended in Brazil, Ecuador, Bolivia, Argentina, Uruguay, Chile, and several of the Central American countries.

In Nicaragua, internationally monitored elections saw the defeat of the candidate of the ruling Sandinista party, and, even more remarkably, that revolutionary party allowed the opposition candidate, Violeta Barrios de Chamorro, to take office. In Panama, albeit with the assistance of an armed intervention by the United States, strongman Manuel Antonio Noriega fell and the previously elected Guillermo Endara, whom Noriega had not allowed to take power, occupied the presidency. Finally, in Paraguay, Alfredo Stroessner—the longest in power of the Latin American caudillos—fell to a military coup that immediately called for elections. By 2010, of the twenty Latin American countries, only Cuba did not have a democratically elected chief executive, which suggests that democracy had finally arrived as the dominant political system in Latin America.

The Latin American Context for Democracy

As the democratic wave arrived to the twenty Latin American countries, difficulties came from six sources: the Iberian tradition and history, the misuse of "democracy" before the 1980s, pockets of underdevelopment, serious inequities of income distribution, the aftereffects of recent civil wars, and the absence of governments that could effectively implement policies for the nation as a whole.

Challenges to Democracy from the Iberian Tradition and History

Constructing and maintaining a democracy is nowhere an easy matter. As the Latin American countries faced a possible democratic future, difficulties arose from a political tradition unfavorable to limited government, as shown in Chapters 1 and 2. Heralding the demise of Latin America's elitist, authoritarian, top-down, and often antidemocratic political tradition, Mario Vargas Llosa, the Peruvian novelist and unsuccessful presidential candidate in 1990, called for

> the will to modernize, to clean up, and to cut the state down to the proper size for ensuring order, justice, and liberty. It means fostering the right to create wealth in an open system, based on merit, without bureaucratic privileges and interference. It also means that the state must assume responsibility for ensuring that each generation will enjoy that which, together with liberty, is the basis for democratic societies—namely, equality of opportunity.[1]

Those challenges, however, proved to be difficult.

It might be anticipated that the groups who benefited from the old system would resist democracy. Thus, if Latin American history of the 1980s to 1990s is any guide, the two major groups uncomfortable with the new rules of the game were the military and the economic elite. Although evidence suggests that the civilian elites now see democracy as the best hope for stability, it was still possible that if elected governments in Latin America faced serious economic difficulties, some members of the military would think of the traditional way of disposing of misbehaving governments—the military coup. This is demonstrated by the two attempts to overthrow the elected president of Venezuela in the early 1990s, and the *New York Times* reported in January 1994 that many Brazilians were ready for the military to return to power because of economic problems and rampant corruption among civilian politicians. Regardless that with the passing of each year the probability of a military coup seemed lower, in the first five years of the new millennium they nonetheless occurred in Ecuador, Bolivia, and Paraguay.

Previous Misuse of Democracy

Some Latin American countries called themselves "democracies" before 1989, although they in fact were not. Various Latin American dictators, including Anastasio Somoza Debayle in Nicaragua and Rafael Trujillo in the Dominican Republic, among many others, had already shown that a nice electoral facade could make a country appear to be democratic, although fraud only made a mere facade.

The history of elected governments in Latin America surely warns against assuming that having elections means that there is necessarily a democracy. Elections are a good first step, but they are not the whole story. Within a cultural tradition that favored strong leadership more than institutional constraints on power, the region has often had elections without having democracy. Historically this came about for four basic reasons: the limitation of suffrage on gender, educational, or economic grounds; the restriction of voting rights of parties opposing the one in power; the qualification of the power of the elected executive by some other body, usually the military or foreign governments and multilateral institutions; and excessive executive power. But even if those four conditions are met, a consolidated democracy still means much more than elections.

In the first case, suffrage was sometimes restricted by either literacy abilities or property ownership. Of course, in many countries the landless and uneducated tended to be indigenous people, blacks, mulattos, and mestizos, but there were also many whites who had the misfortune to fall into that category. As for the question of female suffrage, Latin American countries tended to be later than the United States in enfranchisement of women. By the 1960s, however, there were few, if any, Latin American countries in which suffrage was not at least theoretically open to all.

Second, many Latin American countries denied the vote to some on the basis of political loyalties. At times this has been done by not allowing members of one political party to vote, while allowing members of another the prerogative to vote more than once (Colombia in the 1950s). In other cases the ability to vote as one pleases was constrained when the voting process was watched closely by the military (Venezuela in the early 1950s). Likewise, there have been instances when press freedoms were so restricted that opposition parties could not effectively get their views out to the electors (Nicaragua and El Salvador in the 1980s). The opposition to Hugo Chávez stated that the same happened in 2009 in Venezuela.

Third, there were countries in which all citizens apparently had the right to vote and there were few constraints on any candidate during the electoral process. Afterwards, however, the elected president was greatly restricted by the military in his policy options. Hence, in the 1960s the Guatemalan military allegedly informed President Julio César Méndez Montenegro that he could do anything that did not affect either the military or the large landowners. In the 1990s the Sandinistas in Nicaragua placed similar restrictions on Violeta Barrios de Chamorro, protecting Sandinista labor unions and the military upon agreeing to let her take the presidency after her election in 1990. Furthermore, sometimes the constraint might come from some foreign government or international organization.

In addition, while internally very democratic in some ways, some Latin American governments were constrained in their economic policies, especially those having to do with foreign businesses, by the U.S. government, the World Bank, the IMF, or the combination of the three. The most notable instance in the 1970s was the government of Salvador Allende in Chile.

After the 1990s the outside constraints had more to do with the continuation of democracy. In 1992, for example, the United States reduced aid to Peru after President Alberto Fujimori suspended the congress and the judicial system. This policy was tempered in the new millennium, especially after terrorism became a priority of the U.S. government. However, the Organization of American States used its influence at times to maintain democracy, as seen in the cases of Ecuador and Paraguay. The Inter-American Democratic Charter, passed by the OAS in 2001, recognized that the countries of the region might confront critical political situations that could lead them to request OAS intervention. After assessing the situation, representatives of the OAS Member States can collectively take the necessary diplomatic initiatives, with the support of the General Secretariat, to prevent or confront an alteration of the constitutional regime, thus protecting or restoring democratic institutions.

Another aberration of democracy in some elective governments was the excessive power of the president, with no real separation of powers or checks and balances. Hernando de Soto and Deborah Orsini wrote the following about Peru prior to the presidency of Alberto Fujimori—although it could have described other Latin American countries:

The only element of democracy in Peru today is the electoral process, which gives Peruvians the privilege of choosing a dictator every five years. Rule making is subsequently carried out in a vacuum, with the executive branch enacting new rules and regulations at a clip of 134,000 every five years (an average of 106 each working day) without any feedback from the population.[2]

De Soto and Orsini argued that the contradictions in the political and economic systems impeded change in Peru. Those incongruities came from the presence of strong, entrenched interests that were defended by a tiny minority of the population, which effectively prevented the majority from taking part in decision-making.

The gridlock of this system led President Alberto Fujimori to disband congress and the courts in 1992, leading to international condemnation for ending "democracy." Guatemalan President Jorge Serrano tried to do the same in 1993. In this case the president failed for lack of support from the armed forces and was removed from power by them. Both cases show that, even though excessive executive power detracts from democracy in Latin America, on occasion the chief executive has attempted to increase his already overwhelming power.

Traditionally almost all Latin American countries had constitutional ways for the president to acquire more power. Whether called "state of siege" or "state of emergency," these stipulations allow presidents to decree policy, in many cases without conferring with the congress or having the decrees subject to judicial review. Although the democratic idea of limited power is found in the constitutions of Latin American, so also are means for the chief executive to rule with almost unlimited authority.

Pockets of Underdevelopment

Although very modern in many ways, all Latin American countries have large pockets of people living in abject poverty. The neoliberal economic changes—the end of protective tariffs, the privatization of state-owned industries, the reduction of support for the poor—that occurred in the area in the last decade of the twentieth century increased, at least in the short run, the number of poor people because they caused unemployment when previously protected industries went bankrupt. In addition, some people with slightly higher living standards, such as owners of small businesses and bureaucrats, opposed further change because they once benefited from the traditional state-capitalist economic system.

These socioeconomic inequalities seemed to some to make democracy unlikely in Latin America. Robert Wesson, for example, after listing the problems of ethnic divisiveness, low standards of living, disdain for politics, a weak or unfree press, poorly organized and narrow parties, unfair elections, politically powerful armies, weak institutions of higher education, traditions of strong leadership, the paternalistic state, and clientelist politics, argued that "one basic condition may account for most of the rest, and it is probably a sufficient condition to explain the difficulty of democracy in Latin America, although by no means the sole cause. This is inequality, the separation of the rich from poor or top from bottom, of educated from ignorant or illiterate, or refined and proud elite from despised masses."[3] The difficulty that this inequality creates for democracy is that "to expect the cultured and well-off would accede to major social changes because they are outnumbered and outvoted in elections of dubious honesty by the ignorant and impoverished—many of whom are undernourished and diseased—is unrealistic. That would require a society of saints with an unlikely degree of loyalty to democratic principles."[4]

Ironically, since neoliberals see democracy and economic reform as interdependent, the poor and others who benefited from the mercantilist system may use the new democratic political regime to elect presidents and members of national congresses who are opposed to neoliberalism. This happened in the elections of Hugo Chávez in Venezuela, Evo Morales in Bolivia, and Daniel Ortega in Nicaragua, among others. Alternatively, the poor may turn to guerrilla violence, as indigenous people did in a post–Cold War revolutionary Zapatista National Liberation Army in early 1994 in Chiapas, Mexico.

The Legacy of Civil Wars

In many Latin American countries thousands have died in recent civil wars. Tension exists between conflict and consensus in any democracy, by its nature a system of institutionalized competition for power. As Larry Diamond argues, "Hence the paradox: Democracy requires conflict—but not too much; competition there must be, but only within carefully defined and universally accepted boundaries. Cleavage must be tempered by consensus."[5] Many Latin American countries have suffered years of war before learning this lesson. Nowhere has the problem of conflict been more serious than in Mexico and Colombia, where there have been bloody civil wars between parties. Other countries have had civil wars at the beginning of their independent history but then moved on to less violent modes of competition. In the 1960s Marxist guerrilla groups chose armed conflict instead of electoral competition, and the resulting civil wars created a series of related problems for a number of Latin American democracies.

It is especially difficult for a democratic government to deal with revolutionaries with different ethical standards. As Gustavo Gorriti has argued about countries with guerrilla challenges,

The authorities in the threatened countries must confront the nightmarish realities that any Third World democracy faces when battling a determined group of ruthless insurgents. A well-planned insurgency can severely test the basic assumptions of the democratic process. While they provoke and dare the elected regime to overstep its own laws in response to their aggression, the insurgents strive to paint the very process they are trying to destroy as a sham. If ensnared in such perverse dynamics, most Third World democracies will find their legitimacy eroding, and may eventually cease to be democracies altogether.[6]

Democracy is abandoned altogether when a government under this pressure becomes involved in a "dirty war." A number of countries have had such wars, in which thousands of people have been murdered or simply "disappeared"—Argentina and Chile in the 1970s, El Salvador and Guatemala in the 1980s, Peru in the 1980s and 1990s, and for the last fifty years in Colombia. In these cases the government, or at least the military, has been involved. Once the dirty war is over and democracy is restored, the question becomes to what extent violators of human rights in the previous period should be punished. Punishing the guilty (from the military, predominantly) may in turn threaten the democracy. As did Raúl Alfonsín in Argentina, many civilian presidents may pardon putative violators of human rights rather than risk making the military subsequently so angry as to intervene again.

Although during the 1960s most Latin American countries faced guerrilla threats, by 2010 only in Colombia were they still numerous. Sendero Luminoso still existed in Peru, but with much less importance than before; and guerrillas still were present in the southern part of Mexico. Where civil wars have only recently ended, the difficult task is to achieve consensus among erstwhile enemies. As has become apparent in El Salvador and Colombia, even though a government may grant amnesty to guerrillas, the people who suffered at their hands may not be ready to forgive and forget.

The Ability to Govern

Charles Tilly has argued, "No democracy can work if the state lacks the capacity to supervise democratic decision making and put its results into practice."[7] Although the degree of state weakness varies in Latin America, few governments have been able to enforce their decisions throughout their countries. As relatively poor countries with serious problems of transportation and communication, many Latin American countries have never been able to ensure the rule of law for the entire nation. Although they might be quite democratic in the way in which their leaders are elected and their laws are written, at best they govern only the major cities.

With the emergence of the drug trade in the 1970s, this weakness of government was exacerbated in Latin American countries. Colombia, Peru, Bolivia, and Mexico were especially affected in this regard. The ways in which the drug trade distorted democracy in her native Colombia were described by María Jimena Duzán, herself a personal victim of it:

> Today in Colombia, we have had to take a stand against drug trafficking. Colombians, especially journalists, who deal with these themes know that at such times our democracy itself is at stake in the form of our freedom of expression and our right to dissent. . . . This is a terrorized political class that has delivered itself to the designs and money of the drug dealers. Those who stand up to the bosses and challenge them have fallen victim.[8]

In Peru the *Sendero Luminoso* (Shining Path), a Marxist guerrilla group, along with the drug traffickers of the Upper Huallaga valley destabilized politics for ten years. Mexico, given its size and apparent stability, at times seemed less affected. However, its location made it a transit point to the United States, and some drug interests have infiltrated its government as much as they have in Colombia. By 2008 Mexican drug groups had replaced Colombian ones as the chief suppliers to the market in the United States. Conflict between rival groups made murder and kidnapping rates sadly reminiscent of Colombia in the 1980s.

The Period of Democracy Since 1978

At no time in history have the Latin American countries had elective presidents as frequently as they have since the democratic wave began in 1978. However, this does not mean that "liberal democracy" has arrived in all the Latin American countries. In addition, "delegative democracy" has replaced the liberal variety in some countries.

Liberal Democracy

Elections are not the only criterion for liberal democracy, with Philippe Schmitter and Terry Lynn Karl suggesting its ten characteristics shown in Table 5.1.[9] First, constitutionally elected officials must effectively control government decisions. Second, the elections for those officials must be frequent and fair. Coercion cannot exist on a large scale if the criterion of free elections is going to be met. Third, almost all adults must have the right to vote in these elections and, fourth, likewise they must have the right to run in them. Furthermore, there must be no danger in either voting or running for public office.

Table 5.1　　Characteristics of Liberal Democracy

1. Constitutionally elected officials must effectively control government decisions.
2. The elections for those officials must be frequent and fair.
3. Almost all adults must have the right to vote in these elections.
4. Almost all adults must have the right to run in them.
5. Citizens must have the right to express themselves about politics without fear of punishment.
6. Citizens must have the right to seek alternative sources of information, and such sources must exist and be protected by law.
7. Citizens must have the right to form independent organizations and groups, including political parties, civil societies, and interest groups.
8. Officials who are elected must be able to govern constitutionally without the veto power of unelected officials, such as the military.
9. Officials must be able to act independently without outside constraints.
10. Power must not be controlled by one branch of government alone; rather, there should be a system of checks and balances.

Source: Philippe C. Schmitter and Terry Lynn Karl, "What Democracy Is . . . And Is Not," *Journal of Democracy* 2, no. 3 (Summer 1991): 75–88.

Fifth, citizens must have the right to express themselves about politics without fear of punishment. Sixth, they also must have the right to seek alternative sources of information, and such sources must exist and be protected by law. This suggests that the media must be allowed to publish and broadcast, unlike many cases in the past when states of siege or emergency have led to censorship. Seventh, citizens must have the right to form independent organizations and groups, including political parties, civil societies, and interest groups. The stipulation of "independent" suggests that the government should not favor certain interest groups over others (as was characteristic of the ones that had been successfully co-opted), and should neither reward some with financial assistance nor punish some by using violence against them. Eighth, the officials who are elected must be able to govern constitutionally without the veto power of unelected officials, such as the military. Ninth, the same officials must be able to act independently without outside constraints. Tenth, power must not be controlled by one branch of government alone, but rather there should a system of checks and balances.

In addition, some argue that a full democracy should also have a considerable degree of egalitarianism, a sense that all people are full citizens, not victims of class, racial, or gender discrimination. All should have a sense of participation, social and economic programs that are more or less just, and a certain civic consciousness that all people deal with each other in fair, impartial, and just ways. With these in mind, although some of the Latin American countries may have the institutional apparatus of democracy, in many respects they are still far from having democratic societies.[10]

A democracy is *consolidated* when people consider it "the only game in town." This means that, no matter how bad things get, the only option is to behave in a "democratic" way—that is, to wait for the next election, contact representatives in government, or use (if available) other constitutional methods such as recall elections. It does not mean occupying key roads and bridges, as happened in Argentina in 2000 to 2002; using the military to overthrow a president who is disliked, such as what occurred in Ecuador several times in the first decade of the new millennium; or using economic power to get rid of a president, or at least pressure him to change policies, as in Venezuela in 2002. Chile, Uruguay, and Costa Rica are the only three Latin American countries that have met these criteria during the entire period, though Argentina, Brazil, the Dominican Republic, and Mexico after the 2000 presidential elections have made notable progress toward that ideal.

The difficulties in many cases come from two paradoxes of democracy. The first is that a democracy must be both representative and efficient. Second, a democracy must be based on a consent that is earned by its effectiveness. The first paradox of democracy lies in pitting representativeness against governability. Democracy implies an unwillingness to concentrate power in the hands of a few, and it therefore subjects leaders and policies to mechanisms of popular representation and accountability. To be stable, however, a democracy must be able to act—sometimes quickly and decisively. Representativeness requires that parties and leaders speak to and for these conflicting interests. Thus, to be able to govern, parties must have sufficient autonomy to rise above them.[11]

A related, important contradiction of democracy in Latin America is between consent and effectiveness. Democracy means literally "rule by the people." To be stable a democracy must be deemed legitimate by the people; they must view it as the best, most appropriate form of government for their society. This legitimacy requires a profound moral commitment and emotional allegiance, but these develop over time and partly as a result of effective performance. Larry Diamond also argues that "democracy will not be valued by the people unless it deals effectively with social and economic problems and achieves a modicum of order and justice."[12] This has been a problem in many Latin American countries as the neoliberal removal of customs barriers has led to large-scale unemployment of individuals who had jobs under the old, protected economies. The 2000 presidential elections in Mexico, for example, demonstrated how this could be a political issue. Even within the party in power, opposition arose to the neoliberal changes as their effects on the poor of the country became obvious.

Table 5.2   Guillermo O'Donnell's Characteristics of Delegative Democracy

1. The President is the embodiment of the nation and the main custodian of the national interest, which it is incumbent upon him to define.
2. What he does in government does not need to bear any resemblance to what he said or promised during the electoral campaign; he has been authorized to govern as he sees fit.
3. Since this paternal figure has to take care of the whole nation, it is almost obvious that his support cannot come from a party; his political basis has to be a movement, the supposedly vibrant overcoming of the factionalism and conflicts that parties bring about.
4. In this view other institutions, such as congress and the judiciary, are nuisances that come attached to the domestic and international advantages of being a democratically elected President.
5. Accountability to those institutions or to other private or semiprivate organizations appears as an unnecessary impediment to the full authority that the president has been delegated to exercise.

Source: Guillermo O'Donnell, "Delegative Democracy?" Kellogg Institute Working Paper #192 (April 1993), http://kellogg.nd.edu/publications/workingpapers/WPS/172.pdf, 7.

Delegative Democracy

The recent wave of democratization in Latin America demonstrates these paradoxes. On one hand, there have been more elective presidents in more nations than ever before. For the first time there is near-universal suffrage. On the other hand, however, there have been limitations and shallowness of democratic practices. Scholars have come up with adjectives such as "low intensity democracy" and "schizophrenic democracy" to describe these circumstances. The most common term, however, has been "delegative democracy." All three suggest that the initial euphoria surrounding the demise of military dictatorships has changed to a growing dissatisfaction regarding the ambiguous character and quality of new civilian regimes.[13]

Guillermo O'Donnell's idea of a "delegative democracy" includes four major characteristics. First, the president is the embodiment of the nation and the main custodian of the national interest, which it is incumbent upon him to define. Second, what he does in government does not need to bear any resemblance to what he said or promised during the electoral campaign—he has been authorized to govern as he sees fit.

Third, since this paternal figure has to take care of the whole nation, it is almost obvious that his support cannot come from a party. Instead, his political basis has to be a movement, the supposedly vibrant overcoming of the factionalism and conflicts that parties bring about. Typically, winning presidential candidates in delegative democracies present themselves as rising above all *parties*—that is, they transcend both political parties and organized interests. How could it be otherwise for somebody who claims to embody the whole of the nation?

In this view, other institutions—such as congress and the judiciary—are nuisances that come attached to the domestic and international advantages of being a democratically elected president.[14]

Although such executive domination is far from new in Latin America, in the first decade of the new millennium "liberal" democracies became "delegative" ones in Venezuela (Hugo Chávez), Bolivia (Evo Morales), Ecuador (Rafael Correa), and perhaps to a lesser degree Colombia (Álvaro Uribe). In all cases necessary constitutional changes were accepted by the voters through referendums or by the national congress through constitutionally mandated procedures.

Some scholars, however, think that the governments are not "democratic" in any way—not even a delegative one. In a study of Venezuela and Paraguay, Paul Sondrol argues:

> But the term democracy, with modifiers, fails to capture these regimes' common essence and defining feature; their purposeful, authoritarian nature. Semi-authoritarian governments are not failed or struggling democracies that, given time, academic compassion, and plenty of foreign assistance, will inevitably, democratically, blossom.[15]

These are, Sondrol says, democratically disguised dictatorships, a particular regime type whereby formal democratic institutions mask and legitimate de facto authoritarian political control. They have four major characteristics:

1. blocking mechanisms limiting electoral transfers of power;
2. democratic trappings and weak institutionalization;
3. policy disconnect between economic and political liberalization, controlled and manipulated by regime elites; and
4. limits to civil society empowerment.

Sondrol concludes that Venezuela's Hugo Chávez represents the new type of revolutionary, messianic strongman, elected by citizens "with eyes wide open." They are "alienated by traditional politics and lured by simple, appealing, populist solutions to cut through the red tape of confusing, corrupt, and tedious pluralist politics." Therefore, "[p]erhaps it is time to stop thinking in terms of the 'democratic transitions' paradigm, and to start calling these semi-dictatorships what they really are."[16]

Conclusions

As the following chapters of this book demonstrate, many Latin American countries have a coexistence of the old system of "living museum" politics, liberal democracy, and delegative democracy. Some might best be called "semi-authoritarian." To the extent that the living museum system exists, the paradigm suggested by Charles Anderson (and presented here in chapter 3) is still useful. If liberal democracy, delegative democracy, or semiauthoritarianism has become the dominant system, new paradigms for interpreting Latin America must be developed. In assessing which system prevails in a country, the factors presented in Tables 5.1 and 5.2 will be helpful.

Two concerns should be kept in mind as one evaluates the politics of the Latin American nations. First, the systems are very dynamic with change occurring constantly. This means that a valid conclusion made on one date might soon change. Second, judgment about the factors in Tables 5.1 and 5.2 is very difficult, as many times sources in the United States do not include adequate information. If Latin American sources are consulted—and many are readily available on the Internet—often information from both governments and oppositions is intentionally reported incorrectly.

Both concerns were clearly shown in Honduras in mid-2009. On the face of it, the country left liberal democracy and returned to the living museum system when the military overthrew President Manuel Zelaya. Both the United Nations and the Organization of American States condemned this, while the Obama administration called for Zelaya's return to office. Some even called this a "return to banana republic politics." On the surface this case might seem simple. Using the terms of this chapter, a president who had been elected in a "liberal democracy" tried to change his country to a "delegative democracy," just as Chávez had in Venezuela or Correa in Ecuador. The military as the representative of the "living museum" system took over power.

However, the matter was not quite that simple. The Honduran constitution limited a president to one four-year term, and Zelaya wished to remain in power and change the country to a "delegative democracy." He wanted to have a "consultation," a vote of the people. The Electoral Commission denied him that right and the Supreme Court declared such a vote to be unconstitutional. Nevertheless, President Zelaya ordered the armed forces to organize the consultation. They refused and instead overthrew Zelaya. After the Supreme Court removed him from his post, the Congress, following the constitution, elected Roberto Micheletti as the new president.

This Honduran case demonstrates the fragility of democracy in some Latin American countries. It also shows that aspects of the "living museum" model—a strong executive and military intervention—could reappear. Yet it also shows that the idea of democracy is strong. In November 2009 the Honduran people elected Porfirio Lobo as their new president.

Suggestions for Further Reading for Chapters 1–5

Anderson, Charles. *Politics and Economic Change in Latin America.* New York: Van Nostrand, 1967.

Burkholder, Mark, and Lyman Johnson. *Colonial Latin America.* New York: Oxford, 2002.

Bushnell, David, and Neill Macauley. *The Emergence of Latin America in the Nineteenth Century.* New York: Oxford, 2002.

Camp, Roderic. *Democracy in Latin America: Patterns and Cycles.* Wilmington, DE: Scholarly Resources, 1999.

Collier, David. *The New Authoritarianism in Latin America.* Princeton, NJ: Princeton University Press, 1980.

Collier, David, and Ruth Collier. *Shaping the Political Arena: Critical Junctures, the Labor Movement, and Regime Dynamics in Latin America.* Princeton, NJ: Princeton University Press, 1991.

Dominguez, Jorge, and Abraham Lowenthal. *Constructing Democratic Governance.* Baltimore, MD: Johns Hopkins University Press, 1996.

Evans, Peter. *Dependent Development: The Alliance of Multinational, State, and Local Capital in Brazil.* Princeton, NJ: Princeton University Press, 1979.

Gwynne, Rober, and Critobal Kay. *Latin America Transformed: Globalization and Modernity.* London: Arnold, 1999.

Kryzanek, Michael J. *U.S.-Latin American Relations.* Westport, CT: Praeger, 2008.

Langley, Lester. *The Americas in the Modern Age.* New Haven, CT: Yale University Press, 2005.

Levine, Daniel. *Religion and Politics in Latin America.* Princeton, NJ: Princeton University Press, 1981.

Lewis, Paul. *Authoritarian Regimes in Latin America.* Blue Ridge Summit, PA: Rowman & Littlefield Publishers, 2005.

Lorrain, Felipe, and Marcelo Selowsky. *The Public Sector and the Latin American Crisis.* San Francisco: ICS Press, 1979.

Loveman, Brian. *Por La Patria: Politics and the Armed Forces in Latin America.* Wilmington, DE: Scholarly Resources, 1999.

Malloy, James. *Authoritarianism and Corporatism in Latin America.* Pittsburgh, PA: University of Pittsburgh Press, 1977.

McClintock, Cynthia. *Revolutionary Movements in Latin America.* Washington, DC: U.S. Institute of Peace Press, 1998.

McDonald, Ronald, and Mark Ruhl. *Party Politics and Elections in Latin America.* Boulder, CO: Westview Press, 1989.

Needler, Martin. *The Problems of Democracy in Latin America.* Lexington, MA: Lexington Books, 1987.

Pastor, Robert. *Democracy in the Americas: Stopping the Pendulum.* New York: Holmes and Meier, 1989.

Peeler, John. *Building Democracy in Latin America.* Boulder, CO: Lynne Rienner, 1998.

Skidmore, Tom, and Peter Smith. *Modern Latin America.* New York: Oxford, 2001.

Smith, Peter. *Democracy in Latin America.* Oxford: Oxford University Press, 2005.

Veliz, Claudio. *The Centralist Tradition in Latin America.* Princeton, NJ: Princeton University Press, 1980.

Wiarda, Howard J., ed. *Authoritarianism and Corporatism in Latin America—Revisited.* Gainesville: University Press of Florida, 2004.

Wiarda, Howard J. *The Soul of Latin America.* New Haven, CT: Yale University Press, 2001.

Wynia, Gary W. *The Politics of Latin American Development.* 3rd ed. New York: Cambridge University Press, 1990.

Notes

CHAPTER 1

1. Robert C. Williamson, *Latin American Societies in Transition* (Westport, CT: Praeger, 1997), 127.

CHAPTER 2

1. David Collier and Ruth Berins Collier, *Shaping the Political Arena: Critical Junctures, the Labor Movement, and Regime Dynamics in Latin America* (Princeton, NJ: Princeton University Press, 1991).

CHAPTER 3

1. Charles W. Anderson, *Politics and Economic Change in Latin America: The Governing of Restless Nations* (New York: Van Nostrand, 1967), especially chapter 4.

2. See David Collier, ed., *The New Authoritarianism in Latin America* (Princeton, NJ: Princeton University Press, 1979).

3. Peter H. Smith, *Democracy in Latin America: Political Change in Comparative Prospective* (New York: Oxford University Press, 2005), 103.

4. "Notification of the Works of Father John Sobrino," Zenit, The World Seen from Rome, www.zenit.org/article-19147?l=english.

5. José Nun, "The Middle Class Military Coup," in *The Politics of Conformity in Latin America*, ed. Claudio Véliz (London: Oxford University Press, 1967), 66–118.

6. James Petras, "Strategies of Struggle: The Centrality of Peasant Movements in Latin America," *Counterpunch*, June 4–5, 2005, www.counterpunch.org/petras06042005.html.

7. This section is based on Dr. Donna Lee Van Cott, "Latin America: Indigenous Movements," in the *Encyclopedia of Nationalism*, vol. 2, ed. Alexander J. Motyl (San Diego: Academic Press, 2000).

8. Mala N. Htun, "Women's Political Participation, Representation, and Leadership in Latin America," in Women's Leadership Conference of the Americas, Issue Brief, www.iadiaglo.org/htunpol.html, 9/22/99.

9. Mayra Buvinic and Vivian Roza, "Women, Politics and Democratic Prospects in Latin America," Inter-American Development Bank, December 2004, www.iadb.org/SDS/doc/women.pdf.

10. This section is based on suggestions from Dr. Vanessa Gray. Our thanks go to Dr. Gray for her assistance in this section.

11. Smith, 176.

12. Anthony Leeds, "Brazilian Careers and Social Structure: A Case History and Model," *American Anthropologist* 66 (1964): 1321–47.

CHAPTER 4

1. "Washington Consensus," Global Trade Negotiations Homepage, Center for International Development at Harvard University, April, 2003, www.cid.harvard.edu/cidtrade/issues/washington.html.

2. Robert Vargas, "The Pink Tide: Socialism Sweeping Across Latin America," @hora Depaul IX (Spring 2006), www.depaulasu.net/Ahora2006Winter.pdf, last viewed, June 2, 2009.

3. Alan Gilbert, "The Latin American Mega-city: An Introduction," www.unu.edu/unupress/un upbooks/uu23me/uu23me03.htm.

4. "Latin America: Nations Must Address Urban Pollution, U.N. Says," Interpress Service, October 16, 2007, www.goliath.ecnext.com/coms2/gi_0199–7115864/LATIN-AMERICA-NATIONS -MUST-ADDRESS.html.

5. Peter Saundry (contributing author), Central Intelligence Agency (content source), and Mark McGinley (topic editor), "Latin America and Caribbean Population Growth Rates," in *Encyclopedia of Earth*, ed. Cutler J. Cleveland (Washington, D.C.: Environmental Information Coalition, National Council for Science and the Environment, 2009).

6. Raymond Vernon, *The Dilemma of Mexico's Development* (Cambridge, MA: Harvard University Press, 1963).

CHAPTER 5

1. Mario Vargas Llosa, "The Culture of Liberty," in *The Global Resurgence of Democracy*, eds. Larry Diamond and Mark F. Plattner (Baltimore, MD: Johns Hopkins University Press, 1993), 86.

2. Hernando de Soto and Deborah Orsini, "Overcoming Under-Development," *Journal of Democracy* 2, no. 2 (Spring 1991): 106.

3. Robert Wesson, *Democracy in Latin America: Promise and Problems* (New York: Praeger, 1982), 125.

4. Ibid., 130–31.

5. Larry Diamond, "Three Paradoxes of Democracy," *Journal of Democracy* 1, no. 3 (Summer 1990): 49.

6. Gustavo Gorriti, "Latin America's Internal Wars," *Journal of Democracy* 2, no. 1 (Winter 1991): 86–87.

7. Charles Tilly, *Democracy* (Cambridge: Cambridge University Press, 2007), 15.

8. María Jimena Duzán, "Colombia's Bloody War of Words," *Journal of Democracy*, 2, no. 1 (Winter 1991): 105.

9. Calling anything with elections democracy, despite fraud, was labeled "electoralism" by Philippe C. Schmitter and Terry Lynn Karl, "What Democracy Is . . . And Is Not," *Journal of Democracy* 2, no. 3 (Summer 1991): 78.

10. A study of Latin America that added other criteria to the institutional ones of democracy was Jorge I. Domínguez and Abraham F. Lowenthal, eds., *Constructing Democratic Governance: Latin America and the Caribbean in the 1990s* (Baltimore, MD: Johns Hopkins University Press, 1996).

11. Diamond, 49.

12. Ibid., 49.

13. Kenneth M. Roberts, *Deepening Democracy? The Modern Left and Social Movements in Chile and Peru* (Stanford: Stanford University Press, 1998), 1.

14. Guillermo O'Donnell, "Delegative Democracy?" Kellogg Institute Working Paper #192 (April 1993), http://kellogg.nd.edu/publications/workingpapers/WPS/172.pdf, 7.

15. Paul Sondrol, "Semi-Authoritarianism in Latin America," www.allacademic.com/meta/p_mla_apa_research_citation/0/9/8/8/8/pages98880/p98880–1.php, 1–2.

16. Ibid., 25.

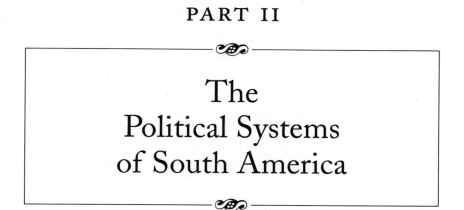

PART II

The Political Systems of South America

SOUTH AMERICA

6

Argentina in the Twenty-first Century

Linda Chen

Argentina began the twenty-first century in political and economic chaos. An economic crisis precipitated by the failure of neoliberal reforms, commonly referred to as the "Washington Consensus," led to a period of political instability that brought three different presidents to office over a two-week period in late 2001. A caretaker government, led by Peronist Eduardo Duhalde from 2002 to 2003, was replaced by Peronist rival Néstor Kirchner in elections held in 2003. Kirchner succeeded in halting the economic decline and serving his full term in office. Still, this bright spot in Argentine politics has been overshadowed by Kirchner's machinations to build a political dynasty. In 2007, he stepped aside in favor of his wife, Cristina, who handily won the presidential elections. This move was widely viewed as attempting to prolong the Kirchners stay in power well beyond the next presidential elections scheduled for 2011.

Cristina Fernández de Kirchner's tenure in office, to date, has been a turbulent one, as it coincided with the global economic downturn. Orchestrating early mid-term legislative elections in June 2009 led to voter repudiation of the Kirchners. As a result, Argentina, at the end of the first decade of the millennium, sees its economy headed for crisis and the political ambitions of the Kirchners in tatters.

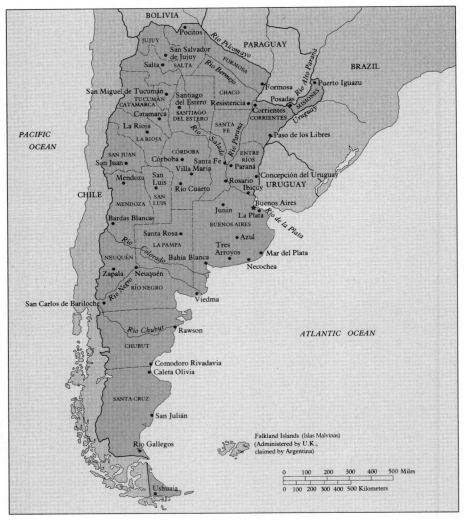

ARGENTINA

The Land

Argentina's size—1.1 million square miles, or 2.77 million square kilometers—is about four times the size of Texas. Located in the southernmost part of South America in the area known as the Southern Cone, it faces the Atlantic Ocean to the east and has the Andean Mountains at its back. Its northern border, which it shares with Paraguay and Bolivia, is mostly tropical. Its southern area, which includes Patagonia, Tierra del Fuego, and (according to Argentine claims) a part of Antarctica, lies in the subpolar and polar zones.

Embracing so many climates as it does, Argentina is easily divided into many different regions, each with its own economic and social character. Most of the population and economic activity are found on the Pampa, a flat, open plain of rich soil, moderate rainfall, and temperate climate lying along the Atlantic coast and running into the country's midsection. This is where Argentina's principal exports—wheat, corn, and beef—are produced. It is also where Argentina's major cities and industries are located. Buenos Aires, the nation's federal capital and chief port, is an extensive metropolis of over three million people in a province of fifteen million. It dominates the rest of the country politically, economically, financially, and culturally. The porteños, as the residents of Buenos Aires are known, consider themselves quite superior to their fellow citizens in the provinces, and indeed to all of Argentina's neighbors. Whatever may be the accuracy of such a claim, it is certain that Buenos Aires does tend to draw in much of the talent of southern South America. In addition to Buenos Aires, the Pampa includes other large industrial hubs such as La Plata (approximately 650,000 people), the capital of Buenos Aires Province; Córdoba (about 1.5 million), where much of the automobile industry is located; and Mar del Plata (about half a million), a popular beach resort on the Atlantic.

North of the Pampa lies another fertile plain, known as the Littoral because it lies between the Paraná and Uruguay Rivers. It is slightly warmer than the Pampa but still produces beef and grain crops. Having been settled later than the Pampa, it exhibits more evidence of planned colonization in the sense that there are fewer large estates and more medium-sized farms. The city of Rosario (about 1.3 million), situated on the Paraná River, is another major industrial center with a number of important oil refineries.

Beyond the Littoral is the tropical Northeast, much of it a frontier region only recently settled. The population is a mixture of Paraguayans, with their unique Guaraní language and customs, and Europeans. Traditionally, the economic mainstay of this region was yerba maté, a bitter green tea grown on large plantations that is very popular in southern South America. More recently, however, cotton and citrus crops have also been introduced.

Proceeding west from the Pampa the traveler encounters a range of low mountains, similar to the Appalachians, in the western part of Córdoba province. Beyond these is the desert, as the land falls increasingly under the rain shadow of the Andes Mountains. There are oases lying due west, however, in a region known as Cuyo. The main city here is Mendoza (approximately one million), and the principal economic activities are wine-growing and the cultivation of olives. Much of this is done by small producers, many of them Italian immigrants.

North of Cuyo, the Andes Mountains spread out to form the Bolivian altiplano. This is Argentina's least developed and most impoverished region, cut off by the mountains from the Pacific coast and too far from the Atlantic. Much of the population is ethnically and culturally similar to Bolivians and lives on isolated farms in the mountain valleys. In the lowlands of Salta province, along the Bolivian border, there is some oil industry. Tiny Tucumán province, just south of Salta, was once the sugar-growing center of Argentina, but antiquated practices and the withdrawal of government subsidies caused this industry to go into a sharp decline, much of it moving to more modern plantations in Salta's lowlands.

Going south from the Pampa brings one to Patagonia, Argentina's largest, coldest, and least populated region. Upper Patagonia is a transitional zone in which cooler-temperature fruit such as apples and pears can be grown. Farther down in Patagonia, however, the land becomes a bleak, windswept plateau, often buffeted by Antarctic storms. With the exception of oil fields located along the coast in Comodoro Rivadavia and against the Andes Mountains in Neuquén, this area's economic activity is limited to fishing, mining, and the raising of sheep for wool on enormous *estancias*, Argentina's sheep and cattle ranches. Mining consists of exploiting mainly low-grade coal and iron deposits.

The People

Argentina's population of just over forty million is overwhelmingly urban (92 percent), with approximately one third living in the greater Buenos Aires metropolitan area. It is also overwhelmingly of European descent—mainly Spaniards and Italians—and also Roman Catholic, at least nominally. Argentines are relatively healthy, although some deterioration in living standards due to the economic crisis of 2001–2002 has been evident. Infant mortality stands at eleven per one thousand live births, life expectancy is seventy-three years for males and seventy-nine years for females, and the literacy rate is 97 percent for Argentines fifteen years and older (schooling is compulsory until age fifteen).

Argentina's ethnic mix—97 percent European, 3 percent mestizo and others—is a product of its unusual pattern of settlement. As a colony it produced little wealth for the Spanish crown and therefore remained sparsely settled. The indigenous population was made up of small, nomadic, hostile tribes that were gradually driven off the Pampa by the settlers, down into Patagonia. By the end of the nineteenth century they were practically eliminated. At the same time Argentina's cattle-raising culture required little importation of African slaves to work the estancias. Then, in the last two decades of the nineteenth century there was an enormous influx of European migrants, drawn by the attraction of vast tracts of cheap land, that significantly reconstituted the population. Today, Italian, French, German, English, Irish, Slavic, Jewish, and Arabic last names are common, as are Spanish.

Social structure in Argentina has allowed for movement both upward and downward. The upper classes consist of two kinds of elites. First is the traditional large rancher/farmer *estanciero* elite. Although very wealthy, this is by no means a closed aristocracy. Many successful immigrants joined it during the late nineteenth and early twentieth centuries. Alongside and overlapping with it is the more modern group of bankers, merchants, and industrialists. The two elites mingle socially in the highly prestigious Jockey Club and tend to congregate in the fashionable neighborhood of Barrio Norte in Buenos Aires.

The middle classes range from a very well-to-do upper stratum that is positioned just below the elites to a petit bourgeoisie consisting of small farmers and businesspeople, white-collar professionals, and lower-level bureaucrats. Top military officers, Catholic clergy, lawyers, doctors, and managers of corporations form the upper middle class. Sometimes their control of the government may make some of them as powerful as the elites.

The upper levels of the working classes consist of white-collar workers (*empleados*) and the skilled laborers (*obreros calificados*). Skilled laborers often make more money than white-collar workers, but they lack the latter's social status. Empleados go to work in a coat and tie, and although they may own only one of each, they do not get their hands dirty. Obreros, on the other hand, do sweaty work. Most working-class parents dream of getting their children enough education to move them up the social scale from obrero to the empleado category, if indeed not into the middle class. Below these two groups are the semi- and unskilled urban workers, and below them are the unskilled rural workers. Joining them are the members of the informal labor force, or "cuentapropistas." These are unregistered workers who work, part or full time in economic activities that official statistics do not capture. The ranks of these workers in the informal economy have exploded in the past twenty years, with some estimating that they now constitute nearly half of all workers in the country.

The Economy

Argentina has a sophisticated economy based on plentiful natural resources (especially oil); a highly skilled labor force; an efficient, export-oriented agricultural sector; and a great variety of industries. Its exports consist mainly of wheat, corn, soy, beef, and oilseeds. Argentina's chief trading partners are Brazil, the United States, and Italy. In 1991 it joined Brazil, Paraguay, and Uruguay to form a regional trading bloc called MERCOSUR, which has proved to be an important boost to foreign trade. Economic growth in the early 1990s averaged between 6 and 8 percent a year, following a period in the 1980s of economic contraction and hyperinflation. Unfortunately that period also left Argentina saddled with a huge foreign debt that continues to plague the Argentine economy. As structural problems, international crises, and domestic policies all worked to undermine Argentina's ability to grow and prosper, the Argentine recovery of the early 1990s did not last. By the late 1990s the economy was in recession and the years from 2000 to 2002 saw the Argentine economy contract and economic crises take hold. The situation began to improve starting in 2003 as the administration of Néstor Kirchner managed to arrest Argentina's decline and steer it on the road to recovery. However, the worldwide recession of 2008–2009 has again led to a slowing of Argentina's economy.

The Argentine economy has a long history of "stagflation," a combination of stagnant growth and runaway inflation. The causes were structural and arose mainly from excessive government intervention in the economy. Populist administrations, beginning in the 1940s, based their electoral support on a combination of heavy social spending, trade protectionism, and ubiquitous economic regulation. Such an inward-oriented, "hothouse" economy was designed to guarantee high living standards for labor and to subsidize a large number of small, labor-intensive businesses that would provide plenty of jobs.

Traditionally Argentina's economy was characterized by the dominance of large estancias in the countryside and small businesses in the towns and cities. Naturally there were many exceptions to this general rule. Small and medium-sized farms and ranches produced profitably for the market, and there were even well-off tenant farmers. In certain industries, such as automobiles, pharmaceuticals, and rubber—or rather, any large enterprise requiring heavy capital inputs and advanced technology—big foreign companies dominated. The state was in control of "basic" or militarily strategic industries—energy, transportation, mining, oil, armaments, utilities. Often that meant the armed forces' direct ownership and management. The domestic private sector therefore tended to concentrate on manufacturing light, nondurable consumer goods, such as food products, textiles, home furnishings, and small appliances. In addition, domestic private capital controlled most wholesale and retail commerce, as well as the service sector. With a few notable exceptions, these locally owned private companies were small, employing fewer than ten people on the average. Many simply worked with their own, unpaid family members. In short, Argentina had an urban economy of mainly small capitalists, or a "shopkeeper society."

This society began showing signs of breaking down in the 1960s. Argentine industry was inefficient, and its products were therefore both costly and often shoddy. Protected by tariffs and manipulated exchange rates, however, it had a captive market to exploit. Because most people lived in the cities and depended directly or indirectly on this industry, politicians hesitated to challenge it. The money to support public services came mainly from sales taxes, tariffs on foreign goods, and tariffs levied on Argentina's agricultural exports. The tariffs were greatly resented by the farmers and ranchers, but because they were only a minority of the population, they were unable to change the policy. Nonetheless, these added costs were pricing Argentine beef and grains out of world markets, and as they did so the government's treasury began running low on foreign exchange.

By the 1980s Argentina was in a real crisis: deeply in debt, with banks and businesses failing, agriculture stagnant, and capital fleeing the country. Population trends added to the crisis. Like many other socially advanced countries, Argentina's birthrate had fallen greatly, to a little over 1 percent—not enough to replenish itself. Young people with skills were leaving for Europe or the United States, while the elderly and retired were becoming an increasingly large portion of the population. A slight increase of women in the workforce helped to alleviate the situation somewhat, but with the growing recession and unemployment, there was little incentive to seek regular work. On the other hand, the informal economy—where people worked for below minimum wages, evaded social security payments and payroll taxes, and flouted most other labor laws—grew rapidly. By the end of the 1990s it was believed to account for at least 60 percent of all economic activity, although no records exist to prove that assertion.

Following the election of Carlos Menem to the presidency in 1989, the old system came under full-scale attack. The Peronist orthodoxy that supported state-dominated economic policymaking was no longer viable, especially as the socialist model was collapsing in the Soviet Union and elsewhere. Menem's economics minister Domingo Cavallo instituted a set of neoliberal reforms that sought to insert Argentina into the global economy on terms promoted by the U.S. and international lending agencies. These Washington Consensus reforms advocated cutbacks in government spending, privatization of state-owned industries, and liberalization of trade.

The impact on Argentina's urban middle and working classes was devastating. Stripped of protection and subsidies, many small businesses disappeared, gobbled up by larger foreign and domestic companies. Within a few years the "shopkeeper society" was transformed into one dominated by large private conglomerates. Because these were capital-rather than labor-intensive, unemployment rose in the working classes as well, especially among women and youth.

The lynchpin of Menem's neoliberal economic project was the "convertibility plan," which pegged the peso's value to the dollar so that one peso equaled one dollar. While early results from the convertibility plan were positive and international creditors and lending agencies were impressed, the structural flaws in such a plan began to take hold after 1994. The overvaluation of the Argentine peso meant that Argentine goods were not competitive on the world market. This plan also depended on access to available credit, a situation that would turn sour after the Mexican financial crisis of 1994 caused a shrinking of external investment. Along with problems of political corruption, infighting in Menem's government, profligate spending by the provincial governments, and the chronic problem of tax evasion, by the end of the 1990s the Argentine economy was headed toward crisis.

In 2001 Argentina defaulted on its US$100 billion debt, plunging the country into economic and political chaos. Neoliberal reforms were in a shambles. The next two years saw the unprecedented contraction of the economy and severe impoverishment of the Argentine population. Between 1999 and 2002 the GDP shrank by 20 percent, unemployment reached record-high levels of 18 percent, and over 50 percent of the population saw their lives descend into poverty. International lending agencies all but abandoned the country.

The election of Néstor Kirchner to the presidency in 2003, however, effectively brought a halt to Argentina's economic decline. In a departure and perhaps rejection of the Washington Consensus, Kirchner reasserted the role of the state in managing economic policy and promoted a nationalist-tinged argument for economic recovery. In what is often referred to as neodevelopmentalism, Kirchner sought to prioritize social welfare spending with the continued need for global integration. In his four-year term ending in 2007, Argentina's economy rebounded. Economic growth averaged 9 percent per year and private consumption increased by 52 percent. Unemployment and poverty rates saw sharp declines: Unemployment declined from a high of 20 percent in 2002 to 9 percent in 2007. Poverty rates went from a high of 50 percent in 2002 to 27 percent by the end of 2007. Kirchner also resuscitated collective bargaining among labor unions, and workers saw a rise of 70 percent in real wages. Without a doubt, the economic reforms pushed forward by Kirchner brought much relief to millions of Argentines.

Kirchner's ability to carry out such drastic reforms was facilitated by a period of high prices for Argentine exports, especially in commodities, fuels, and processed agricultural goods. The Argentine peso also enjoyed relatively favorable terms on global exchange markets. Tax revenues were raised and foreign investment began to flow back into the country. Kirchner also succeeded in renegotiating Argentina's foreign debt on positive terms for Argentina. Still, these favorable conditions for Argentina's global economic position could not last forever.

Cristina Fernández de Kirchner's election in 2007 coincided with the global downturn in the economy. In her first year in office Fernández de Kirchner did battle with the agroexport sectors in her quest to raise tax revenues—a fight that she lost. Inflation was creeping into the economy and export prices had begun to decline. Fernández de Kirchner's decision to take over billions of dollars of private pension funds set off new concerns about the government's fiscal solvency. Many analysts argue that Néstor Kirchner failed to undertake economic reforms that would have cushioned the effects of the downturn the country faced by 2009. The situation was not helped by the fact that Néstor Kirchner, and then Cristina after him, manipulated official economic data about economic conditions. This practice was another indication that Argentina's economy was heading into another crisis.

Argentina's Early Development

Argentina's history has been shaped by conflict and division. Once Spanish rule was overthrown, the leaders of the independence movement quickly fell out among themselves over what sort of government they would have. The city of Buenos Aires, the former capital of the old Viceroyalty of La Plata, wanted a centralized government and advocated for a form of liberalism emphasizing free trade, encouraging European immigration, promoting modernization, and reducing the power of the Catholic Church. Led by Bernardino Rivadavia, they created a Unitary Party and sought to concentrate power in a central government dominated by Buenos Aires.

Opponents from the interior provinces of Argentina bridled under the dominance of Buenos Aires. Their interests were basically local, and what united them was a desire to promote their own interests and limit the power of a central government. Aside from this, among the federalists many disagreements would arise. For instance, while the interior provinces were open to foreign trade, each wanted to do so on its own terms by encouraging inland navigation by foreign ships. Buenos Aires federalists were opposed to this idea. Still, when Buenos Aires caudillo Juan Manuel de Rosas sought to unify the country under a "federalist scheme," many of the provinces went along. A federalist scheme, even if promoted by a caudillo from Buenos Aires, was better than anything the Unitaries advocated.

A powerful estanciero who represented the cattle interests, Rosas had adopted the ways of a gaucho and had gained prestige in a series of frontier wars against the Indians. With his own cavalry, in 1829 he drove the Unitaries out of the country, and from then to 1852 he ruled as the caudillo dictator of Buenos Aires. Rosas governed as a strong nationalist, so all aspects of liberalism were repressed. The Catholic Church was given control over education, censorship suppressed any criticism, and those suspected of Unitary sympathies were intimidated—and sometimes murdered—by a paramilitary organization known as the Mazorca. Most people with liberal opinions went into exile.

Rosas was defeated in 1852 by a combination of rebellious caudillos and exiles. The following year the Argentine Federation adopted a constitution patterned closely after that of the United States. Its liberal principles included the separation of powers, checks and balances, the right to private property, and the guarantees of free speech and press. It also encouraged the government to foster immigration. Because it provided for a federal system, however, the city of Buenos Aires would not accept it. Armed clashes followed. In 1862 Buenos Aires finally agreed to join the federation, and in 1880 the city itself was detached from the province and made a federal district.

From 1852 to 1916 Argentina was ruled by a "liberal oligarchy" who believed that governing should be left in the hands of the educated and the propertied. To control electoral outcomes, various provincial gentry formed a single official party, the National Autonomist Party (Partido Autónoma Nacional, PAN), and ruled by fraud and corruption. Under the liberal oligarchy, Argentina's foreign trade grew rapidly, and the proceeds were plowed into internal developments: roads, bridges, ports, and an excellent system of public education. New methods of agriculture were adopted, cattle breeding and pasturage were improved, and new lines of production were introduced: grain-growing and sheep-raising. Foreign capital brought in the railroads, the telephone and telegraph, gas and electric power, the refrigerated steamship, modern meatpacking, and modern sanitation. With the commercial boom also came an increase in banking, insurance, and construction. The port of Buenos Aires became one of the busiest in the world, and the city was transformed from a dull colonial-looking town into a modern European-type capital whose broad boulevards and imposing buildings reminded travelers of Paris.

Along with these radical changes came a huge wave of immigration from Europe. Many came originally as seasonal farm workers, saved their earnings, and bought their own farms out on the expanding frontier. Others moved to Buenos Aires or smaller cities, where they started small factories or commercial shops as well as provided services to meet the growing demands of a rapidly rising population. Between 1869 and 1895 Argentina's population had more than doubled, from 1.7 to 3.9 million. By 1914 it would more than double again, to over 7.8 million, with about half the gain due to immigration and settling on the Pampa or in the Littoral. In that same period the city of Buenos Aires grew from only about 100,000 inhabitants to over 1.5 million, and fully half of the latter were foreign-born.

The massive influx of immigrants had far-reaching consequences. To begin with, it greatly increased the size of Argentina's middle classes. In 1914 the economic census showed that two thirds of all the proprietors of industrial establishments and three fourths of owners were foreign-born. The vast majority of these businesses were small, averaging fewer than seven workers. Nevertheless, industry and commerce were beginning to take their place alongside agriculture as important economic activities, and a new entrepreneurial class was emerging. Rising in tandem with these small capitalists was a new urban industrial working class. The same 1914 census found that half of all industrial workers were foreign-born, many of whom had experience in Europe's socialist, anarchist, or syndicalist movements.

These new elements would soon tear apart the liberal oligarchy's monopoly on government. In 1889 the Civic Union (*Unión Cívica Radical*, later called the Radical Party) launched as a reform party, which called for universal suffrage, honest elections, and good government. Its leaders were progressive members of the oligarchy, but the bulk of its following came from the middle classes. The Radicals attempted to overthrow the oligarchy on two occasions, in 1890 and 1905, but failed. Their leader, Hipólito Yrigoyen, denounced PAN's continual resort to fraud. At the same time, the labor movement divided into a moderate socialist wing and a revolutionary anarchist wing. The liberal oligarchy, now organized under the Conservative Party, sought to repel these pressures from below. However, progressive members, including Roque Sáenz Peña, accepted the need for reform. In 1910 Sáenz Peña won the presidency and pushed through Congress an electoral law (that bears his name) granting suffrage to all males who performed a year of military service as well as the institution of the secret ballot. It also included a new electoral law, called the "incomplete list" system, under which the party with the most votes in a district would receive two-thirds of the representatives, while the one coming in second would get the other third. The era of mass politics had begun.

Mass Politics

The election of 1916 brought Yrigoyen to power and ushered in fourteen years of rule by the Radical Party. Yrigoyen and his successors, however, did little to transform the economic priorities of the era. The economic interests of the elites, still concentrated in the export cattle industries, were little threatened under Radical rule. Even so, elements of the conservative elites grew increasingly unhappy sharing power with middle-class interests. The Radicals did not have a particularly good relationship with the rising ranks of the working classes either. Although Yrigoyen seemed to tolerate the socialist-oriented unions, he had disdain for the anarchists. A number of labor strikes during Yrigoyen's presidency were met with police force and repression. In 1919 labor repression reached an all-time high with the events of the "Tragic Week," when the police, the army, and armed groups of members of a right-wing paramilitary organization called the Patriotic League attacked strikers at a steel mill. They then proceeded to the Barrio Once, where many workers and Jews lived, and killed an estimated one thousand people. Two years later the army crushed an anarchist-led strike in Patagonia, executing over two thousand workers and torturing many more.

With the Great Depression of 1929, the era of the Radicals came to an end. Conservative elite interests, who had never been supportive of "opening up the political system," saw their chance to oust Yrigoyen, who had been re-elected for a second term but who seemed incapable of handling the economic dislocation brought about by the Depression. Agitation among the military, who had their own grievances against the Radicals, led to a military coup that deposed Yrigoyen in 1930.

The leader of the coup was army General José F. Uriburu, an admirer of Benito Mussolini, who advocated an ultranationalist state that favored elite rule under a corporatist state. Ousted after two years in power, he was re-placed by General Agustín P. Justo, who had the support of a broader array of interests—Conservatives, dissident anti-Yrigoyen Radicals, and maverick so-cialists. Economic policymaking in the 1930s led to inroads in industrial-ization. The Great Depression laid bare the vulnerabilities of Argentina's dependence on commodity exports, so the small industrial base began to ex-pand. Bereft of markets from which to import manufactured goods, urban middle-class entrepreneurs began production of light manufactured goods. Argentina's industrial base thus expanded under this import-substitution-industrialization model. Foreign investors played a key role in this expansion.

The 1930s were also a time of social upheaval. European immigration had ended with World War I, never again to reach its former volume, but now came a great wave of migrants from Argentina's rural interior to the cities, pushed off the land by the Depression and pulled into urban centers in search of factory jobs. Metropolitan Buenos Aires alone doubled its population to over six million. Most of these newcomers were unskilled and could not find steady work and instead scrambled for low-paying peripheral jobs. Nor were they welcomed by the older working class. The latter were Europeans or their descendants, and they looked down on these rural, dark-skinned migrants. In return, the "little blackheads" (*cabecitas negras*), as they called them, had no interest in the foreign-sounding ideologies like communism and socialism, then dominant in the labor movement. They would take any work at any pay, and thus avoided the labor unions, who likewise avoided them. So the Argen-tine working classes divided: the relatively well-off skilled workers with their Marxist-oriented unions, on one side, and a much larger, un-unionized, un-skilled, insecure mass of recent migrants living in sprawling, squalid, makeshift slums on the city's edge, on the other. This was the soil from which Peronism would emerge.

The Peronist Watershed

The political scene in Argentina in the early 1940s was dominated by the external events of World War II. The army, many of whose officers were German-trained, supported an alliance with the Axis powers. A group of high-level officers conspired to implant a government modeled after Mussolini's Italian fascist regime. Calling themselves the Group of United Officers (GOU), they successfully took power in 1943. Among its members was a little known army colonel named Juan Domingo Perón. When the events of World War II made it clear that the Axis powers were losing, the military establishment in power began a search for an exit strategy.

Meanwhile, in 1943 Perón had asked to take over the management of the Secretariat of Labor and Social Welfare. Previously he had served as Minister of War, a position he used to build a support base within the army. As minister of labor, Perón began to settle disputes in labor's favor. He reversed longstanding antilabor legislation and actively promoted legislation to improve workers' lives. Old-age pensions, accident and health insurance, annual paid vacations, factory safety codes, minimum wage and maximum hour legislation were all expanded and enforced. Labor unionists were given positions in his ministry; others were freed from jail. Employers who had fought the creation of labor unions were now forced to accept them. Perón's support base among labor grew.

Some within the military began to view with alarm the policies of Perón. The conservative elites and industrial groups were also resentful and suspicious of Perón's courting of workers. The growing opposition to Perón led a group of officers to oust him from all government posts and put him under arrest on a naval base in the La Plata River. What happened next is still the stuff of Peronist legend. Labor unions and workers' organizations mobilized to protest the jailing of Perón. Thousands of workers descended on the capital of Buenos Aires and converged on the Plaza de Mayo, demanding Perón's release. Not having an alternative, the military finally agreed to release Perón. On October 17, 1945, Perón appeared on the balcony of the Casa Rosada (Government House) and saw the results of his hard work of organizing the working classes. As he gestured in victory to thousands of workers cheering him, it was clear that the working classes had forced their way into the political arena. The Peronist Era had begun.

The election of 1946 passed the mantle of power and legitimacy to Perón. In the run-up to the election Perón organized his own political party, the Labor Party, which organized his many supporters under his leadership. He had the solid support of the labor unions, many of which had organized within the past three years; factions of the military from whose ranks he came; and the Catholic Church, for which Perón had promised to retain their right to control education and to prevent divorce legislation. The Conservative Party, landed elites, urban industrialists, middle-class radicals, and an array of socialists and communists were opposed to Perón. Nevertheless, Perón's victory in the 1946 election was decisive: 1,479,517 votes for the Labor Party and 1,220,822 for the opposition Democratic Union, a coalition of anti-Peronist interests. Perón's allies also swept the two houses of Congress, the provincial governorships, and all but one of the provincial legislatures.

Perón came to power with a number of factors in his favor. He had won a fair and open election with the support of a broad coalition of groups, including elements of the military and the Catholic Church. The state treasury was full, as Argentina had been able to capitalize on the sale of supplies to the Allies during World War II. Furthermore, international prices of food and raw agricultural materials were rising relative to industrial goods. His development policies focused on expanding basic industrialization, expanding social welfare benefits, a certain redistribution of wealth, and promoting nationalism.

Perón continued to pursue his pro-labor policies by promulgating legislation covering all aspects of workers' lives. Real wages and fringe benefits went up. Under the Secretariat of Labor and Prevision, Perón created an extensive network for the administration of labor affairs. He gradually concentrated labor matters under the General Direction of Labor and Direct Social Action (DGTASD). All aspects of labor relations, including collective bargaining, labor law enforcement, union registrations and dues, workplace conditions, and employer-union conflicts came under the purview of the DGTASD. To ensure labor compliance with Peronist policies, the General Confederation of Labor (CGT) was given a monopoly of control over labor unions. The CGT was the only legally recognized labor confederation in the country, and any union that wished to be legally recognized had to fall under its control and oversight. In classical corporatist fashion, the CGT was the vehicle by which Perón transmitted his policies down to labor rank and file.

Perón's pro-labor policies were part of his economic project to further industrialization. Profits from the agricultural sector were transferred to the industrial sector. Agriculturalists were forced to sell all their commodity exports to a government agency called the Argentine Institute for Production and Trade (*Instituto Argentino de Producción y Intercambio*, IAPI) at government-set prices. The idea was for IAPI to buy at the lowest possible price and then sell the goods on the world market at the highest possible price. The profits would then be used to finance industrialization.

Perón's industrial project sought to expand import substitution industrialization. To that end, he nationalized the central bank, railroads, telephone, electricity and gas, and urban transport. The state began development of an aviation and a steel industry. Compensation for the nationalizations came from state treasury funds, leading to a severe depletion of state funds for promoting industrialization beyond that of light manufactured goods. As a result, capital-intensive industrialization never really took off. Parallel to the CGT controlling labor, Perón set up the General Economic Confederation (CGE) to represent industrialists, merchants, and agriculturalists.

Perón's political style was clearly populist as he continued to direct his words and deeds to the working classes. With his wife, Eva Duarte, Perón sought to elevate the working classes from their historic second-class status. Eva Perón (Evita), in particular, served as an effective interlocutor between Perón and the people. Her own biography, emphasizing her illegitimate upbringing in a dusty provincial town and her rise to political fame, served as an inspiration to millions of working-class and poor Argentines. Adopting a glamorous style, Eva Perón took an active part in dispensing social welfare funds to the working class and poor.

Perón's populism, though, also had its authoritarian side. Soon after taking office he renamed the Labor Party as the Peronist Party so as to solidify his own personal power base. He and his allies set about purging Argentine politics and society of anyone who opposed Perón, whether they were independent-minded labor leaders or newspaper publishers. Political parties other than the Peronist Party were harassed and repressed. Perón used censorship and outright strong-arm Mafioso brutality tactics to reinforce his power. Political corruption also was endemic, as the Peróns surrounded themselves with relatives and friends, many of whom saw access to the Peróns as an invitation to seek personal and material gains.

From 1946 to 1949 the Peronist project produced economic growth and a substantive improvement in people's lives. The real incomes and quality of life of Argentine workers and the middle classes increased, and for all the loathing the economic elites expressed toward Perón, they did not suffer much under his redistributive policies. Regardless, industrialization did not lead to sustained economic growth, and by 1950 the state treasury was running out of monies to continue supporting its own state-run, inefficient industries and its expanded social welfare expenditures. When Eva Perón died in 1952 from cancer, Perón's decline began.

Facing pressure from a deteriorating economic situation, Perón sought even greater controls over society. He attacked the Catholic Church, an early Perón supporter, when they refused to canonize his wife as a saint despite popular demonstrations on her behalf. Then the clergy provoked a confrontation when it began to organize Christian Democratic trade unions in competition with Perón's. Perón went on the attack, forbidding religious processions and expelling priests. Street clashes escalated until finally, on the night of

June 16, 1955, Peronist fanatics set fire to several downtown churches, including the Cathedral and the Archbishop's Palace. Meanwhile, anti-Peronist opposition had been growing in the military. The navy had always been a center of resistance, but now the army, one of Perón's main pillars of support, was restive. Its professionalism was insulted by mandatory courses in Peronist political indoctrination at the Academy and by the regime's new program of encouraging the sergeants and enlisted men to join the Peronist Party. The officers feared that their own men would be encouraged to spy on them. With the Catholic Church and important factions of the military allied against Perón, a military coup, led by General Eduardo Lonardi, forced Perón from office in September 1955. Perón took refuge initially in Paraguay and ultimately made his way to Spain. The first Peronist experiment was over.

The legacy Perón left Argentina in 1955 was expanded group interests vying for political power. The Peronist Party–supported labor unions and working classes vied for political power alongside the agricultural elites, the armed forces, the urban middle-class interests, and industrialists. To the state he left a huge bureaucracy with responsibilities to nationalized industries and social welfare policies. To the economy he left a depleted state treasury and a shaky industrial base. Perón neither destroyed the power of the traditional economic elites nor did his government gain enough strength to check their power. Rather, the next eighteen years would see attempts to defeat Peronism, all of which would fail at high social and political cost.

Peronism in Exile

The military coup of 1955 opened a period of political and economic turmoil in Argentina. The military regime, led first by coup leader Lonardi and then by General Pedro Aramburu, set about de-Peronizing Argentine society. It outlawed the Peronist Party and purged the labor union leadership of all Peronists. Strikes by workers were quashed as well. De-Peronization also involved attacking the symbols and historical memory of the Peróns. Aramburu embarked on a campaign to expose the excesses and corruption of the Peróns by displaying the material goods they amassed. He was also responsible for kidnapping Evita's body and having it sent to Milan, Italy, so as to deny the Peronist movement of a "sacred" symbol.

Aramburu was committed to returning the government to civilian rule, and so in 1958 elections were called. Aramburu had hoped that a resurrected Radical Party would lead the country out of its Peronist nightmare. Unfortunately for him the Radicals split internally and a left-wing faction, led by Arturo Frondizi, attempted to win the support of the labor unions by advocating a populist platform very similar to Perón's. The Peronist Party, however, was denied the right to field candidates. Because voting was and is obligatory,

Perón, from his place in exile in Venezuela, ordered his followers to cast blank ballots in the provincial elections that were a prelude to national elections. A full 25 percent of the votes cast were blank, attesting to Frondizi and everyone else the popular support Perón still enjoyed.

So as to ensure his success in the presidential election, Frondizi entered a pact with Perón to legalize Peronism in return for Peronist votes. Frondizi won in a landslide and initially promoted pro-labor policies. This stance would not last, however, and for the next four years Frondizi sought to carve out a middle position between Peronism and anti-Peronism. He failed and instead managed to alienate both Peronists and anti-Peronists. When Frondizi attempted to adopt a mediating stance with the Cuban Revolution, the military ousted him from power. The next Radical experiment would be Arturo Illia, who represented the right-wing faction of the Radicals. An elderly doctor from Córdoba province, Illia was ineffectual, and in 1966 he was replaced by a military coup. Factions of the military then decided to give up on civilian rule and take power themselves for the long term.

General Juan Carlos Onganía took power in 1966, and like most of his military colleagues he no longer viewed democracy as viable for Argentina. Peronism still remained strong, a fact that was viewed as preventing Argentina from addressing its most pressing economic problems. According to the military, Argentina suffered from "stagflation," a combination of stagnant production and inflation. Free-market reforms such as austerity, competition, and privatization were needed, all of which would result in social unrest. Only a military dictatorship could enforce such harsh policies.

Onganía's economic policies were successful for the first two years. Inflation dropped from 40 to 5 percent, productivity rose, and exchange reserves were at their highest level in years. The unions were forced to suffer a wage freeze, and their strikes were brutally repressed. The press was censored and the universities were placed under tight control. Then, in mid-1969, workers in the city of Córdoba struck and were joined by university students. Four days of urban warfare left more than a dozen people dead. Known as the "cordobazo," this event inspired antigovernment demonstrations throughout the country. That same year a leading collaborationist labor leader, Augusto Vandor was assassinated and a group of urban guerillas, the Montoneros, kidnapped former President Aramburu and executed him. Onganía, having lost control of the political situation, was forced from office.

For the next few years political forces converged to enable Perón to return to power. Political violence became commonplace as left-wing terrorism was met with right-wing terrorism. The military was finding it increasingly difficult to repress Peronism; labor unions continued to overwhelmingly support Perón; the Montoneros wanted Perón's return; and other classes in society viewed Perón's return as a way out of the chaos and violence plaguing society. After a bit of political machination, Perón returned triumphant to Argentina in 1973. This time, his wife was Maria Estela (Isabel) Perón.

Now a frail old man, Perón could not manage the forces he had supported from exile. The Montoneros who had demanded his return as a condition for ending their violent tactics were rejected by Perón once he returned to power. Within his own inner circle Perón was very much dependent on his personal secretary, José López Rega. A confidant of Isabel Perón, López Rega became minister of social welfare, which gave him control of a large budget that he used to build a private terrorist army of his own, known as the Argentine Anticommunist Alliance (AAA). It targeted left-wing guerilla movements, including the Montoneros, who responded in kind with their own violence.

Perón's death in 1974 brought further violence and chaos to Argentina. His widow, Isabel, who had been his vice president, was incapable of running a government, much less able to deal with Argentina's serious social and economic problems. Erratic economic policymaking, the rising militancy of the labor unions, and the increasing fears of the military brought an end to Isabel's regime. Once again, the military stepped into power. On March 26, 1976, to most Argentines' relief, Isabel was removed from power in a military coup.

Military-Sponsored Terror

The coup of March 1976 heralded a return to military rule that would be a departure from past military interventions. Calling its mission the "Process of National Reorganization," the military junta, made up of representatives of the army, navy, and air force, with Army General Jorge Rafael Videla as its head, committed itself to ending the political chaos and to setting the economy on a stable course. To achieve the former, the military undertook draconian measures to purge Argentine society of subversive elements that were impeding Argentina's development. It was not enough to rout the guerilla forces that had plagued Argentine society for the past decade; what was needed was to attack the root causes of Argentina's political instability. According to the military junta, Argentina's woes went beyond the problems of Peronism and an intransigent labor movement. To the military junta the entire fabric of Argentine life had been poisoned and diseased by leftist subversion, leading to a sick society rent with chaos and corruption. The solution was a concerted campaign to purge Argentina of those subversive elements and to reassert the "true" values of Argentine life. One of the self-proclaimed mottoes of the military junta was "Tradition, Family, and Property," borrowed from the ultraconservative Catholic Opus Dei organization that was popular with some in the military. The Argentine Catholic Church hierarchy became a staunch supporter of the junta.

The methods used by the military junta are by now famous. Green Ford Falcons with no license plates chauffeured by nondescript men sped through the streets of Buenos Aires both day and night in search of specific individuals believed to be subversives. Illegal detention centers were set up all over the country, equipped with both sophisticated and primitive means of torture. Basic civil liberties were severely restricted as Argentine society found itself gripped in fear and terror by the military junta's actions. All groups representing civil society (political parties, labor unions, civic associations) were repressed and their leadership went underground.

Although no sector of Argentine society was immune from this war against subversion, the hardest hit were the working classes, students, labor-movement activists, and urban professionals. The words "*los desaparecidos*" entered the Argentine lexicon to signify that persons were "being disappeared" by shadowy forces rather than disappearing of their own accord. Most of the disappeared were never found (all told, an estimated 30,000 persons lost their lives between 1976 and 1983 to this war), although mass graves are periodically uncovered in contemporary Argentina, filled with skeletons that show signs of violent deaths such as bullet holes, bashed-in skulls, and broken bones. In addition to dumping torture victims in mass graves, people were burned alive in ovens, and others were thrown into the La Plata River in the hopes that their bodies would be eaten by sharks. Some remains, however, would end up on the beaches of the river.

Among those who were kidnapped and disappeared in this "Dirty War" were women who were pregnant. It is estimated that approximately four hundred babies were born in captivity by women who were subsequently killed after giving birth. The babies were "adopted" by the families of military men or were sold on the black market. The whereabouts of these children of the disappeared continues to play out in contemporary Argentina.

Although all sectors of Argentine society were repressed, it is noteworthy that a group of women whose children were disappeared organized to defy the military junta's policies. The Mothers of the Plaza de Mayo captured the imagination of the international media beginning in 1977, when a few brave women decided to demonstrate publicly against the repressive policies of the regime. Covering their heads with white scarves and holding up placards with pictures of their missing children, the Mothers held weekly marches around the Plaza de Mayo, calling attention to the regime's human rights abuses. Several of the original founders of the group were themselves disappeared, but the group persevered and were an important voice in ensuring that the human rights abuses of the junta not be ignored once it left power.

Part of the motivating drive for the repression was the military junta's economic priorities. Under the direction of José Martínez de Hoz, Argentina's economy was to be "reorganized" so as to promote growth, competitiveness, and global integration. Argentina's economy suffered from too much state intervention and the dominance of trade unions. In order to fix Argentina's economy, labor unions needed to be tamed and state-run industries needed to be privatized. In these ways foreign investment could be attracted so as to restart the Argentine economy.

With respect to the organized labor movement, the military junta attacked the central labor confederation, the CGT, and jailed many prominent labor leaders. Factory floors were occupied by military men to coerce workers to work. Trade union activity was banned, union elections were disrupted by the military, and control over union dues reverted to the government. Organized labor's fortunes were also eroded due to the free-market policies of the regime that led to the closing of state-run and inefficient industries, thereby causing massive unemployment.

The long-term impact of Martínez de Hoz's policies was a disaster. Neither economic growth nor inflation was tamed, and by 1980 the days of Martínez de Hoz were numbered. As the economic situation took a downturn, the military junta sought ways to maintain power. In 1981 General Videla ceded power to General Roberto Viola, who in turn was replaced by General Leopoldo Galtieri at the end of the year. By this time human rights groups in Argentina and newly radicalized labor unions began to agitate against the military regime. To quell the rising domestic discontent, Galtieri took Argentina into the ill-conceived war against Great Britain for control of the Falklands—or the Malvinas, as the Argentines call this group of islands in the South Atlantic. It was hoped that enflaming a longtime conflict with Great Britain would rally Argentine nationalism toward the regime. What Galtieri did not bargain for was Great Britain's response: It sent its famed naval fleet and Royal Air Forces to retake the islands. Argentina's defeat led to the hurried exit of the military junta from political power.

Transition to Democracy

The election of Raúl Alfonsín to the presidency in December 1983 was a watershed event in Argentina's political history. For the first time in a freely contested election the Peronistas did not win. The people's preference for the Radical Civic Union candidate, who himself had been jailed under the military, signaled a desire for a fresh start in Argentine politics, one that was a clear repudiation of past authoritarian regimes. During the electoral campaign Alfonsín promised to bring the Proceso's top military officers to trial for violating human rights, a promise he made good once elected. Alfonsín appointed a special investigative commission whose report was used as the basis for the trials held in 1985. For several months in early 1985 victims and families of victims testified to the extent of the human rights violations. General Videla was handed a life sentence and the other junta leaders were given long prison sentences. The military, fully discredited due to the disastrous performance in the Falklands War, had little recourse to protest. However, when courts and prosecutors began to indict lower-level officers, military rebellions occurred. Three military rebellions took place between 1987 and 1988, events that led to the curtailing of the human rights prosecutions. A "full stop" law was enacted, which limited the time period for when cases could be brought to the courts, all but stopping prosecutions against military personnel. The "due obedience" law then absolved from prosecution those who were "just following orders." Human rights organizations, including the Mothers of the Plaza de Mayo, vigorously opposed this legislation.

In the area of the economy Alfonsín and his economic team embarked on a number of strategies to curb rampant inflation, which had reached a yearly rate of 6,900 percent by 1985. He introduced a reform package called the Austral Plan that consisted of wage and price freezes, spending cutbacks, and raises in utility rates. Although the plan had initial successes, Alfonsín's failure to follow through on all his promises soon led to a resurgence of hyperinflation. Attempts to fix the Austral Plan came to nothing, and in the 1987 congressional elections the Radicals were roundly defeated by the Peronists. Two years later Alfonsín himself would leave office early due to his government's inability to manage the economic crisis. At the time of his resignation in June 1989, inflation had roared back to 4,900 percent, the GDP had contracted, real wages had fallen, and the external debt had reached a record US$63,314 million.

Peronism Without Perón

Carlos Menem, governor of La Rioja province, campaigned as an old-fashioned Peronist caudillo, promising to be the champion of the lower classes, but on taking office he shifted his stance so as not to end up like Alfonsín. Instead of populist economics he embraced a very orthodox neoliberal formula. Foreign capital, free trade, and privatization were promoted with vigor. To keep government spending within budgetary limits, the peso was pegged to the dollar at an exchange rate of one to one, and the Treasury was allowed to print only as many pesos as there were dollars in the Central Bank. Called the "convertibility plan," such measures soon brought inflation down to single digits, and economic growth climbed to around 9 percent. However, the social costs of these reforms were high. Thousands of government workers lost their jobs, as did workers in Argentina's inefficient industries. Local companies, long protected from competition, were either bought by foreigners or were absorbed into Argentine conglomerates. About a third of the economically active population was officially classified as living in poverty. Menem had thus reinvented the terms of debate with regards to the Argentine economy.

While Menem revolutionized the economy, his style of governance in other ways resembled aspects of Peronist *caudillismo*. Seeking to maximize his power, Menem sought a number of changes to Argentine institutional arrangements. He expanded the Supreme Court to nine members from the original five, and thereby set about packing the court with his allies. Under pressure from the military, he granted pardons to convicted military leaders. Although these moves enabled Menem to successfully reduce the size of the military ranks from around 100,000 to 20,000, he engendered the enmity of human rights organizations. He succeeded in instituting legislation that severely weakened the labor movement, including abolishing collective bargaining, enabling employers to have greater flexibility in hiring and firing, and breaking the labor unions' control over social welfare funds. Perhaps Menem's most important political maneuver was to have the constitution amended to allow his reelection as president. Instead of one six-year term, in 1994 the constitution was changed to allow for a four-year presidential term but with possible reelection.

Menem's early success in controlling the economic situation enabled him to make many of the changes cited above, so he easily won reelection in 1995. However, his administration was increasingly beset by scandals (many related to the sale of state-run industries) and allegations of political corruption. Furthermore, Menem's highly public divorce from his wife, his penchant for consorting with movie stars and celebrities, and his use of family members as political advisors who were accountable to no one further compromised his reputation. As the economic situation began to decline, so did Menem's political fortunes.

The election of 1999 brought about Peronism's defeat once again, this time at the hands of a coalition consisting of the Radical Civic Union and the Front for a Country in Solidarity (*Frente del País Solidario*, FrePaso). The latter was a political party formed in 1994 of disaffected Peronists and persons from left-of-center political parties. Calling themselves the "Alianza," Fernando de la Rúa (head of the Radicals) was elected on a platform of promising to end political corruption and to ameliorate the suffering of millions of Argentines whose economic livelihoods were destroyed by the neoliberal policies of the 1990s. The Alianza was short-lived because political differences between the Radicals and FrePaso led to a fracturing of the alliance and instability in the de la Rúa coalition. Economic policymaking failed to arrest the deepening decline of economic productivity, and poverty rates increased.

By the end of 2001 the political and economic situation was chaotic. De la Rúa resigned from the presidency, thereby plunging Argentina into its worst political crisis since the era of military rule. Congress selected a succession of three presidents in a two-week period. Finally, Eduardo Duhalde, a Peronist Party boss from Buenos Aires Province, was elected president in early 2002. Instead of calling for early elections, Duhalde opted for elections in 2003 (what would have been the end of de la Rúa's full term).

Democratic Consolidation—A Mixed Record

The 2003 presidential election brought Néstor Kirchner, Peronist governor of Santa Cruz province, to office. An ally of Eduardo Duhalde at the time, Kirchner won the presidency with only 22 percent of the popular vote after his closest rival, former President Carlos Menem, dropped out of second-round balloting. Kirchner then succeeded in stabilizing the economic situation and oversaw four years of economic recovery. Legislative elections in 2005 delivered to him huge majorities that allowed him to pursue a number of political and economic reforms. Kirchner's policies strengthened democracy in Argentina in a number of ways. They also, however, reinforced long-standing tendencies that concentrated power in the hands of the executive and did little to further institutional stability.

In strengthening democracy, Kirchner reformed the Supreme Court by basically overturning the changes made under Menem, who had packed the Court with political cronies. Kirchner forced the resignation of six out of nine justices and replaced them with respected jurists. He eventually reduced the Supreme Court back to its original five members as a show of support for the Supreme Court's independence. Kirchner also had Congress repeal the amnesty laws that had all but shut down prosecutions of individuals from the 1976–1983 military junta responsible for human rights violations—a demand long called for by the human rights community. The pardons of the former military leaders were also annulled. Additionally, Kirchner appeared to respect civil liberties, allowed for clean elections, and engendered greater public trust in the government. He served out his entire term in office, a feat that is noteworthy considering the long history of civilian presidents forced from office early either by military coup or economic crisis.

On the negative side, Kirchner, as with his predecessors, concentrated power in the executive. After the 2005 legislative elections Kirchner forced the Congress to grant him vast discretionary authority over the budget in the "superpowers law." He abolished open primaries (a practice in effect since 2002) for the nomination of presidential candidates. Moreover, even as he reformed the Supreme Court, his heavy-handed efforts to do so reinforced the primacy of presidential power. He intervened in the once-independent state statistical agency, INDEC, by firing technocrats and manipulating the procedures by which inflation was measured. This blatant politicization of economic data has all but discredited any claims by the government of how well the economy is faring. Finally, in a blatant attempt to prolong his stay in power, Kirchner's decision to step aside after one term to have his wife stand for the presidency, was seen as an attempt to run for reelection after Cristina's term is up, thereby continuing the Kirchner political dynasty into the future.

Cristina Fernández de Kirchner was elected on the popularity of her husband's economic policies. The fact that the economic situation in Argentina began to decline just as she took office complicated her ability to maintain power. On the heels of several crises in her first year, her popularity plunged. In order to arrest her declining popularity Fernández de Kirchner moved midterm legislative elections originally scheduled for October 2009 to June. Her husband then put himself forward for a seat from Buenos Aires, so the election was largely a referendum on the Kirchners' popularity and policies. They lost this political gamble as Néstor Kirchner failed to win a seat and the Kirchner wing of the Peronist Party lost majorities in both houses of the legislature.

The Kirchners' political viability remain very much in doubt. Whether Fernández de Kirchner will succeed in serving out her entire term remains an open question. Some analysts hope she will open her administration to greater consultation and compromise, while others fear that the emerging economic downturn will once again result in political instability.

The Government

The 1853 constitution, which though revised is still basically the law of the land, was modeled after that of the United States. It provides for a federal republic with twenty-three provinces and a federal district. The national government is divided into three branches: the executive, a bicameral Congress, and a judiciary. There is a strict separation of powers and a classic system of constitutional checks and balances. The constitution also contains a lengthy section outlining citizens' rights and guarantees, including the rights of petition, assembly, free speech, and free press. Freedom of religion is guaranteed, as is the right to own private property. An individual may not be arrested without a warrant, may not be forced to testify against him-or herself, and has a right to a lawyer and to a speedy and fair trial. The sanctity of the home and personal privacy are to be protected.

There is often a wide gap, however, between the written constitution and how Argentina actually is governed. For example, rights and guarantees may be suspended in times of emergency. Serious internal commotion or the threat of a foreign attack may be used by the president to justify declaring a state of siege. Although the president is supposed to obtain the Senate's approval, which is given only for a limited period of time and only for specific purposes, in practice both dictatorial and democratic governments have found it relatively easy to evade these restrictions, especially if the president has a congressional majority.

By the same token, Argentina's federal system is a great deal more centralized than a formal reading of the constitution would indicate. The federal government has specific, enumerated powers; the provinces are left with unspecified "reserve" powers, which in practice are quite whittled down. Provinces are referred to in the constitution as "the natural agents of the Federal Government, to see that the laws of the land are obeyed." Federal law and treaties always trump provincial law. The real sources of provincial weakness, however, are their financial dependence on the federal government and the latter's right to intervene in a province to maintain order. Concerning finances, the provinces are restricted in their ability to levy taxes. By contrast, the federal government has the revenues derived from the port of Buenos Aires and other, mostly indirect, taxes. What's more, given the widespread practice of tax evasion, even those are hardly sufficient to cover its responsibilities, so there is little left over for revenue sharing with the provinces. As for the federal government's power of intervention, this frequently has been abused. Citing electoral fraud or financial mismanagement, past presidents have often replaced opposition-party governors or provincial legislatures with their own hand-picked interveners.

Despite the tripartite division of powers at the national level, the president dominates the political system. Neither Congress nor the courts have been allowed to develop as powerful, independent institutions. At various times both have been abolished, suspended, or ignored. Even under democratic rule, a president whose party enjoys a comfortable majority in both houses of Congress usually has no trouble getting any legislation passed.

Congress consists of two houses, a Senate and a Chamber of Deputies. Each of Argentina's twenty-three provinces has three senators, as does the federal district of Buenos Aires, for a total of seventy-two. Since 2001, they have been directly elected for six-year terms, with one third of the seats up for reelection every two years. The Chamber of Deputies is based on population, and it currently has 257 members, directly elected for four-year terms, with one half up for reelection every two years. Seats are distributed on the basis of proportional representation.

The Argentine Congress historically has been weak, and during the present era of democracy dating from 1983 it has "delegated" a great deal of power to the executive in the form of "emergency powers," which has enabled the president to enact budgetary and regulatory laws without congressional oversight. Very few politicians appear to make a "career" out of serving in

Congress, and the result is that its institutional capabilities are quite under-developed. There exist few experienced legislators in the Congress, committees are weak, technical expertise is low, and oversight bodies are ineffectual.

Legislation may originate in either house, except for bills that deal with taxes or appropriations, which must start in the Chamber of Deputies. Bills must pass both houses, after which they go to the president for his approval. If he signs them, they become law, but if he vetoes them in whole or in part (he has the line-item veto), only a two-thirds majority of both houses can override him.

The president and vice president are directly elected by the voters for a four-year term. Presidents may be reelected once. Their patronage powers are wide ranging: Judges, ambassadors, cabinet officers, and the top military posts require Senate approval, but lower administrative officials are appointed by him alone. Beyond that, they are charged with seeing that the laws are faithfully executed, acting as commander-in-chief of the armed forces, and opening each annual session of Congress with a state-of-the-union message.

The real source of the president's dominance lies in certain extraordinary powers, which presidents traditionally have interpreted in such a way as to overwhelm the other branches of government. First, there is the state-of-siege power, which can temporarily release a president from constitutional restraints. Second, the power to intervene in the provinces has enabled presidents in the past to cancel the mandates of their opponents. Third, the president may issue rules and instructions that are "urgent and necessary" for the execution of the laws. This innocuous phrase has been the source of presidents' increasingly common use of executive orders to bypass the regular legislative process. Some of the most controversial economic reforms of the Menem administration were put into effect in this way. Nor does the Congress usually act as a watchdog over such overexpansion of executive power. For President Néstor Kirchner, his coming to office in the midst of one of Argentina's worst economic crises enabled him to demand—and get—from Congress extraordinary emergency powers to issue legally binding decrees.

Political Parties and Pressure Groups

Argentina had been an essentially two-party system since popular elections were introduced in 1912. In the first decade of the twenty-first century, however, it has been the Peronist Party that has dominated national politics, with the Radical Civic Union (UCR), the Peronist Party's historic rival, failing to rebuild after the debacle of Fernando de la Rúa's resignation from the presidency in 2001. The UCR, founded in 1889, had been the party that represented the middle classes. Although it continues to maintain a national institutional structure, it has not shown any signs of revitalization in the past several elections.

It is the Peronist Party (or the Justicialist Party as it is known by its official title) that has weathered the political and economic misfortunes of the past twenty-five years. Justicialismo's institutional development was marked by the fact that it began as Perón's personal vehicle, the Peronist Party. Even so, the party has often been a coalition of various interests. Besides the trade union movement, its membership consisted originally of dissidents from the Radicals who liked Perón's statist program as well as right-wing authoritarians with fascist leanings. When Perón granted women the vote, Evita Perón helped form a feminine wing to the party. Translated into practical terms, Justicialismo was a version of the corporate state, in which business, farmers, labor, the professions, and students were required to belong to officially sanctioned organizations. Its highly regulated economy, which aimed at national self-sufficiency, encouraged the growth of three powerful interests that became the permanent basis for the Peronist coalition: a highly centralized trade union movement, a class of rent-seeking capitalists living off state subsidies and protection, and a large government bureaucracy. These interests survived Perón's fall in 1955 and continued to resist all attempts by successive governments to eradicate Peronism.

In the 1970s the left-wing Montonero guerrillas added themselves temporarily to the Peronist coalition, so that ideologically its supporters spanned the entire political spectrum, from extreme left to extreme right. In the 1990s President Carlos Menem then moved the Justicialist Party decisively to the right with his neoliberal program, doing so at the cost of alienating a large number of working-class supporters.

President Néstor Kirchner resurrected some traditional populist rhetoric during his term in office, but at the same time he did not fully reverse the neoliberal reforms of Carlos Menem. Kirchner did, however, pay more attention to the social needs of the population and challenged international lending agencies to be more cooperative. The Menem and Kirchner presidencies represent the wide diversity that exists within the Peronist Party with regards to economic decision-making. Néstor Kirchner lost to a Peronist rival in the June 2009 legislative elections, one who advocated closer adherence to the neoliberal reforms championed by Carlos Menem in the 1990s.

In all cases the dominance of the Peronist Party raises serious questions concerning the institutionalization of democracy. Healthy political party competition is a necessary requirement of democracy, for it promotes accountability, oversight, and offers meaningful alternatives to voters. Minor political parties have often not survived past an election and in most cases, have been vehicles for personalities rather than social movements. Polls indicate that

Argentina's middle classes do not support Peronism but are at a loss in their search to find alternative political representation. As the nation heads into the presidential elections scheduled for 2011, it remains to be seen whether Peronism will remain dominant (albeit with its intense factionalism) or if new political movements will emerge out of the heterogeneous disaffected sectors of society who are anti-Peronist.

Future Prospects

Since the transition to democracy in 1983, Argentina has experienced periods of political stability marked by free and open elections, the transition of power from one political party to another, and after some initial tensions, military willingness to be subordinated to civilian power. At the same time, Argentina has at times seemed to seesaw out of control, as the political crisis of 2001 that led to the resignation of Fernando de la Rúa illustrates.

The economic stability of Argentina has been even more problematic. Hyperinflation, massive external debt, defaulting on the foreign debt, and monetary and fiscal crises have all plagued the Argentine economy for years. The economic meltdown of 2001–2002 caused massive unemployment, impoverishment, and the contraction of the economy. The much vaunted reforms of neoliberalism championed by Carlos Menem failed, and the economic crises it precipitated served to reverse decades of development in Argentina.

Perhaps one of the lessons of the recent past is that neither neoliberal nor left-leaning, state-driven redistributive polices provide the answers to Argentina's quest for sustained economic growth. Néstor Kirchner offered up his own brand of populist social welfarism by emphasizing the need to respond to citizens' suffering before meeting the demands of the international lending agencies. His tough stance worked, but he failed to institutionalize economic reforms that would have insulated Argentina from the effects of the current global economic crisis.

As Argentina enters the second decade of the twenty-first century, it continues to struggle with a number of political challenges. Putting the economic house in order will remain the central focus of the Cristina Kirchner administration—all the more so since it remains to be seen whether economic crisis will lead to political crisis, as has been the pattern in modern Argentine politics. Argentina has had a habit of changing the political rules of the game when crisis occurs, thereby weakening the institutionalization of policies, procedures, and offices. Hyperpresidentialism remains a problem and, with it, the lack of a viable opposition to the Peronists. While other areas of Argentine democracy appear to be healthy—such as the continued civilian control over the military, widespread respect and observance of civil rights and liberties, and continued national support for democracy—Argentina's path toward democratic consolidation remains a work in progress.

Suggestions for Further Reading

Auyero, Javier. *Flammable: Environmental Suffering in an Argentine Shanty Town*. New York: Oxford University Press, 2009.

Bonner, Michelle. *Sustaining Human Rights: Women and Argentine Human Rights Organizations*. University Park: Penn State University Press, 2007.

Cleary, Matthew, and Susan Stokes. *Democracy and the Culture of Skepticism: Political Trust in Argentina and Mexico*. New York: Russell Sage Foundation, 2006.

Epstein, Edward, and David Pion Berlin, eds. *Broken Promises?: The Argentine Crisis and Argentine Democracy*. Lanham, MD: Lexington Books, 2006.

Fiorucci, Flavia, and Marcus Klein, eds. *The Argentine Crisis at the Turn of the Millennium: Causes, Consequences and Explanations*. Amsterdam: Aksant, 2004.

Helmke, Gretchen. *Courts Under Constraints: Judges, Generals, and Presidents in Argentina*. New York: Cambridge University Press, 2004.

Levitsky, Steven, and Maria V. Murillo, eds. *Argentine Democracy: the Politics of Institutional Weakness*. University Park: Penn State University Press, 2005.

Lopez-Levy, Marcela. *We Are Millions: Neo-Liberalism and New Forms of Political Action in Argentina*. London: Latin America Bureau, 2004.

Nouzeilles, Gabriela, and Graciela Montaldo. *The Argentina Reader: History, Culture, and Politics*. Durham, NC: Duke University Press, 2002.

Spiller, Pablo, and Mariano Tommasi. *The Institutional Foundations of Public Policy in Argentina*. New York: Cambridge University Press, 2007.

Tedesco, Laura. *The State of Democracy in Latin America: Post-transition Conflicts in Argentina and Chile*. New York: Routledge, 2004.

Veigel, Klaus. *Dictatorship, Democracy, and Globalization: Argentina and the Cost of Paralysis, 1973–2001*. University Park: Penn State University Press, 2009.

Wright, Thomas. *State Terrorism in Latin America: Chile, Argentina, and International Human Rights*. Lanham, MD: Rowman and Littlefield, 2007.

7

Brazil's New Way

The BRIC Road to Progress

Iêda Siqueira Wiarda

Brazil's commemoration of its five hundred years of existence in 2000 was followed by the euphoria of the 2002 elections when a barely literate but heroic union leader, Luiz Inácio Lula da Silva, fifty-eight, won an overwhelming popular mandate over the government-supported candidate.[1] Proclaiming a "Brasil: Um País de Todos" (Brazil: A Country for Everybody), Lula, as he likes to be called, celebrated not only his electoral victory but also the promises inherent in an embrace of multiethnic society. To most seasoned observers in and out of Brazil, the following years demonstrated Lula as an adept national and international politician. He moved beyond his left base toward the center, chose good cabinets, and signed a number of well-received international economic and diplomatic agreements. Not surprisingly, with an approval rating above 80 percent, he handily won a second term in 2006.

As is often the case in the history of this enormous country, Lula's presidency has been marked by a number of alleged scandals linked to some of the president's closest associates. The president himself was not touched. Major investment companies in 2008 endorsed Brazil as a significant emerging market, a BRIC—*B*razil, *R*ussia, *I*ndia, *C*hina. Brazil was well on its way to finally being seriously considered a country deemed worthy of international attention.[2]

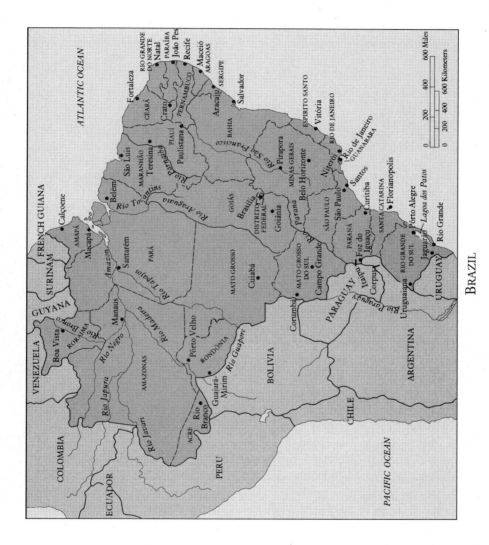

BRAZIL

Yet, it is well to remember that both the promises and the disappoint-ments, the renewal of well-placed hope and the travails of everyday life did not start with Lula but reflect the vast panorama of Brazil's multifaceted resources—both human and geographic—and a history both intriguing and unique in Latin America. It is thus incumbent to examine the cultural and po-litical underpinnings as we begin to assess whether this giant country, richly endowed in so many ways, is able to indeed achieve what it senses it deserves: respect and weight within world councils. One should also note that Brazil, in contrast to other BRICs, does not have to cope with major ethnic and reli-gious divisions, a variety of languages and dialects, harsh winters and large deserts, and, for now, huge population burdens.

The largest of Latin American countries, Brazil covers nearly half of South America and is the fifth largest country in the world. Except for a few islands, it consists of one single, unbroken land mass. Given its size, it is not surprising that Brazil has distinct regions and that Brazilians enjoy touting their state of origin as the best. Historically, its population ranges from those living at the level of the Stone Age to those who are comfortable in the great metropolises of the world. Throughout this largest Portuguese-speaking country in the world, the language is surprisingly uniform. While different ac-cents are detectable, Brazilians of all classes, all colors, and all regions under-stand each other. Thus, although Brazil faces many complex problems, a high degree of cultural integration among the overwhelming majority of its citi-zens remains a major source of strength—"A Country for Everybody" indeed.

Brazil's 4,500-mile Atlantic coast facilitates trade with the world. Its pop-ulation, approaching 200 million[3] and concentrated along that coast, has now slowed its growth to a little over 1 percent per year, thus making it the world's fifth most populous nation, which is a relatively low demographic density in comparison to other countries. Even though the country (3.29 million square miles) is only slightly smaller than the United States, most of its citi-zens live on 10 percent of the land, a 200-mile-wide zone bordering the At-lantic from Fortaleza to the Uruguayan border. The country shares borders with all South American countries with the exception of Ecuador and Chile. Controlling the world's eighth largest market-based economy, Brazil was the economic miracle from the mid-1960s through the mid-1970s until the eco-nomic disaster of the 1980s. Hyperinflation in the early 1990s was tamed by the ambitious "Real Plan" of the late 1990s, and inflation was estimated around 5.9 percent at the end of 2009. Although it is still high, it is certainly better than the nearly 13 percent when Lula became president.

Globalization has meant that Brazil's products can be found everywhere, from orange juice, coffee, bran and oils, soybeans, cocoa, and beef to transport equipment and metallurgical products. Brazilian engineers and technicians supervise and complete major construction projects in Africa and the Middle

East. São Paulo's stock exchange, Bovespa, is quoted in the economic sections of most newspapers. The Internet and the World Wide Web have enmeshed the country with the rest of the world, as seen in the linkages formed between human rights groups and indigenous councils. Globalization has also meant that Brazil has had to divest itself of its long-held protectionist garb. More liberal and flexible interpretations of the 1988 constitution's restrictions have served as inducements for great foreign capital participation. Moreover, others feel that some of the restrictions have helped Brazil in the economic crisis of 2008–2009.[4]

Under former President Fernando Henrique Cardoso, Brazil strengthened its economic ties with Argentina, Paraguay, and Uruguay under the Southern Common Market (MERCOSUL), of which Chile and Bolivia have also become associate members. Early in 2005 Brasília was the site of a South American and Arab country summit. This was another indication that President Lula had gone beyond traditional ties to Portuguese-speaking African countries to Muslim countries and China in particular, and because of this, under President Lula, a number of international deals have been signed.[5] The heightened economic and international profile gave Brazilians a renewed sense of direction and cause for nationalistic pride. But this sense was tempered by the realization that the riches of Brazil have not as yet been fully and humanely explored and that corruption may be still rampant. The country's entrepreneurs, among the most highly paid in the world, have failed to turn much of their abundance toward the improvement of some of the most impoverished people in the world. One of President Lula's best-known initiatives, the Family Purse, is slowly beginning to address major economic difficulties by subsidizing food, school, and housing.

Brazil is now a major player in the economic and strategic worlds, but some social and political problems persist. This is particularly true in the educational and health situation of most Brazilians.[6] The promise of democracy and reform, so firmly held in 1985 when power passed into civilian hands after decades of military regimes, has slowly begun to deliver a better life for all Brazilians. Thus, as Brazil celebrates five hundred years of existence, its citizens rightly ask about their past and speculate about their future. It is to this past history and speculation about the fulfillment of promises in the second decade of the new millennium that this chapter is devoted.

History, Background, and Political Culture

Brazil stretches across three time zones, and the Atlantic island of Fernando de Noronha territory lies in a fourth. Most of the country's landmass is east of the United States, the Equator crosses Brazil's northern border, and the area south of Rio de Janeiro is outside the Tropical Zone. Mountains, geologically old and not very high, moderate the climate, and nights are relatively cool. Rainfall is generally plentiful, but precipitation in the Northeast is irregular, so that region, plagued by droughts as well as floods, is the poorest in Brazil. Some twenty mountains are higher than 5,000 feet, but none is as high as 10,000 feet. Half of the country is a plateau running from 500 to 3,000 feet above sea level. The Amazon carries more water into the ocean than any other river in the world. This immense river can be plied by oceangoing vessels as far as Peru, and many of its tributaries are navigable by major ships. Despite having no great lakes, Brazil contains one fifth of the world's fresh water. For a country that has only recently found a great deal of oil, it is fortunate that Brazil has great hydroelectric potential. The country's overall energy production, however, is considered inefficient and expensive compared with that of other countries.

Brazilians usually divide their country into five regions: North, Northeast, Southeast, South and West Central. The North, stretching across the northern third of Brazil, is the largest and the least populated region. Dominated by the Amazon, it is an area of legendary wealth and potential, mostly still untapped. Manaus and Belém are the major cities in the largest rain forest in the world.

The Northeast, with 18.2 percent of the land, occupies the eastern bulge and has become notorious in recent years for recurring droughts, floods, and human hardship. It is tropical in climate and has a narrow coastal plain where traditional crops such as sugarcane and cacao have been grown for centuries. It is a region of old Portuguese names and proud political traditions, but being poor and far away from the center of power, it is sometimes labeled "Brazil's Bangladesh." The world demand for ethanol, however, is giving this region a new lease for better lives.[7]

The densely populated Southeast represents 10.86 percent of Brazil's territory and close to half of the nation's population. It has long been the political and economic center of the country, contributing more than 60 percent of the country's gross national product (GNP). Large numbers of Japanese, Italians, Lebanese, and impoverished Northeasterners have come to São Paulo and prospered, making that city and the state the cosmopolitan heart of Brazil. Industry in this region has attracted millions, and its mild climate and abundant rainfall have reinforced it as a magnet. The highlands, rugged and mined for gold and precious and semiprecious stones in colonial days, are now mined for high-grade iron ore and other minerals. Former President Cardoso is a *paulista* and São Paulo is President Lula's adopted home state.

The South, stretching from Paraná to Rio Grande do Sul, has attracted a large number of Northern European immigrants. It occupies 6.79 percent of the national territory. Important agriculturally and the home of national political leaders such as Presidents Getúlio Vargas and General Ernesto Geisel, the South has for decades been a haven for separatist ideas. The climate is temperate though with occasional frosts that damage the coffee crop.

The West Central region includes the states of Mato Grosso (North and South) Goiás, and the federal district. This region has grown tremendously since the establishment of Brasília as the country's capital in 1960 and the development of lucrative agribusiness. Rainfall is sometimes sparse, and the climate is tropical to mild in the highlands. In the north the region resembles the Amazon area, with dense forests and heavy rains, but its savannas are ideal for cattle-raising. Some rivers flow north toward the Amazon, whereas others run south to join the Plata Basin. With 22.08 percent of the territory, the West Central region is contributing relatively more than previously. With the increasingly populous capital, it is reminiscent of the American Far West, with extensive cattle ranches, soy farms, tourism, and a wealth of minerals.

The Southeast and the South have composed the undisputed economic and political heartland for decades. São Paulo, a state with a population larger than Argentina, has a GDP second only in Latin America to all of Mexico. The Northeast is the proverbial land of history, poverty, and intermittent droughts and floods. The North is the Amazon land of the jungle and promise, and the West Central is the brash political and growing agribusiness center. What links these varied regions is the Portuguese language and, progressively, a national communications grid. Railroads are scarce, highways are somewhat less so, and rivers are used when not interrupted by falls. Airplanes now link most cities throughout the country, as do television, the telephone, the Internet, and radio.[8]

Brazil's history sets it apart from Spanish America.[9] Brazil can be said to have existed before it was formally discovered by the Portuguese explorer Pedro Álvares Cabral in 1500. In 1494 the Pope, in an attempt to avoid subsequent disputes between the then-major empires of Spain and Portugal, divided the South American continent into an eastern portion, to belong to Portugal, and a larger western portion, to belong to Spain. Before long it was clear that the Pope's Tordesilhas line would be breached and the Portuguese would proceed to colonize the Brazilian landmass and impart to it their own Iberian traditions and language. The Tordesilhas line had granted Portugal only the easternmost bulge of today's Brazil, but Portuguese and later Brazilian explorers pushed the line westward to the present borders. However, land wars seldom erupted between the Portuguese and the Spanish colonizers and their heirs. Instead, often expansion occurred naturally as Brazilian pioneers went beyond the Tordesilhas line—in fact, most of them had never heard of any such line—to settle new land and populate new areas, and then their offspring moved even farther west. Thus, from the beginning of its history, Brazil's concept of a "living frontier" has been a major aspect of its existence as a nation and has defined the character of its relations with other South American countries.

In the very early decades, however, the Portuguese seldom ventured beyond a few scattered outposts on the Atlantic shore. Portugal, in contrast to Spain, was more interested in its lucrative trade with India than in exploring the primitive land where early promises of gold and precious stones had gone unfulfilled. The only attraction of the new colony seems to have been a red wood that produced a brilliant red dye. From this red wood—the color of glowing coals, and thus *brasil* wood in Portuguese—came the name of Brazil. In the middle of the sixteenth century the French twice tried to settle near present-day Rio de Janeiro and were driven off, but their bold challenge proved to be the catalyst to Portugal's interest, and Emperor João III finally decided that he needed to secure Cabral's discovery. The king parceled out the coastline in the form of fourteen royal grants (*capitanias*) to wealthy Portuguese. The capitanias gave Brazil its first formal shape and laid the basis for the country's enduring federalist tradition.

The capitanias grew slowly and became less stagnant only as the Portuguese started raising sugarcane later in the sixteenth century. Sugar required a great deal of labor in its production and Brazilian Indians were not well suited to this strenuous labor, preferring death to slavery. The Portuguese captured blacks at trading posts along the African coast and took them to tend the sugarcane fields and refineries. For the next three centuries, then, over three million young blacks were forcibly brought to the colony. Intermarriage between Portuguese, Indians, blacks, and the growing number of Brazilians (i.e. Portuguese subjects born in Brazil) was not uncommon, and the basis for Brazil's racial mixture was established.

Jesuit missionaries attempted to protect the Indians by gathering them into villages organized around a church, with the aim of Christianizing and educating them. Although the missionaries' intentions may have been good and they did save the Indians from enslavement and slaughter, most of the Indians died from European diseases to which they lacked immunity, such as small pox, measles, tuberculosis, and the common cold. Their unique culture was largely lost or slowly blended with the culture of the far more numerous blacks and whites, and today only around two hundred thousand Indians remain in Brazil.

A sense of distinctly Brazilian national identity first emerged with the expulsion of the Protestant Dutch. For two decades they had controlled the northeastern coast, but Portuguese and Brazilians drove them out in 1654, a triumph for the Catholic Church and for a Portuguese Brazil. The event that brought about the opening of the interior, however, was the discovery of gold and plentiful precious and semiprecious stones just before the onset of the eighteenth century. In Minas Gerais (literally "general mines") the development of the interior was given a major thrust by the exploits of the daring *bandeirantes*, mostly pioneers from São Paulo. These descendants of Portuguese and Indians traveled in bands and brought along flags (*bandeiras*), families, cattle, and Indian slaves. If confronted by Jesuits, they were likely to pillage the missionaries' villages. Cruel and energetic, they ventured far from the coast and established the first settlements of the present-day states of Goiás and Mato Grosso. Diamantina in Minas Gerais, now almost unknown outside of Brazil, was at one time the diamond capital of the world. These early mining towns saw the first stirrings toward independence from Portugal—tragic and abortive attempts to emulate the North American independence movement and the republican form of government.

Brazil's independence came about in a different way from that of its Spanish neighbors. The other South American countries rebelled against Spain and eventually formed separate republics, but Brazil stayed intact and its "war" of independence does not merit that label. Historically speaking, Brazil owes its independence to the fact that Napoleon's army invaded Portugal in 1807, and under British pressure and protection the Portuguese court moved to Brazil. João VI enjoyed the colony so much that he raised it in rank to a kingdom within the Portuguese empire and stayed in Rio de Janeiro long after the Napoleonic threat was past. When the British finally persuaded him to return to Lisbon, he left his son Pedro as his regent. Shortly afterward in 1822, Dom Pedro proclaimed Brazil's independence, and from this, the Portuguese prince became Brazil's first monarch.

After this rather uneventful independence, Brazil experienced minor civil wars, slave rebellions, and attempts at secession, including some in the South in favor of a republican form of government, but the former Portuguese colony somehow managed to survive all struggles intact. The best explanation is that Brazil, in contrast to Spanish America, did not struggle through a protracted and divisive war of independence. The Portuguese House of Bragança ruled until 1889, and even today there are Bragança pretenders to head the Brazilian government. The 1988 constitution allowed voters to choose a monarchial form of government, if they wished, in 1993. Although Brazilians rejected monarchy, many nonetheless debated its merits. In the 1993 referendum 12 percent of the participants voted in favor of a monarchial-parliamentary system.

The easy separation from the colonial power and the long period of relative stability gave Brazil a strong feeling of national unity and nearly a century of enlightened rule. In fact, it can be argued that it was the farsightedness of Brazil's second emperor, Pedro II, which brought his reign to a close. His daughter Isabel's approval of the abolition of slavery in 1888 robbed Pedro II of the crucial support of the landed gentry, and shortly thereafter a republic was proclaimed and the heartbroken king went into exile.

However, other forces also helped bring about the republic, many of them nurtured by the king's policies. A greater opening to the world made it possible for the Brazilian elite to become familiar with democratic and republican forms of government elsewhere, and a trip by the emperor to the United States, which was fully reported back home, made educated people familiar with the thriving republic to the north. In the meantime, especially during Pedro II's prolonged reign from 1840 to 1889, people in the southern portion of the country were feeling neglected by the government in Rio de Janeiro. Of even greater significance, younger military men were becoming increasingly politically involved and restless under the emperor's rule. Brazil's war against Paraguay, which lasted from 1864 to 1870, was fought with a mixture of pride and shame, because it pitted a giant against a determined but extremely weak opponent. Paraguay was ruined for decades by the consequences of the war, and even though Brazil and its allies, Argentina and Uruguay, were victorious, the war had been expensive and divisive for them. The war debt, the doubts about the war itself, a desire for greater say in the form of government, and the abolition of slavery converged to make change a foregone conclusion. Yet Pedro II was personally respected, and the overthrow of the monarchy came as a surprise to most Brazilians. On November 15, 1889, the Republic of Brazil was proclaimed. The emperor departed for Europe with his family and a few friends, refusing to accept the substantial compensation that the revolutionaries offered. His wife died shortly thereafter, and Pedro himself died two years later.

Pedro II's long reign provided Brazil with decades of stability, but at the turn of the century the country was almost empty. Its sparse population was mostly illiterate and divided into a minuscule rich elite, a large poor class, and a nearly nonexistent middle class. The freed people were hardly better off than they had been as slaves. Wealthy Brazilians sent their sons to Europe—mostly to France—to get an education because Pedro II's legendary love of learning had not been translated into the establishment of even a basic educational system. The few schools that did exist were run by the Catholic Church, and most offered only a rudimentary education to the children of the elite.

Since 1889 the form of government has been that of a federal republic, but Brazil has never had a truly federal system. The president has traditionally been stronger than governors or mayors, checks and balances have not always applied, and the republican system itself has been tempered by a degree of authoritarianism. The 1988 constitution did, however, attempt to give greater power to Congress. Furthermore, although the 1992 impeachment of President Fernando Collor de Mello seemed to indicate new congressional authority, in the 2000s corruption of major congressional leaders who have not faced expulsion could once again show flawed legislative powers and, above all, the weakness of the party system.[10]

The military, a power behind the throne during the monarchy, is still influential, and between 1964 and 1985 it governed the country with very few challenges. Revealingly, the latent powers of the military to intervene were not fully eliminated in the liberal constitutional charter of 1988. In the 1990s political and economic turmoil have caused many Brazilians to look again to the military as the ultimate stabilizer. It is to the credit of the military that it has not taken advantage of the situation to reenter the political arena as it did during the chaos of 1964.

The middle class has expanded, especially since the 1930s, but it cannot compete in terms of sheer political and economic power with the military and economic elites. The poor still form the largest group, but they have gained some welfare protections since the 1930s. The 1988 constitution extended and expanded many of their protections and welfare entitlements, but, again, many promises remain on paper. Constitutional revisions sought to review the plight of the poor pragmatically and find the money to implement social justice provisions. Presidents Cardoso and Lula both launched new programs, but these remain still mostly untested.

The lingering economic gap is somehow bridged—even transcended—by Brazil's vibrant culture. Television viewers worldwide are familiar with the spectacular pageant of carnival in Rio de Janeiro, in which the most daring and imaginative (as well as expensive) displays are staged by slum dwellers. Popular music, similarly highlighted during carnival, reaches many countries in toned-down versions of samba and bossa nova that has been transformed into the all-pervasive Muzak. Brazilian movies have competed well in world festivals and in box office appeal; television shows are technically advanced and innovative; and a great many *telenovelas* (soap operas), first shown in Brazil, are routinely seen in Portugal; in Lusophone, Africa; and throughout Spanish America and Spain itself.[11]

From an international perspective it is not far-fetched to consider Brazil the cultural center of the Portuguese-speaking world because of its vastly superior number of writers, actors, painters, and artists in comparison with other Lusophone countries. Jorge Amado, whose works fictionally depicted life in Bahia and the Northeast, saw several of his novels, among them *Gabriela* and *Dona Flor*, become bestsellers and then movies in the United States. The visual arts are likewise noteworthy, with some of their best-known interpreters reflecting the ethnic mix of the country. Candido Portinari's murals portray the suffering of Northeastern migrants and the urban poor; the paintings of Manabu Mabe, another paulista, are viewed around the world. The cities of Salvador and Ouro Preto feature some of the hemisphere's best examples of Baroque architecture by early artisans. Brasília is well known for its futuristic design, and its architecture has been emulated on all continents.

Sports, particularly soccer, occupy an important position in Brazilians' lives. Life comes to a stop when the World Cup soccer competition takes place every four years, and politicians vie with each other to show their devotion to a winning team. When, in 2009, the Brazilian team won over the American counterpart, there was a great deal of celebration. Brazilian players, such as Kaka, are among the highest paid in the world. Volleyball, water sports, track and field, basketball, car racing, and tennis are other major sports in which Brazilians have done well in international meets.

A love of telenovelas, a penchant for emotional and earthy sambas, a cynical approach to religion and other ponderous matters, and a perennial optimism in the face of daily disappointments seem to characterize the Brazilian personality. In the words of Elizabeth Bishop, a Pulitzer-prize winning writer who made Brazil her home for decades,

> Brazilians are very quick, both emotionally and physically. Like the heroes of Homer, men can show their emotions without disgrace. Their superb *futebol* players hug and kiss each other when they score goals, and weep dramatically when they fail to. Brazilians are also quick to show sympathy. One of the first and most useful words a foreigner picks up is *coitado* ["poor thing"] . . . [There is the great] Brazilian belief in tolerance and forbearance . . . [with] the greatest tolerance . . . extended to love, because in Brazil that is always the most important emotion. Love is the constant element in almost every news story, street scene, or familiar conversation.[12]

Few Brazilians would quarrel with the poet's understanding of their soul.

At the time when Bishop wrote, she had in mind a mostly rural country. By the 2000s, on the other hand, around 75 percent of the population had become urban. Greater Brasília, which many thought would never amount to more than a backwater capital, now has a population over two million and is a major magnet in the West Central region. Porto Alegre, with over two million inhabitants, is the major center in the South. Urban growth has been spectacular. It has aided economic development and brought more people to work in the great and expanding industries, but has also created serious social and political problems. Cities are chronically short of funds to provide even the most rudimentary services, such as water and sewer facilities. Nevertheless, various attempts to lure the peasants back to the land have been dismal failures.

Whether in the cities or in the countryside, four major groups make up the Brazilian population: the original Indians; the Portuguese, who began colonizing in the sixteenth century and who again came in large numbers after their own "revolution" in the 1970s; Africans, who were brought as slaves to work on the plantations and in the mines; and the various European, Middle

Eastern, and Asian immigrants, who have settled since the middle of the nineteenth century, particularly in the Southeast, where they have made São Paulo one of the most cosmopolitan cities in the world. The states of Santa Catarina and Rio Grande do Sul have been havens for waves of German immigrants, so much so that it once prompted the unfounded fear that they might subvert Brazil to Hitler's cause. It is conservatively estimated that about five million Europeans settled in Brazil between 1875 and 1960, and millions of Japanese and Middle Easterners have likewise come to Brazil to find a land of opportunity. These immigrants struggled for a long time but eventually succeeded beyond all expectations. Many highly placed politicians, professionals, and entrepreneurs are second- and third-generation hyphenated Brazilians. Most immigrant families have become fully integrated, having adopted the Portuguese language and often the Catholic religion as well. The sense of being Brazilian is strong, so much so that ethnic strife is minor, and when it does occur openly it is not condoned officially and is ridiculed and condemned by the media. President Lula's "Um País de Todos" is not an empty slogan.

Most Portuguese explorers usually came without their families and often intermarried with Indians and later with African slaves. Thus, although the basic ethnic stock of Brazil was once Portuguese, miscegenation and the subsequent waves of immigrants have resulted in a rich ethnic and cultural heritage. Traditionally, Brazilians are adamant in denying any racial or ethnic prejudices. It is true, however, that the farther one progresses up the socioeconomic and political ladder, the whiter one is likely to be (although not necessarily carrying a Portuguese name, as presidential candidate Paulo Maluf and presidents Juscelino Kubitschek and Ernesto Geisel attest). By the same token, attempts to organize black movements have not been very successful, and perhaps revealingly, the labels used in these attempts are not Portuguese but imported from abroad. The leadership of these movements is as likely to be foreign as Brazilian.

The Indians have been far less fortunate than blacks or immigrants. Located mainly in the northern and western border regions and in the upper Amazon Basin, there are now only around two hundred thousand Brazilian Indians, and they are considered an endangered group. Their numbers have been declining for years, but recently, increased contact with the outside world, the expansion of agribusiness, and road projects have accelerated the process. The government has programs to establish reservations and to provide assistance, but it has likewise promoted or at least condoned the expansion of roads, mining, and commerce onto hunting and tribal lands, and this has had disastrous results for the dwindling numbers of indigenous people. Tragic stories of farmers and miners despoiling Indian villages are not unusual. Meanwhile, the efforts of private groups and the Catholic Church to help the Indians survive are subject to controversy, and most Brazilians feel that the Indians should "integrate"—or else.

The fact that the few Indians who have survived often cannot communicate in Portuguese has not helped their cause, because the Indian languages are wholly foreign to the vast majority of Brazilians.[13] Indeed, Portuguese is one of the main strands that holds the overwhelming majority of Brazilians together. It is true that Brazilians who live near the borders can communicate in Spanish and that educated Brazilians know English, but Portuguese is the language of Brazil. North American-Brazilian cultural centers are popular, and a knowledge of English is avidly sought as a key to professional, business, and social betterment. With the economic recession of the early 1990s, some professionals went to the United States, Portugal, and Japan seeking better opportunities, only to find themselves unwelcome aliens; many returned to their native country disillusioned. With the advent of the Internet and global communications, most groups have established links with similar ones in the United States, Europe, and Asia.

Another main cultural strand is the Roman Catholic Church, but regardless that this is the largest Catholic country in the world, Catholic tenets have traditionally been lightly respected and the number of religious vocations has never been high. Protestant churches, notably charismatic and fundamentalist ones, have grown tremendously in recent years, especially among the poorer urban dwellers. By now Protestants have their own informal *bloque* in Congress, and a governor of Rio de Janeiro, an *evangélico*, had the very Brazilian name of Anthony William Garotinho Matheus de Oliveira. A possible presidential candidate, former minster Marina Silva, is an *evangélica*. Furthermore, many Brazilians, even if nominally Catholic, are also devoted to various spiritualist and voodoo rituals. There are Jewish groups, mostly in Rio de Janeiro and São Paulo; Moacyr Scliar, a well-known novelist and essayist from Porto Alegre, has written extensively on Brazil's Jewish community and its role in national life. Overall, religious tolerance is the norm, and persecution for one's beliefs has been rare, although the Catholic Church is accorded a special place in religious festivals, family traditions, and everyday life.[14]

Interest Groups, Parties, and Political Organizations

With its size and economic, political, and regional diversity, it is not surprising that Brazil has always had a variety of interest groups, parties, and organizations. This variety has become even more pronounced in recent decades. Because Pedro II's empire represented stability and provided for a great deal of freedom, the transition from monarchy to republic in 1889 did not bring about an outcropping of popular groups overnight. Indeed, the republic emerged as a continuation of oligarchic rule, one in which the landed interests were the most powerful, the states of São Paulo and Minas Gerais continued their preeminence, and the top military officers exerted the moderating power (*poder moderador*) that the emperor had represented. Outstanding civilians such as the great jurist Rui Barbosa were sometimes brought to the fore, and it was he, rather than the military leaders, who wrote the decree that brought about the separation of church and state in 1890.

World War I then brought the first major challenge to the Brazilian rulers. The loss of European markets was disastrous: Farmers were unable to sell their crops, and only toward the end of the European conflict did trade improve somewhat as the warring nations sought to import foodstuffs. Brazil officially opted to side with the Allies in 1916, and this choice helped the country's trade situation. Even this improved trade, however, was not enough to cure festering problems. The coffee plantations, which had supplanted sugar plantations as the major export activity, were overproducing, and prices continued to drop. Even more ominous was that the southern states, which had long felt alienated from Rio de Janeiro, were becoming more restless, and the old dream of secession persisted.

Issues of civilian-military relations were a constant source of aggravation to people in and out of government. Although civilians managed to keep the military out of the presidency, discontent within the army was a concern for all presidents. The impact of the Great Depression was felt acutely in Brazil as exports continued to drop. Influential Brazilians, powerful farmers, and young military officers began to look for a forceful president as the 1930 election approached. The incumbent president contributed to the search for alternatives by favoring a presidential candidate from his own state of São Paulo in defiance of an informal tradition whereby presidents from São Paulo and Minas Gerais had taken turns. This proved to be the catalyst for *mineiros'* support of another candidate, Getúlio Vargas, a popular governor from the southern state of Rio Grande do Sul. When the official candidate won the election, many Brazilians felt that Vargas had been deprived of a legitimate triumph, and he was urged to rebel. Feeling that he had enough military and popular support to succeed, Vargas and his followers moved by train toward the capital. Support grew as he traveled north, and by the time he reached Rio de Janeiro the president had fled and Vargas was able to assume power with a minimum of force.

Between 1930 and his resignation in 1945, Vargas ruled with a combination of cunning, ever-changing political coalitions, a vaguely corporatist Estado Novo concept, and a brand of populism that endeared him to many Brazilians, who came to call him "the father of the poor." Under him, women were granted the right to vote. However, with little regard for rule, Vargas instituted extra-constitutional policies and programs and was not averse to ruthless suppression of people who opposed him. Power was centralized, and federalism, already weak, was practically abolished when he used his powers to intervene in the states, appointing his own governors. Education became centralized and controlled, censorship was imposed, and the legislative assembly was not convened. Although many of Vargas's decrees were softened in their application, other policies he instituted were to have lasting effects. His social security system, a novelty in Brazil that made him very popular with workers, still forms the core of today's social welfare system. He garnered a great deal of support from nationalists of different political stripes with extensive nationalization of economic institutions and natural resources. Characteristically calling himself "apolitical," he presided over a regime that lacked a coherent ideology and even political parties. He counted on the support of labor while also making sure it had little independent strength.

During World War II, after some initial hesitation, Brazil joined the Allied side in 1942 and contributed troops and officers who saw action in Italy alongside U.S. forces. The United States was allowed to use Brazilian bases in the Northeast, and the country prospered because of the great demand for its products. Furthermore, World War II, fought for the preservation of democracy, had the unsurprising effect of calling into question Vargas's authoritarianism. In October 1945, military officers, responding to popular demands for a freer system, stepped in and sent Vargas home to Rio Grande do Sul. In January 1946 the second republic, with a former minister of war, General Eurico Gaspar Dutra, as president, was ushered in.

Then in September 1946 a new constitution was adopted and, although it guaranteed free elections and civil liberties, it nonetheless preserved the greatly enlarged executive built up by Vargas and his centralized institutions. President Dutra continued investments in public works and expanded the health and transportation systems. Inflation, however, was a constant menace. Brazil expected greater trade and economic help from the United States, especially in view of Brazil's role in World War II, but these expectations were disappointed. The massive Marshall Plan for European economic reconstruction was not paralleled in Latin America. Brazil was equally disappointed when it was not given a seat in the UN Security Council—an issue that persists today.

Vargas was popularly elected to the presidency in 1951 as the candidate of the Labor Party, but he no longer commanded the respect or the affection he had enjoyed during his earliest years in power. He had lost much of his popular appeal and was unable to deal with economic problems any more successfully than had Dutra. Some of his closest associates were implicated in charges of corruption, and when his aides appeared to have been directly involved in assassination attempts against members of the opposition and in the death of an air force major, the armed forces were prepared to push Vargas to resign. Faced with the possibility of a coup or perhaps in an effort to avoid possible bloodshed, Vargas committed suicide.

The election of 1955, in which Juscelino Kubitschek was chosen as president and former Vargas minister of labor João Goulart vice president, was made possible by the military's willingness to play its *poder moderador* role to the hilt and serve as the guarantor so that the duly elected officials could take office. Kubitschek, who had been a popular governor of Minas Gerais, vowed to give Brazil "fifty years of progress in five," and in many ways he fulfilled his promise, but at a heavy price. He pushed for the hasty completion of hydro-electric plants and a variety of public works, the establishment of several new universities, medical schools, and economic institutions, and the opening of major highways and airports. He launched Brazil's automobile and aircraft industries and built the long-planned new capital, Brasília, in the central state of Goiás. All of these projects could be justified as serving as the building blocks for a modern Brazil, but they were pushed too hastily and involved tremendous cost overruns. By the time he left office, Juscelino (as he preferred to be called) was still a very popular man, but inflation had become a major burden. The successful presidential candidate in 1960, the former mayor and governor of São Paulo Jânio Quadros, ran on a pledge to balance the budget, end inflation, protect Brazil from foreign greed, curb corruption, and launch all independent foreign policy.

Quadros was elected with the largest plurality in the history of Brazil, but he soon ran afoul of Congress and alienated even some of his strongest supporters by his aloof and erratic behavior. He did push for measures designed to reform exchange controls, end consumer subsidies, and curtail the printing of worthless money, but these measures took away much of his support among the poor people and others who were most negatively affected. He publicly praised the Soviet Union, even though little trade was possible between the two countries and a communist system held little appeal for most Brazilians. He also pinned a medal on Fidel Castro, even though it was common knowledge that the Cuban dictator had just presided over a period of terrorism and indiscriminate killings at the infamous *paredón* (wall).

Quadros became a more enigmatic figure as he exhibited a number of eccentricities, among them wearing a uniform and requiring others around him to wear them too—to ward off "germs." His economic measures did not seem to be working, his popularity evaporated, and his peculiarities led people to believe he was unstable. No longer adulated as a savior, he resigned abruptly and left Brazil before completing a year in office. His irresponsible tantrum was to cost Brazil's democracy dearly.

Quadros's vice president, João Goulart, had been picked for that position almost as an afterthought and because people felt he would bring to the ticket whatever remained of the old Vargas machine. Goulart, like Vargas, was from the South and was a landowner and a politician with close ties to labor. At the time of Quadros's unexpected resignation Goulart happened to be in the People's Republic of China. Politicians favorable as well as unfavorable to him counseled that he return to Brazil by a long route so that the military, Congress, and other influential groups could work out a compromise that would enable him to become president. The eventual compromise created the post of prime minister who would share power with Goulart (and probably be close to the people who most objected to him), and Goulart became president. But almost from the very start the relations among the president, the military, and the old-line politicians were strained. Goulart prevailed in getting rid of the prime minister, but this was a Pyrrhic victory.

For the people who were already suspicious of his intentions, it confirmed their fear that Goulart wanted to become a second Vargas, only more so: more populist; more to the left, and more demagogic. His populist economic policies proved more inflationary than beneficial, and, being unable or unwilling to control his one base of support, the unions, he allowed strikes and threats of strikes to become a daily occurrence. For many Brazilians, who traditionally had opted for their flag's motto *Ordem e Progresso* (Order and Progress), the spectacle of a demagogic president unable to provide at least a measure of economic and political certainty engendered a longing for a more stable president.

Much has been written about the U.S. involvement in the coup that eventually drove Goulart from the presidency. A fair appraisal would conclude that many North Americans felt uneasy about the turn of events. This uneasiness was compounded by Goulart's vague, inflammatory threats against "foreign powers" and by the suggestion that some of his more radical advisers may have had links to Brazil's small Communist Party. However, to conclude that the United States engineered a coup is to be blind to the realities of Brazilian traditions and politics in 1964. The United States probably knew about and did not discourage a coup. For a variety of good and not so good reasons, the U.S. embassy was supportive of the people who wanted to get rid of Goulart. After all, a number of highly placed North Americans in Brazil were close friends with influential Brazilians who were active in the opposition, especially those in the military.[15]

The actual unraveling is beyond dispute. The final catalyst came from Goulart himself when he undermined military discipline by siding with groups of mutinous soldiers. With the growing middle class already bitter because of inflation and the daily uncertainties caused by strikes, the military was urged to fulfill its constitutional duty to act as the poder moderador and ensure that "order and progress"—as well as discipline—prevailed. Unhappy governors of powerful states such as Minas Gerais joined with generals in insisting that Goulart resign or face the prospect of a protracted civil war.

The "revolution" of March 31, 1964, was virtually bloodless. There was practically no support for Goulart, and even his base, the labor unions, failed to rise in his favor. Most political leaders regarded military rule as the only alternative to strikes fomented by the president, mutinies, and daily chaos. The army chief of staff, Marshal Humberto Castelo Branco, who had seen combat duty in Italy alongside U.S. forces, was chosen president. A quiet, intellectual man, he sincerely believed that his term in office would be a mere transition to another, more reliable civilian president. But Castelo Branco was in the minority among his fellow officers, most of whom—along with a great many civilians in Brazil—felt otherwise and thought that the country needed a strong "apolitical" government. The military was destined to rule Brazil for over twenty years, and even in the liberal 1988 constitution, its traditional power as a moderating force was not eliminated.

Regardless of the debate about the constitutionality of the military takeover in 1964, few anticipated what came after the coup. Instead of a transitional regime, the military consolidated its power. Politicians who had initially sided with the officers were banned from politics or sent into exile; the still-popular Kubitschek was among those who were proscribed. Political parties were considered unnecessary or a nuisance, and thus the thirteen that did exist were abolished. Eventually the military saw the need to promote a more "popular" image, and two political organizations, the pro-government National Renovating Alliance (ARENA) and the opposition Brazilian Democratic Movement (MDB) were formed under government auspices. As their names indicate, they were coalitions of parties and ideological factions rather than political parties in the U.S. sense.

For a time, especially between 1968 and 1972, the military leaders in power were prone to disdain any effort at democratization. Their idea seems to have been to provide an economic miracle that would, in turn, expand the economic pie and eventually the number of pieces that could be given away to the populace. The emphasis was on technocratic rather than political advice, on economic development rather than preparation for democracy and popular participation. Censorship was the order of the day, and the regime in power was not hesitant to show who was boss and to use threats and outright brutality if it felt that was needed to "sanitize" the system.

As long as economic expansion continued and inflation was kept fairly low, demands that the military give up power were muted, but the oil shock of 1973 changed the situation. Coming from outside and completely out of the control of the government, the skyrocketing oil prices meant a drastic reduction of the economic forecasts. The economic miracle was no more, the pie was no longer growing, and the people who were demanding more than the merest of crumbs were becoming less intimidated and more vocal. With the economy faltering, the military leaders saw the wisdom of moving for an *abertura*, an opening toward the eventual resumption of democratic forms.

Under an administration-sponsored bill, Congress abolished the two-party system and a multiparty system was put into place. Five parties were recognized under the reorganization law; two of them were actual continuations of those allowed previously. The opposition MDB became the Brazilian Democratic Movement Party (PMDB), based in part on the old Brazilian Labor Party (PTB) and a few smaller political groupings, as well as whatever remained of the more progressive elements of President Dutra's Social Democratic Party (PSD). In its new incarnation the PMDB counted among its supporters the expanding urban middle class, intellectuals, and workers. Its program called for greater control of the economy, income redistribution to help disadvantaged groups in society, full political democracy, and direct elections.

The pre-1964 PTB suffered much infighting in its attempt to regain its preeminence, and out of the struggle emerged the Democratic Workers' Party (PDT). The PDT was most active in the state of Rio de Janeiro, where it was led by Governor Leonel Brizola. The governor, closely associated by family, state, and political ties with the deposed Goulart, sought to model the party on the European social-democratic parties, but most observers saw the PDT as a personalistic vehicle for the ambitious governor rather than an ideological one. Another party in search of the labor vote was the Worker's Party (PT), which competed primarily with the PMDB and the PDT for the votes of industrial workers and for the ideological backing of urban intellectuals.

The Liberal Front Party (PFL) was led by former Vice President Aureliano Chaves of Minas Gerais, who split from the PSD in the 1984 presidential campaign to support the PMDB and the fellow mineiro presidential candidate Tancredo Neves. In fact, most of the PFL, which in 1985 became a junior partner in President José Sarney's democratic alliance, was composed of politicians who had been elected in 1982 on the Democratic Social Party ticket but who had subsequently broken away from that party to support Neves. Regardless of its capable young leaders, the PFL nonetheless fared poorly in the 1986 election, giving rise to the joke that it was a party of great leaders and a tiny following. Its modest strength lay in small and rural enclaves, and this support worked to its disadvantage in a country increasingly urban and urban oriented.

President Sarney himself had been one of the original PFL leaders before he formally joined the PMDB to become Neves's new running mate. The PMDB-PFL coalition enabled Neves to upset most predictions and defeat the government-backed PSD opponent, Deputy Paulo Maluf of São Paulo, in 1984. Neves commanded a wide margin in the electoral college and was a popular, grandfatherly figure. He had accomplished the nearly impossible task of assembling a variety of ideological groups intent on replacing the military and launching a democratic system. For its part the military had stacked the game to favor Maluf but, faced with the popularity of Neves, opted to accept Neves as someone too politically cunning to attempt radical progress without a good measure of order. All prognostications came to naught when Neves fell fatally ill on the eve of his inauguration.

With Neves near death, the specter of a military coup or the passing of the presidency to Ulysses Guimarães, the congressional leader, were only two of the many possibilities. But Guimarães, a longtime opposition leader, could not count on the goodwill of the military, and vice president-elect Sarney had, after all, been a former president of the promilitary Democratic Social Party. After a great deal of political maneuvering, Sarney was confirmed as the new president. He had the support of the PSD and the PFL, but he was not a popular figure. The military did not fully trust him because he had switched sides instead of supporting its candidate, Maluf; the democratic forces that had so enthusiastically supported Neves could not forget that Sarney had been added to the ticket as a last-minute gesture toward people who had supported the military but were now willing to jump onto the civilian bandwagon.

Opposition to Sarney came mainly from the left—from the PDT of Rio de Janeiro and the PT of São Paulo. The PDT mixed populism and machine politics as part of Leonel Brizola's perennial struggle to attain the presidency; the PT, on the other hand, had really been an umbrella for a variety of socialist groups, often based on unions and on the Catholic Church's liberation theology wing. Both the PDT and the PT assumed that worsening economic problems would bring them victory. Their calculations, however, initially backfired because of the short-term maneuvers of the president and his supporters. The early success of the anti-inflationary economic Cruzado Plan, launched in February 1986, buoyed Sarney's popularity and ensured an easy victory for those aligned with him. It mattered little in the election campaign that the Cruzado Plan proved to be an ephemeral respite and that it had to be abandoned shortly after the 1986 elections; in fact, cynics said that the plan worked only long enough to ensure the socialists' defeat in those elections.

By 1988, however, Sarney no longer could hide the economic debacle or influence or even buy many voters. In the November election for mayors and municipal assemblies, Sarney's policies were overwhelmingly rejected. Sarney and the old-line politicians, including presidential hopefuls Maluf and Guimarães, were the great losers, and the undisputed great winner was the PT, closely followed by Brizola's PDT. It could be said that the 1988 election, in which an unpopular and arguably illegitimate government paid the price for an inflation rate of more than 700 percent in the preceding year, reestablished populist Brizola and socialist Luiz Inácio Lula da Silva (better known as simply Lula) as serious candidates for the presidency in 1989. The possibility of either man's winning the elections was viewed with deep misgivings by the armed forces and the conservative business establishment, and both the alternatives were not much more reassuring for an orderly transition to democracy and a renewal of "progress."

As it turned out, the 1989 contest proved the volatility of a large, young, and inexperienced electorate. More than twenty candidates waged a vigorous campaign. Some of them were old political names—not only Brizola but also Maluf, Guimarães, and Chaves. Others represented the new forces of organized labor and liberation theology; Lula found his greatest strength here. Just days before the elections, all polls were rendered meaningless when a popular television star announced his candidacy and immediately became one of the front-runners. Then, in a twist of the proverbial *jeito* (a creative maneuver), the supreme electoral court found him ineligible to run. That left Lula and Brizola as the major contenders, along with Fernando Collor de Mello, a young former governor of one of Brazil's smallest states.

Disdaining to affiliate with any major party, Collor came out of nowhere to lead the race. He survived the first ballot contest and narrowly edged out Lula in the runoff elections in December 1989—53 percent to 47 percent. Collor came to prominence when, as governor of Alagoas, he led a campaign against highly paid civil servants. He turned this campaign into a national crusade against corruption and incompetence. His vigorous denunciation of Sarney struck a responsive chord among Brazil's poorest, the rural population, and also business people who were fed up with the state's dominance of the economy. With the backing of the powerful Globo news network, Collor succeeded in undermining Lula's appeal. As most of Brazil's intellectuals supported Lula and agreed with his Marxist prescription for curing the country's ills, Collor called for a vague modernizing and restructuring of the economy.

Collor—a young president, forty years of age—promised to bring back some order and progress to the economically troubled nation. His program included cutting the inflation rate, which ran at a record 1,800 percent in 1989; prosecuting tax evaders; cutting the number of ministries in half; and selling money-losing state companies. He hoped that foreign creditors would not take the 1988 constitutional restrictions too seriously but instead would be willing to swap their debt titles for shares in Brazilian companies and that debt could be renegotiated. To enact even a portion of this ambiguous plan, however, Collor needed the cooperation of a powerful and hostile Congress. Lula, Brizola, and other disappointed presidential hopefuls counted on increasing their supporters' share of the congressional seats in the October 1990 elections. In fact, the PMDB obtained 21 percent of the vote, the PFL 17 percent, the PDT 9 percent, the PSD 8 percent, the PRN (National Reconstruction Party) 7.9 percent, and the PTB and the PT 7 percent each, with "other" comprising 23.1 percent of the 503 seats. In the federal Senate the results gave the PMDB twenty-seven seats, the PFL fifteen seats, the PDS ten seats, the PTB eight, and the PDT five, and the "other" occupied sixteen seats. In so fractionalized a Congress, much of it bitterly frustrated by Collor's victory, the goal was not greater order and progress but rather more chaos and confrontation.

Collor played into the hands of his enemies and disgraced himself even in the eyes of those who had supported him. By early 1992 it became clear that the president, who had come into government under the banner of austerity and probity, was deeply enmeshed in a scandal of corruption and favoritism. Congress moved to remove the president through an unprecedented impeachment process, with the result that, by December 29, 1992, Collor was removed from the presidency. In his place Vice President Itamar Franco, the physical, political, and generational antithesis of Collor, became president.

The specter of a coup lurked in the wings. The military, some members of which opposed both Lula and Brizola, had been uneasy over Collor's proposal to abolish the National Information Service (SNI), Brazil's foreign and domestic intelligence agency, and to shut down Brazil's nuclear program. Two small Communist parties, illegal during the military regimes, were also eager to discredit both the youthful Collor and the avuncular Franco, but with the dissolution of the former Soviet Union, Marxist parties were having a hard time justifying their own existence. Possibly thirty thousand Communists were said to exist in Brazil, so the fact that social-democratic ideas and ideals were embraced by a large percentage of the population was of far greater relevance. A small Green Party objected to Collor's development plans, but a wide variety of ecologically minded groups received a world forum during the proceedings of the Earth Summit in 1992, which garnered a great deal of praise for the Collor government's ability to hold a major international gathering.

Overall, the exuberant political ferment of the 1980s had some positive results. Since 1985, Brazilians, regardless of their ideological leanings, have fully participated in vigorous partisan politics, informed by media reporting that reflects a broad range of political views and ideologies. One can speculate, however, that the two dozen or so political parties will eventually coalesce into three to five major fronts or umbrella organizations that fit into the pattern of right, center, and left, with Brazil's political center being considerably to the left of the U.S. one. Less speculative are polling results that show increasing disenchantment with all political parties and politicians, so much so that those vying for leadership roles are careful to stress their "independent" and nonpartisan credentials. The PMDB, if literally translated, is the Party of the Brazilian Democratic Movement, but its adherents stress "movement" rather than "party."

The political system is notable for the fragmentary nature of parties, as governments struggle to keep their own supporters in line. Even the very popular Lula has often had to work through party coalitions and special favors and funds for politicians nominally in the opposition. A good example is former president Sarney, currently the senate leader and the focus of many scandal stories, who still counts on Lula's support even though Sarney himself is listed as being of the opposition. What may be more significant, regardless of whether Sarney is pressured to leave the Senate's presidency, is the fact that he represents the last generation of politicians who counted on machine politics led by influential families who dispensed favors and garnered loyalty. It is noteworthy that Sarney and his daughter Roseana have both served in the Senate and been governors of Maranhão. But Maranhão is "old" not "new BRIC" Brazil—a country no longer rural, with over 75 percent of the population urban and with new aspirations and a different set of loyalties.[16]

As political parties and loyalties are changing, so are a number of interest groups that compete for popular support. Some of these groups predate the latest democratic opening and even go back to the Vargas era, when the president subsidized and assisted such groups in exchange for political support. Among them is labor, whose members first banded together in mutual aid societies in the very early years of industrialization. It was not until Vargas's first time as president in the late 1930s and early 1940s, however, that these workers were organized into unions that received benefits from the government while avoiding strikes and other destabilizing tactics. In effect, labor rights and social security provisions were provided at the price of collaboration or, at the very least, apathy.

After the 1964 coup the military abolished the largest labor confederation, the General Worker's Command (CGT), which had been a major supporter of Goulart, himself a former labor minister under Vargas. Under all the military administrations the labor unions were strictly controlled and subject to government intervention. Union leaders were chosen by the government to ensure industrial peace, because it was essential to the military's plan for attracting domestic and foreign investment that labor not agitate for raises or go on strike.

While the economy was booming in the late 1960s and early 1970s, coinciding with the most stringent military controls, the system of state-imposed industrial peace worked well in that strikes seldom took place, much less succeeded. After the downturn in the late 1970s, labor was not as easily tamed, and about this time the military itself was beginning to question the wisdom of remaining in power indefinitely. Eventually the new unions and new leaders emerged outside of government control or, at the very least, with tacit acceptance by the military administration. After the abertura, which also began in the late 1970s, it was possible to strike even though strikes could still be ruled illegal. In 1980 metalworkers in São Paulo managed to shut down the powerful automobile industry there for several weeks. Their leader, Lula, was jailed, but the strike showed that workers were again willing to take risks. From this fairly successful strike action emerged the new PT, the Workers' Party, which remained the most coherent opponent of the government. It takes an anticorruption stance and espouses state-led economic development, but it also continues to be plagued by internal strife and, on occasion, charges of corruption.

Brazilian businesspeople, either as individuals or through their organizations, encouraged or welcomed the 1964 coup. They had reason to fear Goulart's increasing sympathy for labor demands, and they had disliked the general economic and political uncertainty, which made investment planning difficult if not impossible. Their euphoria over getting rid of Goulart, however, proved short lived, because the military proceeded to consolidate the government's role in the economy. Military and civilian technocrats moved into various new economic areas without consulting the private sector, and the old tradition of having the government protect weak companies was rendered obsolete by the government's determination to achieve economic growth as fast as possible. Foreign companies were lured to invest in Brazil, often at the expense of less-efficient Brazilian enterprises, and the lowering of tariffs made it easier to import certain items than to produce them at home. Tax collection was tightened and thus another traditional way of financing business was removed. Their growing disappointment with and even resentment of the military made businesspeople, for their own reasons, ready to welcome and support the abertura along with the workers and old-line politicians.

Business support for an end to the military regime coalesced with that of other groups who had challenged the authoritarian system for years. One of these groups was the Catholic Church. Brazil is the most Catholic country in the world in terms of the number of church members, and the Church has a special position as an interest group. In contrast to many Spanish-speaking countries in Latin America, Brazil has not experienced long and bitter fights in relation to the Catholic Church. The first republican constitution in 1891, under the inspiration of Positivism, took away the Church's special privileges without causing major trauma. For decades after the advent of the republic, the Brazilian Catholic hierarchy concentrated on running schools for the Brazilian elite and performing its theological and pastoral duties. Vatican II, between 1962 and 1965, did move the Church toward greater involvement in social and political matters, but this was not a radical departure because, especially in the 1940s and 1950s, a number of lay and Catholic groups had become active among students, workers, and even clearly political organizations. Vatican II did, however, give a new impetus to this refocusing of the Church, and it also gave Brazilian theologians the opportunity to advocate liberation theology and greater attention to the poor.

In the early 1960s this refocusing coincided with President Goulart's call for populist measures such as agrarian reform and the expansion of the welfare system. At the time of the 1964 coup the Church was deeply divided, with some members of the clergy supporting Goulart and others seeking to undermine him. Some supported his populism, but others saw it simply as a demagogic appeal. Many people feared that the Church's growing political involvement would entangle it in matters that were not crucial to it as an institution and as a church. Large parades in the major cities often had the tacit approval and support of the Church, with parishioners calling for moral renewal and decrying the chaos of everyday life. In the Northeast, priests were among those who helped landless peasants take over large and often unused tracts of land. The possibility of a divided Church did not help Goulart's cause.

After the advent of the military regime in 1964 this split continued. At first many people continued to be wary of what they perceived as the politicization of the Catholic Church. Others, however, increasingly denounced government repression and accused the government of failing to conform to Brazilian tradition by refusing to return to the barracks and give power back to civilians. By the 1970s much of the Brazilian Church hierarchy supported the effort to organize popular Catholic base communities in order to obtain greater social justice and respect for human rights, and the churches were even providing sanctuary for striking workers being pursued by the military. With the abertura, Church leaders and laypeople alike were involved in the formation of political parties and eventually in the drafting of the new constitution. Perhaps not by coincidence, the greater political involvement of the Catholic Church occurred simultaneously with a growing challenge to Catholicism by a variety of Protestant churches, especially the more charismatic and evangelical ones and those concentrating their proselytizing efforts on the poor, the illiterate, and the displaced in the urban areas. President Lula and his party, the PT, continue to have good relations with those theologians who espouse liberation theology and who support the popular "Family Purse," which subsidizes food and school. Regardless, the number of Brazilians who consider themselves Catholic has fallen sharply to less than 75 percent in 2000, the time of the last census. Many have moved to Pentecostal churches, and more significantly, Brazilian Catholics often espouse a religion that is deeply embedded with African rites.[17]

Besides the churches, unions, military, business sector, and political parties, a number of other organizations acted as pressure groups, with varying degrees of success. The Brazilian Order of Lawyers was active during the military regimes in seeking the restoration and enforcement of legal protections. The Brazilian Press Association opposed censorship and publicized, especially abroad, the plight of persecuted journalists. A number of women's organizations emerged, particularly after the 1975 International Women's Year. The National Student Union, abolished at the time of the 1964 coup, continued to operate underground and sometimes fairly openly. Race-based groups, a novelty in Brazil, emerged and began to demand "real" versus theoretical equality for all. With the abertura and the holding of elections, literally hundreds of issue-, policy-, and candidate-focused groups emerged and began to compete, although most of them were transitory. More focused and militant African-Brazilian groups did coalesce in more recent years. Benedita da Silva Sampaio, a former PT federal senator and vice-governor of Rio de Janeiro at the end of the 1990s, is probably the best known voice for these groups. Furthermore, the Movement of the Landless (*Movimento dos Trabalhadores Rurais Sem Terra*, MST) makes national and international news with the invasion of nonproductive and agribusiness farms.

One organization that continues to exert influence is the Superior War College (ESG). Founded in 1949, the ESG has been a center for training military and civilian elites. Somewhat similar to a think tank except that it is sponsored and subsidized by the government, it trained several presidents, including Castelo Branco, Geisel, and the presidential adviser Golbery do Couto e Silva. The ESG's slogan, "Security and Development," became a banner for anticommunism during the military regimes, but the organization goes far beyond mere anticommunism. It has been at the forefront of a great deal of sophisticated economic and strategic planning, and because it stresses that it aims to educate and inspire leaders, whether they be military or civilian, it is likely to remain a formidable institution. Its extensive network of alumni serves as a recruiting source for both government and private enterprises, with many male and female ESG alumni in key positions.

Government Institutions, Bureaucracy, Main Policy Issues

Russell H. Fitzgibbon, one of the most astute observers of Latin America, said that "the organization of the Brazilian political system is largely distinguished by its federalism, which provides a backdrop for the performance of various political functions."[18] It has also been said that Brazil is the most federal of Latin America's regimes, but these statements do not mean that it is "really" federal in terms of the U.S. model.

Given the size and diversity of Brazil, federalism made sense to the people who drafted the first republican constitution in 1891. The Rio de Janeiro government was weak and unwilling to challenge powerful regional centers, and although the central government remained vulnerable, for the next three or four decades the states had a great deal of freedom. São Paulo, Minas Gerais, and Rio Grande do Sul showed so much independence that they maintained diplomatic relations with foreign governments, displayed their state flags above the national one, and called their state governors "presidents."

The Vargas era lessened these centrifugal pulls. The 1934 constitution gave preeminence to the national executive, state flags and anthems were abolished, and most economic functions were handled by the national government. Vargas's Estado Novo strengthened and reinforced centralization to the extent that, even after his departure in 1945, the national government's powers far outstripped states' rights. Only during the turbulent and short Goulart years did some states again act on their own, perhaps secure in the knowledge that the federal government had enough other problems that it could not worry about states' initiatives. Governor Leonel Brizola of Rio Grade do Sul expropriated U.S.-owned utilities in that state, and an economic development organization in the Northeast, SUDENE, managed to receive funds directly from AID (Agency for International Development). Military units based in Rio Grande do Sul, Minas Gerais, and São Paulo were crucially involved in the civilian-military coup that deposed Goulart in 1964.

From 1964 to 1985 the military regimes revised the constitution with institutional acts and decrees, which sometimes gave the national executive carte blanche in the restructuring of the government and in the proclamation of all types of policies. The taxing powers of the federal government ensured that all governors and mayors, even those of powerful states and metropolises, would comply with the wishes of the president if they hoped to get any funding for essential services. Even after the ushering in of a civilian regime, however, the president still holds a great deal of power: He chooses and heads a cabinet, coordinates the actions of all ministries, and selects thousands of positions.

In an attempt to curb some of the presidential powers and to meld federalist and antifederalist impulses, the 1988 constitution became a monstrous hybrid. It promised greater freedom and power to states and local administrators, but it did not reverse the decades-old trend toward centralization. It gave Congress greater power than ever before and strengthened civil liberties, labor rights, and social benefits. Its proclamation, in October 1988, abolished the authoritarian charter of 1967. It ensured the right to strike, set the voting age at sixteen, abolished censorship, and gave more power and income to state and municipal governments.

Under the new constitution, Brazilians in November 1989 elected a president by direct popular vote for the first time since 1960. In what turned out to be a major source of domestic and international wrangles, questions concerning the international debt were debated by the entire Congress, and the president and the minister of finance were no longer able to settle by themselves on a course to resolve Brazil's international obligations. Since 1992, major constitutional amendments have been adopted, mostly pertaining to economic issues. Many of the more restrictive clauses in the constitution have been implemented in a more liberal way so as to make possible both privatization of state-owned enterprises and greater influx of foreign investors. Yet, unless and until the constitution is fully revised, the possibility of interference by federal and/or state government in business ventures is very much alive, as seen in the actions of a state governor who challenged not only the constitutionality of some contracts but also even the payment of governmental debts. In the political realm, a 1997 constitutional amendment permitted the president and vice president, who are elected for four-year terms, to serve a second consecutive term.

Under the constitution Brazil remains a federative republic composed of twenty-six states and a federal district where the capital of the country, Brasília, is located. Each state has its own government; their structures mirror the federal ones, with powers that are not reserved for the federal government nor are they assigned to municipal councils. Governors are elected by direct popular vote and the state legislatures are unicameral. The state judiciary similarly mirrors the federal model, and its jurisdiction is defined to avoid conflicts with federal courts. Brazil has some 5,560 municipalities, and their councils handle local affairs.

While the political fighting continues as a daily occurrence, the revision of the 1988 charter has been piecemeal and sporadic. Ambiguity continues to surround the role of the military as the guarantor of the constitutional order. The left complains that the proposed changes further protect large private landowners and undermine the sputtering efforts to distribute plots to landless peasants at a time when 5 percent of the country's population owns half the arable land.

Regardless of the constitutional tinkering and the travails of a disordered democracy, some structural mainstays are not likely to change. Thus, traditionally, Brazilian ministries have been very large bureaucracies with a plethora of subcabinets, councils, and other agencies—many of them powerful in their own right—plus institutes, autonomous agencies, and the like attached directly or indirectly to the ministries themselves. In this bureaucratic maze personal and political linkages are of great importance and often override considerations of merit, efficiency, or organizational rationalism. With so many people involved, many of them moving toward contradictory goals and policies, it is not surprising that Brazilian bureaucracy is notorious for its *papelada* (red tape), unpredictability, and penchant for corruption. Antibureaucratic czars have been appointed, but to no avail. Throughout the system, from top to bottom, the sheer dead weight of a myriad of legal rules and enacted codes that have long ago outlived their usefulness remains untouched.

Systematic inefficiency and the opportunity for favoritism are not mitigated when presidents, members of Congress, and governors themselves routinely appoint cronies and family members to important posts, regardless of their qualifications. Thus, with little relevance to the constitution du jour, only the proverbial ability of the Brazilian bureaucrat to bend the rules just a little or apply a little humor or a jeito so that some business can be transacted daily has kept the whole machinery of government from coming to a grinding halt.

A conservative estimate places the federal civil service at three-quarters of a million people. This figure is meaningless because it does not take into consideration the countless independent and semi-independent bureaucracies and the many civil servants who have more than one full-time job. Presidents Collor, Cardoso, and Lula have applied regimes of austerity and tried to shrink the federal payroll, with some success. Longtime employees lost one of their many jobs, but many of those who dropped from the rolls did so because they were entitled to generous pensions and retirement benefits. The Foreign Ministry (Itamaraty) is one of the better-run ministries, with a reputation for well-trained career officers, some continuity, and a relative insulation from political vagaries. Interestingly, it is also the ministry that is the least popular, with Brazilians and foreigners alike complaining about its inflexibility and its mind-numbing respect for the most minute and meaningless details.

Brazil has traditionally had a bicameral legislature, and this tradition remained unchallenged in the 1988 constitution. Although the number of legislators has varied, the usual provision calls for three senators from each state and the federal district for a total of eighty-one members. The Chamber of Deputies, 513 strong, is chosen on a population basis and favors the least-populated rural states. The chambers have legislative committees, but their staffing patterns vary a great deal, and thus their ability to draft legislation is hard to predict. Throughout history the president has been the chief legislator, and the legislation proposed by the executive branch has almost always been approved by Congress by overwhelming margins. This has been somewhat moderated by the 1988 charter, which gave greater powers to the Congress and denied the presidency its former wide decree powers. It was no longer possible for a strong dictatorial president to dismiss the legislature, as had been done several times in the past. The realities, however, have remained far more powerful than any constitutional provisions. The presidency was somewhat weakened when President Collor was impeached for malfeasance; old-timers recalled that his father had, with impunity, killed a fellow senator in chambers. Congress has likewise been discredited when many of its members are tarnished by grand larceny, rampant favoritism, and even the crude elimination of estranged wives and inconvenient enemies.

The legislature under the 1988 constitution can sanction the president, alter the national budget, and determine international treaties. The text of the constitution was sufficiently ambiguous concerning the power of Congress that it made it possible for the legislative branch to assert itself against the president and vice versa. In the presidential debacle of 1992, with the removal of President Collor, there was little doubt that Congress was preeminent. But in reality congressional powers ebb and flow. To obtain the constitutional amendment that allowed for a second presidential term, President Fernando Henrique Cardoso had to barter powers and funds with legislators and governors. His initiatives toward fiscal reforms were stymied by congressional objections, but Congress was equally frustrated in obtaining presidential implementation of some of its adopted measures. The weakness of the political parties ensures that neither president nor representatives will be able to count on the loyalty of most of their partisans.

Government structure and policymaking up to the first decade of the 2000s have seen small and major adjustments, but there is a rising skepticism about the benefits of democracy and a constant despair over the inability of politicians to govern. Yet, if one relies on history and tradition as guides, the 1988 constitution, like the others that preceded it, will be "reformed" through its daily encounters with Brazilian realities just as policymaking, regardless of the mountains of regulations and degrees, will ultimately remain at the mercy of the most skilled bureaucrat or the most imaginative Brazilian's jeito.

However, even a new constitution and the proverbial jeito have not been able to ameliorate some of the country's policy issues. On the one hand the risk of armed conflict per se is low and no guerrilla groups pose a threat. In fact, more worrisome are the threats posed by private militias that are hired by landowners to deter the Movement for the Landless members from encroaching on their properties or the very well-armed groups that protect one or more of the many drug lords. A great deal of international attention was focused on the killing of an American nun in the Amazon region. It is likely that her assassins had been paid off by those who wanted to continue clearing the rain forest, which she opposed. The government promised to investigate and punish, but most Brazilians remain skeptical.

In reality, far more problematic for Brazil is the rising level of crime, especially in major cities such as São Paulo and Rio de Janeiro. The growing incidence of poverty and the increased occurrence of drug abuse and drug commerce are often reflected in the kidnapping of tourists and wealthy Brazilians. The country's police force, for its part, remains badly trained and poorly paid, which helps promote corruption and deficiencies in law enforcement.

In long range terms, the policy areas that concern Brazilian governments the most have been the weaknesses inherent in Brazil's educational system. Indicators tend to compare Brazil unfavorably to its neighbors Argentina, Uruguay, and, farther away, Chile. Presidents Cardoso and Lula have promoted greater funding and attention to primary education. At the upper end,

Brazil does have an excellent system of public universities, but most students who are able to meet the stringent entrance requirements come from middle- or upper-class families.

Poor health indices reflect poverty, inadequate sanitation, low levels of education, and ecological degradation. The constitution provides for many health benefits, but these mostly remain on paper. More promising has been the government's proactive programs toward Brazil's HIV-AIDS population, and these have been hailed as some of the most successful efforts of their kind in the world.[19]

The International Arena

Even in colonial times Brazil's relations with its neighbors were characterized by accommodation and expansion: accommodation in the sense that Brazil seldom went to war with its neighbors (the major exception being its war with Paraguay) and expansion dating back to the disregard of the 1493 Tordesillas line and the continuing assumption of "living frontiers." In more recent years Brazil has been a leader among the Latin American nations and has played a prominent role in security efforts and in economic cooperation with the Western Hemisphere. During World Wars I and II Brazil aligned itself with the Allies, and in the 1940s Brazilian soldiers played a distinguished and decisive role in the Allied victory at Monte Castelo, Italy. Many of the generals behind the 1964 coup were involved in that campaign and formed close professional and personal relations with their North American counterparts. A man who later became president, Castelo Branco, shared a tent with the American Vernon Walters, and the two men became lifelong friends.[20]

Brazil is a signatory of the Rio Treaty, the Inter-American Treaty of Reciprocal Assistance, and the Organization of American States (OAS), which is sometimes headed by a Brazilian diplomat. Brazilian career foreign officers have distinguished themselves in international bodies, and some of them have been chosen to head such organizations, as was the case in the World Health Organization a few years ago. More recently Brazil has given priority to strengthening its ties with other South American states and has become a member of the Amazon Pact and the Latin American Integration Association (ALASI). President Sarney and Argentine President Raúl Alfonsín overcame the traditional enmity between their two countries with several understandings and protocols to ensure cooperation in a number of areas, including nuclear armaments and research. Brazil is a charter member of the United Nations and has been an active participant in several of its specialized agencies. It has contributed troops to UN peacekeeping efforts in the Middle East, in the former Belgian Congo (now Democratic Republic of Congo),

Cyprus, Mozambique, and especially in Haiti. Brazil helped mediate the resolution of the Angolan civil war.

Brazil's booming economy, trade, and international debt have caused it to become increasingly involved in international politics and economics. It is a member of the General Agreement on Tariffs and Trade (GATT), the Committee of Twenty of the International Monetary Fund (IMF), several World Bank organizations, the Inter-American Development Bank (IADB), and many international commodity agreements. The United States, Western Europe, and Japan are the primary markets for Brazilian exports and the main sources of foreign lending and investments. In value Brazil is the third-leading trade partner of the European Economic Community (EEC). Brazil's earlier dependence on imported oil had forced it to strengthen its ties with the oil producing nations in the Middle East, and a number of technical barter arrangements have been worked out whereby Brazilian technicians and laborers exchanged their expertise and their work for oil from Middle Eastern countries, especially Iraq. The Gulf War, for example, found thousands of Brazilian contracts in a variety of jobs in Iraq. Brazil has often voted with Arab countries rather than with Israel in international organizations.

Beginning in the 1970s Brazil expanded its relations with black African countries. In 1986 it introduced a proposal at the UN General Assembly to establish a zone of peace and cooperation in the South Atlantic. Because of its own large black population and its longstanding integrationist record, Brazil consistently voted for resolutions calling for an end of apartheid in South Africa. With the democratization of that country, Brazil has joined and strives to lead in the formation of a South Atlantic security and economic zone.

Brazil has diplomatic relations with most countries in the world, among them the former Soviet Union, all the East European countries, and Cuba. What's more, the country's relations with the United States are unique. The United States was the first country to recognize Brazil's independence in 1822. Dom Pedro II admired Abraham Lincoln and visited the United States during the 1876 centennial. President Dwight Eisenhower was given a hero's welcome when he visited Brazil in 1960, and presidents Franklin Roosevelt and Harry Truman were cordially received. President Jimmy Carter visited in 1978, but at the time there were major strains between the two countries regarding questions of human rights, and Brazilians were incensed by the attempts of the United States to interfere in Brazil's nuclear program. President Ronald Reagan visited Brazil in 1982, and President Sarney was received in the United States in 1986. President Bill Clinton visited Brazil in 1997 and maintained warm relations with former President Cardoso, whom he entertained at Camp David and in the White House. Lula met with President George W. Bush and recently with President Barack Obama.

In the 1950s and 1960s Brazil received about US$2.4 billion in U.S. economic assistance through AID, PL480 (Food for Peace), and the Peace Corps. During Brazil's military administrations, the Peace Corps and the International American Foundation (IAF) were accused of interfering in domestic affairs and were told to leave the country; however, IAF has since resumed its large program. After 1972 U.S. aid efforts emphasized, among other programs, the training of young Brazilian technicians and social scientists in graduate schools in the United States. In view of Brazil's economic development and its ability to obtain loans and technical assistance from private and multilateral sources, the U.S. assistance programs were phased out in the 1970s. The Department of State and other departments have small contingents in Brazil that collaborate on science and technology projects; respond to endemic diseases, emergencies, and natural disasters; and may be of technical assistance in family-planning efforts.

Although the United States is still Brazil's most important commercial partner, the trading relations have become less friendly since Brazil actively sought other partners and refused to open its markets to U.S. products and vice versa. Nationalism and simple tradition reinforced Brazil's insistence on continuing export subsidies and protectionism; nowhere were these clearer than in the 1988 constitutional provisions that actively discriminated against foreign investors and, in effect, closed certain industries to foreign firms. By the new millennium tradition and protectionism, shaken by the cold realities of tough global competition, were giving way to privatization and a friendlier response to international economic overtures. The Cardoso and Lula administrations have been characterized by higher international profiles. Both have vigorously pursued expanded relations within South America and have promoted an expansion of the Southern Common Market to include free trade agreements (FTA) with Chile (1996) and Bolivia (1997). Brazil continues to campaign to become a permanent member of an enlarged UN Security council.

The more formal agreements between Brazil and the United States include a treaty of peace and friendship; an extradition treaty; a joint participation agreement on communication satellites; and scientific cooperation, civil aviation, and maritime agreements. The two countries exchange academic personnel under Fulbright and other scholarly programs and carry out university cooperation projects. Under the popular Partners of the Americas program, several U.S. states have active exchanges with their counterparts in Brazil. Increasingly, Brazil has sponsored artistic groups to visit the United States as well as other countries in order to promote better relations and to publicize Brazil's cultural achievements.

With respect to this international debt, there are both encouraging signs and signs that do not seem to augur well. On the plus side, in September

1988 President Sarney formally ended the country's nineteen-month-old moratorium on payments on its then-US$121 billion foreign debt. At the time the Brazilian president warned that Brazil could not permanently export capital and called on creditors to do their part as Brazil was doing its part. Brazil's return to orthodox strategies and its rapprochement with the IMF marked the end of a roller-coaster period of economic experiments that included a wage and price freeze, a promising boom, and the moratorium on payments enacted shortly after the 1986 elections.

The 1988 constitution, however, has complicated the picture by giving Congress wide powers to decide on external payments and policies affecting Brazil's relations with international banking institutions. Those developments were but the most recent chapters in the long-simmering dispute between Brazil and its creditors. The oil shocks of the 1970s and 1980s and the world recession that followed were keenly felt in Brazil because of its crucial need to maintain ever-higher levels of exports to finance its economic development. By 2008–2009, Brazil appeared to be weathering the world recession better than the more economically developed countries. Ironically, some restrictions in trade and banking were assisting Brazil's recovery.

Brazil has been celebrating an unexpected oil boom since 2007, when Petrobrás, the government-controlled energy company, discovered the Tupi oilfield. With an estimated eight billion barrels of oil, the Tupi discovery places Brazil among the biggest oil producers in the world. Following the discovery, Lula used an old proverb, "God is Brazilian," and he vowed to pump billions of petrodollars into his war on poverty by creating a social fund.

In a broader sense, relations between Brazil and the United States have had an uneven track record. Although tensions and disagreements remain on charges that Brazil "dumps" (i.e., sells below cost) products such as steel, both countries became more engaged in day-to-day consultations after Cardoso and Lula took office. On the U.S. side, there seems to be a realization that the health of the Brazilian economy is vital to the overall health of South American economies, while on the Brazilian side, given the stiff competition linked to globalization, there has been a corresponding realization that the United States is too big a customer to annoy with obsolete nationalistic posturing. However, old attitudes do not change easily. Presidential aspirants denounce Cardoso and Lula's more liberal economic policies. They echo the popular sentiment that the United States is the country that could—but does not—help this significant (in resources and strategic terms) partner in the hemisphere to overcome its economic and international problems, and has appeared to thwart Brazil in its efforts to become a world power and serve in the UN Security Council.

Brazil's relations with other North and South American countries have their own uniqueness. Brazil and Mexico agreed in 1983 to complete a barter deal that would provide for the exchange of up to US$1 billion of goods each way. Brazil has concluded agreements for hydroelectric dam systems in the Plata Basin, and the Itaipú Treaty, signed with Argentina and Paraguay, makes Brazil the owner of the second largest hydroelectric dam in the world. Better relations now exist between Argentina and Brazil after decades of suspicion on both sides. President Sarney advocated a common market between the two countries, and although this idea is probably far from realization, they are trading much more than before, with Brazil exporting a large variety of manufactured goods in exchange for agricultural products.

Brazil is a leading player in the World Trade Organization's Doha Round negotiations and continues to seek to bring that effort to a successful conclusion. To further increase its international profile (both economically and politically), the Lula administration is seeking expanded trade ties with developing countries as well as a strengthening of the Mercosul customs union with Uruguay, Paraguay, and Argentina. In 2004, Mercosul concluded free trade agreements with Colombia, Ecuador, Venezuela, and Peru, adding to its existing agreements with Chile and Bolivia to establish a commercial base for the newly launched South American Community of Nations. In 2008 Mercosul concluded a free trade agreement with Israel. Mercosul is pursuing free trade negotiations with Mexico and Canada and has resumed trade negotiations with the European Union. The trade bloc plans to launch trilateral free trade negotiations with India and South Africa, building on partial trade liberalization agreements that concluded with these countries in 2004. In July 2006 Venezuela officially joined the Mercosul trade bloc. Furthermore, China has increased its importance as an export market for Brazilian soy, iron ore, and steel, becoming one of Brazil's principal trading partners and a potential source of investment.

Brazil was never a major partner with the former Soviet Union, but it has remained interested in increasing its exports to that region. The Soviet Union was quite active in promoting cultural exchange at all levels, and a number of young, promising Brazilians were provided with scholarships to study in Moscow. Of far greater significance currently are the growing economic relations between Brazil and China, from export of minerals to import of manufactured goods.

Overall, Brazil has been pragmatic in the conduct of its foreign affairs. Unless a clear benefit can be derived, Brazilians seldom take the lead. It is content with and comfortable in pursuing its own interests without unnecessarily antagonizing the countries it deeply depends on, but it will stand firm when it feels that its nationalism and sovereignty are not being given the attention they deserve. The best example of this was Brazil's strong stand in obtaining nuclear technology from West Germany in spite of President Carter's insistent and eventually counterproductive pressure.

The overly specific and detailed provisions in the 1988 constitution might have affected Brazil's conduct of foreign policy to a greater extent than they actually did, given Brazil's internal political disarray and governmental turnovers. It is clear that for the time being and in the prolonged period of transition, Congress will have much more to say in this area than before. Once a popularly elected and determined president comes on the scene, however, the pendulum may swing again toward the executive as the major player. As the country approaches 2010, no major changes are expected. What is a possibility is that two women will vie for the presidency for the first time. Dilma Rousseff, chief of staff for Lula, is the PT likely candidate, but she lacks her mentor's charisma and is undergoing cancer treatments. A more intriguing possibility is Marina Silva, a former ecology minister who broke with the PT and will run under the Green Party flag. José Serra, governor of São Paulo, will likely run for the PSDB; Aécio Neves may trump Serra because he is more charismatic and is a popular governor of Minas Gerais. Lula, under the Constitution, cannot run a third time.

Conclusion

Brazil's growing sense of importance and impact on the world scene goes beyond mere posturing. If it were not so diverse, so potentially rich, and so culturally integrated, its assertiveness would be empty indeed. Robert Harvey, a longtime observer of Brazil, said it best:

> Brazil is the unstoppable colossus of the south; a major regional power already; the first big third-world country knocking on the door of the club of developed democracies; and a potential United States in the next century. . . . Brazil's long-term prospects are glowing; its very bravado is one of the main reasons why it can look forward to the future as much as, say, bankers, investors, potential migrants and, not least, governments ought to be looking at Brazil as carefully as their precursors did at the United States in its early maturity. . . . Brazil has reached major power adulthood, although not yet the responsibility—and caution—of middle age.[21]

In fact, most careful observers usually echo this correspondent's conclusions. They agree that despite Brazil's present economic and political problems, it is not too rash to predict that the next decades will witness Brazil's rise first to an unchallenged status within Latin America, then to a predominant status within the South Atlantic community, and finally to major world power status.

The potential is there, but so also are the burdens of a chaotic and overly bureaucratized system, constitutional arrangements still untried, and a fragile and discredited democracy. General Emílio Garrastazú Médici, who presided over the so-called economic miracle, is reputed to have said, "The country is doing well, the people not so well." In spite of over a decade of democracy this assessment is still mostly true, because although in the 1990s a new order was indeed taking shape, progress has often been slow and fitful. If anything, because in the 2000s it is a maturing democracy, more is expected of Brazil, its leaders, and its system by the average Brazilian. This is the same average Brazilian who is indeed proud of seeing fellow Brazilians reach international pinnacles in sport, culture, and fashion, but who has to deal with the daily indignities of unemployment, corrupt civil servants, a chaotic party system, and inadequate health and educational institutions. In the new millennium, will the average Brazilian see the potential and the reality finally meld into one? Will Brazilians no longer be, at one and the same time, among the poorest and richest people in Latin America? Time alone will tell.

Suggestions for Further Reading

Ames, Barry. *The Deadlock of Democracy in Brazil: Interests, Identities, and Institutions in Comparative Politics*. Ann Arbor: University of Michigan Press, 2001.

Avritzer, Leonardo. *Participatory Institutions in Democratic Brazil*. Washington, D.C.: Woodrow Wilson Press, 2009.

Baer, Werner. *The Brazilian Economy: Growth and Development*. 5th ed. Westport, CT: Praeger, 1999.

Cardoso, Fernando Henrique, and Mauricio A. Font. *Charting a New Course: The Politics of Globalization and Social Transformation*. Boulder, CO: Rowan and Littlefield, 2001.

Diplomacia, Estratégia, Política Fall, no. 9 (January/March 2009).

Font, Mauricio A., and Anthony Peter Spanakos, eds. *Reforming Brazil*. Lanham, MD: Lexington, 2004.

Gordon, Lincoln. *Brazil's Second Chance: En Route Toward the First World*. Washington, D.C.: The Brookings Institution, 2001.

Roett, Riordan, ed. *Mercosur: Regional Integration, World Markets*. Boulder, CO: Lynn Rienner, 1999.

Skidmore, Thomas E. *Brazil: Five Centuries of Change*. 2nd ed. New York: Oxford University Press, 2010.

Telles, Edward E. *Race in Another America: The Significance of Skin Color in Brazil*. Princeton, NJ: Princeton University Press, 2004.

Notes

1. The votes of 110 million Brazilians for 367,271 candidates were counted flawlessly across Brazil by electronic machines. Lula's impressive victory was proclaimed within hours of the closing of the polls.

2. Tim Padgett and Andrew Downie, "Brazil's New Way," *Time International* 173, no. 11 (March 2009): 22; David Oakley and Patti Waldmeir, "Developing Nations Shine Amid the Crisis Gloom," *Financial Times*, July 28, 2009, 19.

3. Statistics and indices can be found in *World Bank, Little Data Book* (Washington, D.C.), and various publications by Economist Intelligence Unit (London) as *Country Reports: Brazil, Country Profiles*, and *Latin America at a Glance*, and various publications by IBGE, Instituto Brasileiro de Geografia e Estatística.

4. Jonathan Wheatley, "Historic Rules Help Brazil to Avoid Worst of Crisis," *Financial Times*, June 17, 2009, 3.

5. Jonathan Wheatley, "Brazil Signs Hydro-Electric Deal," *Financial Times*, July 27, 2009, 3; Alexei Barrionuevo, "Energy Deal with Brazil Gives Boost to Paraguay," *New York Times*, July 27, 2009, A10.

6. Alex Bearak, "Poor Man's Burden," *New York Times*, June 27, 2004, 1–7, 30–35, 50, 56–57; and James Scudamore, *Heliopolis* (London: Harvill Secker, 2009). The latter is a portrait of São Paulo's *favelas* (slums).

7. Greg Victor, "First and Third Worlds Coexist Uneasily as Brazil Lurches Toward Global Prominence," *Pittsburgh Post Gazette*, March 24, 2002; Javier Blas, "Sugar Prices Head Towards the Sky," *Financial Times*, July 29, 2009, 22.

8. See the full special report "Brazil," *Financial Times*, July 7, 2009.

9. Thomas E. Skidmore, *Brazil: Five Centuries of Change*, 2nd ed. (New York: Oxford University Press, 2010).

10. Leonard Avritzer, *Participatory Institutions in Democratic Brazil* (Washington, D.C., Woodrow Wilson Center Press, 2009); "Brazil's Scandal-Plagued Senate: House of Horrors," *The Economist*, July 11, 2009, 39.

11. Jonathan Wheatley, "Dancing Through the Economic Crisis," *Financial Times*, July 7, 2009, 1, 3; and "Television in Brazil: Soaps, Sex and Sociology," *The Economist*, March 14, 2009, 42.

12. Elizabeth Bishop, excerpt from "Brazil," *New York Times*, 1963, 12–13.

13. Elizabeth Rosenthal, "An Amazon Culture Withers as Food Dries Up: A Tribal Extinction is Feared as the Rainforest Falls," *New York Times*, July 25, 2009, A1, A6; "The Future of the Forest," *The Economist*, June 13, 2009, 27, 29.

14. "An Unruly Bunch," *The Economist*, May 16, 2009, 47.

15. Brazilian Embassy, *Brazil and the USA: What Do We Have In Common?* (Washington, D.C., 1999). Much has been written on this issue. One of the best and shortest pieces is the analytical article by Glaucio Ary Dillon Soares, "The Rise of the Brazilian Military," *Studies in Comparative International Development* 21, no. 2 (Summer 1986), 34–62.

16. Alexei Barrionuevo, "Scandal Puts Pressure on a Brazilian Leader to Step Down," *New York Times*, August 7, 2009, A8.

17. Rowan Ireland, *Kingdom Comes: Religion and Politics in Brazil* (Pittsburgh: University of Pittsburgh Press, 1991).

18. Russell H. Fitzgibbon and Julio A. Fernandez, *Latin America: Political Culture of Development* (Englewood Cliffs, NJ: Prentice-Hall, 1981), 270.

19. "AIDS: No Carnival" and "Roll Out, Roll Out," *The Economist*, July 30, 2005, 71–72.

20. Soares, *op. cit.*

21. Robert Harvey, "Brazil: Unstoppable," *The Economist*, April 25, 1987, 3.

8

Chile

Paul E. Sigmund

What is it about Chile that is so fascinating to the foreign observer? A long (2,600-mile, 4,200-kilometer) "string bean" of a country of nearly seventeen million inhabitants squeezed between the Andes and the sea, it is one of the most important copper producers in the world. It exports fine fruits and wine and has a literate, relatively large middle class. Evidence of its cultural sophistication is the substantial number of world-class Chilean writers and poets, including two Nobel prizewinners. Its topography is varied, ranging from deserts in the north to a fertile 600-mile (966-kilometer) Central Valley—not unlike the valley of the same name in California—to heavily wooded mountains and fjords in the farthest southern regions. Chile's strategic value is limited, except for its control of the Strait of Magellan. None of these factors, however, accounts for foreigners' extraordinary fascination with the country.

Chilean politics is the reason for the great interest in that country. Until the 1973 coup it was one of the oldest constitutional democracies in the world. Since 1833, with only two interruptions—a short but bloody civil war in 1891 and a period of military intervention and plebiscitarian rule between 1925 and 1932—its political system followed regular constitutional procedures, with civil liberties, the rule of law, and periodic contested elections for a bicameral legislature and a directly elected president.

In recent decades successive governments have attempted to implement a variety of approaches to address Chilean underdevelopment. Between 1958 and 1964 a conservative government headed by President Jorge Alessandri

PERU

Arica

Iquique

BOLIVIA

Chuquicamata

Antofagasta

PARAGUAY

0 100 200 300 400 Miles

0 200 400 Kilometers

Copiapó

La Serena
Ovalle Coquimbo

Valparaíso
★ Santiago

Rancagua
Talca

ARGENTINA

Concepción Chillán

Angol

Temuco

Valdivia

Osorno

Puerto Montt
Ancud

Castro

Isla de Chiloé

Puerto Aisén

ATLANTIC

OCEAN

Península de
Taitao

PACIFIC

OCEAN

Strait of Magellan

Punta Arenas
Porvenir

Cape Horn

CHILE

tried to resolve Chile's problems of inflation, unemployment, and slow growth by emphasizing market incentives along with government programs in the areas of housing and limited agrarian reform. The Christian Democratic government of Eduardo Frei Montalva (1964–1970) initiated a Chileanization program for a partial government takeover by purchase of the U.S.-owned copper mines, adopted a much more radical agrarian reform law, promoted programs to organize and benefit peasants and "marginalized" sectors, and cooperated actively with the U.S.-sponsored Alliance for Progress in attempting to carry out what Frei called a "Revolution in Liberty." A three-way election in 1970 led to the victory of Salvador Allende, the candidate of the Marxist-dominated Popular Unity coalition. Allende tried to initiate a "transition to socialism," which involved takeovers—sometimes of questionable legality—of industry and agriculture, income redistribution, and accelerated class polarization.

In 1973 the three armed services and the national police (*carabineros*) overthrew Allende, and what had begun as an institutional coup to save democracy from Marxism soon became a personalist dictatorship under General Augusto Pinochet, the head of the army. Pinochet closed down the political system but allowed a group of free market–oriented economists, many of whom (known as "los Chicago boys") had been trained at the University of Chicago, to open up what had been a highly protected economy and drastically reduce government intervention in a controversial experiment in economic—but not political—libertarianism. In 1980 Pinochet appealed to Chilean legalism and constitutionalism to legitimate his power by calling and winning a snap plebiscite on a constitution that enabled him to continue in office until 1989 but required another plebiscite on a new mandate for an additional eight years. Then, on October 5, 1988, he lost that plebiscite by a vote of 55 percent to 43 percent.

In the elections that followed, a multiparty, anti-Pinochet coalition (the *Concertación por la Democracia*) elected a Christian Democrat, Patricio Aylwin, to a four-year term ending in March, 1994. He was succeeded by Eduardo Frei Ruiz-Tagle, the son of the former Christian Democratic president. In 2000, after a very close election, Ricardo Lagos from the Socialist Party, the other major partner in the coalition, narrowly defeated the candidate of the conservative coalition. Then in 2006, another Socialist, Michelle Bachelet, the daughter of an Air Force general who had opposed the 1973 coup and landed in prison, was elected as the first Chilean woman president, defeating Sebastián Piñera, the multimillionaire candidate of the National Renovation party. Then, in January 2010, the twenty-year rule of the Concertación was ended when Piñera, the candidate of the right, in turn defeated former president Frei Ruiz-Tagle.

The contrasting approaches to development adopted by successive Chilean governments have produced a large and controversial literature. Conservatives, reformists, revolutionaries, and authoritarians have cited the accomplishments and failures of the various Chilean governments in order to defend or attack more general ideological approaches to Third World politics. The Allende experiment in particular has spawned an enormous literature—probably one thousand books in many languages—but the other governments also have both their defenders and their critics. The Pinochet dictatorship in particular was characterized by a dramatic opening of the economy, accompanied by violations of human rights that drew worldwide attention. The policies of the post-Pinochet democratic governments, which have combined economic growth based on private and foreign investment, export promotion, and low inflation with increased social equity and a dramatic reduction in poverty (from 40 percent in 1990 to 13.7 percent in 2006) have been seen as a model for the rest of Latin America.

Citizens of the United States have reason to be interested in Chilean politics because of the deep involvement of the U.S. government in that country between the 1950s and the 1990s. Because Chile had the oldest and, outside of Cuba, largest Communist party in the Western Hemisphere, the United States began in the 1950s to take a strong interest in its political life. The United States supported, both overtly and covertly, the reformist Christian Democratic regime in the 1960s; opposed, overtly and covertly, the Allende government in the early 1970s; and was ambivalent about the Pinochet regime, being repelled by its human rights violations (which led to a cutoff in 1976 by the U.S. Congress of all military aid and sales to Chile) but supportive of Chile's free-market approach to development and willingness to respect its international economic obligations. Beginning in the mid-1980s, for both ideological and pragmatic reasons, the Reagan administration began to promote a democratic transition in Chile and an end to the Pinochet dictatorship. Before the 1988 plebiscite the U.S. Congress went even further, appropriating one million dollars to support free elections in Chile. Since the return of democracy in 1990, U.S.-Chilean relations have improved dramatically, and in 2004, after many years of negotiation, the two countries signed a free trade agreement.

Interest in Chile revolves around three general questions. First, how is it that, in contrast to most other Latin American countries, Chile has been able to develop and maintain pluralist civilian constitutional rule throughout most of its history? Second, why did what appeared to be a strong, stable democracy give way to repressive military rule in 1973, and what was the role of the U.S. government before and after the coup? And third, what lessons can be drawn from the contrasting approaches of recent Chilean governments for achieving a successful combination of democracy, economic growth, and social justice?

Political History to 1973

To answer the first question we must look at Chile's history and political culture as well as the self-image held by the Chileans themselves. Most accounts of the origins of Chile's constitutionalism begin with the early postindependence struggles for control of the government between the conservative *pelucones* ("bigwigs") and the more liberal *pipiolos* ("upstarts"). After the autocratic ways of "the Liberator," Bernardo O'Higgins, had led to his resignation in 1823, a period of conflict ensued that ended with the triumph of the pelucones in the Battle of Lircay. The 1833 constitution adopted under their auspices created a strong role for the president, elected by property holders for a five-year term with the possibility of reelection for a second term, but it also gave the Congress a role in approving the budget. To this day Chilean conservatives look back to the 1830s, when Diego Portales established a strong centralized state operating under the rule of law as a governmental ideal that is still valid. They argue that the strong presidency and state not only continued cultural patterns inherited from the Spanish monarchy but also maintained the rule of Castillian-Basque landowners in a way that prevented the breakdown of authority and military intervention that characterized many other newly independent Latin American states. Others maintain that the development of civilian constitutionalism owes more to the presidency of Manuel Bulnes (1841–1851), the hero of the 1837 war with Peru and Bolivia, than to Portales. Bulnes sharply reduced the size of the army and built up a civilian-based national guard as a counterweight to it while strengthening the state bureaucracy so that it provided effective administration and loyalty to the institutions of the state. In addition, he was willing to work with Congress even when it opposed his plans; he relied on changes in his cabinet to keep in touch with elite opinion; and, most important, though still personally popular, he left office in accordance with the constitutional timetable.

In the two-term, ten-year presidency of Bulnes's successor, Manuel Montt (1851–1861), the Liberals reemerged, now reinforced by the influx of progressive ideas from Europe after the liberal revolutions of 1848. As in other Latin American countries the Liberal-Conservative split focused on centralism versus federalism and the relations between church and state. The federalist tendencies of the Liberals reflected the opposition of the mining interests of the north and the medium-sized landholders of the south to the political dominance of the large landowners of the Central Valley around the capital, Santiago. Revolts against Santiago domination in 1851 and 1859 were put down, but what Chileans call the Oligarchic Republic (1830–1861) gave way to the Liberal Republic (1861–1891), in which factions of the elite combined and recombined in the Congress and the presidency so as to open the system by limiting the presidency to five years (1871) and abolishing the property requirement for voting (1874). A small but expanding middle class then found political expression in the founding in 1861 of the Radical Party, which was committed to Freemasonry, reducing church influence, promoting public education, and establishing universal male suffrage. However, Conservative control of elections in the countryside in what was still largely a rural country meant that the large landowners were able to use electoral democracy to maintain their dominance rather than resorting to military intervention to stem the effects of increased popular participation. Church-state issues, such as who should control clerical appointments, cemeteries, and education, still divided the political class, but after 1859 all groups now agreed on elections and peaceful competition rather than on the use of force to resolve their differences.

The Liberal-Conservative split was papered over during the War of the Pacific (1879–1883) against Peru and Bolivia. Chile's victory gave it a one-third increase in territory involving the rich copper and nitrate areas of the north, but it also led to border disputes with Peru (which were resolved only as late as 1929) and with Bolivia over its access to the Pacific (still an issue today). The victory vastly increased government revenues from export taxes and produced not only a period of economic prosperity but also the beginnings of an inflation problem that was to continue for almost a century. When President José Manuel Balmaceda (1886–1891) began to take measures to end currency depreciation, promote small landholding, and establish state control over the largely British-owned nitrate deposits, he encountered fierce resistance from landowners and foreign interests. When Congress refused to approve his budget, he attempted to rule alone, and a civil war ensued in which ten thousand Chileans died, including Balmaceda himself, who committed suicide after his forces were defeated.

The Chilean constitutional system was fundamentally transformed as a result of the 1891 Civil War. During the period of the Parliamentary Republic (1891–1920), power passed from the president to Congress, and the center of political attention shifted to the local bases of the notables who controlled the Congress. National governments (a total of 121 cabinets between 1891 and 1924), rose and fell, depending on shifting congressional majorities, while weak presidents presided over unstable coalition governments.

Following the end of the War of the Pacific in 1883 a Prussian captain, Emil Körner, was invited to organize the Chilean Academy of War, and he began a program to professionalize the army along Prussian lines. (The goose step and the army's strict hierarchical structure and professionalism mark the continuing effects of the original Prussian influence.) So effective was Körner that Chilean military missions were subsequently invited to train armies in Colombia and El Salvador.

In the economy, nitrate, coal, and copper mining expanded (in the last case, by U.S. companies), and labor agitation increased. Labor began to organize, and the massacre of two thousand nitrate workers and their families at Iquique in 1907 became a part of the collective memory of the labor movement. Luis Emilio Recabarren, a labor leader, was elected to Congress in 1906 but was not allowed to take his seat. In 1912 Recabarren founded the Socialist Workers' party, which in 1921 became the Communist Party of Chile. The expanding middle class found its political expression in the Radical Party, which in addition to its traditional endorsement of the separation of church and state, began to adopt programs favoring social welfare legislation.

The development of cheap synthetic nitrate during World War I dealt a serious blow to Chilean prosperity, which had been based on mineral exports. The election of 1920 brought to the presidency a new populist leader, Arturo Alessandri Palma. Although Alessandri's supporters secured a majority in the congressional elections of 1924, Congress resisted his proposals for social legislation and labor rights. These proposals were adopted only under pressure from young reformist military men in the galleries—the so-called "rattling of the sabres." Alessandri left the country in protest against military intervention but returned in 1925 to preside over the writing of the 1925 constitution. The constitution provided for a strong president, elected for a six-year term, but it denied the possibility of immediate reelection. Members of Congress were elected at a different time and for different terms (four years for the Chamber of Deputies and eight years for the Senate), and Congress was obliged to choose between the top two presidential candidates. Legislators were elected according to a system of proportional representation that accentuated the proliferation of parties that had already begun to take place. Church and state were separated, and labor and social welfare guarantees were included in the constitution. Chile was thus well ahead of most other Latin American countries in the establishment of the welfare state.

Alessandri resigned three months later, and his successor was forced out by Colonel Carlos Ibáñez, who ruled by plebiscite and decree until 1931. Following a series of short-lived military governments, Chile returned to elected governments in late 1932. The military largely withdrew from politics, and four decades of civilian rule ensued.

One of the many unstable governments in the period from 1931 to 1932 was a military-dominated "Socialist Republic" that lasted one hundred days from June to September 1932. Marxist intellectuals, students, and military men then joined to form a new leftist party, the Socialist Party of Chile, which was formally established in April 1933. In late 1932 Arturo Alessandri returned as president, but he now followed a much more conservative policy than earlier. The period that followed has been described by some Chilean writers as the *Estado de Compromiso* (the compromise state)—that is, one in which there was something for everyone and no interest group was directly threatened. The combination of staggered elections and proportional representation meant that it was difficult to get a stable majority for any program, especially if it involved fundamental reforms.

In 1938 Pedro Aguirre Cerda, the candidate of a Popular Front coalition of Radicals and Socialists with Communist support, won the presidential elections. He faced a hostile legislative majority, and the coalition lasted only two years. The Popular Front succeeded in securing the passage of a few social welfare laws, but its principal accomplishment was the establishment of the Chilean Development Corporation (CORFO), which provided the legal basis for a larger state role in the economy. The period from 1938 to 1952 was characterized by the dominance of the Radical Party, which governed through shifting coalitions and policies along with generous patronage to the party faithful. One such shift was from an alliance with the Communists in 1938 to the outlawing of the party by the Radical-sponsored Law for the Defense of Democracy in 1948. (The Communists were legalized again in 1958.)

When the country looked for an alternative to the Radical Party in 1952, it turned to none other than the old military strongman Carlos Ibáñez, who won by a landslide under the symbol of a broom to sweep out the corrupt and ineffective Radicals. Ibáñez did not deliver on his promises, however, and the traditional parties returned to the fray in 1958. A new party, the Christian Democrats, which had been formed by successive reformist splits from the Conservatives, made a surprising showing in the 1958 elections. The Christian Democrats divided the centrist vote with the Radicals, while the leftist alliance of the Socialists and Communists came close to electing Salvador Allende as president. Allende was narrowly edged out by Arturo Alessandri's son, Jorge, the candidate of the Liberals and Conservatives. (There were no longer any significant differences between the Liberals and Conservatives, since the church-state issue had been settled in 1925, and overlapping rural and urban interests in both parties rendered obsolete the old divisions between the landowner and merchant classes.) The 1958 election, with its three-way split between left, center, and right, marked the beginning of a recurrent problem in Chilean politics—how to get majority support for presidents and parties when the electorate was divided into "the three thirds" (los tres tercios).

When it looked as if the 1964 presidential elections might give Allende a chance to win by a plurality in a multicandidate race (and thus, by tradition, to be elected in the congressional runoff), the right threw its support to the charismatic Christian Democratic candidate, Eduardo Frei Montalva, whose program for a "Revolution in Liberty" was offered as a democratic response to the challenge of the Cuban Revolution. Frei won the popular election with the first absolute majority in modern Chilean history—55 percent to Allende's 39 percent. But when he began to implement his program of accelerated agrarian reform, expanded welfare legislation, and higher taxes, the right withdrew its support.

Frei's reforms had strong U.S. backing inasmuch as they coincided in aims and methods with the Alliance for Progress, but they ran into congressional opposition (because of staggered elections, the Christian Democrats never controlled both houses) and created inflationary pressures. After a successful first three years Frei faced an increasingly hostile Congress, and in 1969 he had to put down a local military revolt, the first since the 1930s. The right was optimistic that it could win the 1970 presidential elections with Jorge Alessandri, now eligible to run again, since the Christian Democrats had lost support and did not put forward a strong candidate. On the left, meanwhile, the Socialist-Communist alliance backing Allende was broadened to include a left splinter group from the Christian Democrats as well as the main body of the Radical Party (which had also split).

The result was a narrow victory by Allende (36.2 percent, lower than his vote in 1964) over Alessandri (34.9 percent) with the Christian Democratic candidate a distant third with 27.8 percent. Chile was thrown into a constitutional, political, and economic crisis as Congress, which was over two-thirds non-Marxist, was asked to elect a Marxist as president in the constitutionally mandated runoff between the top two candidates. The crisis was intensified by U.S. covert efforts to create turmoil in the economy and to promote a military coup as well as by the assassination by a rightist group of the army commander-in-chief. It is a testimony to the legalism and constitutionalism of the Chilean military and people that after lengthy negotiations, the constitutional tradition was followed, and in November 1970 Salvador Allende became president.

In the case of the Allende government, the pattern of three good years followed by three bad ones that had characterized previous administrations was telescoped into eighteen months for each period. In 1971 the U.S.-owned mines were completely nationalized by a widely supported constitutional amendment (although the compensation procedures, which in most cases amounted to confiscation, immediately got the Allende government into trouble with the United States and the copper companies); a boom, produced by the granting of large wage raises while price controls were strictly enforced, buoyed the economy; and the Allende coalition received nearly 50 percent support in the municipal elections. However, by 1972 runaway inflation had set in; violence was increasing in the countryside; shortages of foodstuffs and essential goods occurred; and class polarization, encouraged by a government that was trying to broaden its base of support among the lower classes, exacerbated personal and political relations. Using among other "legal loopholes" legislation from the 1932 Socialist Republic, the government took over and "intervened" or "requisitioned" five hundred firms—and industrial and agricultural production dropped. Further exacerbating the economic problems, opposition-dominated professional and occupational groups (*gremios*) called strikes that paralyzed the country in October 1972 and again in July 1973.

Despite several attempts at negotiations with the Christian Democrats, Allende was not able to work out an agreement with the opposition-dominated Congress. (The left wing of his Socialist Party opposed any agreement, as did the right wing of the Christian Democrats.) By the time the congressional elections of March 1973 took place, the three-thirds had become two intransigent pro- and anti-Allende blocs. The center-right Democratic Confederation won 55 percent of the congressional vote, compared with 43 percent for Allende's Popular Unity Federation, and the division of the country only intensified. Violence increased as extremists on both sides (the Movement of the Revolutionary Left [MIR] and the rightist *Patria y Libertad*) carried out assassinations, blackouts, and bombings. To the concerns of the military over the collapse of the economy and the breakdown of law and order (symbolized by a widely circulated picture of a policeman being beaten by a masked and helmeted revolutionary) were added fears of Marxism, as the government announced that all schools would be required to give government-mandated courses in socialism.

Yet the army still considered itself to be "professional, hierarchical, obedient, and non-deliberating" as required by the 1925 constitution. The armed forces did not move until the Supreme Court had written open letters to Allende protesting the government's refusal to carry out court orders to return seized property, the Congress had passed a resolution accusing the government of "habitually" violating the constitution and the law, and the other army generals had forced out their constitutionalist commander-in-chief, Carlos Prats (later assassinated in exile by Chilean intelligence agents).

On September 11, 1973, the army, air force, navy, and national police overthrew the Allende government in a one-day coup that included the bombing of La Moneda, the presidential palace (the traditional symbol of civilian rule), and the suicide of Allende (following the example, which he often cited, of President Balmaceda in 1891) as army troops stormed the burning palace.

Despite reports, never proven, of CIA involvement in the coup (a 1975 U.S. Senate investigation concluded that between 1971 and 1973 CIA money supported the opposition media, some of the strikers, an extreme-right group, and anti-Allende propaganda among the military), the coup was an authentically Chilean product. The armed forces moved only when it became clear that the civilian politicians were unable to run the economy or to maintain a constitutional consensus and that the military monopoly on the instruments of coercion was being threatened by armed groups. Allende had been able to use the constitution to defend himself against military intervention as long as the economy was functioning and law and order prevailed. However, once it appeared that the legality and constitutionalism that Allende had proclaimed as essential to the *via chilena* to socialism no longer existed, the armed forces broke with their tradition of nonintervention. Many factors contributed to the breakdown of constitutional democracy, but the most important ones seem to have been the sharp increase in violence and polarization as well as the collapse of the economy.

Military Rule

Most observers had assumed that if the armed forces intervened, it would be for a short period during which they would outlaw the Marxist parties, stabilize the economy, and call new elections. They were wrong. It is now clear that 1973 was a turning point in Chilean history. The leaders of the coup—especially General Augusto Pinochet, who used his position as head of the senior branch of the armed services to centralize political power in his hands—were determined to change the pattern of Chilean politics. They spoke of eradicating the "cancer of Marxism," creating a "protected democracy" that would not be subject to the demagoguery of the politicians, and making sure that the breakdown of law and order as well as the threats to national security that occurred during the Allende administration would never be repeated.

Yet as clear as their determination to change Chilean political culture might have been, the specifics of how to do so were not evident at the outset. The leftist parties were outlawed, the Communist Party headquarters was burned, and the other parties were declared "in recess." Thousands of suspected leftists were rounded up, tortured, and in many cases killed. (The best-known case is that of Charles Horman, a U.S. citizen. It is the subject of the book and film *Missing*, which accurately portray the atmosphere of postcoup Chile, although the basic thesis of *Missing*, that Horman was killed because "he knew too much" about the U.S. role in the coup, is incorrect.) Many of the leaders of the left went into exile or took refuge in foreign embassies. Those who did not were transported to Dawson Island in the frigid south and were later allowed to go into exile as well. The constitution, in the name of which the coup had been carried out, was simply ignored as the government began to function in accordance with a series of decree-laws that gave legislative and constitutional power to the four-person junta and executive power to its head, Pinochet. (At the time of the coup there had been discussion of rotating the presidency of the junta among the armed forces, but it was soon clear that Pinochet intended to stay in that post, and a decree-law in June 1974 made him President of the Republic and Supreme Chief of the Nation.) The judiciary remained in place and supinely recognized the legal validity of the decree-laws, refusing to issue writs of habeas corpus (*recursos de amparo*) for all but a minuscule number of the thousands who were arrested. A committee of conservative jurists was appointed to revise the constitution, but it worked very slowly and did not report out a draft until five years later.

The effort to remove what the military viewed as the sources of subversion meant not only that the parties who were members of Allende's Popular Unity Federation were outlawed, but also that the universities were put under military rectors and leftist professors were purged; the newspapers and magazines of the left were closed (along with the theoretical journal of the Christian Democrats); labor unions, many of which had been Marxist-led, were dissolved; and peasant organizations were disbanded. Foreigners who had been assisting the Allende government were expelled and, in a few cases, tortured or killed. Diplomatic relations were broken with Cuba and the Soviet Union (but not with China, a principal customer for Chilean copper).

The most important change, in terms of its lasting impact on Chilean society, was the opening of the economy carried out under the auspices of "los Chicago boys." Departing from the usual statist tendencies of the Latin American military, the junta decided to entrust economic policy to a group of free market–oriented civilian economists, most of whom had received graduate training in economics at the University of Chicago. Reacting to the socialist interventionism of the Allende years, their program called for opening Chile to internal and external competition by relying on private enterprise, competition, and market forces. It removed price controls, reduced tariffs dramatically, expanded exports, moved toward the establishment of more realistic exchange rates, and returned landholdings and businesses that had been illegally seized. (The copper nationalization was not reversed both because it had been carried out by a constitutional amendment and because part of the foreign exchange earnings of copper was earmarked for military purchases.) At first the program was adopted in a gradual fashion, but two years later it was applied in a drastic "shock treatment."

The new regime engaged in campaigns of violence and repression against its enemies. Military missions moved to the north and the south to carry out summary executions of leftists. The report of the National Commission on Truth and Reconciliation in February 1991 and subsequent investigations identified by name 3,197 Chileans who had been killed or had disappeared between 1973 and 1990, most of them victims of "agents of the state or persons in its service." The reports of the National Commission on Political

Imprisonment and Torture, chaired by Bishop Sergio Valech, published in 2004 and 2005, listed 28,456 cases, often involving physical abuse, rape, electric shock, and other forms of torture.

The violation of human rights in Chile led to a serious deterioration in relations with the United States, and in 1976 the U.S. Congress imposed a ban on Chilean arms aid and purchases, which was not lifted until 1990. Relations worsened when President Jimmy Carter made human rights a central element of U.S. foreign policy. In the United Nations, reports to the General Assembly about Chile were prepared each year by a special rapporteur, and the UN Human Rights Commission continued to discuss Chilean abuses.

Within Chile Pinochet managed to transform what had been an institutional coup by the four services into a personal dictatorship. The system of promotions and retirements was altered so that his protégés could remain beyond retirement age while those who were a possible threat to his power could be retired. The intelligence branches of the armed services were consolidated into a single National Intelligence Service (DINA), which established computerized files and conducted a national system of terror. DINA killed General Prats, in exile in Argentina, and wounded Bernardo Leighton, a Christian Democrat with good relations with the left, in Rome. Its most heinous crime was to blow up the car of Allende's former ambassador to the United States, Orlando Letelier, in the heart of Washington, D.C. The U.S. investigation that followed led to the extradition and conviction of the immediate perpetrator, a rightist U.S. citizen who had been living in Chile, and continuing pressure on Chile to extradite the higher-ups involved. After the return of democracy, the head of DINA, Manuel Contreras, was tried and sentenced to seven years in prison for ordering Letelier's death. (After his release he was tried and sentenced to life imprisonment for other human rights crimes.)

As a result of the Letelier investigation, Pinochet removed Contreras and reorganized DINA as the National Information Center (CNI), which wielded less independent power than DINA had exercised. In 1978, when General Gustavo Leigh, the air force member of the junta, began to call for more rapid progress toward civilian rule, Pinochet removed him and appointed a low-ranking air force general as his successor. This action led to the resignation or forced retirement of eighteen air force generals. With his triumph over Leigh, Pinochet's personal control of the armed forces was complete.

Meanwhile, the economy, which had suffered a drastic contraction as a result of the shock treatment, was now beginning to be described as the "Chilean economic miracle." From 1977 until 1981 it expanded at rates of 6 to 8 percent a year. With tariff rates down to 10 percent (from an average of 100 percent during the Allende period), cheap foreign imports flooded the country. The exchange rate was fixed at 39 pesos to the dollar, and nontraditional exports such as fruit, lumber, and seafood reduced the share of copper in earning foreign exchange from 80 percent to less than 40 percent. It was possible to take out dollar loans at the overvalued exchange rate, and Japanese cars and scotch whiskey could be purchased more cheaply in Chile than in their countries of origin. It was in this heady atmosphere that a plebiscite was held on a new constitution.

The 1980 Constitution

In late 1978 the Committee for the Study of a New Constitution produced a draft that was submitted to the advisory Council of State, which had been created by Pinochet in 1976. On July 1, 1980, the Council submitted a revised draft that proposed a five-year transition, with an appointed Congress until 1985 and a full return to civilian rule at that time. In the next month Pinochet and his advisers completely rewrote the transitional provisions of the draft to produce a quite different timetable that would enable Pinochet to remain in power until at least 1990, and possibly until 1997. With only one opportunity for public criticism—a public meeting at which Frei spoke and leftist slogans were chanted (by CNI agents, some said)—the draft was submitted to a vote on the seventh anniversary of the coup, September 11, 1980, and the government-controlled media announced that it had been approved by a 67 percent vote. Later there were charges that the vote had been artificially inflated in the more remote areas, with more votes reported than there were voters. (The voting rolls had been destroyed after the coup, and there were no independent poll watchers to check on the voting.)

One of the transitional provisions added in July 1980 was that approval of the constitution also constituted election of General Pinochet for an eight-year presidential term beginning March 11, 1981. The transitional articles also called for a plebiscite in late 1988 on an additional eight-year term for a presidential candidate nominated by the junta. In the event that the junta candidate lost the plebiscite (as in fact happened), competitive elections for the presidency and for Congress were to be held in late 1989, with the elected government taking office on March 11, 1990.

The 1980 constitution attempted to remedy the defects of the 1925 constitution by providing for the simultaneous election of the president and the Congress (thus removing the adverse effects of staggered elections) and establishing a two-round runoff system for the popular election of the president (so that he would have the mandate of a popular majority—a system that almost certainly would have led to the election of Jorge Alessandri in 1970). The constitution also created a strong Constitutional Tribunal with the power to "control" (that is, review) the constitutionality of all important laws and to make definitive judgments on all constitutional disputes. The Chamber of

Deputies was to have 120 members elected for four-year terms, and there would be 26 senators (later increased to 38), elected for eight-year terms, with half chosen every four years. In addition, all ex-presidents who had served six years were to be senators for life, and there were to be nine appointed senators—two former members of the Supreme Court, one ex-controller general, one former university rector, one ex-cabinet member, and one former commander from each of the four armed services. (The nonelected senators were abolished in August 2005, but in the initial years of the transition to democracy they gave the right the power to block government legislation in the upper house.)

The "Modernizations"

With the apparent success of the government's economic policy Pinochet's advisers began to extend the principle of free choice to the area of social policy by means of the so-called "modernizations." Labor unions were now permitted, but they were restricted to the local firm or factory, and their right to strike was limited. The National Health Service was reorganized and decentralized, and private health services were authorized to receive payments from the compulsory health insurance deduction, leading eventually to the enrollment of about 30 percent of Chileans in private health plans. Private universities and educational institutions were authorized, and tuitions were raised, which could be financed by low-interest loans that were immediately payable if a student failed or was expelled from the university (e.g., for political activities). Local education was reorganized on the basis of contracts between the municipality and private educational corporations so that teachers ceased to be civil servants and lost tenure rights. Housing policy was reoriented to encourage private contractors to build low-cost housing, and the government provided low-interest loans and grants to the poor only if they had saved enough to make a small down payment.

The most fundamental shift was the privatization of the complicated and bankrupt social security system. A reduction in premiums persuaded Chileans to place their compulsory social security deductions in publicly regulated but private and competitive pension funds resembling the individual retirement accounts (IRAs) in the United States. Unlike IRAs, however, the pension funds replaced rather than supplemented the public social security program. The government still maintained a basic social security safety net for those people who, for reasons such as poor health or insufficient contributions, could not participate in the system. Over the next several years, however, the government's responsibility for most of the social security program ended.

The "modernizations" and the opening of the economy to internal and external market forces were part of a broader view that was influenced by economically conservative (Latin Americans would call them "neoliberal") thinkers in the United States and Europe. Friedrich Hayek and Milton Friedman visited Chile, and think tanks and publications began to project a vision of a new Chile with a consumer-oriented and prosperous economy like those of South Korea and Hong Kong. This economy would gradually move toward democratic and decentralized politics that would replace the statism and socialism of the past.

In March 1981 when Augusto Pinochet entered the newly reconstructed presidential palace as "constitutional" president of Chile, he was able to feel secure. The original legitimization of the coup (the prevention of a Marxist takeover) was no longer viable, but it had been replaced by a constitution that had the support of the armed forces and of many members of the upper and middle classes. Furthermore, the new prosperity of the "economic miracle" was even beginning to trickle down to the lower classes as employment and wages began to rise and inflation declined. A state of emergency in various degrees and a limited curfew were still in force, and police roundups in the poor areas and occasional political murders of leftists still occurred. But some opposition magazines and books (although not newspapers or television) were tolerated and the more visible aspects of the repression were no longer evident.

The Protests

The sudden collapse of the Chilean economy in 1982 shattered this optimistic view of the prospects of the regime. External factors such as excessive indebtedness at rising interest rates and a low price for copper exports, combined with internal weaknesses such as an overvalued exchange rate and the existence of underfinanced paper financial empires involving interlocking banks and industries, led to a wave of bankruptcies and widespread unemployment. As unemployment figures rose to include nearly a third of the workforce (including those enrolled in the Minimum Employment Program), Chileans began to engage in public protests against the government for the first time since 1973. Beginning with the copper workers' union in May 1983 and soon joined by the illegal but nonetheless newly revived parties, the protests escalated monthly until August, when President Pinochet had to call out 17,000 members of the regular army to keep order.

Pinochet, however, was able to keep his hold on power by pointing to the timetable outlined in the constitution and appealing to fears of disorder and violence. (The Manuel Rodríguez Patriotic Front [FPMR], a terrorist movement associated with but more committed to violence than the Communist Party, had begun to engage in acts of sabotage, bombings, and blackouts.) In 1986 Pinochet's position was strengthened when large arms deposits destined for the FPMR were discovered, and when the group carried out an unsuccessful assassination attempt against him.

The 1988 Plebiscite

In contrast to the plebiscite on the 1980 constitution, the 1988 plebiscite was organized well in advance. Laws were published concerning electoral registration, recognition of political parties, and the method of carrying out the plebiscite itself. The problem for the opposition was to decide whether, by participating, they would give implicit recognition to the 1980 constitution, the legitimacy of which they had always questioned. The Communist Party called for a boycott, but later, under pressure from its membership, it permitted its adherents to register. The Christian Democrats eventually complied with the legal requirements for party registration, and the Socialists had it both ways by refusing to seek recognition while registering a Party for Democracy (PPD), which was open to all who opposed the regime.

The conservative parties, the center-right National Renovation Party, and the pro-Pinochet Independent Democratic Union (UDI), had already been recognized, and they urged their members to register and vote. The government pressured the military and public employees to do the same. At the beginning of 1988, when it was rumored that Pinochet was urging the junta to call a plebiscite in March, it looked as if he could get a new eight-year term without difficulty. However, several factors turned the situation around.

First, sixteen opposition parties from the center and the left (minus the Communists) formed a unified Command for the No, published a program calling for a return to democracy and an end to ideological proscriptions, and insisted that a democratic government would respect private property and the economic rules of the game. Second, church-related groups conducted massive registration drives throughout the country, resulting in the registration of 92 percent of the eligible voters by the time the electoral registries were closed. Third, the Constitutional Tribunal ruled that the opposition must be given access to the state-owned television—and fifteen minutes of prime time were given free of charge to the opposition for twenty-seven days. With the assistance of the Center for Free Elections (COPEL) of the Organization of American States and the U.S. National Endowment for Democracy, the opposition developed an effective television campaign as well as poll-watching and vote-counting techniques that made fraud almost impossible. The result was that, despite massive government propaganda arguing that a "no" vote would mean a return to the chaos and communism of the Allende period,

Pinochet was defeated by a vote of 55 percent "no" to 43 percent "yes" on his continuation as president for another eight-year term.

The Return to Democracy

On December 14, 1989, Patricio Aylwin, a Christian Democrat who was the candidate of the center-left Concertación por la Democracia, defeated the candidate of the pro-Pinochet parties and took office on March 11, 1990. Pinochet continued as army commander for an eight-year term as permitted by the transitional provisions of the 1980 constitution. Along with the heads of the other armed services, he also had a seat on the National Security Council, and thereafter, as an ex-president, he could be a senator for the rest of his life.

Thanks to their years of exile in Europe and the United States, the Aylwin cabinet contained the largest number of ministers and deputy ministers with graduate degrees of any modern government. The government announced that it would give priority to primary education and job training. Government spending on education, adjusted for inflation, doubled between 1990 and 1997. Health spending increased by 75 percent, although substantial inequalities between the public and private health care sectors remained. Between 1990 and 1997 foreign investment and exports doubled, and inflation and unemployment dropped to 6 percent. Economic growth averaged 7 percent a year in the same period, with an 11 percent growth rate in 1992. The percentage of the population living in poverty dropped from 39 percent in 1987 to 23 percent in 1994, and the living standards of all groups rose as average wages increased by 22 percent, although income distribution remained highly skewed. The U.S. embargo on military aid was lifted, and negotiations for free trade agreements with the United States, Canada, and Mexico were begun.

The Aylwin government moved quickly in the area of human rights. To investigate human rights abuses, Aylwin appointed a Commission on Truth and Reconciliation, headed by Raúl Rettig, a former Radical senator, and including Gonzalo Vial, a conservative historian and former education minister in the Pinochet government. The Commission had no judicial powers and did not identify the perpetrators, but it listed the victims by name and called for moral and monetary reparations to the families of the victims. In April 1991 an additional politically inspired murder was added to the list with the assassination by the leftist Manuel Rodríguez Patriotic Front of Senator Jaime Guzman, the founder of the rightist UDI party.

The Aylwin government was pressured by members of the Socialist and PPD parties as well as by the Association of Families of the Detained and Disappeared (AFDD) to take further action in the human rights area. Political cases were moved from military to civilian courts, nonviolent political prisoners were released, and the Communist Party was legalized, but Pinochet continued to insist that he would protect "my people" (*mi gente*) from prosecution. In December 1991 he issued a low-level mobilization ("call to quarters") that was intended to deliver a message to the government. Cases that involved murders and disappearances that had taken place after the amnesty declared by Pinochet in 1978, as well as the Letelier murder in Washington that, at U.S. insistence, had been exempted from that amnesty, proceeded at a slow pace through the court system.

The human rights cases were among the first problems of the new administration of Eduardo Frei Ruiz-Tagle, who took office on March 11, 1994, following a record win—58 percent of the votes—over Arturo Alessandri, a nephew of the former president. In retrospect, it now appears that the jurisdiction of the civilian courts over human rights cases involving the military was finally established in November 1993 with the sentencing of retired General Manuel Contreras, the former head of the DINA intelligence agency, and his assistant, Pedro Espinoza, for their part in the Letelier assassination. After many months of resistance, including a stay at a military hospital by Contreras, the two former officers began in September and October 1994 to serve their sentences in a specially-constructed jail for members of the military.

The Pinochet Case

In accordance with the 1980 constitution Pinochet went out of office as commander-in-chief of the army in March 1998 and decided to accept his seat as a senator for life. There were protests at his swearing-in as well as an unsuccessful attempt by Socialist, PPD, and some Christian Democratic members of Congress to deny him his seat. His only significant legislative activity was involvement in the resolution of a dispute over ending the status of September 11th, the anniversary of the coup, as a legal holiday by replacing it with a Day of National Unity on the first Monday in September.

In October Pinochet went to London for back surgery, and on October 16, while he was recovering in a hospital, he was arrested by Scotland Yard in response to warrants issued by a Spanish judge requesting that he be extradited for trial for the murder of Spanish citizens as well as for acts of "genocide, terrorism, and torture." The case went through many judicial bodies, including the House of Lords. Then on March 28, 1999, the Law Lords dismissed most of the charges on the grounds that they had not been crimes in Britain at the time they were committed, but they upheld the charges of torture for the acts carried out after December 18, 1988, the date that Britain ratified the International Convention Against Torture. On October 8, 1999, the Magistrates Court ruled that Pinochet could be extradited to Spain to stand trial on those charges.

In August and September Pinochet's health (he was now eighty-three) deteriorated with a series of minor strokes, and he was reported to be suffering as well from diabetes, asthma, circulatory problems, and depression. The Chilean government had already appealed to the British Home Secretary to return him to Chile on humanitarian grounds, and after a government-appointed board of doctors declared him unfit to stand trial in January 2000, he was returned to Chile on March 4, 2000. Awaiting him were fifty-eight cases of human rights abuses being considered by a Chilean judge.

The Frei government, made up of opponents and in some cases victims of Pinochet, had argued for his return, claiming that Chile, as the country in which the crimes had been committed, had original jurisdiction. That claim was initially unconvincing because of the slow pace of human rights cases in the Chilean courts, Pinochet's congressional immunity as a senator, and the amnesty that he had declared in March 1978 for crimes committed between 1973 and the date of the amnesty. However, during his detention in England there had been a turnaround in the personnel and actions of the Chilean courts, as the Pinochet appointees began to retire. The judges began to take up more and more of the human rights cases, including those committed before 1978, which were now considered capable of being tried under the novel judicial doctrine that if the bodies of the disappeared had not been found, a crime of "ongoing kidnapping" (*secuestro permanente*) was still being committed. Cases such as the infamous "Caravan of Death"—the murders of political prisoners in central and northern Chile in October 1973 about which a best-selling book had been written—the assassination of a leading labor leader in 1982, and the 1974 murder of General Prats in Buenos Aires began to be pursued actively in the Chilean judicial system, and military commanders were called on to testify.

Pinochet's successor as army commander protested against the new judicial activism and reinterpretations of the law, but then took no further action. Frei's minister of defense organized a series of dialogues on human rights that included both members of the military and human rights activists, but there was no talk of military action. Clearly Pinochet's arrest and detention had changed the nature of politics in Chile.

The 1999–2000 Presidential Election

Proof that the Pinochet era had been left behind came with the presidential elections of December 1999 and January 2000. Ricardo Lagos, a Socialist who had been education minister and public works minister in the Aylwin and Frei governments, won the Concertación primary election (a new feature of Chilean politics), resoundingly defeating the Christian Democratic candidate. The rightist Alliance for Chile, comprised of the National Renovation Party (RN) and the Independent Democratic Union (UDI), nominated Joaquín Lavín from the more conservative UDI. Lavin had become nationally visible because of his innovative administration as mayor of Las Condes, the upper-class suburb of Santiago, where he had promoted public works, health clinics, housing for the poor, and centers for the elderly. Neither Lavín's earlier association with the Pinochet government nor Lagos's participation in the Allende government was discussed in the campaign, which focused principally on issues of education, health care, public safety, and the economy. After a well-financed campaign in which he projected an image of youth, vigor, and charisma (and outspent the Concertación by a reported US$50 million to US$10 million), Lavín came within 34,000 votes of defeating Lagos in the elections of December 12, 1999, winning a majority of the women's vote and carrying many of Chile's regions. He lost the runoff on January 16, 2000, by 2.6 percent. Political observers attributed Lagos's margin to the votes of some or all of the 3 percent who had voted for the Communist candidate in the first round and to a shift to Lagos in the women's vote as a result of the organization of women voters by the popular Christian Democratic minister of justice, Soledad Alvear.

Lagos appointed a cabinet that included, besides his Socialist/PPD fellow party members, a significant number of Christian Democrats—especially at the assistant minister level—and a minister of finance who had been a director of the International Monetary Fund. The economy, adversely affected by the world crisis of the latter 1990s, recovered dramatically with growth rates around 6 percent in 2005 and 2006. Foreign investment poured in, copper prices rose to all time highs, and Chile became the world's second largest exporter of salmon. Chile signed free trade agreements with the European Union, South Korea, and the United States, adding them to those with Canada and Mexico concluded under the previous administration. Although Chile's distribution of income remained among the most inequitable in the world—with the top 10 percent of the population receiving 42 percent of income and the bottom 20 percent only 3.3 percent—the expanding economy led to a decline in poverty to 13.7 percent in 2006 and to a reduction in unemployment. While other Latin American countries suffered inflation, government instability, and budget deficits, Chile's budgets and balance of payments remained in surplus, its price levels stable, and its level of corruption the lowest in Latin America.

The Lagos government modernized the judicial system, replacing the inefficient "inquisitorial" system, in which the judge also carries out the investigation and indictment, with the adversarial system in use in the United States and Britain. Augusto Pinochet's senatorial immunity was lifted after he returned from Great Britain. A number of judges ruled that he was fit to stand trial, despite his illnesses, and he was repeatedly placed under house arrest—but because his lawyers were able to engage in appeals until his death in December 2006, no actual trial took place.

In November 2004 the commander of the army accepted the institutional responsibility of the army for the human rights abuses of the Pinochet period. At the end of the month the Commission on Political Imprisonment and Torture, headed by Bishop Sergio Valech, gave gruesome and detailed accounts of the tortures inflicted as a matter of policy. Its report and a later follow-up demonstrated that over 28,000 Chileans has been subjected to rape, torture, and physical abuse. It proposed that the victims receive health and education benefits as well as a pension equivalent to US$180 a month.

In 2004 and 2005 a subcommittee of the U.S. Senate investigating money laundering found evidence that the Riggs Bank has assisted Pinochet in setting up fictitious accounts to hide dollar deposits. Further investigation revealed that the Pinochet family had 125 bank accounts holding in excess of US$17 million in nine American banks under false names. Legal proceedings against the family included the arrest of Pinochet's wife and one of his sons, who were accused of involvement in the cover-up as well as income tax evasion. The cases were later dropped.

The political and social consequences of these developments were considerable. Lavín lost support and the conservative vote was split as the other rightist party, the military-dominated National Renovation, nominated as its presidential candidate Sebastián Piñera, a wealthy businessman who had voted against Pinochet in the 1988 plebiscite. In contrast, the Concertación avoided a primary fight when Soledad Alvear, the Christian Democratic candidate, bowed out in view of the commanding lead in the polls of Michelle Bachelet, the Socialist/PPD nominee. The fact that both candidates were women was an indication of the cultural liberalization that had taken place in Chile.

In August 2005 Congress passed a series of constitutional amendments removing the antidemocratic provisions of the 1988 constitution, such as the nonelected senators and the prohibition of presidential removal of military commanders without the consent of the military-dominated National Security Council as well as returning the national police to the Ministry of the Interior. It also shortened the presidential term to four years, thus assuring that henceforth the president, the Chamber of Deputies, and half the Senate would be elected simultaneously. However, it was not able to agree on abandoning the "binominal" congressional electoral system of two-member districts.

With the abolition of the appointed senators, the Concertación secured a legislative majority in both houses in the December 2005 legislative elections. In the presidential election Bachelet secured 46 percent of the vote against a divided opposition but, lacking a majority, was forced into a runoff against Piñera in January 2006—which she won handily.

As a relatively new figure in national politics, Bachelet promised to make significant changes. She named a cabinet that initially included half women. She worked with the parties of the Concertación but brought in different advisers and announced that her government would emphasize and expand popular participation in politics.

Her initial popularity was diminished by a nationwide strike of public school students, demanding improvements in the quality of their education. The "penguins," as they were called because of their uniforms of dark jackets and white shirts, received wide support, and Bachelet responded by appointing a large study group to recommend reforms. A second problem that emerged in her first year was a badly planned and executed reform of public transportation in Santiago ("Transantiago") that substantially increased travel time to work.

In other areas, however, promised reforms were carried out, including the establishment of a national system of child day care, an extension of health care to many new ailments, new housing that effectively eliminated the shantytowns of Santiago, and an expansion of access to higher education. The most significant reform was the expansion of pension coverage to those who had not been able to participate in the contributory scheme initiated under the Pinochet regime—including for the first time housewives of retirement age.

In foreign policy the Bachelet government continued to send troops to the UN force in Haiti; led UNASUR, a new organization of South American governments; and supported the opposition by the Organization of American States to the coup in Honduras. Chile also attempted to mediate the split in the Latin American left between its populist wing headed by Hugo Chávez of Venezuela and those that followed a social democratic model such as Chile and Brazil.

In the last year of her term Bachelet's approval rating rose to 72 percent, the highest of any Chilean president. Much of the improvement was due to Chile's response to the world economic crisis. At the beginning of her administration, the price of copper, one of Chile's principal sources of government revenue and foreign exchange, soared to unprecedented heights. Bachelet's Finance Minister, Andres Velasco, resisted pressures to spend the surplus, arguing that it should be saved for periods when the price was low. When the worldwide financial crisis of 2008–2009 hit Chile, thereby resulting in unemployment, a drop in the price of copper, and an increase in poverty, the government was able to draw on the surplus to support low-income and impoverished Chileans with monthly cash payments and to finance stimulus programs in housing, education, and public investment. Chile thus was able to weather the crisis more successfully than other Latin American countries.

Yet the personal popularity of Bachelet, who was not permitted to succeed herself, could not be transferred to the Concertación government coalition. Partly because it wanted to appeal to centrist voters who were being wooed by Sebastián Piñera, the candidate of the right, it chose former President Eduardo Frei Ruiz-Tagle from the Christian Democratic Party. Due to defections and expulsions, however, the Concertación had lost its legislative majority. It was further damaged by the sudden emergence as a candidate of Marco Enríquez-Ominami, a thirty-six-year-old Socialist congressman who was the son of a guerrilla leader killed after the coup. Splitting the Concertación vote, Enríquez-Ominami appealed to previously apathetic young voters and to those disillusioned with the government coalition after twenty years in power. Piñera was therefore able to win the first round of the presidential election handily and to defeat ex-president Frei in the runoff by a narrower margin. The Concertación did maintain a narrow majority in the Congress, which meant that Chile would have a divided government for the next four years.

Political Parties

The Right

Before 1973 the right was dominated by the National party, which had been formed in 1966 by a fusion of the old Liberal and Conservative parties. The National Party declared itself dissolved after the coup, and during the 1980s two center-right parties were formed—the Independent Democratic Union (UDI), which was initially based on the anti-Allende *gremialista* movement at the Catholic University, and the Party of National Renovation (RN), which is somewhat more secular in inspiration and less committed to the personal and institutional defense of Augusto Pinochet. The electoral system encouraged the two parties to present joint candidates for the presidency and congress. Joaquín Lavín's near-victory in 1999–2000 seemed to make the UDI the dominant party of the coalition, but strong personal enmities between the leaders of the two parties led them to present separate presidential candidates in 2005. In 2009–2010, however, both parties came together to support the presidential candidacy of Sebastián Piñera.

The Center

The most significant centrist party is the Christian Democratic party of Chile. The government party in the 1960s, it maintained its internal structure and youth, student, labor, and women's branches during the period of military rule. Drawing their welfare state–human rights–mixed economy political philosophy from Catholic social thought, the Christian Democrats were once the strongest party in Chile, but their share of the vote has declined in recent years. Having abandoned the policy of going it alone (*camino propio*) that it pursued in the 1960s, the party is strongly committed to working with other parties in order to maintain stable progressive governments in Chile.

The Christian Democratic Party is supported by the Chilean middle class, but it also has an important labor component. The party has long since abandoned the communitarian socialism with which it briefly flirted during the Allende period, and it now accepts the importance of the market as an allocator of resources, although it criticized the regressive social effects of the economic policies of the Pinochet regime. The Christian Democratic government of the 1960s adopted a strong agrarian reform law, but the party now advocates other means (e.g., technical assistance and access to credit) to raise living standards and production in the countryside. It supports the encouragement of foreign investment and the promotion of exports, but combines this with a strong commitment to the expansion of educational opportunity, health care, and the reduction of poverty. The Party has lost much of its early dynamism, evidenced by Eduardo Frei's poor second finish in the 2005–2006 presidential election.

The Radical Party, now renamed the Radical Social Democratic Party, was once the fulcrum of the Chilean center, but it has been seriously weakened by frequent splits on the left and right. Although there are still Radical supporters in the provincial towns and rural areas, and the party has international recognition as, for example, a member of the Socialist International, it has received less than 5 percent of the vote in recent elections.

The Left

In the past the left has been dominated by the Socialist and Communist parties, which were allied in the Popular Action Front (FRAP) between 1957 and 1970 and formed the core of Allende's Popular Unity coalition between 1970 and 1973. In the late 1960s the Socialists adopted an increasingly radical position so that, during the Allende period, they represented the most "revolutionary" party in Allende's coalition, often taking positions to the left of Allende himself. After the coup most of the Socialist leaders went into exile in Europe. By the late 1970s a split had emerged between those (mainly in Western Europe) who favored a more moderate position similar to the positions of the French and Spanish Socialists and those (mainly in Eastern Europe and the Soviet Union) who favored continued close cooperation with the Communists and commitment to Marxism-Leninism. With the opening of politics in Chile, the two groups again united to reestablish the Chilean Socialist party, which abandoned Marxism, thereby becoming an important partner in the electoral coalitions and governments of Aylwin and Frei and nominating the successful presidential candidates of the Concertación in 2000 and 2006, Ricardo Lagos and Michelle Bachelet.

When the more moderate wing of the Socialists decided to form the Party for Democracy (PPD) as an "instrumental" party to defeat Pinochet in the 1988 plebiscite, its president, Ricardo Lagos, achieved national prominence as he denounced Pinochet on television. (Lagos ran as the presidential candidate of both the Socialists and the PPD in 1999.) The PPD has thus abandoned its quasi-Marxist roots and now emphasizes the need to modernize Chilean economics, politics, and society. It continues to field its own candidates but cooperates with the Socialist Party. Like the Christian Democrats, the Socialists have suffered from defections, most notably of Marco Enríquez-Ominani, who left to run as an Independent in the 2005–2006 elections.

The Communist Party was outlawed after the coup, and many of its leaders persecuted and murdered. Nonetheless, it continued to be active among workers and in the shantytowns. Although it endorsed the via pacífica to power between 1957 and 1973, in 1980 it began to advocate "all forms of struggle," including "acute forms of violence." For this reason the other parties were unwilling to work with the Communist Party against Pinochet, although they supported its right to participate in the democratic process by nonviolent means. After the party was legalized in the 1990s it secured only 3 to 6 percent of the vote, compared with the 15 to 18 percent that it had received before 1973. However, in alliance with other leftist groups it has received more votes in municipal elections, and the Communists still have strength among the trade unions and in university student politics. The Manuel Rodríguez Patriotic Front, an offshoot of the party, carried out violent actions in the 1980s, but it split in the early 1990s on the issue of the continued use of violence and is no longer significant. Furthermore, the two-member district electoral system has been successful in preventing Communist candidates from being elected to Congress. In recent presidential elections the Communists helped to form coalitions that presented candidates who received about 5 to 6 percent of the votes. Then, in 2009 the Communist party elected three deputies because of an agreement with the Concertación.

After twenty years of democratic government the classic "three-thirds" division of the Chilean parties into left, center, and right no longer describes the Chilean political scene. It has been replaced by a bipolar division between the governing Concertación, composed primarily of the Christian Democrats, the Socialists, and the PPD, and the conservative opposition, made up of National Renovation (RN) and the Independent Democratic Union (UDI). That division has been encouraged by the electoral system for the Congress that in effect only allots seats to the first- and second-ranking parties or coalitions, but there is now support for a return to a modified proportional representation system that is considered more democratic.

The Armed Forces

It has been said that Chile has a British navy, a U.S. air force, and a Prussian army. The navy has an aristocratic tradition, the army and air force draw many of their officers from the upper-middle class, and members of the national police often come from lower- to middle-class backgrounds. There were tensions among the services within the junta, especially over Pinochet's dominance and even concerning the advisability of his candidacy in 1988. Nevertheless, he was able to use his control of the army and after 1980 draw on the military tradition of legalism and constitutionalism in order to maintain a facade of unity and support. He remained as army commander until March 1998, and when his intelligence agency, the National Information Center (CNI), was dissolved in January 1990 many of its members and activities were transferred to the army intelligence unit.

As long as Pinochet was army commander the threat of military action could not be discounted. After his arrest and detention in October 1998, however, a much younger group took power and accepted the legitimacy of civilian control of the military. With the official apology in 2004 by the army commander for its institutional involvement in human rights abuses of the dictatorship, the break from the Pinochet-dominated past was complete.

Business and Agriculture

Chilean industry and business have long been formally organized into the Society for the Promotion of Manufacturing (SOFOFA) and the Confederation for Production and Commerce. However, it was altered fundamentally by the policies of the Pinochet government. Inefficient companies protected by high tariffs went bankrupt while new export-oriented businesses handling everything from kiwi fruit to rosehip tea flourished. Ownership became concentrated in a few financial-industrial *grupos* after the sell-off of state enterprises following the coup. In 1982 some of the largest groups went bankrupt and were taken over by the government. They and most other state enterprises (except the state-owned copper mines) were privatized later in the decade, sometimes through dubious transactions that enriched Pinochet supporters.

In agriculture, too, a process of restructuring has taken place. Seized lands were returned to their owners after the coup, and the land that had been distributed into cooperatives under the 1967 agrarian reform law was divided into individual holdings. Many of the small holdings were later sold to agrobusiness entrepreneurs, resulting in a process of reconcentration—though often under owners different from the traditional landowner families. The landowners are organized into the National Agricultural Society (SNA), one of Chile's oldest interest groups. Other groups such as shopkeepers, truckers, and others are represented by organized occupational groups, as are lawyers, doctors, nurses, and architects. However, their legal right to set rules for the professions was withdrawn in the late 1970s, and their influence has diminished since the return to democracy.

Other Groups

The Roman Catholic Church

Sixty-six percent of Chileans claim to be Catholic—although the percentage of Chileans who actively practice that faith is much lower—and 17 percent are Protestant. There are significant numbers of Lutherans descended from earlier German immigration, a small Jewish colony, and a rapidly increasing number of evangelicals and fundamentalist Protestants. Although church and state have been separated since 1925, the Catholic Church retains considerable national influence. Several of the elite private secondary schools are church-related, and the Catholic universities in Santiago and Valparaiso are important educational institutions. Church publications are influential, and the declarations of the Chilean Bishops' Conference are given wide publicity by the media. The bishops repeatedly criticized the human rights abuses of the Pinochet government, and the Church-sponsored Vicariate of Solidarity actively assisted the victims of repression. In the past a progressive majority dominated the Bishops' Conference, but more recent Vatican appointments have substantially increased conservative influence. Opus Dei, the conservative lay Catholic group, has become influential, with its own university, secondary schools, and in the case of Joaquín Lavín, presidential candidate. The Church opposed efforts initiated by Christian Democratic legislators to enact a divorce law to replace the existing fraudulent annulment procedure, but after many years of debate, legal divorce became possible in 2005. Abortion is illegal in Chile, although women's groups and others argue for allowing "therapeutic" abortions. The Church opposes the "morning-after" pill, but in 2009 both Frei and Piñera supported its distribution by public health agencies.

Labor Organizations

The Marxist-dominated Unitary Labor Central (CUT) was dissolved after the coup and its leaders were persecuted, though the Christian Democratic labor leaders were treated less severely. In the late 1970s limited union activity was permitted, and in the early 1980s a National Labor Command (CNT) was organized, later renaming itself the CUT. With the return of democracy new legislation expanded the rights of labor, but the labor movement is much weaker than before 1973, with only 16 percent of workers enrolled as union members. The Lagos government reintroduced collective bargaining, but there are still limits on the right to strike.

Students and Intellectuals

The 2006 strikes and the presidential candidacy of Marco Enríquez-Ominami reversed the political apathy of students. Chilean intellectuals were highly critical of the Pinochet government. Two Chilean novels—*La Casa de los Espíritus* (The House of the Spirits), by Isabel Allende, the niece of the former president, and José Donoso's *Desesperanza* (Curfew)—were international bestsellers that attacked the dictatorship. Ariel Dorfman's play, *Death and the Maiden*, which concerns torture under the Pinochet regime, has been presented in many countries. Furthermore, *Machuca*, a fictionalized account of the impact of the Allende government on an exclusive private school, is the most successful Chilean film in recent years.

Foreign Influences

Chileans have always tried to overcome their geographical isolation by keeping up with developments in Europe and the Americas through the media or, if they can afford it, foreign travel. There are significant foreign colonies in Chile as well as English, French, and German schools. With the opening of the Chilean economy, foreign banks and financial institutions established branches in Chile, and foreign investment soared. Nearly all the economic technocrats of the Pinochet and Concertación governments were trained at American universities. There are major UN regional offices in Chile, the most important of which is the UN Economic Commission for Latin America and the Caribbean. The Chilean left was an active participant in the rethinking of radical, especially Marxist, ideology that occurred in Europe in the 1970s, and the Chilean right, also influenced by international ideological currents, moved from a traditionalist hierarchical corporatism to more modern libertarian and economically oriented modes of thinking.

Governmental Structure

The 1980 constitution was clearly designed to limit the power of Congress. The president can call a plebiscite on constitutional amendments rejected by Congress. Presidential budgets must be voted on within sixty days or they automatically go into effect. New expenditures must be matched by new taxes, and the Central Bank may not borrow money. All takeovers of property must be compensated in cash at full value. The Constitutional Tribunal automatically reviews important legislation, and its decision is final. Additionally, to reinforce the Pinochet government's intention to keep Congress out of the way, a new Congress building was constructed in Valparaiso, an hour and a half from Santiago. (The Congress will return to the capital in the near future).

In addition, local government has been strengthened, taxing power has been given to the *comunas* (municipalities), education and health care have been decentralized and partially privatized, and social security has been turned over to private pension funds—although a safety net has recently been considerably expanded for a large number of Chileans who were not able to participate. The number of state enterprises has been reduced from five hundred at the time of the coup to fewer than twenty, and even the state-owned copper mines are likely to be opened to foreign capital by the Piñera government.

Toward the Future: The Lessons of Chile

Many lessons have been drawn from the Chilean experience. An obvious conclusion is the importance of maintaining the institutional and constitutional consensus and the willingness to compromise that characterized Chile for so many years. Chile's civilian political leaders have learned from the sad recent history of their country the desirability of avoiding the ideological dogmatism of the right, the left, and even the center that characterized the politics of the 1960s and early 1970s and ultimately led to military intervention. A second general lesson is the importance of maintaining a healthy growing economy, which in recent years has meant opening Chile to foreign investment and integrating it economically into regional and global markets.

However, an open economy is not enough, Chile tells us. Both for ideological and pragmatic reasons it is necessary to improve education on all levels and to upgrade living standards through health, housing, and social security programs, which often involves collaboration between the public and private sectors. Unemployment is still relatively high, educational opportunity has expanded but is still limited, and a regressive distribution of income continues to be the Achilles' heel of what appears to be a thriving economy.

In the twentieth century, Chile experienced more than its share of political and economic upheavals. It became a laboratory for the application of the models of development proposed by liberals, radicals, and conservatives, and these often provided both negative and positive lessons. It has modernized and globalized its economy, carried out a peaceful transition from military rule, and moved in the direction of greater social justice, tolerance, and democracy. No institutional model is perfect, but Chile does seem to have found a successful combination of democracy, economic growth, and social equity.

Suggestions for Further Reading

Angel, Alan. *Democracy after Pinochet: Politics, Parties, and Elections in Chile*. London: Institute for the Study of the Americas, 2007.

Arriagada, Genaro. *Pinochet: The Politics of Power*. Boston: Unwin Hyman, 1988.

Barahona de Brito, Alexandra. *Human Rights and Democratization in Latin America: Uruguay and Chile*. New York: Oxford University Press, 1997.

Barros, Robert. *Constitutionalism and Dictatorship: Pinochet, the Junta, and the 1980 Constitution*. New York: Cambridge University Press, 2002.

Borzutsky, Silvia. *Vital Connections: Politics, Social Security, and Inequality in Chile*. Notre Dame, IN: University of Notre Dame Press, 2002.

Branch, Taylor, and Eugene M. Propper. *Labyrinth*. New York: Penguin, 1983.

Cavallo, Ascanio. *La historia oculta de la transicion: Chile 1990–1998*. Santiago: Ediciones Grijalbo, 1998.

Cavallo, Ascanio, et al. *La historia oculta del régimen militar*. 2nd ed. Santiago: Editorial Antartica, 1989.

Chile, Comision Nacional sobre Prision Politica y Tortura (Valech Commission). *Informe*. 2004. www.gobiernodechile.cl/comision valech.

Chile, National Commission on Truth and Reconciliation. *Report*. Trans. Phillip E. Berryman. Notre Dame, IN: University of Notre Dame Press, 1994.

Collier, Simon. *Chile: the Making of the Republic, 1830–1865*. New York: Cambridge University Press, 2003.

Davis, Madeleine, ed. *The Pinochet Case: Origins, Progress, and Implications*. London: Institute of Latin American Studies, 2003.

Davis, Nathaniel. *The Last Two Years of Salvador Allende*. Ithaca, NY: Cornell University Press, 1985.

Dinges, John. *The Condor Years: How Pinochet and His Allies Brought Terrorism to Three Continents*. New York: New Press, 2004.

Drake, Paul, and Jaksic, Ivan, eds. *The Struggle for Democracy in Chile, 1982–1990*. Lincoln: University of Nebraska Press, 1995.

Ensalaco, Mark. *Chile Under Pinochet: Recovering the Truth*. Philadelphia: University of Pennsylvania Press, 2000.

Falcoff, Mark. *Modern Chile, 1970–89: A Critical History*. New Brunswick, NJ: Transaction Books, 1989.

Franceschet, Susan. *Women in Politics in Chile*. Boulder, CO: Lynn Rienner, 2005.

Haughney, Diane. *Neoliberal Economics, Democratic Transition, and the Maphuche Struggle for Rights*. Gainesville: University of Florida Press, 2006.

Hauser, Thomas. *Missing: The Execution of Charles Horman*. New York: Touchstone Books, Simon and Schuster, 1983.

Hilbink, Lisa. *Judges beyond Politics in Democracy and Dictatorship: Lessons from Chile*. New York: Cambridge University Press, 2007.

Huneeus, Carlos. *The Pinochet Regime*. Boulder, CO: Lynn Rienner, 2007.

Kornbluh, Peter. *The Pinochet File: A Declassified Dossier on Atrocity and Accountability*. New York: New Press, 2003.

Loveman, Brian. *Chile: The Legacy of Hispanic Capitalism*. 3rd ed. New York: Oxford University Press, 2001.

Meller, Patricio. *The Unidad Popular and the Pinochet Dictatorship: A Political Economy Analysis*. New York: St. Martin's Press, 2000.

Moran, Theodore. *Multinational Corporations and the Politics of Dependence: Copper in Chile.* Princeton, NJ: Princeton University Press, 1974.

Muñoz, Heraldo. *The Dictator's Shadow: Life under Pinochet.* New York: Basic Books, 2008.

Nunn, Frederick. *The Military in Chilean History: Essays on Civil-Military Relations, 1810–1973.* Albuquerque: University of New Mexico Press, 1976.

Oppenheim, Lois Hecht. *Politics in Chile: Socialism, Authoritarianism, and Market Democracy.* 3rd ed. Boulder, CO: Westview Press, 2007.

Pollack, Marcelo. *The New Right in Chile, 1973–97.* New York: St. Martin's Press, 1999.

Remmer, Karen. *Party Competition in Argentina and Chile, 1890–1930.* Lincoln: University of Nebraska Press, 1984.

Roberts, Kenneth. *The Modern Left and Social Movements in Chile and Peru.* Stanford, CA: Stanford University Press, 1998.

Schamis, Hector. *Re-forming the State: The Politics of Privatization in Latin America and Europe.* Ann Arbor: University of Michigan Press, 2002.

Scully, Timothy. *Rethinking the Center: Politics in Nineteenth- and Twentieth-Century Chile.* Stanford, CA: Stanford University Press, 1992.

Sigmund, Paul E., ed. *Chile 1973–1998: The Coup and Its Consequences.* Princeton, NJ: Princeton University Program in Latin American Studies, 1999.

———. *The Overthrow of Allende and the Politics of Chile, 1964–1976.* Pittsburgh: University of Pittsburgh Press, 1977.

———. *The United States and Democracy in Chile.* Baltimore, MD: Johns Hopkins University Press, 1993.

Smith, Brian H. *The Church and Politics in Chile.* Princeton, NJ: Princeton University Press, 1982.

Stallings, Barbara. *Class Conflict and Economic Development in Chile, 1958–1973.* Stanford, CA: Stanford University Press, 1978.

U.S. Senate. *Staff Report on the Select Committee on Intelligence Activities: Covert Action in Chile.* Washington, D.C.: Government Printing Office, December 18, 1975.

Valdes, Juan Gabriel. *Pinochet's Economists: The Chicago School of Economics in Chile.* New York: Cambridge University Press, 1996.

Valenzuela, Arturo. *The Breakdown of Democratic Regimes: Chile.* Baltimore, MD: Johns Hopkins University Press, 1978.

Verdugo, Patricia. *Chile, Pinochet and the Caravan of Death.* Miami: North-South Center Press, 2001.

Weeks, Gregory. *The Military and Politics in Postauthoritarian Chile.* Tuscaloosa: University of Alabama Press, 2003.

Whelan, James R. *Out of the Ashes: Life, Death, and Transfiguration of Democracy in Chile, 1833–1988.* Washington, D.C.: Regnery/Gateway, 1989.

9

Colombia

Violence, Resource Wealth, Transnational Forces, and a Vibrant Civil Society

Vanessa Joan Gray

When Álvaro Uribe Vélez took office in August 2002, leftist insurgents had been active in some parts of Colombia since the early 1960s. Before then, the country had suffered over a century of intermittent civil wars between the Liberal and Conservative political parties. Landowners had employed private armies to protect or expand their wealth and power since the founding of the republic. Then a fourth source of organized violence, drug trafficking groups, emerged in the 1970s when intense foreign demand for marijuana and cocaine spurred illicit drug production in regions of Colombia with inadequate law enforcement and chronic unemployment. When the drug traffickers' fortunes and penchant for counterinsurgency began merging with the interests of agribusinesses and other sectors of the legal economy, the use of paramilitary-style private armies reached unprecedented levels. For generations, then, Colombians have been losing their family members, property, and livelihoods to organized violence.

Because Colombia has endured successive forms of violent conflict for many decades, the criminality and social problems associated with postconflict settings exist even though war is still being waged. Thus Colombia has some

Map labels (as they appear):

Caribbean Sea

0 50 100 150 Miles
0 50 100 150 Kilometers

Santa Marta
Riohacha
Barranquilla
ATLÁNTICO
LA GUAJIRA
MAGDALENA
Cartagena
SIERRA NEVADA
DE SANTA MARIA
CÉSAR

P A N A M A

Sincelejo
SUCRE
Montería
CÓRDOBA
NORTE
DE
SANTANDER
Turbo
Cúcuta
Pamplona

Río Atrato
Río Cauca
Río Magdalena
Bucaramanga
Río Arauca
Arauca
ANTIOQUIA
SANTANDER
ARAUCA
Medellín

V E N E Z U E L A

Quibdó

PACIFIC OCEAN
RISARALDA
CALDA
Tunja
BOYACÁ
Río Meta
Pereira
Manizales
CUNDINAMARCA
CHOCÓ
Armenia
Bogotá
Río Upía
VICHADA
QUINDÍO
Ibagué
ORINOCO PLAINS
Buenaventura
VALLE DEL CAUCA
TOLIMA
Villavicencio
Puerto López
Río Guaviare
Cali
DISTRITO
ESPECIAL
META
GUAINÍA
CAUCA
Neiva
HUILA
Popayán
ANDES MOUNTAINS
Río Guainía
NARIÑO
VAUPÉS
Pasto
Río Vaupés
Ipiales
PUTUMAYO
CAQUETÁ
AMAZON REGION

E C U A D O R
Río Caquetá
B R A Z I L
AMAZONAS
Río Putumayo

P E R U
Leticia

COLOMBIA

of the highest rates of "common" crime in the world, and many homicides and kidnappings are committed without political motives or links to the narcotics trade. Rates of violence within families are also extremely high. This chapter will argue that violence is an integral feature of Colombian society because the government has never fully succeeded at administering the rule of law in all parts of the territory.

During President Uribe's first seven years in office, the government has achieved important security gains by reducing urban assaults by illegal groups, making transit safer, and protecting major production areas. The largest guerrilla group, FARC, is now much weaker, and thousands of paramilitary fighters have been demobilized. But Uribe's achievements follow a pattern seen repeatedly in Colombia's history: One form of violence is tackled by negotiations or hard-line government action, while other forms of organized violence remain endemic. Like its predecessors, the Uribe government has not sufficiently integrated former combatants into the legitimate economy or provided justice for all citizens. Strides in reducing some forms of violent conflict notwithstanding, the "skills" needed for organized violence remain in demand by other armed groups, and too many Colombians possess those skills and lack alternatives to participating in the perpetuation of violence.

The Land

Though Colombia ranks only fifth among Latin American nations in terms of territorial size, it is a country of spectacular geographic diversity. Influenced by climate patterns from two oceans and two continents, Colombia has three ranges of the Andes Mountains, plains in the Orinoco River basin, large expanses of Amazon forest, and coasts on the Caribbean Sea and the Pacific Ocean. Among the diverse habitats found in Colombia are mangroves, deserts, rain forests, cloud forests, and snow-capped mountains. In fact, Colombia is one of the most biologically rich places on the planet: It has more bird species than any other nation, and ranks second in the number of amphibian and plant species it harbors. Conservation biologists contend that the only nation to surpass Colombia in endowment of biodiversity is Brazil—a nation that is seven times larger.

Colombia has four main geographic regions: the Andean highlands and their valleys, the Caribbean lowlands, the Pacific lowlands, and the lowlands of the Orinoco and Amazon River basins. Historically, the nations' population and its economic and political activity have been concentrated in the Andean region and the Caribbean cities of Barranquilla and Cartagena. The capital, Bogotá, has over seven million inhabitants, and four other cities, Medellín, Cali, Barranquilla, and Cartagena, contain several million inhabitants each.

Colombia does not have seasons like the ones found in nations farther north or south of the Earth's equator. Rather, climate varies widely with altitude. Bogotá, at 8,530 feet (2,600 meters), is known for cool nights and abundant rain, but its average temperatures have risen noticeably in the last few decades. Medellín, at 4,852 feet (1,479 meters), calls itself the "city of eternal spring," and has temperatures in the sixties at night and the low eighties during the day. Cali and Bucaramanga, at slightly lower elevations, are warmer. The hottest cities are located at sea level on the coasts of the Caribbean and the Pacific, in the plains of the Orinoco, or in the Amazon basin.

Agricultural products also vary with elevation. The higher areas produce grains and potatoes; the middle altitudes are best suited to the cultivation of coffee and flowers; and the lowlands favor tropical crops such as sugarcane and bananas. In recent decades, Colombia's booming cut-flower industry extended its operations to higher elevations using state-of-the-art greenhouses. Production in the Orinoco plains (*llanos*) includes cattle-ranching, rice and palm oil plantations, and petroleum extraction. Additionally, major emerald deposits are mined in the Andes and extensive coal resources are mined in the Guajira Peninsula.

Parts of the Amazon region and the Pacific Chocó, formerly places of rubber extraction and small-scale mining, became colonization frontiers spurred by logging, fishing and shellfish extraction, and then land speculation. Since the late 1980s these regions have also experienced enormous growth in the petroleum, mining, and agribusiness sectors. Coca cultivation and processing has been concentrated in the lowlands of the Orinoco and Amazon as well as the southern Pacific coast, while marijuana is cultivated mostly on the Caribbean coast. The opium poppy is grown at higher elevations in the Andes. Since the 1990s the trend has been for the petroleum, mining, illicit drug, and biofuel industries to increase output and extend into new regions. New investment has also made it possible for Colombia to exploit its abundant hydrological and natural gas reserves for domestic energy use. Finally, Colombia is an important producer of gold, iron ore, emeralds, nickel, platinum, silver, and copper.

A key feature of Colombia's geography is the challenges the landscape presents for nation-building. Relative to many nations at a similar level of development, Colombia's rich and geographically dispersed natural resource endowment provides more opportunities for political rivals and illegal economies to prosper and avoid being eliminated. At the same time Colombia's topography makes it more costly and difficult for the government to extend services and full citizenship rights to remote areas, and such efforts are vulnerable to violent attacks by illegal armies. Some people assume that armed groups are challenging the Colombian government where it once held control, but there are regions where such control has never existed. Even before the Spanish Conquest, topography hindered efforts by Bogotá elites to rule over other regions. Chronicles from colonial times to the present are rife with descriptions of the deadly animals, insects, and diseases, not to mention the steep slopes, fast-flowing rivers, and impenetrable jungles and swamps that have thwarted attempts to administer the territory. Today, trucking and aviation link the nation's population and production centers, but getting from Bogotá to some destinations still takes many days and requires travel by boat or on foot.

The other crucial issue is that a resources-and-conflict dynamic exists in parts of rural Colombia. Before the late 1980s, climate and topography had made it unfeasible to use resources in the Chocó, the Amazon, the eastern plains, or the forested remnants of the high Andes in a sustained fashion. Then a transnational mix of new technology, investment capital, and increased demand fueled cultivation and extraction booms in legal and illegal resources in remote places with weak or no government presence.

There are many ways in which resource operations can fuel violence in Colombia. The presence of income-generating resources such as emeralds or illicit drugs can erode trust and discipline within armed groups, intensify competition among rival groups, and prolong conflict by giving weaker groups the means to keep fighting. Controlling access to resources that can be smuggled, mined, or logged allows an armed group to provide jobs to supporters. The coal, oil, and gas sectors are vulnerable to obstruction and sabotage by armed groups, meaning that energy firms may pay off whichever armed group holds power locally.

When large-scale resource use comes to a locality, local residents often face infiltration by armed actors and may become pawns and targets in lethal rivalries. Rural Colombians report being subjected to abuse in association with many types of resource exploitation, regardless of whether the resident armed group was paramilitary, guerrilla, or soldier. Armed actors demand information, services, lodging, payments, labor, and most of all, compliance. Moreover, resource bonanzas tend to benefit outsiders while locals are left with damage to their environment, the erosion of previous livelihoods, and the disruption of social relations. In Colombia legal mechanisms exist for denouncing illicit resource activities, grieving damages from licit ventures, or claiming a small portion of the earnings from large projects for the benefit of the local community. Such democratic innovations, however, exist alongside a terrifying lack of protection for the physical security of people who challenge powerful interests. Individuals and communities who invoke their rights in resource conflicts risk and frequently incur violent reprisal.

A final point to consider regarding Colombian territory is that reports on the number of municipalities where guerrilla, paramilitary, or government forces are active give the impression that an area is under the "control" of an armed group. Colombia's landscape, however, makes it difficult for any group to consolidate its rule by force decisively. Rough terrain and abundant resources offer so many opportunities to rivals and resisters that in some hotly contested areas neither the central government nor any other armed group has established enduring authority structures. When a rival group encroaches on an area, the armed group that is already present finds its capacity to provide services and protect unarmed supporters diminished. It becomes more inclined to plunder than to spend resources to build local support. As the incumbent group grows more abusive, some locals may begin collaborating with the rival group. Violence intensifies as dominance shifts from one group to another, and then abates after perceived enemies are driven out or killed. The cycle repeats itself in some regions.

Yet, as bad as the security problems are, the prospects for high returns from investment in Colombia's resources remain strong, and hence business continues. Courageous individuals and organizations—Colombian and from abroad—are dedicated to trying to expand the rule of law in these regions, but their work is extremely dangerous.

The People

Colombia has 45 million inhabitants, the third largest population in Latin America and the twenty-ninth largest in the world. Over three-quarters of Colombians reside in urban areas. The government does not keep statistics on religious affiliation, and estimates by other sources vary. Among respondents to a 2007 poll by the daily newspaper, *El Tiempo*, 80 percent identified themselves as Catholic, 13.5 percent belonged to non-Catholic Christian faiths, 2 percent were agnostic, and the remaining 4.5 percent belonged to other religions, including Islam and Judaism.

The population has been ethnically diverse since the Conquest, when consensual and forced unions of indigenous peoples, Africans, and Europeans were common. Most Colombians today are a mixture of European and indigenous, European and African, African and indigenous, or all three. The main indigenous group at the time of the arrival of the Spanish, the Chibchas, was a large, sedentary, agricultural civilization. Spanish colonial practices, including enslavement, combined with European diseases and the destruction of food supplies by nonnative livestock to cause massive loss of life and the near complete assimilation of the Chibcha people. Today, Chibcha descendants inhabit the central Andean region, but their culture no longer exists. Other indigenous cultures survive in the departments of Nariño and Cauca, in the Chocó, the Amazon, the Guajira Peninsula, the Catatumbo region, and the Sierra Nevada de Santa Marta. In these regions, groups ranging in size from a few hundred to tens of thousands speak indigenous languages, practice traditional faiths, and use pre-Columbian techniques to grow food and produce goods for household use and markets. Colombia's indigenous population is made up of more than 80 distinct ethnic groups living in 638 reserves that encompass nearly 120,000 square miles found in almost all of the nation's departments.

African slaves were brought to Colombia to labor in mines and on plantations during the colonial era. Today their descendants comprise the majority of the population in coastal areas, a large portion of the people of the Cauca Valley region, and a significant minority in the largest cities. In regions where Afro-Colombians are the majority, distinct cultural practices are evident, and throughout Colombia, African influences can be heard in the music and observed in popular forms of dance. A key facet of ethnic politics in Colombia is that in the 1990s the nation legally designated 132 collective territories as traditional "black communities," most of which are located in the Pacific region and cover about 18,000 square miles.[1]

Afro-Colombians and indigenous peoples together constitute a sizeable minority of Colombia's population. In the 1970s indigenous peoples began forming identity-based organizations to claim legal, territorial, and cultural rights. Subsequently Afro-Colombian organizations were formed and both types of groups have achieved important material and political gains. The Constitution of 1991 and other laws issued in the 1990s grant special rights to indigenous and black communities, such as the right to territory and the resources therein, cultural autonomy and identity, self-government, and the right to be consulted about legislative and administrative decisions affecting them. Advocates for minorities assert that 27 percent of Colombia's population self-identifies as Afro-descendent, and 2 percent of Colombians define themselves as indigenous. Government statistics, however, cite lower figures for these ethnic groups.

Colombians of pure Spanish lineage take pride in their ancestry and are disproportionately represented in affluent circles. Descendants of more recent arrivals from Europe and the Middle East also figure prominently among economic and political elites. A relationship between race and poverty is evident in Colombia in that the people with the greatest wealth and power rarely have dark skin or non-European features. Moreover, according to a 2009 report on minorities by the UN refugee agency, Colombia's Afro-descendant and indigenous populations have an illiteracy rate nearly three times that of the rest of the population, and 72 percent of Colombia's indigenous people and 87 percent of Afro-Colombians over the age of eighteen have not completed primary school. Ethnic disparities also infuse the armed conflict's impact on civilians. The rural poor—who are predominantly mestizo, Afro-descendant, or indigenous—constitute the vast majority of conflict victims. As recently as February 2009, eighteen members of the Awá indigenous group were massacred in the department of Nariño.

The type of violence that affects the largest number of Colombians is forced displacement. Every year from 2000 to 2008, the Norwegian Refugee Council ranked Colombia as having the second largest population of internally displaced persons (IDPs) in the world. Estimates of the present number of Colombian IDPs range from three to four million people. Violence also displaces Colombians across borders. Southern Panama receives tens of thousands of fleeing Colombians, and in 2009 the number of Colombian refugees in Ecuador was estimated to be 130,000. Venezuela is the most affected: In September 2009 the UN High Commissioner for Refugees reported that 200,000 Colombians had taken refuge in Venezuela and warned that the number was rising at an increasing rate. Finally, IDPs and refugees living in makeshift camps in border regions are not the only Colombians "voting with their feet" and leaving homes and livelihoods: Millions of Colombians reside in the United States, Europe, and Canada. The nation's ongoing security problems are clearly a contributing factor in this migration.

The Economy

The Colombian economy occupies a middle tier in global terms. World Bank statistics for 2008 indicate that Colombia's gross national product was the 36th largest in the world, exceeding, for example, that of Israel. In terms of GNP per capita, however, Colombia's rank falls to 104. This is because Colombia ranks third in income inequality among countries in Latin America and the Caribbean.

According to the Colombian trade ministry, the nation's exports grew by 25 percent in 2008, surpassing the export growth of Brazil, Mexico, and Chile that year. In 2007 Colombia's top ten exports were petroleum, coal, coffee, flowers, textiles, ferronickel, bananas, chemicals, pharmaceuticals, and gold. Colombia is Latin America's third largest oil exporter, after Venezuela and Mexico. Colombia used to be highly dependent on coffee exports—coffee was 79 percent of Colombia's exports in 1964 and 32 percent in 1987—but the nation's export profile is now more diversified. Fluctuations in global coffee markets no longer wreak havoc on national accounts, but Colombian-grown coffee, which has always been cultivated in the shade, maintains an international reputation for quality.

The impact of illegal drug production on the Colombian economy dates to the 1960s, and by 1979 receipts from marijuana and cocaine exports brought more foreign currency into the country than all of the nation's legal export earnings combined. The drug trafficking industry remains strong in spite of a series of vigorous antinarcotics campaigns waged by the government backed by massive U.S. assistance for those efforts.

Colombia's five top-ranking imports in 2007 were machinery, grains, chemicals, mineral products, and consumer products. While Colombia's principal export destinations are the United States, Venezuela, and Ecuador, its primary sources of imports are the United States, China, and Mexico. The Uribe government has encouraged exporters to diversify away from the U.S. and Venezuelan markets. The government has achieved greater policy success in creating incentives for foreign direct investment (FDI). These measures include removing capital controls, improving protection of intellectual property rights, rewriting the mining and forestry codes, facilitating emergency credit lines from multilateral banks, enhancing the nation's free trade zone mechanisms, enforcing stability contracts, and pursuing bilateral trade agreements. In 2007 new FDI to Colombia totaled US$9 billion—more than triple the amount in 2002. Most of the new investment goes to the manufacturing, mining, and energy sectors, and the United States is Colombia's largest source of new FDI, particularly in petroleum and coal.

Colombia's liberalization of its petroleum sector increased the number of exploration and production contracts from large and small hydrocarbon firms. New security policies and increased drilling activity during the Uribe years slowed a decline in national petroleum production, and it is projected that Colombia will continue to export oil through 2015. Colombia is currently the world's fifth largest exporter of coal and the largest producer in Latin America. Not long after the development of coal, large reserves of natural gas were also identified, which are expected to be a relatively long-term source of energy. Colombia has likewise dramatically increased production of biofuels (from oil palm and sugarcane) since Uribe took office. Whereas natural gas and hydro power are destined more for internal use, biofuels are being developed for export in response to European demand and incentives from U.S. antinarcotics and energy policies. From the U.S. perspective, Colombia's role as an energy supplier became much more crucial when major producers such as Venezuela and Iraq grew less reliable.

Colombia has signed free trade agreements with Chile, Mexico, and Venezuela. A NAFTA-like accord, the U.S.-Colombia Trade Promotion Agreement (CPTA), was signed by President Bush in November 2006. The Colombian Congress passed the CPTA in 2007 despite organized opposition from civil society groups. As of September 2009 the agreement still awaited U.S. congressional approval. The CPTA will institutionalize existing trade relations between the two countries, making it more difficult for future governments to reverse Uribe's economic policies. The passage of the agreement is a major goal of the Uribe government and appears to have the support of the Obama administration.

Although many countries in Latin America have suffered macroeconomic calamities, the Colombian economy has performed extremely well, enjoying strong, steady economic growth from World War II to the late 1990s. From the early 1950s to the 1980s, Colombia's GDP grew on average 6 percent per year, and real per capita GNP gains were achieved. When the recession of the 1980s devastated most of Latin America, Colombian growth rates slowed, but the economy did not experience the profound reversals suffered throughout the region. Moreover, Colombia maintained creditworthiness with international lenders and received new loans without an IMF standby loan.

Colombia's robust and steady growth rates can be attributed to the presence of a relatively stable political regime that was less subject to the populist and military demands for expenditures that influenced policymaking in other Latin American nations. One can also credit Colombian technocrats who, in addition to being relatively insulated from political pressures, had the foresight and consensus to pursue policies that encouraged investment and growth while avoiding excessive indebtedness, protectionism, or economic openness. Examples of Colombia's economic policy successes are the early application of a crawling-peg devaluation, an export-led growth strategy, and the development of national coal and petroleum resources through joint ventures.

For decades Colombian political elites took pride in having a "mixed" economy in which the government played a larger role than in the United States. This orientation began changing in the late 1980s. Since the presidencies of Virgilio Barco (1986–1990) and César Gaviria (1990–1994), Colombian governments have been implementing the neoliberal policies promoted by Washington and adopted throughout Latin America, albeit after the process was already complete in some countries and when others were reversing the policies. Privatization represented less of a dramatic shift for Colombia than for some of its neighbors because fewer industries were state-owned in the first place. Nevertheless, over time the "economic opening" has profoundly reshaped the political economy of Colombia. The lowering of tariffs provoked the first dramatic shifts, which were then followed by the privatization of numerous agencies including banking, credit, housing, telecommunications, transport, public works, utilities, and agricultural credit. The most recent wave includes rewriting national legislation. As in the rest of the world, economic restructuring in Colombia favors some groups (consumers with money to buy imported goods and large national and foreign firms with the capacity to compete globally) to the disadvantage of others (workers in formerly protected industries, smaller and medium-sized producers for domestic consumption, and lower-income groups who lost subsidies or who lack the skills, capital, or social access to take advantage of new opportunities).

Colombian political elites nonetheless have remained committed to neoliberalism, though some politicians pin responsibility for the unpopular outcomes associated with specific policies onto rivals. When the economy sunk into recession in the late 1990s, the legitimacy and solvency of the political system were in jeopardy. Political elites responded by accelerating the neoliberal restructuring, and by the time the Uribe government took office, macroeconomic trends had begun to improve. In 2003 real economic growth doubled over the previous year and the annual growth rate hit 7.7 percent in 2007. The growth rates of the Uribe era were interrupted in 2008, however, when the contraction of the global economy and recession in the United States reduced demand for Colombian products. Nevertheless, due to the combined effect of Uribe's gains in securing production and transit areas, rising commodity prices, and record levels of foreign investment, the economy rallied in the first two-thirds of 2009 and a positive economic outlook is predicted through the end of the decade.

At the same time, the economy is now more vulnerable to global forces, as the 2008 contraction illustrated. Other trends also warrant concern. First, more than ever before, the performance of the Colombian economy is dependent on military spending and U.S. aid. A "garrison" economy weighted toward security measures, armaments, and armed personnel carries not only social and ethical disadvantages, but also economic ones. Policies to offset the social dislocations of economic restructuring have been insufficient, adding to the number of potential recruits for the groups causing the nation's public order and security problems. Investment and production in Colombia remain contingent on the continued pacification of armed groups, and as the next section will show, there is reason to be less than optimistic that peace and the rule of law have been definitively established. Finally, an open, resource-based, capital- and technology-intensive export economy that favors large, globally competitive producers carries political and environmental costs that may someday galvanize enough opposition to reverse the neoliberal orientation of Colombia's economic policy.

Illegal Armed Groups

Three types of illegal forces challenge the Colombian political system: guerrilla groups, drug traffickers, and paramilitaries. The three have very different goals: seizing power and wealth from foreign interests and national elites; producing and trading marijuana, cocaine, and heroin; and defeating guerrillas and opponents of progress. But they all use similar methods such as assassinating government officials and community leaders; extorting, kidnapping, torturing and murdering civilians; and aggressively recruiting lower-income young people. All three group types derive at least part of their financing from drug trafficking activities, earnings that amount to hundreds of millions of dollars per year for each category of group.

Guerrilla Groups

Since the early 1960s guerrilla groups have filled a power vacuum in remote parts of Colombia, organizing the construction of infrastructure and maintaining order, albeit an authoritarian and self-serving kind of order. In the 1980s four main guerrilla groups operated in Colombia: the Revolutionary Armed Forces of Colombia (FARC), the Army of National Liberation (ELN), the Nineteenth of April Movement (M–19), and the Popular Army of Liberation (EPL). The latter two groups demobilized in 1990; FARC, ELN, and fragments of EPL remain in combat today, sometimes collaborating and sometimes as lethal rivals. In 2009 the ELN was under attack by FARC forces in the departments of Norte de Santander and Arauca.

FARC is Latin America's largest, wealthiest, and best-trained guerrilla force; at its peak in the early 2000s it had some twenty thousand armed combatants. From its origins in self-defense forces in the 1940s, FARC had close ties with the Communist Party, and some members still invoke Marxist rhetoric. FARC strongholds arose in lawless frontier regions where FARC forces provided protection to colonists and peasants growing illicit crops,

In the 1990s civilian support for FARC fell for three reasons. First, the dissolution of the Soviet Union ended a key source of financing and caused more Colombians to view Marxist ideology as anachronistic. Second, FARC made up for the lost revenue by relying more on the cocaine and heroin sectors, and it then intensified its longstanding practice of kidnapping for ransom and extorting ranches and businesses. Third, FARC responded to intensified attacks from paramilitary groups and the national military with actions that hurt civilians: using landmines and gas-cylinder bombs, hijacking commercial jets, assassinating elected officials, murdering community activists, and bombing an upscale family recreation center in the heart of Bogotá. Despite losing popular sympathy, until just a few years ago FARC continued to gain territory, build its arsenal, and expand its fighting forces.

At the end of the 1990s the government of Andrés Pastrana (1998–2002) granted FARC a large cease-fire zone to facilitate peace talks. FARC used the area to strengthen its forces, which enraged the military as well as many civilians and raised alarm in Washington. For decades, Colombian presidents had negotiated with guerrilla groups (despite opposition from some military and civilian elites), but FARC was now seen as engaging in reprehensible conduct, acting in bad faith, and having a shot at victory.

Toward the end of his term Pastrana called off the talks and the military invaded the ceasefire zone. In the next election, Colombians voted for Álvaro Uribe, who promised a hard line and proceeded to wage the largest military campaign in Colombian history against FARC, whose forces retreated from keys areas with their ranks declining. In 2008 the organization suffered three more blows. First, the government bombed a FARC camp just over the Ecuadorian border, killed the guerrillas' international spokesperson, Raúl Reyes, and acquired his laptop for intelligence purposes. Then the septuagenarian FARC leader Manuel Marulanda died of natural causes. Finally, government forces rescued kidnapping victim Ingrid Betancourt, a presidential candidate FARC had held since 2002. Nevertheless, in 2009 FARC was down but not out: The group was still estimated to have over 10,000 combatants based in several regions.

The M–19 was once Colombia's second largest guerrilla group. Formed by middle- and upper-class young people frustrated by accusations of fraud in the 1970 presidential election, the M–19 was less doctrinaire than the FARC. It gained notoriety for the theft of Bolívar's sword and for taking a group of foreign diplomats hostage. In the late 1980s the M–19 leadership was decimated by clashes with the army and police, and in 1989 the group signed an agreement with the government whereby leader Carlos Pizarro and eight hundred militants turned over their arms, demobilized, and were reincorporated into civilian life. Leading a new political party called AD-M19, Pizarro entered the 1990 presidential race and became an articulate spokesman for peace policies, but was assassinated just forty-five days after having laid down arms.

Inspired by the Cuban Revolution and supported by Havana, ELN is another Marxist group formed in the 1960s. It is the second largest guerrilla group in Colombia today. but its membership has fallen since the late 1990s from 5,000 to about 3,500. The ELN is responsible for hundreds of bombings of the pipeline carrying Colombia's export petroleum, consequently damaging the national economy, ruining local ecosystems, and incinerating at least one village. The tactic did not garner public support for the group.

In the early 1980s the large sums that the ELN extorted from pipeline construction operations allowed the guerrilla group, which had dwindled in size at that point, to re-arm and expand its ranks dramatically. The coal and oil sectors were lucrative targets for the ELN's kidnapping and extortion activities until the mid-1990s, when the ELN lost territory to challengers. Today, firms in the energy sector are more likely to pay protection money to security services with paramilitary links rather than be extorted by the ELN. Also, U.S. participation in the Colombian conflict has prioritized the energy sector, placing the ELN on the defensive. Both the Pastrana and Uribe governments have pursued talks with the ELN, so far without result.

The small Maoist-oriented EPL was active in the Magdalena River valley and linked with a wing of the Communist Party. Numbering less than 1,500, it was known for strict discipline and its critique of FARC's involvement in drug trafficking. The EPL financed its activities with kidnappings and extortion of landed elites. The EPL accepted a 1984 cease-fire and demobilized in 1990, but subsequently reappeared.

Drug Traffickers

Colombian drug-trafficking organizations—heirs to a contraband tradition dating back to colonial times—emerged in the late 1960s and recruited couriers and assassins in slums populated by people displaced by civil strife and counterinsurgency campaigns. The meteoric growth of the trafficking industry went largely unchecked by the government until the mid-1980s. At that time a decade of intense combat between the government and traffickers based in the city of Medellín followed. Traffickers bombed the headquarters of the Colombian equivalent of the FBI, assassinated a justice minister and four presidential candidates, waged an extended car-bombing campaign in major cities, and shot down a passenger jet. The traffickers' goal was to murder leaders committed to curtailing their power and to terrorize the public into opposing extraditions to the United States. The government, however, defied the traffickers and worked more closely with the United States. Hundreds of public officials and tens of thousands of soldiers, policemen, and citizens lost their lives in this struggle. The Colombian government ultimately emerged the victor, but help from the United States—and the Medellín traffickers' rivals in the city of Cali—was required for the government to prevail.

In the early 1990s President Gaviria initiated a kind of plea bargaining that allowed traffickers who surrendered and confessed to receive a reduced sentence (a Constituent Assembly had just prohibited extradition). Gaviria's policy resulted in the surrender of the notorious drug lord Pablo Escobar, but he escaped after a little over a year in prison, evaded capture for fifteen months, and then was killed by government troops in 1993. Escobar's death marked the end of the Medellín cartel, the most brazen, violent, and politically ambitious trafficking group. The leaders of the Cali cartel either surrendered or were captured during the Samper years.

The defeat of the two cartels did not, however, end the drug trade. Hundreds of smaller, more mobile trafficking groups emerged, drug exports did not decline, and global demand rose. Abundant evidence has documented the investment of drug earnings into legitimate businesses in Colombia, and cases of corruption have surfaced involving high-level politicians and officials in the armed forces and police, not to mention a U.S. military attaché and a circuit court judge in Florida. Considering that drug trafficking has produced at least six Colombian billionaires and some 160 millionaires, one can expect a continuing supply of would-be traffickers no matter how many individuals the government captures or kills. One potential source of change—a rejection of the prohibitionist approach—is politically unfeasible on the U.S. side, but Colombians have debated decriminalization for years. Though the direct contribution of drug trafficking to violence in Colombia has declined, its role in undermining the rule of law remains a critical problem for Colombia.

Paramilitaries

According to sources that include the U.S. State Department, paramilitaries have committed far more massacres and murders than any other armed group in Colombia. Paramilitaries existed before the drug trade, though some notorious paramilitaries were once on trafficker payrolls. In the 1980s drug traffickers and emerald merchants built private armies that were equipped with sophisticated weapons and trained by foreign mercenaries. Drug barons collaborated with landowners and military officers to create *Muerte a Secuestradores* (Death to Kidnappers, MAS), a paramilitary death squad whose mission was to kill the kidnappers preying on landowners and ranchers. MAS operatives did not succeed in killing many guerrilla kidnappers, but they did kill thousands of leftist civilians, individuals accused of associating with guerrillas, and people they declared socially undesirable, such as street children, drug addicts, muggers, and prostitutes.

During the 1990s, paramilitary groups took control of strategic corridors and regions where they could extract large protection and extortion rents and that previously had a guerrilla presence. Their ranks soared to over 15,000. In 1997 hundreds of paramilitary groups from around the country loosely affiliated under the *Autodefensas Unidas de Colombia* (United Self-Defense Groups of Colombia, AUC), an organization founded by Carlos Castaño. After AUC leader Castaño was murdered by his rivals in the organization, its internal coherence weakened even further. During Castaño's tenure, however, paramilitaries improved their public image, an impressive feat given their record of using tactics of terror, such as invading small towns with lists of names, torturing and grotesquely murdering targeted residents in public, and driving survivors to abandon their homes.

Paramilitaries are not insurgents or rebels because they only rarely engage in combat with government forces, and they do not aim to overthrow the government. They have, at times, attacked specific government officials and public agencies, but they function mainly as militias allied with elements of the armed forces and some economic elites, both licit and illicit. In some regions, paramilitary groups have conducted joint operations with government forces, while other entities of the same government often attempt to bring paramilitaries to justice. Paramilitary impunity reveals the weakness of prosecuting agencies relative to the military and the civilian elites who support paramilitary actions. These discrepancies show the fragmentation of the

Colombian state apparatus and the insufficient power, at least so far, of civilian elites who oppose paramilitary goals and methods.

The paramilitary phenomenon has partial origins in a self-defense tradition whereby rural Colombian communities organize and arm themselves in response to physical attack or threats to their livelihood. Today many paramilitary fighters claim they took up arms in reaction to guerrilla abuses or predation by criminal gangs. More importantly, landowners and large firms hire armed groups to protect their property and interests. These manifestations of privatized security occur because the government cannot or will not prevent them or has not managed to effectively reduce the demand for such services.

Worse, paramilitary groups are partly the result of government policies. A 1964 counterinsurgency decree authorized self-defense units until 1989, when state-sponsored militias were declared unconstitutional after an outcry over the atrocities they committed. Despite the change in the law, human rights groups documented continuing collusion between paramilitary groups and specific military brigades. Moreover, the government has authorized new forms of paramilitarism twice since 1989. Thus the government has both acquiesced when private elites have employed their own armies and succumbed to using private groups to battle its enemies.

Beginning in 2003 the Uribe administration successfully negotiated a mass demobilization of over 30,000 paramilitaries and incarcerated hundreds of illegal combatants. These achievements notwithstanding, troubling patterns exist: High-level drug traffickers have used the program to avoid prosecution, former paramilitaries have legalized properties they acquired by violence, civilians have been victimized by reconstituted and newly formed paramilitary groups such as the *Águilas Negras* (Black Eagles), and reports of government forces committing human rights abuses, including summary executions, have risen.

Political History

History to 1930

As a Spanish colony, Colombia was neither a backwater nor an administrative or economic center like Mexico, Peru, and Cuba. Colombia was part of the viceroyalty of Peru until 1739, when Bogotá became the center of a new viceroyalty that included present-day Venezuela, Panama, and Ecuador. The war for independence from Spain was waged by high-ranking elites and was finally achieved after the Battle of Boyacá in 1819. Colombia's liberator, Simón Bolívar, went on to assist Ecuador, Peru, and Bolivia in their independence struggles. Initially, the newly independent Colombia was part of a confederation with Venezuela and Ecuador, but that union lasted only ten years. Panama was a province of Colombia until 1903, when the United States helped secessionist elites break away from Bogotá and form a separate republic.

In the aftermath of the war for independence Colombian politics were, as in many other parts of Latin America, violent and chaotic. By 1850, however, a distinct pattern had emerged in Colombia: civilian rule by two political parties, one calling itself Liberal and the other Conservative. Both parties were controlled by elites and did not arise from or respond to political pressures from the masses. The parties differed as to how much federalism, free trade, or power for the Roman Catholic hierarchy they considered desirable, but they shared the same fundamental ideology regarding the social and economic order. A change of party in the presidential palace resulted in only minor policy shifts, but it also replaced one vertically integrated network of *patrónes* and clients for another.

For this reason, party competition was fierce and extended beyond the ballot box. There were six civil wars between the two parties in the nineteenth century, some of which were lengthy and bloody. To fight their wars, party bosses mobilized peasants (*campesinos*) who were economically and socially dependent on them. Thus a campesino was a Liberal or Conservative soldier due to his ties to a *patrón*, not because of interests that could objectively be called his own. The wars inculcated partisan hatred among lower-income groups, which meant that other cleavages—social, economic, ethnic, and regional—were much less salient than political party affiliation. While the population suffered casualties, elites in both parties reaped benefits.

Political History Since 1930

Before 1930 Colombia's economic development did not produce social groups that sought access to the political system via electoral politics. A small middle class emerged as the government bureaucracy and private industry expanded, but it never managed to form a new political party. Members of middle-income groups identified first and foremost as Liberals or Conservatives based on their family affiliation, and their political weight was felt within the traditional parties, not as an external challenge to them. A long period of Conservative Party rule ran into difficulties toward the end of the 1920s because of tensions created by the Great Depression, divisions within the party, and challenges from a growing labor union movement, to which the government responded with brutal force. When the new president, Enrique Olaya Herrera, was elected president in 1930 by a coalition of Liberals and Conservatives, civil war broke out between Liberal and Conservative campesinos. This time the violence was only partly directed by the leaders of the parties. Modernization of the agrarian sector was consolidating land holdings, intensifying struggles over arable land and water rights, and displacing rural labor, which fueled conflicts.

Other important developments marked the 1930s. A faction of the Liberal Party advocated an activist government role in economic development. This group led the party during Alfonso López Pumarejo's "Revolution on the March" (1934–1938), when various reforms were begun (social welfare legislation, agrarian reform, and import-substitution industrialization) and labor organization was encouraged. In reaction to Liberal activism, a faction of the Conservative Party led by Laureano Gómez took an extremist stance. When centrists in the leadership of both parties joined in coalition with Gómez, the reforms were stymied and López left office before completing his second term. In the next election the Liberals were divided and the Conservatives won the presidency. In rural areas, partisan violence was instigated by Conservative party bosses seeking to consolidate power and win a majority in upcoming congressional elections. Liberals fought to prevent those gains. Conservative campesinos seized lands that had been taken from them by Liberals sixteen years earlier, believing correctly that the government in Bogotá would support them.

The civil war that followed, known as *La Violencia*, exceeded previous wars in scope and brutality. Aggravated by the April 9, 1948, assassination of Jorge Gaitán—a populist Liberal challenger in the 1946 election who became head of the party and the odds-on favorite to win the presidency in 1950—the war was most intense in areas experiencing land conflicts. Over the next twenty years more than two hundred thousand Colombians (in a country of ten million) were killed. In some parts of the country almost everyone became a victim, perpetrator, or firsthand witness to carnage.

As warfare directed by party elites spun out of control, other forms of organized violence were spawned. Selective assassinations and economic plunder were carried out for personal gain, ruthless bandits of lower-class origins prospered, cruel vendettas cycled back and forth, and persecuted Liberals and communists organized themselves into armed self-defense forces. The period also witnessed the only military government in Colombia of the twentieth century, that of Gustavo Rojas Pinilla, from 1953 to 1957. Rojas came to power supported by party leaders, with the exception of Laureano Gómez (1950–1953), whose presidency was terminated by the coup.

Under Rojas, a combination of military force and populist spending succeeded in pacifying areas affected by partisan violence, banditry, and feuds, but pockets of resistance survived where the peasantry had become radicalized. Moreover, the government's public works effort fell short of nation-building. Much of Colombia remained isolated and without formal governance. When Rojas grew more repressive and showed an interest in remaining in power, the leaders of the two parties joined forces to oust Rojas and implement a power-sharing agreement called the National Front. The agreement included the following stupulations for the sixteen-year period from 1958 to 1974:

- The presidency would alternate every four years between the two traditional parties;
- All legislative bodies would be divided equally between the Liberals and the Conservatives regardless of the electoral results within a district;
- All high-level administrative appointments, such as ministers, governors, and mayors, would also be divided equally between the two parties, as would bureaucrats not under civil service law;
- No new political parties could participate in elections during the period; and
- National legislation could only be enacted with a two-thirds majority in the national congress.

The National Front was an elite pact that mandated power-sharing between the two traditional parties. The two parties did not have to compete with each other in elections, and voters' options were limited to candidates supported by one of the traditional parties. The president's power to implement change was also severely restricted. As a result, party organization languished precisely when millions were migrating to cities, and party leaders failed to incorporate voters from the growing ranks of the unemployed. The parties did manage, however, to exclude alternative organizations from politics. Over time, the power-sharing arrangement reduced the capacity of the state to govern the nation, creating conditions that favored the growth of guerrilla movements, drug trafficking, and a black-market economy.

Since the 1920s, then, generations of Colombians have been forcibly displaced by violence and large-scale economic changes. Some migrants to cities end up indigent or resort to crime, and some of the many people who seek refuge on the frontier join armed groups or work in the drug trade. Occasionally, members of Colombia's political elite have recognized these feedback loops and attempted to address the root causes of conflict. Land reform is a case in point, but the two best attempts made by Colombian presidents (in the 1930s and the 1960s) were both defeated by intransigent elites.

Some Colombian presidents have pursued policies that address one facet or another of the nation's predicament. President Julio César Turbay (Liberal, 1978–1982) allied closely with the Reagan administration, pursued a hardline approach to law and order, and repressed dissent, but he failed to curb the growth of narcotrafficking, leftist insurgencies, or the underground economy. In contrast, President Belisario Betancur Cuartas (Conservative, 1982–1986) shifted Colombia toward a more nonaligned foreign policy and negotiated amnesties, truces, and the reincorporation of guerrillas into society. One outcome of the Betancur peace process was the founding of a political party, the Patriotic Union (UP, or *Unión Patriótica*), of former FARC insurgents who had laid down arms. The peace and democratization efforts of the Betancur government were sabotaged by regional elites and elements of the armed forces command, who, among other things, commissioned the assassination of thousands of UP members by paramilitary groups, thereby successfully driving the party from relevance. Betancur did, however, institute other important democratization reforms that unfolded during subsequent presidencies, such as direct mayoral elections, but his policies were financially constrained by unfavorable global economic trends, and his government faced structural impediments to mobilizing popular support.

The next president, César Gaviria, negotiated with guerrillas and other armed groups. Major drug traffickers surrendered and plea bargained, and some paramilitaries also turned themselves in. The government held elections to select a constituent assembly that debated and wrote a new constitution. With U.S. assistance, the government systematically eliminated the Medellín drug traffickers. Nevertheless, at the end of Gaviria's term the level of violence in Colombia was higher than before his term began.

The Ernesto Samper government did not pursue a policy of negotiating with guerrilla groups. Their numbers, victories, and territory grew substantially during the period, mostly from their burgeoning finances from their protection and extortion of Colombia's booming drug trade and energy sector. The Samper presidency was wracked by a scandal arising from the accusation (first made by Andrés Pastrana, his opponent in the presidential campaign) that the Cali drug group had donated US$4 million to Samper's electoral campaign. The scandal led the U.S. government to impose sanctions that debilitated the Samper government. It was during the Samper years that almost all of the leaders of the Cali cartel either surrendered or were captured. Regardless, other trafficking groups formed, cocaine production rose, and the Colombian drug trade diversified to include heroin production and distribution.

In the mid-1990s Colombia's guerrilla forces grew so powerful that analysts warned an insurgent victory was possible. Large firms, both national and foreign, complained bitterly about soaring security costs, and foreign investors began to turn away from Colombia. President Pastrana sought negotiations with guerrilla groups and granted FARC forces control of an area the size of Switzerland. FARC combatants, recalling the fate of comrades who disarmed during the Betancur years, were not inclined to disarm. Moreover, FARC leaders were disinclined to bargain, presumably because their treasury, arsenal, and troops were larger than ever and because the FARC's worst adversaries, the paramilitaries, were multiplying their forces and territory. The

Pastrana government did not pursue policies that reined in the power of the paramilitaries. Despite much rhetoric and many meetings, the Pastrana peace talks failed completely. The very idea of negotiating with FARC came to be discredited, high-profile kidnappings soared, and guerrilla attacks on cities intensified.

Then, President Álvaro Uribe took office in 2002, rejecting the peace policies of predecessors and pouring unprecedented effort into the war against guerrillas. He revamped the military with historic levels of assistance from the United States. Under Uribe some indices of violence improved. Travel within the country became less dangerous, and many urban Colombians experienced a greater sense of security than they had had in years. The Uribe government signed a cease-fire with the paramilitary umbrella organization and thousands of paramilitary troops demobilized, but paramilitary operations continued in various regions and impunity for crimes committed by paramilitaries remained widespread. The government's ability to bring paramilitaries to justice was limited by the fact that paramilitaries demobilized without having been defeated militarily and were not about to volunteer to be prosecuted. War with the FARC continued, and there was little progress in negotiations with the ELN.

Violence in Colombia: Long Duration and Multiple Forms

The principal victims of the Uribe government's military offensives are rural civilians, who are displaced to urban shantytowns, new regions, and neighboring countries by occupation and combat operations. Colombians also are displaced by the fumigation of drug crops, the construction of infrastructure such as hydroelectric dams, and large-scale resource development. In one of Colombia's longstanding and deeply destructive patterns, from the ranks of displaced, new belligerents are recruited to fight and kill. Social services to counteract this tendency are woefully inadequate. Most disturbing, however, is the incidence of child soldiers. In mid-2006 the U.N. development program estimated that fourteen thousand children under the age of eighteen were active members of Colombia's guerrilla and paramilitary groups, and it reported that many of these children observed or were victims of domestic violence and violent crime before they joined an armed group.

Studies of nations with protracted civil conflicts demonstrate that previous episodes of collective violence significantly increase the risk of recurrence in some form. Large-scale conflict changes a society by creating economic incentives for violence and increasing the supply of the material and skills used to inflict that violence. The links between violence past and present in Colombia can be quite macabre, as in the way paramilitaries dismembered victims using techniques favored by the Medellín drug cartel, whose methods of cutting up human bodies were reminiscent of tactics used in La Violencia. Thus, when new forms of violence emerge in Colombia, they interact with earlier forms but often do not replace them. This problem was identified in the early 1990s by Colombian academics known as "violentologists," but policymakers in Washington and Bogotá continue to underestimate the spillover and feedback dynamics of violence. Instead, they focus on one or two forms of Colombian violence in isolation and even meld together the categories of, for example, guerrillas and drug traffickers. This perspective oversimplifies the problem and therefore is unlikely to produce meaningful solutions.

The Role of U.S. Policy in the Colombian Conflict

It is important to recognize the role of U.S. policies in the dynamics of violence in Colombia. By supporting military responses to problems that might be better addressed with social policies, strengthening armed parties to the conflict, and inadvertently aggravating problems that fuel violence in Colombia, the United States has diminished the prospects for nonviolent conflict resolution in that country. U.S. involvement in the Colombian conflict dates back to the early 1950s, when Colombia was the only Latin American nation to send troops to assist the U.S. effort in the Korean War. A battalion of professional soldiers volunteered for the assignment, and in return Colombia received equipment and training. The collaboration created close ties between the two nations' armed forces and strengthened the Colombian military relative to civilian government agencies. Anticommunist ideology was not new to Colombian military officials, as they had been fighting a small Communist resistance since the 1940s, but their virulently antileftist stance has been reinforced by the institutional relationship formed in this period.

In the 1960s, U.S. counterinsurgency aid to Colombia included helicopters, napalm, and advice on using terrorist actions and paramilitary squads to fight guerrillas. The United States supported Colombian elites who opposed the land reform efforts of President Carlos Lleras Restrepo (1966–1970) and those who advocated the use of military force against a small leftist insurgency and a large, highly mobilized, and mostly nonviolent peasant movement. The Cold War tendency of U.S. policymakers was to treat as enemies of the United States leaders and organizations who advocated for the redistribution of wealth and power. A hallmark of this mindset was to view state repression, even of civilians, as a lesser evil than allowing leftist political groups to gain influence in the region.

From the 1970s through the end of the century the priority of the U.S. government in Colombia was supply-side drug policies, which criminalize and militarize the issue in source countries. The goal is to disrupt trade and curb production so that illicit drugs will be scarcer and costlier for U.S. users.

In pursuit of this goal the U.S. government has applied intense diplomatic and economic pressure on Colombia. U.S. drug war policy expanded the mission of Colombian security forces and supplied them with training, sophisticated hardware, and intelligence capabilities. Critics argue that as a result, Colombian forces became less transparent and accountable.

The U.S. approach to its drug problem has also affected Colombia indirectly. The demand for illegal drugs by U.S. citizens fed the rise of Colombian traffickers in the first place. Decades later, purchases by U.S. drug consumers have the effect of financing criminal, guerrilla, and paramilitary activity in Colombia. At the same time, the prohibitionist U.S. stance on the drug issue reduces the policy options available to Colombian elites for mitigating the violence, corruption, and social problems that stem from the *illegality* of the drug trade. The U.S.-led drug war has combined with global market forces to cause other indirect impacts, such as when crop eradication in Peru and Bolivia in the 1980s triggered a surge in coca cultivation in Colombia. The U.S. military campaign in Central America was another U.S. policy that played an indirect role, bringing millions of weapons to the isthmus just north of Colombia in the 1980s and becoming Colombia's major source of illegal arms in the 1990s.

In 1998, when Colombia's guerrilla forces had grown to unprecedented levels, the Clinton administration responded with Plan Colombia, a US$1.3 billion package to expand existing policies: fumigate more hectares; disrupt more processing operations; and supply more technology, weapons, helicopters, and surveillance. It made Colombia the third-largest recipient of U.S. military assistance in the world and marked a shift toward aiding the Colombian military. (In the past, U.S. aid was primarily directed toward Colombia's police forces.) Critics argue that Plan Colombia intensified conflict in target areas; displaced small farmers and thus spread drug cultivation to new regions; and strengthened the security forces in ways that undermined efforts to improve democratic governance.

After September 11, 2001, the administration of George W. Bush shifted the rhetoric on policy toward Colombia to emphasize counterterrorism, but in the actual theater the distinction between counternarcotics and counterinsurgency had long since blurred. For example, Plan Colombia under Clinton specifically targeted FARC regions, while the key development during Bush's presidency was greater emphasis on the military defense of Colombia's oil industry. Then in 2002 the U.S. government authorized an additional US$98 million in annual assistance to Colombia for protection of the Caño Limón oil pipeline, and U.S. forces now maintain bases in oil production areas in Arauca and Caquetá.

There are indications that U.S. policy toward Colombia will continue in a similar direction under the Obama administration. The Minister of Defense,

Gabriel Silva, announced in August 2009 that Colombian Special Operations combat troops, created and trained by the United States, would soon be deployed in Afghanistan. In 2009 the governments of Colombia and the United States also negotiated and signed an agreement that would grant U.S. forces the right to use and upgrade existing Colombian military bases. Specifically, U.S. aircraft, naval vessels, and personnel could be stationed at three Colombian air bases, two Colombian ports, and two Colombian army bases. Up to eight hundred U.S. military personnel and six hundred private contractors would be permitted to use the bases, reaching the maximum of fourteen hundred that was set by the U.S. Congress in 2000 and roughly doubling the current U.S. military presence in Colombia. For the agreement to take effect, it will have to be approved by the appropriate bodies of the two governments.

The Government

Not many Latin American countries have had a longer tradition of civilian government, fewer military governments, or more elections held without incident than Colombia. Nevertheless, Colombian democracy is compromised by endemic violence and the uneven application of the rule of law. Efforts at democratization include the 1991 popular election of governors (previously appointed by the president), following the popular election of mayors that began in 1988. Institutional reform culminated in a constituent assembly in 1991 to rewrite the 1886 constitution. Seventy-four delegates—elected by proportional representation and including former guerrillas, representatives of indigenous peoples, and civil society activists—wrote the new charter.

Colombia's national government remains similar in structure to the U.S. model of three branches of government with a separation of powers and checks and balances. The executive remains the most powerful branch of government. Though the Constitution of 1991 gives more power to the Congress, that potential has yet to be realized. Efforts to strengthen the judiciary with the creation of a National Prosecutor's Office and the delegation of judicial review to both the Supreme Court and the Constitutional Court have produced more substantive results.

The new constitution also decentralized administrative functions. Departments and municipalities now have weak powers of taxation, and the national government is obliged to share revenues from income and value-added taxes with local governments. There are provisions for the recall of elected officials, citizen-initiated legislation, class-action suits, and the collective rights of indigenous communities. Measures were also adopted to reduce nepotism and place limits on official travel.

The Uribe government, however, has worked to rescind a number of democratization measures, and it successfully led efforts to amend the constitution to allow a sitting president to be reelected. Congress passed the amendment, and in 2005 the Constitutional Court ruled that the amendment had been adopted in a procedurally correct manner. After a referendum approving the change, Uribe won his second term in 2006.

The current electoral system is one of proportional representation for both houses of Congress, departmental assemblies, and municipal councils. Additionally, the new constitution has an unusual feature: the hundred-member Senate is elected from a national constituency and given proportional representation: Any party that receives 1 percent of the national vote receives one senator. This change was intended to give representation to parties other than the Liberals and Conservatives.

In 2006 Colombia implemented a new electoral system in the congressional elections. With the old system of proportional representation, party lists were given a number of seats according to the proportion of the vote received. The candidates elected were then chosen by the order in which the party had placed them on the list. Under the new "preferential" system, voters can choose any candidate on the party list from which they vote. After it is determined how many seats a party list has received, the votes for the individual candidates are counted, and those receiving the most votes are elected to the Congress.

A bill to hold a referendum on whether Álvaro Uribe can run for a third term as president of Colombia passed the legislature in August 2009 and was signed by the president the following month. In September 2009 an Invamer/Gallup poll reported that a majority of the public supported a third term for Uribe. Nevertheless, for Uribe to become Colombia's first three-term president at least three requirements must be met. First, the referendum will have to be approved by the Constitutional Court. Second, at least 25 percent of eligible voters will have to turn out for the referendum—not a small achievement when one considers that the writing of a new constitution in 1991 motivated just over 26 percent of the electorate to participate and given that a referendum cannot be held at the same time as another election without a change of law. Finally, Uribe would then have to win his third presidential election. As popular as Uribe is, the alteration of electoral laws twice for his personal political advantage may lower enthusiasm for his remaining in power. At the same time, the process can be expected to galvanize opposition by Colombia's social organizations and elicit concern from the international bodies that track democratization trends in Latin America.

Organized Political Groups

Two political parties, the Liberals and the Conservatives, dominated Colombian politics from the mid-nineteenth century through the end of the twentieth century. Neither of the parties fit the "mass party" model, though they mobilized support without such a structure. Party leaders often split into factions, sometimes along programmatic lines, other times along personalist ones. Today the ideological differences of the Liberal and Conservative party positions are about as great (or meager) as those of the Democrats and Republicans in the United States.

Throughout the twentieth century a majority of the Colombian electorate identified with the Liberal Party. During the National Front period, more people voted for Liberals for Congress than for Conservatives (although parity rules awarded each party 50 percent of the seats). The successful presidential bid by Liberal Alfonso López Michelsen in 1974 received 56 percent of the vote, and Liberal Gabriel Turbay Ayala received a smaller majority over his Conservative opponent in 1978. A Conservative president, Belisario Betancur, was elected in 1982 when the Liberals presented two candidates, underscoring the tendency for the minority party to win when the majority party is divided. In 1986 and 1990, a united Liberal party won the presidency overwhelmingly. The constitution of 1991 introduced the requirement of an absolute majority for election to the presidency, and the elections of 1994 and 1998 went to a second round. In 1994 a Liberal Ernesto Samper defeated Conservative Andrés Pastrana, but in 1998 Pastrana then won. The framers of the constitution intended for the new rules to curb the dominance of the Liberals and Conservatives, but this did not occur in presidential elections until 2002.

Since the dismantling of the National Front, third-party movements have slowly become more important in Colombian elections. When the ex-dictator Gustavo Rojas Pinilla founded the National Popular Alliance (ANAPO) in 1961, rules created by the two dominant parties required calling it a "movement" rather than a party and obliged it to present Liberal and Conservative candidates for office. ANAPO had its greatest success in 1970 when it garnered 14 percent of the national Liberal vote and 21 percent of the national Conservative vote. Rojas then lost the presidential election to his Conservative opponent by a margin of only 3 percent. The fortunes of ANAPO declined as Rojas aged, and leadership shifted to his daughter. She ran for president in 1974 but received only 9.4 percent of the popular vote.

The party that emerged from the Betancur government's democratic opening, the Patriotic Union (UP), was founded by the Communist Party and by demobilized FARC guerrillas. The UP attracted followers from the unarmed left as well as community organizers, idealists, and young people. The 1986 elections became the first in Colombia in which a leftist coalition ran a presidential candidate. The UP candidate received only 4 percent of the presidential vote, but the party did elect twelve members to the Congress as well as scores of local officials in regions throughout the country. In the presidential campaign of 1990 the UP candidate was assassinated. It is possible that over time the UP might have developed in a manner similar to that of the Brazilian Workers Party, gaining experience by governing at the municipal level and building a mass membership. However, over six thousand members of the UP were murdered in the years following its regional victories, and paramilitary violence thus terminated the UP's role in politics.

The demobilization of the M–19 guerrilla group in 1990 produced another leftist party, the Nineteenth of April Democratic Alliance (AD M–19). Despite losing a presidential candidate to yet another assassination in 1990, the AD M–19 finished second in the elections for the Constituent Assembly later that year, winning nineteen delegates and playing a major role in the writing of the new constitution. The party's showing in the 1990 presidential election (13 percent of the vote) was impressive, but its influence waned as the decade wore on. One of its leaders, however, Antonio Navarro Wolff, continues to be a national political figure, and in 2010 he was the governor of the department of Nariño.

Over the last decade several trends are evident in Colombian party politics. The two largest parties in Congress remain the Liberals and Conservatives, but there are dozens of other political parties, sixty-eight of which have won congressional seats. Party discipline continues to be weak, and voter enthusiasm for the traditional parties continues to decline. The traditional parties are rife with internal and personalist divisions. In 2002 Álvaro Uribe ran successfully as an independent Liberal candidate for the presidency, unofficially separating himself from his party despite lifelong membership and having served two terms as a Liberal senator and one as a Liberal governor. In 2005 individuals from various parties created an Uribista party, known as the Social Party of National Unity, but commonly called *La U*, to support the reelection of Uribe in 2006.

In 2009 a change of law made it easier for elected officials to change their party affiliation, resulting in a number of individuals moving from one party to another. The greatest beneficiary, at least initially, was La U. Another spin-off party, Cambio Radical, supported Uribe and won twenty seats in the Chamber and fifteen in the Senate. The president of the national directorate of the Conservative Party supported the 2006 reelection of Uribe, but Conservatives were divided between those who favored conceding that no Conservative had much chance of defeating Uribe and others, such as former president Pastrana, who vehemently opposed such a strategy.

In his second term Uribe's estrangement from leaders of the Liberal party became more pronounced. In June 2005 President Uribe accused former president César Gaviria, a fellow Liberal and the former secretary general of the Organization of American States, of being "sectarian." Uribe publicly attacked Gaviria again in mid-2008. Liberal Party leaders responded by denouncing Uribe and called on the attorney general to take action against the president. Shortly after, the Liberal party declared its formal opposition to Uribe's reelection in 2006, but he won anyway. In mid-2009 it appeared likely that Uribe would run for a third term. Politicians from several non-Uribista parties were supporting his bid, though many prominent Liberals and the opposition party Alternative Democratic Pole boycotted votes on the issue.

In contrast to the disunity among traditional politicians, the leaders of two leftist parties—the Independent Democratic Pole (*Polo Democrático Independiente*, PDI), and the Democratic Alternative (*Alternativa Democrática*, AD)—met in 2005 to join forces and form the Alternative Democratic Pole (*Polo Democrático Alternativo*, PDA). These unification efforts followed the 2003 election of the PDI's Luis Eduardo "Lucho" Garzón, a former communist union leader, as mayor of Bogotá. Another PDI candidate won the mayoralty in the petroleum-refining city of Barrancabermeja, and a third candidate linked to the PDI won in Bucaramanga, the capital of the Santander department. The PDA appears to have programmatic consensus and vigorous competition over electoral lists. In 2006 Carlos Gaviria edged out Francisco Cordoba of the AD and defeated Antonio Navarro Wolff to be the PDA presidential candidate. In the legislative elections of 2006, the PDA won 9 out of 166 Deputies and 11 out of 100 senators. In the presidential elections of May 2006 Carlos Gaviria came in second to Uribe with 22.04 percent of the vote. Then in February 2009 the PDA convened its second national congress in Bogotá. Some fifteen hundred delegates met in committee to form policies on internal party governance, unity, ethics, and finance, and to develop strategies for electoral contests, peace-building, opposing the Uribe government, addressing economic problems, and pursuing relations with the rest of Latin America.

Sectoral Organizations, the Military, the Church, and Organized Labor

Along with the traditional parties, groups representing economic elites have formal access to the Colombian political system. Associations of large landowners, industrialists, media interests, and financial groups are the most powerful. The National Association of Industrialists (ANDI), founded in 1944, counts more than five hundred of Colombia's largest enterprises as affiliates. Its influence comes from the wealth and prestige of its members, its active role in policymaking, and the overlapping of its interests with those of large agricultural producers. Also powerful is the National Federation of Coffee Growers (FEDECAFE). Founded in 1927, this private association is dominated by the larger coffee producers and exporters. Relations between the coffee growers and the government are close. A recent president of

FEDECAFE, for example, previously served as ambassador to the United States, adviser to a Colombian president, and is now the minister of defense. Colombian society has many other interest groups at the upper- and middle-income levels that are represented by organizations licensed by the state and granted some formal input in the political process.

The political role of the Colombian military has a long history, though it has been one of the least interventionist in Latin America, and civilian control of the armed forces has been relatively high. In the nineteenth century each party controlled its own army. The "national army" supported the party in power while the opposition party maintained a separate army. The professionalization of the military commenced when the army and naval academies were founded in 1907, and a war college followed two years later. During the National Front the partisan identification of the military ended, but since the early 1960s the military has deployed personnel and equipment in civic projects. Consequently, military expertise in some areas exceeds that of the civilian bureaucracy. Moreover, the high command has tremendous influence over policies concerning guerrillas.

On a few occasions, the military has taken actions that raise questions about the extent of civilian control. In the 1930s López Pumarejo, during his "Revolution on the March," transferred military officers who opposed him to remote posts and promoted those who supported him. During his second term he was briefly taken prisoner in a coup attempt. Then in 1990 the military attacked FARC's headquarters on precisely the same day as the nation was electing a Constituent Assembly. In November 1985, when the M–19 guerrilla group seized the Palace of Justice and took its occupants hostage, the military stormed the palace, defeating the takeover but also killing more than one hundred innocent people—including all the justices of the Supreme Court—and incinerating the contents of a building that housed a vital branch of government. In 2009 new evidence came to light regarding gross violations of human rights by the military against employees of the Palace during the siege.

Since the late 1990s the trend has been for the Colombian military to grow more powerful relative to the national police force and civilian government agencies. The Uribe government has increased the armed forces by 30,000 and the police forces by 10,000, reorganized the structure of the armed forces, created new combat units, and adopted advanced weapons, communications, and intelligence technologies. It has made the armed forces more mobile and facilitated closer collaboration with U.S. personnel. It has set up zones of "rehabilitation and consolidation" that are administered under the direction of the military and where civil liberties, such as the right of assembly, are restricted. The Uribe government has also created a network of civilian informers using security fronts in neighborhoods and businesses as well as taxi, bus, and truck drivers to monitor streets and highways. Peace activists and some scholars of civil-military relations consider these trends ominous, but William Aviles[2] argues that neoliberal policymakers in Colombia have successfully mitigated the emergence of antiglobalization or antidemocratic factions within the military while also reducing the institutional prerogatives of the armed forces.

Historically, the Roman Catholic Church in Colombia was among the most powerful in Latin America, partly because of the religiosity of the masses and partly because of the Church's extensive landholdings and explicit alliances with political and economic elites. Until the National Front, ties between the Church hierarchy and the Conservative party were very close. During La Violencia, for example, bishops threatened to excommunicate anyone who voted for Liberal candidates, and some priests refused the sacraments, including burial, to Liberals. Colombia is also known, however, for rare but dramatic instances of radical priests, such as Camilo Torres. Torres was a sociologist from an affluent Bogotá family who concluded that being a good Christian in Colombia required working for fundamental change. After frustrating experiences trying to promote reform first as a priest and then as a government official in the agrarian reform agency, Torres left the clergy and joined the guerrillas in the late 1960s. Soon afterward he was killed in combat. Another example of a radical priest is Manuel Pérez Martinez, a defrocked Spaniard who from the 1970s until his death in 1998 was a leader of the ELN guerrillas.

Urbanization and secularization in the late twentieth century eroded the Church's power, and the hierarchy became less emphatic in its support of the status quo. Under the leadership of political and ecclesial hard-liner Cardinal Alfonso López Trujillo, the Colombian hierarchy was considered the most conservative in Latin America, but this changed in the 1990s when the cardinal took a post in Rome and more Colombian Church officials began to address the new cycle of violence afflicting the country. Though Church officials critique the violence, they tend to refrain from condemning specific actors and are particularly reticent about criticizing the government.

In contrast to the hierarchy, since the late 1980s Colombian priests, religious workers, and laypeople have led efforts to document human rights atrocities, defend and assist victims, and promote nonviolence in high-conflict areas. These activities can and do involve confronting government entities. Of the many faith-based organizations that promote human rights, social and economic development, nonviolence, and dialogue in Colombia, the most influential ones are either affiliated with the Catholic Church or founded by Church officials. The NGO Center for Popular Education and Research (CINEP) runs the most comprehensive data bank on human rights violations and political violence statistics. Additionally other Catholic organizations provide accompaniment to people in conflict and trafficking regions and act as intermediaries and information sources for international aid groups. Sometimes the Catholic Church is the only institution with a presence in a high-conflict rural area or IDP encampment, and through its Social Pastoral agency, it provides critical services. The work is dangerous. According to the international nonprofit Catholic Relief Services, since the late 1980s some sixty Catholic priests, nuns, seminarians, and even bishops have been assassinated, and the number of pastoral agents and Protestant pastors killed is higher.

Unlike Argentina and Chile, Colombia does not have a history of militant labor unions. The exception was in the 1920s, when mass strikes were held against the United Fruit Company and were quelled with brutal repression. In subsequent decades Colombian labor organizations were divided along party lines. The Confederation of Colombian Workers (CTC) was founded in 1935 under the auspices of a Liberal government, and the Union of Colombian Workers (UTC) was formed in 1946 with close links to the Conservative party and the Church. A third federation, the Syndical Confederation of Workers of Colombia (CSTC), was formed in the 1970s. In 1986 leftist unions formed the United Workers Central Organization (CUT), which has since become the largest and most influential federation. In addition to being moderate, fragmented, and allied with the traditional parties or Church, the labor movement never represented more than a third of formal wage earners. Repression has limited the growth of the movement from the beginning, and neoliberal restructuring has reduced the ranks of organized labor since the 1990s.

A 2005 study reported that 4.8 percent of the Colombian workforce is unionized. Roughly 856,000 workers are members of Colombia's 2,357 registered labor unions. Trade unions are most prevalent in the public sector, education, health care, mining, and the petroleum industry. Organization in the agricultural sector is generally low, but one union, SINTRAINAGRO, is the largest banana workers' union in Latin America and represents eighteen thousand banana workers. Of Colombia's three national trade-union umbrella organizations, the CUT is the largest and is unaffiliated abroad, the CTC is affiliated to the International Confederation of Free Trade Unions, and the CGTD is affiliated to the World Confederation of Labor.

The political sympathies of Colombian trade unions span a wide range, but they are unified in their opposition to the privatization of state entities and to efforts by the government and employers to weaken the labor code and change the social security system. Individual unionists may have ties to guerrilla organizations or, less frequently, paramilitary organizations, but the large federations emphatically reject all the armed groups. Instead, they advocate civil society participation in peace negotiations and an end to structural social inequality, which they contend is the root cause of the armed conflict.

Colombia has the highest rate of assassinations of trade unionists in the world, and paradoxically, violence against labor activists has afforded Colombian unions a bit of political leverage thanks to pressure exerted on Colombia via transnational networks. International labor groups cite the figure that over two thousand labor activists have been killed in Colombia since 1991. As recently as 2005, 70 trade unionists were murdered, 260 received death threats, 56 were arbitrarily detained, seven survived attacks in which explosives or firearms were used, six were kidnapped, and three were disappeared. Labor activists acknowledge that Colombia's high murder rate overall partly accounts for mortality among unionists, but the fact remains that members of labor unions are more likely to be killed than members of the general population. It has been calculated that Colombian journalists are similarly at higher risk because of their profession. Violence against trade unionists is an issue that activists have used to heighten the visibility of the Colombian conflict internationally as well as to oppose Uribe government policies, the free trade agreement, and U.S. military and drug assistance to Colombia. The cause of trade unionists in Colombia has been taken up by groups such as the AFL-CIO in the United States and the ILO headquarters in Europe. Violence against unionists also is a key element in the lawsuits that have been filed against U.S. firms accused of violence against civilians or collaboration with armed groups in Colombia. The plaintiffs in these suits include Coca-Cola, Drummond coal, Dole, and Chiquita, but as of the fall of 2009 only in the Chiquita case had there been admissions of illegal conduct or payments of damages.

Future Prospects

The Uribe government's stated goals—advancing government control, the rule of law, and legitimate institutions throughout the country—remain well short of fulfillment. Though insurgencies fueled by ideology have been marginalized, criminal operations have gathered strength. Civil society leaders continue to be targets for death threats and assassination. Several million people are refugees in their own country, and Colombia still supplies the vast majority of the cocaine consumed in the United States.

Colombia's near-term prospects are likely to be more of the same. Even if the FARC were vanquished, its demise would not end organized violence in Colombia. Given the abundance of resources in Colombia's difficult-to-access mountains, plains, and forests—not to mention the powerful external demand for those resources—eliminating all adversaries and criminal operations by force may not be possible. The Uribe government's expanded military forces cannot replace the need for a representative, embedded state that enjoys voluntary compliance and administers justice effectively in all parts of the territory.

Colombia's flawed version of democracy and neoliberal economic policy orientation can be expected to endure, and a close alliance with the United States will probably facilitate that continuity. Drug trafficking and paramilitary violence are unlikely to be curbed. Violence will undermine the quality of life for the middle and upper classes, prompting some to emigrate, but most individuals and organizations will carry on as usual. Opportunities for predatory and illicit economic gain will continue to provide powerful incentives for antisocial behavior. The poor will remain in dire circumstances, many suffering harrowing violence, and their children will continue to be pressed into service by armed groups and criminal gangs.

There is little threat of drug traffickers or paramilitaries openly seizing power, but the insidious influence of these groups is likely to continue. The chances that the guerrillas will achieve military victory are very remote, but the guerrilla phenomenon will not go away in the near future. A military coup is highly improbable, but should order collapse, the chances of a coup would increase. Such a collapse is hard to imagine, however, given the U.S. commitment to shoring up the Colombian government. For now, few prospects exist for the rise of a mass movement like those seen in Ecuador, Argentina, and Bolivia.

Over the medium term it is possible that both significant reform and substantive peace can be achieved by a successor to Uribe. A more responsive democracy and more effective judiciary have been emerging since the constitution of 1991, and some Colombian leaders aspire to transform their country via the rule of law. Colombian civil society groups have demonstrated courage, resilience, and creativity, and innovative mayors in Bogotá have illustrated the potential for remarkable progress. Formidable challenges, of course, still exist. First, protections for political participation and accountability have to be strong enough so that assassination is no longer an effective way to block change. Second, economic rights must be defended more widely and opportunities distributed more fairly.

Colombia has suffered from various types of organized conflict for an unusually long time, and state weakness, unique landscape features, and transnational influences aggravate the problem. The lesson is that the factors driving violent conflict in Colombia adhere to a certain logic, and hence policies that address factors in isolation or out of context cannot bring about an enduring peace for all Colombians. Because the country's geography and resource endowment make the classic "dominate and pacify" route to political order unlikely to prevail, it is time to start providing much greater social investment and supporting the self-determination of populations in high-conflict zones. At the very least, policies should be avoided that further degrade livelihoods and violate physical security in the sectors of society from which Colombia's many armed groups derive their manpower.

Suggestions for Further Reading

Bouvier, Virginia, ed. *Colombia: Building Peace in a Time of War.* Washington, D.C.: U.S. Institute of Peace Press, 2009.

Kirk, Robin. *More Terrible than Death: Massacres, Drugs, and America's War in Colombia.* New York: Public Affairs, 2003.

Kline, Harvey F. *Chronicle of a Failure Foretold: The Peace Process of Colombian President Andrés Pastrana.* Tuscaloosa: University of Alabama Press, 2007.

———. *Showing Teeth to the Dragons: State-building by Colombian President Alvaro Uribe Vélez, 2002–2006.* Tuscaloosa: University of Alabama Press, 2009.

Molano, Alfredo. *The Dispossessed: Chronicles of the Desterrados of Colombia.* Chicago: Haymarket Books, 2005.

Rappaport, Joanne. *Intercultural Utopias: Public Intellectuals, Cultural Experimentation, and Ethnic Pluralism in Colombia.* Durham, NC: Duke University Press, 2005.

Richani, Nazih. *Systems of Violence: The Political Economy of War and Peace in Colombia.* Albany: State University of New York Press, 2002.

Roldan, Mary. *Blood and Fire: La Violencia in Antioquia, Colombia, 1946–53.* Durham, NC: Duke University Press, 2002.

Tate, Winifred. *Counting the Dead: The Culture and Politics of Human Rights Activism in Colombia.* Berkeley: University of California Press, 2007.

Taylor, Steven L. *Voting Amid Violence: Electoral Democracy in Colombia.* Lebanon, NH: University Press of New England, 2009.

Notes

1. *Comunidades negras* are defined as a group of families of African descent that share culture, history, and traditional customs within a rural, community relationship that preserves an awareness of identity distinct from other ethnic groups (Law 70 of 1993, and Article 50 of the Constitution). The Constitutional Court affirmed in 2001 and 2003 that black communities are deserving of rights included in ILO Convention 169 regarding tribal peoples.

2. William Aviles, "Despite Insurgency: Reducing Military Prerogatives in Colombia and Peru," *Latin American Politics and Society* 51, no. 1 (2009): 57–85.

10

Peru

Authoritarian Traditions, Incomplete Democracy

David Scott Palmer

Even in a region known for its diversity, Peru stands out. Within its borders are more subclimates than in any other Latin American country. A coastal desert gives way inland to imposing peaks of the Andes, high plains, and inter-mountain valleys, which in turn fall off to the dense tropical rain forest of the Amazon Basin. The population of twenty-eight million is equally varied, from large clusters of highland Indo-Americans and scattered communities of jungle counterparts to descendants of the Spanish conquerors, colonists, and Afro-American slaves; European, Middle Eastern, Chinese, Japanese, and Korean immigrants; as well as a majority of mixed-race *mestizos*. The economy includes a significant export sector based on the extraction of copper, gold, iron ore, zinc, and oil; fish and fish meal; and farm products from recently modernized, totally irrigated coastal agriculture. Illegal drug production in jungle areas, mostly coca leaf and cocaine paste, is rebounding after a sharp decline in the late-1990s. Politics may be characterized over Peru's more than 185 years of independence as alternating between one form of authoritarian rule or another, with occasional forays into formal democracy.

In recent years, Peru has experienced the region's most reformist and state-expanding military rule (1968–1980) as well as one of its most open

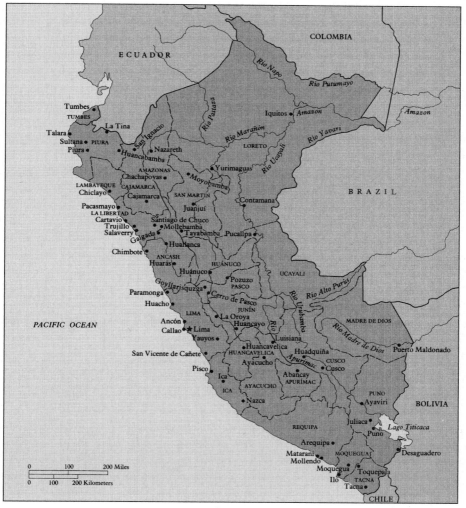

PERU

democracies (1980–1992). The country has also suffered a most virulent insurgency, led by Shining Path (1980–1995), and one of only two lasting unconstitutional breaks (1992–1993) following Latin America's generalized restoration of democracy. During the 1990s Peru also moved abruptly from high levels of state economic control to become one of the most open economies in the hemisphere and developed one of Latin America's most successful programs of extreme poverty reduction. At the same time, political leadership instituted an array of arbitrary controls that led many observers to characterize Peruvian politics of the late 1990s as a "democratic dictatorship." Beginning in late 2000, with the return to an open political process democratic practices have been fully restored and a market economy further deepened. Nevertheless, important issues remain unresolved, and Peru's democracy is still a work in progress.

Political Culture

Key among factors shaping Peru's political culture and history is almost three hundred years of Spanish colonial rule, which included authoritarian political institutions and mercantilist economic structures. Both gave colonialists little experience in handling their own affairs. The carryover into the postcolonial period was greater in Peru than in most other Latin American republics, both because control was imposed more consistently and because of the nature of the independence movement itself. The belated struggle for independence was more a conservative reaction to liberalizing forces in Spain and elsewhere than a genuine revolution, and it came largely from outside, formally succeeding in 1821.

Not surprisingly, therefore, authoritarian rule continued long after independence. No civilian president was elected until Manuel Prado in 1872, although there were some enlightened military leaders such as Ramón Castilla (1845–1851, 1854–1862). Also continuing were neomercantilist economic policies, with Great Britain replacing Spain as Peru's major trading partner and the source of most capital and investment. Of the few local entrepreneurs who emerged in this context, most acted as agents for British interests. Peru did experience its first economic boom during this period, based on the extraction for fertilizer of the rich deposits of guano (bird droppings) on islands off the coast. The economic benefits were short-lived, however, because of the outbreak of the War of the Pacific (1879–1883).

The war forced the break with the past that independence had not provided. Chile wrested from Peru the coastal department of Tarapacá, with its immense nitrate deposits, and occupied a large portion of the country, including Lima. Politically, this disaster demonstrated the weakness of existing institutions and contributed to the emergence of Peru's only sustained period of limited liberal democracy (1895–1919). Economically, the war bankrupted the country and the traditional elite. Because many of Peru's basic resources were mortgaged, Peru became even more dependent on British interests. This coincidence of sharply increased economic dependence and liberal democracy set the pattern for a limited state and private foreign enterprise that continued until the 1968 military coup.

Furthermore, Peru's independent political life has been marked by flamboyant leadership styles that garnered support on the basis of personal appeal rather than institutional loyalty. Many leaders have tended to place personal interests above obligation to any political party organization or even to the nation. As a result, most parties have been personalist vehicles, and most presidencies have involved tumultuous struggles among contending personalities, often ending in military coups. In addition, until recently a large percentage of the national population was not integrated into national economic, political, or cultural life. The Indo-American population of Peru, although in numbers predominant until the 1970s, has participated in national society only in the most subordinate of roles, such as peon, day laborer, and maid. Historically, the way open for this population to escape repudiation by the dominant society was to abandon their own heritage and work their way into that of the Spanish. Among the most important changes in contemporary Peru is large-scale Indo-American migration to towns and cities, where the new arrivals feel they or their children can become a part of the dominant culture: Catholic, Hispanic, and Spanish-speaking. Only with the Constitution of 1979 did illiterates—predominantly native American—gain the right to vote for the first time in national and municipal elections.

As to the economy, Peru was much slower than most of Latin America in shifting from the liberal model of a limited state and an open economy to one marked by greater state intervention. The liberal model endured for several reasons: Domestic elites were willing to retain strong foreign economic control; the military was largely under elite dominance; political leadership kept its personalistic and populist character; a non-Communist, mass-based political party absorbed most emerging social forces; and Indo-American culture slowed the flow of new elements into national society. As a result, neither politics nor the economy changed in any significant way until 1968, when a military coup ushered in a period of unprecedented reform.

Historical Background

Peruvian political history may be divided into several distinct periods: consolidation (1824–1895); limited civilian democracy (1895–1919); populism, mass parties, and veto coups (1919–1968); reformist military rule (1968–1980); full civilian democracy (1980–1992); *autogolpe* (self-coup) and its aftermath (1992–1993); "direct democracy" (1993–2000); and the return to full, if incomplete, civilian democracy (2000–present).

Consolidation (1824–1895)

Several issues kept Peru from the early establishment of a reasonably stable political and economic system. Because Peru had been the core part of a larger viceroyalty during the colonial period, it took some time simply to define the country's national territory. The boundaries were roughly hewn out between 1829 and 1841. Augustín Gamarra and José de la Mar failed to capture Ecuador for Peru in 1829. In the Battle of Yungay in 1839, Andrés Santa Cruz lost his post as protector of the Peru-Bolivia confederation when defeated by a Chilean army, causing the confederation's collapse. In 1841 in the Battle of Ingavi, Gamarra was killed in his attempt to annex Bolivia to Peru.

Once the boundaries were more or less settled, there remained the key problem of establishing reasonable procedures for attaining and succeeding to political office. Peru had at least fifteen constitutions in its first forty years as an independent country, but force remained the normal route to political power. Of the thirty-five presidents during this period, only four were elected according to constitutional procedures, and no civilians held power for more than a few months. Regional *caudillos* often attempted to impose themselves on the government, which by the 1840s was becoming an important source of revenue because of the income from guano.

Unlike much of Latin America during the nineteenth century, Peru was divided politically less by a conservative-liberal cleavage and more by the issue of military or civilian rule. By the 1860s partisans of civilian rule were beginning to organize themselves into a *civilista* movement. The War of the Pacific dramatically demonstrated the need for professionalization of the Peruvian military and helped provoke the formal establishment of the Civilista Party, as well as a number of more personalistic contenders. The eventual result was Peru's first extended period of civilian rule, starting in 1895.

The War of the Pacific also more firmly embedded the tendency to depend on foreign markets, entrepreneurship, and loans. War debts of more than US$200 million were canceled by British interests in 1889 in exchange for Peru's railroads, the Lake Titicaca steamship line, a large tract of jungle land, free use of major ports, a Peruvian government subsidy, and large quantities of guano.

Limited Civilian Democracy (1895–1919)

Peru's longest period of civilian rule began in 1895. While the military reorganized itself under the guidance of a French mission, a coalition of forces among an emerging commercial elite gained control of the government. Embracing neopositivist ideals of renovation, modernization, and innovation, the civilians also advanced the classic liberal precept of a government that would serve to enhance the capacity of the private sector. Their main political objective was modest: keeping civilians in power through increased government expenditures for communications, education, and health. These were financed by taxes on rapidly expanding exports, revenues from new foreign investments (largely U.S.), and new foreign loans after Peru's international credit was restored in 1907.

The civilian democratic interlude, ensured when President Nicolás de Piérola (1895–1899) provided for the direct election of his successors, was undone by various factors. First, the Civilista Party, although reasonably well organized, suffered periodic severe internal divisions. Other parties, such as the Liberal, Democratic, and Conservative, were personalistic, rising and falling with the fortunes of their individual leaders. Second, there was severe domestic inflation precipitated by the international economic crisis accompanying World War I. Third, there was the growing unwillingness of elite-oriented parties to respond to a wide array of demands from new groups entering the political system as the result of expanded government services, especially education.

Also corrosive to civilian rule were the actions of some leaders themselves. In particular, Presidents Augusto B. Leguía (1908–1912, 1919–1930) and Guillermo Billinghurst (1912–1914) operated in self-serving and personalistic ways. Billinghurst, once elected, eschewed Civilista Party support to make populist appeals to the Lima "masses."

Although he was beholden to the commercial elite, Billinghurst did not try to work within the party or the economic elite to try to bring about some quiet accommodation that might have avoided a confrontation. Growing dismay among elite members gradually drew them to the military, which intervened just long enough in 1914 to remove Billinghurst from office. Leguía, after ruling constitutionally during his first presidency, ended once and for all the shaky civilian democracy in 1919. Rather than work out a behind-the-scenes accommodation with opposition elements in 1919, after he had won democratic election he led a successful coup of his own and ruled without open elections until being ousted by the military in 1930.

Populism, Mass Parties, and Veto Coups (1919–1968)

The populism of this period took two forms: civilian, exemplified by Leguía, and military, best illustrated by General Manuel Odría (1948–1956). Both forms were characterized by efforts to stymie political organizations and to encourage loyalty to the person of the president through favored treatment for the elites and by the distribution of goods, jobs, and services to politically aware nonelites. Both forms were also marked by favorable treatment for foreign investors and lenders, thereby maintaining external dependence relationships.

Both civilian and military populism had a number of important effects on the Peruvian political system. They permitted elites to retain control through their narrowly based interest group organizations (the National Agrarian Society, SNA; the National Mining Society, SNM; and the National Industrial Society, SNI) and their clubs (*Nacional* and *La Unión*). When confronted after 1930 with Peru's first mass-based political party, the American Popular Revolutionary Alliance (APRA), the elites were forced to rely on the military to carry out their political will because they had no comparable party to which to turn. The military, in turn, found it could accomplish its own objectives through veto coups to keep APRA out of power. Thus populism, by discouraging political parties, contributed significantly to continued political instability.

Between 1914 and 1984, the only elected civilian to complete a term, his first, was Manuel Prado (1939–1945, 1956–1962). Why he did so is instructive. He was of the elite and accepted by it. He did not try to upset the status quo. He gained the military's favor by supporting its material and budget requirements. He reached an implicit modus vivendi with APRA. Finally, he happened to be president during a period when foreign market prices for Peruvian primary-product exports were relatively high and stable.

Perhaps the most important political event in pre-1968 Peru was the organization of APRA. Although founded in Mexico by exiled student leader Víctor Raúl Haya de la Torre in 1924, APRA soon became a genuinely mass-based political party in Peru with a fully articulated ideology. By most accounts APRA was strong enough to determine the outcome of all open elections held in Peru after 1931. For more than fifty years, however, the military ensured that the party would never rule directly.

Although APRA has had a strong popular appeal, the party's importance for Peruvian politics rests on its reformist ideology and its organizational capacity. With the exception of Lima, APRA absorbed most of the newly emerging social forces in the more integrated parts of the country between the 1920s and the 1950s, most particularly labor, students, and the more marginal middle sectors of the north coast. The party's appeal thus helped prevent the emergence of a more radical alternative. Furthermore, even though APRA was an outsider for most of the period from its founding to 1956, it never overthrew the status quo. At key junctures the party leadership searched for accommodation and compromise to gain entry even while continuing to resort to assassinations and abortive putsches in trying to impress political insiders with its power.

Between 1956 and 1982 APRA became a center-conservative party will-ing to make almost any compromise to gain greater formal political power. In 1956 APRA supported the conservative Manuel Prado in his successful bid for a second term as president and worked with him throughout his adminis-tration in what was called in Peru *La Convivencia* (living together). When APRA won open elections in 1962 but was just shy of the constitutionally re-quired one-third, the party made a pact with its former archenemy, Odría, to govern together. At this point the military intervened and ran the country for a year before facilitating elections, which were won by its favored candidate, Popular Action's (AP) Fernando Belaúnde Terry. During the Belaúnde ad-ministration (1963–1968) APRA formed an alliance with Odría forces in congress to obtain a majority and block or water down many of AP's reforms. Although such actions discredited the party for many, APRA remained Peru's best organized and most unified political force.

The AP, founded in 1956 by Belaúnde, brought reformist elements into the system just as APRA had done before. AP's appeal was greater in the sierra and south, where APRA was weak. Thus, the two parties comple-mented each other by region, and between them they channeled into the sys-tem virtually the entire next wave of newly mobilized popular forces.

In spite of APRA-Odría political obstructionism, important reforms were carried out between 1963 and 1968 under AP, including the establishment of various new agricultural programs; expansion of secondary and university education, cooperatives, and development corporations; and reinstitution of municipal elections. For all intents and purposes the extremist threat to Peru-vian institutions was stillborn. The opposition in congress, however, often blunted initiatives or refused to fund them. In addition, the U.S. government, anxious to assist Standard Oil Company's settlement of the investment-expropriation dispute between its Peruvian subsidiary, the International Pe-troleum Company (IPC) and the Peruvian government, withheld for more than two years Alliance for Progress funds badly needed by the Belaúnde ad-ministration to help finance its reforms. Growing economic difficulties in 1967 and 1968 eroded public confidence, and a poorly handled IPC national-ization agreement sealed Belaúnde's fate. On October 3, 1968, with a blood-less coup, the armed forces began long-term, institutionalized military rule in Peru.

Reformist Military Rule (1968–1980)

"The time has come," stated the new military regime's first manifesto, "to dedicate our national energies to the transformation of the economic, social, and cultural structures of Peru." The underlying themes of the military's ma-jor statements during the *docenio* (twelve-year rule) included a commitment to change, national pride, social solidarity, the end of dependency, a worker-managed economy, and "a fully participatory social democracy which is neither capitalist nor communist but humanistic." Past governments had declared their intention to change Peru, but this one was prepared to act. What was surprising, given Peru's history of military intervention on behalf of the elites, was that a major reason the 1968 coup occurred was because the Belaúnde government had failed to deliver on promises of significant reform.

Why did the military become an instrument for reform in Peru? The answer lies mostly in developments related to the military itself. One was the officers' educational experience after the mid-1950s in the Center for Higher Military Studies (CAEM). Another was a small but intense antiguerrilla campaign in 1965. Third was the effect on military institutional development of continuous U.S. military training from the 1940s through the 1960s. Fourth was the U.S. government's decision in 1967 not to sell jet fighter planes to Peru, which crystallized nationalist sentiment. Last was a vigorous and successful army-led civic action program after 1959. These factors prompted most of the officer corps, at least within the army, to conclude that the best protection for national security was national development. In their view, civilian politicians and political parties had failed to meet the development challenge in the 1960s. Many officers concluded that only the military, with its monopoly on legitimate force, was capable of leading Peru toward this goal.

Once in power the military called itself revolutionary but practiced reform. Almost without exception, the 1968–1975 policy initiatives were based on the twin assumptions of continued economic growth, with improved distribution of this growth, and the willingness of economic elites to accept incentives to redirect their wealth toward new productive activities. Significant changes occurred. One of the most important was the rapid expansion of state influence and control. New ministries, agencies, and banks were established; basic services were expropriated, as were some large foreign companies in mining, fishing, and agriculture, with compensation and reinvestment incentives; and state enterprises or cooperatives were established in their place. Important areas of heavy industry were reserved for the state, new investment laws placed various controls on the private sector, and government employment mushroomed. At the same time Peru pursued the objective of enhancing development by diversifying its external relationships, thereby reducing the country's economic and political dependency.

Another significant initiative was a large-scale agrarian-reform program, which effectively eliminated large, private landholdings. About 360,000 farm families received land between 1969 and 1980, most as members of farm cooperatives. Commitment to cooperatives illustrated the regime's concern for popular participation at various levels. Neighborhood organizations, worker communities, and cooperatives of several types proliferated after 1970, as did various coordinating bodies. All of these changes represented substantial adjustments in past practices and for a time appeared likely to succeed.

By 1971 the military's model for the future political system of Peru had emerged in more or less coherent form: corporatism. This model perceived Peruvian social and political reality in terms of an organic whole, organized by functional sectors and hierarchically within each sector. Government was to serve as the overarching body to initiate, coordinate, and resolve disputes. It was apparently assumed that the new model would eventually replace the old, political party-based one through the dramatic increase in the size and capacity of government and the incentives provided to popular sectors to relate to it. This assumption proved false.

Four major factors led to the regime's undoing. First and most fundamental was that the military's reform plans were much too ambitious. Leaders wanted to do too much in too many areas in too short a time. Second, success was premised on continued economic growth, which stopped after 1974 when economic difficulties multiplied. With locally generated resources not available as expected, the military government turned to foreign loans, often short-term ones, to keep up the momentum, which produced a severe debt crisis by 1978. Third, those in power failed to consult with the citizenry, the presumed beneficiaries of the reforms. This neglect contributed to popular resentment and mistrust. Finally, the illness after 1973 of the head of state, General Juan Velasco Alvarado, contributed to a loss of the institutional unity of the armed forces themselves, which his dynamic and forceful leadership had helped to instill. The eventual result was a mixture of old and new programs in yet another overlay, which was increasingly ill-financed, confusing to citizens, and ultimately unsuccessful.

An August 1975 coup, led by General Francisco Morales Bermúdez and supported by the military establishment, gently eased out the ill and increasingly erratic General Velasco and ushered in the consolidating phase of the *docenio*. With the exception of the agrarian reform, initiatives were quietly abandoned or sharply curtailed. By 1977 mounting economic and political pressures prompted the military regime to initiate a gradual return to civilian rule.

The resulting Constituent Assembly elections in 1978 represented another political milestone because they included participation by an array of leftist parties, which garnered an unprecedented 36 percent of the vote although APRA won the most seats. The Assembly itself was led by APRA founder, Haya de la Torre—another first given the long-term animosity of the military. These elections also marked the beginning of significant involvement in the system by the Marxist left. The Assembly produced the constitution of 1979, which set up national elections every five years and municipal elections every three years, beginning in 1980. One irony of the elections was that they returned to the presidency the same person who had been so unceremoniously unseated in 1968.

Full Civilian Democracy (1980–1992)

This time Belaúnde's AP was able to forge a majority in Congress, in coalition with the small Popular Christian Party (PPC), and won the first plurality in the municipal elections as well. However, events conspired once again to make life difficult for the governing authorities. Inflation continued to increase, reaching 60 percent in 1980 and exceeding 100 percent by 1984. The recession deepened so that in 1983 the GNP actually declined by over 10 percent, and real wages eroded during Belaúnde's second administration (1980–1985) by over 30 percent. World market prices for Peru's exports—copper, oil, sugar, fishmeal, and minerals—remained low or declined even further. Devastating weather accompanied the arrival in 1982 of the El Niño ocean current, and crops and communications networks in the northern half of Peru were destroyed by rain and flood, while in the south, crops withered as a result of drought.

Given such unfavorable economic developments, the foreign debt burden became even more onerous, from US$8.4 billion in 1980 to over US$13 billion by 1985. International Monetary Fund (IMF) agreements provided new funds and debt refinancing, but they also imposed economic restrictions. With the domestic controversy that ensued, Belaúnde hedged on IMF strictures, which provoked a breakdown in the agreement and left a substantial burden for the next administration.

Another major challenge for the government was the Shining Path guerrilla movement. Originally based in the isolated south-central sierra department of Ayacucho and headed by former professors and students from the local University of Huamanga, Shining Path advocated a peasant-based republic forged through revolution. The group's ideology was Marxist-Leninist, based on the principles of Mao and José Carlos Mariátegui, a leading Peruvian intellectual of the 1920s who founded what became the Communist Party of Peru. After some fifteen years of preparations—which included study groups, control of the University of Huamanga, leadership training in China, and work in the Native American peasant-dominated local countryside—Shining Path launched its people's war on the very eve of the May 1980 national election that ended the military docenio.

The Belaúnde administration did not take the group seriously for almost three full years. Only in December 1982 did the government declare Ayacucho an emergency zone and send the military to deal with the problem. By the end of Belaúnde's term thousands had perished in the violence, human rights violations had skyrocketed, and over US$1 billion in property damage had occurred. The emergence in 1984 of a new guerrilla group, the Tupac Amaru Revolutionary Movement (MRTA), added to popular concerns over the spreading political violence.

Such economic and political difficulties substantially weakened popular support for Belaúnde and the AP in the 1983 municipal elections. In the 1985 presidential vote the AP candidate was routed, gaining only 6 percent of the total. The largely Marxist United Left party (IU) garnered 21 percent for its candidate, Alfonso Barrantes, and a rejuvenated APRA won with 46 percent with its youthful (thirty-six years old) standard bearer Alán García Pérez (1985–1990).

The García victory was doubly historic: After a fifty-five-year struggle APRA had finally gained both the presidency and a majority in both houses of congress. Additionally, for the first time since 1945 and only the second time since 1912, an elected civilian president handed power over to an elected successor. The 1986 municipal elections also saw substantial APRA gains, including for the first time ever, the mayorship of Lima.

Alán García's forceful, nationalistic leadership put the international banking community on notice that Peru would be limiting repayments on its debt (now over US$14 billion) to 10 percent of export earnings. Domestic initiatives, especially in agriculture, contributed to long-overdue economic growth at rates of 9 percent in 1985 and 7 percent in 1986. But the recovery ran out of steam in 1987. The economy never did recover from the surprise presidential bank nationalization that year, even though this ill-considered attempt ultimately failed.

The second half of García's term was an unmitigated disaster. Peru suspended all foreign debt repayments, which resulted in international credit drying up. Inflation skyrocketed to 1,722 percent in 1988, 2,600 percent in 1989, and 7,650 percent in 1990. The economy declined by more than 20 percent during this period. Political violence, which had ebbed between 1985 and 1987, surged anew. By the end of the García government in 1990 casualties exceeded fifty thousand and direct and indirect damages were more than US$14 billion. Total foreign debt with arrearages was over US$23 billion. Not surprisingly, García's popularity plummeted from an 80 percent favorable rating early in his term to single digits near the end.

In this challenging context, parties across the political spectrum competed aggressively for support in the November 1989 municipal elections and the April 1990 presidential and congressional vote. In 1989 the IU divided badly, squandering a historic opportunity. From virtual oblivion, Peru's right reemerged, centered on the capacity of the novelist Mario Vargas Llosa to galvanize popular concern over President García's failures. A new coalition, the Democratic Front (FREDEMO), was formed among conservative and centrist parties, and it was able to win more mayoralties in 1989 than any other group.

However, Shining Path also used the elections to step up its terror campaign by killing over a hundred candidates and local officials and forcing scores of others to resign. As a result, about 25 percent of Peru's two thousand-odd district and provincial councils could not carry out elections at all, and the vote cast in the rest was sharply reduced.

In the run-up to the April 1990 national elections, opinion polls made Vargas Llosa the heavy favorite. Many were stunned when another political newcomer, National Agrarian University President Alberto Fujimori, came from less than 3 percent in the polls a month before the vote to finish second with 25 percent to Vargas Llosa's 28 percent. In June Fujimori won easily in the runoff between the top two contenders. His victory was explained as the product of popular frustration with politics-as-usual and Vargas Llosa's over-identification with politicians of the right.

Once in office President Fujimori launched an economic shock program even more severe than Vargas Llosa's proposal during the campaign. He argued that economic recovery could not be secured until Peru's economic mess had been straightened out and the country's international credit standing restored. In the short run, however, his drastic measures accelerated inflation to historic highs, further reduced domestic economic activity (28 percent in 1990), and pushed twelve to fourteen million more Peruvians below the poverty line (60 to 70 percent of the population). Congress went along for the most part, even though Fujimori's party grouping, Cambio 90, held only about one-quarter of the seats. Surprisingly, most Peruvians also went along; Fujimori's support in opinion polls remained consistently above 50 percent.

By early 1992 such drastic measures began to produce results. Inflation was sharply reduced (139 percent in 1991). International economic reinsertion moved forward after foreign debt payments and negotiations with the international financial institutions (IFIs) were resumed in late 1990. Signs of economic recovery also began to appear. Beginning in October 1991, the United States increased bilateral economic assistance and initiated its first substantial military aid in over twenty years.

Peru's congress became more restive and assertive, particularly with human rights issues, but did authorize emergency executive-branch decree powers and approved most initiatives. Although political violence continued to be a serious problem, government forces had also had some successes against both

Shining Path and the MRTA. Given such positive momentum, few were prepared for Fujimori's April 5, 1992, *autogolpe*.

The Autogolpe and Its Aftermath (1992–1993)

This "temporary suspension" of democracy, dissolving congress and the judiciary with armed forces backing, drew immediate and almost universal international condemnation. The United States immediately suspended assistance except humanitarian and counter-narcotics aid. It also used its influence to ensure postponement of Peru's international economic reinstatement as well as of new aid by most of the dozen countries comprising the Peru Support Group. The Organization of American States (OAS) pressed vigorously for democracy's reinstatement.

Fujimori, chastened by the intensity of the international response, agreed immediately to prompt electoral restoration. This was accomplished with national elections under OAS oversight for a new, smaller, one-house congress–cum-constitutional-convention in November 1992 and municipal elections two months later. Results included marginalization of traditional parties, greater concentration of power in the presidency, and a congressional majority that supported Fujimori. Furthermore, former President García was forced into exile after the autogolpe and lost his leadership role in APRA.

The new constitution was narrowly approved (52 to 48 percent) in an October 1993 referendum. It recentralized government authority, set the bases for privatization and economic liberalization, and allowed for the immediate reelection of the sitting president. As the autogolpe worked out, then, Fujimori was very much the winner.

However, his April 1992 action could easily have been disastrous. Suspension of economic assistance postponed economic recovery in Peru by at least a year. Shining Path expanded recruitment and violence, and it then began to predict imminent revolutionary victory.

What saved Fujimori's authoritarian gamble was the careful police work of a small, specialized antiterrorist group in the Ministry of the Interior, formed under García, which paid off with the dramatic capture of Shining Path leader Abimael Guzmán and key lieutenants on September 12, 1992. Several hundred other guerrilla operatives were rounded up in the following weeks, thwarting what was to have been a massive offensive to close out the year. Tougher antiterrorist decrees issued in the aftermath of the autogolpe permitted rapid trials in military courts and life terms without parole for some two hundred key figures. The fortuitous capture of Guzmán, however, was the key event that legitimated the autogolpe; it gave the Fujimori government the political space to pursue its ambitious national reconstruction agenda.

"Direct Democracy" (1993–2000)

President Fujimori's government engaged in multiple machinations to remain in office, but he also had a broad base of popular support. Such approval stemmed largely from his government's ability to drastically reduce political violence and to restore economic and political stability. Inflation virtually ended (from 57 percent in 1992 to 3 percent by 2000), and with economic liberalization and reinsertion into the international financial community, Peru's economic growth averaged over 7 percent from 1994 through 1997. Between 1993 and 1998, Peru received over US$10 billion in new investment and US$8 billion in new loans, and it signed a Brady Plan with foreign creditors that reduced foreign debt by more than US$5 billion (to just under US$19 billion by 1997). A variety of innovative local microdevelopment initiatives reduced extreme poverty by more than half from 1991 through 1998 (31 to 15 percent) while also creating hundreds of new community organizations that began by administrating the projects.

Over the course of the Fujimori decade, political parties were further undermined by a combination of their own limitations and government actions. Independent groups, including the president's, proliferated and dominated the 1995 national elections and the 1995 and 1998 municipal votes. No traditional party except APRA received over 5 percent of the vote in the 1995 national elections—a dramatic turnaround from the 1980s.

After a clear mandate in 1995 (64 percent of the valid vote and a majority in congress) President Fujimori called for "direct democracy without parties or intermediaries" and increased expenditures for local development as well as initiated monthly stipends directly to municipal governments. However, his government also changed the political rules—often arbitrarily and unconstitutionally—to keep a robust political party system from reemerging and to undermine the opposition's electoral campaigns.

Intimidation tactics included wiretaps, physical assault, and character assassination campaigns orchestrated by the Peruvian National Intelligence System (SIN), directed by Fujimori's closest ally and confidant, Vladimiro Montesinos. The regime also thwarted a 1998 national referendum on a third term (for which 1.4 million signatures had been secured) through a congressional vote not accepting its validity. "Direct democracy," then, as actually carried out, was imposed from the top in ways that were anything but democratic—or even legal.

Having rigged electoral machinery and procedures in his favor, President Fujimori surprised no one by deciding to run for a third, constitutionally dubious term in the 2000 elections. Unlike 1995, however, he did not secure an absolute majority in the first round, nor did his supporters win a congressional majority. He was forced into a runoff with second-place finisher Alejandro

Toledo, a U.S.-educated economist from a humble indigenous background—but without political experience. The best efforts of the international community, led by the OAS Election Observer Mission, to ensure a free and fair voting process for the runoff were not successful. Toledo withdrew in protest, and the incumbent won with just 52 percent of the valid vote (about one-third of all ballots cast were spoiled in protest).

Events soon revealed the pyrrhic quality of this 2000 electoral "victory." Inaugurated amidst massive protest and tear gas in July, Fujimori was gone by November. Precipitating his downfall was the videotaped revelation that SIN director Montesinos was bribing elected representatives of the opposition to ensure a pro-Fujimori majority in congress. In spite of President Fujimori's desperate moves to maintain control—including firing and forcing Montesinos into exile and calling for early elections in which he would not be a candidate—popular indignation overwhelmed his maneuverings. By early November opposition parties had regained control of congress. They refused to accept Fujimori's letter of resignation from Japan, where he had fled in ignominy, but declared the presidency vacant instead on grounds of "moral incapacity." A transitional government led by president of congress and long-time AP representative Valentín Paniagua took the oath of office on November 22. Fujimori's so-called "direct democracy" ended in disgrace.

Full But Incomplete Democracy (2000–Present)

The Paniagua interim presidency (2000–2001), though only nine months in duration, was surprisingly effective in righting the ship of state and putting it back on course. Amidst multiple new revelations of official misdoing during the Fujimori years, hundreds of former high-level civilian and military leaders were tracked down and arrested for corruption and abuse of position, including Montesinos himself from his refuge in Venezuela. A Truth and Reconciliation Commission was established to document the human rights abuses committed during the "people's war." Attempts to bring Fujimori back from exile in Japan to face Peruvian justice were unsuccessful, however, as it turned out that he had Japanese citizenship and could not be extradited.

New elections in April 2001 were as free and fair as those of 2000 were tainted. A hard-fought first round between Lourdes Flores Nano of National Unity (UN) on the right, and Toledo of Peru Possible (PP) and APRA's García on the center-left saw Toledo (with 37 percent of the vote) and García (with 26 percent) having edged out Flores (24 percent) for the runoff. Here, García's efforts to cast himself as a wiser and more experienced leader fell short. Toledo, who had led the opposition to Fujimori in the aftermath of the 2000 electoral debacle, won with 54 percent of the vote, though with only a congressional minority.

The Toledo presidency (2001–2006) stumbled politically from the start. Upon taking office in July he faced a plethora of demands—ranging from opposition to privatization, to seeking a greater share of foreign corporation taxes, to ending coca eradication—from an array of local organizations, which his government handled badly in almost every case. Amidst violence and property damage, promises were made and not kept, decisions reached and reversed, and new programs announced but not funded. The president's disorganization, his libertine personal life, his assertive if talented Belgian wife, and the controversial personal advisors and family members who surrounded him all contributed to growing popular disillusionment with his administration. Toledo's popularity declined to single digits for much of his five-year mandate, even in the context of renewed and sustained economic growth and a major decentralization initiative in 2003–2004 creating elected regional governments.

However tainted Toledo's presidency, there was never a sense that Peruvian democracy itself would collapse. The 2006 elections saw Alán García just edging out Lourdes Flores once again in the first round (24 to 23 percent), with "outsider" Ollanta Humala, a former military officer who had mounted a small abortive revolt against Fujimori in 1999, thus waging a left-populist campaign to win the first plurality (32 percent). In the runoff, García won a much narrower victory over Humala than polls had predicted (53 to 47 percent) by convincing enough Peruvians that he had learned from the mistakes of his disastrous first presidency and would not repeat them the second time around. In a graphic demonstration of the political center's neglect of the periphery, however, almost all sierra and jungle departments favored Humala, while the entire coast went for García—the first Peruvian elections to show such geographical polarization.

Although in his inaugural address President García (2006–2011) proclaimed his determination to deliver a major "economic shock" to develop the sierra, his administration fell far short on actual delivery. Although genuinely "reinvented" as a promoter of continued economic liberalization in his second term and presiding over continuing rapid economic growth in Peru—including the ratification of a Free Trade Agreement (FTA) with the United States in 2007—until the U.S. economic crisis in the last quarter of 2008, most of the highlands saw few of the benefits. As occurred during the Toledo government, local and regional social conflicts increased markedly in both sierra and jungle, almost doubling between 2008 and 2009, and official responses were almost always late, ineffective, and sometimes even disastrous. A regenerated Shining Path armed cadre in coca-growing regions of the Apurímac and Upper Huallaga valleys has embarrassed Peruvian police and army operations on several occasions in 2008 and 2009, with guerrilla incidents at a fifteen-year high. An abortive police effort in June 2009 to dislodge jungle indigenous groups from a two-month blockade of a highway in Bagua resulted in at least thirty-five casualties, most of them police. Even the coast was not spared; two years after a devastating earthquake in Pisco and Ica in August 2007, most of those affected had still not received the assistance authorities had promised.

Another serious manifestation of the center's indifference to the sierra is the failure to implement the recommendations of the Truth and Reconciliation Commission (CVR) for forensic identification of the victims of the violence in some 4,200 common graves—mostly in Ayacucho and most believed to be killings and interments by the military—as well as promised compensation to the surviving family members and their communities. For all of its success in the macroeconomic arena, the García government has repeated the pattern of inattention and both inappropriate and belated responses to the multiple needs and demands of the population of Peru's periphery.

In a major miscalculation Alberto Fujimori decided to leave his safe haven in Japan to go to Chile before the 2006 elections in an apparent attempt to generate support for his political group's congressional candidates. Peru's extradition request was eventually granted by the Chilean Supreme Court, and the former president was repatriated to stand trial for corruption and human rights abuses. In a series of trials both Fujimori and his close associate Vladimiro Montesinos were convicted on multiple counts and will likely spend the rest of their lives in jail.

The decentralization initiatives that were begun with funding of municipal (district) governments by Fujimori and continued with elections and funding for regional (department) governments in the Toledo administration have generated new opportunities for access by local political and social organizations—a dynamic that has continued during the García years. Local and regional elections have generated literally hundreds of local groups competing for mayor, district council, or regional president, and they have reduced the historic concentration of virtually all political power at the national level. Although the quality and competence of such elected officials varies widely, the new array of district and regional governments with resources at their disposal offer many more opportunities for both political access and response to some local needs.

As attention begins to focus on the 2011 elections, early candidates with significant support include the popular mayor of Lima, Luis Castañeda Lossio, Congresswoman Keiko Fujimori, the eldest of the former president's children and former First Lady, and former president Alejandro Toledo Manrique. Although Ollanta Humala is also in the mix, his radical rhetoric and multiple missteps appear to make him unlikely to repeat his strong performance in 2006. Given Peru's recent political history, however, the appearance of a new "outsider" cannot be discounted. The military, still recovering from the scandals of the Fujimori era and still trying to regain a semblance of institutional unity and coherence, shows no signs of political restiveness. Even if imperfect and incomplete, democracy remains the only political show in Peru.

Social and Political Groups

Organized social and political groups have played less of a role in Peruvian affairs than in most other Latin American countries until quite recently. The reasons may be traced in part to the strong patterns of Spanish domination that inhibited growth long after the formal Spanish presence was removed. What emerged instead was a strong sense of individualism within the context of region and family for that small portion of the total population that was actually included within the nation's political system.

In the decades following independence, governments were made and unmade by regional caudillos or officials whose power was based on control of arms, personal appeal, and family or regional ties. The best lands were increasingly controlled by non-Indo-Americans, who took advantage of post-independence decrees and constitutions that removed Indo-Americans and their preserves from state protection. The church also lost some of its land-based financial strength, and *beneficencias* (private welfare societies) took over the ownership and administration of many church properties. Thus, political and economic power was quite fragmented in nineteenth-century Peru. The disastrous War of the Pacific abruptly ended the beginnings of economic consolidation based on the guano export boom.

With the establishment of limited civilian democracy between 1895 and 1919, some of what were to become the country's most important interest groups were founded, including the National Agrarian Society (SNA), the National Mining Society (SNM), and the National Industrial Society (SNI). For a long time, however, the important decisions affecting the country were usually made in the Club Nacional, formed much earlier (1855) and the lone survivor of post-1968 reforms. Even the military operated between 1914 and 1962 largely as the "watchdog of the oligarchy." Thus, elites could determine policy outside the electoral arena when necessary and had limited incentives to operate within any party system.

The changes produced by the reform military governments of 1968 to 1980 overturned the old elites and gave rise to opportunities for new sets of social actors through the rapid expansion of new forms of participation. These included various types of cooperatives in agriculture, neighborhood associations in the squatter settlements, and worker self-management communities in industry and mining. At their peak in the late 1970s such entities incorporated as many as eight hundred thousand workers.

The proliferation of local-participation organizations enabled the military government to provide an alternative for citizen participation at a time when involvement through political parties at the national level was cut off. Although the benefits of participation in these new organizations were often significant, most members were from the upper echelons of the working class. Because growth of these enterprises was predicated on profit generation, and because economic conditions after 1975 did not favor such growth, these organizations never developed as expected. Another problem was that the citizen-participation organizations were generated from the top down through the National Social Mobilization Support System (SINAMOS). As the economic viability of the new organizations faltered in the context of growing national economic problems, SINAMOS's regional offices became lightning rods for popular protests, leading to the agency's dismantling in 1978.

Further manifestations of growing popular opposition occurred during a conflict between the national police and the military in early 1975, when large groups of citizens took to the streets of Lima and several provincial capitals and engaged in massive looting and burning sprees. These events were a key precipitant of the August 1975 coup, which effectively marked the end of the military's reformist phase, including its efforts to build a new structure of citizen participation.

With the restoration of civilian rule in 1980, parties and unions regained their pre-1968 roles, largely supplanting the military's model. Vigorous political participation through a score of parties covering the entire ideological spectrum characterized the 1980s, with power alternating between center-right and center-left groups at the national executive level and with substantial representation in congress by the Marxist left. In municipal elections political organizations won shares of district governments at different times, with pluralities shifting from AP to IU to APRA and back to IU. An unanticipated legacy of long-term reformist military rule, then, was to usher in a historically unprecedented level of partisan politics, institutionalized to a degree that few people foresaw and proceeding apace in spite of profound domestic economic difficulties and a substantial guerrilla movement.

However, with the breakup of IU in 1988–1989 and widespread popular disappointment with party politics as successive elected governments failed to respond to citizen needs, political independents came to dominate national and local elections in the 1990s, and union membership declined. Fujimori's 1990 election and the 1992 autogolpe reflected the shift to "antiparty" politics, as did the independent-dominated 1992 congressional/constitutional assembly elections and the 1993 local elections. The result was a progressive deinstitutionalization of electoral politics and a return to more personalistic approaches at the center. Another outcome was a dramatic increase of popular organizations at the local level, as citizens sought to fill the newly available political space.

These new social actors included neighborhood/community improvement or environmental preservation groups, mothers' clubs, coca growers' associations, and school-parent organizations. Although they were usually focused on gaining official responses to immediate needs or perceived abuses, some also expressed concerns based on ethnic identification. With weakened parties and unions and new, locally directed government and nongovernmental organization programs, such newly mobilized groups filled an important role in articulating citizen demands to improve local conditions.

Over the course of Peruvian political history, elections have tended to be intermittent and tentative, and electoral restrictions kept most Peruvians out of the national political arena. Property ownership requirements were not lifted until 1931, when the secret ballot was also introduced. Women were not enfranchised until 1956, and a literacy requirement remained in effect until the advent of universal suffrage in 1980.

The political party scene in Peru is quite fragmented. Furthermore, it is dominated by personalism across the entire ideological spectrum. AP split into pro- and anti-Belaúnde factions, although it came back together with the Belaúnde victory in 1980, only to divide again after 1985. APRA divided after the death of Haya de la Torre in 1979, but the progressive faction regained control after the election of Haya's protégé, Alán García, as party head in 1982 and president in 1985. The García government's problems after 1987 contributed to new divisions within APRA, now largely resolved with its post-Fujimori–era resurgence and a more pragmatic, market economy support reorientation. A small but influential Christian Democratic party (DC) also divided into a tiny leftist faction allied with IU and a larger conservative group (PPC), which formed part of FREDEMO between 1988 and 1992 and eventually allied with other center-right political actors in the National Union (UN) party.

The Marxist political movement founded by Mariátegui became the Communist Party of Peru (PCP), which retained its Moscow-oriented core while fragmenting almost endlessly into Maoist, Castroite, and Trotskyite splinters. All these splinters shared pieces of equally divided urban and rural union movements, although the PCP controlled the largest portion (about 75 percent). With economic crises and economic liberalization initiatives, union organizations have declined from about 30 percent of the formal workforce in the early 1980s to less than 10 percent two decades later.

The public prominence of Shining Path after 1980 and its recourse to guerrilla tactics evoked an almost universally negative response from Peru's Marxist left, which was not inclined to pursue its goals through violence. When most of its members were joined (however loosely) in the IU during the 1980s, the Communists were the second largest political force in terms of electoral support (peaking in the 1986 municipal elections at 31 percent of the total vote). The rise of an organized left operating within rather than outside the political system was one of the positive legacies of the military docenio. However, IU's breakup in 1989 sharply reduced the role of the left in national politics after 1990 until the surprising resurgence of a new populist left led by Humala and his Peruvian Nationalist Party (PNP) in the 2006 elections.

During the 1990s Peru's parties became even more divided and numerous. In part this was because those who exercised power in the 1980s did it badly, thus discrediting them in the view of most of the public. In part it was because party leadership continued to place personal over institutional concerns. It was also the result of the adroit manipulation of new political rules and procedures by Fujimori governments in which weak new political groups were encouraged over strong parties. In 1995 fourteen groups contended for the presidency and twenty for Congress, with traditional parties capturing less than 15 percent of the valid vote. This pattern was repeated with twelve contenders in 2000, but with a combination of fewer, more established parties and the new populist PNP in 2006.

Municipal elections, however, have been consistently dominated by large numbers of political groups that function only for the vote itself, with a tendency for these to increase over time in the context of local and regional decentralization. Such political fragmentation at the local level is not necessarily a problem because the hundreds of local groups competing for office are broadly representative of community and regional issues and concerns.

At the national level, however, the picture is more mixed, with a combination of traditional and newly organized parties competing for the presidency and congress. Transitional President Paniagua demonstrated that traditional parties were capable of playing a positive role, while Toledo presided over a new party group (PP) that epitomizes a personality-driven alternative. With García's victory, a traditional party regained control of the executive branch, but in a closely contested election with yet another personalist and populist alternative that won more seats in congress. As democracy has become routinized once again in Peru, such a mixed pattern of competition between established and personalist parties is likely to continue.

Government Machinery

The Peruvian government of most of the twentieth century may be characterized as small, centralized, and personalistic. Until the 1960s, government employees constituted a very small proportion of the workforce and were usually selected on the basis of party affiliation, family ties, or friendship. Ministry bureaucracies were concentrated in Lima. Government presence in the provinces was limited to prefects and their staffs, military garrisons in border areas, small detachments of national police, schoolteachers, and a few judges—all appointed by authorities in Lima.

A government monopoly of the guano industry and of tobacco, matches, and salt-marketing were among the few official ventures before 1960. Until the 1960s the central bank was privately controlled, and even government taxes were collected by private agencies. Within the government the executive branch predominated. During periods when congress was functioning, however, the executive's authority was subject to numerous checks, including congress's powers to interrogate and censure ministers and to appropriate funds.

The government's size and scope increased considerably during the first Belaúnde administration with the establishment of new government agencies. Total government employment increased by almost 50 percent between 1960 and 1967 (from 179,000 to 270,000), and the public sector's share of GDP grew from 8 percent to 11 percent.

However, the most dramatic changes in the size and scope of the state machinery occurred between 1968 and 1980 under the reformist military regime, which dramatically expanded government involvement in order to accelerate development. Existing ministries were reorganized and new ministries and autonomous agencies were created. By 1975 total government employment had increased by almost 70 percent over 1967 (to 450,000), and the public sector's share of GDP had doubled to 22 percent. Even with such a rapid expansion of the state, however, central government activities remained concentrated in Lima. Official funding tended to go toward construction, equipment, and white-collar employment in the capital rather than for activities in the provinces.

The political and financial crises of 1975 and the change of government brought to an end the dynamic phase of public sector reforms. Resource limitations, growing popular opposition, and the inability of the military regime to act effectively to implement its own decrees prevented full implementation of the corporatist model articulated between 1971 and 1975. The 1979 constitution, however, drawn up by an APRA-IU majority, retained the statist orientation of the Peruvian political system even as it set the bases for civilian rule.

With the return to democracy in 1980 President Belaúnde announced his intention to restore the dynamism of the private sector and to reduce the role of government. However, continuing economic problems and substantial public resistance made these changes difficult to carry out. The García government moved quickly to implement longstanding APRA decentralization goals, including regional development corporations, expanded agricultural credit, and regional legislatures, while working simultaneously to win the confidence of domestic entrepreneurs. Initial successes were substantial, but by the end of García's term, they had been overwhelmed by an ill-advised nationalization of domestic banks and Peru's worst economic crisis in one hundred years. Central government employment expanded from six hundred thousand employees in 1985 to one million in 1990—but with half the budget.

The Fujimori administration, after implementing drastic shock measures to stop Peru's economic hemorrhaging, began to move the country toward economic liberalization. This process involved selling off state enterprises created or nationalized under the 1968–1980 military regimes, retiring many government employees and reorganizing ministries to be able to dismiss thousands more, and overhauling the legal framework to favor private property and investment. Tax collection was also reorganized so that government could begin to pay its own way again. Collections increased from less than 4 percent of GDP in 1989 to 14 percent by 1995. Over the course of the 1990s over one hundred former state agencies were privatized, generating around US$8 billion in new foreign investment. The 1993 constitution incorporated these changes but also further concentrated power in the presidency and in central government. New government agencies, several designed to emphasize microdevelopment projects in Peru's poorest districts, began to operate in the early 1990s, as did a municipal fund to transfer resources to local governments. Overall, the state did not become smaller during the Fujimori years, although it was dramatically changed and reorganized.

The Toledo government ended some of the Fujimori regime's government agencies and reorganized others but also reduced their efficiency through political patronage. It also embarked on a new decentralization initiative in 2003–2004, with elections of officials at the department level for the first time, along with greater local taxing authority. Since 2006 the García administration has engaged in further reorganization but also sustained the center's commitment to strengthen regional and local governments with additional funding and expansion of personnel. Nevertheless, even with such reinforcement and support, the regional governments in particular have been slow to implement meaningful development programs in their areas of responsibility.

Public Policy

Historically, public policy in Peru may be characterized as limited. Laissez-faire liberalism applied from the 1890s up to 1968 with few exceptions. Most services were privately owned, and the government's role was normally that of facilitator or expediter for the private sector, including foreign enterprises.

Unlike many Latin American countries, Peru did not respond to the challenge of the world depression after 1929 by sharp increases in public services and enterprise. This difference resulted from the simultaneous challenge to elites posed by APRA, with its advocacy of sharply expanded state control. By successfully keeping APRA from power in the 1930s, elites also retained a limited state. By the time APRA finally entered the political arena as a legitimate force in 1956, its position on the role of the state was much more accommodating to elite interests.

The electoral campaigns of 1961–1962 and 1962–1963 raised more explicitly the need for a greater public sector role. The ultimate winners, AP and Belaúnde, worked actively between 1963 and 1968 to make the state a more dynamic force and to create a climate of increased popular expectations regarding what the state could and should do.

Between 1968 and 1980, then, the military government served as the major force for an unprecedented expansion of the state. Such rapid expansion posed challenges of its own, and in trying to do so much so quickly the government spread itself too thin. Although providing new job opportunities for the middle class, the rapidly expanding bureaucracy often had difficulty delivering promised goods and services, especially in outlying provinces. Official announcements and periodic flurries of activity raised popular expectations, but growing economic resource limitations contributed to citizen protests and violent confrontations over unmet demands.

The 1968 takeover of the International Petroleum Company (IPC) demonstrated that the military government was serious about reform. This action served to establish the legitimacy of the new regime with the citizenry and to demonstrate to the U.S. government and foreign investors that Peru would no longer accept the degree of foreign influence that had hitherto prevailed. Other expropriations of important foreign investments also took place, but with compensation. New outside investment was welcomed under stricter regulation and occurred principally in copper mining and oil exploration. Foreign loans were avidly sought and were acquired at record levels.

Thus, even while adopting a radical posture in foreign economic relations, the military government recognized the necessity for continued foreign loans and investments to help accomplish national development goals. However, such heavy international borrowing after 1971, in part a result of the reluctance of the domestic private sector to invest in spite of generous incentives, came back to haunt the government. Prices for some Peruvian exports declined markedly, domestic production of others also dropped, and optimistic forecasts of oil exports proved erroneous. A severe financial crisis resulted between 1975 and 1977. Consequently, many development objectives were compromised, and the very legitimacy of the regime came into question.

Subsequent civilian governments have had to face many of the same problems. Although no new nationalizations occurred under Belaúnde, efforts to sell some enterprises back into private hands and to encourage new foreign investment were largely thwarted by domestic depression, international recession, and large debt-repayment responsibilities. The first García administration adopted a much more nationalistic and government-activist posture, with debt repayments tied to export earnings and some nationalizations, among other measures. Over the last half of APRA rule, however, the economic crisis overshadowed other policy priorities and discredited statist approaches to development.

Fujimori's government, coming to power at a time of unprecedented economic and political problems, reversed the twenty-five-year trend toward larger government in Peru. Privatization and economic liberalization became the watchwords of the 1990s and contributed to the resumption of economic growth after 1993. Government was substantially reorganized—even "reinvented"—and the private sector expanded markedly. Under Toledo, however, popular protest has thwarted most efforts to continue the privatization process. Even so, it has not reversed changes already introduced.

The agrarian reform of 1969 was the most far-reaching of all the military government's policy initiatives. However, given the scarcity of arable land the majority of needy farmers gained nothing. The already better-off coastal farmers received most of the reform's redistributive benefits, and the central government's major effort in the more isolated sierra was too little and too late. Many cooperative enterprises there never operated effectively, which contributed to a move back to private ownership in the 1980s.

A byproduct of the reform was a serious decline in agricultural production, which was overcome only partially by the Belaúnde government's sharp reduction in food subsidies and the resulting increase in food prices after 1980. The García administration sharply expanded agricultural credit until 1988, thus helping to boost production. However, the same agrarian reform problems that led Belaúnde to reprivatize a large number of the agricultural cooperatives also contributed to the ability of Shining Path to expand its influence in the more marginal indigenous-dominated highlands. From the elections of 1980 until the mid-1990s, the sections of Peru with the highest levels of blank and spoiled votes as well as abstention rates were these very areas: Ayacucho, Apurímac, and Huancavelica in particular.

Although the threat posed by Shining Path has passed, the farmers of the Peruvian sierra in particular still lack access to credit and the technical assistance necessary to be able to modernize. As a result of central government neglect in a part of the country that continues to have most of the farm population engaged in traditional, usually subsistence agriculture, the population remains predominantly poor and marginalized. The outward migration to the cities that has resulted from the guerrilla violence between 1980 and 1994 and ongoing limited economic possibilities poses multiple challenges for a country endemically deficient in new employment opportunities.

Official combined unemployment and underemployment figures have ebbed and flowed between 50 and 80 percent of the economically active population. Overall real-wage statistics show a similarly variable pattern, with some improvement during the first half of the García administration, followed by precipitous erosion over the next five years. Without the dynamic informal sector, which is an array of economic activities outside official purview and measurement, the average Peruvian might be even worse off. Estimates suggest that about 60 percent of the nation's economy and two-thirds of the jobs are to be found in this sector. These figures do not include up to three hundred thousand peasant families who live off the coca and cocaine-paste industry, which was concentrated in the 1980s and early 1990s in the Huallaga Valley 250 miles northeast of Lima. Peru was until the late 1990s the world's largest producer of coca leaf (60–65 percent), the raw material for cocaine, and still produces between 20 and 30 percent of total coca leaf output.

Inflation undermined the economic foundations of Peru during the five-year García presidency with a staggering 2,000,000 percent cumulative increase. By 1993 the annual inflation rate was down to 39 percent, the lowest since 1977. Inflation levels ever since have ceased to be a problem for Peru, averaging 3 percent or less since the late 1990s. Economic growth returned as well, averaging over 7 percent between 1994 and 1997 and, after a late 1990s recession, back to 3 to 6 percent growth between 2001 and 2008.

Regardless of its failings as a democracy, what the Fujimori government was able to do in the public policy arena over the decade of the 1990s was to restore a viable state that could mount an effective response to the unprecedented set of problems facing Peru when he first took office. Most particularly, his administration eliminated inflation, restored economic growth, reduced levels of political violence, and developed multiple small programs for the neediest sectors of the population. The Toledo administration then inherited a reasonably well-functioning state and, unlike his predecessor, operated democratically. However, his government was unable to build on this base except for the regional decentralization initiative, and this was largely because of ineffectual leadership. García's second term has represented an almost complete turnaround from his first, with a commitment to retain and deepen the market economy pursued since the early 1990s as well as the decentralization initiatives of his immediate predecessors. The results, at least at the macroeconomic level, have been impressive through 2008, with sustained economic growth, reductions in overall levels of poverty, and even a government fiscal surplus. His major problems, which also bedeviled Toledo, result from an array of ineffective and even counterproductive responses to social conflicts in the sierra and jungle as well as an inability to make good on promises to stimulate the development of the sierra.

Foreign Affairs

Historically, Peru's foreign relations have been conditioned by boundary disputes, diverse natural resources, domestic political and economic objectives, and the Humboldt Current. From independence on, boundaries were a matter of dispute and a prime motivator of Peruvian diplomacy as well as a source of armed conflict. In the south the loss of nitrate-rich Tarapacá and Arica to Chile in the War of the Pacific (1879–1883), ratified by the Tacna-Arica Treaty (1929), has conditioned relations with Bolivia and Chile ever since and has given a certain defensive dimension to foreign policy more generally. In the north, Peru ceded Leticia to Colombia in 1932, an unpopular move, but it then successfully pursued a brief war with Ecuador in 1941 to assert its historic claim to substantial lands in the northeastern Amazon basin. Although Ecuador signed the Rio Protocol of 1942 accepting the new frontier, that country's officials renounced it in 1960, with armed clashes and military mobilizations a frequent occurrence in the disputed area over the next thirty-five years.

Peru's agricultural and mineral resources are numerous and diverse. They include sugar, cotton, rice, asparagus, fish and fish products, and minerals such as copper, iron ore, natural gas, gold, silver, and oil. Such diversity has often served to protect Peru from the uncertainties of international markets and to stimulate a wide variety of foreign investments. Peru joined forces with Ecuador and Chile as early as 1952 to proclaim a 200-mile territorial limit in ocean waters, a claim to the rich fishing of the Humboldt Current that eventually worked its way into international law in the 1970s as a 200-mile economic zone. The Peruvian government was also a driving force behind the Andean Pact, begun in 1969 to expand markets, diversify trade, and apply common foreign-investment criteria among the Andean countries. Economic nationalism joined political nationalism as a major component of Peruvian foreign policy for most of the period between 1968 and 1990, which resulted in expanded state control of previous foreign holdings in agriculture, mining, and fishing and closer regulation of new and remaining enterprises.

The military government's stated objective in international affairs from 1968 to 1980 was the elimination of dependency, a call also taken to heart by the APRA administration of Alán García from 1985 to 1990. This goal led to Peru's taking a number of steps to alter its international economic position, including new trade and diplomatic relationships with the socialist bloc and conscious diversification of Peru's trade, investment, and loan assistance. These policies continued during the Belaúnde administration and may have helped for a time to keep the severe economic problems from being even worse. García then pursued a more nationalistic strategy, which contributed to economic growth in 1986 and 1987 before developing into a new, more severe crisis between 1988 and 1993.

Beginning with the 1968 military takeover, Peru attempted to strengthen its developing-nation position. It took on an important leadership role among the Third World nonaligned countries. Unfortunately, Peru's struggle to diversify its dependence and to achieve a position of Third World leadership was seriously compromised by the country's growing economic difficulties after 1975. In 1978, 1982, and 1984, Peruvian governments were forced to accept stringent IMF conditions for the continuance of economic and loan assistance.

Beginning with Alán García's inaugural address in July 1985, however, Peru committed itself to an independent debt-repayment position. By the end of 1987 Peru was in arrears to governments, international agencies, and foreign private banks. By the end of 1988 economic nationalism had contributed to producing Peru's most severe domestic economic crisis in over a hundred years. The elected reformist APRA government found itself as constrained by international forces as its reformist military predecessor, in spite of equally strenuous efforts to break with past patterns and move Peru along a more independent course in the foreign affairs arena.

Domestic factors interfered with this goal as well. In June 1986 President García hosted the annual meeting of the Socialist International (SI) in a bid to reassert Peru's independent reformist credentials. However, a Shining Path assassination attempt on the Peruvian president during the meeting, followed almost immediately by a coordinated prison uprising of jailed guerrillas, which was brutally repressed with almost three hundred inmate deaths, thoroughly embarrassed the Peruvian head of state and dashed any hopes García held for SI leadership.

The combination of deep domestic economic crisis and changing international realities contributed to a dramatic shift in Peru's foreign economic policies in the 1990s. Privatization and economic liberalization opened up the country once again to private investment. Economic nationalism receded rapidly as a cornerstone of Peru's foreign relations. Over the 1990s scores of public enterprises were privatized, tariffs slashed, foreign debt repayments resumed, and legal foundations for private investment restored. Foreign investment more than doubled—from about US$4 billion in 1993 to over US$9 billion in 1998. Peru led efforts to reconstitute the Andean Pact as the Andean Group on terms much more favorable to private sector activity. Finally, the international financial community became a major source of government development programs once again. Although foreign debt increased to over US$30 billion by 1998, with scheduled repayments running at about half of export earnings, most specialists continued to see Peru as a good credit risk.

Perhaps Peru's most significant foreign policy success in recent decades was the successful negotiation with Ecuador of a definitive border settlement in 1998. The Peru-Ecuador boundary dispute had been Latin America's longest standing and had provoked almost two dozen armed clashes between the countries even after the issue was supposedly resolved by treaty (the Rio Protocol) in 1942. The most violent was the major confrontation between January and March 1995, which cost the two countries over US$1 billion and hundreds of casualties.

Negotiations could proceed under the Rio Protocol aegis, unlike some previous clashes, because Ecuador once again accepted its jurisdiction. However, they were arduous and slow. Only after three and a half years were the heads of state of both countries able to reach an agreement, and only with the arbitration of the guarantors. The final border became the one agreed on in 1942, but with Ecuador having access to and private ownership of a symbolic square kilometer of territory at Tiwinza, an area of fierce fighting in 1995. The agreement also included a separate treaty of navigation and commerce for Ecuador on the Amazon and its tributaries and a commitment by the Inter-American Development Bank (IDB) and the World Bank (WB) to some US$3 billion in border integration and development projects. The remaining seventy-eight kilometers of the previously disputed boundary were fully demarcated by 1999, and over the succeeding ten years, cross-border transit and bilateral trade and investment have increased significantly, even though all provisions of the final accord have not yet been fully implemented.

The role of U.S. public and private participation in Peru has always been quite complex. Private investment grew rapidly in the early twentieth century but was almost exclusively in isolated enclaves on the north coast (oil and sugar, then later cotton and fish meal) and in the sierra (copper, other minerals, and later iron). Successive governments encouraged such investment. Even during the military *docenio*, in spite of some expropriations and a conscious attempt to diversify sources of foreign investment, substantial new U.S. investment took place, particularly in copper (Southern Peru Copper Company) and oil exploration and production (Occidental Petroleum Company).

The Belaúnde government's policy toward private investment was more open but only partly successful owing to international and domestic economic problems. The García administration's nationalistic posture in a context of growing economic and political difficulties discouraged most new investment, both domestic or foreign, between 1985 and 1990. Fujimori's shift to privatization and economic liberalization began slowly, given Peru's grave problems, but gathered momentum beginning in 1993 with several hundred million dollars in portfolio and direct investments. Between 1993 and 1998, over one hundred public enterprises were privatized and over US$6 billion in new foreign investment generated. Spanish investment was the largest, with US$2.4 of the US$9.8 billion total as of 1998; U.S. second, with US$1.6 billion; and British third, with US$1.2 billion. Policies favorable to foreign investment continued during both the Toledo and the García governments, with the 2007 Free Trade Agreement offering added incentives, even though among some sectors of the public there is growing concern over the negative environmental effects of some investments, especially those in mining.

Regardless of how one may debate the issue of foreign dependence, U.S. investment and loans served in Peru before 1930 to balance the country's extreme reliance on Great Britain. The enclave nature of this assistance had both positive and negative impacts: reduction of economic ripple effects on the rest of the Peruvian economy, provision of islands of relative economic privilege for workers in which unions could become established, and creation of small areas of virtual foreign hegemony within Peru.

With growing economic nationalism in Peru in the 1960s, the U.S. government collaborated closely with U.S. businesses to try to work out solutions satisfactory to U.S. interests. The IPC case between 1963 and 1968 illustrates this policy in the extreme. One basis for Peru's desire to expropriate IPC rested on well-founded claims that the concessions giving Standard Oil of New Jersey subsoil rights in La Brea y Pariñas (near Talara) in 1921 and 1922 were illegal. The U.S. government supported Standard Oil's position, and when negotiations bogged down periodically, U.S. government foreign assistance and loans under the Alliance for Progress were interrupted. The Belaúnde government, under duress, finally struck a bargain with the company, but the controversial terms generated public debate and turmoil and provided the immediate precipitant for the 1968 coup.

Within a week after taking power, the military nationalized IPC. This and subsequent periodic expropriations kept most new official U.S. aid suspended between 1968 and 1972, except for relief and rehabilitation assistance after a 1970 earthquake. Eventually, the military regime found itself obliged to resolve expropriations with financial settlements that companies considered fair, in part as a result of U.S. government pressure but also because the Peruvian government wanted and needed continued foreign private investment and loans.

Historically, U.S. government presence in Peru was not a large one. Starting in 1938, however, because of U.S. security concerns with international fascism in the hemisphere and after World War II with international communism, the U.S. government has been a major actor. Between 1945 and 1975, grants and loans to Peru totaled US$1.107 billion, of which US$194 million was military assistance. Aid funds during Belaúnde's first term, when available, went primarily for projects in marginal sectors that the opposition-controlled Peruvian congress was unwilling to fund. A large-scale civic action program for the military in the 1960s helped shape officers' views on the national development mission of the Peruvian armed forces, as well as the U.S. government's refusal to permit the sale of jet fighters to Peru in 1967. This action helped Peruvian officers realize that their own welfare, as well as that of their country, would be enhanced by diversifying their sources of supply and, hence, their dependence.

Actions and reactions by both Peruvian and U.S. governments since 1968—including aid and loan cutoffs, the expulsion of most of the large U.S. military missions, and the end of the Peace Corps presence until its small-scale renewal in 2003—considerably lowered the official U.S. profile in the country. García's prickly relationship with the United States limited U.S. programs to modest economic aid and drug interdiction and eradication assistance. Between 1973 and 1990 Peru had a substantial military sales and assistance relationship with the Soviet Union, in excess of US$1 billion. This included the training of several hundred army and air force personnel each year in Peru and in the Eastern bloc as well as up to a hundred Soviet advisers in Peru.

U.S. government offers to increase economic and military assistance substantially after Fujimori's election as part of the counter-drug Andean Initiative began to be implemented in October 1991. However, all but humanitarian and some counter-narcotics aid were suspended by the United States after Fujimori's April 1992 autogolpe. Continuing concerns over human rights violations delayed aid restoration even further after democratic forms were reinstated in 1993. Gradually, however, U.S. aid to Peru increased over the course of the decade to a level averaging over US$100 million per year, mainly for programs in development, democracy, counter-narcotics, and food assistance.

The U.S. role in counter-drug programs in Peru since the mid-1990s has been controversial. Funds for eradication and alternative development have had an impact on cocaine production, but interdiction of planes that appeared to be transporting drugs was suspended after a U.S. missionary's plane was mistakenly shot down in 1999. During the latter years of the increasingly undemocratic Fujimori administration, U.S. policy favored counter-drug activity over pressure to maintain democratic practice. With both the Toledo and the García governments, continuing counter-narcotics activity has contributed to significant increases in organized resistance by coca growers as well as new activity by a somewhat revitalized Shining Path, which poses additional challenges for Peruvian authorities.

Conclusions

Peru as an independent nation has had great difficulty in overcoming its authoritarian legacy. About three-fourths of the time nondemocratic governments have ruled the country. The Spanish colonial heritage was an important factor impeding the evolution of liberal-democratic institutions in the nineteenth century, but additional considerations—including international market forces, the incorporation of more and more of the population into the national political and economic system, and political leadership perceptions and actions—prevented the emergence of a stable institutional structure in the twentieth century.

The reformist military governments of 1968 to 1980 tried but failed to construct a new participatory model of community-based politics and a new economic model based on a leading role for the state. Their failure had its origin in their inability to appreciate the boundaries within which reformers must operate in order to accomplish development objectives. In particular they did not grasp the degree to which political leaders in a country like Peru are hemmed in by forces largely beyond their control. Then, although full electoral democracy established in 1980 began with great enthusiasm and promise, it soon fell prey to some of the same problems that had undermined its authoritarian predecessors. It also had to cope with Latin America's most radical and violent guerrilla organization, the Shining Path, and it handled that challenge poorly as well. Once again, a combination of circumstances and political leadership predispositions led to the dismantling of democracy in 1992 with Fujimori's autogolpe.

President Fujimori succeeded where his civilian predecessors had failed by pursuing a new strategy to deal with Shining Path and by implementing a new economic liberalization model that ended hyperinflation and restored economic growth. These successes gave him the popular support necessary to set up a new political system under the Constitution of 1993. This system contained democratic forms and procedures, but numerous mechanisms as well that gave untoward control to the head of state. Although many new government agencies and programs worked to benefit the less privileged at the periphery, the quality of democracy and democratic discourse in the center was progressively eroded. Most of the media were cowed, and opponents were often harassed and intimidated. Peru became a prime example in Latin America of a government that manipulates democratic procedures so as to ensure its own continuance in power. The result was democratic in form but authoritarian in substance—Peru's latest manifestation of its long-authoritarian tradition.

President Toledo then restored open democracy in Peru, the crumbling of which was the product of a combination of growing hubris by Fujimori, Montesinos, and key cohorts within business, military, and police, and a remarkable outpouring of popular indignation. Although democratic practice under Toledo was chaotic and problematic, even in the midst of sustained economic growth, the García government has succeeded in stabilizing democratic process in spite of some continuing issues that have not been handled well. Though still incomplete, democracy in Peru seems finally to be replacing the country's authoritarian past.

Suggestions for Further Reading

Burt, Jo Marie. *Political Violence and the Authoritarian State in Peru: Silencing Civil Society.* Basingstoke: Palgrave Macmillan, 2008.

Carrión, Julio, ed. *The Fujimori Legacy: The Rise of Electoral Authoritarianism in Peru.* University Park: Pennsylvania State University Press, 2006.

Dietz, Henry A. *Urban Poverty, Political Participation, and the State: Lima 1970–1990.* Pittsburgh, PA: University of Pittsburgh Press, 1998.

Fumerton, Mario. *From Victims to Heroes: Peasant Counter-Rebellion and Civil War in Ayacucho, Peru, 1980–2000.* Amsterdam: Thela Publishers, 2002.

McClintock, Cynthia, and Fabian Vallas. *The United States and Peru: Cooperation—At a Cost.* New York: Routledge, 2003.

Palmer, David Scott, ed. *Shining Path of Peru.* 2nd ed. New York: St. Martin's Press, 1994.

Quiroz, Alfonso W. *Corrupt Circles: A History of Unbound Graft in Peru.* Baltimore, MD: Johns Hopkins University Press, 2008.

Stern, Steve J., ed. *Shining and Other Paths: War and Society in Peru, 1980–1995.* Durham, NC: Duke University Press, 1998.

11

Venezuela

Can Democracy Survive
Electoral Caudillismo?

David J. Myers

Defiant and beaming with confidence, President Hugo Chávez Frías gazed out over Venezuela's National Assembly on the morning of July 25, 2009. He had come to celebrate the tenth anniversary of the opening of the national constituent assembly that drafted the 1999 constitution. National Assembly deputies cheered their president. All counted themselves as supporters of his Bolivarian Revolution. The opposition's boycott of National Assembly elections in 2005 had left them without a voice in the national legislature. President Chávez was buoyant because five months earlier he had prevailed in the national referendum that ended term limits on elected officials. This increased the likelihood that he and his supporters could hold power indefinitely. President Chávez had weakened his opponents by nationalizing many important businesses, distributing abundant petroleum income to millions of his countrymen, and making Venezuela a major force in Latin American politics. He led a coalition of states in the region that rejected liberal democracy and free trade as well as maneuvered to reduce U.S. influence.

Chávez's discourse promised his supporters that the best was yet to come. It was time to consolidate their rule in a regime he called Twenty-First Century Socialism. The President cautioned that for him to continue this, the

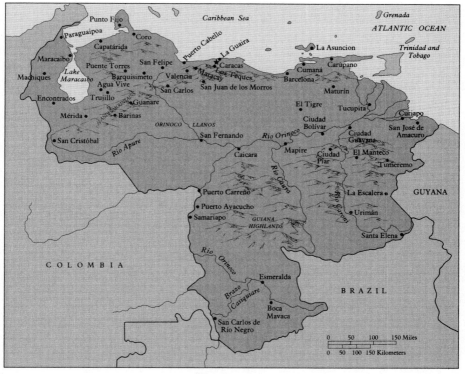

VENEZUELA

National Assembly should consider giving him a new *Ley Habilitante* (Enabling Law). In Venezuelan constitutional law the Ley Habilitante is a kind of blank check that the legislative branch can grant to the executive for designated purposes over a specified period of time. During the time it is in effect the Ley Habilitante allows the president to propose and approve legislation without consulting the legislative branch of government. President Chávez promised that if he were granted the habilitante he would "set loose the process of socialist transformation" and "create the new structures of the Proletarian Bolivarian state."

The President also excoriated his enemies at home and abroad. He cautioned that the United States under President Barack Obama remained the "evil empire." He resurrected charges that the U.S. government had plotted with Venezuelan oligarchs to remove him in the short-lived and unsuccessful *golpe del estado* of April 11–13, 2002. After mocking the oligarchs and their Yankee coconspirators, he thundered that the armed forces and the people were behind him and that he could never be ousted by military means. Oozing sarcasm, he stated that "much less by means of elections" could they remove him from power. In a final rhetorical flourish aimed at his domestic opponents President Chávez boasted: "You believed that the forces of revolution would be in the opposition for all of your lives; well, accustom yourselves to the situation as it is because now it is your turn. You are now the ones that are in the opposition and you will never return to power."[1]

Venezuela's flight from liberal democracy and foreign policy activism are not the only reasons for interest in the country. Between 1945 and 1989 Venezuela changed from a rural to an urban society while appearing to avoid chaos and soften the pain of modernization. Literacy rates rose dramatically, indigenous heavy industry took shape, and for a brief moment Venezuelans enjoyed one of Latin America's highest standards of living. Prosperity ended in the 1980s, however, when falling revenues from the international sale of petroleum undermined the economic and political institutions that, since the late 1950s, had allocated economic and political resources. Post-1958 democracy, the fruit of pacts among elites, allowed new actors to enter the ruling class, expanded the middle sectors, and improved living standards among the poor.[2] Then the government's inability to honor and deepen these pacts in the 1980s led to constitutional crises in 1992 and 1993, the discrediting of political and economic elites, and the election in December 1998 of Hugo Chávez as president.

Land and People

Geography and history have shaped contemporary Venezuelan politics. Nestled in the northeastern quadrant of South America between 1 and 13 degrees north of the equator, Venezuela is hot and tropical. Cool temperatures predominate only at altitudes above 3,280 feet (1,000 meters). The country's 28.1 million inhabitants live in an area of 352,150 square miles (912,050 square kilometers), roughly the size of Texas and Oklahoma combined. Stretching some 1,750 miles (2,816 kilometers) along the Caribbean Sea and the Atlantic Ocean, Venezuela extends south into continental South America. It encompasses snow-covered mountains rising to 16,427 feet (5,007 meters, Pico Bolívar) and reaches into the Orinoco and Amazon jungles. Some 3,000 miles (4,800 kilometers) of continental borders form frontiers with Colombia, Brazil, and Guyana. The Orinoco River, one of the largest and most navigable rivers in the world, drains four-fifths of the country. But the mountains, not the river or the plains, have historically been Venezuela's most influential geographical features. The dominant colonial settlements, agricultural estates, and urban centers are nestled in cool mountain valleys, and until 1925 when petroleum extraction became Venezuela's most important economic activity, these valleys formed the unchallenged economic, administrative, and social heartland of the nation.

Geographers divide Venezuela into five regions: the Guyana Highlands, the Orinoco Lowlands, the Northern Mountains, the Maracaibo Basin/ Coastal Lowlands, and the numerous small islands along the Caribbean coast. These regions vary immensely in size, resources, climate, population, and historical input.

The Guyana Highlands, encompassing 45 percent of the national territory, is the largest region. Historically remote, poor, and sparsely populated, Guyana became a symbol in the 1950s of the nation's drive to industrialize. Guyana's industrial and mining centers remain oases of modern civilization surrounded by tropical forests. Ancient plateaus, some extending for 125 miles (200 kilometers), rise more than 3,280 feet (1,000 meters) above the jungle floor. From their heights tumble breathtaking waterfalls, including the planet's highest uninterrupted one, Angel Falls. On these plateaus flourish flora and fauna that exist nowhere else. Until the 1950s Guyana exerted little influence on national affairs, but subsequent government investment in the region has made Guyana's industrial infrastructure central to Venezuela's development aspirations.[3]

Lying between the southernmost part of Venezuela and the coastal mountains are the great grassland prairies (*llanos*) of the Orinoco Lowlands. Occupying 33 percent of the national territory, the Llanos support 20 percent of the population. For six months of the year this vast, featureless plain, 620 miles (1,000 kilometers) long and 400 miles (645 kilometers) wide, is subject to rainfall so heavy that much of it lies under water. As the ensuing dry season progresses, the mud turns to deep layers of dust, vegetation shrivels, the heat becomes intense, and streams dry up. Although the region is far from ideal for raising cattle, a type of culture based on that industry has grown there and continues to be managed by a rough—and for many years lawless—breed of man (*el llanero*) for whom cattle-raising is a way of life. President Hugo Chávez is a llanero.

The Northern Mountains constitute the third major geographical region. Although they encompass only 12 percent of Venezuela's land area, they support roughly two-thirds of the country's population. The principal mountain chain consists of the coastal range and the Sierra Nevada de Mérida. In the coastal range are found the capital city of Caracas, the Valencia-Maracay industrial center, large coffee holdings, sugar *haciendas*, and rich farmlands surrounding Lake Valencia. Because of its agricultural importance this region was for many years dominated by a rural oligarchy and large estates maintained by cheap peasant labor. Although coastal-range political leaders have played a central role in Venezuelan history, they have often lost to more aggressive rivals from less-favored regions.

The high and rugged Sierra Nevada de Mérida is a western spur of the Andes. With peaks rising to 16,400 feet (5,000 meters), its early inaccessibility discouraged great agricultural estates (*latifundios*). The Venezuelan Andes were thus characterized by medium-sized landholdings and populated by small clusters of people, both *mestizos* and Indians. Despite the presence of an influential university in the city of Mérida, Andean Venezuela remained isolated until the rise of coffee as a commercial crop. It is a region where religion and family ties are strong, as are the historic values of Hispanic culture.

Ten percent of Venezuela's national territory consists of a narrow, partly arid, partly swampy belt of lowland lying between the steeply rising coastal mountains and the Caribbean Sea. This region comprises the Maracaibo Basin and the Coastal Lowlands. Most of Venezuela's oil is found in the Maracaibo Basin, and the region's drained swampland has been transformed into rich farms and cattle ranches. However, over 80 percent of the Basin's inhabitants are classified as urban. Most reside in Greater Maracaibo, the country's second-largest metropolitan region. Beginning in the 1920s oil exploitation transformed the Maracaibo Basin into a thriving commercial, industrial, and educational center. In contrast, tourism is the most important economic activity of the eastern Coastal Lowlands. Here are located the best Caribbean beaches, and the climate is clear and dry. African influence is stronger in this region than anywhere else in Venezuela.

In addition to the mainland, there are seventy-two islands of varied size and description. The most important and best known is Margarita, in the state of Nueva Esparta. The site of some of the oldest Spanish settlements in Latin America, Margarita is a thriving free port and tourist center.

Most Venezuelans are an amalgam of Caucasian, Amerindian, and black. They have a common culture, predominantly Hispanic but with important Amerindian and African strands. Overwhelmingly Roman Catholic (85 percent) and Spanish-speaking, Venezuelans view themselves as members of a single ethnic mixture. The national census does not classify according to race or ethnicity (except for Amerindians in the Orinoco and Amazon jungles), so it is only possible to make educated guesses. Pure Caucasians comprise between 10 to 15 percent of the total population. A small number belong to proud families who trace their ancestry to renowned Spanish names, some came from the former Ottoman Empire in the 1920s, but most of the pure Caucasians immigrated to Venezuela from southern Europe between 1945 and 1958. Perhaps 10 percent of Venezuelans are black, less than 3 percent are pure Amerindian, and between 70 and 80 percent are of mixed ancestry. Ethnic mixing has occurred at all social levels, and ethnicity does not serve to distinguish either separate groups or classes. Nevertheless, Caucasian features are valued, and their predominance is greater among the higher social and economic strata.

Internal migration since World War II has transformed Venezuela from a rural society into one that is highly urbanized. First, peasants abandoned the countryside and rural villages for regional market towns. Then, townspeople subsequently moved to the large cities. Initially, Caracas received a disproportionate number of these migrants, mushrooming from a metropolitan region of about five hundred thousand in 1945 to a diverse metropolis of over five million in 2009. Four other cities—Maracaibo, Valencia, Barquisimeto, and Barcelona-Puerto/La Cruz—boast populations of more than one million. In contrast, large areas of rural Venezuela are depopulated. Census estimates in 2000 placed the total urban population at just over 80 percent of the total national population.

Historical and Political Economy

The history of Venezuela is one of progressive integration into the North Atlantic area. Integration began when Christopher Columbus landed in eastern Venezuela during his third voyage in 1498. The Venezuelan mainland was the first area of South America to be explored by Spain, but the region proved a disappointment, especially when contrasted with the riches discovered in Peru and Mexico. Disappointment led to neglect, and Venezuela remained a colonial backwater until the latter half of the eighteenth century. At that time Spain's Bourbon monarchs concluded that Venezuela had become more valuable, so they updated their imperial organization to increase control and collect taxes.

Consolidating Political Order and
the Transition to Liberal Democracy

The war for independence destroyed Venezuela's colonial bureaucracy in a clash of bandit armies who confiscated and reallocated property. Old methods of defining legitimacy and right were replaced by a new system based almost entirely on force and favor with those who controlled force. This modification of the colonial order came as a logical extension of political authority being militarized. Militarization also confirmed the primacy of Caracas. After Venezuela separated from Gran Colombia in 1830, control over Venezuela, more than ever, meant control of the capital city.

Between 1830 and 1920 Venezuela evolved into a commercial bureaucratic outpost of the industrializing North Atlantic. After decades of civil strife there was a consolidation of political order during the late nineteenth and early twentieth century. Crucial in this process were the pacification and development programs initiated by General Antonio Guzmán Blanco (1870–1888) and consolidated by General Juan Vicente Gómez (1908–1935). Gómez took the essential relationships inherent in Guzmán Blanco's programs for exploiting Venezuela's niche in the international arena and—by applying ruthless logic aided by a monopoly of technology and communications—developed them to their conclusion. He fixed the bureaucratic commercial pattern in its final form before Venezuela succumbed to the overwhelming pressure of what historian John Lombardi has labeled the "petroleum-based technological imperium."[4]

Over the final decade of Gómez's rule (1925–1935) the "petroleum-based technological imperium" overpowered the commercial bureaucratic system. This arrangement was and is the product of opportunities and complexities endemic to petroleum exploitation. Transformation involved creating modern systems of transportation and communication and diffusing industrial technology into the oilfields. It also facilitated the intervention of foreign interest groups and ideologies into Venezuela's internal politics.

Caracas, measured by any set of variables, gained disproportionately from the new economic regime, although not until after Juan Vicente Gómez passed from the scene. The long-lived dictator disliked and distrusted *caraqueños* (residents of Caracas) and ruled from Maracay, a small settlement some sixty miles to the west of Caracas. Gómez's successors then launched a major effort to bring standards of comfort in the capital up to those of urban North Atlantic countries. University education, art, culture, social services, architectural and urban grandeur—whatever the North Atlantic imitation, Caracas residents monopolized it to an ever-growing degree. Thus, Venezuela's capital acquired the trappings of modernity while the rest of country remained much the same. Caracas attracted the ambitious, the wealthy, and the young from other regions. The distance separating Caracas from the interior grew greater until no other center could compare with it.

The "petroleum-based technological imperium" was arguably the single most important factor shaping Venezuela's twentieth-century political development. It played a key role during Venezuela's journey from primitive dictatorship (1935–1958) through party-centered democracy (1959–1999) to the current "Twenty-First Century Socialism." This journey began in the late 1920s, even before the passing of General Juan Vicente Gómez. At that time the demands of managing the new extractive economy exceeded the capabilities of the nineteenth-century commercial bureaucratic structures to broker social, economic, and political conflict. This prompted the search for new institutions, and growing U.S. influence throughout the Caribbean led Gómez's successors to experiment with limited political democracy. However, the elitist tenor of this experiment proved its undoing.

On October 18, 1945, junior military officers joined with working- and middle-class reformers from the interior to seize power in a short but bloody coup d'état. Democracy for the few gave way to democracy for the masses. The new system's dominant radicals used their leftist political party, Democratic Action (*Acción Democrática*, AD), to gain total control of the government and then to pass legislation that began to redistribute wealth, power, and cultural authority. The upper and middle classes panicked, turning to the military for protection.

On November 24, 1948, the armed forces overthrew the popularly elected government of Rómulo Gallegos, outlawed the dominant AD political party, and imposed a military junta to govern the country. Governments presided over by Colonel Carlos Delgado Chalbaud (1948–1950) and General Marcos Pérez Jiménez (1952–1958) favored importers and merchants at the expense of the industrialists. They took advantage of the strong global demand for petroleum so as to increase exports of crude oil by 7.4 percent and petroleum products by 14 percent per annum. For a brief period this reliance on the oil industry's growth to fund import-driven economic development appeared to be working: The increase in Venezuela's domestic product averaged an extraordinary 9.4 percent per year during the middle 1950s.

However, economic and political circumstances deteriorated after 1956. The condition of having a dynamic enclave petroleum economy surrounded by inefficient agricultural production had long been a source of political stress. The basic problem lay in the contrast between the living standards (high and increasing versus low and stagnating) of those who enjoyed the fruits of the technologically based petroleum imperium and those on the outside. The economic situation became critical in 1957, leading financial elites to criticize the military regime openly. General Pérez Jiménez attempted to counter declining support with increased repression, which only stiffened the resolve of his enemies, who received assistance from the U.S. government. Early in the morning of January 23, 1958, after he lost control over Caracas, Marcos Pérez Jiménez fled the country.[5]

Fair and open elections occurred at the end of 1958. Rómulo Betancourt (AD) won the presidency and AD gained control of Congress. The opportunistic Democratic Republican Union (URD), the Social Christian party (COPEI), and the Venezuelan Communist Party (PCV) elected significant delegations. The three major political parties (AD, URD, and COPEI) learned from their earlier failures and agreed to share power. The Pact of Punto Fijo[6] gave to militants from the major political parties important bureaucratic positions and a place in the leadership of each major interest group organization (e.g., the Labor Confederation, the Peasant Federation, and professional associations such as the Engineering Guild). In addition to sharing power, the leaders of AD, URD, and COPEI agreed to build support for economic pluralism before undertaking far-reaching wealth redistribution. Agreement on this reformist agenda was a critical first step in building legitimacy for post-1958 democracy.

Traditional elites and the leaders of the mass-based political parties opted for the Punto Fijo reconciliation system in 1958 because of their disastrous experience with military rule and because they anticipated that distributive politics funded by ample resources would be the norm. They calculated that income from the foreign sales of petroleum, if not squandered (here the example of General Pérez Jiménez loomed large), would provide the resources with which they could successfully broker the demands of traditional elites and previously excluded groups. Leaders of the Labor Confederation and Peasant Federation were to be incorporated into this expanded distributive process and empowered to service their clients. Punto Fijo democrats calculated that this system would avoid the widespread revolutionary violence that had convulsed Cuba and culminated in Fidel Castro's imposition of communism.

The Petroleum Roller Coaster and Institutional Stress

The flow of revenue from petroleum to Venezuela's central government between 1958 and the present has experienced sharp ups and downs, like the ride on a roller coaster, and these ups and downs shaped the development of Venezuelan political institutions. Escalating petroleum revenue helped to consolidate liberal democracy in the 1970s, and sharp declines in the 1990s contributed to its unraveling. This reduction, which dramatically reduced the distributive capability of the state, opened the door for the "Bolivarian Revolution" of Hugo Chávez Frías.

More than 80 percent of the total income that Venezuela received between 1945 and 1989 came during the administrations of Carlos Andrés Pérez

(1974–1979), Luis Herrera Campíns (1979–1984) and Jaime Lusinchi (1984–1989). Benefiting from international events over which Venezuela had no control, these three governments and their economic allies administered unprecedented wealth. The quadrupling of the market price of a barrel of petroleum in 1973 allowed the government of Carlos Andrés Pérez (CAP) to create a potpourri of state corporations and to initiate a multitude of infrastructural development projects. CAP also nationalized, with mutually agreed upon compensation to foreign investors, the iron and petroleum industries. However, he invested in many projects whose payoff would be only in the long term, and he continued to spend massively on importing food. By the end of his term the state had yet to extend its economic largesse on an equitable basis to large numbers of people, and charges of corruption swirled around the government. Thus, in 1978 voters entrusted the presidency to the opposition COPEI Party.[7]

President Luis Herrera presided over a volatile economy. At the time of his inauguration in February 1979 Venezuela appeared headed for a period of prolonged budgetary deficits. Before austerity programs could be implemented, though, new increases in the price of petroleum doubled the government's income. Unprepared for this favorable turn of events, President Herrera was unable to take advantage of it. Improvised policies and corruption led to economic stagnation. These conditions, in conjunction with declining petroleum revenue, led to Black Friday (February 13, 1983). On this day President Herrera devalued the currency and announced drastic austerity measures. However, the conditions that led to Black Friday proved intractable. They ushered in a string of economic disasters that devastated COPEI and fatally weakened Punto Fijo democracy.

Jaime Lusinchi of AD won the 1983 presidential elections, and his government would be the last hurrah for traditional distributive politics. Lusinchi made a fundamental mistake in economic policy when he opted to restructure only at the margins. After some initial successes Venezuela's economy resumed its decline. The government then ran a balance-of-payments deficit of US$4 billion in the election year of 1988 in order to avoid an economic recession. The economy responded by growing at a rate of 5 percent, and AD's Carlos Andrés Pérez won a second presidency. However, Lusinchi's refusal to come to grips with Venezuela's reduced circumstances restricted the options open to his successor.

The New Departure and Its Consequences

On February 2, 1989, Carlos Andrés Pérez became president for the second time. Three weeks later Venezuelans were stunned when their new leader announced that foreign reserves were severely depleted; that in 1988 the country had run a fiscal deficit exceeding 9 percent of the GDP; that the current account of the balance of payments had its largest deficit in history; and that all prices in the economy, from interest rates and black beans to medicines and bus fares, were artificially low and impossible to maintain. President Pérez warned that only bitter medicine could cure these maladies, but when he administered the first dose, three days of rioting and looting left more than three hundred dead and the country overwhelmed with panic, perplexity, and rage. It was the worst outbreak of violence since the early 1960s, when the then-struggling liberal democracy clashed with Castroite guerrillas. Fallout from the 1989 riots weakened President Pérez, doomed efforts by his successor to restore the regime's legitimacy, and brought to power its most intractable enemies.

In the immediate aftermath of the February 1989 rioting there was reason to hope that Carlos Andrés Pérez might correct the foundering political regime. Venezuela settled into a deceptive calm even though conditions screamed that the petroleum-fueled distribution network could no longer sustain existing institutions.[8] President Pérez used this calm to initiate a neoliberal economic package, *El Gran Viraje*, the Great Turnaround. This radical departure from the past relied on four sets of policies: macroeconomic stabilization, trade liberalization, privatization, and deregulation.

Trade liberalization and privatization brought profound change. Government planners removed nontariff barriers covering 94 percent of local manufactures and eliminated special permits for exports, simultaneously restructuring the tariff system, and thus bringing the country's average tariff level down from 35 percent in 1988 to around 10 percent in 1990. Entry into GATT consolidated the freest trade regime of the post-1958 era. The foreign commercial banks responded by reducing and restructuring US$20 billion of Venezuela's public debt. Finally, a new foreign-investment policy eliminated most restrictions on foreign investors and minimized bureaucratic interference in their financial, commercial, and technological transactions. For the first time the stock market was opened to overseas investors.

The Pérez administration took concrete steps to privatize state enterprises whose survival depended on capital infusion from the government. By the end of 1992 four commercial banks, the national airline, the telephone company, as well as the cellular telephone system, a shipyard, the ports, sugar mills, and several hotels had all been sold. Other activities slated for privatization included horse-racing tracks, a second airline, additional hotels, the Caracas water-supply system, regional electric distribution facilities, and the public television network. These changes, dramatic reversals for a president who had nationalized petroleum and led the Latin America Social Democratic Movement, confirmed the serious loss in capability that Venezuela's distributive network had experienced.

The repercussions of President Pérez's economic restructuring were felt throughout the 1990s. Early in the decade Venezuela's economy set world records. These records, however, masked the deterioration of state institutions, which became less capable of acting on the basis of technical and professional criteria. Carried into policy areas such as health care, transportation, housing, and agriculture, poor performance by the state further undermined the quality of life for most Venezuelans. Purchasing power also declined. Decay seemed pervasive, which damaged the government's legitimacy even more. The societal deterioration that eroded support for Pérez also extended to the armed forces. As early as the 1970s the professional military promotion system of the early democratic system was relaxed and politicized. This spurred partisanship and rivalries inside the officer corps, thereby creating significant incentives for aspiring officers and their protégés to block or even sabotage the career development and possibilities for promotion of their rivals. Until the fiscal crisis of the 1980s those who lost in this Byzantine competition received middle-level executive positions within the myriad of state enterprises. However, this even became the exception as budgets tightened and the public sector contracted. Incentives then increased for the losers to overturn the political regime.

Another consequence of the 1980s fiscal crisis for the armed forces was that the daily needs of enlisted soldiers and junior officers became grossly underfunded. Tensions between junior and senior officers were also exacerbated by the fact that the former had received extensive opportunities to complement their military training with professional education at home and abroad, thus differentiating their experience in the profession from that of older officers. The latter belonged to a generation that came of age in the 1960s, when the fight against leftist insurgents was all-consuming.

To summarize, reduced economic circumstances after the devaluation of "Black Friday" and distinct generational experiences combined to create distrust between junior and senior officers, erode discipline within the armed forces, and undermine their cohesion. Given these conditions, the military as an institution ceased to be a bulwark of support for liberal democracy.

The crisis broke on February 4, 1992, when a group of junior military officers calling themselves the Bolivarian Military Movement attempted a coup that almost succeeded. Although much in the Bolivarian Military Movement's program was confused, its call for the affluent and dishonest to be tried for crimes against the nation struck a responsive chord among the majority who had suffered during economic decline. Thus, although the coup failed, it emboldened the opponents of President Pérez, his austerity plan, and even long-forgotten enemies of post-1958 liberal democracy.

The fifteen months that separated the February 1992 coup attempt from President Pérez's suspension from office in May 1993 proved remarkable for their turbulence and intensifying opposition to the government. Former President Rafael Caldera stopped just short of proclaiming that the Bolivarian Military Movement's cause was just, and President Isaías Medina's last minister of the interior, Arturo Uslar Pietri, suggested that forcing Pérez from office before the end of his term might make amends for the revolution of 1945. In late November 1992 the military (this time the navy, air force, and marines) mounted a second unsuccessful coup, and Venezuela's once-robust macroeconomic indicators faded. During May 1993 the attorney general, Ramón Escobar Salom, assembled persuasive evidence that President Pérez had misused government funds. The Supreme Court then found "merit" in these charges, and the Senate suspended Pérez from office to face trial before the Supreme Court.

The eight months that followed raised more questions than they answered. After AD and COPEI came to an agreement, their senators selected one of their own, Ramón J. Velásquez, to serve as interim president. Velásquez, a political intellectual, oversaw free and open elections in December 1993 for president, congress, and the state legislatures. However, during his brief stewardship the economy failed to recover, privatization stalled, and bitterness over declining living standards intensified. The Velásquez legacy to his successor, Rafael Caldera (1994–1999), was perhaps an even chance of preserving Punto Fijo democracy.

For almost two years Rafael Caldera endeavored to set the clock back to a past that he viewed positively—the years of his first presidency (1969–1974). He blamed corruption and the neoliberal policies of Carlos Andrés Pérez for the country's ills. Soon after taking office President Caldera moved against CAP's backers in the financial community. The unintended consequence of that decision was the collapse of the entire banking system, a turn of events that severely damaged the government's capability to grow the economy.

In July 1996 President Caldera made a complete turnaround and negotiated an agreement with the International Monetary Fund that reinstated many of the neoliberal reforms (as a program called Agenda Venezuela) that he had previously criticized. The fruits of Caldera's earlier policies, despite their popularity when first announced, were an inflation rate of 103 percent (1996) and an increase in the foreign public debt to US$26.5 billion. In addition, the government had not built mechanisms of participation likely to generate support for the return to a more market-oriented development strategy. When it came to implementing Agenda Venezuela President Caldera actually increased centralization. He and Luis Alfaro Ucero, the secretary general of AD, allied in the Congress to give the national executive new powers to amend the consumer protection law and intervene in the foreign exchange market, which unmasked AD as a silent partner in the government. Neither Caldera nor AD had much credibility after that.

The opportunity to make dramatic changes in the political system came with the national elections of 1998. Voters went to the polls to choose the president and members of congress. COPEI and AD nominated presidential candidates with fatal flaws, which underscored their isolation. Just prior to the presidential voting, AD and COPEI abandoned their nominees and threw their support behind the promising but ultimately unsuccessful candidacy of Enrique Salas Römer, the independent governor of Carabobo. The real story of the presidential election campaign, however, was the meteoric rise of Hugo Chávez. He personified opposition to post-1958 liberal democracy, and on December 6 voters elected him president by a decisive margin.

Chávez rewrote the rules of Venezuelan politics in 1999. At his February inauguration he vowed to replace the existing "moribund" and "unjust" order with a new and responsive democracy. He quickly organized a referendum in which 85 percent of the voters authorized elections that would select delegates to a Constituent Assembly whose charge was to draft the new constitution. Delegates favorable to President Chávez controlled the Constituent Assembly, and on December 15, 1999, the government submitted the new constitution to voters for their approval. Seventy-two percent voted in favor.

Neither President Chávez nor his opponents were satisfied totally with the 1999 constitution. Opponents felt that it gave too much power to the national executive, especially after President Chávez implemented its provisions in ways that allowed his followers to dominate most of the state apparatus. The opposition claimed that this domination unfairly restricted their ability to compete in the political arena. Conflict between the opposition and the government intensified in November 2001 when President Chávez enacted a package of forty-nine special laws designed to reverse the neoliberal trends of the 1990s. This package signaled the radicalization of the Chavista movement.

Seven months later opposition forces attempted an unsuccessful *golpe del estado* (April 11–13, 2002). In December 2002 and January 2003 the opposition again attempted to force President Chávez from office, this time through massive demonstrations in Caracas and Maracaibo. With the economy contracting and societal violence a real possibility, the government allowed the process to go forward whereby signatures would be collected to implement provisions in the 1999 constitution (Articles 72 and 233), which provided for a recall referendum. On June 8, 2004, following a contentious signature-collecting process that lasted for more than eight months, the National Electoral Council certified that the petition for a recall referendum had obtained the requisite number of signatures for the referendum to take place. The referendum was held on August 15, 2004. More than 58 percent of voters expressed the preference for Hugo Chávez to remain as president. Defeat stunned the opposition and allowed President Chávez to increase his domination over the country.

Two subsequent referendums initiated by President Chávez reveal his dissatisfaction with constraints imposed on his rule by the 1999 constitution. The first, which took place on December 2, 2007, followed by a year his election to a second six-year term as president. The paramount political change proposed by this referendum was the abolition of presidential term limits and the allowance of the indefinite reelection of the president (but this was not allowed for any other political post). Other important changes expanded social security benefits to workers in the informal economy, ended the autonomy of the central bank, prohibited large land estates while allowing the state to provisionally occupy property slated for expropriation before a court has ruled, reducing the maximum working week from forty-four to thirty-six hours, prohibiting foreign funding for political associations, and prohibiting discrimination based on sexual orientation. In addition, the referendum provided for reorganization of the country's administrative districts and empowered the president to control elected state governors and mayors by an unelected "popular power" that was dependent on the national executive.

Voters narrowly rejected the proposal (51 to 49 percent). It was Hugo Chávez's first major electoral defeat since his election as president in December 1998. Initially the President conceded defeat and congratulated the opposition for this victory, while adding "for now we could not do it." Two days later he characterized the results victory as a "*victoria de mierda*" (shitty victory), and chastised the opposition for "covering it (the victory) in shit." Manuel Rosales, the most important opposition candidate in the 2006 presidential election, had a different response. He proclaimed, "Tonight, Venezuela has won."

Defeat of the proposal to amend the constitution undercut President Chávez's power and authority. Inside of the Chavista movement speculation sprang up over who would succeed the president when his term expired in February of 2013. The opposition took heart, waged vigorous campaigns in the subnational elections of November 23, 2008, and scored some surprising victories. Even more ominously, petroleum prices fell as the global recession deepened. Within the President's inner circle there was concern that the impact of this decline inside Venezuela would be to increase dissatisfaction with the government.

Seven days after the subnational elections President Chávez seized the initiative. He announced that he would open a new wave of discussion on the proposal for allowing postulation without limits for the presidential candidate. The initiative, however, received a mixed reception. Inside the Chavista camp, individuals with presidential aspirations and their supporters grumbled. Opponents called the proposal "illegal and unconstitutional," pointing out that Article 345 of the 1999 constitution states that, "A revised constitutional reform initiative may not be submitted during the same constitutional term of office of the National Assembly." President Chávez finessed the constitutional issue by declaring that the change to the constitution would be in the form of an amendment, instead of a constitutional reform. He defused reservations within his own movement by redefining the amendment to apply to all popularly elected positions (state governors, mayors, National Assembly deputies, and state legislators), not only to the president. The National Assembly overwhelmingly approved the proposal, which opened the way for the referendum.

On February 15, 2009, 54 percent of voters (abstention was 30 percent), backed the proposed amendment. Students and others took to the streets in protest, but the police quickly dispersed them. Most of the international observers found the voting to have been clean, transparent, and fair. Success strengthened President Chávez's authority within his United Socialist Party of Venezuela (*Partido Socialista Unido de Venezuela*, PSUV), the armed forces, and among lukewarm supporters. It also disheartened the opposition. Following passage of this referendum President Chávez accelerated the implementation of measures to consolidate "Twenty-First Century Socialism."

Political Parties and Elections

Events between 1998 and 2009 transformed the political party system. AD and COPEI had been the core of post-1958 liberal democracy. Both had strong indigenous roots, although the former maintained ties to the European Social Democrats and the latter to the Christian Democrats. For many years AD and COPEI efficiently performed the functions most often associated with modern political parties: mobilizing supporters, recruiting individuals to fill government positions, mediating the demands of competing interests, and creating symbols that strengthened support for the political regime. However, on the eve of the 2006 presidential election identification with the AD had fallen to barely 5 percent, and COPEI teetered on the brink of extinction.[9]

The decline of AD and COPEI in the 1990s allowed Hugo Chávez Frías to transform the political party system. In 1997 he organized the Fifth Republic Movement (*Movimiento Quinto República*, or MVR) as an electoral vehicle to advance his candidacy in the 1998 presidential election. Once the Punto Fijo establishment realized the magnitude of Chávez's appeal they coalesced behind the presidential candidacy of Enrique Salas Römer, the Yale-educated governor of Venezuela's richest and most industrialized state, Carabobo. Nevertheless, Hugo Chávez Frías won the December 6, 1998 presidential election with just under 57 percent of the popular vote.

Twenty months later on July 31, 2000, Venezuela held elections for the first time under the new 1999 constitution. In those elections voters chose the president, all governors and mayors, and all members of the new unicameral National Assembly. AD and COPEI declined to contest the presidency. Chávez's only significant challenger was Lieutenant Colonel Francis Árias Cárdenas, his second-in-command during the unsuccessful military coup of February 4, 1992. Árias had split with Chávez over the president's leftward drift and emerging anticlericalism. Chávez then captured 60 percent of the total vote, slightly more than in 1998. The MVR and its allies secured 46 percent of the seats in the National Assembly, while AD and COPEI together held only 21 percent. The remaining third of the seats were controlled either by allies of the MVR or regional political parties.

Hugo Chávez's supporters, though controlling the National Assembly, lacked the two-thirds majority necessary for modifying the constitution. This changed on December 4, 2005, when opposition political parties abstained from the election for deputies to the National Assembly. That decision was in large part a reaction to the decisiveness of President Chávez's victory in the recall referendum of August 2004. Opposition leaders were demoralized. They also doubted the veracity of the referendum results reported by the National Electoral Council and did not trust the Council to report accurately the results of the National Assembly elections. In addition the opposition felt disadvantaged because of the government's aggressive patronage activities. Opposition leaders called for abstention in hope of discrediting the elections and forcing President Chávez to accept ones that would be internationally supervised. It proved a disastrous miscalculation. The rate of abstention did approach 75 percent, but without opponents the Chavistas captured all 167 seats in the National Assembly. The opposition was left without representation in the legislative branch of the national government.

There was never any doubt that Hugo Chávez would run in the presidential election of December 3, 2006. After much debate the opposition came together and participated. Their unity candidate was Manuel Rosales, governor of the oil rich state of Zulia. Chávez proclaimed the election a contest between the candidate of the revolution and a tool of the U.S. government. Rosales attacked the President for his international giveaway programs, especially the publicized discounted sales of petroleum to Cuba. Rosales also promised to reduce crime, increase public safety, and replace much of the government's social spending with direct grants to individuals. The Governor of Zulia made a respectable showing, but President Chávez received almost 63 percent of the popular vote. The rate of abstention fell to 25 percent.

President Chávez made no secret of his intention to speed up the pace of revolutionary transformation during his 2007–2013 term of office. He decided that the undertaking required an institutionalized political party that could organize the masses, recruit candidates for political office, and socialize citizens to support the revolution. The proto-party that had run Chavista candidates for office since the 1998 elections, the MVR, was a loose movement of supporters who lacked permanent institutions. Thus, ten days after being elected to a second six-year term President Chávez announced his intention to create a new political party, the United Socialist Party of Venezuela (PSUV).

On March 7, 2007, Chávez presented a phased plan, lasting through November, for establishing the PSUV. This plan called for creating a system of "battalions," "platoons," and "squads" that would be responsible for organizing militants into a hierarchy of groups. Party leaders at the apex would choose candidates to run for governmental positions and rally militants in support of the revolution. Eleven relatively insignificant political parties that had backed President Chávez in the 2006 election quickly indicated that they would join the PSUV. Three small supportive political parties with a personal identity that transcended that of the President (Fatherland for All, *Patria Para Todos,* PPT; For Social Democracy, Podemos; and the Communist Party of Venezuela, *Partido Comunista de Venezuela*, PCV) stated that they would remain autonomous until after the PSUV took shape, at which time they would decide on their membership based on the party's program. This led President Chávez to characterize the three as "almost in the opposition."

The PSUV came together in three phases. The first, which began on March 5, 2007, ended on June 10 with the announcement of a timetable for completing the process. Members of the MVR and the Francisco Miranda Front, the president's personal youth organization, worked together in a membership drive that resulted in 5,696,305 signing up as "aspirants to become militants." This number was roughly 80 percent of the votes received by Hugo Chávez in the 2006 presidential election. The second phase began on July 31, 2007, when twenty-two thousand base organizations (known as *batallones socialistas*) held assemblies to organize and elect representatives to the Foundational Congress. The Congress, attended by 1,681 delegates, met on January 12, 2008, in Caracas. President Chávez subsequently approved a list of sixty-nine candidates for provisional posts in the PSUV. In elections held on March 9, 2008, party militants chose fifteen from this list of candidates. Ninety-four thousand PSUV militants cast their ballots.[10]

The first electoral test for the PSUV came on November 23, 2008, when voters choose 22 regional (state) governors, the "High Mayor" of Metropolitan Caracas, and 265 mayors. The PSUV won 17 governorships, roughly 80 percent of the mayoralties, emerging by far as the most important political party. However, the opposition did score some important victories. Opposition candidates won the governorships in some of the most populous states (Zulia, Miranda, Carabobo, and Táchira) while also capturing the "High Mayor" of metropolitan Caracas. Manuel Rosales, the defeated candidate in the 2006 presidential elections, won the contest for Mayor of Maracaibo, the country's second largest city. Nevertheless, the PSUV gained a level of domination at the regional and local levels that had never been achieved by a single party during the forty years of Punto Fijo democracy.

Opposition to the PSUV in 2008 was concentrated in four small political parties and allied independents. The opposition was strongest in Caracas and the more urbanized states of the West and the Andes. It was weakest in the small towns, rural areas, and the eastern region—precisely the regions where AD had been most dominant between 1946 and 1998. After ten years of the Bolivarian Revolution voter identification with AD hovered around 3 percent. Less than 1 percent identified with COPEI and MAS, the other two political parties that boasted significant followings in the Punto Fijo years. Only when all opposition forces united behind a single candidate did they stand any chance of winning elections.

The three important opposition political parties in 2008 lacked national followings. The middle class *Un Nuevo Tiempo* (A New Time) had some appeal to unionized workers, especially in the petroleum industry, and emerged as the strongest political force in the western state of Zulia. Manuel Rosales (the leader of Un Nuevo Tiempo) attempted to build the party into a national force following his defeat in the presidential election of 2006. This effort was largely unsuccessful. In December 2008 Rosales was elected Mayor of Maracaibo, but soon afterward President Chávez forced him into exile.

The second important opposition political party, *Primero Justicia* (Justice First), attracted young Catholics who had become disillusioned by the prolonged internecine warfare between the second generation leaders of COPEI and the party's founder, Rafael Caldera. Initially Primero Justicia attracted a broad spectrum of Catholic youth from the middle class of Caracas, Barcelona, and some affluent neighborhoods in cities of the Central region. Before long, however, the party's elitist clerical orientation and bias toward Caracas reduced its appeal.

The third important opposition political party, *Proyecto Venezuela* (Project Venezuela), depended on the once-dominant COPEI political organization in the industrial state of Carabobo. After his unsuccessful run against Hugo Chávez in the 1998 presidential election Proyecto Venezuela founder Henrique Salas Römer passed control of the party to his son, Henrique Salas Feo. In spite of winning the governorship of Carabobo in the regional elections of November 2008, Salas Feo has been unable to expand Proyecto Venezuela beyond the boundaries of his native state.

In summary, the Venezuelan system of political parties is fluid. Little remains of the strong two-and-a-half system of institutionalized political parties that dominated between 1970 and 1998. During that time three-quarters of Venezuelans identified with either AD or COPEI. As of mid-2009 the PSUV controlled most electoral offices, although the party depended on funding from the national government as well as organizational manpower on the Francisco Miranda Front (whose first loyalty is to the person of Hugo Chávez), and it lacked leaders of note apart from Hugo Chávez. The opposition political parties were no less personalistic than the PSUV. Unlike the PSUV, however, opposition political parties lacked a national presence. Thus, in a little more than a decade Venezuela has gone from boasting one of the strongest systems of competitive political parties in Latin America to having one that is feckless and subservient.

Interest Groups

Bolivarian Venezuela is less supportive of demand-making by organized interests than was the Punto Fijo polity. Hugo Chávez has stated on more than one occasion that he views the checks and balances of liberal democracy as a smoke screen that allows the upper and middle classes to perpetuate their domination. Chávez's advocacy of "direct democracy" reflects his populistic personalism and affinity for Rousseau. Nevertheless, some institutional and associational interest groups retain influence.

The military, along with the church and the landed elite, dominated Venezuela from independence until General Pérez Jiménez fled the country on January 23, 1958. The provisional junta that replaced him faced nationwide strikes supported by business, labor, and other groups demanding civilian political rule. Confused and dispirited, the army acquiesced to the election as president of its nemesis, Rómulo Betancourt. The Betancourt government endured threats from right-wing traditionalists and an insurgency mounted by leftists. The counterinsurgency effort that defeated the guerrillas forged a bond between the armed forces and civilian democratic leaders. Until the urban riots of February 1989, this bond remained a formidable obstacle to direct military intervention in politics.

After 1989 the armed forces could not be depended on to make demands through constitutional channels. Instead, they became institutions that, under conditions judged favorable by the officer corps, might intervene directly in politics. There are several reasons for this transformation. First, simmering frustration with party-based governments' management of the economy made violent protests increasingly common, and the last two Punto Fijo governments called on the army to assist the police in preserving order on several occasions. Second, the armed forces faulted liberal democratic governments for not maintaining police capabilities, and this raised questions about how budgets had been spent. The experience of using force against protesting civilians led many in the military to question their support of an unpopular, party-centered regime dominated by gerontocracies that appeared unscrupulous and isolated.

Finally, as suggested earlier, the opulent lifestyles of young politicians and businessmen during the 1990s, when contrasted with the economic difficulties experienced by junior officers, created resentments in the armed forces against the political and economic establishment. President Pérez sought to address these grievances after the unsuccessful coups of February and November 1992, and in early 1994 President Caldera made his own special overtures to the officer corps. Neither was able to return the armed forces to their earlier regime-supportive stance.

In the first years of the Chávez government the military was divided into three factions. One supported the Bolivarian Revolution, another was vehemently opposed, and a third argued that the armed forces should remain apolitical and focus on professional enhancement. President Chávez, however, was determined to transform the armed forces into a pillar of support for his regime. He also saw the bureaucracy as corrupt and incompetent. Correspondingly, he launched Plan Bolívar 2000, an improvised departure that funneled funds for infrastructure maintenance and development through regional military garrison commanders. Some officers opposed this policy, while others used the opportunities that accompany the construction of public works for personal enrichment. In general, Venezuela's physical infrastructure deteriorated under military stewardship.

Early in 2002 factions in the military opposed to President Chávez viewed with increasing concern his leftward drift. On April 11, 2002, a march in Caracas by hundreds of thousands of government opponents ended in shootings that killed and wounded more than fifteen individuals. Opposition leaders and government security forces blamed each other. This incident became an excuse for military officers opposed to President Chávez to remove him from office. They replaced Chávez with Pedro Carmona Estanga, president of the umbrella business confederation, Venezuelan Federation of Chambers of Commerce (*Federación de Cámaras y Asociaciones de Comercio y Producción de Venezuela*, FEDECAMARAS). However, the perpetrators of the coup could not agree on how to organize a government. Disillusionment and confusion gave supporters of President Chávez the opportunity to regroup. In less than forty-eight hours factions loyal to the president took control and returned him to the presidency.[11]

Since the coup of April 11 President Chávez has never trusted the armed forces. As a result, not only did he purge officers suspected of having sympathized with the coup, he also marginalized all who were not seen as active supporters of the Bolivarian Revolution. In addition, he organized militias of reserves among unemployed slum dwellers and changed official military doctrine to take advantage of these reserves. On January 29, 2005, the secretary of the National Defense Council (*Consejo de Defensa de la Nación*) announced the adoption of a new military doctrine that gave priority to preparing for asymmetric warfare. This doctrine conceded that Venezuela could not resist a conventional invasion by the United States (now seen as Venezuela's most likely military opponent). However, it held out the possibility that once invaders had landed and occupied territory, the newly formed militias could mount an insurgency that would turn the tide. This doctrine also gave the government a national security rationale for strengthening forces composed of individuals from strata most supportive of the president.

On July 31, 2008, acting under authority given to him by the National Assembly, President Chávez promulgated a new Organic Law of the Armed Forces. The renamed *Fuerza Armada Nacional Bolivariana* (Bolivarian National Armed Forces) boasted a strengthened chain of command that allowed the president more direct control over all four services. The law also enshrined protection of the Bolivarian Revolution as a primary obligation of the armed forces. Each service was now to be composed of three basic kinds of units: combat, logistic, and intelligence. In addition, the law gave formal recognition to the Bolivarian National Militia in which the entire population is required to serve at the discretion of the president. This reorganization appears to have reduced the combat capability of Venezuela's armed forces, as was demonstrated during the crisis with Colombia in March 2008. At that time President Chávez ordered eight thousand troops to the Colombian border as a demonstration of his outrage over President Álvaro Uribe's raid across the Ecuadorian border to attack units of the Colombian FARC. Many units never arrived at the border with Colombia, and those that did appeared in piecemeal fashion.

The Roman Catholic Church has long been an important political actor in Venezuela. In the 1960s, after a two-decade conflict with the AD party over state control of education, the Church reached an accommodation with AD.[12] However, accommodation did not prevent the ecclesiastical hierarchy from expressing its disapproval of corruption, decay in the judiciary, cronyism, inequality, and moral deterioration. The *Centro Guimilla*, a Jesuit think tank, leveled especially biting criticism at AD and COPEI in the 1970s and 1980s. After the urban riots of February 1989 and two unsuccessful coups in 1992, the Episcopal Conference issued public statements intended to put distance between the church and the neoliberal policies of President Carlos Andrés Pérez. Church leaders gave strong backing to the second Caldera government and maneuvered behind the scenes to effect a reconciliation of the president and the COPEI political party.

The bishops viewed the rise of Hugo Chávez with alarm, especially his reliance on advice from militant leftists whose antagonism toward parochial education predated the revolution of October 1945. Nevertheless, the ecclesiastical hierarchy took no official position in the referendum that approved the 1999 constitution that increased central government power. After the unsuccessful coup of April 11, 2002, relations between the ecclesiastical hierarchy and the government deteriorated. President Chávez opined on more than one occasion that the church had supported the coup, while influential clerics condemned government policies as undermining democracy. This led President Chávez into a brief flirtation with evangelical Protestantism. However, his enthusiasm for this option cooled when Rev. Pat Robinson, a well-known fundamentalist preacher in the United States, suggested on his *700 Club* television program that President Bush should use the Central Intelligence Agency to "take out" the Venezuelan leader. President Chávez responded with a novel strategy to weaken established religious interests. He imported *babalaos*, or shamans of the Santería religion from Cuba, and installed them in the shantytowns.

Private-sector interests in Venezuela are diverse, ranging from local agribusinesses to multinational manufacturers. During the Trienio (1945–1948), the revolutionary interlude between military dictatorships, businesspeople were united in their opposition to AD's militant Marxism with its emphasis on regulation and state intervention in the economy, but like the military and the church, the business community adjusted to Punto Fijo democracy and prospered.

Private-sector leaders anticipated developing similarly profitable arrangements with the Chávez government. However, as the Bolivarians revealed their sympathy for socialism, government-business relations cooled. When the president of the most important private-sector organization, FEDECA MARAS, agreed to serve as provisional president in the short-lived military government of April 2002, relations turned frigid. In 2007, following his re-election to a second six-year term as president, President Chávez nationalized a number of private enterprises, and the pace of nationalization quickened in 2008 and 2009.

Two hundred individual groups comprise FEDECAMARAS, but the institution is dominated by four pivotal interests: industry, trade, cattle-raising, and agriculture. Each possesses its own chamber: CONINDUSTRIA for industry, CONSECOMERCIO for commerce, FENAGAN for cattle-raising, and FEDEAGRO for agriculture. Because these key interests have different and sometimes conflicting priorities, the single-interest or intermediate chambers are as important as centers of political demands as FEDECAMARAS.

Multinational corporations have long been important players in domestic Venezuelan politics. Exxon, Royal Dutch Shell, and Gulf invested massively to make Venezuela one of the most important producers of petroleum. After President Carlos Andrés Pérez implemented the "Great Turnaround" in 1989, a torrent of foreign capital flowed into Venezuela from the United States and Western Europe. It then left almost as rapidly following the unsuccessful coups in 1992, and it returned in force in 1996, when the state petroleum company (*Petróleos de Venezuela*, PDVSA) signaled a willingness to accept overseas assistance to implement plans that would double Venezuela's oil production capability. Private foreign investment again fled in 1999 when newly inaugurated President Hugo Chávez voiced criticisms of profit repatriation and multinational corporations in general. However, Chávez did sign contracts with selected multinationals to exploit reserves of viscous petroleum in the Orinoco tar belt. In other matters of infrastructure development, such as the subways in Caracas and Maracaibo, President Chávez has contracted engineering firms based in Brazil, China, and elsewhere in the developing world.

Organized labor and peasants, two associational interest groups, played important roles in Punto Fijo democracy. As part of their strategy to wrest political power from the entrenched Andean cabal in the 1940s, AD and COPEI created labor and peasant organizations.[13] A third interest group, professionals, then fell under the domination of political parties in the 1970s. The leaders of all three groups were subject to party discipline during the liberal democratic era. Building on these controls, AD and COPEI exercised decisive power and influence over unionized workers, peasants, and professionals until 1999.

Following the approval of the 1999 constitution the leading labor organization, *Confederación Venezolano de Trabajo* (Venezuelan Confederation of Workers, CTV) opened negotiations with President Chávez, offering to eliminate the influence of AD and COPEI in their unions in return for recognition by the national government. This was not acceptable to the President, who began to organize his own Bolivarian trade unions. Consequently, the CTV joined with FEDECAMARAS and other opponents of the government in a series of strikes that convulsed the country in 2002 and 2003. In March 2003, after breaking the final and most virulent strike, President Chávez discharged sixteen thousand workers belonging to the Federation of Petroleum Workers (FEDEPETROL), as well as six thousand of the petroleum company's elite staff. Contracts with other CTV unions were simply ignored. The CTV carries on, but as a shadow of its former self. Furthermore, government-supported Bolivarian trade unions smother all competitors with the help of Chavista operatives from the Francisco Miranda Front.

Until the mid-1980s Venezuela's urban poor were only weakly integrated into the Punto Fijo system. This was largely because the political parties having the greatest appeal to slum dwellers during the decade of regime consolidation (the 1960s) lost out to AD and COPEI, both of which treated the shantytowns with benign neglect. The demand-making structures that eventually crystallized among shantytown inhabitants were different from the party-dominated associations of workers, peasants, and professionals. Initially, the most important organization to represent Venezuela's urban poor was the Center at the Service of Popular Action (CESAP). During the 1980s CESAP settled on the strategy of working within the existing party-centric regime. This choice undermined the legitimacy of CESAP when the second Pérez and Caldera governments adopted neoliberalism.

The perception of having been abandoned by AD and COPEI drove the support that slum dwellers gave Hugo Chávez Frías in the presidential elections of 1998 and 2000. Soon after taking office in 1999 President Chávez began organizing shantytown residents into *Círculos Bolivarianos* (Bolivarian Circles). These Circles were multifaceted. On the one hand, they taught young women to sew, manage small businesses, and provide needed child care. On the other, they assisted the government in identifying its supporters and discrediting opponents.

Círculos Bolivarianos remained active in many locales throughout the first decade of Bolivarian rule. However, other revolutionary organizations such as the electoral *Comando Maisanta*,[14] the irregular asymmetric warfare battalions, and the Communal Councils have become the cutting edge of the regimes' hold on the shantytowns.[15] In 2005 the addition of resource-allocating *misiones* (missions), administered directly by President Chávez, gave the government a broad range of geographically dispersed institutions to control activity in slums and reward supporters. In July 2007 Chávez appointed a commission that proposed constitutional reforms for the purpose of streamlining the potpourri of resource-allocating bureaucracies. As discussed earlier, these arrangements, packaged as constitutional reforms, were narrowly defeated in the referendum of December 2007.

Government Structures

Venezuelan state organization has been in flux since 2000, when the shift toward institutions envisioned by the constitution of 1999 began. That document provides for a presidential system with five separate branches of government: the executive, the legislative, the judicial, the electoral, and the people's power. Twenty-three states and a capital district comprise a polity in which the President has recentralized many powers that in 1989 and 1993 were distributed by law among the regional and local governments. The 1999 constitution envisioned a Federal Council of Government, presided over by the vice president, which would oversee subnational governments. Because President Chávez did not want to deal with an institution in which regional and local leaders could articulate their interests freely, he never established the Council. In January 2007 he advanced the idea of dividing Venezuela into five regions. A vice president, named by the president, would administer each region, with regional governors and mayors reporting to the vice president. The details of this plan are unknown at the time of this writing. However, the approach is in keeping with the centralistic tradition of Hispanic and Roman Catholic constitutional development.

Venezuela's current national executive is more powerful than its predecessor, which when compared with other liberal democracies, was a strong presidency. Chosen by a plurality of the popular vote and eligible for indefinite reelection to terms of six years, the President presides over the national government. He is commander-in-chief of the armed forces and appoints a cabinet, composed of twenty-eight ministers (as of May 2009). The president can freely remove members of the cabinet and create new cabinet positions. The current constellation of cabinet ministries reflects the Bolivarian Revolution's preference for state control. They range from the powerful Ministry of Interior Relations and Justice to the recently created Ministry of Tourism. The president also is empowered to name and remove the vice president at will, who assumes the presidency if that office falls vacant.

The use of numerous Misiones to allocate resources is a unique feature of the current national executive. After the unsuccessful military coup of April 2002 President Chávez began establishing Misiones, which he oversaw personally. For example, the Ministry of Education was bypassed to establish special programs for literacy (*Misión Robinson*), accelerated high school degree programs (*Misión Ribas*), and revolutionary Bolivarian Universities (*Misión Sucre*). Other high-profile Misiones include programs that provide public health services to the slums (*Misión Barrio Adentro*) and distribute food to the poor at subsidized prices in popular markets (*Misión Mercal*). There is even a mission to construct socialist cities, *Misión Villanueva*. In July 2009 the official Web site of the Venezuelan government listed twenty-seven such Misiones. The Misiones budgets are closely guarded, although to fund them the president can draw freely on the more than US$31 billion that the Venezuelan government is estimated to hold abroad.

The 1999 constitution substituted a unicameral National Assembly for the bicameral Congress that under the 1961 constitution was the font of central government lawmaking. However, this National Assembly has less autonomy and fewer prerogatives in relation to the national executive than its predecessor, which in some measure reflects the disrepute into which Congress had fallen at the end of the Punto Fijo era. The 1999 constitution allows the president to dissolve a recalcitrant National Assembly and call for new elections. In addition, legislation can be introduced into the National Assembly from seven sources: the national executive, the Delegative Commission of the National Assembly, any three members (Deputies) of the National Assembly, the Supreme Tribunal, the Electoral Power, the Citizen's Power, and by petition bearing the signature of 0.1 percent of registered voters.

When the first National Assembly was elected in the mega-elections of July 31, 2000, the MVR and its allies gained roughly 55 percent of the seats. The second National Assembly, elected in 2005, has 167 members. Each state, regardless of population, has at least three deputies. In a departure from tradition, the Amerindian community elected three deputies. Deputies were elected in a mixed system for terms of five years and, following the referendum of February 15, 2009, are eligible for indefinite reelection. Sixty percent of each state's deputies come from single-member, winner-take-all districts, and 40 percent are elected on the basis of proportional representation by party list. The opposition abstained from the 2005 elections for the National Assembly, which allowed the MVR and allies of President Chávez to capture all 167 seats. The Assembly itself is presided over by a president with help from two vice presidents. Proposed changes to the electoral law would increase the proportion of deputies to be chosen in single-member, winner-take-all districts for the 2010 National Assembly elections.

The 1999 constitution placed the Supreme Judicial Tribunal at the apex of the judicial system. Like its predecessor, the Supreme Court, the Supreme Judicial Tribunal meets in several kinds of "chambers": plenary, political-administrative, electoral, and ones that deal with civil, penal, and social matters. The National Assembly elects justices to the Supreme Tribunal for terms of twelve years and they cannot run for reelection. During their term in offices the constitution prohibits justices from engaging in partisan political activity. Indeed, drafters of the 1999 constitution went to great length to shield the entire judiciary from the influence of political parties. Initially the twenty Supreme Judicial Tribunal justices enjoyed limited autonomy, and in several chambers opponents of President Chávez had the majority. After the 2004 Recall Referendum failed to remove President Chávez he increased the number of justices by twelve. The National Assembly then elected individuals as justices who have rubber-stamped his positions. Finally, the constitution of 1999 established separate courts for the military. This practice has its roots in Castilian tradition of the military *fuero* (right), which shields members of the armed forces from being tried by civilian courts.

The 1999 Constitution established the Electoral Power as a separate branch of government in reaction to domination of the Supreme Electoral Council (CSE) by political parties. During Punto Fijo the CSE funded the political parties and their election campaigns. The CSE also oversaw tabulation of the votes at local polling places prior to the transfer of ballots to a central location by the armed forces. In some polling centers only AD and COPEI had observers, and evidence exists that on occasion the two divided among themselves the votes of third political parties where those parties had no observers. The worst excesses of this kind occurred in the 1993 national elections, but five years later the reorganized CSE eliminated these problems by mobilizing a random sample of citizens as poll watchers. Under the 1999 constitutional regime the Supreme Electoral Tribunal has supervised all elections, and most observers agree that voting has been free and ballots have been counted accurately. However, the Tribunal has refrained from intervening in disputes during electoral campaigns when opposition parties charge that the government is assisting government supporters.

The Citizen Power, a second new branch of government, was established in reaction to the widely held perception that during post-1958 democracy, government had become abusive and corrupt. The Citizen Power is a kind of ombudsman and watchdog. The maximum authority of this branch of government is the Moral Republican Council, an institution composed of three individuals: the public prosecutor (*Fiscal*), the national comptroller (*Contralor General de la República*), and an official known as the People's Defender. The People's Defender "promotes, defends and watches out for" constitutional rights and guarantees. By a two-thirds vote, the National Assembly designates the People's Defender, who serves for a single period of seven years. Like other institutions of the central government under Chávez, the People's Defender is highly responsive to the President's desires.

Policymaking

Policymaking in Venezuela is personalistic and fluid. After President Chávez's reelection on December 3, 2006, he quickened the pace of transformation to twenty-first century socialism. Voter rejection in December 2007 of the President's constitutional reform proposals slowed the pace, but it picked up following voters' approval of indefinite reelection for the president and other elected officials on February 15, 2009.

Since then the assessment of policies based on their capability to advance the Bolivarian Revolution as defined by President Chávez has intensified. Equally important and predating the current regime is the availability of income from petroleum to implement preferred policies. For example, in 2004 petroleum income soared, so President Chávez expanded the role of the state. Other salient characteristics of Venezuelan policymaking include the Hispanic tradition of centralized and hierarchical authority, nationalism, and influences from abroad, especially the North Atlantic. These characteristics shape the four central issue areas of policy: service delivery, economic development, public order and safety, and foreign and national defense.

Service Delivery Policy

Service delivery immediately and directly affects quality of life, and its diverse components include housing, infrastructure development, health, sanitation, food, environment, social security, education, urban development, culture, and transportation. Until the revolution of 1945 only the upper class enjoyed access to quality services, and one of the most attractive dimensions of the AD's early program was its promise to use the state so as to extend high-quality services to all. The making and implementation of service delivery policies as Venezuela transitions to "Twenty-First Century Socialism" is fluid and often confused. As of 2009 it was centered in five kinds of institutions: ministries of the national executive, regional governments, municipal bureaucracies, and corporations managed by the state, and the Misiones. Eliminating duplication in the area of service policy delivery is one of the most important challenges facing the Bolivarian regime.

Economic Development Policy

Economic development encompasses activities that expand the capacity to produce goods and commodities for internal consumption as well as for export. Its impact on quality of life, although just as important as service delivery, is less immediate and direct. Like service delivery policy, economic development policy's issue areas are highly diverse, including mineral extraction, industry, commerce, finance, and planning. Venezuela's private sector coexisted with AD and COPEI governments between 1958 and 1990, even though the party elites and business leaders remained suspicious of each other. Throughout the Punto Fijo years governments reserved large areas of the economy for state enterprises. In the neoliberal decade of the 1990s Presidents Pérez and Caldera privatized many important public entities. Hugo Chávez's 1998 presidential campaign suggested that he would end the most flagrant abuses of the new economic order rather than change it. As of mid-2009, however, only three of Venezuela's top thirteen companies remained in private hands.

Venezuelan mineral extraction, despite the importance of gold, iron, and bauxite, revolves around petroleum. Nationalization of the multibillion-dollar oil industry, the product of a broad national consensus, occurred on January 1, 1976. To manage and coordinate the newly nationalized petroleum industry, the government created Petroleum of Venezuela (*Petróleos de Venezuela*, PDVSA), a state corporation attached to what is now the Ministry of Energy and Petroleum. One of President Chávez's first decisions was to replace the president of PDVSA with an individual from his inner circle. In early 2003, when PDVSA workers and executives sided with demonstrators seeking to remove the President, he discharged almost nineteen thousand PDVSA employees. PDVSA production of petroleum fell and has remained at almost 20 percent below the level attained prior to the dismissal.

With PDVSA in turmoil the government looked increasingly to petroleum from the concessions given to multinational companies for exploitation of the Orinoco Tar Belt's heavy reserves. These concessions themselves became controversial when the soaring price of petroleum allowed the companies to profit mightily from their activities. In 2007, when the Venezuelan government increased the tax rate on these profits, Exxon-Mobile and Conoco-Phillips rescinded their concessions. However, other multinationals remained, and ample income from petroleum sales enabled President Chávez to fund his Misiones through the previously discussed term-limits referendum on February 15, 2009.

Finance and commerce are issue areas that involve especially intensive public-sector/private-sector interaction. The Ministry of the Treasury and the Central Bank set the broad financial parameters within which governments pursue economic development. The 1999 constitution gave the national executive limited authority to intervene in the Central Bank, but President Chávez has pushed intervention far beyond what was envisioned by the constitution's framers. On July 3, 2009, he assumed control of the influential Spanish-owned *Banco de Venezuela*. Combined with other state banks, this purchase gave the government control over about 21 percent of deposits, 16 percent of loans, a payroll of 15,000 employees, and 651 bank branches.

Public Order and Safety Policy

Public order and safety policy are comparatively homogeneous and revolve around the recently consolidated Ministry of Interior and Justice. This ministry serves as the president's right hand in exercising political control. It also oversees the National Identification Service, policing, and the Office of Immigration. In the Bolivarian Republic, as during the Punto Fijo era, the president gives this ministry to one of his closest political confidants.

Responsibility for public order leads to the Interior Ministry's being entrusted with control of a national police force, called the Directorate of Intelligence and Prevention Services (DISIP). The director of DISIP, although under the minister's direct supervision, has unhindered access to the president. Popularly referred to as the political police, DISIP is responsible for gathering political intelligence, safeguarding political order, supervising foreigners within the country, and, in coordination with the National Guard, narcotics control. The National Guard operates as a second national police force; in rural areas it is the most important agent for law enforcement and it patrols the borders and the coast. A third national police force, the Technical and Judicial Police (*Policía Técnica Judicial*, PTJ), is charged with protecting the rights and liberties of citizens. It resembles the U.S. Federal Bureau of Investigation in purpose, and it has primary responsibility for criminal investigation and the arrest of suspects. In the aftermath of decentralization legislation in the early 1990s, governors and mayors created important subnational police forces. A new "organic" Law of the Police proposed by President

Chávez in April 2009 would give control of these forces to the Ministry of the Interior and Justice.

National Defense and Foreign Policy

Foreign and defense policymaking is centered in the ministries of Defense and Foreign Affairs as well as in the institutes and state entities attached to them. The Ministry of Energy and Petroleum, because of Venezuela's heavy dependence on international petroleum markets, also plays an important role in foreign policy. The focus here is on traditional national and foreign policy concerns: defense of the frontiers, control of the national territory, relations with foreign powers, and an array of nonpetroleum international economic issues.

National Defense.   Despite substantial overlap in the assigned tasks of the ministries of Defense and Foreign Affairs, coordination between them was minimal until the 1980s. The most important explanation for this shortcoming is that, since independence, the critical missions of the armed forces have been internal. Presidents Rómulo Betancourt (1959–1964) and Raúl Leoni (1963–1968) strengthened relations between AD and the military during their successful campaigns against leftist insurgents. Subsequently, until the ascent of Hugo Chávez, the primary mission of the military was to exercise control over the national territory in a manner that discouraged dissidents from waging guerrilla warfare. Furthermore, the armed forces seldom attracted individuals belonging to the economic and political elite. All four branches (Army, Navy, Air Force, and National Guard) provided a path for upward mobility. The officer corps attracted middle- and working-class youths, while peasants and shantytown residents filled the enlisted ranks.

The 1999 constitution envisions unification of the armed forces under a single Chief of Staff.[16] It also attempts to minimize the capability of civilians to intrude into military affairs. President Chávez has selected key members of his cabinet from among his former comrades in arms; many regional governors elected under the banner of the PSUV are retired military. Since the military coup of April 11, 2002, President Chávez has purged the officer corps of individuals suspected of disloyalty. He has also imposed the doctrine of asymmetric warfare, in large part to justify the creation of popular militias as a counterweight to the regular armed forces.

On July 31, 2008, the new Organic Law of the National Bolivarian Armed forces entered into effect. This law committed the military to defending the Bolivarian Revolution and made the National Bolivarian Militia (*Milicia Nacional Bolivariana*) an integral part of the armed forces. The Militias, acting with the Defense Committees of the Communal Councils, are empowered to determine which citizens are "patriotic." The Organic Law also increased the president's authority over maneuver units of the armed forces and gave him the power to order any citizen to serve in the military. In summary this legislation transformed the military from a professional force at the service of the nation into the guardian of Hugo Chávez's Bolivarian polity.

Foreign Policy. Foreign affairs, also a constitutionally mandated presidential responsibility, center on the Ministry of Foreign Relations. During the Punto Fijo era presidents often selected prominent independents for the position of foreign minister as a way of building broad societal support. Over time AD and COPEI each formed a cadre of foreign policy experts. The professional foreign service was co-opted into these cadres, which also managed the Foreign Trade Institute (*Instituto de Comercio Exterior*, ICE). Established in the early 1970s, ICE oversees and stimulates Venezuela's nonpetroleum exports. President Chávez has appointed some of his most reliable collaborators to the position of Minister of Foreign Affairs. One of the most important charges given early appointees was to purge the foreign service of diplomats with longstanding ties to AD and COPEI.

Venezuelan diplomacy since the second government of Rómulo Betancourt (1959–1964) has sought to reduce the importance of relations with North Atlantic countries, but early successes were meager and fleeting. Cooperation within OPEC to set the price of petroleum acquired great importance during the 1960s, and it gave Venezuela an influential voice among producers of petroleum. In the 1980s coordination with other debtor countries in negotiating repayment terms with OECD-country banks became a priority. Both issues presented opportunities for Caracas to resurrect rhetoric associated with such anti-European and anti-U.S. themes as Latin American unity, international social justice, and Hispanic cultural superiority. President Hugo Chávez has taken these themes to new heights.

From the beginning Hugo Chávez voiced his unease with U.S. influence over Latin America in general and Venezuela in particular. Chávez clashed with President George W. Bush at the April 2001 Quebec summit over free trade in the Americas. He also opposed the U.S. invasion of Iraq in 2003 and took the lead in organizing UNASUR (the Union of South American Nations), a regional organization designed to resolve political and military conflicts in South America. UNASUR pointedly excluded the United States, and President Barack Obama's efforts to improve relations between Caracas and Washington have been largely unsuccessful.

Hugo Chávez excoriated Presidents Álvaro Uribe and Barack Obama for signing the treaty on July 16, 2009, which gave the United States access to three Colombian air bases to facilitate efforts to stop the flow of drugs out of South America. These bases were to substitute for the Manta facility in Ecuador that President Rafael Correa closed. Chávez charged that the presence of U.S. armed forces at Colombian bases could facilitate an invasion of Venezuela, and he brought these concerns to the August 28 meeting of UNASUR in Bariloche, Argentina. Brazil and Chile as well as Chávez's allies—Ecuador, Bolivia, and Argentina—did express concern over the basing agreement between Colombia and the United States but rejected calls for sanctions against Colombia.

The final high concern of Venezuelan foreign policy is relations with Cuba. Hugo Chávez's affinity and cooperation with Fidel Castro stands in sharp contrast to Venezuela's Punto Fijo–era policy. Chávez supports Cuba's communist regime through sales of petroleum at deep discounts. These sales have freed Fidel and Raúl Castro from accommodating to pressures intended to make Cuba more pluralistic as a condition for increased trade and investment from countries in the North Atlantic. Venezuela and Cuba also formed the Bolivarian Alternative for the Americas (*Alternativa Bolivariana para las Américas*, ALBA) trading group, which provides states opposed to the U.S.-supported Free Trade for the Americas Initiative an institutional home. Other members of ALBA include Ecuador, Bolivia, Nicaragua, Honduras, and Dominica.

Prospects

Venezuelan politics changed dramatically after the referendum of February 15, 2009. The removal of term limits on all elected officials set the stage for Hugo Chávez to acquire a degree of control not achieved since the days of Juan Vicente Gómez, and it led followers of the President with personal ambitions for national power to resign themselves to rule by Hugo Chávez for the foreseeable future. The opposition—harassed, marginalized, and subject to selective thuggery—grows ever more desperate. Nevertheless, the Venezuelan president's legitimacy rests in large measure on his ability to win elections. Of this he is acutely aware. The playing field that he offers opposition candidates is so unbalanced that only under extraordinary circumstances do they stand any chance of more than isolated successes.

Several policies sustain the unbalanced playing field that favors President Chávez and his supporters. First, he dispenses ample patronage in ways that allow him to gain and retain clients. During Chávez's rule the national government has received US$475 billion in revenue from exports, largely from the sale of petroleum. This enabled him to fund missions to aid the poor, purchase the loyalty of a cadre of professionals (the *Boli-burguesía*), and proceed with the nationalization of Venezuela's largest private corporations. It also allowed the Venezuelan president to assemble a coalition of states to confront the United States in the international arena. Finally, on the chance that Venezuela's economy undergoes catastrophic collapse, Chavista rallies, such as those supporting the February 15, 2009 referendum, feature militants chanting, "Even though we might be hungry and out of work, we will stick with Chávez."

Media control and restrictions on freedom of speech have also played an important role in President Chávez's campaign to control the political arena. In June 2007 he took control of Radio Caracas Television (RCTV), the country's most important opposition channel. After the December 2008 elections for governors and mayors the government began proceedings against *Globovisión*, the only remaining television station that criticized his rule. Soon afterward Minister of Public Works and Housing and Director of Telecommunications Diosdado Cabello began reviewing the operating credentials of 240 regional and local radio stations. On August 1, 2009, Cabello announced that the first group of 34 stations had ceased operation and other closures would follow.

On the same day Attorney General Luisa Ortega Díaz made known the text of the Law against Media Crimes that she would submit to the National Assembly within the week. Article 5 of the law stipulated that "Any person who discloses false news through a mass media outlet, causing serious disruption to public tranquility, panic or anxiety in the population, disruption of public order or a prejudice to the interests of the State, shall be punished with imprisonment from two to four years." Stunned opposition politicians, journalists, and academics proclaimed that the law amounted to thought control and ended any pretense that Venezuela was a democracy. The Attorney General replied that "it is necessary for the Venezuelan State to regulate freedom of expression [in the context of] our legal instruments."[17]

To summarize, Venezuelan liberal democracy died in the aftermath of the unsuccessful recall referendum of August 2004. Electoral caudillismo, a process by which the president uses his charisma to win elections and curtail individual liberties, undid the direct democracy that was taking shape between 2004 and 2008.[18] However, it must be kept in mind that widespread support exists for President Chávez's efforts to improve the lot of the poor. Furthermore, many applaud his success in challenging U.S. influence in region. Given the prevalence of poverty, the number of people who believe that President Chávez's policies have empowered the masses, and the difficulties that liberal democracies have experienced in reducing poverty, the prospects of Venezuelan-type populism are as good as those of the so-called third wave democracies.[19]

Suggestions for Further Reading

Alexander, Robert J. *Rómulo Betancourt and the Transformation of Venezuela.* New Brunswick, NJ: Transaction Books, 1992.

Canache, Damarys. *Venezuela: Public Opinion and Protest in a Fragile Democracy.* Miami: North-South Center Press of the University of Miami, 2002.

Coronil, Fernando. *The Magical State: Nature, Money, and Modernity in Venezuela.* Chicago: University of Chicago Press, 1997.

Crisp, Brian F. *Democratic Institutional Design: The Powers and Incentives of Venezuelan Politicians and Interest Groups.* Stanford, CA: Stanford University Press, 2000.

Ellner, Steve, and Miguel Tinker Salas, eds. *Venezuela: Hugo Chávez and the Decline of an "Exceptional Democracy."* Lanham, MD: Rowman & Littlefield, 2007.

Friedman, Elizabeth J. *Unfinished Transitions: Women and Gendered Development of Democracy in Venezuela, 1936–1996.* University Park: Penn State University Press, 2000.

Gil Yepes, José A. *The Challenge of Venezuelan Democracy.* New Brunswick, NJ: Transaction Books, 1981.

Hawkins, Kirk A., and David Hansen. "Dependent Civil Society: The Circulos Bolivarianos in Venezuela." *Latin American Research Review* 51, no. 1. (2006): 102–32.

Karl, Terry L. *The Paradox of Plenty: Oil Booms and Petro-States.* Berkeley and Los Angeles: University of California Press, 1997.

Lombardi, John V. *Venezuela: The Search for Order, the Dream of Progress.* New York: Oxford University Press, 1982.

Martz, John D., and David J. Myers. *Venezuela: The Democratic Experience.* Rev. ed. Westport, CT: Greenwood Press, 1986.

McCoy, Jennifer L., and David J. Myers. *The Unraveling of Representative Democracy in Venezuela.* Baltimore, MD: Johns Hopkins University Press, 2005.

Nelson, Brian. *The Silence and the Scorpion: The Coup Against Chávez and the Making of Modern Venezuela.* New York: Nelson Books, 2009.

Trinkunas, Harold A. *Crafting Civilian Control of the Military in Venezuela: A Comparative Perspective.* Chapel Hill: University of North Carolina Press, 2005.

Zuquete, Jose Pedro. "The Missionary Politics of Hugo Chávez." *Latin American Politics and Society* 50, no. 1 (2008): 91–122.

Notes

1. President Chávez's speech before the National Assembly on July 25 is discussed at length in *El Universal,* July 26, 2009.

2. Venezuela's post–1958 democracy was popularly known as "Punto Fijo" democracy, the designation derived from the name of the house (belonging to Rafael Caldera) where party leaders signed a political pact to share power in the wake of the overthrow of General Marcos Pérez Jiménez.

3. Lisa Peattie, *Rethinking Ciudad Guyana* (Ann Arbor: University of Michigan Press, 1987).

4. John V. Lombardi, "Patterns of Venezuela's Past," in *Venezuela: The Democratic Experience,* rev. ed., eds. John D. Martz and David J. Myers (Westport, CT: Praeger-Greenwood, 1986), 7–21.

5. Judith Ewell, *Venezuela: A Century of Change* (Palo Alto, CA: Stanford University Press, 1984), 124–27.

6. Terry Lynn Karl, "Petroleum and Political Pacts: The Transition to Democracy in Venezuela," *Latin American Research Review* 22, no. 1 (1987): 63–94.

7. David J. Myers and Robert E. O'Connor. "The Undecided Respondent in Mandatory Voting Settings: A Venezuelan Exploration." *Western Political Quarterly* 36, no. 3 (1983): 421–33.

8. Moisés Naim, "The Launching of Radical Policy Changes, 1989–1991," in *Venezuela in the Wake of Radical Reform,* ed. Joseph S. Tulchin (Boulder, CO: Lynne Rienner, 1992), Chapter 4.

9. Other political parties played major roles in the Punto Fijo political regime, but until the elections of 1993, only the nominees of AD and COPEI had captured the presidency. For an excellent

overview of the evolution of Venezuela's system of political parties see José Molina, "The Unraveling of Venezuela's Party System," in *The Unraveling of Representative Democracy in Venezuela,* ed. Jennifer L. McCoy and David J. Myers (Baltimore, MD: Johns Hopkins University Press, 2004), chapter 8.

10. The official Web site of the PSUV is www.psuv.org.ve/. There are no scholarly accounts of the development of the PSUV available. A detailed description of the process that confirms with my personal observation is available at www.wikipedia.org/wiki/United_Socialist_Party_of_Venezuela.

11. Brian A. Nelson, *The Silence and the Scorpion: The Coup Against Chávez and the Making of Modern Venezuela* (New York: Nation Books, 2009).

12. A more comprehensive discussion appears in Daniel H. Levine, *Popular Voices in Latin American Catholicism* (Princeton, NJ: Princeton University Press, 1992), 65–91.

13. Two rival labor confederations, the Unified Center of Venezuelan Workers (CUTV, estimated membership eighty thousand) and the Confederation of Autonomous Unions (CODESA, estimated membership sixty thousand) provided alternatives to the CTV during post–1958 democracy.

14. President Hugo Chávez swore in members of the newly created Comando Maisanta on June 9, 2004. The Comando's purpose was to organize the president's supporters and take them to the polls so they could vote against his removal in the recall election of August 15, 2004. After the recall failed, the Comando continued to play an important role in the government's efforts to organize supporters and mobilize them on behalf of initiatives advanced by President Chávez.

15. Steve Ellner. "A New Model With Rough Edges: Venezuela's Community Councils," *NACLA Report for The Americas* (May/June 2009), 11–14.

16. Early in the Punto Fijo period, President Rómulo Betancourt replaced the centralized General Staff with a Joint Staff (Estado Mayor Conjunto), which was an advisory rather than a centralizing organ.

17. The Attorney General's speech before congress, when she introduced the Special Law against Media Crimes, is discussed and analyzed in El Universal (31 de Julio, 2009). For a useful examination of this speech in English, including the quote that appears in the text, see the August 4, 2009 edition of *Reuters Market Wire*.

18. For a useful discussion of electoral caudillismo, see David Close, "Undoing Democracy in Nicaragua," in *Undoing Democracy: The Politics of Electoral Caudillismo,* eds. David Close and Kalowatie Deonandan (Lanham, UK.: Lexington Books, 2004).

19. Coined by Samuel Huntington (*The Third Wave: Democratization in the Late Twentieth Century* [Norman: The University of Oklahoma Press, 1991]), the term "Third Wave Democracy" refers to the liberal democracies that replaced the bureaucratic authoritarian regimes that predominated in Latin America during the 1970s.

12

Uruguay

Balancing Growth and Democracy

Ronald H. McDonald and Martin Weinstein

Uruguay is the smallest of the South American republics, but the distinctiveness of its political experience and innovations far transcends its size.[1] It is perhaps best known today as a longstanding democracy that "failed," one that is now struggling to reaffirm and redefine its democratic traditions. However, it is also a country that in the nineteenth century created democracy out of chaos and translated its traditional corporatist values and realities into democratic institutions. It experienced a profound disillusionment with the modern premises of economic growth and stability as well as a period of escalating political instability and incremental military intervention. In 1985 Uruguay reestablished democratic government and politics, and since then it has been preoccupied with defining the meaning of "normalcy" in this new context.

Uruguay often has been viewed as a historical exception to the general pattern of politics in Latin America, an isolated instance of enlightened pluralistic politics in a region of corporatist authoritarianism. Uruguayans, in fact, have shared the same corporatist values as most of their neighbors but, almost uniquely, have shaped them into distinctive democratic processes and traditions. They have borrowed selectively from the experiences of Europe and the United States and, as necessary, made innovations to suit their own environment. Today Uruguay has reestablished its democratic heritage and revitalized

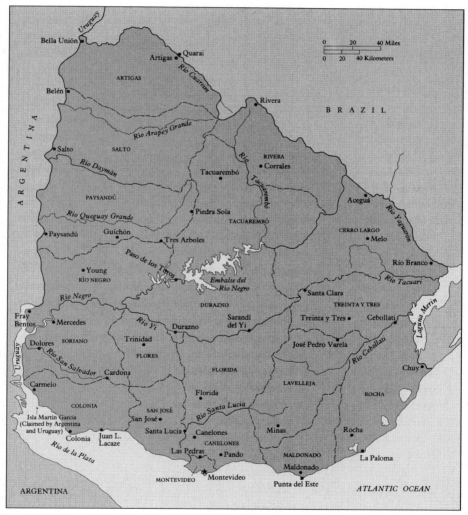

Bella Unión

Artigas • • Quarai

ARTIGAS

Río Cuareim

Belén

Rivera

A R G E N T I N A

Río Arapey Grande

Salto

SALTO

RIVERA

Río Daymán

Corrales

Tacuarembó

Río Tacuarembó

PAYSANDÚ

Piedra Sola

Río Queguay Grande

Aceguá

Río Yaguarón

Paysandú

Guichón

Tres Arboles

TACUAREMBÓ

CERRO LARGO

Melo

Paso de los Toros

Río Branco

Young

Embalse del
Río Negro

Río Tacuari

RÍO NEGRO

Río Negro

DURAZNO

Santa Clara

Fray
Bentos

Mercedes

TREINTA Y TRES

Laguna Merín

Río Yí

Durazno

Sarandí
del Yí

Treinta y Tres • Cebollati

Dolores

SORIANO

Trinidad

José Pedro Varela

Río Cebollati

Chuy

Río San Salvador

FLORES

Cardona

FLORIDA

Carmelo

LAVELLEJA

ROCHA

COLONIA

Florida

SAN JOSÉ

Río Santa Lucía

Isla Martín García
(Claimed by Argentina
and Uruguay)

San José

Minas

Rocha

Colonia

Santa Lucía

Canelones

Juan L.
Lacaze

CANELONES

MALDONADO

La Paloma

Río de la Plata

Las Pedras • Pando

Maldonado

Carmelo

MONTEVIDEO • Montevideo

Punta del Este

ATLANTIC OCEAN

ARGENTINA

0   20   40 Miles
0   20   40 Kilometers

B R A Z I L

Uruguay

URUGUAY

its historic values, and in the process it has cautiously explored new forms of organization and reevaluated the failed premises that eroded its traditional democracy previously.

The unique qualities of Uruguayan democracy have been little known—let alone understood—outside the country. Outwardly the country seems to have many similarities with other democracies, including regular and meaningful elections, a rule of law that respects and protects individual liberties and freedoms, and a policymaking process that is responsive to public opinion and scrutiny. Yet these qualities exist within a distinctively Latin American context, which recognizes and incorporates corporatist assumptions in the democratic processes, utilizing such familiar devices as co-optation, parity, coparticipation, and charismatic leadership. Many of the premises, which were the logic of the country's traditional democracy, proved unreliable, and in the mid-twentieth century Uruguay went through a period of sustained political and economic decay, violence, and ultimately authoritarian military rule.

The establishment of Uruguayan democracy originally was the result of an armistice between contentious landowners and provincial *caudillos* who came to recognize the potential for significant profits from increased exports. The politicians also saw democracy as a way to create political stability and gain political support from a rapidly expanding urban middle class committed to consumerism, consumption, and the benefits of state-provided services and welfare. Uruguayan democracy was based on an important economic assumption: Economic growth was inevitable, irreversible, and largely a spontaneous process that could subsidize the expanding and increasingly costly demands of a democratic society—an assumption common to other liberal democracies, including the United States.

The political ideas that underlay Uruguayan democracy were forcefully and explicitly articulated by its most influential statesman, José Batlle y Ordóñez. These included the belief that political stability was essential for prosperity and growth; that it would be achieved only by allowing free but balanced access to political power under a rule of law; that it could be sustained only by responding to the needs and demands of the masses; and that it must be protected from the pernicious influences of ambitious executives, politicians, and international opportunists while guaranteeing a strong role for the state. Batlle was also strongly anticlerical. He believed that the church and Catholicism were an organized threat to secular control and progress and that the church and state should be totally separated.

What is important about the Uruguayan experience is its relevance to other democracies whose processes, welfare, and stability are based on similar assumptions. The reexamination in Uruguay of fundamental democratic premises and values, particularly within a context of economic stress, was not an easy task, nor were the questions of blame and retribution for individuals and institutions that were culpable for the collapse of the democratic system. The concerns ultimately raised the issue of how normalcy would be defined within the new and reevaluated contemporary context. It is still unclear how much the result will borrow from the past, from neighboring societies in Latin America, or from new premises and new values. Uruguay has dealt with crises and dilemmas that would test any democracy, and for that reason its experience, both the universal and the parochial dimensions, merits careful evaluation.

Economic History and Social Context

Uruguayan economic history is particularly important for understanding the country's politics and government. Early in the twentieth century Uruguay became a largely middle-class country with one of the highest standards of living in Latin America, but it subsequently experienced a protracted economic decline that challenged and eventually helped destroy its democratic politics. Uruguayan exports failed to remain viable and competitive internationally; its domestic economy became heavily dependent on services rather than agricultural and industrial activities; its dependency on imports, particularly for energy, created massive financial problems; and its commitment to consumption rather than productivity distorted national priorities and created an escalating international debt and uncontrolled inflation. Uruguay's economic success and its subsequent decay were both influenced by international economic realities, most of them beyond the country's control.

Uruguay's wealth was generated by the export of traditional commodities, principally wool, mutton, lamb, cattle, and grains. The economy was too small to industrialize rationally or efficiently, and the effort to do so encouraged import-substitution-industrialization (ISI) and protectionist trade policies, which in turn created inefficient monopolies, both foreign and domestic, along with equally inefficient state-owned enterprises. The domestic economic situation was complicated by high production costs and profit expectations resulting from high-risk industrial ventures. It was also complicated by modern but unrealistic economic expectations of workers, who effectively organized and created politically influential labor unions.

By the end of the nineteenth century the worldwide demand for Uruguayan exports had grown dramatically. Traditional fibers like wool had not yet been challenged by synthetic ones, and by the mid-1870s the technology of refrigerated ships had made the export of fresh meat possible. The rural sector provided the capital on which the nation's development and wealth were based, thus subsidizing the industrial, commercial, and financial interests of the capital city, Montevideo. Export revenues allowed the importation of consumer goods demanded by the urban dwellers and helped supply the capital for Montevideo's own inefficient industrialization. Because the small-scale industrialization was inefficient, expensive, and monopolistic, industrial products could not compete in export markets or domestically in either quality or price with imports. However, the workers who the industries employed, concentrated in and around the capital city, grew in number and became more highly organized and politically active than their rural counterparts: For them the process of industrialization was popular. There emerged an inevitable conflict between the rural and urban interests in the country, one in which the capital city eventually prevailed by virtue of its greater population. The situation was a corrosive and dangerous one in which the affluence, growth, and consumption of the urban areas were being subsidized by the rural areas, whose economy was slowly deteriorating.

By the end of World War II the demand for Uruguayan exports had begun to decline. Other supplies of fresh meat were available in international markets, particularly for Uruguay's largest trading partner, Great Britain, and wool fibers were being replaced by synthetic ones. Rather than responding to these changes, the traditional rural economy continued producing the same export commodities, and so export revenues decreased within a context of shrinking demand.[2] Uruguay's failure to renovate its export economy and to recognize and respond to major shifts in international demand and new technologies set in motion a slow process of economic decay, which went largely unnoticed by the public until, after decades, its cumulative effects were clearly visible. The eventual political implications were disastrous.

At the end of World War II neighboring Argentina and Brazil, not to mention Mexico, were effectively industrializing at rapid rates, but industrial growth in Uruguay had slowed dramatically. The worsening imbalance between export revenues and import costs, an imbalance seriously aggravated by the sharp rise in the cost of imported energy in the 1970s, severely strained the country's financial solvency and encouraged two further and ultimately disastrous economic decisions. To sustain economic growth and financial liquidity the civilian governments expanded the money supply, inducing rapid and at times rampant inflation, while the country increasingly borrowed money from international sources to subsidize its worsening trade deficit.

The first policy eroded the confidence of Uruguayan investors and encouraged an accelerating capital flight along with decline in investment. It also destroyed the ability of the urban middle and working classes to save or maintain (not to mention improve) their living standards, which eventually alienated a substantial portion of the electorate and eroded confidence in the economic system. The second policy created a massive international debt, which by the mid-1980s was equal to about half the annual national per capita income. In the decade from 1977 to 1986 the level of international debt in Uruguay increased by more than 400 percent, one of the highest rates of increase in the hemisphere, and that was largely under a military government committed to economic austerity and willing to endure the response to unpopular policies.

However, economic decay was not an unpredictable, catastrophic experience that instantly devastated living standards and economic activity. It was slow, incremental, and entirely predictable, but the difficult political decisions required to reverse it were not or could not be made, even by a military government. As economic conditions deteriorated following World War II and a brief boom brought on by the Korean War, increasing demands were imposed on the government to provide compensatory services and subsidization, which in turn created more public spending and inflation, further discouraged domestic and foreign investment, and ultimately reinforced the general pattern of economic decline and the political problems associated with it. Although the country had achieved one of the highest standards of living in Latin America, Uruguay began to face apparently unsolvable economic problems, which continue to frustrate the nation's politics and politicians today.

The country's economic performance in the 1990s was strong by historical standards, thanks for the most part to the creation of the Southern Common Market with its significant increase in intraregional trade. Gross domestic product grew by 7.9 percent in 1992, 3.0 percent in 1993, and 6.3 percent in 1994. It then slid to a negative 1.8 percent in 1995, but moved back nicely with a 5.3 percent increase in 1996, 5.1 percent in 1997, and 5.3 percent in 1998. Brazil's currency crisis put Uruguay in recession in 1999. The big news on the economic front was that Uruguay's decades-old battle with inflation was finally close to victory. Inflation was only 4.5 percent for the first six months of 1998, making that year the first in memory with single-digit inflation. Since 1998, the inflation rate has continued to trend downward.

The government deficit was reduced to 1.4 percent of the GDP in 1997, with a reduction to 1.2 percent for 1998, but an increase in 1999 due to the recession. Net public foreign debt as a percent of GDP declined from a high of 44 percent during the debt crisis of the 1980s to a manageable 13 percent of GDP in 1996. Private investment in machinery and equipment more than quadrupled (admittedly from very low levels) from 1986 to 1996. However, Uruguay continues to have a poor investment and savings rate and an unfortunate record of attracting foreign investment.

Imports and exports grew at about 13 percent in 1996 and 1997, again reflecting increased trade with Argentina and Brazil. Only 7 percent of Uruguay's exports are destined for the United States, which only supplies 12 percent of its imports. On the other hand Argentina and Brazil together accounted for 46 percent of exports in 1996 and some 43 percent of imports, with Brazil alone the destination of over one-third of Uruguay's exports.

Unemployment in this security-conscious country remains stubbornly high, at about 11 percent of the workforce. Unemployment rose significantly in 1996, but strong economic growth in 1996–1997 reduced the average to 9 percent in the 2007–2009 period. Nevertheless, this relatively high unemployment rate has helped the left in terms of its credibility and criticism of the government.

When all is said and done the tiny Uruguayan economy, coupled with the state's historic commitment to welfare policies, allows a homogeneous population of some 3.2 million people to maintain the highest Physical Quality of Life Index (PQLI) in Latin America, according to the United Nations.

The Uruguayan people are themselves a distinctive mixture. During the colonial period the country had virtually no indigenous population. Most immigrants were from Spain and Italy, the latter primarily in the late nineteenth and early twentieth centuries. These were largely middle- and working-class people from urban areas, attracted to the prosperous and expanding Uruguayan economy, who remained in the capital city of Montevideo. They brought with them European political attitudes and economic expectations, which were absorbed into the country's party politics. Today about half the national population resides in the capital city. Rural life, perhaps because of its historic economic importance, spawned a mythology of its own centered around the gaucho, but the reality of rural life has little in common with the myths. During the period of economic decay following World War II and the Korean War there was a substantial migration of urban Uruguayans out of the country, many of them to Argentina and Brazil, a process that was reinforced by the turbulent political conditions of the 1960s and the subsequent military dictatorship.

Uruguay was one of the first nations in Latin America to make a major commitment to public education, with the result that a high level of literacy was achieved at a relatively early time historically. With literacy came high levels of political awareness and participation along with modern socioeconomic expectations.

Political Organization in Uruguay

Uruguay is a highly organized society with clearly defined interest groups and complex political parties, but the society is organized in organic rather than pluralistic ways. The framework for this organization was devised by José Batlle in order to achieve political stability out of the chaotic experience of civil wars, international intervention, and party-organized conflict.

The nineteenth century produced two political parties: the Colorado Party and the National Party, more commonly known as the Blanco Party (the parties originally were identified by the color of the brassards their adherents wore during armed confrontations). After generations of fighting for national hegemony, often with international provocation from Brazil, Argentina, and Great Britain, the possibility of economic prosperity, which came in the 1870s with the potential for a rapid expansion of exports, dramatized the advantages of cooperation rather than armed conflict for advancing the economic interests of both sides. The resolution of the civil conflict was promoted and eventually achieved by José Batlle.

Batlle was a descendant of a politically prominent and influential Uruguayan family who has produced many important political leaders. He was elected president twice, in 1903 and 1911, and he established the framework for modern Uruguayan politics and government. After defeating the Blancos in the last of the civil wars he established a political compromise with them based on the concepts of parity and coparticipation. Parity recognized the "legitimate" interests of the Blancos in the rural departments where they were strong, and Batlle all but ceded these departments to their control. He also accepted their participation in the national government, proportional to their share of the national vote, and allowed them a share of government patronage and revenues. The Blanco Party won only three subsequent national elections—in 1958, 1962, and 1989—and became virtually a permanent minority. Batlle's Colorado Party consistently attracted more voters nationally than the Blancos, but it was willing to share with the Blancos the exercise and benefits of power. The 1952 constitution went so far as to formalize coparticipation by awarding two of five positions on the boards of all state enterprises to the minority party.

Batlle designed an electoral system that incorporates parity and coparticipation both within and between the nation's political parties.[3] The Uruguayan electoral system regulates parties, elections, and the distribution of legislative seats, establishing *lemas* and *sublemas*, which are equivalent to parties and party factions. Lemas are composed of sublemas, factions that are the supporters or political machines of individual leaders. Anyone can form a sublema, acquire formal identification within a lema, and in effect create a personal political organization with a separate identity. The electoral strength of a sublema and its leader adds to the total vote of a lema, which in turn determines both lema and sublema legislative representation. From this process ambitious political leaders are thereby permitted into the political system and can exercise political influence proportional to their ability to attract votes. Their organizations are integrated into the larger lema, or party coalition, and they have a vested interest in the success of other sublemas, which they nonetheless campaign against because their representation is determined by their share of the cumulative vote for the lema. Presidential elections used to have the effect of combining a primary election with a general election.

Sublemas in Uruguay form the nucleus of political organization and encourage a clientele relationship between the party leaders and the voters.

Constituents with problems can request help from sublema leaders and their organizations, and in Montevideo sublemas maintain neighborhood clubs and organize campaigning. Through cross-endorsement, cross-listing, and a sharing of candidates, they form additional coalitions among themselves within the lemas, coalitions that constantly shift from one election to another.

The lema system is formalized by proportional representation, which allocates legislative representation according to the size of the popular vote. Campaign costs are also subsidized for sublemas according to the size of their vote. For the voter the system encourages a general identification with a lema and a personal identification with a sublema. The general electoral system also reinforces the Colorado and Blanco parties, which benefit principally from it, and it restrains the growth and success of new or smaller parties.

José Batlle built the Colorado Party into the majority political organization by mobilizing the urban classes of Montevideo and appealing to their interests. He proposed—and while president implemented—vast public programs of education, culture, welfare, and social security. He encouraged industrialization and resisted foreign penetration of the country's economy. Batlle advocated abolishing the presidency as an institution and replacing it with a rotating collegial executive, an idea he borrowed from Switzerland. His reasoning was that the dictatorships that were so common in Latin America were the result of an inevitable greed for power, and because one could not change human nature the only way to prevent dictatorships was to abolish the presidency and replace it with an institution that dispersed power. Batlle was by profession a journalist (he founded *El Día*, the largest daily newspaper in Montevideo), and he used his journalistic interest to further his political objectives, a process that continues today in Uruguay. Opposition to his leadership arose within the Colorado Party, and anti-Batllista factions (sublemas) were formed.

Batlle's ideas were visionary for their time: He initiated a modern welfare state in Uruguay long before it had been tried elsewhere. He was a consummate politician, but his political pragmatism was tempered by his idealism. Batlle believed he could eliminate instability and turmoil by expanding and organizing the political base of the country and by responding to the basic needs of the Uruguayan people.

In spite of his influence and success Batlle's ideas were based on two vulnerable assumptions, both of which proved to be erroneous and eventually contributed to the decay of Uruguayan democracy. The first was the assumption of continued economic growth and prosperity, a common perspective among industrializing nations during the nineteenth century. This assumption was drawn from the experiences of large nations, specifically Great Britain, France, Germany, and the United States, and it proved inappropriate for Uruguay. The second was the assumption that a collegial executive could prevent authoritarian governments. Uruguay did not experiment with a pure form of the collegial executive until the 1950s, perhaps the worst possible moment because the economy was in the process of decline and strong leadership was desperately needed. Ironically, for eight of the twelve collegial executive years the government was controlled by the Blanco Party, which was the first time in the twentieth century that it had prevailed in national elections. The experiment with a collegial executive, combined with the economic dilemmas for which no answers could be found, contributed to the political paralysis that encouraged a revolutionary group known as the Tupamaros and, ultimately, military intervention. The Tupamaros did not succeed in taking power, but they did provoke the military to do so.

There have always been minor political parties in Uruguay. One of the oldest was the Civic Union (UC), a conservative Catholic organization that provided an alternative to the prevailing tradition of anticlericalism that Batlle sponsored. By the 1960s several small parties combined with a dissident liberal sublema of the Colorado Party to form an electoral coalition, originally known as the Leftist Front of Freedom (FIDEL) and ultimately as the Broad Front (*Frente Amplio*). Included in the Broad Front were the Communist Party of Uruguay, the Christian Democratic Party, the Socialist Party, and List 99 of the Colorado Party, established by Zelmar Michelini. By combining the strengths of small parties in the 1971, 1984, and 1989 elections, the coalition posed a serious threat to the two traditional lemas, which in many ways are themselves political coalitions. Civic Union disappeared following redemocratization, having been replaced by New Space (*Nuevo Espacio*), an organization of radical Catholics and social democrats, some of whom had supported the Broad Front.

Like the political parties, economic interests have been well organized in Uruguay. The organizations include national associations of ranchers, business enterprises, and labor. Labor organizations emerged very early in Uruguay and were modeled after their European counterparts. The largest labor organization, the National Confederation of Workers (CNT), is Marxist, but its strength has not necessarily been translated into votes for Marxist parties. Organized workers were a principal target for Batlle's policies, and a large proportion have been Colorado Party supporters in spite of their union's orientation. The CNT was outlawed under the dictatorship, but a new organization, the *Plenario Intersindical de Trabajadores* (PIT), formed in the early 1980s and subsequently merged with the CNT after the reestablishment of democracy.

The political scenario that eventually produced a military dictatorship is a long and complex one. Military intervention occurred gradually, although by mid-1973 the military was fully in control of the government. The Tupamaro revolutionary movement, specializing in urban terrorism in the capital city, became a highly destabilizing influence during the 1960s. The government retaliated with a state of siege, massive arrests, torture, suppression of political leaders and groups, and censorship. Regardless, these actions were ineffective and even counterproductive. The military gradually assumed responsibility for the Tupamaro threat and brought the civilian institution under its control.

The military regime had both successes and failures in managing the economy, but the experience proved unpopular with Uruguayans and divisive for the military. No single military leader was able to consolidate his control, although one (Gregorio Álvarez) tried. The military response to the Tupamaros was brutal and, for Uruguay, unprecedented. The movement was crushed, but at exceptionally high costs to Uruguayan legal and political values. In fact the guerrillas were crushed before the military took control of the government in June 1973. The military ruled until 1985.

By the early 1980s the military leaders had begun to recognize the inevitability of restoring civilian rule and began looking for a way to maximize their continuing influence and minimize any retribution against them—individually and institutionally—after leaving power. They looked for inspiration to Brazil, whose officers were methodically and gradually returning that country's government to civilian control, and they were aware of the chaotic experience occurring in Argentina, where the military was leaving power in disgrace and facing civilian retribution.

The military regime decided to hold a referendum in 1980 on a new constitution that would protect the military's political influence, a referendum held under conditions of tight controls and censorship. Not only was the measure defeated, it was so decisively defeated that the regime had no choice but to acknowledge its failure. At that point military officers began negotiating with civilian political leaders—at least those they were willing to talk with—about conditions for a return to civilian rule. This change was formally achieved in March 1985 after elections the preceding November in which two of the major presidential contenders, Wilson Ferreira Aldunate of the Blanco Party and Liber Seregni of the Broad Front, were prohibited from being candidates.

The victor in 1985 was a Colorado Party candidate, Julio María Sanguinetti. Party voting and the resulting legislative representation were very similar to what they had been in 1971—the last election before the total military takeover. The Colorado regime encountered difficulties and controversies in its quest for normalization, and in the 1989 elections the Blanco party, for only the third time in history, prevailed, winning a plurality in the two legislative chambers and electing a president, the moderate Blanco leader Luis Alberto Lacalle. In 1994 the Colorados again won the presidency, but only barely, with the Blancos and the Broad Front close behind. National politics seemed to have been transformed by that election—perhaps permanently—to a three-party system.

Government Structure and Policies

Uruguay has a centralized government and is divided into nineteen departments, including the capital city of Montevideo. Virtually all decisions in the country are made at the national level. The 1966 constitution allows departments to elect local legislatures comprising thirty-one members and an *intendente*, the departmental administrative officer.

The president is popularly elected for a five-year term, and all elections in the country are held simultaneously. The legislature is bicameral, with ninety-nine representatives in the Chamber of Deputies, elected from districts, and thirty-one in the Senate, with the nation as a single district. All are elected by proportional representation. The current constitution was adopted in 1966 in the aftermath of the twelve-year experiment with a collegial executive. The legislature has considerable power and is organized through a system of committees.

In December 1996, after years of discussion, a reform was narrowly approved by the voters in a constitutional plebiscite. Under the new system each party can run only one presidential candidate, who will be chosen by primaries conducted in each party and ratified at a party convention. To be elected president the successful candidate must receive at least 50 percent of the total vote or face a runoff (*ballotage*) against his nearest competitor. Given the 1994 electoral results, such a runoff appeared all but a certainty for 1999, which in fact turned out to be the case, as discussed below.

This constitutional reform, which passed by the barest margin (50.3 percent) in a national referendum, represents a revolutionary change in the electoral system. In brief, the most significant features are as follows:

1. Although elections will continue to take place every five years, unlike the old system each party can now have only one presidential candidate.
2. A primary system was established to determine each party's candidate. The successful candidate must obtain at least 40 percent of the primary vote, with a 10 percent difference between the winner and the nearest competitor. If not, a party convention will choose the candidate.
3. To win the presidency the successful candidate must obtain an absolute majority of the votes. If not, a second round (ballotage) will take place between the top finalists. The first round will take place the last Sunday in October. If a second round is required, it will take place the last Sunday in November.
4. Local elections are now separated from national elections. Elections for intendentes of the nineteen departments and their local legislative bodies will take place in May of the year following the presidential and congressional elections.

There are several major implications of these reforms. First, the elected president will be able to claim majority support, a result unheard of under the old system. Second, voters may have to choose from candidates not of their party—or even of their liking—in the second round. Third, the primary system may help produce a real party leader as opposed to the historical norm of leaders of party factions. Finally, local governments will be elected at a different time from the national government, allowing ticket-splitting for the first time in history. This may help generate more power at the local level and, with it, more demands on the central government.

The Uruguayan economy is a distinctive mixture of private and public enterprises. Most of the economy is privately owned and managed, but about 20 percent of the gross domestic product (GDP) comes from state-owned companies. The largest of the state-owned monopolies is the *Asociación Nacional de Combustibles, Alcohol y Portland* (ANCAP), which refines petroleum and manufactures alcohol and cement. That agency alone accounts for 4 percent of the GDP. In the 1970s there was an effort to encourage international banking in Uruguay in order to provide "offshore" benefits to foreign banks and investors and stimulate economic development by encouraging new investments in the country. The policy was partially successful and was supported by the military regimes and the subsequent civilian governments.

What has historically given Uruguay the appearance of a welfare state has been not so much the direct participation of the government in the economy but the benefits provided by the government. Nowhere is this situation more apparent than in the social security system, which partially supports over 350,000 retired Uruguayans, a number equal to almost one-third of the active workforce. Low population growth means Uruguay has the highest proportion of retired persons of any Latin American nation, and this fact, combined with state-provided retirement benefits, creates an enormous financial burden on the people who are economically active.

The economic problems facing the Sanguinetti government in 1985 were formidable. The rural economy needed revitalization, both for export objectives and for food production; Uruguay had one of the highest per capita international debts in the region; national investment and economic growth were low; and the foreign trade situation was critical, with exports failing to provide sufficient revenues to pay for the energy, resources, and manufactured goods the country needed to import as well as to service its international debt. The only course the government had available was economic austerity, which is not a policy designed to cushion the return to civilian, democratic government. Besides these economic problems the erosion of public services and programs and a decline in real income and savings during the twelve years of military control had stimulated new demands, which were difficult for political leaders to ignore in the restored democratic environment, but even more difficult for them to meet. Economic performance during the Colorado administration of President Julio Sanguinetti was better than most expected, based on a policy of economic liberalism.

The next president, Blanco leader Luis Alberto Lacalle, continued that policy, significantly reducing the foreign debt, renegotiating debt payments, attracting new investment, and repatriating fugitive capital. Efforts to privatize state corporations, however, met considerable opposition, resulting in another plebiscite in 1993 that overturned with 72 percent of the vote a legislative decision to sell the state telephone monopoly (ANTEL). Plans to privatize the state natural gas monopoly, the state fishing corporation, and the state electric utility seemed at least temporarily moribund. After the vote, president Lacalle sarcastically observed, "Uruguay is a country that has been very happy for a very long time, and prefers a little with security rather than a lot with risk." Normalcy in Uruguay apparently meant public enterprises and service as usual, but Lacalle did cut Uruguay's high tariffs and joined the regional Southern Common Market, consisting of Argentina, Brazil, Paraguay, and Uruguay.

The Uruguayan military is professional by Latin American standards and, except for the recent dictatorship, it stayed out of politics for most of the twentieth century. During the dictatorship the size of the military grew at least 400 percent, and defense expenditures rose appreciably to a percentage of the GDP far exceeding that of Brazil, Argentina, or Mexico.

One of the principal objectives of normalization following redemocratization was to bring the military under the control of civilians, and the major issue was how to deal with military leaders who were responsible for human rights violations during the dictatorship. The issue plagued the Sanguinetti government, which was otherwise preoccupied with economic problems, and impeded the normalization of national politics. In late 1987 the legislature passed an amnesty bill that prevented prosecution of military and police personnel for human rights violations during the dictatorship. The legislation was very unpopular and provoked a petition campaign to hold a referendum on the legislation and the question of immunity. Public opinion polls showed that a majority of Uruguayans believed that military personnel did commit human rights violations during the dictatorship and that those who did should be punished. The petition campaign forced a referendum, which was held in April 1989, but the effort to overturn the immunity legislation failed by a negative vote of 53 percent. The majority of voters in Montevideo, however, voted in favor of the referendum. The fate of the disappeared continues to be an issue in Uruguayan politics.

The Uruguayan military never engaged in the mass killings for which their Argentine and Chilean comrades are so infamous. They did, however, arrest thousands and subject them to torture while also imposing a draconian rule on Uruguay's citizens from 1973 to 1985. The number of disappeared in Uruguay totaled a few dozen, with some 140 Uruguayans sharing the same fate in Argentina. The whereabouts of these individuals has never been clarified by the Uruguayan military. Children born to captive and subsequently disappeared Uruguayans are being sought by their relatives in much the same manner as the mothers and grandmothers of the Plaza de Mayo in Argentina. President Batlle was directly involved in this issue and planned to convene a commission to investigate and issue a report on the matter.

Many government leaders had felt that it was necessary to end the bitter recriminations and focus on the task of economic development. They also wanted to finesse an issue that might create a confrontation with military leaders and raise the possibility of another military intervention. Their efforts seem to have had the desired effects. Former Tupamaros have been largely reintegrated into national politics through the Broad Front. Their former leader, Raúl Sendic, died in Paris shortly before the plebiscite. The military has remained out of politics and under civilian control, but it is unclear whether its political influence has been permanently contained.

The first truly open national elections since the end of the military dictatorship were held on November 26, 1989. The Blanco Party won a plurality of the vote with 38 percent, and one of its leaders, Luis Alberto Lacalle, was elected president. Colorado candidates received less than one-third of the vote, and the Broad Front about one-fifth. The latter did, however, receive a plurality (34 percent) in the municipal elections for the city of Montevideo, electing a Socialist mayor, Dr. Tabaré Vázquez, and a majority of the municipal council. The failure of the Colorados to mobilize their traditional support in Montevideo was critical to their loss, but the results were ambiguous on the question of electoral realignment. At the least they seemed to imply that there would be a three-way party competition in the future.

National elections held in November 1994 confirmed that implication. Former President Julio Sanguinetti (1985–1989) barely won the election as the Colorado Party presidential candidate, and his party received only about 32 percent of the vote. The Blanco Party received somewhat more than 31 percent and the Broad Front, in a coalition known as the Progressive Front, only slightly less. The election signaled the end of the traditional two-party dominance of Uruguayan politics and a new balance between the three political forces. The Broad Front won the majority of Montevideo for the second consecutive time. After his inauguration in March 1995, President Sanguinetti stressed the need to reform the burdensome social security system in the country, in which there is now one retired person for every two workers, and thus consumes almost 40 percent of the national budget.

The 1999 party primaries proved no contest for the left, where Tabaré Vázquez easily won the nomination, and for the Blancos, whose former president, Luis Lacalle, also won handily but found himself with a bitterly divided party. The Colorado primary was hard fought, but in the end perennial candidate Jorge Batlle, son of one president and grandnephew of another, won the nomination.

In the first round of the elections the left, in a historic breakthrough, finished first with some 39 percent of the vote. The Colorado candidate finished second with 32 percent, and the Blancos finished a dismal third with only 22 percent. The Broad Front thus emerged as the single largest political force in the country, with high hopes of capturing the presidency in a runoff election with the Colorados. The Blanco leadership threw its support to Batlle, but no one could be sure that the rank and file would follow suit. Up until ten days before the second round all the polls showed Vázquez with a slight lead, but the final poll results showed that Batlle had pulled into a statistical dead heat. Uruguayans were both apprehensive and excited as election day approached. The undecided voters broke heavily for Batlle, who prevailed by 52 to 45 percent.

Uruguay began the new century with a wake-up call to its traditional parties. The voters indicated that although a majority still favors the rule of Colorados and Blancos, they wanted more creative solutions to the country's endemic problems of high unemployment and mediocre growth. They also wanted politicians who do not feel they are entitled to their power and get too comfortable as they share its spoils with friends and family.

Even before the events of September 11, 2001, it was a difficult year for Uruguay. President Batlle's first full calendar year in office confronted him with a worsening of Uruguay's economic situation exacerbated by an outbreak of hoof-and-mouth disease (*Aftosa*) that seriously disrupted Uruguay's meat exports. The government had hoped that 2001 would bring modest economic growth after two years of recession. Unfortunately, the continued devaluation of the Brazilian currency—the *Real*—and the deepening economic and political crisis in Argentina had adverse effects on both Uruguayan exports and tourism. With these internal and external conditions, unemployment skyrocketed to some 16 percent and the GDP was a negative 1.1 percent for the first half of the year. The only good news on the economic front was the continued low inflation rate of 4 to 5 percent.

Unfortunately, 2002 was a year of worsening economic crisis for Uruguay.[4] The financial meltdown in Argentina and the political and economic instability in Brazil caused by the election of the leftist candidate Luiz Inácio Lula da Silva (Lula) led to a deepening recession in Uruguay.

The most negative effect on the Uruguayan economy was produced by the freeze on deposits in Argentina caused by the collapse of the Argentine peso when that government abandoned its convertibility plan, which pegged its currency at one-to-one with the U.S. dollar. This forced many Argentines to withdraw dollars from their bank accounts in the traditionally safe haven of Montevideo. The subsequent collapse of two banks in Uruguay had many Uruguayans fearing for the safety of their banking system, leading them also to withdraw funds. The result was that in the first seven months of the year Uruguay lost 81 percent of its foreign reserves. The country's sovereign debt abruptly declined from investment grade to junk status during the same period. The Gross Domestic Product fell 7.8 percent in the first half of the year and was expected to contract some 10 or 11 percent for the year as a whole. Uruguay's GDP then declined some 20 percent since the recession started in 1999, and unemployment climbed to a record 17 percent. Inflation, which was a mere 3.59 percent in 2001, hit 24 percent by September of 2002 and was expected to go slightly higher by the end of the year.

President Jorge Batlle of the ruling Colorado Party tried to contain the damage but was obliged to accept the resignation of his Minister of the Economy, Albert Bensión, and replace him with the more highly respected Alejandro Atchugarry. The good will Batlle enjoyed in Washington helped him obtain a US$1.5 billion bridge loan from the United States in order to keep the banking system solvent until over US$3 billion in funds could arrive from the IMF, the World Bank, and the Inter-American Development Bank (IADB). Politically, the left appeared to be gaining strength as a result of the economic crisis. By October, polls showed that the leader of the leftist coalition, Dr. Tabaré Vázquez, would receive some 50 percent of the vote.

The following year proved no less difficult for the Uruguayan economy, but it was not as disastrous as the previous one. After a fall in Gross Domestic Product of over 10 percent in 2002 and a further decline of 6 percent in the first half of 2003, data for the second half pointed to enough economic strengthening to lead to the expectation that Uruguay would record no growth or a modest decline for the year as a whole. In May Uruguay successfully renegotiated its private debt with an innovative bond exchange that stretched out the repayment schedule, thus giving some breathing room for the last two years of the Batlle Administration and the first year of the next government. The banking system remained deeply depressed with nonperforming loans running at 25 percent at private banks and a staggering 50 percent at such key public institutions as the *Banco de la República* and the Mortgage Bank (*Banco Hipotecario*). The later institution lost US$1.1 billion in 2002.

Then, the year 2004 was an exciting and pivotal time in Uruguay. After nearly four years of sharply negative growth, the economy—aided by recovery in Argentina, strong growth in Brazil, and excellent commodity prices—grew by a robust 13.6 percent in the first half of the year. Unfortunately for the ruling Colorado Party, little of this positive macroeconomic performance filtered down to Uruguay's poor or to the middle class. Unemployment remained above 13 percent, and more than one-third of Uruguayans lived in poverty.

In this context the presidential and congressional elections that took place on October 31 marked a sea change in Uruguayan politics. Throughout the year the polls showed that the leftist coalition known as the Broad Front-Progressive Encounter was the largest party in the country. The question that remained was whether it would secure the 50 percent plus one vote it needed in order to avoid a runoff with one of the traditional parties—the Blanco Party (PN) or the Colorados. In the last two weeks before the election all of Uruguay's polls agreed that the socialists had reached the magical number needed to avoid a second round and that Tabaré Vázquez would be president. Dr. Tabaré Vázquez (known as Tabaré) was a sixty-four-year-old oncologist who had been the political leader of the Broad Front leftist coalition since he was their presidential candidate in 1994. Tabaré had been elected mayor (intendente) of Montevideo in 1989 in what was a breakthrough election for the left. A Socialist Party militant, Tabaré is photogenic and charismatic and has carefully juggled his coalition, which includes social democrats, democratic socialists, socialists, communists, and ex-Tupamaros.

In the election itself, the left received 50.4 percent of the vote, followed by the Blancos (34 percent) and the Colorados (10 percent). Vázquez assumed office on March 1, 2005. The historic victory by Vázquez and the left was seen by many to further strengthen the hand of Brazilian President Luiz Inácio Lula da Silva as he sought to turn Mercosur into the major voice for Latin American economic integration and the chief interlocutor with both the European Union and the United States in trade negotiations. Vázquez's victory was the latest example in South America of a move to the left and center-left.

Five years of leftist rule proved very positive for Uruguay. With the appointment of Danilo Astori as Minister of Finance, the Vázquez administration quickly signaled its willingness to accept the rules of international finance and investment. Early on Vázquez made it clear that he would keep an eye on budget deficits and inflation. The country enjoyed four years of exceptionally solid economic growth after the Broad Front victory, with average annual increases of some 7 percent. Inflation continued to be manageable during the same period. Exports boomed due in no small measure to the voracious appetite of China and India for raw materials and foodstuffs, which propelled a hugely successful economic recovery in Argentina's and Brazil's emergence as major economic players. The good times enjoyed in the Southern Cone also translated into a tourist boom for Uruguay. Foreign investments also grew exponentially, thanks in part to a billion dollar investment in Uruguay's forestry and paper pulp industry. This latter project, however, proved a bone of contention between the Uruguayan and Argentine governments.

President Néstor Kirchner fought the paper pulp plant all the way to the World Court. When Argentina lost there, the government continued to support environmental groups that closed the highways and bridges between the two countries, thereby causing an economic loss estimated at several hundred million dollars for Uruguay. In the end, the plant was completed and is functioning.

The Vázquez government took advantage of its majority in both Houses of Congress to pass legislation on same-sex partners' rights and health care coverage for poor children. The latter program was paid for by an increase in the minuscule personal income tax. This move proved deeply unpopular with the middle and upper class, even those members of these groups who were supporters of the left. The 2009 presidential and parliamentary elections, which are held for all positions only once every five years, will be an exciting affair. President Vázquez refused all efforts to have him run again under a constitutional reform proposal permitting him to serve consecutive terms. A hard fought primary in June 2009 resulted in the candidacy of the former Tupamaro leader José Mujica, head of the *Movimiento de Participacion Popular* (MPP) faction of the Broad Front. Mujica turned to his main rival, Danilo Astori, as his vice presidential choice, but this marriage was not made in heaven.

The Blancos (*Partido Nacional*) saw their primary won by ex-President Luis Lacalle who quickly asked his main competitor to join him on the ticket. The Colorado Party—the dominant party in Uruguay for much of the twentieth century—continued to fare incredibly poorly. Its standard bearer, Pedro Bordaberry, received only 17 percent in the October election. Lacalle received 29 percent, while Mujica led with 48 percent. Because Uruguay's constitution requires a majority for victory, a second round took place the last Sunday in November to decide a winner between the top two candidates. José Mujica won with 53 percent, and thus the leftist government continued.

Globalization, the Challenges for Economic Growth, and the Consolidation of Democracy

Globalization and regionalization under Mercosur has shown mixed results for Uruguay. The neoliberal model adopted by Blanco president Luis Lacalle (1989–1994) and Colorado president Julio Sanguinetti (1994–1999) brought decent growth and an explosion of consumer credit in the mid- and late-1990s along with a boost in tourism and trade with its two large neighbors, Argentina and Brazil. Unfortunately, Jorge Batlle, Colorado President from 2000 to 2004, presided over the worst financial crises since the depression after the 1999 Brazilian devaluation led to a financial meltdown in Argentina that, not surprisingly, spread to Uruguay. The economic crisis in the first three years of the new millennium was a key factor in the left's electoral victory.

China and India may have an increasingly important role to play in Uruguay's future. Already, the Indian software giant, Ta-Ta Consultancy, is guaranteeing a job to all computer science graduates in Uruguay. Additionally, China's huge demand for food and raw materials is already benefiting the Southern Cone, and Uruguay should get a piece of this export boom.

The 2008–2009 world financial and economic crisis has affected Uruguay, but not as dramatically as it might have in the past. Nevertheless, with little or no economic growth in 2009, the incumbent leftist government may pay the electoral price for an economic slowdown, which will certainly feel like a recession after the strong economic performance of the 2003 to 2008 period.

Uruguay has undoubtedly achieved democratic consolidation. The 2009 election is the seventh since democracy was restored in 1984–1985. Since then all three major political forces have enjoyed at least one term in the presidential office. Elections are clean, fully contested, and voter fraud is virtually impossible. As we move into the third decade since the 1973–1984 dictatorship, it is clear that the sadly unpleasant rupture of constitutional democracy was an anomaly for Uruguay's proudly democratic political culture and political history.

Suggestions for Further Reading

Campiglia, Nestor. *Los Grupos de Presión y el Proceso Político.* Montevideo: Arca, 1969.

Garcé, Adolfo. *Donde hubo el fuego: el proceso de adaptacion del MLN-Tupamaros a la legalidad y la competencia electoral (1985–2004).* Montevideo: Editorial Fin de Siglo, 2006.

Garcé, Adolfo, and Jaime Jaffe. *La era progresista.* Montevideo: Editorial Fin de Siglo, 2004.

Gillespie, Charles G. "Activists and Floating Voters: The Unheeded Lessons of Uruguay's 1982 Primaries." In *Elections and Democratization in Latin America, 1980–1985,* edited by P. W. Drake and E. Silva. San Diego, CA: Center for Iberian and Latin American Studies, Center for U.S.-Mexican Studies, Institute of the Americas, 1986.

Gonzales, Luis E. *Political Structures and Democracy in Uruguay.* Notre Dame, IN: University of Notre Dame Press, 1991.

Handelman, Howard. "Prelude to Elections: The Military's Legitimacy Crisis and the 1980 Constitutional Plebiscite in Uruguay." In *Elections and Democratization in Latin America, 1980–1985,* edited by P. W. Drake and E. Silva. San Diego, CA: Center for Iberian and Latin American Studies, Center for U.S.-Mexican Studies, Institute of the Americas, 1986.

———. "Uruguay." In *Military Government and the Movement toward Democracy in South America,* edited by H. Handelman and T. G. Sanders. Bloomington: Indiana University Press, 1981.

Kaufman, Eli. *Uruguay in Transition.* New Brunswick, NJ: Transaction Books, 1978.

McDonald, Ronald H. "Legislative Politics in Uruguay: A Preliminary Analysis." In *Latin American Legislatures: Their Role and Influence,* edited by W. H. Agor. New York: Praeger, 1971.

———. "Redemocratization in Uruguay." In *Liberalization and Redemocratization in Latin America,* edited by G. Lopez and M. Stohl. Westport, CT: Greenwood, 1987.

———. "The Rise of Military Politics in Uruguay." *Inter-American Economic Affairs* 28 (1975): 25–43.

———. "Uruguay." In *Political Parties and Elections in Latin America,* edited by Ronald H. McDonald and J. Mark Ruhl. Boulder, CO: Westview Press, 1989.

Rial, Juan. "The Uruguayan Elections of 1984: A Triumph of the Center." In *Elections and Democratization in Latin America, 1980–1985,* edited by P. W. Drake and E. Silva. San Diego, CA: Center for Iberian and Latin American Studies, Center for U.S.-Mexican Studies, Institute of the Americas, 1986.

Taylor, Philip B. "The Electoral System in Uruguay." *Journal of Politics* 17 (1955): 19–42.

———. "Interests and Institutional Dysfunction in Uruguay." *American Political Science Review* 58 (1963): 62–74.

Weinstein, Martin. *Uruguay: Democracy at the Crossroads.* Boulder, CO: Westview Press, 1988.

———. *Uruguay: The Politics of Failure.* Westport, CT: Greenwood, 1975.

Notes

1. The bulk of this chapter was co-authored with Ronald H. McDonald. The material from 2001 on is my (Martin Weinstein's) sole responsibility.

2. By comparison Argentina has been reasonably successful in adjusting its rural exports—balancing cattle and grain exports—as international demand and prices have changed.

3. The discussion in the next several paragraphs is adopted from my (Martin Weinstein's) entries on Uruguay in the 2002–2004 editions of the *Britannica Book of the Year.*

4. For a more extensive discussion see Ronald H. McDonald and J. Mark Ruhl, *Political Parties and Elections in Latin America* (Boulder, CO: Westview Press, 1989), 91–110.

13

Paraguay

Challenges in Democratic Consolidation

Paul C. Sondrol

The 2008 electoral defeat of the entrenched Colorado Party was a milestone in Paraguay's long trek toward democracy. After sixty-one years, Paraguay transformed from a hegemonic party system into a multiparty one manifest in the coalition government of President Fernando Lugo. Undeniable positive changes have occurred in Paraguay since the 1989 coup that ended the thirty-five-year dictatorship of Alfredo Stroessner, including widespread acceptance of free elections, enhancement of civil and political rights, and greater press freedoms. Nonetheless, these newer democratic values coexist with remaining authoritarian and praetorian proclivities, rampant corruption, and impunity that often prevail over justice and the rule of law. "Democratizing" Paraguay suggests many tasks yet undone.

Semitropical Paraguay is bordered by Argentina to the south and west, Bolivia to the north, and Brazil to the east. The country's name comes from the river dividing the fertile grasslands of the east from the drier Chaco region of the north and west. Slightly smaller than California (157,047 square miles) and located in the heart of South America, Paraguay, with six million people, is one of the least densely populated countries on earth.

Paraguay, like Uruguay, is a buffer state, historically ensnared between the combined and conflicting ambitions of Argentina and Brazil. The history of Paraguayan foreign relations is one of attempts to maintain sovereignty by

BOLIVIA

Fortín Ingavi

Fortín Madrejón

Villazón

Fuerte Olimpo

Puerto Guarani

BRAZIL

Puerto Sastre

Bella Vista

Mariscal
Estigarribia

Minas-cué

La Esmeralda

Filadelfia

Puerto Casado

Pedro Juan Caballero

Rio Pilcomayo

Rio Verde

Horqueta

Concepción

Rio Paraguay

Puerto Ybapobó

San Pedro

Rio Bermejo

Rio Pilcomayo

Rosario

San Estanislao

Villa
Hayes

Itaipu

Asunción

Coacupé

Coronel Oviedo

Hernandarias

ARGENTINA

Paraguari

Villarrica

Puerto
Presidente
Stroessner

Foz do
Iguaçu

Caazapá

Boquerón

Rio Alto Paraná

Corpus

Pilar

San Juan
Bautista

Capitán Meza

Desmochados

Yacireta

Encarnación

Rio Paraná

GRAN CHACO

0   25   50   100 Miles

0   25   50   100 Kilometers

PARAGUAY

counterbalancing the covetous influences of its powerful neighbors. Like Bolivia, Paraguay is landlocked, and this status and remoteness as well as the problems that are a direct consequence of this isolation continue to impact foreign policy.

Paraguayans are the most racially and culturally homogeneous peoples in Latin America (95 percent of the population is *mestizo*), thus avoiding the racial/class cleavages found in other Hispanic countries. Seventeen kinds of indigenous peoples constitute 3 percent of the population and remain the most marginalized sector of Paraguayan society. Paraguay is one of the few bilingual countries in the Western Hemisphere and the only one where an aboriginal language, Guaraní, is spoken more widely than a European tongue. Government and most business are conducted in Spanish, but 90 percent of Paraguay's 6,831,000 people speaks Guaraní. The extremely arid Chaco region, bordering Bolivia, contains about 60 percent of Paraguay's territory but only 3 to 4 percent of the population. Most Paraguayans live east of the Paraguay River on isolated farms or in small villages or towns in the lush arcadia.

History and Political Culture

In the early sixteenth century both Portuguese and Spaniards explored Paraguay, fruitlessly looking for gold. Asunción, the oldest city in the Rio de la Plata basin, was founded in 1537 by the Spanish explorer Juan de Salazar y Espinosa after hostile Indians forced the Spanish to abandon fortifications near present-day Buenos Aires. Asunción became the administrative center of Spanish colonial power over southern South America between 1537 and 1617, but the lack of precious metals and its remoteness soon relegated the town to little more than a fortified trading post and bulwark against the Portuguese in Brazil.

Spaniards in Paraguay quickly found that survival in such a poor, isolated place required independence, and they developed their own ways and resented interference by neglectful Spanish authorities. Overwhelmingly dependent on a subsistence agrarian economy that lacked easy access to markets, the colony lapsed into a stagnant backwater. With the transfer of colonial government to Buenos Aires in 1617, Spanish interest in Paraguay virtually ceased.

Spanish settlers in Paraguay developed a cordial relationship with the native Guaraní. Within a generation Spaniards were incorporated into the Indian lineage system on a kinship basis. The extensive polygamy influenced subsequent cultural developments in colonial Paraguay and produced a different social order than that elsewhere in South America. Acculturation, intermarriage, and racial miscegenation resulted within a few generations in a unique racial culture amalgamated from Spanish and indigenous influences, with few sociocultural distinctions separating rulers from the ruled. Paraguay evolved into a homogeneous, egalitarian society whose citizens claimed a higher degree of internal cultural unity than most other Latin American nations. This early sense of collective identity was a strong point in Paraguay's bid for independence and early nation-building.

In 1776 Paraguay was placed under the larger jurisdiction of the newly created Viceroyalty of the Rio de la Plata, seated in Buenos Aires. In 1810 independent Paraguayans refused to give allegiance to Argentine leaders who were declaring independence from Spain. Paraguayans subsequently beat back invading Argentine armies in two decisive battles in early 1811, ending both Spanish and Argentine control over the country.

Nineteenth-Century Politics

Since its independence in 1811 Paraguay has experienced two protracted periods of extreme tyranny (1816–1870 and 1940–1989) sundered by one semidemocratic intermission (1871–1939). The dictatorships of three successive tyrants who ruled Paraguay for almost sixty years following independence is at least partially responsible for a political-cultural environment conducive to authoritarianism and militarism.

The dictatorship of José Gaspar Rodríguez de Francia (1814–1840) set the tyrannical tone. Although he ruthlessly quelled internal dissent, Francia also set Paraguay's finances on a sound basis and constructed a national army. He maintained Paraguayan independence by fending off blockades and border skirmishes from Argentina and Brazil. He further responded to these threats with a policy of isolation and autonomous development, sealing Paraguay's borders and restricting foreign contact. Francia created a socialist state from lands expropriated from his hated aristocratic Spanish and *criollo* enemies. From these lands he built state farms and factories for armaments and ships, while income from the land expropriations and state monopolies on *yerba maté* provided consistent profit.

Francia further eroded the Spanish colonial base by banning marriages between whites, thus accelerating the *mestizaje*, or ethnic mixing and homogenization of the population. Via mass arrests and executions, the Spanish were obliterated as a ruling class in Paraguay. Francia managed to maintain Paraguay in peace and stability while other South American states were paralyzed by civil wars and political chaos in the early postindependence period, but the scope of his police-state control was far more pervasive and penetrative than brutal-but-chaotic *caudillo* governments elsewhere.

Francia's successors were the father/son dictatorships of Carlos Antonio López (1841–1862) and Francisco Solano López (1862–1870). Carlos Antonio López ended Francia's surreal solitude and reopened Paraguay to international trade and commerce. He established diplomatic relations with numerous countries, including the United States; built the first railroad in South America; and modernized the Paraguayan military. By the time López died in 1862 Paraguay was a regional power in southern South America.

Carlos Antonio's son, Francisco Solano López, became national dictator in 1862. Fancying himself as a Latin Napoleon, Solano López aimed to forge an alliance with Uruguay to counter the might of Argentina and Brazil in the Plata basin. However, Paraguay's meddling in the realm of these giants plunged the nation into the most savage war in the history of Latin America.

The Triple Alliance War (1865–1870) combined the armies of Argentina, Brazil, and Uruguay against Paraguay, which lost over half its prewar population of 525,000, of which only approximately 28,000 men survived. Paraguay also surrendered 25 percent of its national territory. After five years of slaughter, including the sacking of Asunción and Solano López's death in battle, Paraguay's utter defeat ended the nationalist era of autocratic development.

An extremely repressive brand of tyranny was ingrained into the national consciousness during those formative generations of Paraguay's history, perpetuating a tradition of intolerance to opposition and dissent and exaggerated adulation of strong-man rule. But as unbridled as were these three early autocrats, they also brought Paraguay sovereignty, stability, and economic development during the first six decades of national life.

This experience stands in sharp contrast to the petty bosses and would-be democrats who dotted the next sixty years of the so-called "Liberal Republic" (1876–1936). This era witnessed the reverberations of military defeat in the Triple Alliance War. The years between 1870 and 1932 saw political confusion, economic collapse, and foreign domination. A new, alien, liberal constitution, limiting the power of the state and expanding individual rights, was established by the occupying Brazilians, as was a provisional government representing neither the history nor spirit of Paraguayan political culture. Novel notions of citizen participation and self-government lacked resonance in a nation unfamiliar with democracy and reeling from the demise of so many of its people and most of its male leadership. The chronic political instability of the postwar years in Paraguay reflected the jarring impact of one of the greatest military disasters in modern history.

After 1870 a dozen years of anarchy and violence involving various military chieftains precluded any real recovery from the war's devastation. In a climate of assassinations and intrigue the political agenda of Paraguayan leaders who survived the war was rather basic: rebuild a shattered economy, settle boundary disputes and indemnification questions, get foreign troops off Paraguayan soil, and control the national government. Paraguay's party system began to take shape in 1887, when the political elite divided into two groupings. The Colorados, officially the National Republican Association (*Asociación Nacional Republicana*, ANR), dominated government between 1876 and 1904 and claimed lineage to the *Franciata* and López dictatorships. The Liberals proclaimed themselves the vanguard of limited government and civil liberties, but they suffered an antipatriotic stigma via their collaboration with the occupying Brazilians.

Paraguay's traditional multiclass, two-party system is one of the oldest in the world. Yet despite the institutionalized nature of the traditional parties and their extreme partisanship, Colorados and Liberals are both personality-driven patronage machines of political bosses and supporters. For 140 years these parties have played an often violent game over national power and control—not necessarily ideology. Control of the national government means control of the few sources of wealth in an impoverished state like Paraguay. As a result, the Colorado and Liberal parties have long remained malicious toward one another over generations.

As neither Colorados nor Liberals had much regard for democratic ideals, the net result after 1870 was a cycle of repression and revolt over decades of instability. Following thirty years of Colorado rule dominated by party founder General Bernardino Caballero, the Liberal "revolution" of 1904 wrested power, ruling then for the next three decades in the most unstable era in Paraguayan history. Between 1870 and 1938 Paraguay had thirty-four presidents, two of whom were assassinated and three overthrown.

After 1870 Argentine, Brazilian, and British speculators were the main beneficiaries of Paraguay's bankrupt economy. Foreign capital bought up vast tracts of land sold by Paraguayan governments at low prices as revenue for the destitute nation. The old state-owned lands of the Franciata and vast tracts owned by the López family were parceled out in the Land Law sales of 1883 and 1885. By the time sales were curtailed in 1915 ninety thousand square miles of land in Paraguay, comprising fully 35 percent of the area of the country, had been sold to foreigners. Prosperity was nurtured by the land sales, and by 1900 Paraguay finally began to recover from the devastation of the Triple Alliance War, regaining its prewar population of around five hundred thousand people living mainly in rural areas. At the beginning of the twentieth century, however, Paraguay remained a crude, insular, backward economy and polity.

The Twentieth Century

Although prosperity and trade increased in Paraguay after 1900, endemic political instability, notably civil wars in 1904, 1922, and, most seriously, in 1947, hindered sustained economic and political development. By the mid-

1920s Paraguay was again threatened from without, this time from the north. Bolivia, deprived of its Pacific coastline from its defeat in the War of the Pacific against Chile (1879–1883), now looked east to find an alternate outlet to the sea. Bolivia capitalized on Paraguay's political instability in the early 1900s in order to build a series of forts in the disputed territory of the Chaco desert, thereby beginning a relentless thrust southward toward the Paraná River, running south through Argentina to the Atlantic. When war came in 1932 Bolivia's German-trained army held every statistical advantage. However, Bolivia sent an army of largely highland Indians into the mud, swamp, and tropical heat of the Chaco lowlands, where they were annihilated in battle against a highly mobilized Paraguayan military, fighting on its own terrain against a foreign aggressor. Over the next two years the Paraguayans won a string of bloody confrontations and were at the steppes of the Andes when a truce was signed in 1935.

The Gran Chaco War heightened social mobilization in Paraguay, generating demands by various classes and economic sectors that the existing Liberal regime could not meet. Standards of living in Paraguay in the mid-1930s were woefully low. Working conditions, especially in the yerba maté plantations, were atrocious, and Paraguay's educational system was the poorest in South America. In the 1930s Asunción remained a somnolent boondocks, largely lacking paved roads, running water, or even electricity in other than a handful of homes and government buildings. On February 17, 1936, a military coup led by war hero Colonel Rafael Franco removed Liberal President Eusebio Ayala. The "Febreristas" were a motley crew of Fascists, Social Democrats, and Marxists who revivified the old images of the Francia and López dictatorships and advocated an authoritarian, corporatist, one-party state modeled on Mussolini's Italy.

With the Febrerista coup of 1936, civilian supremacy in Paraguayan politics ended for the next half-century. Another military uprising toppled the Febreristas in August 1937. Chaco War veteran General José F. Estigarribia seized power in 1940 and formally scrapped the 1870 Liberal constitution, replacing it with a new document enshrining presidential dictatorship and a powerful, regulatory state. When Estigarribia died in an airplane crash months after taking power, his successor, General Higinio Morínigo, became military dictator.

Morínigo's regime (1940–1948) was far more repressive than its predecessors. Morínigo outlawed the Liberal Party in 1942 and ruled over an openly pro-Nazi regime as Paraguay became a nest of Nazi intrigue during World War II. The war brought prosperity to Paraguay in response to world demand for agricultural exports, but the defeat of the Axis powers and pressure from the United States prompted Morínigo to liberalize his dictatorship in 1946.

When Morínigo tried to reintroduce authoritarian controls in 1947 a military rebellion plunged Paraguay into a bloody, five-month-long civil war. Although 80 percent of the officer corps went over to the rebel side, Morínigo's outgunned forces nevertheless won. It was a pyrrhic victory, however. Morínigo was deposed by the ascendant Colorado Party in early 1948. Now civil service positions in the bureaucracy and promotion within the armed forces were contingent on Colorado Party affiliation. Meanwhile, the military, divided by factions loyal to various officers jockeying for power, revolted and seized control in 1948, three times in 1949, and finally in 1954, when General Alfredo Stroessner carried out his *golpe*.

The Stroessner Regime

Stroessner consolidated his dictatorship, becoming by 1989 the longest-ruling leader in Paraguayan history. Stroessner built his tyranny on the Colorado Party and the military, with himself as *caudillo* over both institutions. Unlike the more faceless military juntas surrounding Paraguay, Stroessner secured a popular base for his dictatorship, bringing the Colorado Party (the primary instrument of patronage) under his formal control and penetrating society via a national network of party branches and block wards. The Colorados acquired "official" status, sponsoring Stroessner's eight successive presidential candidacies, building a personality cult for the dictator, and providing a mass base to counterbalance the military. By 1967 Stroessner's purges had left the Colorados monolithic, *stronista*, with immense grassroots support and representing one of Latin America's most powerful political movements. To the preexisting ultranationalism of the Colorado Party, *stronismo* added a demagogic, populist tone as well as a newer, maniacal, anticommunist national security doctrine.

Along with the Colorados, the armed forces were the other key pillar—and ultimate guarantor—of the regime. Loyalty to Stroessner by the officer corps formed the basis of *caudillismo*: personalist rule supported by loyal retainers, rewarded with wealth and power. A notorious web of corruption developed in the officer corps, now solidly Colorado. Stroessner also adroitly appealed to their corporate interests by reorienting their role and mission to one of guaranteeing the regime against "Communist" insurgency. High military spending and public acclaim by Stroessner added luster to the armed forces. Unlike neighboring military regimes, Stroessner also shielded his military from controversy, leaving most repression and human rights abuses to the secret police. The *Stronato* continually utilized the shopworn menace of "Communist subversion" to move against any sign of independence or militancy among peasants, students, workers, or the church before any of these challenged the regime. The 1992 discovery of detailed documentation from the regime's intelligence agencies reveals the pervasiveness with which the dictatorship's lidless eye cast a penetrative gaze over almost all social institutions, belying stereotypes that Stroessner's was simply an old-fashioned, poorly organized autocracy.

By 1988 when Stroessner won his eighth reelection, the dictator's sclerotic detachment from day-to-day decision-making, a growing succession crisis, and a worsening economic situation all served to rot the regime. Paraguayans themselves had also changed. They were a more mobilized, expectant population, no longer overwhelmingly rural and atomized. White-collar professionals outside the regime chafed at the ongoing centralization of power and corruption. The international context was also different, as Paraguay was now surrounded by new democracies in Argentina, Brazil, and Uruguay. Divisions emerged in the once-monolithic Colorado Party, threatening its symbiotic axis with the military. A "militant" faction remained fanatically devoted to Stroessner as president-for-life and ultimately to his son, Colonel Gustavo Stroessner. The "traditionalist" Colorados argued for a nonpersonalist transition after Stroessner to ensure continued Colorado Party hegemony. A violent coup d'état in early 1989, led by military rebels loyal to traditionalist General Andrés Rodríguez, deposed Stroessner, sending him into exile in Brazil.

Paraguay in Transition

General Rodríguez quickly consolidated power, purging the Colorados and army of high-ranking militants. Rodríguez released political prisoners, relaxed press restrictions, and allowed Paraguayan exiles to return. Snap elections in May 1989, three months following the coup, were won by Rodríguez and the Colorado juggernaut with a lopsided 74 percent of the vote. Rodríguez was inaugurated on May 15, 1989, for a four-year term.

Under Rodríguez Paraguay experienced significant political reforms, taking remarkable steps toward rejoining the international community after decades of ostracism and isolation. The new constitution in 1992 prohibited party membership for new military officers (but not those already serving). Corruption, integral to Stroessner's kleptocracy and deeply engrained in Paraguayan culture, skyrocketed after 1993, when the country entered a deep recession. Paraguay's enormous black market represents a large sector of the economy, and ranking military officers hold lucrative side interests in narcotics, contraband, prostitution, and money-laundering. Rodríguez himself was reportedly involved during his entire career in parasitic rake-offs and graft.

Colorado divisions continued into 1993 over the party's presidential candidacy. Conservative construction magnate Juan Carlos Wasmosy ultimately prevailed, becoming the first civilian president in almost sixty years, but represented the continuing alliance between the military, dominant economic groups, and Colorado politicians that formed the triad of the Stronato. Intimidation against opposition parties and open intervention by the military preceding national elections in May 1993 showed that party/military elites would only accept a Colorado victory.

In the "cleanest-dirty" vote in forty-eight years, Wasmosy won the election on May 9, 1993, with 40 percent of the vote, beating Domingo Laíno of the Partido Liberal Radical Auténtico (PLRA, 32 percent) and Guillermo Caballero Vargas of the new independent movement Encuentro Nacional (PEN, 23 percent). The failure of both opposition candidates to unite, unseat the ruling Colorados, and initiate a practice of party coparticipation was a historic opportunity lost.

With strong remnants of the military/Colorado alliance remaining, movement from authoritarianism to some form of democracy was problematic in Paraguay. Citizen participation, in the form of strikes and protest marches by peasants, workers, and government employees, became more visible, and social groups began to network and organize. Yet regime elites, most of whom had supported Stroessner for decades, paid only lip service and remained uncommitted, beyond expediency, to democracy.

Political crisis erupted in April 1996 when President Wasmosy dismissed army commander General Lino Oviedo, who refused to step down. With Oviedo in revolt and threatening to kill the president, Wasmosy was temporarily forced to take refuge in the U.S. embassy. Crucial to ending the crisis without bloodshed was the massive show of support Wasmosy received from the Clinton administration, the Organization of American States, and Paraguay's trading partners Argentina, Brazil, and Uruguay, in the Southern Cone Common Market (*Mercado Común del Cono Sur*, MERCOSUR). The renegade Oviedo was finally forced to resign. Paraguay's shaky electoral system triumphed, but Oviedo's barracks revolt was a dark reminder that ingrained praetorian tendencies do not suddenly disappear with regime change.

Tension again mounted in September 1997 when the Colorados nominated Oviedo as their party candidate for the presidential elections in 1998, despite internal party opposition and negative reactions in Washington. When Wasmosy ordered Oviedo's arrest on charges of "insulting" the president, the general went into hiding and campaigned as a fugitive for forty-one days. As Paraguay continued its madcap course to the May 1998 national elections, Oviedo surrendered and campaigned from jail. The MERCOSUR giants Argentina and Brazil again arbitrated Paraguayan politics by threatening the country's membership in the free trade bloc if Oviedo were elected.

By the 1998 elections, politics was so helter-skelter in Paraguay that after General Oviedo was sentenced to ten years in prison for his 1996 coup attempt, he continued to run for president and led in the polls until the

Supreme Court nullified his candidacy. Oviedo's running mate, civilian engineer Raul Cubas, then became the Colorado Party presidential candidate, and his archenemy, Luis María Argaña, an old *stronista*, became the vice-presidential nominee. Colorado upheaval was still not enough to help opposition Democratic Alliance (Liberal Party) candidate Domingo Laíno. But by February 1999 Cubas was locked in a power struggle with his own vice president and faced impeachment for defying the Supreme Court and freeing Oviedo from prison as his very first act as president. The Colorado Party now extended its control over national government past a half-century.

On March 23, 1999, Vice President Luis María Argaña was machine-gunned in downtown Asunción. Argaña's faction of the Colorados immediately blamed Cubas and his puppet-master, Oviedo. Cubas was impeached by Congress a week later, after Asunción's central square became a bloody battleground in response to Argaña's murder, with rooftop snipers killing six and wounding hundreds in battling rival blocs. Coup rumors swirled in the capital and prodemocracy demonstrations flooded the streets. The ambassadors of Brazil, the United States, and the Vatican met with Cubas and negotiated his resignation in the face of mounting street demonstrations. A new Colorado-dominant coalition government, headed by former senate president Luis González Macchi, took power.

The August 2000 vice-presidential elections resulted in a narrow but astounding victory for the Liberal (PLRA) party. This was the first time a Liberal was elected to Paraguay's executive since 1939 and the first time any opposition candidate had won an executive position via election since before the Colorado party came to power in 1947. González Macchi's "national unity" administration soon fell apart when the PLRA withdrew from the government, but the ruling Colorados remained split between *argañistas* and *oviedistas*.

The economic picture was equally murky. The government drastically downgraded Paraguay's growth estimates for 2001 from the original 3.5 percent to only 1.5 percent, and the country's fiscal deficit was a record US$257 million. The social deficit was worse. Proclaiming that Paraguay's economic and social crisis had reached extreme limits, the Catholic Church denounced the government's insensitivity and ineffectualness in addressing poverty. Waves of protest marches and highway blockings by peasant associations and trade unions were launched in March against the administration, increasingly seen as incompetent in the face of mounting land invasions by *campesinos*, a prolonged banking crisis/scandal, a police abduction/torture scandal, privatization (of state monopolies) fiascos and concomitant pressure from the International Monetary Fund, escalating crime (especially kidnappings), and pervasive corruption and cronyism.

In September 2002 the nongovernmental organization Transparency International rated Paraguay as the most corrupt country in Latin America and the third most corrupt in the world. This was no surprise to Paraguayans, 23 percent of whom in an opinion survey responded that the country was being run by the mafia. A 2001 UN study had already underlined "the absence of a culture of legality" in Paraguay. Responding to the charge, Colorado mandarins were outraged . . . outraged! With masterful irony, party bigwigs organized rallies demanding "action" against corruption.

In February 2003 President González Macchi survived his second impeachment attempt and prepared to wait out his unremarkable term, ending in August. The winner of the April 27 presidential election was no surprise: Nicanor Duarte of the Colorado party, 14 percent ahead of the PLRA candidate. The Colorados, in power uninterruptedly since 1947, seemed impervious to the collapse of the Stroessner dictatorship in 1989.

The new Duarte administration faced heightened expectations and growing demands to respond to Paraguay's social crisis. Colorado governments since 1989 fomented political liberalization but failed to address chronic economic and social concerns—especially corruption—thus displaying little difference in this regard from the Stroessner regime. Continuing Stroessner's model, Duarte, despite populist blandishments, supported the interests of large landowners, the business class, and the military in their dealings with peasants, workers, and civil society.

Duarte's presidency witnessed the further splintering of the Colorado party, engaged in bitter infighting over the party's candidate in 2008. When his efforts to amend the constitution to allow him to seek reelection failed, Duarte's party faction endorsed Education Minister Blanca Ovelar over his own vice president, Luis Alberto Castiglioni. Castiglioni had the support of the stronista faction of the Colorados led by Alfredo "Goli" Stroessner, grandson of the dictator. With the Colorados in civil war and coup-monger Lino Oviedo running under his UNACE (*Unión Nacional de Ciudadanos Eticos*) banner, the beneficiary was former Roman Catholic bishop Fernando Lugo, head of a disparate coalition of leftist parties termed the APC (*Alianza Patriótica para el Cambio*), who emerged as the frontrunner, winning the presidency on April 20, 2008. Lugo won with nearly 41 percent of the vote compared to 31 percent for Blanca Ovelar of the Colorado party. The era of Colorado party domination in Paraguay was over.

Political Groups

The Colorado Party clung to power for sixty-one years and was the official party of the Stronato, only splintering in 1989 over the succession issue rather than any notions of democracy. Infighting among various factions clustering around political bosses led to its electoral defeat in 2008. As the largest party in both houses of congress, President Fernando Lugo's coalition government will have to deal with the Colorados in order to push through his legislative proposals.

The Liberal Party (*Partido Liberal Radical Auténtico*—PLRA), out of power since the end of the Chaco War, was illegal from 1942 to 1967. Despite claiming "democratic" ideals, during their years in power (1904–1936) the Liberals showed themselves to be the same elitist, exclusionary group as the Colorados. In exchange for recognition the Liberal Party provided token opposition during the dictatorship. The PLRA is the largest party in Lugo's APC coalition, with competing factions expecting recognition and power after so many decades of repression and marginalization.

The *Alianza Patriótica para el Cambio* (APC) is the disparate coalition of nine leftist political parties and dozens of social movements headed by center-left President Fernando Lugo. In his first year of office Lugo found it difficult to satisfy the often competing interests of elements of the coalition, resulting in *inmovilismo* in addressing Paraguay's staggering array of problems. With nothing concrete to show on campaign promises of land reform, tackling corruption, and, the centerpiece, renegotiating the terms of the Itaipú treaty with Brazil (regarding the giant binational hydroelectric dam on the Paraguayan-Brazilian border) as well as paternity suits battering the ethical credentials he emphasized in his campaign, Lugo operated from an ever-weakening position of strength.

Paraguay's two main peasant organizations, the *Mesa Coordinadora Nacional de Organizaciones Campesinas* (National Coordinating Table of Peasant Organizations, MCNOC), and the *Federación Nacional Campesina* (National Peasant Federation, FNC) pressure the government to improve access to credit, land reform, and an end to official harassment of peasant activists. These groups have become radicalized in recent years, staging sporadic, sometimes violent, land invasions, as Brazilian soybean farmers have bought up huge tracks of land in eastern Paraguay. Although production and export of soybeans and soy-related products has boomed over the past few years, the economic benefits have not trickled down to the more than 250,000 families who depend on subsistence farming, maintaining only marginal ties to the larger productive sector of the economy.

The Catholic Church and Church-related groups constituted a moral challenge to the Stroessner dictatorship in the face of unbending repression, thus calling attention to human rights abuses, corruption, and the extreme concentration of landholdings in the hands of regime elites. Following the 1989 coup a rapprochement developed between the government and the Church, with the latter remaining a persistent voice for social justice in the "new" Paraguay. The clergy also remain traditional defenders of church prerogatives concerning abortion, education policy, and religious orthodoxy. President Fernando Lugo's confession of breaking his vow of celibacy and fathering an illegitimate child while still a bishop—along with other paternity suits (including statutory rape) pending—have disillusioned Paraguayans and politically damaged Lugo's claim to moral authority and transparency in this still-traditional Roman Catholic country.

Organized Labor is scrawny in Paraguay. During the Great Depression Paraguayan governments never initiated import-substitution-industrialization (ISI), instead depending on the country's agricultural exports—mainly cotton, soybeans, tobacco, and yerba—for national income. Moreover, Stroessner reasoned that limited industrialization obviated the rise of an industrial working class and unions capable of threatening the regime. Therefore an urban proletariat with class consciousness never developed. Most economic enterprises, located in and around Asunción, are family-owned firms where personal, not professional, patron-client relations prevail. The Stroessner regime curtailed both the size and potential influence of the labor movement by co-optation, repression, and thorough Colorado Party penetration of Paraguayan industry, as well as policies discouraging large enterprises. Fewer than 50,000 of Paraguay's two million wage earners are confederated, and the small size of the domestic market ameliorates the demand to support a consequential industrialization program.

Public Policy

The rise of newer social movements and of a free press publicizing group concerns illustrates both the changes and continuities in Paraguay. For example, given the durability of an authoritarian and patriarchal political culture, public policies designed to combat gender inequality and discrimination (domestic violence, reproductive rights) were nonexistent until 1992. Modernizing values are reflected in the notable increase in political participation by women and expansion of legal rights via reform of the civil code. As the Colorado party's candidate for president, Blanca Ovelar is a testament to how far women have come in this traditional society. Still, the women's movement in Paraguay remains a largely urban, middle-class affair.

The inequality of land ownership and pressures for landholdings by landless peasants (Paraguay's largest social group) remains another problem area of public policy. Land concentration in the countryside is one of the highest in the world. The top 10 percent of the population controls 65 percent of the land, while 30 percent of the rural population is landless. Peasants, believing that Stroessner's downfall entitled them to land, began an upsurge in land invasions after 1989. Successive Colorado governments, with strong links to landholding elites, responded with sometimes violent repression while rejecting demands for policies of redistribution and the amelioration of rural poverty. Agrarian reform, promised by then-candidate Fernando Lugo, took oblique shape in January 2009 with vague pronouncements for "rural development projects"—but not land distribution. The latter will be extremely difficult without alienating the big soybean producers in eastern Paraguay, who are primarily Brazilians. Violence against them would certainly disquiet Brazil and put talks to renegotiate the Itaipú treaty in jeopardy.

Lugo's coalition government also faces growing demands by state and municipal governments and social movements to respond to the social deficit in health, public housing, and education. Furthermore, judicial reform away from the Colorado-politicized courts as well as reforming the military (merit promotion instead of seniority) and its image as a corrupt, repressive apparatus of the Colorados is also on Lugo's agenda.

An extremely poor nation like Paraguay pays a high price for the rampant corruption, sloppy organization, endemic patronage, and stifling inefficiency of its public sector that absorbs scarce resources, wastes opportunities, and distorts market prices. Paraguay's membership in the MERCOSUR economic integration accord of two hundred million people is viewed, as was the giant binational Itaipú hydroelectric project a generation ago, as a panacea to generate economic growth. That growth has bypassed most Paraguayans.

The International Arena

In international affairs Paraguay negotiates from a weak position. Paraguay's landlocked isolation in the interior of the continent deprives it of strategic importance. Its small population is largely poor and uneducated. The economy is underdeveloped and bereft of important mineral resources. Paraguay possesses little in the way of vital financial, social, or natural attributes needed to give it some heft in international affairs.

Paraguay's history of violent conflict with threatening neighbor-states imbues its foreign policy with a determination—not always met—to maintain friendly relations with them, especially Argentina and Brazil. Paraguay was overwhelmingly dependent on Argentina until the 1970s when, as late as 1969, all of Paraguay's road, rail, and river links with the outside world passed through Argentine territory.

Beginning in the 1950s, however, the Stroessner regime began to approach Brazil for developmental assistance and to counteract Argentine influences. Brazil built a bridge between the two countries over the Paraná River at the border town of Ciudad del Este that offered an alternative export route with a free trade port at Paranaguá, and they then built a highway from Paraguay to the Brazilian coast. The enormous Itaipú project, a joint Brazilian-Paraguayan venture (with Brazil providing the financing and know-how) solidified the changed regional axis of power. By 1982 Argentina's share of Paraguayan exports fell to less than half, while Brazil's share rose from nothing to 58 percent.

By the early 1980s increased Brazilian economic penetration into Paraguay began to alarm the nation, as well as Argentina—Brazil's archrival—of the possibility of Paraguay becoming an economic satellite of Brazil. Paraguayans began to complain about Brazilian capital taking over Paraguayan firms, and Brazilian food, goods, and even music replacing Paraguayan products. Increasing immigration by Brazilian peasants into eastern Paraguay (so-called *Brasiguayos*) and economic domination by big Brazilian soybean-producing farms displacing small Paraguayan farmers added to the resentment. The bedrock issue of Lugo's presidential campaign was vituperative criticism of and demands for renegotiation of the Itaipú dam treaty in order for Paraguay to receive more money for exportation of hydroelectric power to Brazil as well as freedom to export to other countries (prohibited by the treaty). Lugo's nationalist, anti-Brazilian rhetoric, however, only hardened the administration of President Lula da Silva against any renegotiation—not that Paraguay has much, if any, leverage.

Since World War II foreign relations between the United States and Paraguay have been conditioned by mutual interests involving national security, trade, and investment. After using economic and military aid to buy the Morínigo regime's alignment against the Nazis in 1944 the United States continued to use leverage over Paraguay during the Cold War. In return for generous amounts of economic and military aid and political legitimacy, General Stroessner became a staunch defender of U.S. foreign policy. Stroessner broke diplomatic relations with Castro's Cuba and supported the U.S.-engineered expulsion of Cuba from the Organization of American States. Paraguay outlawed the Communist Party, refused to establish relations with communist countries, and voted slavishly with the United States in the OAS and the UN.

Paraguayan-U.S. relations during the Stronato were cordial and reliable during the 1950s and 1960s, but they became more troubled over democracy and human rights issues from 1976 to the end of the regime in 1989. Relations deteriorated rapidly during the Carter administration, which announced that it would no longer ignore human rights violations in Paraguay. With Ronald Reagan's election in 1980, expected improvement in bilateral relations did not materialize, as human rights policy had become an essential component of U.S. foreign policy.

Rodríguez's political liberalization considerably improved U.S.-Paraguayan relations after 1989. High-level U.S. governmental and military officials visited Asunción, praising the positive changes in government and increasing U.S. economic and technical assistance. The first Bush administration pressured Paraguay to create an antidrug agency in Asunción, but Paraguay's fight against drug trafficking deteriorated as General Lino Oviedo's power increased and Paraguay verged on near-anarchy. The culture of corruption in Paraguay further hinders progress in antidrug operations. Paraguay partners with the U.S. in initiatives to combat money laundering, protect intellectual property rights, and fight terrorism. In particular, the United States is concerned about terrorist financing by the influx of Arab-dominated *mafiosi* at the triple border where Paraguay, Argentina, and Brazil meet. The U.S. strongly supports Paraguay's democratization, helping to resolve the 1996 barracks revolt and the 1999 crisis culminating the resignation of Raul Cubas.

Paraguay's relations with Europe continue to expand. Contacts with France, Germany, Great Britain, Italy, and Spain focus on trade, technical assistance, and cultural exchange. After Argentina, Brazil, and the United States, Western European nations are the largest importers of Paraguayan goods, such as tobacco and tannin. Paraguay imports more goods from Germany than from any other European nation. Germans are undoubtedly the most important non-Spanish-speaking European immigrant group in Paraguay in terms of business enterprises and agricultural colonies.

Paraguayan contacts with Asia are also growing. Relations with Japan are longstanding. Thousands of Japanese have settled in Paraguay since the 1930s, and today Japanese capital, technical aid, and industrial investment surpasses that of the rest of Asia together. During the Cold War Paraguay maintained strong diplomatic relations with anticommunist regimes in South Korea and the Republic of China (Taiwan), but today Paraguay is also expanding links with the People's Republic of China.

Paraguay-African relations are minimal except for South Africa and Egypt. Because of their shared pariah status, Stroessner's Paraguay and Apartheid South Africa developed strong bilateral relations beginning in the 1970s. With regard to the Middle East, Israel's outcast status was understood in Stroessner's Paraguay, which appreciated intelligence training by the Mossad in its shopworn "fight against communism." Aside from Egypt, Paraguay has little contact with the rest of the Arab world.

Regarding international organizations, by virtue of her last-minute declaration of war against the Axis powers in World War II, Paraguay was entitled to sign the Declaration of the United Nations, becoming a charter member. But Paraguay's small size and relative unimportance in international affairs works against gaining much influence in the UN. In the Organization of American States Paraguay's status as a lesser-developed country has obtained it special trade/aid concessions, but, in all, Paraguay plays a minor role in hemispheric politics.

The Consolidation of Democracy

Until the defeat of the Colorado party in 2008 Paraguay was a semi-authoritarian regime in which the Colorados claimed a commitment to democracy while attempting to perpetuate themselves in power indefinitely. Paraguay was neither a full-blown dictatorship nor fully democratic, instead displaying characteristics of each. It was a hybrid regime in that generally free elections were held and democratic institutions were in operation, but elections did not transfer substantive political power, and institutions operated so weakly as to provide the Colorados with a more elaborate and believable democratic disguise. If the Colorados had their way, the system would have continued forever.

Lugo's election profoundly changed all that. For the first time in three generations an opposition defeated the entrenched Colorado party, moving Paraguay closer in its long process of democratization. As President Lugo is finding out, Paraguay today is a potpourri of upstart students, haranguing newspaper editors, and militant campesinos in which *políticos* must wheel and deal in a more open political environment. However, Paraguay also remains praetorian with its continual involvement of the military in politics. Since the 1930s the Paraguayan armed forces have made and unmade Paraguayan presidents, and the army is a permanent factor in any calculus of power. Paraguay is a consolidating democracy, but not one fully consolidated.

The Effects of Globalization

Post-Stroessner Colorado governments proved responsive to the "advice" of the Agency for International Development, the World Bank, and the International Monetary Fund as well as external forces advocating more market-oriented policies (financing decisions conditioned, of course, to the government's economic policies). Following the 1989 coup President Rodríguez's technocratic economists privatized some money-draining public-sector boondoggles, reduced government spending, simplified the tax code, eliminated controls on interest rates and foreign exchange transactions, and, portending MERCOSUR, relaxed tariffs and other trade barriers. In recent years, Paraguay has also made steps toward more fiscal transparency. The government also eliminated most tax exemptions.

But trade liberalization has hurt small and medium-sized domestic manufactures of shoes, furniture, textiles, and clothing, thereby forcing many to close. Despite submitting to neoliberal policies and enmeshing itself in the world economy, internal economic conditions in Paraguay continue to deteriorate for the masses. Although the economy grew by 6.4 percent in 2007 and

5.8 percent in 2008, approximately 2.1 million, or 35 percent of the population, remain poor. Unemployment in 2008 was officially pegged at one million or approximately 16 percent of the population, but it is considered much higher by most experts. With a GDP per capita of US$1,928, Paraguay remains the second poorest country in South America. The persistence of grinding poverty and joblessness suggests that, twenty years in, the effects of the Washington Consensus's neoliberal economic policies on the majority of Paraguayans are far less positive than promised. Antimarket backlash was at least in part responsible for President Lugo's historic 2008 election, continuing a line of center-left presidential victories in Bolivia (2005), Brazil (2002/06), Chile (2000/06), and Ecuador (2006).

However, Paraguayan's disillusionment does not stop with the effects of the Washington Consensus. Data from the Americas Barometer 2006–2007 Latin American public opinion surveys show that although support for democracy as a form of government is widespread, satisfaction with how democracy works is not. While Uruguay had the highest satisfaction rate, roughly equivalent with the United States (62.2 percent), Paraguay had the lowest level of satisfaction (27.5 percent). Measuring system legitimacy (respect for political institutions, protection of basic rights, pride in the political system), while Costa Rica (64 percent) and Uruguay (64.3 percent) exhibited the highest levels of system support in Latin America, Paraguay was next to last with only 39.1 percent of respondents supporting their political system.

This is the backdrop to Fernando Lugo's troubled first year as president of Paraguay. Although his election signaled a shift away from neoliberal economic policies and a move toward introducing some redistributive and welfare policies, he has little concrete to show for it. Lugo's defeat of the interminable Colorado party shows the prospects for consolidation of democracy in Paraguay are brighter than they have been since the fall of the Stroessner dictatorship, but the stability of the system remains threatened by gross socioeconomic inequities, weak political institutions, popular discontent, and lingering authoritarian impulses that, with a few unexpected twists and turns, could result in political turmoil.

Suggestions for Further Reading

Kelly, Phillip, and Thomas Wigham. "Democracy in Bolivia and Paraguay." In *Assessing Democracy in Latin America*, ed. Philip Kelly. Boulder, CO: Westview Press, 1998.

Lambert, Peter. "A Decade of Electoral Democracy: Continuity, Change and Crisis in Paraguay." *Bulletin of Latin American Research* 19 (2000): 379–96.

Lambert, Peter, and Andrew Nickson, eds. *The Transition to Democracy in Paraguay*. New York: St. Martin's Press, 1997.

Lewis, Paul H. *Political Parties and Generations in Paraguay's Liberal Era, 1869–1940*. Chapel Hill: University of North Carolina Press, 1993.

Mora, Frank O. "From Dictatorship to Democracy: The U.S. and Regime Change in Paraguay, 1954–1994." *Bulletin of Latin American Research* 17, no. 1 (1997): 59–79.

Sondrol, Paul. "Paraguay: A Semi-Authoritarian Regime?" *Armed Forces and Society* 34, no. 1 (2007): 46–66.

Zagorski, Paul W. "Democratic Breakdown in Paraguay and Venezuela: The Shape of Things to Come for Latin America?" *Armed Forces and Society* 30, no. 1 (2003): 87–116.

14

Bolivia

From Neoliberal Democracy to Multiethnic, Plebiscitarian Politics

Fabrice Lehoucq

By the first decade of the twenty-first century Bolivian politics had reverted to chronic instability. Social protest and legislative opposition forced presidents to resign in 2003 and 2004. After the historic election of Evo Morales, the leader of the leading coca growers' confederation and a self-proclaimed indigenous candidate, to the presidency in December 2005, divisions between the western highlands and eastern lowlands fueled strikes, protest marches, and the violent birth of a new constitutional order.

For much of its history the political system of Bolivia has been one of the most unstable in Latin America. Between 1900 and 2009, for example, there were twenty-nine coup attempts, nineteen of which succeeded in overthrowing the president.[1] In 1952 the military disintegrated before an assault organized by the National Revolutionary Movement (MNR) and radicalized mine-workers, who aimed to capture the presidency that had been denied to their candidate, Victor Paz, in the 1951 elections. In subsequent years the MNR and its allies spearheaded a revolution that enfranchised all adults and legalized the radical redistribution of rural property led by peasant unions.

Since the overthrow of President Gonzalo Sánchez de Lozada in 2003, governments have reversed many of the neoliberal policies that he and his

BRAZIL

Rio Abuná PANDO

Cobija •

Rio Madre de Dios

Rio Beni

Rio Mamoré

BRAZIL

Rio Iténez

Rio Guaporé

PERU

EL BENI

LA PAZ

Trinidad •

Lago Titicaca

Rio San Miguel

★ La Paz

Guaqui •

Rio Desaguadero

Rio Chaparé

Rio Grande

Charaña •

COCHABAMBA

Rio Ichilo

GRAN CHACO

Cochabamba •

Oruro •

Mizque •

Santa Cruz •

SANTA CRUZ

ORURO

Rio Lauca

Lago de Poopó

★ Sucre

Puerto Suárez •

Potosí •

CHUQUISACA

Uyuni •

POTOSÍ

Rio Pilaya

Villa Montes •

PACIFIC OCEAN

CHILE

Tarija •

TARIJA

Rio Pilcomayo

PARAGUAY

ARGENTINA

BOLIVIA

predecessors pioneered. During his short term in office (October 2003-June 2005), Carlos Mesa, the former vice president, renegotiated contracts with multinational energy corporations to increase the state's share of gas revenues. In early 2006 President Morales and his Movement Toward Socialism (MAS) "nationalized" the administration of gas and oil deposits by nullifying these contracts and recreating the state's energy state corporation. Nationalistic energy policies are part of the return of statist economic policies, ones that aim to reassert the state's role in the economy while deepening key social policies pioneered during the 1990s. In a January 2009 referendum the Morales's presidency also gained overwhelming popular support for a new constitution, one that creates important economic functions for the central state, advances the rights of indigenous peoples, and decentralizes state authority to a plethora of lower-level institutions and oversight bodies.

Both changes in political economy and in constitutional arrangements have polarized the country between a majority of citizens in the poorer and more indigenous western highlands and the smaller number of citizens in the richer, less indigenous eastern lowlands. For the regime's numerous supporters, President Morales is reasserting sovereignty over natural resources and "founding" a more plebiscitarian democracy. For the regime's opponents, President Morales's short-sighted economic policies are ruining the country's export economy and have created a populist autocracy. Taking power at the beginning of an unprecedented gas-induced boom—one that has reignited economic growth, reduced unemployment, and turned a serious fiscal shortfall into a healthy surplus useful for expanding social spending—has helped the MAS to stabilize its rule and take Bolivia in new, revolutionary directions. Whether the new constitutional order will outlive Morales and accelerate historically low rates of economic growth, however, is far from assured.

Geography and Social Groups

Bolivia's nine departments span the Andes mountain ranges in the west, which surpass 12,000 feet (3,657 meters) in some places; Amazon rainforest in the east; and a dry, sparsely populated, lowland Chaco region in the south. The lack of navigable rivers and the difficulty and expense of building highways and railroads across dramatic changes in elevation have impeded the economic and political integration of the country and generated sharp interregional rivalries and hostilities. Bolivia's geography and climatic extremes presented barriers to European settlement, resulting in a small population for such an extensive geographical territory—the sixth largest country in South America. Approximately nine million Bolivians are spread throughout a territory of 424,000 square miles (1,098,580 square kilometers).

Bolivians belong to one of three social groups. The vast majority of Bolivians are descendants of the small number of indigenous peoples who survived the conquest. The 2001 Population Census indicates that thirty-three different Native American languages are spoken, although 95 percent of people who speak them are either Aymará or Quechua. Until the late twentieth century most indigenous peoples lived in rural areas. Being a peasant, in fact, has been synonymous with being Indian. Bolivians who speak a pre-Columbian language have been targets of discrimination and, until 1952, could not vote in national elections. The second group of Bolivians is of European descent who, because of their education and wealth, have monopolized positions of power in Bolivian society. The third group consists of people of mixed ancestry or those belonging to a Native American ethnic group that, for economic reasons, learned Spanish and adopted European customs. With time, *cholos* or *mestizos* ("mixed blood") gradually grew in number.

Ethnic identity is complex and fluid in Bolivia. The 2001 Population Census indicates that approximately half of Bolivians speak a non-European language and that 63 percent identify themselves as members of an indigenous group. The 2008 Americas Barometer survey finds that the latter figure has risen to three-fourths of survey respondents.[2] This survey, however, suggests that 68 percent of adults also call themselves mestizos, 21.4 percent identify as indigenous or "original" peoples, and 8.2 percent identify as white. Depending on how questions about ethnicity are asked, Bolivians identify in different ways, suggesting that they have multiple identities, even in the midst of parties that seek to activate (or ignore) ethnic identities.

Interest Groups

Historically Bolivian interest groups mirrored the structure of an economy based on mineral and agricultural exports. Since the 1990s two-thirds of the population has lived in departmental capitals. More than half of the economically active population labors in the informal economy, largely located in these urban centers. Only a small share work in the mineral or petroleum sectors, which are responsible for most export revenue.

The Confederation of Private Entrepreneurs of Bolivia (CEPB) is the oldest organization of businessmen in the country. It includes importers, exporters, and firms producing for the domestic market. In recent years, however, the CEPB has weakened. Businessmen in Santa Cruz no longer participate in the national Confederation. Many of them have diversified away from producing for the limited domestic market that was protected until trade liberalization in the mid-1980s. Since the 1980s Santa Cruz–based businessmen have invested in export agribusiness of soybeans and grains. In the eastern lowland departments of Beni, Pando, Santa Cruz, and Tarija, businessmen have gravitated to Civic Committees based in each of their cities to press for infrastructure, fuel subsidies, and other favorable policies. They have also used the Civic Committees to lobby departments and the national government to obtain and distribute royalties on mineral production that accrue to departments where such resources are located.

The Bolivian Workers Central (COB) and the Confederation of Teachers of Bolivia (CMB) are not as influential as they once were. The decline of formal sector employment has deprived both groups of membership. Gone are the days when mine-workers employed in state companies, which were privatized in 1985, helped to seat and unseat governments. Teachers battled the 1994 education reform, which created bilingual education, and they remain an organized force with which to be reckoned.

Since the late 1990s several social movements have become the dominant interest groups of Bolivian politics. Coca growers organized powerful federations in the Chapare, a tropical region in the Department of Cochabamba that not only raised taxes and provided, at their height, 45,000 coca grower families with basic services, but also battled the army in a U.S.-financed war to eradicate its coca fields. It is widely recognized that coca grown in the Chapare is destined for the illegal trade in cocaine. Estimates from the U.S. government suggested that the 30,000 hectares (74,132 acres) of coca in Los Yungas, a region outside of La Paz, were for domestic consumption, and native Americans have chewed coca leaves, which have a mild stimulate effect, for centuries. President Morales remains the head of the coca federation and deploys its members in protest marches around the country. Political mobilization gradually ended the central government's eradication campaigns, and in 2008 the Morales administration expelled both the U.S. Drug Enforcement Administration and the U.S. ambassador. As a result, there has been an expansion of coca growing lands and the illegal trafficking of coca for cocaine production.[3]

Both highland and especially lowland indigenous peoples have organizations to mobilize on their behalf. The Landless Movement has occupied unused lands since the late 1990s. Neighborhood associations in the cities of Cochabamba and El Alto spawned a plethora of organized groups. In the El Alto case (a city, on the outskirts of La Paz, at fourteen thousand feet above sea level filled with rural migrants), the groups organized in the late 1990s to undo the privatization of their water resources.

Social movements have become the vanguard of revolutionary change. Their power derives from leading protest marches, organizing blockades of highways, and threatening to topple elected governments. By occupying a handful of roads, protesters from El Alto can strangle access to La Paz, where the elected branches of government sit. This is a peculiar piece of the country's political geography that empowers the social movements. Pro-MAS protesters also have representatives in the congressional delegation of the MAS and throughout the state apparatus.

Political Parties and Elections

Since the 1952 revolution three different party systems have existed in Bolivia. The first postrevolutionary party system was between 1952 and 1966, during which the MNR tried to consolidate a one-party system by incorporating peasants, mine-workers, and leftists. The MNR's bid for hegemony came to an end in 1964 when Generals Alfredo Ovando and René Barrientos overthrew Victor Paz's second government. Until the early 1980s military dictatorships outlawed the MNR and other leftist parties. After twenty-two years of military governments, and fraud-tainted and/or inconclusive elections, Hernán Siles, of the left-wing United Democratic and Popular Unity (UDP) coalition, became president in 1982. The second party system was between 1982 and 2002, which was the multiparty system known for its stability and its commitment to market-friendly policies. Since 2003 the MAS has dominated a new party system.

Neoliberalism and Multiparty Politics

When Víctor Paz became president for the third and final time in 1985, inflation in Bolivia was more than 4,000 percent. The government had a fiscal deficit of 23.4 percent of GDP and the country had given up paying interest on its foreign debt. The collapse of Bolivia's tin-led export economy, along with the inability to forge stable governing coalitions, had forced Siles (October 1982–August 1985) to cut his presidential term short by one year. If the revolution stood for nationalizing the means of production, establishing universal franchise rights, and radical agrarian reform, President Paz's final term in office initiated a series of reforms that would make Bolivia one of the model countries for neoliberal reform in the developing world.

Radical macroeconomic stabilization or shock therapy, advised by none other than Jeffrey Sachs, did eradicate inflation. First-generation reforms were followed by a wave of wide-ranging structural reforms during the presidencies of Jaime Paz (1989–1993) and Sánchez de Lozada (1993–1997). Under Jaime Paz the government granted the Central Bank formal independence, reformed public administration, and had begun the privatization of small state-owned enterprises. In a concession to widespread support for nationalized industries, Sánchez de Lozada's administration did not privatize state corporations in petroleum and gas, the railroads, air transport, or any of the other areas that the

Bolivian state had come to control. Instead, it created an innovative program whereby a private sector buyer would purchase a 50 percent–controlling share of a state company (originally, Sánchez de Lozada's government had proposed that investors be granted 49 percent, but the objections by bidding companies led to the percentage point increase). Private pension funds would then become responsible for the remaining 50 percent of the "capitalized" firm's stock, one that would end up paying dividends in the form of an annual pension to elderly Bolivians (the *Bonosol*). His administration also obtained legislative support for ambitious social goals, including a bilingual education system, the creation of more than 310 municipalities that would receive 20 percent of central state revenues, and administrative decentralization. Bolivia's extensive economic reforms came to be touted as a model worthy of emulation because they combined responsible macroeconomic policies with institutional reforms that would lay the basis for sustained and equitable growth.[4]

The transformation of Bolivian politics not only made structural reform possible, but it also raised hopes that political instability was a thing of the past. Both left and right in the country's multiparty system agreed to abide by election results. When a congressional coalition between the rightist Democratic Action Party (ADN) and the Leftist Revolutionary Movement (MIR) made the latter's candidate, Jaime Paz, president in 1989 (though he came in third place), neither the MNR nor its candidate, Sánchez de Lozada (who came in first place), organized street protests or encouraged military factions to overthrow the government. The depth of the economic crisis and dependence on multilateral financial institutions had led to a convergence around market-friendly policies and liberal democratic institutions.

Two features of the political and party system made it possible to stabilize politics and to support structural reform. First, electoral laws reduced temptations to defect from the new policy equilibrium. The 1967 Bolivian constitution maintained a long-term provision empowering Congress to select the president should no candidate obtain an absolute majority of the popular vote. Equally important was the fused ballot system that forced voters to cast ballots for the presidential and legislative candidates of the same party. Straight-ticket voting limited voters' choices as it secured seemingly predictable shares of the vote for a stable average effective number of parties of 3.92 between 1985 and 2002. Both also contributed to cooperative executive-legislative relations. The same congressional coalition of parties that elected a president also obtained seats in his cabinet, whose control of ministerial portfolios was contingent on a complex bargain that allowed strong-minded and wily presidents to produce legislative majorities for their bills. To avoid getting locked out of the cabinet and a share of the spoils, parties learned to support the newfound policy consensus.

Multiparty Politics and Its Critics

Several factors undermined the political foundations of the liberal policy consensus. First, the shift to a Mixed Member Proportional (MMP) system from a closed-list PR system in 1994 expanded voters' choices and thus fueled a market for antiestablishment parties. With the change to a German-styled system, voters could select a representative in one of sixty single-member plurality districts (SMPDs) and still use fused ballots to select another sixty deputies in multimember PR districts. First used in 1997, the MMP system allowed SMPD candidates to bypass the leadership of existing parties and appeal directly to voters. Morales's initial foray into electoral politics came from winning one of these seats with the largest majority of any deputy in the 1997 elections.

Second, by the late 1990s social movements throughout the country began to revive a nationalist and antiestablishment discourse. As the MAS began to organize, it built bridges between existing organizations to assemble a broader movement with revolutionary ambitions. The MAS and its allies incorporated their specific demands into a common platform that targeted "neoliberalismo," a catch-all term of scorn that blamed fifteen years of economic and social reform for all of the country's economic and social ills.

Surveys indicate that a constituency exists for radical politics in Bolivia. The Americas Barometer's first, nationally representative poll of Bolivians in 1998 revealed that only slightly more than 10 percent of survey respondents were highly supportive of the political system and highly tolerant of the political rights of individuals who make negative comments on the Bolivian system of government. Nearly half of those polled had low levels of system support and political tolerance. This biennial poll reveals that these percentages barely changed between 1998 and 2006.[5]

Three structural conditions turned many Bolivians against the liberal policy consensus. Macroeconomic facts did not help the established parties make their case before a skeptical electorate. Though inflation was low and social indicators were gradually improving, the Bolivian economy was growing very slowly. If the country's GDP per capita had grown at an average annual rate of 0.6 percent between 1952 and 1982, extensive structural reform had not done much to accelerate an anemic growth rate. Between 1985 and 2000 the economy only grew in per capita terms an average of 0.9 percent per year.[6]

Next, second-stage liberal reforms had not overcome long-term political weaknesses. Daniel Kaufmann of the World Bank's Governance Indicators project and two colleagues used sophisticated econometrics to understand the institutional roots of "tepid" growth.[7] Their surveys of firms and of Bolivian public officials showed that cronyism, corruption, and the general disregard for the rule of law reduced the profitability of companies as well as the transparency and effectiveness of the public sector. Although there were pockets of excellence in the private and public sectors, firms had to be large and politically well connected in order to benefit from being formal and thus pay taxes. So even when, as in the 1990s, inflation was low and the exchange rate was stable, a weak state did little to lift the country's growth rate. A weak state was also at the root of the legitimacy crisis, one that made—and continues to make—it hard for elected officials to elicit cooperation from society to pay taxes, stop importing and consuming contraband goods (that deprived the state of US$430 million by 1997), and refrain from toppling governments.

Finally, poverty and ethnic discrimination combined to turn many Bolivians against the state. Unimpressive growth rates indicated that most Bolivians lived in poverty. Between 1990 and 2006 an average of 67.8 and 59.3 percent of Bolivians of the western and eastern lowlands, respectively, lived in poverty. Between 1990 and 2002 infant mortality rates had fallen from 109 to 77 per thousand live births, demonstrating that social conditions, at best, were only improving slowly. The Americas Barometer showed that poor Bolivians were also more likely to be targets of ethnic prejudice: In the 2008 survey 31 percent of Bolivians reported being discriminated against in the previous year, by far the highest rate in the western hemisphere.[8] Respondents also indicated that government offices and public places were the two sites where they were most likely to be treated offensively.

Changing commodity markets, however, created a golden political opportunity for the social movements to appeal to a national-level audience, one that would offer them a credible political alternative to the increasingly discredited party system. As the price of gas and oil began to climb with the start of the new millennium, foreign energy companies began to cash in on several years of investment that a liberalized energy policy regime had encouraged. By 2000, international energy markets realized that Bolivia had proven gas reserves second to Venezuela's in South America. Since Bolivia has no coastline, the gas would have to be exported through Chile, but Bolivia had lost in the War of the Pacific (1879–1883) to Chile. The absence of diplomatic relations with Chile meant that gas could not be exported through this neighbor. Antisystemic forces then latched onto these issues to stoke nationalist sensibilities. Increasingly larger numbers of Bolivians believed that the terms provided to foreign energy companies (when the price for gas was low, a point often forgotten in domestic debates) were overly generous and depriving them of their rightful share of resource rents.[9]

Social protest began to escalate by the late 1990s. From a low of an average of thirteen protest events per month during Sánchez de Lozada's first presidency (1993–1997), the social movements then organized an average of twenty-eight protest events per month during the second presidency of Hugo Banzer of the Democratic Action Party (ADN) (1997–2002, though Vice

President Jorge Quiroga became president once Banzer died in 2001).[10] For the social movements, marches and blockades were a way to speak truth to power and part of a more general struggle to rid the country of "neoliberal-ismo." For the MAS's critics these tactics revealed the MAS's double-edged commitment to democracy. Many social protestors, in fact, were not simply aiming to pressure the government, but also to force an extra-constitutional change in government or even to spark another social revolution.[11] While participating in elections and taking seats in Congress and in municipal councils, the MAS was also using the institutions of democracy to undermine democracy itself.

By October 2003 protest marches demanding the nationalization of gas deposits and the president's resignation turned violent, and the army fired on protestors, killing more than fifty. The government split over how to react to yet another regime crisis. Vice President Carlos Mesa, a popular television anchorman and published author, counseled negotiations while Sánchez de Losada holed himself in a bunker known as the war room. Once the military, police, and Congress abandoned the president, he resigned his post and turned power over to Vice President Carlos Mesa.

Bereft of congressional support, Mesa relied on high popularity ratings to amend the constitution to create referendums. The first was held in 2003 and revealed that more than 90 percent of the voters wanted to renegotiate inter-national energy contracts.[12] Street protests demanded that energy contracts be nationalized, which led legislators to hike taxes and royalties on gas com-panies. Despite efforts to find the middle ground, Mesa proved no more ca-pable of navigating the challenges of daily marches and frequent blockades. Protest events soared, reaching an average of forty-nine per month during Mesa's presidency. By early June 2005, Mesa had publicly committed himself to resigning on several occasions before finally turning power over to Ed-uardo Rodríguez, President of the Supreme Court. Even though the consti-tution mandated that the President of the Senate, Hormando Vaca Diez, assume the presidency, the social movements vetoed Vaca Diez's assumption of the presidency.[13]

The December 2005 election of Morales was the definitive end of the market-friendly multiparty system. Leftist and nationalist protest movements had managed to convert a plethora of local and regionally based sectoral movements into a political project that obtained the support of slightly more than half of all Bolivian voters. Former ADN President Quiroga (2001–2002), representing a coalition of establishment parties known as the Demo-cratic and Social Power Party (*Podemos*), obtained just 28.6 percent of the vote. The ability to appeal to voters from a variety of ethnic and class back-grounds indicated that the MAS had outgrown its social movement and in-digenous origins. In a country where two-thirds of the adults identified with one of several ethnic groups and called themselves mestizos, the MAS had successfully mobilized indigenous and rural as well as urban and mestizo voters. It had become a credible, national-level political force that appealed to an increasingly leftist electorate, one that was strongly in favor of asserting more sovereignty over the country's recently discovered gas reserves.[14]

Hegemonic Party Politics

The election of Morales to the presidency produced a new party system, one where MAS was dominant or even hegemonic. The December 2005 election gave them 55 percent of the seats in the lower house of Congress as well as a plurality just two seats shy of controlling the twenty-seven-member Senate. This was the closest thing to a unified party government that Bolivia had seen since the one-party governments of the immediate postrevolutionary period. The effective number of parties in the lower house of the legislature fell to 2.33 from 4.76 in the 2002 legislative elections. As a result, the ideological pivot of the party system therefore moved substantially to the nationalist left.

Morales believed that his government had won a far-reaching mandate. In his inaugural speech the new president informed his country, "especially [his] brother indigenous peoples of the Americas," that "we will take power for 500 years." In the aftermath of the "nationalization" of gas reserves on May Day 2006, the president's popularity ratings soared to 80 percent, seemingly confirming that the electorate wanted MAS to overhaul Bolivian society. MAS wanted to have a majority large enough to produce a new constitution unilaterally, as was seen when the party proposed that elections for the Constituent Assembly award all delegates in three-member constituencies to the party that obtained a plurality of the vote in each of these constituencies.

In the Constituent Assembly elections of early July 2006, MAS came close to accomplishing its objective. With 50.9 percent of the vote, the MAS got 137, or 53.7 percent, of the Assembly seats, most of which were awarded to the plurality winner in three-member constituencies.[15] It could count on the support of another dozen or so deputies, but it remained short of controlling a two-thirds majority in the Assembly. MAS supporters also defeated an accompanying referendum that would obligate the Assembly to grant more autonomy to the country's nine departments.

Results on the autonomy-seeking referendum also revealed that the opposition to the MAS was as much national as it was regional. The measure won overwhelmingly in the eastern departments of Beni, Pando, Santa Cruz, and Tarija, where between 1990 and 2006 an average of 34.3 percent of the population resided and where 45.7 percent of the GDP was generated. Much of the country's (legal) agricultural exports are produced in the eastern lowlands, and, most importantly, 80 percent of proven gas reserves are located in the southern department of Tarija.[16]

A seven-month long procedural struggle over the Assembly's internal rules of order not only revealed the depth of distrust between the MAS and its critics, but also that MAS could not decide whether to compromise with or to overwhelm the opposition. The existing constitution stated that two-thirds of Congressional members present during any session could convene a Constituent Assembly. The March 2006 law echoed the key phrase, which required two-thirds of Assembly members to approve a draft constitution. In late November, however, after several months of arduous negotiations with the Podemos, MAS replaced the two-thirds with an absolute majority requirement in the Assembly's internal rules manual in a midnight session and without the presence of opposition delegates. Opposition boycotts then paralyzed Assembly deliberations, held in Sucre (the country's capital), because a quorum could not be satisfied. Opposition parties also organized hunger strikes and boycotted congressional deliberations in La Paz. In negotiations led by Vice President Álvaro García, MAS agreed to reinstate the two-thirds requirement in mid-February 2007.

By early August 2007 convention delegates agreed to postpone their deliberations so that the national Congress, based in La Paz, could issue a new law granting Assembly delegates a six-month extension on their work. Arguments about rules of order delayed substantive work on a new constitution, and the early August deadline was missed. MAS supporters concluded that the opposition's procedural objections meant that it was just stalling for time, and this reaffirmed their belief that the opposition was little more than a creature of Santa Cruz–based oligarchic interests. For its part, the opposition interpreted lack of progress on substantive questions as evidence that the MAS wanted to impose—not negotiate—a new constitutional order on the country. In exchange for accepting that an absolute majority of national voters—rather than a majority in each of the departments—needed to approve the draft constitution, the opposition got MAS to consent to holding two separate referendums on the Assembly-approved draft constitution. While the first referendum would let voters decide, through majority vote, on measures that delegates could not agree on, the second would submit the final draft of the constitution, containing both the results of the first referendum and convention-agreed upon articles, to the voters for final approval.

Disputes between the MAS and its opponents deepened as the new deadline for drafting a constitution approached. Antigovernment groups, especially from and in the eastern departments, began to organize strikes and search for ways to become more autonomous of the central government. Demonstrations in Sucre became violent—ultimately registering two deaths and hundreds more injured—as locals confronted MAS supporters over whether the executive and legislative branches of government should be moved from La Paz, where they had been relocated in 1898, back to Sucre, the de jure capital of Bolivia. Against this backdrop MAS swiftly approved their draft by availing itself of a procedure outlined in the August law extending Assembly deliberations. The first article of this law stated that the Assembly could dispense with the two-thirds requirement if delegates could not reach this level of support for controversial issues and it submitted such matters to Congress, which could then, with a two-thirds vote, ask voters to settle it in a referendum. In Assembly meetings that the MAS had rescheduled in the city of Oruro in early December, progovernment delegates alleged that they had failed to reach consensus on an issue about whether the maximum size of agricultural properties should be 5,000 or 10,000 hectares (12,355 to 24,711 aces). As a reporter for the daily *La Razón* confirmed in conversations with MAS delegates, this was a ruse to promulgate its draft without having to satisfy the two-thirds requirement.[17] It was inconceivable that sessions filled with MAS delegates would split on this or any measure.

Constitutional Breakdown and Regional Polarization

The MAS-dominated Assembly's vote created a constitutional controversy of enormous proportions. Under normal circumstances the opposition would have appealed to the Constitutional Tribunal, created in 1994, to settle this conflict. However, by late August 2007 the MAS-dominated lower house of Congress had, in a stormy session, voted to begin impeachment trials against four of the five remaining magistrates on the Tribunal because earlier that year they had ruled against Morales's use of a Supreme (i.e., unilateral) Decree to fill four vacancies on the Supreme Court while the Congress was in recess. In response, these magistrates resigned, leaving the Tribunal without a quorum to meet. Although an absolute majority of deputies was sufficient to suspend Tribunal magistrates, only a two-thirds majority could approve their replacements.

Efforts to bridge the divide between the MAS and the increasingly regional-based opposition proved fruitless. The early December 2007 congressional decision to reduce the share of gas and petroleum royalties received by departments only complicated these efforts. Even while reaffirming its commitment to "dialogue" with the Prefects, Vice President Álvaro García Linera refused to reconsider the government's decisions. In late February, while progovernment protestors circled the neoclassical legislative palace in La Paz and threatened opposition deputies, the MAS majority in the lower house of Congress violated parliamentary procedures—and its agreement with the opposition—by approving bills to submit their party's draft constitution and one of its articles (fixing the maximum size of agricultural estates to 10,000 hectares) to the voters for approval.

The failure to honor the agreements governing the production of a new constitution polarized political competition. In response, the opposition-dominated eastern departments organized several equally illegal autonomy-seeking referendums. Between early April and late June 2008, departmental electorates of the eastern lowlands approved autonomy-seeking statutes that directly contradicted the MAS's constitutional project and even the existing constitution on several key points. Santa Cruz's autonomy statute, for example, will make its Legislative Assembly and its Governor (formerly Prefect) responsible for administering national resources, education, citizen security, and tax collection. In the absence of a Constitutional Tribunal to arbitrate differences between the national and departmental government—and, by implication, the constitutionality of the MAS's behavior—regional politicians implied that the eastern departments could proceed to increase their power and authority.

The opposition's swift and successful effort to expand its autonomy put the national government on the defensive as it demonstrated the national opposition's irrelevance in political competition. In early May 2008 Podemos Senators unexpectedly joined forces with the MAS to approve an (unconstitutional) recall referendum for the president and prefects. In December 2007 President Morales had submitted such a bill to break the logjam in the Assembly, one that both he and opposition prefects gradually lost interest in enacting. Once he learned of the news, the president rushed back to La Paz from Santa Cruz. After midnight consultations with his advisors in early May 2008, the president accepted the challenge in what remains a perplexing series of events, and one that illustrates the opposition's failure to unify even around a common strategic stance.

The opposition lost the August 2008 recall referendum. Even though they won the vote in the eastern lowlands, President Morales won more than two-thirds of the national vote—67.4 percent—in his own recall election. None of the opposition prefects did as well in their respective departments, and two of them, José Luis of La Paz and Manfred Reyes of Cochabamba, lost their own recall elections. The extent of the government's support demonstrated that it could really claim to speak on behalf of the overwhelming majority of Bolivians. What appears to be little more than factional rivalry drove Podemos to destroy the opposition prefects' hard-won strategic advantage.

The government quickly acted on its victory. When opposition prefects called for a strike to stop Congress from passing a law to hold a referendum on the draft constitution itself, the government sent the security forces to take over petroleum installations once opposition hardliners cut off gas exports to

Argentina. It arrested and (illegally) jailed the opposition Prefect of Pando, Leopoldo Fernández, after progovernment protestors were shot in an exchange of gunfire between MAS and anti-MAS forces on departmental territory. In a series of high-level negotiations between government and opposition leaders, pro- and enough antigovernment legislators (illegally) amended the December 2007 draft constitution that had been (illegally) promulgated by the Constituent Assembly, and they then set a date to hold the referendum for its approval.

The New Constitutional Order

In late January 2008, 61.43 percent of the voters (with a turnout rate of 90 percent of registered voters) approved the 2009 constitution. It expanded the state's control over the economy and promoted the rights of indigenous peoples and social movements. In the hands of a well-disciplined party or tight coalition of interests, it promises to endow the executive with the ability to marginalize the opposition. In the absence of a dominant party, however, it also threatens to fragment the state: The constitution divides power not only between the three branches of government and an array of semiautonomous institutions and oversight bodies, but also between the central, departmental, municipal, and autonomous indigenous communities.

The new constitution drops the congressional runoff system for selecting the chief executive. It opts for a modified Costa Rican approach to elect the president, one that awards this office to the most voted-for candidate who also had received at least 40 percent of the popular vote as well as at least 10 percent more than the first runner-up. If that does not happen, there is a popular runoff between the top two candidates. The constitution also creates a bicameral "Multinational Legislative Assembly." MAS had wanted all deputies to be elected in single-member districts, but it compromised by creating a lower house of 130 members, half of which are elected in such districts and the other half in multimember districts. The constitution also calls for special indigenous districts: In a transitory law, the old Congress set aside seven districts for this purpose in April 2009, a number that MAS promises to increase once the new Assembly is seated and is able to write a new electoral law. The citizens of each department elect four senators, who are elected proportionally. The president and legislators have five-year terms and can only be consecutively reelected once.

Citizens will also get to vote on court judges, including those of the Supreme Tribunal of Justice and of the Constitutional Court. Judicial candidates, however, will first have to receive the endorsement of a two-thirds vote in the Multinational Legislative Assembly. Those so endorsed will then run in popular elections that will not allow partisan affiliations or campaigning of any kind. For MAS, these procedures will ensure that only honest and impartial citizens will become judges, while for MAS's critics, this system is tailor-made to guarantee that progovernment judges will be elected to the bench and thus not contest the majority's policies. Customary laws held by many indigenous communities will have equal footing with conventional Bolivian laws, which the Assembly promises to amend in the coming years.

The new constitution also empowers both social movements and territorial interests to shape the design and implementation of central state policies. It stipulates the appointment of representatives by the social movements to oversee the institutions of horizontal accountability, including that of the National Electoral Court (CNE), the Comptroller, and the Central Bank. While the president and the Assembly select the governing boards of these institutions, "the sovereign people, by means of organized civil society," to quote the new constitution, "will participate in the design of public policies." A specialized body of law, as yet unwritten, will develop the procedures by which social movements participate in and oversee the country's evolving state apparatus. The 2009 constitution also accelerates the territorial fragmentation of the public sector. It devolves important functions not only to departmental governments but also to municipal and autonomous indigenous territories. For the MAS, these oversight bodies and institutional fragmentation maximize the ability of its constituents to protect their interests, even if they should lose their control of the two elected branches of government.

Conclusion

The social movements have built a new political system in Bolivia by destroying the old one. They overthrew presidents in 2003 and 2004, decapitated the judiciary, curtailed regional autonomy, and marginalized the opposition in the national Congress and Constituent Assembly—actions that, on repeated occasions, have been ratified in successive referendums. MAS and its allies have erected a plebiscitarian regime privileging the relationship between the people, the president, and the legislative assembly. These three institutions designate high court justices and the leaders of the rest of the institutions of horizontal accountability. The social movements also oversee the entire state apparatus to ensure that the preferences of the "sovereign people" reign supreme.

MAS embodies an antiliberal consensus, one that a gas-induced economic boom greatly facilitated. Support for the political system has dramatically improved even as the newfound consensus displays little tolerance for the regime's opponents. Although popular support for the political system has improved, more than two-thirds of Bolivian citizens exhibit low levels of tolerance. The fact that 35.8 percent are highly supportive of the new system and politically intolerant suggests that there is an important minority who hold a combination of attitudes, the Americas Barometer reminds us, that is congruent with a stable autocracy.[18]

It is an open question whether the new regime can outlive Evo Morales. The first social revolution spawned a one-party regime and ended with the 1964 military coup before giving way to several military dictatorships. Chronic instability, which inhibits the consolidation of long-term rules to govern political succession, undermined past attempts to create an enduring political order. The booms and busts of commodity exports also turn allies into opponents, because they wreak havoc with the ability of the state to finance social spending and longer-term development. It was precisely the collapse of the tin boom in the early 1980s that led to the failure of the left's (UDP) last attempt to govern the country. Much of MAS's ability to consolidate a new constitutional order therefore depends on weathering a future bust in commodity exports.

Suggestions for Further Reading

Crabtree, John, and Laurence Whitehead, eds. *Unresolved Tensions: Bolivia Past and Present.* Pittsburgh: University of Pittsburgh Press, 2008.

Grindle, Merilee, and Pilar Domingo, eds. *Proclaiming Revolution: Bolivia in Comparative Perspective.* London and Cambridge, MA: Institute of Latin American Studies and David Rockefeller Center for Latin American Studies, Harvard University, 2003.

Klein, Herbert S. *A Concise History of Bolivia.* Cambridge and New York: Cambridge University Press, 2003.

Kohl, Benjamin H., and Linda C. Farthing. *Impasse in Bolivia: Neoliberal Hegemony and Popular Resistance.* London and New York: Zed Books, 2006.

Lazar, Sian. *El Alto, Rebel City: Self and Citizenship in Andean Bolivia.* Durham, NC: Duke University Press, 2008.

Moreno Morales, Daniel E., et al. *The Political Culture of Democracy in Bolivia: The Impact of Governance.* Report Prepared for the U.S. Agency for International Development, La Paz, Bolivia, August 2008.

Silva, Eduardo. *Challenging Neoliberalism in Latin America.* Cambridge and New York: Cambridge University Press, 2009.

Notes

1. Fabrice Lehoucq, "At the Risk of Being Overthrown: Military Coups in Twentieth Century Latin America," forthcoming.

2. Daniel E. Moreno Morales, et al., *The Political Culture of Democracy in Bolivia: The Impact of Governance* (unpublished report Prepared for the US Agency for International Development, La Paz, Bolivia, August 2008), pp. xxx–xxxiii.

3. Eduardo A. Gamarra, "Bolivia: Evo Morales and Democracy," in *Constructing Democratic Governance in Latin America*, 3rd ed., ed. Jorge I. Domínguez and Michael Shifter (Baltimore, MD: Johns Hopkins University Press, 1996, 2003, 2008), 141–47.

4. Useful overviews include Merilee S. Grindle, "Shadowing the Past? Policy Reform in Bolivia, 1985–2002," in *Proclaiming Revolution: Bolivia in Comparative Perspective*, ed. Merilee S. Grindle and Pilar Domingo (Cambridge, MA, and London, England: DRCLAS, Harvard University and ILAS, University of London, 2003) and Benjamin Kohl and Linda Farthing, *Impasse in Bolivia: Neoliberal Hegemony and Popular Resistance* (London: Zed Books, 2006).

5. Mitchell A. Seligson, *The Political Culture of Democracy in Bolivia: 1998* (Unpublished Report Prepared for the U.S. Agency of International Development, La Paz, Bolivia, 1998), 90. The sample size is 3,000 with a margin of error of ± 1.7 percent. Reports and publications of subsequent poll results indicated are available at: http://sitemason.vanderbilt.edu/lapop/BOLIVIABACK.

6. Angus Maddison, *World Population, GDP and Per Capita GDP, 1–2003 AD* (March 2007 update), www.ggdc.net/maddison/, accessed on March 25, 2007.

7. Daniel Kaufmann, Massimo Mastruzzi, and Diego Zavaleta, "Sustained Macroeconomic Reforms, Tepid Growth: A Governance Puzzle in Bolivia?" in *In Search of Prosperity: Analytic Narratives on Economic Growth*, ed. Dani Rodrik (Princeton, NJ: Princeton University Press, 2003), 334–98.

8. Poverty figures are from Luis Carlos Jemio M., Fernando Candia C., and José Luis Evia V., "Reforms and Counter-Reforms in Bolivia," Research Network Working Paper, Research Department, Inter-American Development Bank, 2009. Infant mortality data is from Kohl and Farthing, *Impasse in Bolivia*, 197. Daniel E. Moreno Morales, "Los escenarios de la discriminación en Bolivia," *Nueva Crónica y Buen Gobierno* 27 (24 October–6 November 2008): 17.

9. Kurt Weyland, "The Rise of Latin America's Two Lefts: Insights From Rentier State Theory," *Comparative Politics* 41 (2009): 145–64.

10. Roberto Laserna and Miguel Villarroel, *38 Años de conflictos sociales en Bolivia: descripción general y por periodos gubernamentales* (Cochabamba and La Paz: CERES, COSUDE, and Instituto para la Democracia, 2008).

11. Álvaro García Linera, a former guerilla and the current vice president, has written extensively about these movements. See García Linera, et al., *Tiempos de rebelión* (La Paz: Muela del Diablo Editores, 2001) and *Memorias de Octubre* (La Paz: Muela del Diablo Editores, 2004).

12. Anita Breuer, "The Problematic Relation between Direct Democracy and Accountability in Latin America: Evidence from the Bolivian Case," *Bulletin of Latin American Research* 27 (2008): 1–23.

13. An insider's account of these months is Carlos D. Mesa Gisbert, *Presidencia Sitiada: Memorias de mi Gobierno* (La Paz: Editorial Plural, 2008), 51–116. A detailed chronology is Ricardo Sanjinés Ávila, *De la UDP al MAS* (La Paz: Hans Seidel Stiftung, 2006), 277–328.

14. Raúl Madrid, "The Rise of Ethno-Populism in Latin America: The Bolivian Case," *World Politics* 60 (April 2008): 484–86. Also, see Salvador Romero Ballivián, *El Tablero Reordenado: Análisis de la Elección Presidencial de 2005* (La Paz: Corte Nacional Electoral, 2006).

15. The plurality winner received two of the three seats in the three-member constituencies. Voters also cast ballots for an additional forty-five seats in nine departmental constituencies. The plurality winner received the first two seats in each five-member district. The subsequent runners-up would each receive one of the remaining three seats. See "Ley No 3364 (6 March 2006)," in *Compendio Electoral* (La Paz: CNE, 2007): 285–96.

16. George Gray-Molina, *La economia mas alla del gas* (La Paz: PNUD, 2005): 155. The figures cited in the previous sentence are from Jemio M., Candia C., and Evia V., "Reforms and Counter-Reforms in Bolivia."

17. "El oficialismo apruebe su CPE y la enviará a 2 referéndums," *La Razón* (La Paz), 10 December 2007. This article notes that 164—six fewer than the two-thirds requirement—delegates were present during this session. I have been unable to confirm this with the Assembly's records because its website has been down since late December 2007.

18. Moreno Morales, et al., *The Political Culture of Democracy in Bolivia*, 99–100.

15

Ecuador

From Crisis to Left Turn

Catherine M. Conaghan

Ecuador joined the ranks of Latin American countries that were taking a twenty-first-century "left turn" when Rafael Correa swore in as president on January 15, 2007.[1] Like his counterparts in the Andean region, President Hugo Chávez of Venezuela and President Evo Morales of Bolivia, Correa won the presidency with an ambitious agenda that offered sweeping change to voters weary of the traditional political establishment. Young, charismatic, and tireless on the campaign trail, Correa captured the imagination of Ecuadorians with the promise of what he called the Citizens Revolution (*La Revolución Ciudadana*). His revolution set its sights on a new constitution, ending neoliberal economic policies, and restoring national sovereignty through a foreign policy aimed at curbing the influence of the U.S. and international financial institutions.

President Correa wasted no time in delivering on his promised transformation. Voters rewarded him with their continued support in public opinion polls and at the ballot box. In April 2007 more than 80 percent of the electorate endorsed Correa's plan for a constituent assembly to write a new constitution. In September 2007 voters delivered a solid progovernment majority in the elections for the assembly. A year later the new constitution won the support of 64 percent of the electorate. Then, with redesigned government institutions and new rules in place, a fresh round of national elections ensued

COLOMBIA

Esmeraldas

Rio Mira

Tulcán

ESMERALDAS

Rio Esmeraldas

CARCHI

Rio Putumayo

Ibarra

IMBABURA

Lago Agrio

Rio San Miguel

Rio Quinindé

PICHINCHA

Quito

Papallacta

Rio Aguarico

NAPO

Rio Napo

Rio Daule

MANABÍ

Latacunga

COTOPAXI

Tena

Nuevo Rocafuerte

Portoviejo

Quevedo

Ambato

TUNGURAHUA

Puyó

Rio Nushiño

Rio Cononaco

Isla La Plata

Jipijapa

LOS RÍOS

Guaranda

BOLÍVAR

Riobamba

Rio Curaray

Babahoyo

PASTAZA

Rio Guayas

CHIMBORAZO

Rio Pastaza

Salinas

GUAYAS

Santa Elena

Guayaquil

Rio Tigre

Macas

Playas

CAÑAR

MORONA-SANTIAGO

Isla Puná

Golfo de Guayaquil

Cuenca

AZUAY

Machala

PACIFIC OCEAN

Rio Zamora

EL ORO

PERU

Rio Tumbez

LOJA

Loja

Zamora

ZAMORA-CHINCHIPE

Rio Chinchipe

ANDES MOUNTAINS

0   50   100 Miles

0   50   100 Kilometers

ECUADOR

in April 2009. For the first time in thirty years, a president was elected in the first round of the election, with no need for a runoff. To no one's surprise, the winning candidate was Rafael Correa, who garnered 51 percent of the vote. Correa's victory was historic in another sense: He became the first president in contemporary history to be reelected, thanks to the elimination of the longstanding ban on immediate reelection.

By any standard, Rafael Correa enjoyed remarkable success in his first two years as president. He consolidated executive authority, out-foxed his opponents in the party establishment, and legitimated his aggressive style and leftist policies with a string of electoral victories. No matter what lies ahead, Correa has secured his place in history as one of Ecuador's most skilful and shrewd leaders; his constitution will shape the course of politics for years to come.

However, Correa's early successes were not built on the force of his personality and ambitions alone. In order to understand Correa's meteoric ascent and why he was able to reshape the political landscape in a relatively short period of time, we need to look beyond the man and understand the historical circumstances that made his fiery leadership and leftist appeals so compelling to so many voters. When Ecuadorians elected Rafael Correa, they looked to the future by voting for a candidate who promised to redress past injustices and put an end to chronic political instability.

Elite Domination and Dependence

Ecuador is the second smallest country in Latin America, with territory equivalent to that of the state of Nevada in the United States. With close to fourteen million people, however, it is more densely populated than Bolivia. Located on the continent's Pacific coast, Ecuador shares borders with Colombia and Peru. Its diverse geography includes the coastal plain, a mountainous interior known as the *sierra*, a flat jungle area to the east in the Amazon basin, and the Galápagos Islands in the Pacific Ocean. Its population is diverse. Over forty indigenous nations constitute 25 percent of the population, while Afro-descendants account for just about 3 percent. Approximately 55 percent of the country is comprised of *mestizos* (mixed race), with European and other immigrants making up the remaining 7 percent of the population.

During the period of Spanish colonialism, Ecuador was a relative backwater in the empire. Unlike Peru and Bolivia, Ecuador had no significant mineral deposits to exploit. Ecuador's resource base lay in agriculture, and its labor force was made up of indigenous peoples. Composed of many Kichwa-speaking tribes, the indigenous population became subject to forced labor in the landed estates (*haciendas*) and textile mills owned by the colonial elite. Thus, class and ethnicity were conjoined early in Ecuador's history, leaving a legacy of racism and discrimination that plagues the country to this day. Indigenous peoples were relegated to the bottom of the social hierarchy, along with African slaves and their descendants, while *mestizos* and whites occupied the more privileged positions in society.

Gaining independence in 1822, Ecuador joined the ill-fated Gran Colombia confederation with Colombia and Venezuela. By 1830 the confederation collapsed and Ecuador began its life as an independent republic. Postindependence politics was marked by two features that had lasting effects on the country's political development: elite domination and elite fragmentation. As in many other Latin American countries, the new republic was dominated by an elite minority, a propertied upper class uninterested in promoting a broad-based democratization of the political system. In Ecuador, however, the elite were divided by geography and had contending economic interests. In the sierra and around the capital city of Quito, large landowners lorded over traditional haciendas, exploiting Indian laborers who, in exchange for the right to farm a small subsistence plot, were subjected to working conditions reminiscent of medieval feudalism. Allied with the Roman Catholic Church, these landed oligarchs eventually formed the Conservative party to defend their interests. On the coast, maritime commerce and tropical export agriculture produced a different, more entrepreneurial upper class in the port city of Guayaquil. The coastal elite, interested in free trade and secularization, then became the bedrock of the Liberal party.

The power struggle between these segments of the dominant class was not confined to the ballot box. Throughout the nineteenth century military intervention and political violence were combined with authoritarian styles of leadership. Conservative party founder Gabriel García Moreno turned his presidency into a ruthless civilian dictatorship, using his power to assure the Roman Catholic Church's control over education while modernizing the country's infrastructure. García became a conservative martyr after liberal activists orchestrated his assassination in 1875. Like García Moreno, the career of the legendary founder of the Liberal party, Eloy Alfaro, was steeped in violence. On numerous occasions Alfaro led military forces to topple governments. In the course of serving as president on four different occasions between 1896 and 1911, Alfaro upset García's legacy by enacting the separation of Church and state, but he likewise continued with projects to modernize infrastructure such as the Quito-Guayaquil railway. After feuding inside the Liberal party led Alfaro to attempt another antigovernment insurrection, he was snatched from a Quito jail cell by an angry mob and lynched in 1912.

By the early twentieth century the coastal elite had consolidated its control over the central government via the Liberal party, thanks in part to an economic boom driven by the export of cocoa beans. Enjoying near perfect climatic conditions for growing the delicious product, Ecuador became the world's largest exporter of cocoa, and the port city of Guayaquil reaped the rewards. The class structure began changing as a new urban working and middle class emerged. But economic prosperity and social differentiation did little to change elite attitudes: Democratization was still of little interest to landholders who depended on controlling the indigenous labor force and the cocoa barons of the coast who were determined to keep their own political power intact. In 1922, when hundreds of workers were killed by police during Guayaquil's first general strike, Ecuador's incipient labor movement got its first taste of how far elites were willing to go to retain control.

The weakness and dependency of the Ecuadorian economy set the stage for an important political juncture in 1925. The export boom turned into a bust as worldwide prices for cocoa declined and plant disease wreaked havoc on large landowners who preferred to spend their wealth in Europe rather than invest at home. Liberal governments had spent too much and accrued debts with international bondholders. With the economy unravelling, young military officers seized power in the "July Revolution." Backed by the sierra elite and segments of Quito's expanding middle class, the military set its sights on straightening out the country's finances, thereby creating new mechanisms to regulate the economy, including a Central Bank.

Although the July Revolution in no way dismantled the power of traditional elites, it did succeed in establishing a state bureaucracy capable of governing with some autonomy from oligarchic interests and put an end to the hegemony of the Liberal party. Moreover, the July Revolution set an important precedent for the military itself. Rather than becoming a reactionary and oppressive force in public life, the armed forces identified itself with reform and never resorted to the kind of brutal repression later practiced by militaries elsewhere in the region. One short-lived military regime in the late 1930s granted legal recognition to the trade union movement and tightened restrictions on foreign business investors. Decades later, the pro-reform identity of the military resurfaced. The military junta of 1963–1966 issued the country's first agrarian reform law. The next military government, headed in its first phase by General Guillermo Rodríguez Lara (1972–1976), declared a "Nationalist Revolution" aimed at modernizing the economy, increasing the role of the state in economic development, and redistributing wealth through agrarian and labor reforms. After most of the progressive reforms fizzled in the face of fierce opposition by the business elites, the military retreated peacefully from politics, handing over power to civilians in a negotiated transition in 1979.

Throughout the twentieth century Ecuador's elite demonstrated a remarkable capacity to regroup and reassert its political power when challenged by new leaders or movements. The career of Ecuador's foremost populist leader, José María Velasco Ibarra, offers a case in point. At various points during his long career Velasco attracted the support of elite-run parties when they found it expedient to ally with him. Velasco galvanized middle- and working-class audiences with his moralizing appeals and anti-oligarchic rhetoric: "Give me a balcony, and I will rule Ecuador," Velasco famously said. He did just that, albeit incompetently. Elected to the presidency five times during his lifetime, Velasco served only one complete term. The military removed him from office for his dismal public administration, not because he enacted policies that benefited the lower classes in any significant way. Without a strong party apparatus or roots in trade unionism, Velasco's personality-driven populism did nothing to undo the underlying dynamics of elite domination.

Other populist leaders failed in their bids for national power. Carlos Guevara Moreno, the founder of the Concentration of Popular Forces (*Concentración de Fuerzas Populares*, CFP), served as Guayaquil's mayor but never won the presidency. His successor, Assad Bucaram, born in Lebanon, was banned from running for the presidency by a rule prohibiting naturalized citizens from the ballot. Ecuador's leftist parties, the Socialist party and Communist party, never commanded a base sufficient to constitute an electoral threat. Nor was there a Cuban-inspired guerrilla insurgency in the style of those that appeared in other countries during the 1960s and 1970s. In short, though elites battled each other bitterly at times for the spoils of power, they also united periodically to make sure that would-be reformers or revolutionaries were co-opted or contained.

From 1948 to 1961 Ecuador enjoyed the so-called "democratic parenthesis," a peaceful rotation of elected civilian governments. The period coincided with a new spike in tropical agricultural exports. In response to the promotion policies enacted by President Galo Plaza and the active interest of the United Fruit Company, Ecuador became the world's leading exporter of bananas. However, just as cocoa export failed to generate sustained economic growth, so did bananas. Facing increased competition from Central American banana producers, by the early 1960s Ecuador's export sector faltered and the structural weaknesses of the economy were plain to see. Import-substitution industrialization depended heavily on protectionist policies and state subsidies, but government finances ebbed and flowed with the prices of the country's agricultural exports. Then, by 1972 the discovery of massive oil reserves in the jungles of the Amazon region changed the equation somewhat by generating windfall profits for the government. Nonetheless, Ecuador's economic dependence did not dissipate. Instead, it deepened as Ecuador joined other Latin American countries in taking advantage of the bonanza in international loans during the 1970s and therefore accruing substantial foreign debt.

Parties and Conflict in the Petro-State

The 1979 transition from military to civilian government marked another important juncture in the evolution of Ecuador's democracy: Universal suffrage was finally achieved. Although women had won the right to vote in 1929, prejudice and social conventions kept many women away from the ballot box in the ensuing decades. Even worse, literacy requirements had effectively disenfranchised the poor, indigenous, and Afro-descendant peoples. As late as 1968 the electorate was estimated to be as small as 15 percent of the population. But social change and the new constitution endorsed by voters in a 1978 referendum finally stripped away the old barriers. Adults were not only entitled to vote, but were legally required to do so. Over the next decade, the size of the electorate doubled. However, the growing electorate, full of first-time and younger voters, also proved to be fickle. Ecuador became a country noted for its high incidence of electoral volatility—voters showed little party loyalty, readily switching their vote across parties from one election to the next.

The extremely fragmented multiparty system offered a wide menu of choices, with parties of every ideological stripe along with strong-willed leaders who were frequently more adept at confrontation than compromise. Although remnants of the old oligarchic parties still remained on the scene, electoral competition expanded considerably beyond the traditional range of rightists, leftists, and populists. A new generation of young, middle-class reformers set their sights on modernizing and recasting the party system. In the presidencies that followed—Roldós, Hurtado, Febres Cordero, Borja— the important themes were twofold: the rocky character of executive-legislative relations and their juggling of the first wave of neoliberalism through stabilization packages without real structural reform.

The populist CFP and the Christian democratic Popular Democracy (*Democracia Popular*, DP) joined forces in the 1979 presidential election, winning an upset victory. President Jaime Roldós and Vice President Osvaldo Hurtado had campaigned as the "force for the change," but the obstacles to change surfaced quickly in the form of chronic partisan conflict and a crisis in executive-legislative relations. Roldós's CFP-led majority in congress splintered apart when Congress president Assad Bucaram, Roldós's one-time mentor and father-in-law, tried to control the new president and define the government's agenda. Roldós defied Bucaram, threatening to call a referendum and form a new party of his own. However, Roldós died an airplane crash in 1981. But Congress's confrontational conduct nonetheless continued under the subsequent government headed by President Osvaldo Hurtado, whose principal goal was to avoid a military coup. Every subsequent president also wrestled with the dilemma of how to govern effectively in a system in which legislative coalitions were almost always unpredictable and short-lived. With no single party in command of a solid majority in congress and with little discipline inside parties, presidents were forced to cobble together alliances. But the costs of the improvised and shaky coalitions were high; trading favors in return for legislatives votes became part of the process of coalition formation as did policy incoherence when lawmakers and presidents struck deals that flew in the face of their previous commitments. From the public's point of view, the policy process looked more like an exercise in corruption and political expediency than decision-making in the national interest.

In addition to chronic partisan conflict presidents also faced mounting challenges in managing a troubled economy. With the acceleration of oil exports and soaring prices in the international commodities market in the 1970s, Ecuador had become a petro-state—a nation in which public finances were extremely dependent on this single mineral export. Through the state-owned firm founded in 1972 (now named PetroEcuador), the military governments extracted windfall profits from the oil sector and used these to underwrite consumer spending and private sector expansion through policies that offered subsidies, cheap credit, and an overvalued exchange rate. Like other oil-producing countries ranging from Venezuela to Nigeria, Ecuador fell victim to the "resource curse," which means that although the abundant natural resource generated extraordinary revenues, the boom was not a springboard to equilibrated and sustained economic growth. Instead, it invited corruption and wasteful spending in both the public and private sectors while fueling the public's expectations that expanded consumption would go hand in hand with oil export.

Along with its "resource curse," Ecuador was ensnared in the "debt trap." Starting with the military government, Ecuador borrowed heavily from public and private international lenders to finance its state-centric economic model. By the conclusion of the military government, Ecuador's debt was around US$3 billion. Continued borrowing by civilian governments, along with the costs of interest and rescheduling payments, pushed the debt to more than US$10 billion by the time President Correa took office in 2009.

With a worldwide recession underway in the early 1980s, international financial institutions pressured debtor-governments to repay their loans and revamp their policies. Ecuador was subject to this "new conditionality" stipulated by the International Monetary Fund and the World Bank. In return for continued loan assistance, lending institutions demanded the implementation of austerity programs and neoliberal economic reforms that included the privatization of public firms, business deregulation, and an opening of markets to foreign investors. In Ecuador, presidents responded to the new demands from abroad in piecemeal form, trying to cope with the external pressures while ensuring their own survival in office as they faced stiff resistance from the public and even the business community in the implementation of the reforms. President Osvaldo Hurtado began the process of adjustment with measures that devalued the currency (for the first time since 1970) and increased taxes on consumption goods. The labor movement reacted to Hurtado's measures with a national strike that ended when the government modified the measures.

When León Febres Cordero, head of the rightist Social Christian Party (*Partido Social Cristiano*, PSC), won the presidency in 1984, Ecuador seemed poised to adopt a radical program of neoliberal economic reform. As the leader of the Guayaquil business community, Febres Cordero had been a long-time critic of the state-centric development model. Nevertheless, he was also a pragmatic politician, and when faced with adverse political circumstances, he was forced to abandon his plans to impose neoliberal reform and focus on simply finishing his term in office. The shaky pro-neoliberal majority that supported his initial austerity measures was swept away in the 1986 midterm congressional elections. A conflict involving supporters of dissident air force officer General Frank Vargas ended in a bizarre one-day kidnapping of Febres Cordero in 1987. Although the president escaped unharmed, his government was weakened. Setting his sights on finishing his term in office, Febres Cordero resorted to deficit spending as government finances collapsed under the weight of falling international prices for petroleum and a disruption in Ecuador's production due to an earthquake in March 1987.

Elected in 1988 as a social democrat, President Rodrigo Borja faced the same dilemmas as his predecessors. Petroleum prices continued to plummet, and the IMF pressed for more austerity in public spending. Though Borja had campaigned on a promise to pay the "social debt" owed to citizens by improving education and health care, government finances severely limited social spending. Like Hurtado, Borja tried to appease foreign creditors with limited stabilization measures such as currency devaluation and price increases for gasoline and electricity.

In 1992 former Quito mayor Sixto Durán Ballén won the presidency with the support of a center-right coalition. He made some inroads in enacting an IMF structural reforms' administration, and he had moved ahead with a deregulation of the banking sector and granted important concessions to multinational corporations allowing for oil exploration and production in the Amazonian region. However, his push to privatize many of the state-owned enterprises ran up against congressional opponents and the military who enjoyed stockholding rights in many of the government firms.

In comparative terms, Ecuador undertook far fewer neoliberal reforms than many other Latin American countries. Along with Venezuela and Paraguay, it was one of the region's most "shallow" reformers in areas such as deficit reduction and privatization.[2] Nonetheless, the episodic application of stabilization packages evoked the ire of the Workers' United Front (*Frente Unitario de Trabajadores*, FUT), the umbrella organization of the major trade union groups, as well as other popular movements.

Decades of oil export had failed to lay the basis for diversified and sustained economic growth. By the close of the 1990s, an estimated 63 percent of the population lived below the poverty line: Stagnant economic growth had given way to negative growth.[3] Citizens laid the blame on an incompetent and corrupt political class—the clique of professional politicians who appeared more interested in feuding among themselves than in solving the country's problems.

Contentious Politics

Between 1997 and 2005 public dissatisfaction with politics-as-usual and conflicts inside the political class turned Ecuador into the leader of a continent-wide syndrome that political scientist Arturo Valenzuela dubbed "presidencies interrupted."[4] In that period, three of the country's five presidents were forced to leave office before completing their terms.

The phenomenon began with the tumultuous presidency of Abdalá Bucaram (1996–1997). Bucaram created the Ecuadorian Roldosist Party (*Partido Roldosista Ecuatoriano*, PRE) in the early 1980s and used it to become the mayor of Guayaquil. He ran for president three times, finally clinching a victory in the second-round runoff against the rightist candidate in 1996. Although Bucaram had campaigned as a classic populist promising to soak the rich and enact sweeping social assistance, the faltering economy gave him little room to govern as one. Bucaram's program for handling the country's economic crisis included the familiar recipe of reducing consumption subsidies and increasing taxes along with a convertibility plan aimed at curbing inflation by tying the value of Ecuador's currency to the U.S. dollar. However, Bucaram's call for austerity and patience fell flat as accusations of corruption piled up, implicating the president and his family in schemes ranging from graft in the customs bureau to malfeasance in the handling of charitable donations.

By early 1997 business interests groups joined with opposition parties led by ex-presidents Borja, Hurtado, and Febres Cordero as well as grassroots organizations in demanding Bucaram's resignation. Among the many organizations mobilizing against Bucaram was the Confederation of Indigenous Nationalities of Ecuador (*Confederación de Nacionalidades Indígenas del Ecuador*, CONAIE). Founded in 1986 as an umbrella to unite an array of existing indigenous organizations, CONAIE had become a national political force by the mid-1990s and the leading voice in opposition to neoliberal policies. Working alongside CONAIE in mass mobilizations against neoliberalism was another umbrella for grassroots organizations, the Coordinator of Social Movements (*Coordinadora de Movimientos Sociales*, CMS).

As thousands of protestors took to the streets of Quito in February 1997, opponents in congress looked for a way to remove Bucaram. Lacking the two-thirds majority necessary for impeachment, congressional deputies declared Bucaram to be "mentally incapacitated." With no support from the military, Bucaram had little choice but to flee the presidential palace and seek political asylum. According to the constitution, Vice President Rosalía Arteaga should have succeeded to the presidency, yet political negotiations between congress and the military ended with congressional president Fabián Alarcón appointed to serve as the country's interim president.

Bucaram's unceremonious removal from office set a precedent for resolving government crisis, although in a way that clearly deviated from the rules prescribed in the constitution. The next elected president therefore fell victim to the same dynamic. Taking office in 1998 with the support of a center-right coalition composed of his own DP and the rightist PSC, President Jamil Mahuad governed during what arguably was the worst economic crisis in the country's history. As oil revenues continued to decline with inflation skyrocketing and the deregulated banking system in virtual collapse, Mahuad enacted a series of highly unpopular economic measures that included a temporary ban on withdrawals from bank accounts. That was followed with a controversial plan to combat inflation by making the U.S. dollar the country's official currency.

The dollarization decree triggered a new round of street politics in January 2000. CONAIE leaders organized a march in Quito and supporters stormed the congress building. Supported by dissident junior military officers, the protestors declared the formation of a new "government of national salvation." The aspiring junta included CONAIE president Antonio Vargas and Colonel Lucio Gutiérrez. Facing strong opposition from the U.S. government and the rest of the military establishment, the new government lasted less than twenty-four hours. Nonetheless, the demonstrations were sufficient to force Mahuad's resignation and a succession by Vice President Gustavo Noboa, who kept the controversial dollarization decree in place.

Thus, the same street politics that jumpstarted the political career of Colonel Lucio Gutiérrez figured in his own demise as president. Gutiérrez triumphed in the presidential elections in 2003 as the crusading anticorruption candidate of the left. He allied his newly created Patriotic Society Party (*Partido Sociedad Patriótico*, PSP) with Pachacutik (PK), the indigenous-based party linked with CONAIE. Yet Gutiérrez's left turn was short-lived. In a familiar turn of events, Gutiérrez acquiesced to IMF pressures for debt repayments and public spending cuts. After CONAIE and PK withdrew their support, Gutiérrez once again turned right and struck a deal with the León Febres Cordero's rightist PSC. That alliance also crumbled. Facing accusations of corruption and the possibility of impeachment in late 2004, Gutiérrez sought congressional votes from Bucaram's PRE. In an unconstitutional maneuver, Gutiérrez agreed to the dismissal of Supreme Court judges and allowed PRE to pack the court with new judges. Cleared of all charges by the new court, Bucaram returned to his hometown of Guayaquil in April 2005 and promised his followers that he would run again for the presidency.

In Quito, Bucaram's return unleashed mass demonstrations. But CONAIE, CMS, and labor groups were not at the forefront of the protest this time. Instead, Quito's streets were taken over by students, housewives, businessmen, and middle-class professionals who staged vigils and marches with an angry demand aimed at President Gutiérrez and the political class: "*¡Que se vayan todos!*" ("Throw them all out!") Gutiérrez dismissed the protestors as "outlaws," a name that the demonstrators subsequently embraced as the name of their revolt. When repeated attempts to quell the demonstrations failed, Gutiérrez fled the presidential palace on April 20, 2005, at which time congressional opponents formally removed him for "abandoning" his post. Vice President Alfredo Palacio took over and completed the remainder of the term.

As the 2006 presidential election approached, Ecuadorians were fed up with politicians and their crisis-prone political system. Public opinion polls showed that citizens had virtually no confidence in congress, political parties, or the government at large. Moreover, the poorly performing economy had torn families apart: An estimated three million Ecuadorians had left the country to seek work in the United States or Europe. Tired of political chaos and economic hardships, voters looked for a candidate who expressed their rage toward the political establishment.

Candidate Correa and the 2006 Election

Capitalizing on his lack of political experience, Rafael Correa campaigned as an "outsider" in the 2006 election. Born in a modest middle-class family in Guayaquil, Correa earned scholarships that eventually led to a doctorate in economics from the University of Illinois and a professional career as a university professor in Quito. His only major stint in public service came after Gutiérrez's fall, when President Palacio tapped him as minister of finance. During his fewer than one hundred days in the post, his tough stance toward foreign investors and the IMF helped establish his credentials as a fresh new leader on the left. Yet Correa had no formal ties to any party. A devout Roman Catholic, Correa described himself as a "humanist Christian of the left."

As Correa prepared to run for president in early 2006, evidence of the public's disenchantment with the party system was abundant. Electoral support for all of the major parties that had dominated political life in the 1980s and 1990s had eroded steadily while new personality-driven vehicles such as Lucio Guitérrez's PSP and billionaire Álvaro Noboa's Institutional Renovation National Action Party (*Partido Renovador Institucional Acción Nacional,* PRIAN) had made significant inroads in the 2003 elections. Reaching out to left-leaning intellectuals, technocrats, and leaders from Quito's "outlaw rebellion," Correa created his own vehicle, the Proud Sovereign Country Movement (*Movimiento Patria Altiva i Soberana,* PAIS).

The forty-three-year old Correa led a campaign that played on the public's anger while also offering messages filled with promises of change. He blamed the party establishment, the so-called "partyarchy" (*partidocracia*), for virtually all of the country's ills, ranging from malfunctioning governmental institutions to chronic economic crises and the flight of millions of Ecuadorians abroad. Correa charged that Ecuador was a country "kidnapped"—a nation in the grip of an immoral mafia of politicians, one that acted in its own interests and colluded with the rich, foreign investors and the United States. Correa promised to govern with "clean hands, lucid minds, and passionate hearts," sweeping away corruption, incompetence, and elitism with a new constitution. Correa told voters that he would put an end to the "long and sad night of neoliberalism" by increasing social assistance, rejuvenating the role of the state in the economy, and putting foreign creditors and investors on notice that abuses would no longer be tolerated.

Correa's message was not highly original, but his approach to the campaign was innovative. His aggressive marketing strategy combined catchy television advertising and expansive radio coverage with energetic public appearances. His television commercials parodied opponents as clowns, comic book characters, and clueless visitors from outer space, while Correa was projected as a young redeemer.

As in previous elections the fragmented multiparty system produced a crowded field of thirteen candidates vying for the presidency. With votes dispersed across so many contenders, no candidate was able to meet the threshold stipulated in election law to win on the first round, held in October 2006. Correa placed second, winning 22.8 percent of the vote. Topping the first-round field was Álvaro Noboa, with 26.8 percent of the vote. Noboa was the personal and political antithesis of Correa. In contrast to Correa's story as a self-made man, Noboa was Ecuador's richest man, the heir to a legendary banana-export fortune. While Correa promised an end to neoliberalism and increased intervention, Noboa celebrated the merits of business and the free market.

The campaign in the runoff election of November 2006 turned into a negative slugfest. Toting a Bible and proclaiming himself to be "God's Hero," Noboa slammed Correa as a communist and protégé of Hugo Chávez who would turn Ecuador into a Cuban-style dictatorship. Correa hammered back, depicting Noboa as a traditional oligarch who exploited child labor on his banana plantations. Although the two candidates clearly occupied opposite sides of the ideological spectrum, each dipped into the traditional playbook of populism, offering voters generous credit programs for housing and small business.

The election concluded with a decisive, nationwide victory for Correa with 56.7 percent of the vote. Yet his victory was complicated by one crucial decision that he made during the campaign: In an unprecedented show of disdain for parties and the congress, Correa ran without a slate of legislative candidates. Instead, he promised to render any sitting congress irrelevant by pushing forward with a plan to write an entirely new constitution. The results of the congressional elections, however, which ran concurrently with the first round of the presidential election, gave control of the legislature to Correa's bitterest rivals and opponents of a new constitution, Noboa's PRIAN and Gutiérrez's PSP. Correa's first challenge as chief executive, then, would be to deal with a recalcitrant congress and avoid having his own "presidency interrupted."

The Plebiscitary Presidency and Public Policy

To sweep away existing institutions and establish a new constitutional system, President Correa needed to maintain his popularity, neutralize the incumbent congress, and legitimize his political reforms with public approval at the ballot box. In the course of achieving all three goals, Correa constructed a plebiscitary presidency. Rather than working through existing institutions and seeking compromise, the president advanced his transformative agenda by using direct, unmediated appeals to the public in order to mobilize support. By doing so he successfully set the country on a path of elections that consolidated his power: the April 2006 referendum, the September 2006 constituent assembly election, the September 2008 constitutional referendum, and the 2009 general elections.

Just three months into his administration Correa scored the first victory of his plebiscitary presidency. In the face of intense public pressure and the threat of an all-out confrontation with the president, the Supreme Election Tribunal (*Tribunal Supremo Electoral*, TSE) reversed its previous opposition to holding a referendum on the constituent assembly, contravened congress, and even managed to dismiss members of congress for opposing the referendum on the grounds of "election obstruction." In turn, the Correa administration struck deals with the replacement legislators, effectively routing the antigovernment majority in congress. When the Constitutional Tribunal (*Tribunal Constitucional*, TC), the country's highest-ranking judicial body, voted to overturn the TSE's dismissal of the elected legislators, the newly induced pro-Correa congressional majority voted to dismiss the nine members of the Constitutional Tribunal who had objected. The congress then later acquiesced to its own demise, agreeing to suspend operations prior to being disbanded altogether by the constituent assembly.

If, as critics contended, Correa's political strategy for upending existing institutions was unconstitutional, it did nothing to undermine the president's popularity with the public. At the time of his inauguration in January 2006, Correa was among the most popular presidents in Ecuador's history, enjoying an approval rating of 73 percent. Throughout 2006 to 2008, Correa was able to sustain majority support with approval ratings of 50 percent or higher. He then took to the airwaves with a weekly radio show. Broadcast regularly on Saturday morning, Correa used the two-hour program as platform for trumpeting his government's accomplishments as well as blasting his political opponents. Along with the president's show, the administration deployed a sophisticated advertising campaign with "feel good" messages. At the conclusion of every government-sponsored television commercial, viewers saw an image that readily evoked Correa as a vibrant man, pumping his arms to greet a sunrise over the Andes. Accompanying every ad was the official government slogan with its inclusive message: *"La Patria ya es de todos"* (Now the Country Belongs to Everyone). Along with paid television spots, the government also made use of the free airtime that television stations are obliged to provide for public announcements.

Correa's communications strategy went hand in hand with his own hyperactive approach to the presidency. Traveling tirelessly throughout the country in countless public appearances, Correa was the unquestioned star at the center of his government's "permanent campaign."[5] Echoing his 2006 election campaign, Correa used the presidential bully pulpit to reinforce his optimistic messages about restoring national pride and improving the quality of life for average citizens. Correa dismissed political opponents in harsh language, labelling them as *pelucones* (reactionary big wigs). When several of the largest newspapers and television stations began questioning Correa's authoritarian style and policies, he trashed them as "savage beasts" and tools of the "oligarchy."

However, the Correa administration did understand that good political communication was just one of the pillars necessary for a successful plebiscitary presidency. To maintain credibility and win successive elections, Correa also needed to deliver tangible material improvements. In one of his first decrees, he doubled the monthly assistance payments to over a million impoverished families from US$15 to US$30 dollars a month, and in 2008 the payment was hiked to US$35. Correa doubled the monies available for homebuyers in the government-sponsored credit program. Low-income families got another boost when he enacted subsidies that halved the price of electricity for low-usage consumers. Farmers also benefited from subsidies for fertilizer and other agricultural inputs. Using his power to declare national "emergencies," Correa rapidly expanded public spending on road construction, prisons, and other major infrastructure projects. Additional government assistance programs, from providing free school uniforms and textbooks to free outpatient medical services at hospitals, won widespread popular approval.

Increased government spending likewise expanded the size of the state apparatus. Government bureaucracy grew with the reorganization of the executive branch and the creation of nine new ministries. Millions of dollars in new investment gave birth to a public television network and radio station, and the government took over the bankrupt *El Telégrafo* newspaper of Guayaquil. The new proactive role of the state was also evident in enhanced government intervention and regulation of business. In 2007 Correa imposed a hefty windfall tax of foreign multinationals in the oil sector. In 2008 he ordered the military to confiscate the assets of a Brazilian construction firm for failing to complete their contractual obligations. Correa intervened directly into contract negotiations with a Mexican telephone company, which eventually led to its exit from Ecuador. To recover debts owed to the state, the president authorized the confiscation of two hundred enterprises owned by fugitive bankers Roberto and William Isaías. After the government threatened to default altogether on its foreign debt, international bondholders resold their debt paper back to the government at a considerably reduced price. By 2009 Ecuador's foreign debt had been reduced to just over US$7 billion—the lowest amount in a decade.

Institutions and the 2008 Constitution

Ecuador has a long history of constitution-writing as a cure for the ills of the body politic. From 1830 through to the twenty-first century, Ecuador had been governed under nineteen different constitutions. The centerpiece of Correa's 2006 campaign was his call for a constitution to replace the one enacted in 1998. In Correa's view the 1998 constitution epitomized everything that was wrong with Ecuador. Correa argued that it laid the legal basis for neoliberalism by emphasizing the role of the market in the organization of the economy.

After winning more than 82 percent of the vote in an April 2006 referendum on whether a constituent assembly should be held, the Correa administration scored a second stunning victory in the election for representatives to the assembly in September 2006. With a slate of candidates led by leftist economist Alberto Acosta, Correa's PAIS ticket won 80 of the 130 seats in the new assembly, thus ensuring that opposing parties such as Noboa's PRIAN and Gutierrez's PSP would have no input in the deliberations.

The assembly deliberated from November 2007 to July 2008. The constitution then emerged as one of the longest-ever produced in Latin American history, with 444 separate articles and being nearly 150 pages in length.

Focusing on the promotion of "good living" (a concept taken from the Kichwa term, *sumac kawasay*), the new constitution enshrined a broad array of social and economic rights ranging from universal rights to social security, free legal counsel and health care to rights to water, adequate housing, the use of public space, and even the practice of sports. Along with extensive provisions stipulating the rights of indigenous groups and Afro-Ecuadorians, the document identified "priority groups" deserving special attention in government programs: children, youth, seniors, pregnant women, prisoners, and persons with catastrophic illness.

The constitution clearly established the legal basis for expanding the state's role in the economy. No longer designated as "market" based, the economy is now framed as "social and [one of] solidarity." In this new economy, the state is assigned rights to "administer, regulate, control and manage" the strategic sector of the economy, which includes energy, telecommunications, nonrenewable natural resources, transportation, hydrocarbon refining, biodiversity, and water. Among the state's powers is the option to expropriate and redistribute land that is not being put to productive use.

Restructuring institutions and intergovernmental relations was also part of the agenda of the new constitution. Enhancing the powers of the presidency and trimming the powers of the unicameral National Assembly figured prominently in the reforms. For the first time, a president is allowed to be re-elected in two successive terms of four years each. Moreover, if a president faces an uncooperative legislature, he/she has the power to dissolve the congress one time during the term and call for new elections. Although the president would also have to run in the special election, the reform gives the president a powerful threat to wield in any executive-legislative conflict, making it near impossible for the congress to remove a president in the kind of legal maneuvers used against Bucaram and Gutiérrez.

Among the most controversial provisions in the constitution was the creation of a new fourth branch of government under the heading, "Transparency and Social Control." The key institution in this branch is the Council of Citizen Participation and Social Control, a body composed of nine nonelected representatives drawn from social movements and grassroots organizations. In a complicated process that includes representatives from the other three branches of government, the Council plays a central role in overseeing appointments to the executive branch that includes election officers, the national ombudsman, attorney general, the comptroller, and other officials involved in making judicial appointments. The radically revised appointment processes stripped the legislature of the powers of appointment that it enjoyed in previous constitutions, thereby eliminating one of the traditional sources of executive-legislative conflict.

In September 2008 64 percent of the public endorsed the new constitution in a referendum. However, Correa's victory was neither untarnished nor uncontested. Groups on the left, including CONAIE and environmentalists, were disappointed by Correa's refusal to include a provision that would give local communities the right to block mining ventures deemed to have adverse economic or environmental impact. On the right, the Roman Catholic Church hierarchy objected to what it viewed as vague language on the family, fearing that it would open the door to abortion and gay marriage. In Guayaquil, center-right opponents led by Mayor Jaime Nebot scored a moral victory when the constitution suffered a narrow defeat in the city.

Nationalism and International Politics

Restoring national pride, asserting the country's sovereignty, and fomenting regional integration are the key components of Correa's approach to foreign policy. In rhetoric and in substance, Correa has demonstrated his readiness to distance Ecuador from its traditionally compliant relationships with the U.S. government, international financial institutions, and foreign investors. At the same time, Correa moved to strengthen ties with President Hugo Chávez, with whom he shares a commitment to the ideals of Bolivarianism, the pan-American unity doctrine inspired by Independence leader Simon Bolívar.

Shows of the government's willingness to flex its muscle in foreign relations took various forms. Correa refused to renew a ten-year-old lease with the U.S. Air Force that allowed an air base in the coastal city of Manta to be used for antinarcotics surveillance operations. Facing major disputes with foreign firms such as Chevron-Texaco, the government canceled its membership in the International Center for Settlement of Investment Disputes (ICSID), the entity that oversees business-government arbitration proceedings. Angry over loan decisions, Correa ordered the envoy of the World Bank to leave the country. He did the same with a U.S. embassy official whom he accused of meddling in intelligence-gathering operations. Demonstrating his independence from the United States, he invited Mahmoud Ahmadinejad, Iran's controversial president, to attend his 2007 inauguration, and in 2008 Correa then became the first Ecuadorian president to visit Iran. After a fifteen-year lapse, Ecuador rejoined Iran and other oil-producing countries in the Organization of Petroleum Exporting Countries (OPEC). Seeking new allies, Correa courted China and secured a two-year petroleum export deal in return for a US$2 billion advance payment.

In July 2009 Correa announced Ecuador's entry in the Bolivarian Alliance of the Peoples of America (*Alianza Bolivariana de los Pueblos de América*,

ALBA). Launched by presidents Hugo Chávez and Fidel Castro, the new organization is conceived as an alternative mechanism for regional integration, and it is in blatant opposition to the U.S.-proposed plan for a Free Trade Association of the Americas. ALBA's ambitious agenda includes strengthening commercial trade among its members, mounting a regional bank, and even launching a regional currency. To date, only a handful of Central American and Caribbean nations have signed onto the venture with Venezuela, Cuba, Bolivia, and Ecuador. Meanwhile, the major continental powers such as Mexico and Brazil remain conspicuously uninterested in the endeavor.[6]

Correa's solidarity with Chávez and other leftist leaders stands in stark contrast to the outright hostility that developed between Ecuador and Colombia when Colombia's longstanding war against guerrilla insurgents spilled across the border dividing the two countries. On March 1, 2008, Colombian president Álvaro Uribe ordered a military raid on a clandestine camp of the Revolutionary Armed Forces of Colombia (*Fuerzas Armadas Revoluconarias de Colombia*, FARC) located inside Ecuadorian territory. Uribe did not seek permission of the Ecuadorian government for the military operation, nor did he advise President Correa in advance. Killed in the aerial bombing of the camp was Raúl Reyes, a top FARC military commander.

The surprising military incursion triggered a regional crisis. In retaliation for Colombia's violation of Ecuador's sovereignty, Correa broke diplomatic relations with Colombia and deployed troops at its northern border. Expressing solidarity with Ecuador, President Hugo Chávez massed Venezuelan troops along its own Colombian border. Although all three countries backed away from an all-out military confrontation, the event marked an important juncture in Ecuadorian-Colombian relations. These relations between the two countries remained tense as Colombian authorities released information found on Reyes's computer that documented contacts between officials of the Correa government and Reyes. President Correa denied accusations that his leftist government was turning a blind eye to FARC's presence inside its own territory and denounced the move as a smear concocted by Colombian intelligence. Chilly relations between the two countries continued through 2009. Then, more questions about the government's alleged relationships with the FARC loomed when a video surfaced that showed FARC's chief military commander discussing his organization's financial contributions to Rafael Correa's election campaign. Once more, Correa denied any wrongdoing.

Conclusions

To date, President Rafael Correa has been successful in achieving many of the objectives that he outlined as part of his Citizens Revolution. In his first two and a half years in office, Correa secured a new constitution, laid the foundation for a state-centric model of economic development, and staked out an activist foreign policy.

As successful as Correa has been thus far, however, he has not vanquished all of Ecuador's traditional political and economic problems. Economic dependence still constricts development, and the puzzle that is the "resource curse" remains. Correa's capacity to finance a state-centric model is predicated to a great extent on the rise and fall of petroleum prices on the international market. In the political realm Correa's plebiscitary presidency has eclipsed the powers of other institutions, tamped down groups in civil society, and defused the disruptive street politics that undid his predecessors. Although the consolidation of executive power means that Correa has resolved the problem of "presidencies interrupted;" at least in the short to medium term, it comes at the cost of an executive branch that is not subject to the normal checks and balances of democracy. Under these circumstances, accountability is likely to be in short supply and the temptation to abuse executive power is substantial.

Suggestions for Further Reading

Clark, A. Kim, and Marc Becker, eds. *Highland Indians and the State in Modern Ecuador*. Pittsburgh, PA: University of Pittsburgh Press, 2007.

De la Torre, Carlos, and Steven Strifler, eds. *The Ecuador Reader: History, Culture, Politics*. Durham, NC: Duke University Press, 2008.

Pineo, Ronn. *Ecuador and the United States: Useful Strangers*. Athens: University of Georgia Press, 2007.

Sawyer, Suzanne. *Crude Chronicle: Indigenous Politics, Multinational Oil and Neoliberalism in Ecuador*. Durham, NC: Duke University Press, 2004.

Notes

1. Jorge G. Castañeda, "Latin America's Left Turn," *Foreign Policy* 85, no. 3 (Sept/Oct 2008): 28–46.

2. Javier Corrales, "Market Reforms," in *Constructing Democratic Governance in Latin America*, 2nd ed., ed. Jorge I Dominguez and Michael Shifter (Baltimore, MD: Johns Hopkins University Press, 2003), 90–91.

3. Liisa North, "State Building, State Dismantling, and Financial Crises in Ecuador," in *Politics in the Andes: Identity, Conflict and Reform*, ed. Jo-Marie Burt and Philip Mauceri (Pittsburgh, PA: University of Pittsburgh Press, 2004), 202–03.

4. Arturo Valenzuela, "Presidencies Interrupted," *Journal of Democracy* 15, no. 2 (2004): 5–19.

5. Catherine Conaghan and Carlos de la Torre, "The Permanent Campaign of Rafael Correa: Making Ecuador's Plebiscitary Presidency," *International Journal of Press/Politics* 13, no. 3 (July 2008): 267–84.

6. Catherine Conaghan and Carlos de la Torre, "The Permanent Campaign of Rafael Correa: Making Ecuador's Plebiscitary Presidency," *International Journal of Press/Politics* 13, no. 3 (July 2008): 267–84.

PART III

The Political Systems of Central and Middle America and the Caribbean

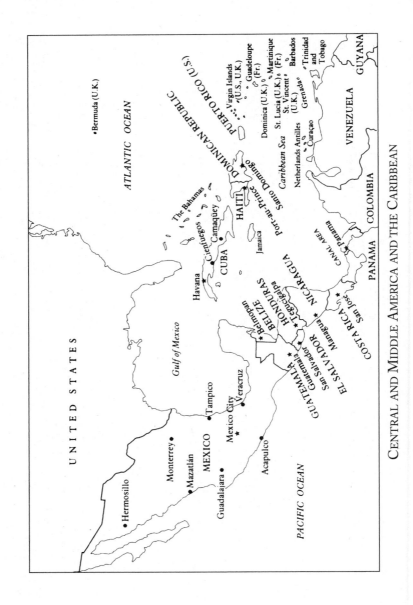

CENTRAL AND MIDDLE AMERICA AND THE CARIBBEAN

16

Mexico

Democratization, Development, and Internal War

Judith A. Gentleman

Mexico's young democracy currently faces pressures from multiple forces that make governance and the continued development of the democratic order exceptionally difficult. To begin with, Mexico's relationship with its neighbor to the north, the world's lone superpower, complicates the governing elite's political agenda—that of further opening Mexico's economic system—while at the same time honoring the cardinal political obligation of all Mexican national leaders of protecting national sovereignty. Second, the economic crisis that first emerged in 2008 in the United States and went on to engulf the world economy has hurt the Mexican economy, in large part because of Mexico's extraordinary interdependence with the ailing U.S. economy. Finally, Mexico is in the throes of an internal war that some have labeled a civil war. Criminal organizations are fighting with each other and the Mexican state to seize effective control of portions of Mexico's national territory in order to freely run drug trafficking and other criminal operations. To accomplish their objective, these criminal forces have succeeded in undermining what are in some cases already weak national and local institutions such as law enforcement and the judiciary.

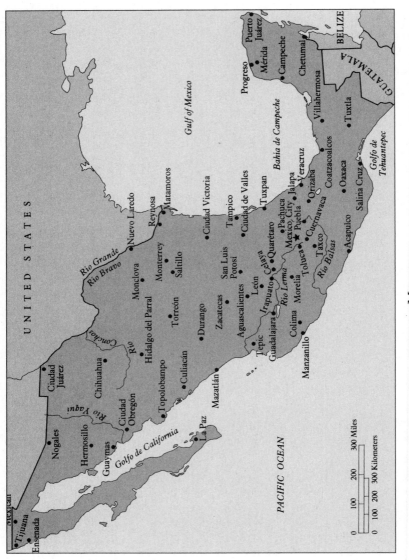

MEXICO

Although Mexico doesn't begin to approach the "failed state" category that some have invoked in discussing the current threat to Mexico, the nation faces real peril to the core of its law enforcement, judicial, and political institutions. In many respects, Mexico's democracy is threatened. Enrique Krauze, one of Mexico's leading historians and political commentators, argues that Mexico has strong institutions that have shown an ability to weather crisis. At the same time, he does not discount the problems that Mexico now faces, admitting that "This may be the most serious crisis we have faced since the 1910 Mexican Revolution."[1] The concern over what to do in response to this threat has yielded divided opinion. Denise Dresser, another prominent Mexican political commentator, worries that Mexico is becoming a "lawless country" but fears that the current strategy to regain control of the country is a flawed approach based chiefly on the "increased militarization of Mexico."[2]

Mexico is no longer the land of the peasant, although the *campesino* occupies an important place in the nation's core identity. It is now a middle-income country with fully 80 percent of the population living in cities. Most Mexicans, 59 percent, are employed in the services sector, both in formal and informal employment, constituting 61 percent of the GDP. After that, industry employs 25.7 percent of the workforce and produces 35.2 percent of GDP, while agricultural activities employ 15.1 percent of the work force, accounting for 3.8 percent of national product. Only 12 percent of national territory is cultivated, and much of that area has been dependent on irrigation projects that date from several decades ago. Mexico's territory includes an arid northern area, coastal lowlands, a central high plateau, mountains, and tropical forested areas. Its coastline is extensive and presents a very considerable management challenge.

Mexico is rich in natural resources including oil and mineral resources, but it has limited agricultural potential due to the arid climate and increasing environmental damage to these fragile areas. It is one of the leading oil producers in the world and is a major supplier of oil to the United States. By mid-2009 Mexico ranked as the third supplier of both crude oil and total oil imports to the United States behind Canada and Venezuela. Mexico imports natural gas, as it has never harnessed its own potentially valuable natural gas that is produced as a byproduct at the well-head. Other resource issues that will need to be addressed in the near future include intensifying water shortages, deforestation, and extensive soil destruction.

The population growth rate of 1.13 percent per annum has declined significantly from what were formerly much higher levels. Mexico's population is approximately 60 percent *mestizo*, 30 percent indigenous, and 9 percent Caucasian. Most Mexicans are Roman Catholics, although evangelical Protestantism increasingly has found appeal among the traditionally Catholic population. The population of the country is concentrated in the nation's major cities including Mexico City and its metropolitan area, where an estimated twenty-two million citizens reside. Other major cities include Guadalajara, Monterrey, Puebla, Ciudad Júarez, Tijuana, Acapulco, Mérida, Leon, and Veracruz. Spanish is the predominant language, although there are also scores of indigenous languages spoken primarily in the southern states of the country.

Despite Mexico's ranking as the thirteenth largest economy in the world based on GDP, fully half of the current estimated population of 111 million is considered poor. Fifteen percent of the population lives in what is deemed to be extreme poverty. It is estimated that approximately half of the 47 million Mexicans counted in the nation's economically active population (EAP) suffer employment problems, which means they are either experiencing underemployment, unemployment, or employment only in the informal sector. Approximately 11 percent of Mexico's total population lives outside of the country, chiefly in the United States, having left in search of opportunity. The U.S. Census bureau reports that 11.7 million persons who were born in Mexico now reside in the Unites States.[3] Mexico's GDP per capita calculated in terms of purchasing power parity (PPP) ranges from estimates of over US$7,000 to US$12,700. Although globalization generally and NAFTA specifically have generated an explosion in trade for Mexico, even workers in more advanced sectors are waiting for the benefits to begin to pour in. In the automobile sector, where jobs have been arriving from the United States, new wage agreements provide for starting wages as low as US$1.50 per hour. According to officials at Volkswagen, workers may now take seven years to reach what was once a starting salary at their Puebla plant. Mexico admits to being in a race with China and that low cost labor is a key to "victory."[4] Illustrative of the wage problem is the case of the auto workers employed at the Daimler-Chrysler plant in Toluca (where the soon-to-be defunct PT Cruiser was produced), who could not afford to buy cars themselves.

Income inequality in Mexico is extreme, and although the per capita GDP figures may appear relatively impressive, in fact income and wealth are poorly distributed. The top 20 percent of the population owns 60 percent of income, while the bottom 20 percent owns 3 percent.[5] The results of this inequality are found in shortfalls in housing, health care, education, and overall opportunity. It is not surprising, for example, that despite Mexico's wealth the country's educational deficit is significant, with Mexico's secondary school performance ranked the lowest of all OECD countries.[6] Mexicans over the age of fifteen now average eight years of schooling, although the problem of disruptions in attendance, poor teachers, and poor facilities leave students with achievement levels below a full eight years of education. Traditionally, the Mexican government has targeted higher education for substantial support at the expense of other educational levels, which then directly benefits elites whose children attend national universities. Private universities have become more attractive in recent years, however, and this has led to some reconsideration of the financial emphasis placed by the state on public universities and higher education at the expense of support to other educational levels. Since 2000 the government has therefore devoted more resources to basic education and has developed social support mechanisms to help families keep their children in schools. Mexico's economic competitiveness is stymied by its educational deficit and by the fact that only 22 percent of the population enjoys access to broadband Internet services, and even that is sometimes of substandard quality.

Mexico is an important country not only because of its economic prominence as one of the world's largest economies and as a major oil producer, but also because Mexico occupies a special place in world history. Its early twentieth-century revolution counts as one of the world's first modern revolutions. In that sense, Mexico occupies a unique place in world social and political development along with France and Russia. Mexico's revolution produced a modern, highly centralized state apparatus that, while nationalist and authoritarian in construct, embraced a corporatist formula that brought the broad Mexican population into relevance in the national political arena. Though not a democracy, this postrevolutionary political order brought all sectors of Mexican society into the national political equation, thus differentiating the new order from traditional autocracies.

Mexico also occupies an important place on the world stage owing to its remarkable cultural and artistic tradition and national cultural inheritance. The pre-Colombian civilizations of the "Teotihuacános"—the Maya, the Aztecs, and numerous other indigenous peoples—have influenced the tapestry of global society in numerous ways. From astronomy to religion, from art to foodstuffs, from administration to warfare—the contributions of Mexico's indigenous groups to our global social inheritance have been remarkable. Contemporary Mexico's influence on the study of archaeology and anthropology, reflecting the nation's rich cultural legacy, has been significant as have been Mexico's art, music, and religious life. Mexico's artists, both in the fine arts and folk art, have won world renown. In the time of global media and mass culture, one may even point to the financial success and worldwide appeal of Mexican-produced *telenovelas* (nighttime soap operas) as testament to Mexico's adaptive and continuing creative energy that finds new outlets and global appeal.

Although Mexico has not played a major role in defense and security matters internationally, the current challenges it faces in combating narcotrafficking and related crime have placed increased international attention on the Mexican state. For the United States and for Central America, there are few more direct, compelling problems than the threat posed by spillover effects from Mexico's drug war. Beyond the critical issue of the drug war, for the United States Mexico's significance is heightened as both a market and a source of migratory labor. The flow of goods, services, and labor between the United States and Mexico constitutes one of the most dynamic and interdependent relationships that may be found anywhere in the world. So significant has the impact of this migratory labor flow been that the preponderance of population growth in the United States can now be traced to migrants, chiefly from Mexico.

The forces of globalization have led Mexico to significant levels of integration with the United States beyond the traditional arenas of trade and investment. The influence of culture and media from the United States and the push of cultural influences from Mexico into the United States via migrating populations have brought these two nations increasingly closer together despite the political distance that still paradoxically divides them and far beyond the integration that historically characterized the Mexico-U.S. borderlands. At the same time, both states actively—and even jealously—guard their own national prerogatives and sovereignty while pursuing economic and policy integration under the terms of the 1994 North American Free Trade Agreement (NAFTA) and the 2005 Security and Prosperity Partnership (SPP). These binding agreements also tie Canada, the third North American state, to its other North American neighbors. Mexico enjoys a close bilateral relationship with the United States, and for some foreign policy analysts on both sides of the border, there is no more important relationship for either state than the one they have with each other. Arguably, Mexico has once again drawn as close to the United States as it was in the prerevolutionary period of President Porfirio Díaz's rule, when intense economic ties bound the two countries together.

Cultural integration between the United States and Mexico has been seen most especially in the borderlands region, but cultural influences in both countries can be found far from the border. In the United States, the *Cinco de Mayo* holiday, popularized in the United States by the Corona beer company (its parent, *Grupo Modelo,* is now 50 percent owned by Anheuser-Busch), has become part of the routine of U.S. cultural life. Less known is the experimentation now taking place in some U.S. communities with the *Quinceaneara* tradition, a practice in which fifteen-year-old girls are introduced by family as now having reached the age of marriagability. Although feminists on both sides of the border may cringe at such practices, bilateral cultural exchanges and influences pose challenges for both societies. Conservative Mexican society may find distasteful the sensationalized and often offensive material produced by the U.S. entertainment industry for television, movies, and the Internet, including violent video games. On the other side of the border U.S. animal rights groups confront the prospect of heightened interest in animal blood sports resulting from Mexican cultural influences, and environmentalists find few signs of progress for borderlands management on the Mexican side. For Mexico the appetite for drugs and the gun culture on the U.S. side of the border that arms Mexico's criminal syndicates are further evidence of the challenges and even price to be paid for globalization and interdependence.

Interdependence has also extended the reach of Mexico's influence into traditional and growing Mexican communities in the United States via telecommunications (the U.S. Spanish-language broadcaster, Univision, for example) and by means of the rapidly growing system of Mexican government consulates in the United States, now numbering nearly fifty. Candidates for political office in Mexico now routinely campaign in the United States in Mexican communities, some of which constitute larger regionally specific communities than exist in Mexico, where entire villages and regions have been all but depopulated as a result of migration to *El Norte*—the United States. On a more ominous note, Mexico's drug cartels have aggressively infiltrated U.S. society, where their customers are found, and have put down roots in major cities, with Atlanta and Los Angeles among the more prominent.

Background: History, Political Culture

Mexico's pre-Colombian past was characterized by the spread of a host of nomadic indigenous groups who are believed to have made their way to the area from northern North America. Indications are that settlements were created as early as 20,000 BC. The development of more settled communities that were focused on agriculture dates to 1,500 BC. More advanced societies then came into existence between 200 BC and 900 AD, and these included the sites known today as Teotihuacán in Central Mexico, Monte Albán in Oaxaca state, and the Mayan sites in Quintana Roo, Yucatán, Chiapas, and elsewhere. These settlements from the so-called "Classic" period were notable for their level of development in architecture, astronomy, language, and regional trade. Explanations for the collapse of these societies vary. Too often, however, the implicit suggestion is that the "Maya" or other indigenous groups "disappeared." This is hardly the case, however, as contemporary Mexican society is built from its varied indigenous population groups, who today remain present in one form or another.

Spain's conquest of Mexico, led by Hernán Cortés, led to the destruction of the Aztec empire by 1521. The Spanish imposed an order that sought to destroy all remnants of indigenous culture and to create a new religious and political authority. Building the new Spanish colonial order atop the central plaza of Aztec authority in Tenochtitlán, the Spanish even used the stones that had been part of Aztec construction to build their new cathedral. Mexico's population traded the old order of warrior-state oppression for a new political order that was also oppressive, harnessing the population to the economic interests of the Spanish mercantile state and to the ambitions of the Roman Catholic Church.

Mexico's war of independence was fought in the late eighteenth century with independence recognized by the Spanish crown in 1821. The independence movement stemmed chiefly from the complaint of the *criollos* against the *peninsulares*. The criollos, many of whom were in fact mestizos, as native-born citizens in the colony, fought against what they saw as discrimination. Opposition to continued Spanish rule was widespread, however, as both indigenous groups and mestizos also fought against the crown. Following independence, the remainder of the nineteenth century was a time of remarkable upheaval and conflict. During this period, under the incompetent leadership of General Santa Ana, Mexico lost 55 percent of its national territory to the United States in exchange for compensation of US$15 million dollars. This territory included what is now California, Arizona, New Mexico, Texas, and portions of Utah, Nevada, and Colorado. In addition, Mexico was forced to accept the loss of another sizeable piece of territory in 1853 under the terms of the so-called Gadsden Purchase, which facilitated the construction of rail transport in the U.S. Southwest. The Mexican-American War of 1848, which eventually led to Mexico's catastrophic loss of territory, brought U.S. troops to Mexican soil, ultimately leading to an eleven-month-long U.S. military occupation of Mexico City and the presence of U.S. troops occupying various parts of the country, including Chihuahua and Veracruz.

The weakness of the Mexican state and its susceptibility to external intervention was also reflected by France's invasion of Mexico in 1861 that led to the establishment of French rule under Maximilian beginning in 1864. British, French, and Spanish troops had occupied Mexican ports in 1861 in order to collect debts owed to these states by Mexico. Once present in Mexican national territory, and as a reflection of the complex geopolitical conflict in Europe at the time, France took the opportunity to establish an empire in Mexico. France's rule lasted only until 1867, but the cooperation of some Mexican elites in this venture testified to the profound confusion that gripped the society concerning its political identity and objective. The long-term rule of Porfirio Díaz grew directly from this political chaos and the dismal performance of national elites in Mexico's postindependence period.

The contemporary Mexican state was built on a platform of convulsive revolutionary upheaval and the subsequent political authoritarianism that established a strong state. Mexico's political culture has been traditionally characterized by conservative values derived from the Iberian culture of the Spanish colonial power. Order, hierarchy, respect for "natural" elites—especially the Roman Catholic Church, a political power in its own right—and governing authority were all principal features of postcolonial society. Although the revolution that was fought from 1910 to 1920 sought to overthrow the ruling authority and to eliminate the influence of the Roman Catholic Church, Mexico remained deeply traditional with respect to its inherited conservative religious traditions and subordination to autocratic rule.

The causes of Mexico's revolution are complex. Essentially, revolutionary forces emerged from different sectors of society in opposition to Porfirian rule. The dictator Porfirio Díaz governed Mexico from 1876 to 1910. His rural policies brought severe hunger to the countryside, triggered appeals for land reform, and ignited calls for a return of national control over natural resources and national production in addition to demands for the end of dictatorship. The array of insurgent forces eventually came into conflict with each other and civil war resulted. Rural and urban interests opposed each other as did conservatively minded elites. Ultimately, Mexico's revolutionary fires were doused with little agreement as to the direction that would be taken. Over many decades, national leaders would return to the issues that had stirred the revolution and seek to respond to grievances such as with the case of the landless peasantry, even if inconsistently. It was not until the government of General Lázaro Cárdenas in the 1930s that a serious land reform was initiated. The creation of a strong state remained an enduring point of consensus among Mexico's postrevolutionary elite, and in this sense Mexico's revolution paralleled other modern revolutions.

The new state was led by the military leaders who emerged as winners from the revolution that began in 1910 and concluded by 1920. The losses suffered by Mexico during its revolution were significant, with the loss of life estimated to be 1.5 million people or 10 percent of the population. An estimated one million Mexicans also fled the country during the conflict, for the most part settling in the United States. The consolidation of the revolution continued from 1920 through 1940. Mexico's new leaders constructed a state that was authoritarian and led by a single official party that declared itself to be revolutionary in nature. This party would rule for seventy years and in time came to be known as the Institutional Revolutionary Party (*Partido Institucional Revolucionario*, PRI.) The new government established full control of the military even as many of its early leaders were generals. Defying Latin American tradition, Mexico's military would be the instrument of the new revolutionary ruling elite and would not serve as an independent "guarantor" of the state, as was typically the case elsewhere in the region.

Although Mexico's political system evolved over time, moderating in some respects, it nonetheless remained highly authoritarian. The official party's political control of society was based on clientelism and a system of patrimonial relationships that flowed from the corporatist, authoritarian model of governance. Elections served the purpose of managing competing interests within the party's corporatist organization, forestalling the development of alternative political centers, and conferring legitimacy on the system. They were not designed to provide for political pluralism. Over time, despite the fundamentally fraudulent nature of Mexico's "elections"—until the 2000 election all successive presidents had been hand-picked by their predecessors—the system provided some veneer of international acceptability for Mexico. By the 1980s the government gradually had begun to take steps toward cooperating with the emerging international norms of democratic process.

The fact that Mexico turned inward in the twentieth century resulted not only from the country's revolutionary exhaustion, but also from the rejection of the internationally focused commercial and investment patterns laid down during the *Porfiriato*. This inward orientation also stemmed from Mexico's experience of foreign interventions, including the Mexican-French War of 1862, the conflicts with the United States including the Mexican-American War of 1846–1848 that led to the loss of national territory, and the U.S. interventions during the period 1914–1916 on behalf of the Constitutionalist side in the Revolution.

Society, Economy, and Interest Groups

Having embraced globalization and pursued a very considerable opening of its economy, Mexico was hit hard by the global economic recession of 2008–2009. As a result of the close economic ties between Mexico and the United States, Mexico felt the pain of the U.S.-based recession more than many other states in Latin America. Fully 85 percent of Mexico's exports are destined for the United States, and as a result the U.S. recession and the collapse of import demand in the United States had a devastating impact on Mexico's fortunes. Mexico's international trade declined by one-third in the first half of 2009. Over 800,000 Mexicans lost their jobs by the first quarter of 2009. By contrast, Brazil and Chile were far more insulated from the effects of the global recession as a result of their more diversified trade profile.

Mexico's industrial production fell by over 13 percent and the economy shrank by over 11 percent. Foreign investment, particularly from the United States, dropped significantly. Manufacturing output fell by nearly 20 percent, in large part as a result of the crisis in the U.S. automotive industry that reduced demand for Mexico's automotive parts and assembly industry. Auto sector exports fell by almost 57 percent over the period January 2008 to January 2009. As a result, workers suffered significant layoffs, and those who still had jobs worked fewer hours. The electronics sector was also seriously affected. Some analysts argued that Mexico would see the beginning of recovery in the second half of 2009.

Mexico's economy was also hurt by the decline in remittances received principally from citizens working abroad in the United States. Remittances declined by nearly 18 percent in the second quarter of 2009, continuing a dramatic downward trend. Added to that was the outbreak of the H1N1 virus in Mexico that depressed tourism, an important source of foreign currency. Fears surfaced that the severe economic contraction would lead to a rise once again in the poverty level and a reduction in the number of children attending school. Unemployment in the formal sector rose dramatically, with the loss of an estimated 5 percent of jobs in that sector due to the recession. The financial shock produced by the recession not only left the national government facing budgetary pressures, but also made it difficult for state and local governments to pay their employees and support services. Expectations are for a slow recovery, with the Mexican government predicting that real GDP would decline by 5.5 percent in 2009 with an expected growth rate of 3 percent in 2010. Analysts predicted an average growth rate of under 4 percent beginning in 2011, far below the growth rate necessary in order to respond to the stubborn poverty levels that continue to afflict Mexico.

The global recession aggravated preexisting tendencies in the Mexican economy that contributed to limits on development progress. Although Mexico took important steps in the 1990s to liberalize its economy, some key sectors remain shielded from competition, including telecommunications, electricity, and petroleum. Despite the success measured in some sectors of Mexico's economy as a result of NAFTA, though Mexico initially saw a rising surplus in trade following the treaty's implementation, it now registers a significant trade deficit with the United States. The agricultural sector faced increasing competition from U.S. producers as the full implementation of NAFTA opened Mexico's economy further. This pressure generated increased unemployment among Mexico's rural poor, adding to migratory pressures on Mexico's cities. Mexico's successful integration into the world economy was further impeded by the effects of corruption and the lack of public security. Mexico ranks at number seventy-two between Peru and Bulgaria in the Transparency International Corruption Perception Index, signifying a very substantial level of corruption. The additional costs imposed on business by the public security problem are estimated to add roughly 25 percent to the costs of doing business. Finally, the failure to place sufficient emphasis on education, science, technology, and infrastructure development continues to plague the system, rendering Mexico less and less competitive in the process of globalization.

Any insulation that Mexico had from the U.S.-induced recession derived from the oil revenues that had buoyed the economy from 2000 to 2008. During these years Mexico's oil revenues had risen dramatically, enabling the government to spend ambitiously. The petroleum sector generated 4 to 5 percent of Mexico's GDP but accounted for 40 percent of national government revenues. In 2009, however, oil revenues sank 24 percent. The Mexican government's diminishing ability to pump oil due to aging and inadequate infrastructure posed additional financial problems that required resolution down the road. Mexico's Petróleos de Mexico, PEMEX, the state petroleum monopoly, planned to build its first new refinery in thirty years, but that facility would not open until 2015. Corruption also substantially undermined PEMEX's performance, with estimates from the mid-2000s of upward of US$1 billion dollars per year lost. PEMEX not only served as a leading source of revenue to the state, but it is also said to have provided illicit financial support for years to the PRI and the Petroleum Workers Union.

Major interest groups in Mexico include state workers, teachers, organized labor, rural workers, religious groups, professional groups, indigenous groups, women, law enforcement agencies, the military, private media, and of course business interests including foreign business and financial interests. Traditionally, state workers, organized labor, teachers, and peasants were organized under the umbrella of the state, and they exercised considerable leverage, with some groups enjoying considerable benefits so long as they operated within the confines of the system. Mexican labor confederations, including the Mexican Regional Labor Confederation (*Confederación Regional Obrera Mexicana,* CROM) and the Confederation of Mexican Workers (*Confederación de Trabajadores de México, CTM*), were among the more powerful interests. More recently an independent umbrella union, the National Union of Workers (*Union Nacional de Trabajadores,* UNT) formed to challenge the state's power in labor organization. Other powerful members of the PRI's organized labor system included the Petroleum Workers Union (*Sindicato de Trabajadores Petroleros de la Republica Mexicana,* STPRM), the Electrical Workers Union (*Sindicato Mexicano Electrecistas,* SME), the Teachers Union (National Education Workers Union, SNTE), and the Peasant Confederation (*Confederación Nacional Campesina,* CNC).

Under the land reform introduced during the government of President Carlos Salinas, the dissolution of the *ejido* system (collective farms) diminished the power of the CNC, as its principal role had been to represent *ejidatorios.* Farmers are now more often represented by rural producers' associations. Unions that were created and maintained within the state system remained powerful, in exchange for which their members were required to be members of the PRI. These workers understood that their jobs depended on their loyalty to the state and that all benefits they enjoyed would derive from their status as clients of the official party and the state.

For much of Mexico's modern history, civil society remained weak and dependent on the state. With the advance of economic liberalization beginning in the 1980s, with the privatization of significant areas of the economy and the end of many subsidies to workers, the private sector and civil society took on new importance. By no means has organized labor and its association with the state been eclipsed, however. Examples of the continued power of the state-labor association can be found in the energy sector, where reform efforts have been stymied by the opposition of major interests concentrated in these economic arenas, including unions. Another interest group that continues to enjoy enormous clout is the teachers' union, which has been widely criticized for what some feel has been opposition to desperately needed reform. Recent testing by the federal government found that 75 percent of Mexico's aspiring teachers were unable to pass a skills exam, an indicator of the problem that is plaguing Mexico's educational system. Mexico's classrooms are too often staffed with unqualified but loyal union activists.

Economic liberalization, including privatization, deregulation, and the opening of the market to increased foreign investment, has also meant the growth of the influence of private sector organizations such as the Mexican Businessmen's Council along with the influence of independent business interests. With the privatization of hundreds of formerly state-owned enterprises, selected entrepreneurs who had been close to the Carlos Salinas group were enormously enriched. Carlos Helú Slim, now one of the world's richest men, benefited from the privatization arrangements governing the telecommunications sector. He and others who similarly grew enormously wealthy as a result of these "opportunities" have come to wield great power in society and have been able to impede further decentralization and competitive reform within Mexico's economy in sectors where they hold overwhelming market power. The Televisa media empire has come to dominate televised news and entertainment in Mexico along with the much smaller Azteca national network. This concentration of media power (Televisa enjoys over 70 percent "share" in TV-ratings parlance) raises concerns about media-government relations and news coverage, as it would in any society. Despite the fact that hundreds of newspapers are published throughout the country, their readership is low when compared to television viewership, thus reinforcing the problem of media concentration. Civil society has seen the growth of a host of new interest associations representing women, the environment, human rights, and others.

Within the state sector it may be the security sector that is growing in clout as a distinct interest as it shoulders the burden of battling the rising criminal threat to society. Although neither the military nor law enforcement is an independent actor, their resource requirements are such that their influence is likely to grow. For its part, Mexico's military already stands as the second largest military in Latin America, and its clout is likely to continue to grow as the prior arrangement of single-party authority fades and Mexico's government becomes the arena for more competitive political exchange among increasingly powerful actors. This political opening will likely enable security interests to build new alliances with emerging political power centers.

Parties, Elections, and Democracy

Mexico's democratization process grew out of the change in the society's system of values, beliefs, and political attitudes as support for the democratic ideal grew along with opposition to the old authoritarian order. Peru's novelist and former Presidential candidate, Mario Vargas Llosa, famously described Mexico's longstanding political system as "the perfect dictatorship." This is due to the fact that Mexico's political leaders had for years promoted the facade of pluralist democracy, particularly in its last decades of power, all the while maintaining a deeply authoritarian system. In power for nearly seventy years, the PRI ruled as the official party with strong-arm tactics, fraud, repression, and, importantly, financial incentives for cooperation. Embracing the mantle of revolutionary justice and social reform, governing elites placed great emphasis on their role as defenders of Mexico's national sovereignty and proclaimed their advocacy of the rights of the downtrodden and of social justice. In so doing the system claimed popular legitimacy, enjoying the compliant support of co-opted social groups, including peasants, organized labor, teachers, and public sectors employees. Once invested in the system, some within these groups became ardent supporters of the ruling party and the corporatist system. Many were directly employed in state bureaucracy or state enterprises and counted on the considerable security that the system offered. At the same time, the system was one designed not to preclude private capital but to promote it, while the government often determined winners and losers in the market arena. Externally, the regime championed all manner of leftist causes, embracing Cuba among others, while simultaneously crushing all domestic opposition at home against the rule of the official party and the regime.

The convulsive protests of 1968 and the government massacre of hundreds of student protesters in the Plaza of the Three Cultures at Tlatelólco in Mexico City seemed to mark a turning point when the governing elites began to lose popular legitimacy. As the government sought to ensure a flawless start for the Olympic Games on October 12, 1968, student protests against the government seethed throughout that summer. Finally, on October 2, security forces attacked student demonstrators at Tlatelólco. The particular targets of the regime's wrath were students from the National Polytechnic Institute, located nearby, and high school students, all of whom tended to be drawn from more humble circumstances. By contrast, the government ordered troops to be withdrawn from the National University of Mexico (UNAM), where the children of the nation's elite attended school and had also been demonstrating. Although the regime charged that foreign agitators were responsible for student militancy, there was never evidence to that effect.

Further weakening support for the system were a series of destabilizing events. Among these was the insurgency in Guerrero during the 1960s and 1970s led by Lucio Cabanes Barrientos, who headed the Party of the Poor. Cabanes was killed in 1974 by the Mexican military, but Guerrero remained under a de facto state of siege for some time thereafter. Cabanes inspired a number of organizations also in Guerrero and the Sierra Madre region. There was devastating financial crisis of 1982 soon after the government announced the presence of tremendous new oil reserves and had constructed massive new oil production facilities, and this led to what was termed the "forgotten decade" in Mexico. The government's poor performance (the military as an exception here) in the aftermath of the catastrophic 1985 Mexico City earthquake shook the public's confidence. Then in 1994 and 1995 the system was first hit by the January 1994 Zapatista/EZLN uprising in Chiapas, led by the charismatic *Subcomandante Marcos*, and then the 1995 banking crisis that led to a U.S. financial bailout that was pushed, at great political risk to himself, by President Bill Clinton and his Treasury Secretary Robert Rubin.

The events in Chiapas and the banking crisis/U.S. bailout were particularly problematic for Mexico's government, as both involved the United States. The Zapatista attack was planned to coincide with the implementation of NAFTA and seemed to catch the government by surprise, particularly in terms of the Zapatistas' brilliant use of media as the new weapon of choice. The uprising inevitably raised questions about the state's ability to function effectively in managing internal security. The military's incompetent performance in quelling the uprising further eroded the government's credibility. This criticism was added to the complaints that had been lodged about abuses perpetrated during the militarization of the nation's southern region to counter illegal entry from Guatemala and to control emergent insurgent forces in Chiapas and Oaxaca. The banking crisis and bailout were both humiliating to the regime insofar as the United States was viewed as having had to rescue Mexico's incompetent leadership regardless that the loans were subsequently repaid fully even before coming due.

The assassination of the PRI's 1994 presidential candidate, Luis Donaldo Colosio, in March 2004 starkly exposed problems within the ruling elite itself. Although Colosio was executed at point blank range, the investigation into his murder yielded only the conviction of the gunman himself and left a cold trail with respect to the parties responsible for the political assassination. Furthermore, the suspicious death of a high-profile political leader had not been without precedent. One such incident involved the 1969 death of PRI elder Carlos Madrazo, father of 2006 PRI presidential candidate Roberto Madrazo.

The mysterious crash of his airplane occurred soon after he announced that he was going to leave the PRI and form a new party in reaction to the events at Tlatelólco. Another case involved the 1989 single-car accident that killed the National Action Party's (PAN) popular 1988 Presidential candidate, Manuel Clouthier. The accident aroused considerable suspicion at the time concerning the circumstances of the party leader's death.

Then, in November 2008 President Calderón's Secretary of the Interior, Juan Camilo Mourino (a probable choice to follow Calderón as a PAN candidate for the presidency), was in an unexplained aircraft accident over Mexico City. This raised substantial concern about the true nature of the accident that killed him and others on board who were involved in state security.

Competitive elections for the presidency have been taking place in Mexico since 1988, and multiparty races were held in state and local elections even earlier, but the first victory of an opposition presidential candidate did not occur until the election of President Vicente Fox in 2000. Fox had previously won the governorship of his home state of Guanajuato, but in the highly centralized Mexican presidentialist system, control of the presidency is critical. The question of whether the authoritarian system collapsed or was overthrown is frequently debated. The answer may be "both." On the one hand, the official party faltered as it confronted sequential votes that it appeared to lose. The old techniques of election rigging and intimidation no longer seemed to work in an environment of expanding communication and citizen mobilization. For a time PRI leaders sought to use the tactic of promising a political opening but then slow-rolling the rule-making that would permit the opening. Then, with the passage of rules that permitted multiparty participation, the races would be rigged with the use of elaborate schemes to steal votes. The PRI was the best in the business when it came to these operations.

When cameras began to film and election observers were present to bear witness to electoral malfeasance, however, the utility of such electoral fraud tactics as closed voting stations, *ratón lóco* (voters madly searching for a place to vote after their name disappeared from their local registry), or the "carousel," where vans carried would-be voters to multiple voting stations, diminished. The old dinosaurs of the party began to give way to modernizers who believed they could meet the competition head on. On the other hand, the forces of democratization organized effectively, developed local citizen observer teams, enlisted international observers and assistance from NGOs and IGOs where possible, and appeared to offer the population a convincing alternative. Initially, the PRI responded to the calls for change by permitting electoral competition at the local level. The floodgate had been opened, however, and citizens eventually demanded full democracy.

The Salinas government, installed in power in 1988, introduced some political reform as a complement to the major overhaul of the national economy that was the hallmark of the Salinas period. The Salinas economic liberalization project brought with it costs to many who had been dependent on the state. To compensate for their losses, Salinas introduced the supremely corporatist National Solidarity Program (PRONASOL) in order to mend the tear in the political fabric that his economic reforms had created and to rebuild support for the party. He had absolutely no intention, however, of democratizing Mexico. As was said at the time, *Salinismo* meant *perestroika* without *glasnost*, in a reference often made to comparisons between the Mexican and Soviet reform processes.[7] What the young generation of PRI technocrats found was that market opening inevitably brought pressures for further political liberalization that were difficult to resist. Ultimately, both the old and young guard of the PRI, the politicos and the technocrats, had to learn how to compete in the new political game that was emerging in Mexico. Clearly, PRI party leaders have begun to make this transition, although some of the tried-and-true practices of the past are difficult to abandon altogether.

The struggle to further expand and deepen democracy continues today. Mexico's political system boasts an array of strong functioning parties with comparatively well-developed party cadres, all of whom now have considerable experience. In the initial years of electoral competition the Party of Democratic Revolution (PRD), the major left party, was significantly disadvantaged because it had not had a chance to develop its own party militants. Instead, it included a mix of refugees from the PRI who only knew the "old ways" and newcomers to electoral politics who were lacking in experience altogether. The National Action Party, by contrast, had had regional experience in electoral competition and was well funded. The PRI had experience, but all the wrong kind. Today, these parties of the left, right, and center are joined by the Workers Party (PT), environmental party (PVEM), the New Alliance Party (*Partido Nueva Alianza*), and the Social Democratic and Rural Alternative Party (*Partido Democrácia Social y Alternative Rural*).

The PRI finds support across the country but especially in the southern states and among older voters. The PAN, the right-center, probusiness and pro-Church party, continues to find its stronghold of support chiefly in the northern states, but it has improved its position in the central region of the country. The PRD, the party of the left, finds support in Mexico City and in states across the center of the country. The July 2009 elections showed rising strength for the PRI, particularly as it reached a majority in the Chamber of Deputies, took control of the governorships of Queretaro and San Luis Potosí, and maintained control of Nuevo León where the economic powerhouse Monterrey is located.[8] The PAN and PRD saw some erosion in their strength. The Workers Party, the Green Party, the New Alliance, and Convergencia all maintained viability, although overall voting participation rates were down. The PAN's erosion of support was not surprising given the economic difficulties confronting the country together with the tremendous levels of violence and public insecurity facing voters. Some observers have argued that the PRI's resurgence in popularity is a result of the fact that voters remember the days when the government was able to maintain public order. They recognize that the PRI had its significant faults, but they credit the party with having had the capacity to keep the lid on crime and violence. Some believe that the PRI may once again be able to bring a level of public order back to society. Others fear that this view will lead to a restoration of the PRI that will pose challenges for Mexico's continued democratization.

Although Mexico now has a functioning democratic electoral system, the skepticism that many citizens express about democracy's performance reflects Mexico's good governance deficit. When polled, only a minority of Mexicans agree that democracy is preferable to any other type of government. Despite the great efforts made to build democracy in their country, Mexicans are frustrated with what "democracy" has produced—and failed to produce. In the view of the majority, democracy has not created the public security, economic security, or opportunity for which they had hoped. Instead, Mexicans find themselves in the midst of an economic and public security crisis with many citizens voting with their feet, choosing to depart their homeland in order to look for opportunity in the United States. Although Mexicans do not support authoritarian solutions, in view of the declining support for such an option over the past several years, Mexican citizens do feel deep disappointment with democracy's performance thus far and with politicians in general.

These disappointments notwithstanding, Mexico has continued its democratic transition despite setbacks along the way. That said, Mexico's internal war is placing pressure on that democracy and potentially jeopardizing the consolidation of the new democratic political order. The potential for stresses in the management of public security, on the judicial system, on law enforcement, and on civil-military relations can contribute to the erosion of the government's legitimacy in the eyes of a frightened public. Evidence suggests that this is already happening regardless that President Calderón is personally popular. The consolidation of democracy in any middle-income country with significant inequality of income presents a daunting challenge. For Mexico, with its array of problems ranging from economic recession to internal war, the problem of consolidation is even more difficult. In particular, the increased emphasis on internal security presents difficult challenges for democracies generally in terms of transparency, human rights, and the temptation to use security fears to erode civil rights.

On the positive side, though much has been accomplished in the past two decades to improve transparency and democratic performance in the electoral arena, many issues remain to be addressed. The role of highly concentrated private media in Mexico's national elections is of concern, as is the extraordinary cost of these elections, even as compared to the extravagant spending that takes place in U.S. national elections. The success of the 2009 congressional and state elections in procedural terms did not eliminate the questions that remain unanswered concerning the fairness of the 2006 presidential election. The enormous controversy surrounding the defeat of the PRD candidate Andrés Manuel López Obrador led to demonstrations and López Obrador's refusal to accept Felipe Calderón's victory for the PAN. López Obrador claimed that the election had been stolen and, indeed, Calderón could claim only a razor thin margin of victory. This election raised again the question of whether Mexico's political and economic elites would ever tolerate the election to the presidency of a candidate from the left. That question had remained paramount in Mexico's politics since the outcome of the 1988 election, in which Carlos Salinas was declared the victor over the PRD candidate Cuauhtémoc Cárdenas, the candidate of the PRD. In that election the vote count was suspended for a week due to mysterious computer failures. Salinas was then declared the winner by the slimmest of margins.

Calderón's victory in 2006 surprised many. What was particularly impressive was the support that he won from youthful Mexican voters who embraced his pragmatic approach and his plan to continue to engage Mexico with the global economy. Older voters tended to support López Obrador and his platform that promoted the defense of sovereignty as well as nationalist and statist economic policy.[9]

The election itself raised a number of issues about the strategy used by both the losing and winning political parties. The PRI failed to grasp the fact that their candidate represented the discredited politics of the past. By contrast, the PAN's mastery of media and its massive election expenditure, its successful use of fear tactics in attempting to tie the PRD candidate, López Obrador, to Hugo Chávez, and finally, the failure of López Obrador to fully appreciate the new media age in which Mexican politics were immersed all became important features of the 2006 contest. Although López Obrador had previously been viewed as a media- and public relations–savvy public official when he served as mayor of Mexico City, his failure to appear in the first of the televised presidential debates did much to undermine his candidacy.

Critics argue that the system is still unrepresentative and has failed to continue the process of democratization that must follow the initial institutional steps that have been taken. As a manifestation of rising discontent with the state of politics in Mexico, the 2009 election saw the launch of a relatively successful "Null Vote" initiative, which urged voters to vote a blank ballot rather than to support the unsatisfactory candidates appearing on the ballot who, some argued, offered the voters no real choice.

The State, Government, and Bureaucracy

Mexico's government is a federal republic built on a system of separation of powers. Its 1917 constitution guaranteed an array of citizen rights of both a substantive and procedural nature. The federal system includes thirty-one states and the Federal District, where Mexico City is located. Currently, the public sector accounts for 11 percent of the labor force. The government includes separate and independent executive, legislative, and judicial branches. Although the constitution provided for this arrangement, the true independence of these branches only materialized with the 2000 election. The system has always been characterized by a strong executive and a weak legislature and judicial system, as is typical throughout much of Latin America. The president is elected for a six-year period known as the *sexenio*. The Congress, comprised of a Senate and a Chamber of Deputies has become more powerful since opposition parties first won representation, beginning in 1997. With the advent of democracy the Congress has been in the process of becoming more professional, learning how to legislate in a constructive manner rather than either simply opposing executive initiative or compliantly affirming executive direction. The prohibition of consecutive reelection for the executive and for the Congress arguably diminishes the accountability of either of these institutions to the popular will. The judicial branch includes federal and state court systems as well as the Supreme Court. Justices are appointed by the Senate once having been nominated by the President.

The Judiciary is the weakest of the branches, although it, too, is undergoing considerable reform. Nonetheless, most citizens understand that with the current performance of the judicial branch and public security ministries, crime enjoys impunity in the Mexican system. An estimated 80 percent of crimes are never reported to authorities because citizens either believe that nothing will be done, fear identifying themselves to relevant government officials, and/or fear law enforcement authorities themselves. Law enforcement agencies have been associated with kidnapping and extortion, inducing fear in the citizenry, and leaving the public with a feeling of helplessness.

Mexico's state-level political systems are of considerable importance. State governors, legislatures, and local political leaders are important actors in the nation's political picture, and these arenas serve as platforms for many political leaders who later move to the national level. Recent presidential candidates from the three major parties, Vicente Fox (PAN), Roberto Madrazo

(PRI), and Andrés Manuel López Obrador (PRD), all spent considerable time honing their skills at the regional level.

The national government's budget is substantially funded by oil revenues generated by PEMEX. Taxes, royalties, and receipts from the petroleum sector constitute 38 percent of the government's revenues. By hedging the price of oil per barrel the government managed to keep revenues steady through 2009, but the financial picture thereafter becomes cloudier. Oil production declined in early 2009 by nearly 7 percent, falling below the government's stated goal of daily production of three million barrels per day. Oil revenues were down by 24 percent in the first half of 2009, leading to budget cuts anticipated in 2010. The two largest producing fields in the Mexican system, Cantarell and Ku-Maloob-Zaap (KMAZ) are both suffering major declines in output.

The problems in Mexico's petroleum sector will not be easy to resolve as major reform initiatives put forward by PAN governments have largely failed, although more marginal changes have been approved. Mexico's petroleum and electricity sectors are both in need of major reform that would provide investment, technical expertise, and professional management that diminish those political influences that have bled resources from the system and engendered tremendous inefficiencies. The influence of the PRI-dominated unions in the energy sector and of the party itself represents a major impasse to the fundamental infrastructure modernization that Mexico so sorely needs. The dilemma concerning energy sector modernization raises fundamental unresolved political questions concerning the role of the state and the further integration of the Mexican economy into the global system.

Oil receipts notwithstanding, the government faces a serious problem on the revenue side, and this has been the case for many years. Like much of Latin America, Mexico's political culture has not been supportive of taxation or compliance with tax law. Admittedly few people enjoy paying taxes, the level of noncompliance in Mexico is such that the revenue stream from taxes alone would be insufficient to support the state's operations. In part, this problem stems from the record of corruption that has left many people with a sense that government employees at one level or another have already illicitly had their hands in citizens' pockets. Second, a tradition of noncompliance with tax law and ineffective tax collection procedures have bred a culture of tax evasion that is supported by impunity in the justice system. Third, the government has historically depended on state sector–generated revenues, but with the privatization of so much state-sector enterprise, these revenues have evaporated, thus requiring additional resources. Further, the recession of 2008–2009 brought tax receipts down substantially. Value-added tax or IVA receipts declined by 20 percent, and government fiscal revenue declined overall by 8 percent. To compensate for this revenue shortfall the influential Mexican Businessmen's Council has recommended new taxes on food and medicine—a highly regressive form of taxation. As expected, this suggestion has been met with considerable opposition.

Corruption in the state sector has been another drag on the efficiency of public administration. It has been said often that no president of Mexico ever left office a poor man. In another widely circulated observation of the political practices prevalent during the years of the PRI's rule, a leading PRI figure remarked, "Only a poor politician is a poor politician." Corruption in this instance is defined not simply as stealing from state coffers directly, which certainly occurred, but also as managing public policy in a manner that would anoint financial and economic winners and losers. It also means payoffs to and from crooked businessmen, public sector administrators, congressmen and senators, union leaders, and even criminal elements including drug traffickers. Corruption means protection from prosecution, impunity and the undermining of law enforcement institutions, special privilege, the abuse of average citizens, and the undermining of the public sector in the name of private interest. Some have argued that these methods were simply the necessary glue that preserved Mexico's long-running regime and thus assured national stability and security. Others argue that this corruption has significantly slowed the development of the state and economy.

President Calderón has sought to tackle government corruption, a major problem for the nation. According to Transparency Mexico, an estimated US$2 billion dollars is spent on bribes for public officials every year. In his first year in office President Calderón announced on "International Anti-Corruption Day" that 11,500 public servants had been fined a total of US$300 million dollars for corrupt practices. He has set his sites most particularly on law enforcement agencies.[10] Illustrative of the problem faced by the Calderón government was the revelation in late 2008 that Mexico's drug czar, Noé Ramírez, had received US$450,000 in bribes from a drug cartel. In a related case, also at the end of 2008 the head of Mexico's Federal Preventative Police (PFP), Victor Gerardo Garay Cadena, resigned after being charged with having ties to organized crime.

Related to the Calderón government's effort to tackle corruption has been the effort to begin to eliminate red tape and streamline government procedures. Paradoxically, in the effort to become more transparent via the Transparency Law of 2002, bureaucratic procedure has become more burdensome with even more pieces of paper and official stamps needed to complete a transaction. Efforts to reform the state sector as the next step in the development of Mexico's democracy have been met with substantial resistance. During the years of PANista governance, Mexico suffered from divided government, thereby making change all but impossible. An area where reform efforts have begun to succeed, however, has been in the judicial system. The government expects to see full implementation of this redesign of the system within eight years. Other areas now targeted for future reform include fiscal reform, pension reform, energy reform, and labor law reform.

Some argue that it will take a social revolution to solve one of Mexico's major public policy problems, poverty, and that incremental reform will never lead to real change. The Ernesto Zedillo administration (1994–2000) initiated an antipoverty program know as *Progresa,* later renamed *Oportunidades* by the Fox administration. This cash-transfer program for families was designed to tackle a variety of problems including family income, school attendance, and child health. The program provided for conditional cash support to families who would see to their children's health care and attendance at school.[11] Approximately five million families are enrolled in the program. The program appears to have had considerable success, but the problem of societal-wide poverty remains stubbornly entrenched. Several federal ministries manage programs to improve social health and welfare, but the development impasse that maintains poverty at very high levels has yet to be overcome.

The federal government bureaucracy consists of eighteen cabinet ministries and numerous additional agencies of significance at the subcabinet level. Mexico faces rising budgetary deficit pressure, especially in the face of a weakening peso, declining oil revenue, and the global recession. One area that will continue to find support, however, is the security sector. The security sector is managed by the President together with the "Security Cabinet," including the Attorney General (PGR), the Interior Secretariat (SEGOB), Public Safety (SPP), and the military departments of National Defense (Army and Air Force, SEDENA) and the Navy (SEMAR). Despite a difficult fiscal picture the military and law enforcement will continue to see rising budgets, which reflects the nation's critical security situation. Mexico's defense budget is currently US$4.4 billion (compared, for example, to the fiscal year 2009 U.S. defense budget request of US$881 billion).[12] Mexico's military is now divided between two entirely independent cabinet ministries, SEDENA and SEMAR, leading to competition for resources. A host of political factors explain this division, but there is little prospect that a unified Defense Department under the direction of a civilian Secretary of Defense will emerge any time soon.

In addition to the enormous problem faced by Mexico in its attempts to contend with the drug war and rising levels of crime, the country also faces significant environmental problems. To begin with, Mexico City is quite literally running out of water. Mexico's long-running dispute with the United States over the diversion of waters from the Colorado River is perhaps a better-known problem to U.S. citizens. Although that problem reached a resolution, however satisfactory or unsatisfactory, the problem of Mexico City's water is not subject to dispute resolution. The city was built in a region of lush lakes that have all but disappeared. That resource has been exploited to the point where the ground is now sinking under Mexico City, and even the floating gardens of Xochimilco are greatly diminished. In the spring of 2009 the government began rationing water, and over five million residents were entirely cut off from water supplies. In addition to the water shortage itself it is estimated that 40 percent of the water that is piped through the city's water system is lost through leaking pipes. The government has few options available to respond to these problems and even fewer plans in the works. Finally, the environmental devastation of the delicate northern territories, leading to increasing desertification, is paralleled by the rampant destruction of rainforest in the southern parts of the country. Mexico has had neither the political nor the administrative capacity to effectively respond to these desperate situations. Although a Green Party has emerged, it has acted primarily in alliance with the conservative PRI and has had little or no impact on these issues.

Foreign Policy

Mexico's postrevolutionary foreign policy and international relations have been shaped by the experience of invasion, a sense of the state's own weakness and vulnerability, and its desire to maintain internal stability. These priorities led Mexico's leaders to carve out several key principles in its approach to international relations. As a result of its catastrophic experiences with Spain, France, and especially the United States, it sought above all to protect its sovereignty and to insist on a policy of nonintervention in the affairs of other states and a posture of nonalignment. Above all, Mexico's foreign policy and international relations must be understood as a function of its relationship with its neighbor to the north. The United States paradoxically has constituted Mexico's number one security problem and simultaneously a bulwark, however uninvited, against external intervention by other states.

Although Mexico has chosen to focus on matters of internal security, this does not mean that it has ignored its neighbors or remained uninvolved in international affairs. Currently Mexico is attempting to diversify its relationships with other states despite its close relations with the United States, hoping to forge cooperative relations with center-right states in Latin America. Mexico is actively engaged in a range of international institutions and takes very seriously its membership. As a state with little material power available to influence the behavior of other states, international organizations, law, and agreements are of significance for Mexico in any efforts it may make to influence world affairs.

One early exception to Mexico's decidedly noninterventionist approach to international relations was President Lázaro Cárdenas's decision to join the Soviet Union in supporting the Republican cause in the Spanish Civil War during the 1930s. Cárdenas sent rifles, ammunition, food, and even aircraft to the Republicans, although the materiel support was not significant to the war effort overall. Notably, only Mexico and the Soviet Union provided external support to the Republican side beyond the assistance provided by the International Brigades.

Mexico sought to maintain neutrality during the WWII hostilities, but by January 1943 Mexico's President Avila Camacho concluded that Germany presented a threat, especially to shipping, and became a U.S. ally in opposing the Axis powers. The government established a military draft and created a Pacific Security Zone under the command of General Lázaro Cárdenas, the country's former President. Mexico joined with the United States in creating a joint U.S.-Mexico-North Defense Commission. After the Commission was created, efforts were made to elaborate cooperative plans, but General Cárdenas decisively opposed those in Mexico City who endorsed, among other things, cooperation involving U.S. troops (however small in number) who would enter Baja California for surveillance purposes.

In 1944 Mexico sent elements of what it called an aviation training group from its newly established 201st Mexican Air Force Expeditionary Squadron to San Antonio, Texas, for training. The squadron, known as the "Aztec Eagles," was sent to the Philippines in 1945 and flew fifty-nine missions in Luzon and Formosa. Seven pilots were killed.[13] Notably, 14,849 Mexican citizens fought in the war under the U.S. flag. At the time of the Korean War, Mexico had supported the UN's diplomatic approach to the problem. The United States sought to persuade Mexico to contribute troops to the war effort, but after some discussions and promises by the United States of materiel assistance, Mexico did not agree to support the troop request. This position was far more consistent with Mexico's overall position on international engagement. Mexico's primary interest has been with engagement with international institutions, participation in international forums, but limited involvement in any issues not bearing directly on Mexico.

Mexico sought to avoid becoming a pawn in the Cold War struggle between the United States and the Soviet Union. In this hemisphere Mexico had little to fear from Cuba, despite the fact that the Castro regime had supported insurgent groups in a number of other states in the Latin American region. Mexico enjoyed important ties with Cuba that dated to the 1950s, when Fidel Castro and Ché Guevara spent time in Mexico preparing for the Cuban Revolution at their guerrilla training camp. Mexico expended every effort to avoid appearing to take sides in the Cold War struggle, despite the fact that its internal security program succeeded in exterminating domestic forces that sought to pursue a Marxist or even reformist alternative. Mexico's cultural elite had historically embraced Russian culture, especially art, film, and literature, and this too served to harmonize relations between the Soviet Union and Mexico.

Mexico's efforts to secure an independent foreign policy position largely succeeded and did so without jeopardizing its critical relationship with the United States. In the post–Cold War period, Mexico's foreign policy emphasized engagement with international organizations and postconflict resolution efforts. In the 1960s and 1970s Mexico did actively participate in and seek a leadership position within the nonaligned movement. Following his presidency, Luis Echeverría (1970–1976) competed for the post of Secretary General of the UN, thus positioning himself as a Third World progressive leader even though as Mexico's Interior Minister in the administration of President Díaz Ordaz (1964–1970) Echeverría had been responsible for the massacre at Tlatelólco in 1968. Mexico was a leader in efforts to bring about peace accords during the Central American wars of the 1980s and the Guatemalan civil war that continued into the 1990s. It has also played a role in efforts to resolve the current conflict in Colombia, serving as a host for negotiations and for parties to the conflict. Furthermore, Mexico has been an eager and responsible participant in hemispheric intergovernmental organizations and a host of international organizations that function beyond the Western Hemisphere.

Beginning in the late 1980s Mexico warmed to the idea of increased economic cooperation and exchange, particularly with the United States. Indeed, it was Carlos Salinas who approached the George H. W. Bush administration with the NAFTA concept and later helped bring it to fruition with the Clinton administration. The United States responded favorably, understanding that the NAFTA concept was both a good economic deal for some U.S. sectors and also a security hedge against potential instability in Mexico. With NAFTA, investment moving offshore from the United States, typically to Asia, would now be attracted increasingly to consider Mexico. From the U.S. perspective, the agreement would provide enhanced employment and development for the close neighbor that the United States did not want to see destabilized. After NAFTA Mexico undertook a wide array of economic exchanges and free trade agreements, embracing globalization and interdependence as new operative concepts for Mexican society.

It was not until the Fox administration that Mexico once again launched bold initiatives in the foreign policy realm. President Fox essentially gambled his presidency on one "deliverable"—that he would be able to bring an immigration deal back to Mexico, having persuaded his good friend and former border state governor, President George W. Bush, that Mexico needed such relief. For Fox, the attacks of 9/11 destroyed the hopes on which he had bet his presidency, as the United States moved to seal its borders. Moreover, his own silence following 9/11 coupled with the anti-U.S. sentiments being expressed in Mexico following the attacks did much to distance the two countries, despite all of the formal "architecture" that tied them together. Further, the Mexican Foreign Minister's announcement that Mexico would withdraw from the Rio Treaty following 9/11 appeared to be a slap at the United States, especially when compared with the politically astute Brazilian invocation of the treaty in defense of the United States following the attacks.

Immigration remained a tremendous sore point for Mexico, particularly given the unilateral U.S. decision to build a wall along the US-Mexico border. The offense taken in Mexico over this wall is difficult to exaggerate. That said, Mexico's cooperation with the United States regarding post-9/11 security in the long run proved to be very positive. Mexico has committed to tracking non-Mexicans who might be entering the United States from Mexican territory and to cooperate in a full program of antiterror actions. Officially, the Mexican government now recognizes terrorism as a global threat and has partnered with the United States to take responsibility for monitoring the movement of identified targets in Mexican national territory. It faces a significant challenge in controlling fifty-two ports of entry and monitoring other national territory that affords access by land or sea. Mexico is now undertaking steps to improve cooperation with the United States in border surveillance for counterterrorism purposes.

Mexico also eventually overcame its anger over the creation of the U.S. Northern Command after the 9/11 attacks. Mexico had never been a part of what the U.S. military refers to as a regional command and dealt directly, as it believed it should, with Washington. After 9/11 under the new arrangements U.S. Northern Command had responsibility for military-to-military engagement with Mexico, much to Mexico's irritation. After some considerable period of time and only after the election of Felipe Calderón as President, Mexico agreed to maintain liaisons with the command and to begin to cooperate more significantly with the United States on security matters. This shift in policy was due to the crisis that had emerged in Mexico over the drug war.

What has not changed, however, is Mexico's determination to refrain from overseas engagement of any kind other than support to humanitarian requirements. Mexico has refused to participate in either UN or Organization of America States (OAS)–sponsored peacekeeping operations. Mexico did provide humanitarian support to victims of the horrific 1998 hurricane Mitch that bloodied Central America. Mexico also sent military elements to support humanitarian operations in Texas and Louisiana in the aftermath of Hurricane Katrina in 2005. Outside of this type of involvement, it remains firmly committed to its noninterventionist position and has been historically skeptical of international values regimes that challenge state sovereignty, for example in areas such as human rights, democracy promotion, and drug certification.[14]

With the election of PANista presidents in Mexico, relations with Cuba soured. Although the PRI had always maintained its posture as a charter member of a community of international left-progressive states, the PANistas were no longer eager to play Fidel Castro's game and agreed that they would no longer protect the Castro regime from allegations of human rights violations in international bodies. Even as this chill in the Mexico-Cuba relationship endured for some time, the Calderón administration reestablished dialogue and diplomatic exchange with Cuba. Other changes could also be seen in Mexico's regional posture with the advent of the Vicente Fox government in 2000. Despite the fact that it was once an ardent defender of its identity as a Latin American state, Mexico now began to publicly acknowledge its other identity, that of a North American partner to the United States and to Canada. Soon, however, President Fox found himself branded a lapdog of the United States and a suspect member of the Latin American community of nations. Some of this rancor stemmed from the conflict that emerged between President Fox and President Hugo Chávez of Venezuela, while some stemmed from Brazil's emerging ambition to occupy the senior leadership position in Latin America. Brazil, for example, sought to promote a South American Free Trade Area (SAFTA) at the time that the Free Trade Agreement of the Americas (FTAA), promoted by the United States, was still a concept under discussion. SAFTA would have excluded Mexico from participation in the regional trade agreement along with the United States. Following this period of disagreement and with the election of Felipe Calderón, Mexico sought to moderate its relationships and once again build diplomatic bridges to both the north and the south.

Mexico maintains excellent relations with other states in the region, especially Chile, Colombia, and much of Central America. Mexico's relations with Colombia and Chile in particular have intensified over the past several years, reflecting these states' common perspectives on trade and economic values. Mexico and Colombia have also begun to collaborate in combating narcotrafficking, and representatives from their security agencies have engaged in exchanges to discuss common strategies and intelligence cooperation. Mexico maintains close relations with the states of Central America, and in 2001 the Fox administration launched the ambitious Plan Puebla-Panama to promote development in southern Mexico and Central America. In part a reaction to the instability in Chiapas and Oaxaca and in part a reaction to Guatemala's and El Salvador's postconflict instability, the plan offered detailed development objectives, particularly for massive infrastructure projects, but the plan's sponsors never found the financing or popular support necessary to move the project forward.

Mexico's relations with the United States currently involve a host of difficult issues. At the August 2009 summit meeting that brought together the leaders of Mexico, the United States, and Canada, the issues on the agenda included economic recovery and competitiveness, citizen safety and security, and clean energy and climate change. For the Mexico-U.S. relationship specifically, key issues now on the table include the final implementation of trade treaty issues and, of course, immigration. One particularly thorny issue is the question of Mexican trucks entering the United States. Although the NAFTA agreement provided that Mexico's trucks would be able to enter U.S. territory, a series of issues has impeded the implementation of this provision, much to Mexico's consternation.

The United States and Mexico have exchanged numerous high-level visits including both President Obama and President Calderón. This exchange reflects the vital importance that each country represents for the other in terms of both economic and security issues. Mexico's relations with the Bush administration had been strained after the events of 9/11 and Mexico's tepid response to the attacks. Relations improved dramatically, however, with the crafting of the Mérida Initiative at the end of the Bush presidency. In a remarkable shift in approach, President Calderón proposed a strategic partnership between Mexico and the United States to fight the drug war and related crime. The United States responded positively and with remarkable speed to move a proposal forward. The initiative signaled that both parties would move beyond mutual recriminations as to who was at fault and would begin to partner in problem-solving.

The complexity of the Mexico-U.S. relationship is at least in part illustrated by the fact that there are 250 million legal crossings of the border per year, which is almost one million per day. Many Mexicans are not only pushed to enter the United States by the difficult circumstances at home, but are also pulled by the attraction of wages that are six times greater in the United States than in Mexico. Immigration policy, however, remains a tremendously contentious issue in the bilateral relationship. Mexico maintains that its citizens who enter the United States to work must be afforded protection of their human rights and should not be treated as a different class of workers only because they do not have papers. Mexico reasons that these workers are employed by U.S. businesses and thus deserve to be treated with dignity and respect and should not be relegated to a dangerous and oppressive life in the underground. Although Mexico remains seriously committed to negotiating a new agreement to obtain relief for its citizens, there appears to be little chance of movement in the near future on this issue from the U.S. side, particularly given the U.S. recession and the staggering unemployment numbers in the United States. Based on reports from the U.S. Border Patrol, exceptionally fewer Mexican nationals are being apprehended in their efforts to cross the border, suggesting that migration to the United States may be declining.

Mexico has had its own difficulties with immigration pressure, as it has been faced with intense migration from Central America and the use of its national territory by human traffickers who are paid to bring people from all around the world to the United States. As an example of the problem Mexico faces, having waived the visa requirement for Brazilian travelers to Mexico in order to improve its relations with Brazil, Mexico later reimposed the visa requirement following a U.S. request for assistance because so many Brazilians were using Mexico as a platform to illegally enter the United States. In another example, Mexico now also faces the growing problem of Chinese immigrant trafficking from Mexican territory into the United States.

In addition to President Obama's visit to Mexico in August 2009 for the trilateral summit, the U.S. President also visited Mexico in April 2009 for one-on-one talks with President Calderón. An impressive array of high-level visits to Mexico by U.S. officials—including the Secretaries of State and Defense and Homeland Security, the National Security Advisor to the President, the Chairman of the Joint Chiefs of Staff, and the Attorney General—also marked the early days of the Obama administration. These visits and President Obama's two visits early in his first term testified to the importance attached to Mexico by the new U.S. administration.

Domestic/Intermestic Policy: Mexico's Drug War

The drug war and related public insecurity in Mexico has become the central focus of the government of Felipe Calderón. It is a policy concern that folds together domestic and foreign policy, and it is the domain of what has come to be called "intermestic" policy—a blend of the two. Although drug trafficking and associated criminality have plagued Mexico for decades, by the mid-2000s the level of violence had escalated, as drug-trafficking criminal organizations fought each other for prime access to their market, the United States, and also fought law enforcement. These criminal syndicates had gained power in Mexico and elsewhere with the weakening of Colombian trafficking operations. In their new role Colombian traffickers became suppliers to Mexican operations, and Mexico's syndicates began to control an increasingly greater share of product development, transit, supply, and marketing into the United States. With the increase in operational responsibility and thus in the money involved, Mexico's syndicates grew in sophistication and firepower. Although the drug business was not new to Mexico and dated back as far as the early twentieth century, the stakes had grown more substantial, thus escalating the violence. Some observers suggested that what was transpiring was, in effect, the "Colombianization" of Mexico.

Although President Vicente Fox had declared the drug scourge to be Mexico's number one national security concern, upon taking office President Calderón launched a determined effort to address the growing violence in the country. With the success seen against Colombian drug trafficking organizations, the Mexican cartels had grown in power, and the effects of their criminal enterprise were felt throughout the society. These organizations have been labeled by some as "mafias" and by others "insurgents." Regardless of their precise designation they have expanded their activities beyond drugs to include a broad menu of criminal activity, including extortion, robbery, assault, human trafficking, money laundering, counterfeiting, and so on.

The number one problem faced by President Calderón in dealing with drug-related violence was the level of corruption that existed in Mexican society. Some observers argued that when the society had been under the control of the former official party, the PRI, regional deals had been brokered with cartels throughout the Mexican state, therefore affording a certain amount of peace in the society. With the coming of the PAN to power under Presidents Fox and Calderón, observers argued that the old brokered deals had collapsed, thus opening up a new wave of violence and pressure on local law enforcement organizations and on local officials more generally. Mexico's cartels now move cocaine, methamphetamine, heroin, and marijuana. Ninety percent of the cocaine entering the United States comes from Mexico, principally from coca grown in Colombia and Peru. It is estimated that with the assistance of Mexican cartels, Peru may become the largest coca producer by 2011 or 2012, displacing Colombia. Mexico's cartels are also increasingly engaged in producing both marijuana and methamphetamine in U.S. territory directly.

President Calderón's initiation of a full-scale war against the cartels involved the deployment of forty-five thousand troops throughout the country, chiefly in the northern border states but also, for example, in the President's own home state of Michoacán, home of one of the most vicious of the cartels, *La Familia Michoacana*. The landscape of cartels is constantly undergoing change as alliances shift and leaders are captured or killed. The Mexican government has agreed to extradite drug kingpins to the United States for prosecution, so these numbers have been rising. For now, in addition to La Familia, other major cartels include the Gulf Cartel, the Federation (which includes the *Sinaloa* Cartel), and the *Júarez* Cartel. These cartels also maintain associated organizations that provide armed force for cartel operations. These include the Zetas, the Negros, and the Kaibiles (former Guatemalan special forces soldiers) to name several such groups.

The Calderón government has focused on corrupt local police forces, taking them down on a selective basis and even arresting entire police forces. The government has sought to create new, fully vetted law enforcement organizations at the national level. The use of the military to conduct not only anticartel operations but also antipolice operations has led to an unprecedented level of conflict between the military and the police, leading to the execution of soldiers, including a retired general, by corrupt police officers. These killings have been extremely vicious and have involved displays of tortured, beheaded soldiers in order to terrorize the armed forces and the wider population. The armed forces have experienced desertions at the rate of thirty thousand per year, and those who remain in service are subject to threats and intimidation. Some of these deserters have been recruited by the cartels, who openly advertise for their services (using banners advertising for recruits), especially those who have received training in special operations or intelligence. The military itself has not been immune to corruption, as was demonstrated by the notorious case of General Jesús Gutiérrez Rebollo, Mexico's former drug czar who was arrested in 1997 for his ties to the Júarez cartel. At the time allegations surfaced that both the Júarez and Tijuana cartels had negotiated protection with military commanders in the area in exchange for bribes.

The level of corruption in law enforcement organizations at both the local and national level required a massive response by the government. As troops fanned throughout the country to combat the traffickers, the violence escalated, and narcotrafficking organizations procured increasingly powerful weaponry in order to respond more effectively to government forces. Furthermore, much of this weaponry poured into Mexico from the United States. According to the U.S. Alcohol, Tobacco and Firearms Agency (ATF), since 2006 over 90 percent of the arms that were seized in Mexico and were traced had come from the United States.

Since the beginning of the Calderón administration over thirteen thousand civilians were killed as a result of drug-related violence. During the same period over one thousand Mexican law enforcement officials were also killed. Overall, the killings were of a very gruesome and extraordinarily cruel nature, including massacres, beheadings, torture, and mutilations. It is estimated that over five hundred thousand persons are employed in the illegal drug industry. Although very difficult to assess, analysts suggest that half of the proceeds from the illegal drug trade are devoted to paying off government officials, including politicians and law enforcement entities. Unlike the case of Colombia, where huge swaths of legitimate business and large agricultural assets fell into the hands, legally or otherwise, of illegal armed groups, including drug traffickers, the orderly disposition of proceeds from trafficking in Mexico is still a work in progress.

The Mérida Initiative forged a new strategic partnership between Mexico and the United States in order to share responsibility for responding to the threat posed by the drug trafficking organizations. The new approach was deemed a "strategic partnership" and identified new responsibilities for the United States in quelling the conflict. The agreement also included a commitment from the United States of US$1.4 billion dollars over three years to support materiel acquisition and systems development and upgrades for law enforcement and the military. Although initially some opposition to the plan surfaced in Mexico, once the United States agreed that there would be no true conditionality attached to the funding, such as to include human rights vetting, and once the Mexican government explained that the plan would not involve stationing U.S. troops in Mexico, Mexican legislative and public opinion swung in favor of the plan.

The United States agreed to work on the demand side of the problem and to work on the issue of illegal arms transfers to Mexico. For the United States, the issue of arms transfers presented a difficult challenge, as there were an estimated twelve thousand gun shops located along the U.S. side of the border as well as numerous gun shows, thus providing easy access to weapons. The Obama administration announced its intent to push the U.S. Senate to ratify the Inter-American Convention on Small Arms Trafficking, which has been awaiting action in the Senate since 1997. An agreement was reached in August 2009 to join the U.S. interagency, including U.S. Immigration and Customs Enforcement (ICE) and ATF, with Mexico's Attorney General office (PGR) in order to develop cooperation in investigative methods so as to combat violence and follow arms trafficking and other illegal activity along the border. Finally, the U.S. administration has ordered the creation of checkpoints by the U.S. Department of Homeland Security to look for illegal arms smuggling and to conduct random inspections.

Conclusion

Mexico's elites have been able to avoid paying the real cost of their failure to bring full development to their population because they have relied for years on the safety valve of emigration to the United States. Porfirio Díaz is widely quoted as having said, "So far from God, so close to the United States," as he lamented the impact of the United States on Mexico's national development. Ultimately, he may have been correct in his assessment, as proximity to the United States has not only led to the loss of over half of Mexico's national territory, but also permitted national elites to avoid taking responsibility for national development, particularly after World War II. As the Asian "dragons" and "tigers" grew their economies and reshaped their destinies in states such as Taiwan, Korea, and Singapore—to say nothing of China— leaders in those countries made important public policy decisions about the need to pursue education and to develop infrastructure and human capital. Unfortunately, the same cannot be said about Mexico's leaders.

When those key decisions could have been made in the 1960s and 1970s, Mexico's ruling elites were consumed with preserving their power and amassing great wealth. Over time the system modernized and a market democracy did emerge, but it was one that was characterized by an untrained and comparatively uneducated labor force, little capacity for innovation, and an entrepreneurial class that had become complacent with largely unfettered access to the U.S. market. Unfortunately, poverty and inequality have bred the kind of opportunities that are destructive rather than productive: crime, drug trafficking, and social anarchy.

The Mexican state now faces a monumental challenge as it attempts to defeat the criminal forces that have put the society under siege. Unfortunately, Mexico cannot control the key factor that sets the condition for this situation— the U.S. demand for drugs. It may be that Mexico's best approach, under these circumstances, is to continue the sometimes agonizingly slow process of rebuilding its law enforcement and judicial institutions. In creating a new climate of security, significant additional resources will be needed in order to protect and insulate these new institutions from criminal influences. Mexico has begun this process, but this effort will require a broad and sustained political consensus within the society to continue the struggle over the long haul. The Mexican state will also need to commit to the use of force in a manner that respects human rights, and if they do not, any consensus achieved will be undermined. What is certain, however, is that without a reasonable level of safety and security for the citizenry, the consolidation of democracy and sustained, inclusive economic development will be difficult to accomplish.

Suggestions for Further Reading

Camp, Roderic Ai. *Mexico's Military on the Democratic Stage*. Westport, CT: Praeger Security International, 2005.

Contreras, Joseph. *In the Shadow of the Giant: The Americanization of Modern Mexico*. New Brunswick, NJ: Rutgers University Press, 2009.

Crandall, Russell, Guadalupe Paz, and Riordan Roett, eds. *Mexico's Democracy at Work: Political and Economic Dynamics*. Boulder, CO: Lynne Rienner, 2005.

Davidow, Jeffrey. *The U.S. and Mexico: The Bear and the Porcupine*. Princeton, NJ: Marcus Wiener Publishers, 2004.

Dresser, Denise. "Mexico: Dysfunctional Democracy." In *Constructing Democratic Governance in Latin America*. 3rd ed. Ed. Jorge I. Domínguez and Michael Shifter, 242–63. Baltimore, MD: Johns Hopkins University Press, 2008.

Domínguez, Jorge I., and Rafael Fernández de Castro. *The United States and Mexico: Between Partnership and Conflict*. 2nd ed. New York and London: Routledge, 2009.

Edmonds-Poli, Emily, and David A. Shirk. *Contemporary Mexican Politics*. Lanham, MD: Rowman & Littlefield, 2009.

Grayson, George. *Mexico's Struggle with "Drugs and Thugs."* New York: Headline Series, Foreign Policy Association. No. 331, Winter 2009.

Grayson, George. *Mexico: Narco-Violence and a Failed State.* NJ: Transaction Publishers, 2009.

Joseph, Gilbert M., and Timothy J. Henderson, eds. *The Mexico Reader: History, Culture, Politics.* Durham, NC: Duke University Press, 2002.

Morris, Stephen D. *Political Corruption in Mexico: The Impact of Democratization.* Boulder, CO: Lynne Rienner, 2009.

Preston, Julia, and Samuel Dillon. *Opening Mexico: The Making of a Democracy.* New York: Farrar, Strauss and Giroux, 2004.

Shorris, Earl. *The Life and Times of Mexico.* New York: W. W. Norton, 2004.

Notes

1. Enrique Krauze, "The Mexican Evolution," *New York Times*, March 24, 2009, A-25.

2. Denise Dresser, "Reality Check for U.S.-Mexico Relations," *Los Angeles Times*, January 15, 2009, www.latimes.com/la-oe-dresser152009jan15,0,4310307,print.story.

3. U.S. Census Bureau, "Census Bureau Data Show Characteristics of the U.S. Foreign-Born Population," February 19, 2009, www.census.gov/Press-Release/www/releases/archives/american_community_survey.

4. Mark Stevenson, "NAFTA Hasn't Proved a Vehicle for Prosperity," June 8, 2008, www.signonsandiego.com/uniontrib/20080608/news1b8mexcar.html, accessed 11/14/2008.

5. Emily Edmonds-Poli and David A. Shirk, *Contemporary Mexican Politics* (Lanham, MD: Rowman and Littlefield, 2009), 270–71.

6. *Country Profile: Mexico* (Washington, D.C.: Library of Congress, Federal Research Division, July 2008), 12; U.S. Department of State, *Background Note: Mexico* (May 2009): 1–12.

7. Michael Reid, *Forgotten Continent. The Battle for Latin America's Soul* (New Haven, CT: Yale University Press, 2007): 202–03.

8. Andrew Selee and Katie Putnam, "Mexico's 2009 Midterm Elections: Winners and Losers" (Washington, D.C.: Woodrow Wilson International Center for Scholars, Mexico Institute, July 2009): 3.

9. Andres Oppenheimer, "Mexico's Political Paralysis," in *Saving the Americas* (Mexico City, Mexico: Random House Mondadari, 2007), 296.

10. Sara Miller Llana, "Setbacks in Mexico's War on Corruption," *The Christian Science Monitor*, December 30, 2008, www.csmonitor.com/2009/0113/p06s01-woam.htm.

11. Reid, 233–34.

12. "The FY 2009 Pentagon Spending Request-Global Military Spending," Center for Arms Control and Non-Proliferation, www.armscontrolcenter.org/policy/securityspending/articles/fy09_dod_request_global/.

13. Monica Rankin, "Mexico. Industrialization Through Unity," in Latin *America During WWII*, ed. Thomas M. Leonard and John F. Bratzel (Lanham, MD: Rowman and Littlefield, 2006), 28.

14. Jorge I. Domínguez and Rafael Fernández de Castro, *The United States and Mexico: Between Partnership and Conflict,* 2nd ed. (New York: Routledge, 2009), 60.

This chapter represents the analysis and conclusions of the author and does not necessarily represent the views of any agency of the U.S. government.

17

Cuba

Development, Revolution, and Decay

Juan M. del Aguila

As the only nation in the Western Hemisphere that has adopted revolutionary Communism for its model of political development, Cuba stands separate from other Latin American nations. The revolution of 1959 and its subsequent radicalization have attracted the interest of students of politics as well as that of policymakers, journalists, intellectuals, and ordinary people, many of whom have been inspired by "the Cuban example." In addition, the central role played by President Fidel Castro from the beginning of the revolution is key to understanding developments in Cuba in the years since he and his followers came to power. This is partly because under his leadership Cuba has become an influential actor in regional politics and has engaged in an unusual degree of revolutionary activism abroad. Like other *caudillos* (political strongmen) of his generation President Castro personifies his country to observers the world over, but as will be made clear in this chapter, his own transformation from an impetuous young revolutionary to an aging dictator parallels the course of the revolution itself.

The politics of revolutionary development have moved Cuba through periods of radical transformation in the economy and the social system, through phases when pragmatism and moderation shaped domestic priorities and affected social attitudes, and finally to the stable totalitarianism of the

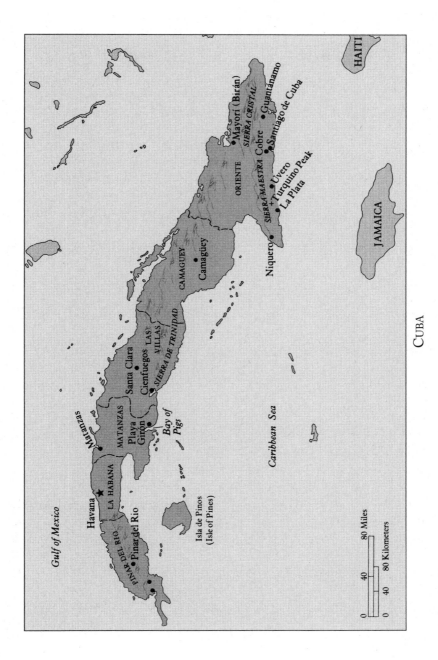

CUBA

1980s characterized by growing difficulties at home and partial retrenchment abroad. In effect, the revolution and its consequences can be understood as an ongoing experiment in the process of achieving mature nationhood, but as with any experiment Cuba's has been characterized by fits and starts, abrupt policy reversals, intense criticism of the real nature of socialism and revolution, and evident exhaustion.

Cuba's limited participation in Latin America, its diminished role in the Third World, and its defunct membership in the former Communist world impose major constraints on its participation in international affairs. Unable to inspire others to carry out revolutions, Cuba sees its influence considerably reduced and is left without powerful friends or allies. Without strategic protection or vital economic support—that is, lacking the resources that facilitated high-profile activism abroad—Cuba's internationalist ventures are a thing of the past. Fewer resources and reduced influence have turned Cuba into a marginal actor in regional and international affairs in the post–Cold War system.

Cuba's economy and social system must now get by without the US$5 to 7 billion in resources from former Communist countries. Because no new sources of wealth are being developed that will fill the gap, living standards are plummeting and social discontent is rising. Growing numbers of Cubans are demoralized, and they have little hope for the future. President Castro believed that unresolved difficulties placed "the Nation, the Revolution and Socialism" in great peril and that the 1990s was "the most difficult decade in History."

History, Political Culture, and Early Development

Cuba, the largest of the Greater Antilles, is located at the entrance of the Gulf of Mexico, some 112 nautical miles (208 kilometers) from the United States. Its 44,218 square miles (114,525 square kilometers) of total surface stretch over a varied topography that includes mountain ranges, rolling hills, plains, and hundreds of rivers and streams. The principal mountain ranges lie in the eastern, central, and western provinces, and the highest mountain, Pico Turquino, rises to some 6,500 feet (1,981 meters) in the Sierra Maestra range.

The country's coastline is indented with several deep harbors and ports: Mariel and Havana in the west; Nuevitas, Nipe, and Santiago de Cuba in the east; and others along the southern coastline. From the colonial period to the present Cuba has relied heavily on foreign commerce for its prosperity, so a sound maritime infrastructure is critical for its trade. After 1959 Cuba shifted its structure of foreign trade away from the United States and toward the Soviet bloc. The Cuban merchant marine has also expanded dramatically since 1959.

Unlike many other developing countries, Cuba has not experienced a dramatic rise in population, and its demographic growth rates remain stable. Population growth averages around 1 percent, which alleviates the burden on employment and services that plagues many countries in the Third World. Of the country's eleven million inhabitants 69 percent reside in urban areas and the rest live in small towns and in the less densely populated rural areas. Most Cubans have lived in large cities and towns since the 1930s, and by the late 1980s over 20 percent of the population lived in the capital city of Havana or its environs. Part of the infrastructure of some of Cuba's larger cities is deteriorating owing to neglect, scarce resources, and the sheer passage of time: Havana was founded by Spanish settlers in 1514, Santiago de Cuba in 1515.

Caucasians, mulattoes, and blacks are practically the only ethnic groups in the country. Whites comprise 66 percent of the population, mulattoes nearly 22 percent, and blacks approximately 12 percent. Whites were the dominant ethnic group during the twentieth century, and many are descendants of the creole elite of colonial Cuba. Intraregional and seasonal migration is a fact of life in Caribbean societies, but although migration to Cuba from other Caribbean and Latin American countries has been low, small numbers of migrants from some Caribbean islands settled in Cuba earlier in the twentieth century. No Indian subcultures exist because for all practical purposes the mostly primitive Indian communities that inhabited the island in precolonial times disappeared early in the colonial period.

Although racial differences were evident in prerevolutionary Cuba, no deep racial cleavages existed between whites and nonwhites. Occupation and income levels established social differences among the races, but they also affected status for blacks, whites, and mulattoes as individuals of a particular race. Racial prejudices were found among many whites and between blacks and mulattoes. Subtle forms of segregation were a manifestation of these basic attitudes, but overt racial conflict rarely erupted. Snobbery and elitism often characterized the behavior of the white upper classes, but more than racism shaped such behavior. Changes in the social system and class structure, which have reduced racial and class differences, have further dampened friction among the races, but they have not eliminated the psycho-social dimensions of racism.

Some scholars, such as Carlos Moore, maintain that "in social, cultural and psychological terms, race pervades the everyday life of every Cuban, white or black," and that "Cuban society was racist prior to 1959 and is steadfastly so today." Moore and others believe that racism is part of a complex cultural legacy rooted in slavery, subsequently exacerbated by social indifference and political neglect, and that revolutionary intolerance has created new racial barriers. He contends that "revolutionary Cuba is a more intolerant and inhospitable environment for the expression of black distinctiveness than was pre-revolutionary Cuba,"[1] and this, he argues, is mostly a consequence of ideological intolerance. On the other hand, the Cuban government considers race and racism to be extremely delicate issues and maintains that the latter is no longer a major social problem. It is evident that the issue of race—rooted in Cuba's history and memory—has not disappeared under socialism, partly because racial harmony cannot be achieved by simply declaring that racism has been abolished.

Columbus discovered Cuba during his first trip to the New World in 1492, but because the island lacked substantial mineral wealth and had not developed an advanced indigenous civilization, it remained sparsely populated well into the eighteenth century. The fifty thousand or so native Indians at the time of the discovery were gradually subdued by Spanish settlers under the *encomienda* system. They were forced to search for precious minerals, work in agriculture, fish, and also engage in primitive forms of trade. Brutal treatment, disease, poor nutrition, and the harmful effects of servitude itself decimated the Indian population, and little trace of their social system remains. Efforts to Christianize the Indians were not entirely successful, and often the Spanish settlers used violence to instill the "proper" attitudes among the Indians. Catholic missions were established and charged with propagating and maintaining the faith, so that friars and priests played important roles in the early life of the colony. The Catholic Church subsequently grew in numbers, wealth, and influence, and its notions of order, faith, spirituality, and salvation pervaded Cuba's cultural foundation.

The Spanish settlers of Cuba were a heterogeneous lot. Many came from Andalucía and other southern regions of Spain, and as was the case elsewhere in Latin America, the lure of gold, a sense of adventure, and the opportunity to escape the Spanish caste system brought thousands of settlers to Cuba and the New World. However, the Cuban colony remained poor, and the prospects of growing fabulously wealthy were greater on the mainland. The colonial regime at this time was weak and ineffective, and Spain itself had little interest in Cuba's development. Franklin Knight writes that "throughout the sixteenth century, the colony [Cuba] virtually stagnated, challenged by pirates, ravaged by hurricanes, plagued by diseases, and depopulated by the magnetic pull of Mexico and Peru."[2] In short, the foundations of Cuba as a colony stemmed from a social system dominated by *peninsulares* and supported by the Catholic Church. The native population failed to resist the impact of a stronger culture and quickly disappeared.

Black slaves were brought to Cuba by the thousands from the 1700s to the middle of the nineteenth century, replacing Indians as laborers on sugarcane plantations, as servants in the larger towns and cities, and as manual laborers in service occupations. A census taken in 1791 showed that out of a total population of 273,000, 56 percent were white and that slaves made up the largest proportion of the black population. A century later another census showed that over the entire colonial period, nearly 375,000 black slaves had been brought to Cuba. It is a fact that the slave trade contributed to the wealth of many planters and traders.

Cuba's economy originally revolved around tobacco and, subsequently, coffee cultivation, but it gradually became a plantation economy geared toward sugar cultivation, production, and export. The island's geographical location offers the right temperatures as well as the necessary rainfall for sugar production, and the terrain of the lowlands is suitable for harvesting cane. Indeed, economists and historians maintain that the island's comparative advantage in sugar production was soon realized and that earnings from sugar exports financed the imports of foodstuffs, textiles, machinery, and other capital goods.

The combination of sugar, slavery, and the plantation economy shaped the colonial social structure and laid the foundation for an economy geared to foreign commerce, but it did not produce a society of small landowners and rural proprietors. Differences among *peninsulares, criollos,* slaves, and *libertos* (slaves who had obtained their freedom) were evidence of a hierarchical system unmindful of any notion of social equality. As depicted by popular novels, books, and documents of the time, colonial Cuba remained unaffected by changes taking place elsewhere and therefore stayed under the tight control of Spain. On the other hand, the benefits of free trade were strongly felt during the English occupation of Havana in 1762–1763, as new markets were found and the economy was further integrated into regional and international commercial networks. Geopolitical rivalries with Great Britain and the United States in time forced Spain to modify the mercantilist regime, and it gradually gave way to a more open trading system. Spain sought to reestablish political control over its colonial domains, including Cuba, in the early nineteenth century, but the impact of liberal ideas, in addition to the introduction of capital and new technology, stimulated new thinking.

An influential group of thinkers and wealthy oligarchs like Francisco Arango and Ignacio Montalvo believed in the promise of positivism and individual will, and educators like José de la Luz y Caballero and the priest Félix Varela engendered an early commitment to political independence and nationhood. Although education was restricted to the creole elite and to the people who could afford it and was influenced by Catholic beliefs, its benefits were felt by a growing number of progressive criollos. A rift between the people who were committed to the preservation of the colonial regime and those who believed in Cuba's gradual emancipation and eventual independence shaped the politics of the period and forced a reassessment of relations between Cuba and Spain. Racial considerations affected each outlook, and Knight maintains that the slave society during the nineteenth century was equally one of ferment and strife. Its strengths created its inherent weaknesses. A divided society was also a divisive society. Tensions existed within the white groups as well as between white and nonwhite. In Cuba, the most enduring of the Caribbean slave societies, the white groups split basically between *peninsulares* and *criollos*.[3]

In summary, the colonial system was marked by inequality and hierarchy, and its economic foundation rested on a plantation economy and slavery. Early advocates of Cuba's struggle for independence faced ideological divisions and clashing interests, which allowed Spain to maintain control over the colony. Lacking clear pro-independence leadership, often fearing the consequences of a social revolution, and without political cohesion or class consciousness, the creole plantocracy accepted its politically subordinate status.

Struggles for Independence, 1868–1901

The emergence of new political currents in the 1860s stemmed from the need to challenge Spanish domination and to improve Cuba's economic position. On the one hand, a nationalistic and clearly separatist movement advocated confrontation and war against Spain if those were the only means of achieving independence. More moderate elements, represented by the Reformist party founded in 1862, advocated representation for Cuba in the Spanish Cortes, administrative reforms, and liberal trade policies. The issue of slavery often divided the creoles, as did class and economic differences between the eastern and western planters. The latter feared a social revolution and tended to be more conservative. Still, Spain's refusal to grant meaningful concessions to the Cubans and its failure to satisfy legitimate political demands led to rebellion in 1868 followed by a decade of bloody and destructive warfare.

The rebels were led by Carlos Manuel de Céspedes, a patriot and moderately wealthy planter from Oriente province. Other political and military leaders like Generals Antonio Maceo and Máximo Gómez fought bravely during the protracted struggle, but latent political divisions among the rebels weakened their effort. Nationalism fed the rebel cause as did the commitment to emancipate Cuba from colonial domination. Spain poured thousands of troops into Cuba and sent one of its best generals, Arsenio Martínez Campos, to lead the Spanish forces. Yet the failure to truly carry the war to the western provinces; the deaths of Céspedes, Ignacio Agramonte, and other leaders; the absence of external help; and the lack of support on the part of many Cubans doomed the rebel cause.

Nearly 250,000 people on both sides lost their lives in the struggle, and Cuba's infrastructure was devastated. The war cost Spain approximately

US$300 million and was both a cause and a consequence of political quarrels among its own elites. Yet Spain and the rebels signed an armistice in 1878 that led to a tenuous peace and a period of self-criticism and questioning on the part of those Cubans who still advocated independence. On the other hand, the Cubans' ability to wage a protracted struggle, endure enormous sacrifices, and exhibit national aspirations demonstrated that a new political consciousness was emerging and that emancipation was achievable. Differences over slavery, regional tensions, and the balance between civilian leaders and military caudillos would have to be resolved before a new war would start—or else Cuba would remain a colony.

Cuba's political economy changed in the last decades of the nineteenth century, partly because the restoration of political stability created economic opportunities for domestic and foreign capital. New technology transformed the sugar industry so that production revolved around foreign-owned industrial complexes, which limited opportunities for local management and participation. A growing worldwide demand for sugar allowed producers to plan with economies of scale in mind, and the industry benefited from new markets, principally the United States. Spain introduced fees and taxes on Cuba's exports in the early 1890s that adversely affected domestic producers, partly because it feared growing U.S. penetration of Cuba, but these measures did not really isolate Cuba from the United States.

A growing dependence on the U.S. market for trade, investment, technology, and industrial inputs characterized U.S.-Cuban relations in the 1880s and 1890s, even while Spain maintained political control. In 1896 U.S. investments in Cuba were estimated at $50 million, concentrated in mining and sugar holdings. Trade between the two countries was valued at $27 million in 1897, and the composition of that trade showed that the United States exported to Cuba manufactured and industrial goods and imported sugar, molasses, tobacco, and a few nonmanufactured products. United States Consul William Elliot Gonzalez publicly recognized that "the Island practically depends completely on the U.S. market for its sugar exports" and that associated industries like the railroads, warehouses, port facilities, and their financial and labor support structures depended directly on the U.S. market.

There is little doubt that this growing penetration of a weak economy dominated by sugar and its derivative production by a growing capitalist, industrial power meant that the colonial regime was subjected to both internal and external pressures. Once again, pro-independence forces gathered to challenge Spanish authority and assert claims for independence and sovereignty and to do so with a new and more compelling sense of unity and national purpose. New leaders, principally José Martí, had forged a more mature vision of political emancipation and nationalism, and the issue of slavery had been laid to rest since its abolition in the 1880s. In short, ideologically and organizationally, the separatists were in a stronger position than in the 1860s, whereas Spain vacillated between granting meaningful reforms and reimposing absolutist government.

As the founder of the Cuban Revolutionary Party (PRC) in exile and as the intellectual force and principal civilian organizer of the war effort, José Martí represented a younger generation of Cubans committed to the total liberation of the country. Martí believed that war was brutal but necessary— "a political process that would definitively resolve a situation in which fear of war is a paralyzing element"—and held that "patriotism is a sacred obligation when one struggles to create conditions in the motherland that would improve the lives of one's countrymen."

In the *Manifiesto de Montecristi,* a critical document issued in 1895, the civilian-military leadership spoke for two generations of Cubans, stating that after the war "the nation would be constituted from its roots, with its own viable institutions, so that a government would be unable to lead it into tyranny." The manifesto asserted that the nation returned to war "with an enlightened and democratic people, cognizant of its own and others' rights" and sure of "its republican education." It is thus quite clear that the people struggling for independence advocated representative government and democratic institutions and were influenced by nationalism, liberalism, and self-determination rather than by absolutism, Marxism, or notions of class struggle.

The war raged back and forth for three years, with the rebels fighting a guerrilla struggle and Spain following a more conventional strategy. Rebel columns moved westward across the countryside, burning and sacking properties and cane fields, attacking small towns, and disrupting the economy. Spain's hated policy of "reconcentration" forced hundreds of thousands of Cubans into fortified towns and military compounds, and hunger, desolation, and brutality decimated the population. Thousands died, including Martí and Maceo, and property losses were valued in the millions of dollars.

A military stalemate between rebel and Spanish forces along with sensationalist accounts of the fighting published in the United States led to U.S. military intervention in 1898. The Cuban question had become an important issue in U.S. domestic politics, and Spain as well as the rebels had attempted to influence U.S. public opinion. There is solid evidence that the McKinley administration preferred a negotiated settlement that would bring independence to Cuba and that it urged Spain to give up its control. Spain rejected diplomatic entreaties and offers of mediation from European powers and obstinately refused to accept either military or political defeat. In April 1898 the U.S. Congress passed a resolution granting President McKinley's request for authority to end hostilities in Cuba, but it also disavowed any interest in exercising sovereignty, jurisdiction, or control over Cuba once Spain had been driven out.

The U.S. occupation of Cuba lasted until 1902, and many students of Cuban politics believe that it created a legacy of resentment and frustration because, in part, U.S. intervention prevented the Cubans from achieving a complete victory over Spain. U.S. military authorities partly rebuilt the nation's infrastructure and brought about significant improvements in public health, education, public administration, and finance, but Cuban nationalists and many intellectuals felt a sense of political impotence and frustration. Subsequently, the inclusion of the Platt Amendment, passed in 1901 by the U.S. Congress, in the Cuban constitution meant that Cuba became a U.S. protectorate rather than a sovereign nation because the amendment granted territorial concessions to the United States, placed financial restrictions on the Cuban government, and allowed the United States to intervene in Cuba's internal affairs.

Cuba's foreign economic relations were subsequently shaped by a Reciprocity Treaty (1903), which granted preferential treatment to Cuban sugar in the U.S. market and reduced tariffs on U.S. exports to Cuba. U.S. investments in Cuba's sugar industry, cattle industry, public services, utilities, and other properties had reached $200 million by 1909, nearly 50 percent of all foreign investment in Cuba. The Platt Amendment and the Reciprocity Treaty facilitated a growing U.S. influence in Cuba and were often perceived as neocolonialist measures aimed at protecting U.S. interests in the island. Many politicians, businesspeople, owners of sugar estates, and some conservative intellectuals felt that the U.S. "tutelage" was not necessarily detrimental. The U.S. presence thus created a significant political cleavage, separating those people who felt it to be beneficial and necessary for Cuba's early development from nationalists who saw it as a direct infringement of genuine self-determination. The views of Ramón Ruiz illustrate a scholarly consensus on these matters, namely, that the Platt Amendment limited Cuba's first experience in self-government and "offered the Cubans a facile way out of domestic difficulties. Reliance on the United States eventually engendered among Cubans a loss of faith in their Republic and in their own nationality."[4]

The Political Development
of Prerevolutionary Cuba

Political competition during the early republican period existed predominantly between the Liberal and Conservative parties. These parties—and others—were essentially controlled by the political caudillos José Miguel Gómez and Mario García Menocal, respectively, and did not articulate clear political philosophies or programs. The political system was based on client arrangements and patronage networks, so partisan loyalties were often exchanged for political favors. Electoral fraud and administrative corruption were common, and elections were often cynically viewed as attempts by manipulative politicians to preserve or expand personal power. Public office was held in disrepute, politics was used as a means of self-enrichment, and the democratic ideals that had motivated Martí and other revolutionary leaders remained little more than abstractions.

On the other hand, respected intellectuals like Fernando Ortiz and Enrique José Varona formed part of an emerging democratic intelligentsia that rejected politics as a means to private gain and advocated civic-mindedness, cultural emancipation, and, above all, honest and democratic government. Varona asserted that "to govern is to watch over compliance with laws, and provide the means for that compliance," and he pointed out that "our public ills are the work of all of us." Ortiz, in turn, criticized the poor conditions found in most of the rural areas, where peasants, seasonal workers, and unskilled laborers toiled under difficult conditions and lived at barely subsistence levels. He attacked the evils of monoculture and the subordination of the economy to foreign capital, and he suggested that the revolutionary generation had betrayed principles articulated earlier. Reformist groups founded the opinion journal known as *Revista de Avance,* and other people joined the Cuban Council of Civic Renovation. Through writing, public speaking, and political organization a cultural revival encouraged debate, much of it focused on the need to cleanse the political culture and establish viable institutions. Finally, many critics framed their charges against the postcolonial regime according to anti-imperialist principles, appealing to students, intellectuals, labor leaders, and others to unite in order to bring about political change.

Gerardo Machado was elected as a popular president in 1924, but he became a virtual dictator following his contrived reelection in 1928 and his violation of constitutional norms. From that point forward, politics took on a violent character. Government and opposition alike engaged in terrorism, shootings, and political assassinations, indicating that institutions were unable to resolve political conflicts and that force was seen as a legitimate arbiter of political disputes.

Then, the Great Depression had a devastating effect on the economy. Plummeting sugar prices affected the livelihood of hundreds of thousands of families, and unemployment, social misery, and rural banditry reflected a deeper structural crisis. The government sought to alleviate the problems by acquiring new loans from U.S. bankers, but the country's creditworthiness was shaky, and it had previously accumulated substantial debts. Cuba's economic and financial dependence on the United States meant that the impact of the Depression was felt in business, finance, public administration, and government itself, so options were limited. Breaking the economic bonds with the United States would wreak havoc and plunge the country into instability and chaos. Managing the crisis through technical approaches and financial legerdemain would only postpone the day of reckoning. Robert Smith describes the complexity of the situation and its interrelatedness:

> During the closing months of 1930 the situation in Cuba degenerated rapidly. The economic picture had been deteriorating for several years and the world-wide depression added problems to an already serious situation. This helped stimulate opposition to Machado, and the threats of disorder mounted.[5]

Student protesters challenged the police in the streets, but resistance to Machado also involved professionals, middle-class elements, labor leaders, and the Communist Party. One of the leading anti-Machado organizations was the University Students Directorate, through which a new generation of activists and revolutionaries advocated a complete and definitive change of regime. The Communist Party attacked Machado from orthodox Marxist positions, depicting him as the instrument of foreign interests and as the enemy of the working class. The party called for popular mobilization, strikes, and urban confrontations, but its calls failed to spark a popular revolution and often led to internecine struggles with other groups. Finally, the ABC, a secret, cellular organization comprised of middle-sector individuals, intellectuals, and students dissatisfied with the politics of the University Students' Directorate, played a prominent role in the struggle against the dictator. The ABC stood for liberty and social justice, and its programs called for economic and political reforms. ABC cells engaged in clandestine activities and were often involved in violent incidents; in fact, the organization's strategy at one point aimed at Machado's assassination. In short, the opposition was unified in its commitment to driving Machado from power and ending the dictatorship, but it was also tactically and ideologically divided. The political agenda of the noncommunist groups called for democratization, socioeconomic change, and a challenge to U.S. interests in Cuba, but their failure to rally mass support against the dictatorship proved to be one of their major weaknesses.

The army proved to be a critical contender because its support was essential for either keeping Machado in power or shifting the balance to his adversaries. The army was structured on parochial loyalties rather than merit, and its military competence was questionable. It remained the pillar of order and stability, but it also felt the violent political fragmentation that ultimately ousted Machado. Some lower-rank members, many of whom came from humble backgrounds and viewed the army as a vehicle for self-improvement and social mobility, demanded higher pay and an end to the politicization of promotions. Such internal pressure, at a time when a crisis of political authority affected the government's freedom of action and paralyzed decision-making, opened the way for an internal revolt led by then-sergeant Fulgencio E.

Batista y Zaldívar. Under his leadership the army sought to contain revolutionary outbursts and directly influence the selection of presidents. This would play a central role during the following decades.

Finally, as had been the case since 1898, the United States played the role of ultimate power broker. In 1933 the new Roosevelt Administration, through Sumner Welles as its special ambassador, shaped a resolution to Cuba's political crisis that preserved U.S. interests and restored stability. Welles succeeded in his mediation efforts, partly because the ABC and other groups accepted his presence and partly because the army failed to support Machado at a critical moment. Through Welles's efforts a weak government under Carlos Manuel de Céspedes succeeded Machado, but that regime was quickly overthrown. A five-member executive committee headed by Ramón Grau San Martín, a physician and university professor, took power briefly, but it too gave way to a more revolutionary government, still led by Grau. Jaime Suchlicki maintains that these events constitute a "turning point in Cuba's history," marking the "army's entrance as an organized force into the running of government and Batista's emergence as the self-appointed chief of the armed forces and the arbiter of Cuba's destiny for years to come."[6]

The revolutionary government ruled amid great agitation and was opposed by the U.S. embassy, powerful business interests, conservatives fearful of administrative anarchy, and the ABC. Its support came from the University Students' Directorate, liberal elements in the press, and, for part of its tenure, Batista and the army. Principally because of the efforts of Antonio Guiteras as minister of government (*secretario de gobernación*), the government established an eight-hour day for workers, required that at least 50 percent of all employees in industry and commerce be Cuban, proclaimed university autonomy, and granted peasants rights to the land they occupied. In addition, the government dissolved all political parties that had collaborated with Machado, reduced rates on utilities, and granted women the right to vote. Guiteras believed in the need for a radical revolution that would uproot the framework of "economic imperialism" affecting Cuba's economic and political development, but neither he nor Grau could effectively centralize power to carry basic reforms forward.

From exile after the revolutionary government's demise and its replacement by a pro-U.S. conservative regime, Guiteras recognized that the "work of a revolutionary government cannot be improvised lightly once in power. It presupposes a preparatory work that [the revolutionary government] could not have had," partly "because it lacked an organized political force able to support it."

One cannot overestimate the impact of the truncated revolution of 1933 on the succeeding generation's psychological makeup, its social agenda, or the political determination of its most able leaders. The incomplete business of

1933 left a sense of frustration among the protagonists of reform and revolution, but in time the goals were rechristened. The failure to democratize politics, achieve economic sovereignty, and cohesively assert a national will shaped the ethos of future reformers and revolutionaries, for whom "the lessons of 1933" laid the foundation for new departures.

Social Democracy and Authoritarianism in the 1940s and 1950s

After the brief revolutionary interlude in 1933 national politics in Cuba went through a period of realignment and moderate authoritarianism characterized by the conservative domination of weak and undemocratic regimes supported by Batista and the army. Taking advantage of improved economic conditions and secure from military threats or revolutionary outbursts, the regimes governed by partially satisfying political demands and reintroducing client arrangements. On the other hand, electoral irregularities, corruption, episodic repression, and the subordination of civil authority to military pressures retarded the development of viable governing institutions, so the system remained personalist and moderately authoritarian.

In his excellent study *Revolution and Reaction in Cuba*, Samuel Farber suggests that "the contrast between the civilian-democratic and the militarist-authoritarian traditions" formed the key political cleavage and that neither the democratic left in exile nor the Communist Party effectively challenged this order. Farber points to relative improvements in civil liberties and a new toleration for moderate domestic opposition groups as evidence of an implicit bargain between the conservative sectors and their opponents, characterized by economic populism and the maintenance of dependent capitalism.[7]

Economic dependence on the United States meant that domestic capital played an increasingly important role, and Cuban interests gradually acquired a growing share of ownership in the sugar industry. Measures like the Reciprocity Treaty and the Jones-Costigan Act, in addition to the policies of the Export-Import Bank, stabilized Cuba's economy and gave confidence to domestic producers, who always looked to the U.S. market as the preferred outlet for Cuban products. U.S.-mandated quotas for sugar guaranteed that Cuba's principal export would enter the United States under a preferential tariff and led to the expansion of acreage and production. The United States supplied 54 percent of Cuba's imports in 1933, a figure that increased to nearly 65 percent at the end of the decade and some 81 percent by 1950. What Cuba bought was purchased in the United States, and although having a dynamic market close by proved to be convenient, it also retarded Cuba's industrial development.

A major threshold in the process of political development was reached in 1940 following the enactment of a democratic and progressive constitution, itself the result of political compromises among the democratic left, conservatives, and Communists. This constitution established universal suffrage and freedom of political organization, recognized Western-style civil rights, and abolished the death penalty. Women, children, and workers received social protection, and racial and sexual discrimination was outlawed. Public education was mandated, and the needs of rural children in particular were identified. Private property was legitimated in a broad social context and the state was charged with "orienting the national economy." Industrial development, agrarian reform, and greater rural-urban integration were set as national priorities, and the state was granted greater powers in national development, public administration, and fiscal and monetary policies.

The constitution reflected a complex bargain between the rising middle sectors and traditional interests, and by explicitly framing a tutelary role for the state in economic and social affairs, it incorporated then-current ideas and political philosophies. If properly observed and enforced, the constitution potentially could have served as the legal and ideological foundation of a lasting democratic order, one that rejected radical approaches but permitted vigorous reformism. Consciously or otherwise, its framers believed that the proper balance between order and liberty had been set and that dependent capitalism could be made to serve broad social interests, not just those of influential elites. Unfortunately, the failure of Cuba's democratic regimes in general and educational institutions in particular to instill the values that a fragile democracy requires if it is to survive a legacy of authoritarianism, corruption, and strongman rule undermined constitutional principles, and violence and gangsterism soon reappeared.

The *Auténtico* (Authentic) administrations of Ramón Grau (1944–1948) and his successor Carlos Prío (1948–1952) initiated reforms in agriculture, fiscal management, labor, and education, while they also maintained respect for civil liberties. National elections were competitive and clean, and Conservative, Liberal, Social-Democratic, and Communist parties received electoral support. Public subsidies, bureaucratic employment, and the creation of new state agencies led to gains among middle-class and professional groups, but agricultural development lagged, and the power of foreign interests was not directly confronted. Worst of all, political violence and urban-based gangsterism threatened the integrity of the democratic regimes, and neither Grau nor Prío was able to stem the violence. Corruption was spawned by a vast system of patronage, payoffs, and bribes, and Grau's minister of education turned his office into a powerful political machine and an illegal financial network. Student activists turned the University of Havana into a haven for gun-toting thugs and criminal factions and often paralyzed the institution through intimidation and brutality. According to Suchlicki,

An entire system of nepotism, favoritism and gangsterism predominated. Despite numerous accomplishments, the Auténticos failed to provide the country with honest government or to diversify Cuba's one-crop economy. The reformist zeal evident during Grau's first administration had diminished considerably in the intervening decade, and Grau himself seemed softened after years of exile and frustration. When confronted with the reality of Cuban politics, the early idealism and reformism of [student leaders and others] gave way to materialism and opportunism.[8]

The political aspirations and national expectations that had been generated were only partially fulfilled by the two Social-Democratic administrations: Modernization through reformism did not curb the power of vested interests or foreign capital, and central authority proved weak and incapable of eradicating violence and corruption. To the unfinished agenda of 1933 were added the unrealized promises of the democratic reformers, and scandals and internecine quarrels in Cuba's leadership class eroded public trust in government. The state, supported by neither a dominant class nor a traditional oligarchy, failed to convert diffuse support into legitimately accepted rule, so the nation simply drifted.

Batista's bloodless but effective coup in March 1952 ended the constitutional regime and restored order superficially through political authoritarianism. Cuba's political development was cut short by the coup, and the system proved vulnerable to force. Proclaiming that worry about the lack of guarantees for life and property had led him to accept "the imperious mandate" to usurp power, Batista and his supporters found little resistance to their actions. Prominent national figures, business organizations, labor leaders, a few church officials, and the leadership of the Popular Socialist Party (PSP, the Communist Party) either endorsed the coup or rejoiced at the Auténticos demise. The Veterans' Association and the Bankers' Association gave their approval, and the Cuban Workers' Confederation pledged to cooperate with the new government. Except for scattered protests by students, denunciations by Catholic lay leaders, and isolated instances of civil resistance, the coup provoked neither massive popular repudiation nor legal-institutional opposition.

During his time in office Batista was unable to legitimate his regime either through elections, good relations with the United States, or negotiations with his opponents. Opposition to Batista included moderate, democratic elements sympathetic to the Auténticos but willing to entertain confrontational approaches; traditional politicians (like those in the Society for Friends of the Republic) who believed that Batista would "come around" if a safe way out of the political stalemate was found; and revolutionaries unwilling to accept halfway solutions or electoral shenanigans. Feeling politically secure, Batista refused calls for new elections and thus spurned a reasonable approach that might have prevented the radicalization of many of his opponents. As a result, insurrection and "armed struggle" became attractive and even justifiable, because there was no viable political center on which a national compromise could be achieved.

Several revolutionary groups, including Fidel Castro's Twenty-sixth of July Movement, participated in the struggle against the dictatorship. Among these, the Revolutionary Directorate (DR) stood out because of its uncompromising ferocity and violent strategy aimed at assassinating Batista himself. Led by the charismatic student leader José Antonio Echeverría, the DR was not the vanguard of a social revolution but rather an organization committed to ending the dictatorship. Ramón Bonachea and Marta San Martín contend that the DR's "immediate task was to overthrow the dictator, establish a democratic form of government, and then carry out a revolutionary program to solve the problems of landless peasants, exploited workers and young people condemned to economic oblivion."[9]

As one of the founders of the Twenty-sixth of July Movement and as its undisputed leader, Fidel Castro played a central role in the insurrection against Batista's dictatorship. A group led by Castro attacked a military garrison in the city of Santiago in 1953, but the attack failed and many of Castro's followers were either killed or subsequently arrested and shot. He was captured and tried for subversion, but as a trained lawyer with oratorical skills, Castro used the trial to issue an indictment of the government. Portraying his cause as just and inspired by patriotism and Martí's ideals, Castro called for a return to constitutional government, agrarian reform, profit-sharing arrangements between owners and workers, and social improvements in rural Cuba. He was convicted and sentenced to fifteen years in prison, but he was subsequently released in 1954 under an amnesty program.

Castro's political beliefs and true intentions before he came to power have been the focus of considerable debate. Some people argue that his commitment to armed struggle reflected the compelling facts that no compromise was possible with Batista and that rebellion itself is justified by lofty principles of Western political theory. Others maintain that Castro harbored Marxist beliefs during his days at the university but that he kept the Communists away from his movement so that it could appeal to the Cuban middle class. Some of his former close associates, like Carlos Franqui, say that Castro's caudillo temperament and his egomaniacal pursuit of personal power raised unresolved questions among his followers regarding what path a Castro-led government would take, but that they realized confronting Castro would not be easy. Finally, moderates such as Mario Llerena collaborated with Castro's movement because they sincerely believed in its democratic nature and could not conceive of Castro either as a Communist or as a future dictator.

Fidel Castro himself has given many contradictory accounts of his thinking at the time, describing himself in 1961 as "a Marxist-Leninist until the day that I die," as "a utopian communist captivated by the incontestable truths of Marxist literature," as a "humanist" who believed in "bread and freedom," and as an anti-imperialist revolutionary. Speaking to the Brazilian Frei Betto in 1985, Castro stated that "before I was a utopian communist or a Marxist, I was a follower of Martí [*martiano*] and a profound admirer of our people's heroic struggles." In the same interview Castro stated, "I had conceived of a revolutionary strategy that would lead to a profound social revolution, but through phases . . . the masses needed to be taken to the revolution through phases" because their consciousness could not be developed overnight. Finally, Castro reveals that he saw the Communists as "isolated, but as potential allies," and that he had good relations with Communist leaders during his student days.[10] Furthermore, at other times Castro praised representative democracy, free elections, and political and economic rights. He purposely understated his most radical beliefs to portray himself as a moderate to the Cuban people and to not frighten the United States. Subsequently, it became clear that he saw himself as the undisputed leader of a radical revolution that would emancipate Cuba and also as the champion of a protracted struggle against the United States.

It is thus unequivocally clear that before he came to power Castro was neither a member of the Communist Party nor a doctrinal Marxist. Rather, he was committed to a radical revolution whose final outcome could not have been foreseen but that placed him in the center of power. In addition, one of his top lieutenants, the Argentine revolutionary Ernesto (Ché) Guevara, was a committed Marxist, as was Fidel's younger brother Raúl Castro. Indeed, the Twenty-sixth of July Movement itself was divided between moderates who rejected communism as well as traditional Latin American authoritarianism and radicals like Guevara who believed that the solution to the world's problems lay behind the Iron Curtain. Finally, one of the key documents of the movement, *Nuestra Razón* (*Our Purpose*), defined the revolution's goals as establishing a free and sovereign country, a democratic republic, an independent economy, and a distinct national culture.

A popular view is thus completely discredited, namely, that U.S. policy failures drove Castro and his regime to communism and forced them into the Soviet bloc. For tactical reasons the rebel leadership did not speak candidly with its own people and uttered deceptive and self-serving statements. At a minimum, *Nuestra Razón* committed the revolutionaries to constitutional government, political pluralism, and respect for civil and property rights. A radical minority led by Castro saw themselves as the self-anointed vanguard of an epic political struggle against capitalism, the Cuban middle class, and U.S. influence in Cuba, and this group launched a mass movement that created an unstoppable momentum.

The guerrilla phase of the insurrection ended successfully for the rebels in December 1958. Domestic isolation, rebel victories in eastern Cuba, and loss of support from Washington convinced Batista that his regime could survive only if the guerrillas were defeated. The army, however, was poorly led, partly because some of its top generals were corrupt and frightened; when a forty-thousand-man army disintegrated when it faced several popular uprisings, this demonstrated a profound loss of morale and an alarming unwillingness to fight a few hundred guerrillas. Cornered and without options, Batista and many of his closest allies fled at dawn on January 1, 1959, paving the way for a total victory by the guerrilla forces.

The breakdown of the authoritarian regime stemmed from its inherent illegitimacy, its refusal to accept an authentic electoral solution during a time of crisis, and its unfounded belief in the use of force and repression. The progressive alienation from the regime of the Cuban middle class reduced the probability that it would become a moderating force and lead a democratic restoration. In a situation in which traditional political forces were discredited and no dependable class base existed, popular support moved toward the revolutionaries. Deeply felt commitments to fundamental change emerged in the midst of an unprecedented vacuum, caused by the collapse of institutions and shifts in the locus of authority over brief spans of time. The guerrillas were able to assume power without direct consent but instead with massive social approval, and national euphoria was the order of the day.

The Cuban Revolution

Neither the insurrection against Batista nor the social revolution that the new regime began to carry out stemmed from deep-seated popular dissatisfaction with the development pattern of Cuba's dependent capitalism. The evidence shows that Cuba had reached a moderate degree of modernization by the late 1950s. Indicators such as literacy rate (75 percent), proportion of the population living in urban areas (around 57 percent), life expectancy (approximately sixty years), and the size of the middle class (between 25 and 30 percent of the population) suggest that Cuba's level of development was comparable to that of other, more advanced Latin American nations.

On the other hand, urban-rural contrasts were marked and the quality of life for the average *guajiro* (peasant) family was well below that of the average urbanite. Health services and educational opportunities were much better in Havana and other larger cities than in the small provincial towns or isolated rural communities, and the best jobs and occupations were not available in rural Cuba. Seasonal unemployment also affected the rural areas disproportionately, and a rural proletariat dependent on the mills for employment saw its economic situation deteriorate once the sugar harvest ended.

In effect, neither the model of Cuba as a chronically underdeveloped society, as depicted by the Cuban government, nor that of an idyllic island characterized by social harmony, a sound economy, and a bustling population fits reality. At the time of the revolution the nation was developing slowly as a dependent capitalist country, in which wealth was not evenly distributed but in which middle sectors and a substantial portion of the working class had made social gains. Although Cuba's political autonomy had remained subject to foreign pressures, the imperatives of capitalist modernization had not obliterated Cuba's cultural integrity, social structure, or economic system.

The success of the revolution can be better explained by political factors than by socioeconomic criteria. The failure of prerevolution governments to develop and nourish viable ruling institutions or to sustain a national ethos of civic-mindedness left those regimes vulnerable to force and strongman rule and to subversion from within. Legal and constitutional norms were not fully developed, and too many people viewed politics and public office as ways to obtain private, selfish gains. No idea of the public good had taken root, and the political culture revolved around traditional notions of order, loyalty, patrimony, and authority.

The new regime was originally divided among advocates of liberal democracy and a mixed economy and the more radical sectors around Castro and Guevara who called for a social revolution. The radicals believed that the basic capitalist system needed to be abolished and the social system uprooted so that the power of vested economic interests, some of them foreign based, could be reduced. To eradicate economic evils associated with a dependent capitalist system, statist practices and antimarket doctrines shaped policymaking, and the revolutionary elite was fully aware that to increase state power meant to increase its own. The agrarian reform of 1959 satisfied longstanding claims of peasants and rural workers, and it also made sense politically. The urban reform of 1960, which socialized Cuban-owned businesses and privately owned real estate, adversely affected the private sector's strength. By 1961 banking, wholesale trade, and foreign trade had been fully collectivized, as had 85 percent of industry and 80 percent of the construction business. This collectivization produced a massive transfer of power and resources from the private economy into the public sector, which was precisely the purpose and intended effect.

Structural changes combined with populist, redistributive measures signaled a willingness to incur domestic costs and foreign anger so as to accelerate the process of radicalizing the revolution. The revolutionary elite believed that to slow down was to court disaster, that momentum itself was proof that the masses supported the regime and enthusiastically joined the assault on capitalism and the private sector. Huge rallies commanded the attention of the populace, and during marathon speeches Castro often mesmerized crowds.

The regime realized that social mobilization could serve as a form of explicit consent. For this purpose, it established mass organizations like the Committees for the Defense of the Revolution, the Federation of Cuban Women, and the Union of Communist Youth to reach the grass roots.

Once it became evident that a radical social revolution committed to socialism was in the making—led by individuals seeking total power—an opposition emerged that attempted to restrain or defeat the revolutionary elite. As often happens in revolutionary situations, a decisive struggle between radicals and moderates ensued, between people committed to some form of democracy and those who would settle for radical socialism and nothing else. Both sides knew that only one would prevail, that no compromise was possible, and that personal risks were involved. The opposition included Catholic organizations, disaffected cadres from Castro's own ranks, respected democratic figures, and other anticommunist elements.

The Communist Party neither carried the Castroites to victory nor became the vehicle on which the revolutionary coalition moved against the private sector and the middle class. Leading Communists like Blas Roca and Aníbal Escalante perceived Castro as an ideological neophyte, unschooled in Marxist verities and unwilling to subordinate his own authority or the power of his movement to orthodox frameworks. The party had criticized the Castroites in the 1950s as "bourgeois adventurers," and its opposition to Batista had been measured, not confrontational. Ideologically, the party still believed in the revolutionary potential of the Cuban working class, and its political work had focused on the labor movement. Needless to say, the party was in no position to assume a leadership role, and its belief that when the revolution came they would become its vanguard was quickly shattered.

In essence, Castro's relationship with the Communist Party stemmed from his desire to limit the damage inflicted on his regime by the defection of noncommunist revolutionaries as well as from the need to enlist Soviet support. The party shrewdly provided organization when Castro's own was being shaken up, and it offered a dialectical explanation for the society's troubles. Andrés Suárez believes that "the Communists played no role, neither in the political leadership of the country nor in the leadership of the students or of the trade unions," but that the party's discipline, support of "national unity," and foreign connections facilitated understandings with Castro.[11]

By the mid-1960s revolutionary changes restructuring class, property, political, and foreign policy relationships had eliminated a dependent capitalist order replete with U.S. influence and moved the country toward radical socialism. The state took over the basic means of production as well as domestic and foreign commerce, industry, transportation, and utilities. Agriculture was reorganized into collective and state farms, but peasants could produce some goods on small, privately owned plots. The mass media were under state control, as was the national system of telecommunications. Party cadres supervised the information network, and Marxism-Leninism shaped the content of public discussion. Dissident intellectuals, nonconformists, and political opponents of the regime were arbitrarily imprisoned, scorned, or forced to leave the country. Nearly five hundred thousand Cubans had left by the mid-1960s, and this number had grown to over 1.5 million by the 1990s.

The regime proscribed dissent and political opposition and forced explicit definitions of loyalty to the system. No opposition parties existed, nor could groups or sectors legally defy the revolutionary state. The legal system came under state control. The court system applied "revolutionary justice" to political offenses, and revolutionary tribunals enforced order and discipline with little evidence of due process. Summary trials of alleged counterrevolutionaries took place, long sentences were imposed on the revolution's opponents, and hundreds were executed. This was a time of social confrontation, characterized by a "we-versus-they" mentality that divided families and intimidated individuals and groups. Thousands of political prisoners served time during the following decades, and many suffered brutal treatment at the hands of guards and prison officials.

The educational system was radically reorganized and centralized, and education was treated as a key to the process of political socialization. National literacy campaigns pushed literacy rates to the mid-90th percentile, but the quality of instruction left much to be desired. Much of Cuba's history was revised and rewritten, and patriotism and national virtues were highlighted. U.S. influence over Cuba's destiny was made the root of many ills. The number of primary schools went from 7,567 in 1958 to 14,807 in 1968, and enrollment doubled during the same period. Thousands of new teachers were trained, rural education in particular was emphasized and supported, and women enjoyed new educational opportunities. Nelson Valdés has noted that students were "required to devote school time to three types of work: educational, productive and socially useful,"[12] which means that pupils worked in agriculture and volunteer campaigns while they studied.

Considerable resources were devoted to public health. Most of the basic medical services were provided free under a government-run health system that included preventive care, specialized services, and even advanced treatment for common or rare diseases. Over the years hundreds of clinics, hospitals, and specialized-care facilities were built and staffed by thousands of graduates in medicine, nursing, and health-related fields. As a result, life expectancy in the 1990s was about seventy-six years of age, and Cuba's infant mortality rate of approximately ten in one thousand ranks among the best for developing countries. However, adverse economic conditions did affect the quality of care. Critical shortages of technologies, medicines, and essential supplies delay treatment and affect the service provided. Without many critical medical imports from the former Communist nations, the system is stressed. Unfortunately, this comes precisely when the demand for medical services is increasing because of economic difficulties. In some instances nutritional deficiencies stemming from food shortages have led to the outbreak of optical neuritis and other diseases that result from low caloric intake. Thus, one of the more notable social achievements of the revolution is increasingly compromised.

The revolutionary development strategy of the 1960s was affected by controversy over economic policy. On the one hand, socialist ideologues led by Ché Guevara argued that a strong moral foundation must be prepared if socialism was to succeed and that egalitarianism, altruism, and collectivism must be its core values. A cultural transformation must accompany structural changes and instill new values and attitudes among the masses. Arguing that the development of revolutionary consciousness was as important as satisfying material expectations, Guevara articulated a utopian view of "the new man" that radical socialism would create. In his famous essay "Man and Socialism," Guevara's thinking is apparent:

> In these countries [including Cuba] there is no form of education for worthwhile social labor, and wealth remains distant from the masses. Underdevelopment and the habitual flow of capital toward "civilized" countries make it impossible to change rapidly without sacrifice. There remains a long road to be traversed in order to construct a solid economic base; and the temptation to follow the paths of material interest, used as a stimulus for accelerated development, is very great.[13]

On the opposite side stood the more pragmatic policymakers and people schooled in "scientific socialism" rather than in Guevara's utopianism. They knew that Cuba was a poor agricultural country without a large industrial base and with little technological innovation on which to launch grandiose development schemes. Consequently, they held that encouraging production and discipline through material incentives and tangible rewards was probably more effective than abstract appeals to altruism and selflessness.

In the end the final arbiter of all disputes, Castro himself, settled the issue and approved Guevara's approach, reversing industrialization policies, accepting moral stimuli, and launching the nation on an all-out campaign against underdevelopment that promised to produce ten million tons (nine million metric tons) of sugar. At its conclusion in 1970 the economy was completely unbalanced, growth rates had plummeted, and scarcity and shortfalls were evident in every sector. Only 8.5 million tons (7.7 million metric tons) of sugar had been produced, and according to Castro the results constituted a moral defeat. Economists like Carmelo Mesa-Lago, Sergio Roca, and others have demonstrated that long-lasting damage was done to the infrastructure by such a colossally wrongheaded approach to development. Although chastened by the losses in production and national morale, the regime and its leader—who offered to resign but stayed on because the crowds still hailed him—survived their first systemic crisis.

In conclusion, regime consolidation came about through sustained mobilization, direct exhortation, and a top-to-bottom direction of an ongoing revolutionary agenda rather than through elections. Rewards and sanctions were utilized to elicit compliance with revolutionary policies, but care was exercised not to alienate key sectors of the working class, peasantry, and urban proletariat. These sectors formed the class basis for the new regime once the middle class had been destroyed and the upper strata had either left the country or accepted a dramatic loss in privilege and status. Daily life became intensely political.

Society and Government in the 1980s and 1990s

Needing to regularize the political process and establish national ruling institutions through which stability could be preserved, the revolutionary elite succeeded in reorganizing the state and the Communist Party and created ruling councils at the local level. Fundamental changes in government became evident, especially in the manner in which central authority is exercised, in President Castro's role as chief decision-maker, in the critical role of the Cuban Communist Party (PCC), and in the organization of social forces. A new socialist constitution was enacted in 1976, defining the PCC "as the leading force in the state and in society," but also outlining the powers of national, provincial, and local organs. Party congresses in 1975, 1980, 1986, and 1991 strengthened the party's hegemonic role, provided forums for discussion of national problems, and set broad strategies for future development.

A new economic model, the System of Direction and Economic Planning (SPDE), framed policies in the late 1970s and early 1980s, taking into consideration criteria such as efficiency, rationality, prices, and other "economic mechanisms." This framework accepted the validity of material incentives and market processes. From this, they introduced wage differentials, production norms, monetary controls, and taxes. Carmelo Mesa-Lago writes that "SPDE takes into account the law of supply and demand and the need of monetary and mercantile relations in the transitional state"—presumably prior to reaching socialism—but that it does not abolish central planning.[14]

The adoption of the SPDE reflected a consensus among planners and technocrats regarding the need for limited market reforms to increase economic efficiency and expand output. At the time other Communist countries were experimenting with "market socialism," and some were suggesting that

Cuba enact policies that would bring its system more into line with that of its major trading partners in the (now defunct) Council of Mutual Economic Assistance (CMEA). Under the SPDE the emphasis would shift from building "socialist consciousness" through voluntarism and ideological appeals to the satisfaction of consumer demands through market mechanisms.

A central question faced by the Cuban regime is the degree to which the satisfaction of consumer demands is essential for regime legitimacy and stability. The economic crisis of the 1990s brings this into focus because the lack of resources and the adoption of ill-advised policies deepen austerity. Promises that socialism would produce abundance and prosperity have never been fulfilled. In fact, what the regime calls "a special period in peacetime" is really an admission of economic failure. Much evidence indicates that the standard of living has declined by nearly 50 percent since 1990 and remains unlikely to improve in the next few years. Such a dramatic deterioration in economic conditions inevitably produces resentment and political disaffection. In short, the social contract between the regime and the masses may be irreparably frayed.

The regime believes, however, that limited economic reform may prevent economic collapse. The new development strategy sanctions capitalist principles without renouncing socialism, but ideology matters less than the compelling need for economic recovery. For instance, the rules governing foreign investment have been liberalized and tourist hotels and other facilities have been built with foreign capital. Joint ventures in specific sectors are now legal and it is likely that some industrial, commercial, and agricultural enterprises will be privatized. Holding dollars is no longer illegal, and in fact special stores where only dollar purchases can be made are now in business. Some forms of private employment are once again permitted, and material incentives are recognized as important factors in making workers more productive. Finally, the government is changing its policy regarding the Cuban community in exile, welcoming those who return as tourists and no longer labeling them "traitors" or "worms."

In all probability these reforms will not produce a sustainable economic recovery. In the end the system's ability to satisfy basic needs and maintain a safety net is severely undermined by a lack of resources, which drives down social consumption and thus the standard of living itself. There is little doubt that economic pain is widespread, indices of social poverty are rising, and grim economic conditions will last for several years. What Cuba is confronting is more than passing difficulties brought about by the loss of economic and technical assistance once available from the Communist world. Rather, the systemic crisis could lead to economic collapse.[15]

At the same time the Cuban regime faces neither ethnic unrest nor expressions of regional supremacy, and this is due to the absence of genuinely oppressed ethnic minorities and because regionalism is simply not a potent

political force. In fact, Cuba has achieved a remarkable degree of political stability and continuity, either as a result of genuine national unity or because its
ruling elite and the Communist Party itself are not completely discredited.
Socialism appears to have engendered widespread political passivity—albeit
laced with discouragement and sullenness—in the present generation, and
nationalism is indeed a galvanizing force. Cubans are constantly told by their
government that unity is the supreme value, social divisions weaken the polity
and create opportunities for "the enemy," vigilance on all fronts is essential,
and "imperialism never sleeps." Although many of these claims are patently
fraudulent and little more than shopworn slogans, their impact is considerable. In the absence of contrary information or any real debate on the merits
of continuity or change, the status quo is preferred.

The Governmental Framework

Cuba's highest-ranking executive organ is the Council of Ministers (CM),
composed of the head of state and government, several vice presidents, the
head of the Central Planning Agency, and "others determined by law." Fidel
Castro is its president, and he is also head of state and government, first secretary of the Communist Party, and commander-in-chief. In fact, all lines of
authority converge on President Castro so that, as Jorge Domínguez and others point out, the "maximum leader's" central role has been formalized. His
brother Raúl is the CM's first vice president as well as minister of defense and
second secretary of the Communist Party. The Castro brothers thus maintain
executive control over the central administrative organs. Their personal power
is nearly absolute.

The CM has the power to conduct foreign relations and foreign trade,
maintain internal security, and draft bills for the National Assembly. It has an
executive committee whose members control and coordinate the work of
ministries and other central organizations. All of its members belong to the
Communist Party, and some—like Minister of Culture Armando Hart and
Armed Forces Vice Minister General Abelardo Colomé—also belong to the
party's Political Bureau.

The Council of State (CS) functions as the executive committee of the
National Assembly between legislative sessions, and it is modeled on the Pre-
sidium of the former Soviet Union's Supreme Soviet. The CS issues decrees
and exercises legislative initiative. Additionally, it can order general mobilization and replace ministers. It has some thirty-one members, including several
of the twenty-five members of the Political Bureau elected at the Fourth
Congress of the Cuban Communist Party in 1991. In addition to the Castro
brothers the CS includes influential policymakers such as Carlos Lage, the
"economic czar"; José R. Machado, an orthodox Communist who oversees

the party's organization; Jorge Lezcano, a Communist Party secretary with some administrative experience; and Roberto Robaina, a former leader of the Union of Young Communists and foreign minister.

The National Assembly of People's Power (NA) is the national legislature. Deputies are elected for five-year terms, but the Assembly holds only two brief sessions per year. In the 1991–1996 *quinquenio* (five-year term) each of its 589 deputies stood for roughly twenty thousand inhabitants. Deputies are directly elected by the people. Among the NA's formal powers, it can decide on constitutional reforms, discuss and approve (but not disapprove) the national budget, plan for economic and social development, and elect judges. In practice, legislative initiative is not exercised, the NA cannot challenge the political leadership, and it is, in fact, a rubber-stamp body. In his study on "the nature of Cuban democracy," Archibald Ritter notes that what partly explains the Assembly's impotence is "insufficient time, support staff, and financial resources to permit individual members to scrutinize problem areas, pieces of legislation, and reports independently and carefully."[16] Some of its work takes place in specialized commissions, such as Child Care and Women's Rights, Defense and Internal Order, and Complaints and Suggestions. Seventeen percent of its members are either educators, health workers, or scientists; 15 percent are presidents of People's Councils; 13 percent work in production and services; and 12 percent are officials from local and provincial Organs of People's Power (OPP). Other deputies are trade union leaders; members of the armed forces and the Ministry of the Interior; high officials in government and the Communist Party; and a few students, athletes, journalists, and religious leaders. Of its 589 members, 506 were elected for the first time in 1993; the average age for all deputies is forty-three.

The underrepresentation of workers, peasants, and women suggests that these groups have yet to transform enhanced status into political influence. For now the typical deputy is a fairly well-educated, probably white male who is either a full-time party bureaucrat or a white-collar employee. The real center of legislative power and initiative lies in the Council of State, and Ritter's conclusion is that "at the level of the National Assembly, a large proportion of the process of leadership selection and policy formulation is carried out by the party within the shell or framework of the National Assembly."[17]

The Organs of People's Power

Cuba's 14 provinces are subdivided into 169 municipalities, each governed by an Assembly of Delegates of People's Power. Their members serve terms of two-and-a-half years, and they are directly elected at the grassroots. The nominating process is carefully monitored by the party and by nominating commissions, which means that a candidate's political attitudes must be acceptable. Democratic-style campaigning is not permitted, and candidates cannot reach their supporters via independently controlled media. Claims that these assemblies constitute "socialist democracy in action" stretch one's understanding of what democracy really means and of what constitutes effective political competition in a one-party state in which basic liberties and freedom of speech are severely restricted.

In 1992 13,432 delegates were elected to these assemblies, 13 percent of them women. A substantial number of these delegates are either Communist Party members or leaders in mass organizations like the Federation of Cuban Women or the Committees for Defense of the Revolution. Membership in the party or any of the mass organizations facilitates political mobility and confers higher status. The assemblies provide a local forum for popular grievances and deal with various problems, such as repairing dilapidated housing, monitoring conditions in day-care centers, distributing health information, and cleaning up local sites. The assemblies' work may either overlap that of mass organizations or take advantage of proximity at the grassroots level. The assemblies depend on national organs for resources, thus often curtailing local initiatives.

The Cuban Communist Party

The PCC has undergone significant transformations since the 1960s, when Castroites took effective control of its organization and eliminated political adversaries. The party atrophied in the 1960s, and by 1969 membership was only fifty-five thousand. Lip service was paid to its leading role, but in fact, the rambunctious politics of the period and the ad hoc manner in which policies were framed forced the party to the sidelines. The "microfaction affair" in 1968, in which orthodox, former PSP cadres led by Aníbal Escalante attempted to sow division in the ranks and provoke Castro's downfall, led to a bitter internal struggle and the subsequent arrest of some thirty-five members of the microfaction. Purges followed and the guilty party members were sent to jail. This affair severely undermined the party's credibility, but it demonstrated that challenges to Castro could be politically fatal. Scholars often speculate that there are divisions among members of the party's top organs, such as the Central Committee, but if so, these divisions have not erupted in a serious challenge to President Castro.

Scheduled congresses were canceled, and the First Congress did not take place until 1975. Party membership went from 202,807 members and candidates in 1975 to some 481,000 in 1981 and 600,000 in the 1990s. The proportions of workers (43 percent) and women (22 percent) are higher than in the past, and the party is making efforts to recruit quality candidates. Its presence at all levels of government and society and in the armed forces suggests that its vertical and horizontal integration has been effective, as are its penetrative capabilities.

On the other hand, substantive questions emerged in the 1980s regarding the ideological rigor of the cadres, their discipline, and their willingness to lead through example and sacrifice. The regime is aware that it must reinvigorate the party at the grassroots level and struggle against atrophy and indolence. President Castro frequently reminds party members of their solemn obligations, their historical mission on behalf of socialism and the revolution itself, and the high personal standards expected of both the leaders as well as the rank and file. Instances of corruption in the party were common in the late 1980s. It suffered from scandals, poor leadership, careless management, lack of discipline, and other deficiencies. Many (perhaps thousands) of party leaders, members, and militants were purged in the late 1980s and early 1990s when the quality of their work was found wanting and abuses of authority and cases of personal corruption were discovered. In short, the party was severely shaken up prior to its Fourth Congress, and there is reason to believe that the purges involved cadres that advocated major economic and political reforms.

Some of the "negative tendencies" found in the party's performance stemmed from its failure to monitor the illegal activities of high officials—many of whom were party members—in the Ministry of the Interior, the armed forces, and elsewhere. In addition, party members were embroiled in the arrest, trial, and execution of Division General Arnaldo Ochoa and three other officers in 1989. General Ochoa, a decorated veteran of the Angolan war and a "Hero of the Revolution," was found guilty of corruption and involvement in drug trafficking. Colonel Antonio de la Guardia, a ranking officer in the Ministry of the Interior and one of President Castro's favorite spies, was found guilty of involvement in drug trafficking, money laundering, and other illegalities. Several officers received long sentences, while others, such as the powerful minister of the interior, General José Abrantes, were subsequently removed from their positions.

It is almost certain that the Castro brothers knew about some of the activities of their subordinates, especially those related to the use of Cuban air space and sea lanes by drug traffickers. Given the regime's highly centralized decision-making structure and the sensitive nature of the group's work, it is most unlikely that top political leaders did not know what was happening. Colonel de la Guardia and his twin brother, General Patricio de la Guardia, serving a thirty-year sentence, were loyal Castroites and friends of President Castro and other leaders. The defendants did not have effective legal representation, nor was due process observed during what became a grotesque "show trial." Abject confessions and instances of self-degradation characterized the defendants' demeanor. President Castro himself instigated the prosecution and asked for the death penalty for Ochoa, de la Guardia, and two others. The quick resolution of the crisis indicates that it was viewed by the leadership as a major political threat, making a summary verdict a foregone conclusion. In the end the Castros succeeded in shifting responsibility for the scandal to their subordinates, meanwhile avoiding any culpability for what they themselves had approved.

Changes made at the Fourth Congress indicate that, although continuity at the top is important, promoting new members to the Political Bureau alleviates some generational pressures and makes way for leaders of important functional groups or sectors. For example, fourteen of the twenty-five members are new, and only six members remain of those elected at the First Congress in 1965. Party secretaries Alfredo Hondal and Jorge Lezcano are new members, as are the division generals Leopoldo Cintra and Julio Casas. Three of the twenty-five members are women, but the well-known president of the Federation of Cuban Women, Vilma Espín, is no longer among them. Some promotions are clearly idiosyncratic, while others stem from the fact that President Castro often rewards his favorites with high-level appointments. Major decisions in domestic and foreign policy are made at this level, and members comprise "the elite of the elite." It can be assumed that decisions are reached by consensus after some discussion, but it is extremely unlikely that, individually or as a group, members can effectively oppose President Castro. New members in particular are unlikely to assert themselves in the rarefied atmosphere of the group, so bringing in new blood is not necessarily indicative of new policy directions. Within this elite the lines of accountability run *from* not *toward* President Castro, so personnel changes seldom affect the elite in general and certainly not the president's absolute power in particular. The leadership is aware that institutional elitism breeds privilege and inequality, undermines the egalitarian rhetoric of socialism, and leads to the formation of what many people regard as "a new class," but these contradictions are generic to socialism itself.

The Lost Decades

The collapse of orthodox communism in the former Soviet Union and Eastern Europe prompted the Cuban leadership to declare a Special Period in Peacetime (SP) in the early 1990s. A strategy of economic survival took shape under conditions of severe austerity and hardship, largely because the $5–6 billion subsidy from former communist allies was no longer available. During the SP, consumption dropped dramatically, services and subsidies provided by the state were reduced or altogether eliminated, and the standard of living for the average individual or household fell precipitously.

Economic hardships multiplied under this strategy. Reliable studies show that Cuba's Gross Domestic Product fell between 35 to 50 percent between

1989 and the mid-1990s, plunging the economy into a depression. For the government catastrophic losses meant downsizing the state bureaucracy; shutting down factories and industries; and reducing or eliminating subsidies to the transportation system, agriculture, construction, housing, and other sectors. Building socialism was going to take longer than expected, so the goal of reaching the communist utopia was pushed into the twenty-second century. Regardless, the authorities ruled out any prospect for a return to capitalism.

Unable to secure oil supplies due to lack of hard currency, the government imposed draconian measures throughout the economy, causing total or partial blackouts on a regular basis. Dwindling energy supplies forced households to burn wood or trash for fuel—a common practice in the least-developed countries of the world. Unemployment and partial unemployment rose as workers saw their jobs disappear and their schedules severely disrupted, all of which adversely affected the standard of living for millions of individuals and households. In sum, for the great majority of Cubans conditions under the SP were similar to those in wartime without the violence. It was nothing less than disastrous and an altogether shattering and traumatizing experience harking back to the days of colonial rule.

President Castro summarily declared the Special Period over in 2004, while the economic contraction that led to it had not abated. The government concluded that the worst was behind them and the government's policies succeeded in containing the damage. Triumphalism resurfaced with a vengeance, and the elites gloated that, unlike their erstwhile communist allies, they had not imploded—yet another great battle in an unending war with imperialism was won. Anyone who predicted that Cuba would be vanquished as an isolated, socialist outpost in a globalized, capitalist world economy was proven wrong. Underestimating the resolve of a revolutionary people, so went the surrealist narrative, once again turned up as a losing bet.

On the other hand, adapting to a new correlation of forces means crushing expectations for a sustainable turnaround. A totalitarian dictatorship with dwindling legitimacy cannot escape that fact, particularly after fifty years of broken promises and in the face of rising, political discontent. The narrative that "only socialism can save the Fatherland" falls on deaf ears and does not motivate the younger generations, who are alienated and altogether repulsed at what their elders left them. To speak to them about *los logros de la revolución* provokes a mixture of contempt and utter disgust that raises serious questions about the level of anger that lies beneath the surface. In short, *la generación histórica* asserts itself through a combination of modest reforms and selective repression at home, all the while mobilizing friends and allies abroad as if it were 1968. Nonetheless, it cannot recover its credibility nor paper over its legacy of failure.

Growth rates have been quite erratic in this decade, and Cuba's unproductive and uncompetitive economy is simply unable to generate the material or financial resources needed to sustain its 11.4 million people. In his major study *The Cuban Economy Today: Salvation or Damnation?*, Mesa-Lago shows that the annual growth rate for 1990–2000 was 1.2 percent—the worst in Latin America. A very modest rebound started with 3.0 percent growth in 2001, 1.5 percent in 2002, 2.6 percent in 2003, and roughly 2.0–2.5 percent in 2004.

On the other hand, the rate of economic growth declined by the end of the decade. The economy flattened out in 2008–2009, and it could slide into negative growth. Despite the fact that President Raúl Castro urges workers and peasants to produce more food and recognizes the need to stimulate food production through higher prices, the domestic supply of basic staples is entirely inadequate. The president is obsessed with food shortages, believing that issue to be politically explosive if solutions are not found. When behavior does not change, the president goes after farmers and workers rather than pointing to his own uninspiring appeals or the underlying causes for shortages. For instance, the president lashed out as evidence came in that new measures he approved allowing land to be leased by individuals were not succeeding, exclaiming, "the land is here, and here are the Cubans! Let's see if we can get to work or not, if we produce or not, if we keep our word. It is not a question of yelling 'the blockade hurts us!' The land is there waiting for our sweat."

Cuba imports 60 percent of its food supply, and foreign purchases have cost the nation up to several billion dollars since 2001. It spent US$2.5 billion importing food in 2008, with several hundred million purchased from U.S. exporters. Revisions made in 2002 to the U.S. embargo now allow Cuba to make cash purchases of food and agricultural commodities in the United States. *The Washington Post* reports that "the United States . . . is the island's largest supplier of food and agricultural products, selling it an average of $350 million worth of rice, beans, and frozen chicken" since 2001.

Declines in the price of nickel and the failure to improve agricultural or industrial production lie at the root of the crisis, which has been further exacerbated by damaging hurricanes in 2007 and 2008. In short, serious studies show that the economy has not recovered from the losses of the last twenty years and that the standard of living is significantly worse than it was in the late 1980s. In the words of independent Cuban economist and critic Oscar Espinosa Chepe: "in the present context of crisis one observes the inexorable deterioration of previous gains in education, public health and social security, as well as the rapid decapitalization" of Cuba's "material and human resources."

One explanation for the economy's abysmal performance is the catastrophic collapse of the sugar industry. The crown jewel of Cuba's political economy lies in ruins, no longer the dominant sector of the command economy. Total output in the 1990s stood around 4 million metric tons (MT) per harvest—regularly falling short of planned targets and not generating adequate levels of hard currency. Precipitous declines in output forced the government to import sugar from Colombia and Brazil to meet export commitments and domestic demand. Output fell from 3.5 (MT) in 2001 to 2.2 million in 2003 and 1.1 million in 2006–07, the worst harvest in Cuba's history. Production in 2007–08 and 2008–09 came in at 1.4 million and 1.3 MT respectively, confirming Oscar E. Chepe's view that "the sugar industry marches on a clear path to its disappearance."

In 2002 the government closed down about half of the sugar mills in order to reduce costs and presumably increase the efficiency of the rest, so that only fifty-six of the country's seventy-five mills were active during the 2004–05 harvest. Furthermore, only fifty-one mills worked during the 2006–07 cycle. Frequent breakdowns led to costly delays that drove yields down, slowed production, and brought unexpected costs for repairs. Thousands of technicians, laborers, administrative personnel, and rural workers who lost jobs due to the closing of the mills did receive some compensation and were urged to train for other jobs. However, acquiring new skills takes time, and thousands formerly employed in the sugar industry have yet to find gainful employment. Thus, unemployment rose in communities affected by the shutdown of the mills, driving an already low standard of living into further decline. The ruins of abandoned sugar mills close to small towns and middle-sized communities throughout rural Cuba vividly stand as social metaphors for what once stood as a world-class industry.

Explanations for the collapse of the Cuban sugar industry include obsolete technology that became too costly to repair, failure to modernize or maintain plants and equipment, recurring problems with inputs that delayed the planting and harvesting cycle, managerial and administrative incompetence at different levels of production, and sporadic labor-related difficulties. Additionally, powerful hurricanes in 2007 and 2008 damaged the crop as well as the economy's physical infrastructure.

President Fidel Castro appointed General Ulises Rosales as Minister of Sugar in 1997 in order to restore morale and impose discipline on an inefficient industry. Gen. Rosales, however, was a career military officer completely untrained for the job, so it is not surprising that his own and the industry's performance were stunning failures. Then, as reward for his incompetence, General Rosales was subsequently promoted to Minister of Agriculture and presumably charged with improving that sector's performance.

As if the government's mismanagement of the industry were not enough, international competition from Australia, Brazil, the Dominican Republic, and other strong exporters keeps worldwide sugar prices volatile. Low prices significantly reduce total earnings from sugar exports for Cuba to a few hundred million dollars, compared to more than US$1 billion in the late 1980s. Nickel exports, revenue from services provided by Cuban professionals abroad, and tourist dollars have since replaced sugar exports as Cuba's main sources of hard currency during this decade.

Cuba's failure to reinsert itself into the evolving global economic system is reflected in its foreign debt, which has escalated dramatically despite the moratorium on part of that debt declared in 1986. As of 2008 Cuba's total hard currency debt stood at US$31.7 billion, a staggering increase relative to its estimated US$20 billion in 2006. Its debt in transferable rubles with several of its former communist allies stood at an estimated US$22 billion in 2006 and at US$21.1 billion in 2008—only a slight reduction. On a comparative basis, for a country of 11.4 million people, its per capita debt is among the highest in Latin America.

The willingness of Venezuelan President Hugo Chávez to provide massive assistance to Cuba has filled some of the gap created when the Soviet Union collapsed. As of 2008 Cuba owed Venezuela US$11.4 billion, a rise of nearly 70 percent since 2006. Debt to Japan rose from US$2.2 to US$2.8 billion in the same period, and debt to Spain rose from US$1.9 to US$3.2 billion. The People's Republic of China is Cuba's third largest creditor, and its debt from Cuba rose from US$1.8 billion in 2006 to US$3.1 billion in 2008. Debt in hard currency with Argentina remained unchanged at about US$2.0 billion. For ideological reasons Cuba does not—and could not—borrow from the International Monetary Fund or the World Bank, and its international credit worthiness ranks among the lowest in the world.

In sum, due to its punishing hard currency debt, the moratorium in effect since the 1980s, and its unreformed and uncompetitive command economy, Cuba finds it extremely difficult to raise fresh loans and credits from sources other than Venezuela, the People's Republic of China, and, to a lesser extent, Russia. For understandable political and geopolitical reasons, those three willingly assume the extremely high risks associated with extending credits to their insolvent Cuban partner.

The Venezuelan Connection

To be sure, a deepening strategic relationship between Cuba and the government of Hugo Chávez in Venezuela pays off handsomely for Cuba. As allies Cuba and Venezuela are bound together politically and ideologically, with former President Fidel Castro and Hugo Chávez becoming strong personal friends and political allies. Despite the occasional press report alluding to tensions in the Cuban-Venezuelan relationship since President Fidel Castro was succeeded by President Raúl Castro (2006–present), there is little evidence that the alliance is weaker today than it was in 2006. In fact, the opposite seems to be more accurate.

During a visit to Havana in 2008 President Chávez publicly declared that he and the Castro brothers "make up one team," adding that "this revolution is more alive than ever and marches forward pounding the drums [because] in the end we are the same revolution." Several bilateral agreements signed on very favorable terms for Cuba since 2001 are in effect in health, education, transportation, energy, science, and technology sectors. Through 2008 the value of Venezuela's investments in Cuba were roughly US$2.5 billion, including US$500 million for completion of an oil refinery in Cienfuegos and US$47 million for a facility to process lubricants and oil derivatives.

In order to protect a friend and ally as well as be in a position to monitor its behavior, the Cuban government has placed hundreds of intelligence and security agents in Venezuela as well. Training for Chávez's personal guard is part of the mission. Cuban operatives work in Miraflores, in key ministries, and in clinics and hospitals throughout the public health system. Top spies and intelligence agents in all likelihood report directly to Fidel Castro. Reports from the U.S. Government and other credible sources show Cuban agents working at the Central Bank, at Venezuela's principal intelligence agency (DISIP), at the Department of Military Intelligence, and in the Ministry of Interior, a key agency involved in domestic security and espionage. One State Department official monitoring an expanding Cuban presence in key administrative and bureaucratic levels declared that "we view an expanding castroite infiltration in Venezuela, Cuban advisors are always a lot more sinister than simple technicians."

With a clear strategic purpose, a Cuban-Venezuelan alliance aims to expand its influence in Latin America and organize opposition to the United States. It is the core axis driving the Bolivarian Alternative (ALBA) to the Free Trade Area of the Americas, which now includes Ecuador, Nicaragu, and Bolivia. One cannot conclude that either the Cuban-Venezuelan alliance or ALBA itself will permanently affect the balance of power in the region or pose serious threats to American interests, but it would be foolish to dismiss what Havana and Caracas are up to. ALBA has already divided the region ideologically, and Chávez in particular is unlikely to lower his profile or give up on his dream of uniting the region under his leadership. In short, flush with petrodollars, energized by delusions of revolutionary greatness and his own toxic rhetoric, and counseled by his idol and mentor Fidel Castro, President Chávez has the will and capacity to spread mischief and potentially destabilize the entire region.

Some ninety-eight thousand barrels are provided per day to Cuba on very generous terms. A few years ago the *New York Times* reported that "Venezuela has been supplying cut-price oil to Mr. Castro in a deal that helps ease Cuba's energy and transport problems." But purchases from Venezuela do not satisfy domestic demand. As a result, lengthy blackouts and interruptions in electrical service ordered by the state repeatedly throughout this decade indicate that imports of oil from Venezuela have not resolved Cuba's energy crisis. Cutting energy consumption is thus a matter of national security.

Imports from Venezuela run well below Cuba's needs and are a fraction of the thirteen million tons the former Soviet Union supplied through the early 1990s. At best, low imports cushion chronic shortages in supply. Furthermore, there is evidence that Cuba resells some of the oil in order to take advantage of high prices, doing so at the expense of domestic consumption and with the approval of the Chávez government. The market value of subsidized Venezuelan oil imported by Cuba in 2008 was US$1.74 billion, up from US$1.1 billion in 2005.

Under the agreements (see above) an estimated twenty-two to thirty thousand Cuban doctors, medical specialists, and health care personnel work in Venezuela, earning Cuba a few hundred million dollars annually. Supplying human capital for an important ally in Latin America replicates the policy of "internationalism" carried out by Cuba in the 1970s and 1980s, which was then and still is focused on the developing world. One report states that more than thirty-one thousand Cuban professionals work abroad in the health services sector of seventy-one countries, generating US$2.3 billion for the Cuban government. Thus, extending medical and health services brings money as well as symbolic and emotional capital for Chávez and Castro in the region as well as from many developing countries.

Though the policies are sold by each leader as "providing services to the poor and oppressed," an unintended consequence is that growing needs in areas of the Cuban health care system go unmet because thousands of providers work elsewhere. Numerous press reports indicate that prestigious Venezuelan professional medical associations energetically protest the presence of Cuban personnel in their country, questioning their ideology, training, and professionalism. The behavior of Cuban professionals working in Venezuela and elsewhere is strictly monitored by officials and agents of state security who work abroad under diplomatic cover. For instance, one Cuban doctor quoted in the cited report deserted while working in Venezuela, saying that "anyone who tells you they came here for ideology is lying. Everyone is here either to earn money to send back to Cuba, to earn dollars, or to escape" (*buscar la manera de irse*).

In the late 1990s Fidel Castro anointed Chávez as his "revolutionary heir"—that is, as the leader willing and able to promote a Bolivarian revolution in Latin America. Presumably, the former *golpista* colonel showed the right stuff and gained Fidel's confidence and affection. The two carry on as if the future is theirs. Castro and Chávez recognize that armed struggle is not the strategy that revolutionaries follow in the twenty-first century. Rather, bankrolling demagogues in Nicaragua, Bolivia, Ecuador, and Nicaragua or subverting democratic countries from within are strategies that look quite promising. El Comandante and El Coronel are fine with that—what matters is that the game of revolution continues in full swing.

Without a doubt the Cuban-Venezuelan alliance was behind rising tensions in Honduras in 2009. Castro and Chávez advised the deposed Honduran President Zelaya to hold a referendum that would pave the way for a constitutional convention that was called for the expressed purpose of lifting the prohibition against the reelection of presidents. The Honduran Supreme Court declared that Zelaya's actions were unconstitutional and issued an arrest order. The Honduran military failed to turn Zelaya in to the proper authorities and, instead, threw him out of the country in a most undignified manner. Subsequently and with the material support of the Venezuelan and Brazilian governments, Zelaya returned surreptitiously to Honduras and found refuge in the Brazilian Embassy in Tegucigalpa.

One cannot be clear about the final outcome of the crisis in Honduras, but Fidel Castro and Hugo Chávez instigated it and played major roles in bringing it about. A negotiated and democratic outcome in Honduras would be a defeat for the Havana-Caracas axis. It would suggest that the region's democratic governments reject "the Bolivarian vision" and—correctly—perceive the axis to be a threat to them and all democratically elected governments that defend individual rights and liberties and eschew populism.

El Chavismo repackages nationalism, anti-imperialism and revolution for conditions in the postcommunist world. In fact, however, it is an old-fashioned doctrine with a heavy dose of reckless populism at its core. Speaking at the World Social Forum in 2005, Chávez referred to himself as "a peasant, a soldier, I'm a man committed to this project of an alternative world which is better and possible, necessary to save the Earth. I am one more militant of the revolutionary cause." Lest his audience did not understand a self-referential delusion, Chávez added: "I have been a Maoist since I entered military school, I read Ché Guevara, I read Bolívar and his speeches and letters, becoming a Bolivarian Maoist, a mixture of all that."

One can dismiss as outdated Chávez's advocacy of "socialism for the twenty-first century," but the view here is that dialectical rhetoric should not obscure what is a serious political threat aimed at destroying Venezuela's middle and upper sectors and what is left of its democratic institutions, private economy, and independent media. Promoting class warfare at home and destabilization in his neighborhood leave no doubt that Chávez aims for *Venezuela hoy y Latino América mañana.*

To sum up, Venezuela's—and the region's—unresolved grievances fuel a visceral anti-American, anticapitalist, antiglobalization, illiberal mentality that generates political capital for protomessianic or populist leaders promising to vanquish hunger, disease, illiteracy, and chronic poverty. Venezuela's neighbors would be well advised to muster the political will to resist anachronistic messianic messages or cynical offers of economic and social assistance. Fidel Castro's illness and retreat from public life have not materially affected his relations with Chávez, the ever-adoring disciple. Whether Castro is convalescing or has regained some of the energy lost to age (eighty-three) or radical surgeries is not as important as the fact that he and Chávez consult regularly on critical domestic and foreign-policy issues. Flattering press releases about Castro's condition issued every time they meet can be deceptive, but what is irrefutable is that their decisions drive a consolidated, strategic alliance in the region.

Tourism, Dollarization, and De-dollarization

A second source of revenue for Cuba is tourism. The industry is moderately rebounding and generating badly needed hard currency. Some two million tourists reportedly visited Cuba in 2008–2009, with net earnings estimated to be in the US$400–600 million range. Expanding tourist facilities is a top economic priority, requiring that long-held ideological prejudices against "contamination from capitalism" be overlooked. The government aggressively looks for ways to bring more tourists to the island, purchasing flashy advertising in Europe and Latin America that portrays sun-drenched beaches, the natural wonders of the countryside, and Cuba's legendary cultural sensuality. *Por favor*, pour me a *Cuba Libre.*

The same factors that lure tourists to other islands in the region bring them to Cuba: lots of sun, white-sand beaches stretching for miles, the prospect of "a romantic getaway," cheap sex, and the certainty that a great time will be had at a nominal cost. Numerous reports in the international media link the rise of prostitution in Cuba to the tourist trade, and it is quite evident that young, single males from Europe and Latin America arrive in droves expecting a fabulous time. Most tourists arrive from Canada, Spain, Germany, Italy, and several Latin American countries via international airlines that provide regular service to Havana. Charters fly directly to Varadero beach and other destinations.

Spanish firms involved in tourism own or lease property along the northern coastline, dotted by world-class beaches and new facilities designed to please visitors. Economist Mesa-Lago reports that gross revenue from tourism went from US$1.9 billion in 1999 to US$2.2 billion in 2004, a modest increase at a time when terrorism had affected international travel substantially. Earnings from tourism have not risen by much this decade, averaging under US$3 billion the last few years.

Tourism is a volatile political issue for a government that failed to take advantage of it as part of its development strategy for thirty years. The first reason for this is, of course, ideological. Second, competition from the tourist industry in the Caribbean, Mexico, and the Dominican Republic cuts into Cuba's earnings once the novelty of "going to the last socialist outpost" wears off. Expansion, in short, is a must. Third, Mesa-Lago points out that "until Cuba is capable of providing its needed inputs domestically the multiplying effect of the tourist industry will not take place." Finally, capitalist enclaves surrounded by a command economy subject to the vagaries of economic conditions in source countries do not constitute the foundation upon which a tourist-based development strategy can be sustained.

Of particular significance is the fact that the government selects those employees that work in the industry and pays their salaries in pesos while it receives dollars from their employers. Placing loyalists, supporters, and even members of the Communist party with foreign firms rewards these persons with a measure of job security and access to goods and services unavailable in the regular domestic economy. A new type of socialist clientelism developing under the auspices of foreign capital serves state interests as well as those of individuals who are "politically safe" and thus see their militancy rewarded. Workers in the tourist industry form part of a privileged sector in the labor force—that is, of workers who see their standard of living improve because they work in the most dynamic sector of the economy from which they draw creature comforts that are unavailable elsewhere.

Because there is no free labor contract in Cuba that defines the relations between a worker and a foreign employer, the state in fact exacts "surplus labor" from workers who automatically see their salaries reduced when they receive pesos that are worth around 25 to $1. Access to tourist venues was highly restricted to outsiders for political reasons until President Raúl Castro ended that prohibition, as it was widely perceived as a blatant form of discrimination against citizens in their own country. The marked contrast between the hardship and sacrifice of daily life for ordinary citizens and the luxury, comfort, and pleasure found in tourist venues illustrates why promoting tourism exacerbates tensions between tourists who enjoy privileges and ordinary citizens who can only dream of "the good capitalist life."

Spanish, Canadian, and other foreign firms operating in Cuba's tourist industry in joint ventures with the state remain silent about what is an extraordinarily exploitative practice, preferring to stay in the government's good graces rather than raise issues that would upset the authorities. However, Cuba has not become the pot of gold that foreign investors expected ten years ago. In fact, as the process of adaptation to external market forces pushes the government into partnerships with foreign firms, attracting foreign capital to the tourist as well as other industries runs into major problems. During this decade the number of joint ventures declined from 392 in 2000 to 236 through 2008. This is presumably because the state is more selective in signing agreements with foreign capital. The state monopolizes foreign commerce and holds small foreign enterprises that meet their goals until Cuba no longer needs them. Cuba's Minister for Foreign Investment says that "we are being more selective" in identifying foreign partners for joint ventures and thus prefer doing business with larger concerns.

Before he transferred the Presidency to Raúl Castro (2006–2008), Fidel Castro's perennial anticapitalist rantings, his decision to freeze the reform process, and poor earnings by foreign firms increased the risks for foreign investors. The main sources of foreign investment are found in the nickel plants operated by Sherritt International, a Canadian firm; Nestle produces soft drinks and ice cream; the Brazilian firm Souza Cruz produces cigarettes, and the French firm Pernod Ricard produces and exports Havana Club rum.

Another source of hard currency are Cuban exiles, who send anywhere from US$300 million to US$600 million annually in remittances to their relatives—although estimates vary greatly and some analysts put the total figure at around US$1 billion. A significant tightening of U.S. policy toward Cuba under the Bush administration made this more difficult, as the new restrictions limited visits to Cuba from Cuban-Americans to one every three years. Furthermore, Bush's policy allowed remittances only to immediate family. With a few exceptions, restrictions were tightened over conventional travel by U.S. citizens as well. The Cuban government denounced what it correctly perceived as an effort to cut into the dollars flowing into the economy, and it shamelessly lamented the fact that Cuban families would suffer as consequence. In fact, the Cuban government's response aimed to divide the Cuban-American community on a very emotional and controversial issue and thus create problems for the Bush administrations from some of its strongest political supporters.

The Obama administration, on the other hand, changed some of the policies enacted by its predecessor with regard to Cuba, which was consistent with the criticisms that candidate Obama had made during his campaign of President Bush's policy toward Cuba. Keeping one of its pledges, the administration eased restrictions on travel, so Cuban-Americans can now visit Cuba several times a year rather than the one visit every three years permitted under the Bush policy. Remittances can be sent to extended members of a family—not just to immediate relatives. Furthermore, the value of those remittances is higher than in the past. Millions of Cuban families depend on those remittances in a country where the average salary is around US$20 a month. Dollars allow Cubans to purchase goods and services that are beyond the reach of households that do not receive assistance from abroad.

On the other hand, rising expectations regarding a fundamental change in U.S. policy toward Cuba have not been fulfilled, and the Obama administration is unwilling to move beyond what it has already done. Policy is rooted in domestic politics, and Cuban-Americans constitute an influential constituency courted by Republicans and Democrats alike. Linking improvements in human rights in Cuba to the possible lifting of the American embargo remains the core U.S. position, and this is rejected by Havana. Havana refuses to entertain any proposal for internal political reform along democratic lines, reiterating long-held positions that its political system is not negotiable, that the Revolution will not sell out to capitalism, and that human rights are not violated in Cuba.

Changing U.S. policy toward Cuba is not a priority for the Obama administration. It would just as soon avoid the bitter polemics and divisive consequences that would surface in Congress and among Cuban-Americans if the administration made unilateral concessions. The new president expects reciprocity from Cuba and has in fact let it be known to Havana that "we are taking steps, but if they do not take steps also, it would be difficult to continue." Consequently, one does not expect either the unilateral lifting of the U.S. embargo nor serious attempts at normalizing relations across the board.

On Cuba's side, it will take the passage of the Castro brothers and their allies before serious bilateral negotiations with the United States begin. The Castro brothers and influential figures from the "historic generation" have amassed fortunes and acquired assets abroad, all in the name of anti-imperialism, revolutionary socialism, equality, and a defense of Cuba's sovereignty. It is foolish to argue that Cuba's "super elite" will surrender its privileges and peacefully exit out of power. Thus, neither the Castro brothers nor their cronies and allies are going to negotiate their way out of power just to please the enemy, nor are these cynical septuagenarians going to dismantle the structures of totalitarianism just to read the glowing press reports that would follow. For them, the collapse of orthodox communism is an object lesson in what happens to ruling elites when they negotiate away their power.

Under President Raúl Castro, the strategic elites that compose the revolutionary coalition include the armed forces, influential members of the Political Bureau and Central Committee of the Communist party, and high-ranking civilians (Ministers, Vice Ministers) with financial, commercial, and managerial responsibilities in the central administration. The armed forces are the dominant elite. From an institutional standpoint, maintaining the loyalty of the armed forces through promotions of officers to top governmental and

Party positions, financial payoffs, and other means are the key to the preservation of the system.

There is no evidence to support the notion that the *nomenklatura* is divided against itself or that it fears the status quo more than it would recoil at the system's collapse. The nomenklatura's vested interest lie with system maintenance, not with facilitating its demise. One's judgment is that the elites are committed to preserving power at almost any cost, regardless of the damage caused from their misguided loyalty or reactionary obstinacy.

The harsh climate surrounding visits by émigrés pits the enduring strength of familial bonds against communist ideology. Thousands of anti-Castro, anticommunist Cuban-Americans return to visit their homeland, spending dollars as well as distributing consumer goods unavailable in the domestic market. A growing minority of Cuban-Americans living in the United States were dissatisfied with the Bush administration's restrictions, particularly many of those coming to the United States since the Mariel boatlift in 1980. Democratic candidate Barack Obama won 35 percent of the Cuban-American vote in 2008, doing better among those voters than John Kerry had in 2004. The desire among a growing minority of Cuban-Americans for lifting the travel restrictions and following through with more serious policy changes was a factor in the 2008 election.

At a time in 1993 when the economy teetered on the brink of collapse, President Castro overcame his rage and legalized the practice of holding dollars, making the U.S. currency the most coveted means of exchange. With greenbacks in circulation, professionals moonlighting as taxi drivers, young women selling themselves as prostitutes (*jineteras*), mediocre academics "invited" by American universities to enjoy the blessings of liberty, and ordinary Cubans hustling tourists all lust after dollars in order to dramatically increase their purchasing power in a country where average salaries run to US$20 per month. Dollarization was seen as a desperate effort at economic survival, and in fact the policy alleviated some damaging macroeconomic tendencies.

Dollarization was abruptly ended in 2004 when the Central Bank declared that purchases in dollars as well as the holding of dollars by ordinary citizens would be illegal. A new currency, the convertible peso (CUC) appeared with a fixed exchange rate, and those holding dollars were urged to change them into convertible pesos. A 10 percent tax was imposed on exchanges from dollars to convertible pesos, thereby affecting Cubans, tourists, banks, hotels, and dollar-only shops. Additional restrictions imposed on state enterprises engaged in trading in dollars as well as on other economic actors in turn forces enterprises to obtain approval for any dollar-based transaction.

Mesa-Lago maintains that such a dramatic reversal of policy stems from "the severe and growing scarcity of hard currency, due to the failure of Cuba's economic policies" and its burdensome external debt. A second explanation is that radical egalitarianism could not be sustained in a dollarized economy driven by forces antithetical to the official ideology. Where "the good life" is reserved for the privileged military, political, and administrative elites with access to dollars, the government's call for "revolutionary sacrifice" is farcical. State priorities trump social or individual consumption because the state needs to increase revenues in hard currency from households as well as all financial and commercial sources. Through dedollarization, the state willfully imposed severe costs on individuals and families holding dollars, therefore sacrificing the general welfare in the hope of ameliorating its own short- and medium-term financial stresses.

With cradle-to-grave protections from the state a thing of the past, a kind of savage, unregulated, and primitive capitalism is making inroads into an unreformed, unproductive, and stifling command economy that is unable to lift households out of permanent austerity. Chasing dollars subverts the social order, undermines the official discourse on the revolution's social achievements (*logros de la revolución*), and definitively eviscerates the memory of Cuban socialism. The transformation of the state into the largest cashier in an economy where the "currency of the empire holds sway," even after dedollarization, indicates as no other fact would that fifty years of radical socialism have ruined the economy, caused widespread impoverishment, and subjected the population to frustration and hopelessness.

To reiterate, regular pesos are worthless and CUC's can only be bought with dollars, so finding dollars (*fulas* in popular argot) is *the* national obsession. A popular refrain once held that *sin azúcar no hay país* (there is no country without sugar), but one's epitaph would be that *los dólares acabaron con la revolución* (the dollars ended the revolution), thus exposing a decayed society and an economic wasteland.

Succession: From Fidel to Raúl, or From an Ailing Messiah to an Uninspiring Administrator

Although the need for major structural and macroeconomic reforms is evident, President Raúl Castro and the gerontocrats in charge of the Communist Party and government (see Table 17.1) refuse to approve the necessary changes for purely political and quite cynical reasons. Formally in charge following a successful transition with an undeniable dynastic character to it, President Raúl Castro remains Second Secretary of the Communist Party. He himself is seventy-seven years old, and the average age of the members of the Council of State (CS) is seventy. An orthodox communist and lifelong crony of the Castro brothers, José Ramón Machado is seventy-eight. He is second (or third, if Fidel Castro is to be considered as first) in line as the first Vice President of the Council. Named Minister of Information and Communications and having been recently promoted once again to the Party's Political Bureau is Ramiro Valdés. A lifelong thug, at seventy-six years of age, *Ramirito* (as his close buddies call him) is feared as a sinister and despised man, responsible for countless acts of repression and brutality against those he branded as "counterrevolutionaries" while he was Minister of the Interior. Among his priorities as Minister is policing the Internet to make sure "contaminated information" is kept out of the hands of those few Cubans with access to new information technology. General Abelardo Colomé, sixty-eight, runs the Ministry of Interior and is a member of the CS. General Julio Casas Regueiro, seventy-two, another hated autocrat, replaced Raúl Castro as Minister of Defense and joins the CS as well. General Casas, a member of the Castro clan, reportedly oversees GAESA, a network of domestic businesses and enterprises run for profit by the Cuban armed forces.

In the words of Cuban historian Rafael Rojas, the Cuban government presided over by Raúl Castro resembles "an olive green oligarchy." The President is surrounded by loyal generals in control of key Ministries and enterprises in strategic sectors of the economy administered by the armed forces. Several of these generals started out as *guerrilleros* (guerrilla fighters) under Raúl's command in the Second Front during the struggle against Batista. Several were promoted to high rank while Raúl served as Minister of Defense. The loyalty of these officers has been proven repeatedly, so there is no reason to expect them or the armed forces to turn on the Castro brothers, demand a transition away from communist rule, or transfer power to democratic reformers.

President Raúl Castro's promise in 2006 that "structural reforms were needed" never materialized. The government fears the emergence of independent, private economic activity and remains committed to a pervasive system of social controls. The President's view is that "it will be our duty in the following years to rise to the maximum the efficiency in the use of our human and economic resources . . . and have the courage to rectify the mistakes made on the side of idealism in the management of our economy." Regurgitating clichés that have lost any motivational impetus, the President's message is aimed at discouraging individual initiative, limiting self-employment, and prohibiting the market-driven distribution of resources in order to perpetuate a dependent relationship between households and the state.

"Raulnomics" does not lead to either the dismantling of the command economy or the systemic introduction of market forces. Measures approved in 2008–2009, such as granting private licenses to taxi drivers, urging farmers to lease land, modestly increasing salaries for some government jobs, and closing cafeterias at government ministries, do not add up to a capitalist counterrevolution. Privatization is not in the cards and neither is the development of domestic sources of private capital. Competition does not drive economic activity, and hiring workers on a private basis is prohibited. Finally, in *Cuba's*

Table 17.1 Members of the Political Bureau of the Cuban Communist Party (PCC) (2008–2009)

Member	Office(s) Held
Fidel Castro (a)	First Secretary, PCC
Raúl Castro (b)	President, Council of State
	President, Council of Ministers
	Commander in Chief
	Second Secretary, PCC
Juan Almeida (died 2009)	Vice President, Council of State
José R. Balaguer	Minister of Public Health
Concepción Campa	Director, Finlay General Institute
Julio Casas	Division General
	Minister of Defense
	Vice President, Council of State
José R. Machado	First Vice President, Council of State
Abelardo Colomé	Corps General
	Minister of Interior
	Vice President, Council of State
Ricardo Alarcón	President, National Assembly
	Member, Council of State
Carlos Lage (c)	Vice President, Council of State
	Executive Secretary, Council of Ministers
Felipe Pérez (d)	Member, Council of State
	Minister of Foreign Relations
Esteban Lazo	Vice President, Council of State
	PCC Secretariat
Ulises Rosales	Division General
	First Vice Minister, Armed Forces
	Minister of Agriculture
	Member, Council of State
Pedro Ross (e)	Member, Council of State
Abel Prieto	Minister of Culture
Leopoldo Cintra	Division General
	Chief, Western Army
Ramón Espinosa	Division General
	Chief, Eastern Army
Yadira García	Minister of Basic Industry
Pedro Sáez	PCC First Secretary, City of Havana
Jorge L. Sierra	Minister of Transportation
Misael Enamorado	PCC Secretariat
Miguel Díaz Canel	Minister of Higher Education
Ramiro Valdés (f)	Commander of the Revolution
	Vice President, Council of State
	Minister of Information Technology and Communication
Alvaro López (f)	Corps General
	Vice Minister of Armed Forces
Salvador Mesa (f)	General Secretary of Cuban Workers Confederation

* The Fifth Congress of the PCC was held in 1997. The Sixth Congress has been postponed indefinitely.
(a) Stepped down from presidency in 2006 due to serious illnesses.
(b) Formally invested as President of Cuba in February 2008. Acted as Interim President from July 2006 until February 2008.
(c) Dismissed from all his positions in government and PCC, March 2009.
(d) Dismissed from all his positions in government and PCC, March 2009.
(e) Ross was appointed Ambassador to Angola in 2007.
(f) Joined Political Bureau in 2008. It is the second time around for Ramiro Valdés.

Aborted Reform, Mesa-Lago and Pérez-López point to the need for "developing a legal framework to establish private property rights and nurture establishment of a private sector, support market behavior, and pursue policies that promote competition."

Rather, it is clear that for the Successor/Administrator and his team of technocrats, stagnation through central control is preferable to sustained growth generated by private initiative or market forces. Totalitarianism vitiated the concept of economic freedom and replaced it with collectivism on the grounds that enforcing equality through central command would promote sustained development. That colossal miscalculation that has been exposed as another fraud cannot be acknowledged by the Successor/Administrator, who in a moment of candor admitted that he was not "elected President to bury socialism, but to improve it."

Thus, the uneven performance of the Cuban economy in the last decades, characterized by low growth rates, unending energy shortages, declines in consumption, and continued state control over broad sectors of the economy is attributable in part to the collapse of preferential relationships with former communist countries. A second explanation stems from the failed doctrines and wrong-headed policies rooted in the command system. A willful commitment on the part of the leadership to continuity rather than systemic change reflects a lack of imagination and, without a doubt, its fears as well. Failure to introduce systemic reforms that would move the economy away from state control and erode the power of bureaucrats and administrators means more of the same. It is unequivocally clear that the Successor/Administrator is neither the aggressive reformer nor visionary who many expected. Instead, he's very much an uninspiring stand-in for a leading role in a third-rate production.

When a final account is rendered, what really trumps all empirical or even ideological explanations are the leadership's stunning subordination of the national interest to its undiminished personalistic and totalitarian vocation and the loyal elites' pathological obsession with the maintenance of personal privileges and political control at the expense of the general welfare. In a new millennium and after half a century of communism, the leader's own demons and his brother's unremarkable initiatives once more frustrate those expecting renewal, thereby leaving broad sectors of the population impoverished, disengaged, and with a grim future.

The International Arena

The key factors framing Cuba's role in the world are revolutionary messianism, an anti-American and anti-imperialistic stance, a legacy of defiance, and Marxist-Leninist ideology. President Castro's revolutionary convictions as well as his shrewdness and episodic demagogic outbursts—often in the midst of crisis and bipolar confrontations—make Cuba an influential actor in regional politics and in parts of the Third World. Still, the country's foreign relations, intended to maximize its international standing and degree of influence abroad, are subject to domestic pressures and external constraints.

In the 1960s Cuba's revolutionary messianism led it to support guerrilla movements in Venezuela, Bolivia, Guatemala, and Nicaragua. Subsequently, Cuba assisted groups like the M–19 in Colombia, the MIR in Chile, the Tupamaros in Uruguay, the Montoneros in Argentina, and the Farabundo Martí National Liberation Front in El Salvador. Cuban support has varied according to political circumstances and the country's own capabilities, but in practically all cases it has involved either training guerrillas in Cuba and sending them out or supplying weapons and logistical assistance to such groups. At times Cuba has provided sanctuary for revolutionaries from various countries, and Sandinista leaders like Tomás Borge and others have spent some time in Cuba. President Castro has repeatedly stated that as a revolutionary country Cuba is obliged to offer moral as well as material support to revolutionaries fighting their own wars of liberation, and the constitution of 1976 includes this principle.

Through a vigorous assertion of proletarian internationalism Cuba once maintained thousands of cadres abroad on various missions. The regime's view has been that through proletarian internationalism Cubans fulfilled their self-imposed revolutionary duties and advanced the cause of socialism and Marxism-Leninism. However, the policy has had explicit geopolitical aims. In the late 1980s approximately eighty-five thousand Cubans were stationed abroad either as combat troops (in Angola and Ethiopia) or as technical and economic advisers (in Nicaragua). Contingents included doctors, nurses, and health care personnel as well as construction workers, teachers, agronomists, and other professionals. Intelligence people, political operatives, and security personnel served abroad—often disguised as *internacionalistas* (internationalist workers)—and supplemented the work of intelligence agencies. In some cases Cuba earned hard currency as a result of these missions, because countries like Libya and Angola paid Cuba in dollars for its services, while the Cuban government paid its people's salaries in pesos.

On occasion fulfillment of these international duties has led to war or confrontation with status quo powers (such as in South Africa) or, as was the case in Grenada in 1983, direct clashes with U.S. forces. In Angola Cuba supported a corrupt Marxist dictatorship and in Ethiopia it backed a brutal Marxist regime. The Angolan war started in the wake of the Portuguese collapse in southwestern Africa in the mid-1970s, and Cuban forces helped turn the tide for Angola's Popular Movement for the Liberation of Angola (MPLA). Cuban troops were stationed in Angola until 1991 and fought against South African regulars and guerrillas connected with the Union for the Total Independence of Angola (UNITA). Official Cuban government casualty sources listed twenty-three hundred dead, including several hundred from diseases and accidents and additional hundreds who were wounded. In all likelihood this figure underestimates the total number of casualties because not all the bodies were recovered from the battlefields. In December 1988 agreements signed among Cuba, South Africa, and Angola formalized an end to Cuba's participation in the Angolan war and established a schedule for South African troops to leave Namibia and Cuban troops to leave Angola. All fifty thousand Cuban combat troops had left by the end of May 1991 when the government and UNITA signed a peace agreement that promised democracy. There is little doubt that improvements in East-West relations, escalating costs at home, and the failure to achieve a military victory forced Cuba (as well as Angola and South Africa) to negotiate seriously.[18]

In the 1980s Cuba resumed diplomatic relations with influential Latin American states such as Argentina, Brazil, and Peru. It appeared that Havana preferred normalization of state-to-state relations in order to active support for some guerrilla movements, and key Latin American governments were seeking ways to bring Cuba back into the Latin American community. A process of reciprocity is under way that allows Cuba to expand critical ties in exchange for pragmatic recognition on its part that democratic processes in Latin America are legitimate. Suspicions regarding Cuba's ties to revolutionary networks and its intrusive behavior moderate Latin America's willingness to renew relations, although sectors of the left sympathize with Cuba and often pressure governments to recognize Havana.

Cuba's relations with Russia are markedly different from its friendly relations with the former Soviet Union. The defeat of hard-line Communists by Boris Yeltsin and the reformers eliminated the prospect that Communists will return to power in Moscow. Second, the values shaping the reform process in Russia (pluralism, free elections, accountability, entrepreneurship) are the opposite of those still dominant in Cuba. Thus, the cultural and ideological framework defining a new bilateral relationship is radically different from what prevailed under Leonid Brezhnev and Mikhail Gorbachev. Third, the reformers know that President Fidel Castro supported the August 1991 coup that aimed to restore Communist rule in Russia. Consequently, they feel no kinship or solidarity with Cuba or Castro. Simply put, Cuba and Castro were outcasts in the eyes of Yeltsin and the reformers in Russia and in Eastern Europe, many of whom view Cuba as an economic basket case and an outdated police state.

Russia, Poland, the Czech and Slovak Republics, Hungary, and others deal with Cuba pragmatically and in a very businesslike manner. Gone are the days when Cuba received preferential economic treatment and strong political support. These nations have adopted Western-style democracy and market economics, while Cuba refuses to liberalize its economy or tolerate political opposition and pluralism. In fact, Cuba's former allies have denounced its abuses of human rights at the UN Commission on Human Rights and have called for an end to repression and political persecution. Because Cuba's internal practices are under international scrutiny, it can no longer count on the protection and "solidarity" of its former allies.

Finally, although U.S.-Cuban relations fluctuate between hostility and tolerance, neither country is prepared to make the crucial political concessions that would lead to a genuine rapprochement. Formal diplomatic relations were broken in 1961, but "interest sections" opened in Washington and Havana in 1977. Issues raised by the United States have included Cuba's strategic relationship with the Soviet Union, its revolutionary activism in Africa and Latin America, and problems in the area of human rights. Historical grievances, nationalism, the U.S. economic embargo, and Cuba's insistence on sovereignty and on earning its powerful neighbor's respect have shaped that country's outlook. The two governments collaborate on matters related to emigration and family reunification, and in 1985 they signed an agreement allowing thousands of Cubans to emigrate to the United States. Restoring relations with Cuba was not a high priority for the Clinton Administration, and Cuban officials repeatedly state that they are prepared to wait for a change of official attitude in Washington.

Prospects for Breakdown and Regime Change

Predictions about the demise of Cuban socialism or about the major transformations that were necessary for the system to survive neither have been realized nor are likely to be met in the foreseeable future. Contrary to what many experts, social scientists, and regime opponents have held, the system has proved to be more resilient than anticipated. Limited economic reforms introduced in the 1990s placed a bottom under what could have been an economic cataclysm, blunting the edge of social pressures that could have exploded into political disorder.

Broadly speaking, that resiliency is rooted in nationalism, not quite yet a spent force. President Fidel Castro's commitment to rule until the very day he dies gives the system inordinate strength as well, notwithstanding the high costs stemming from his absolutist vocation and single-minded intransigence. The loyalty and relative cohesion of strategic elites such as the party apparatus, the armed forces, and younger, proven cadres involved in administration and management limit the probability that a reformist faction would shake up the system.

Finally, repression and fear sustain what a Catholic Church document identified as "induced defenselessness" in the population—namely a widespread sense of fatalism and hopelessness. A credible alternative to Castro's leadership and Communist rule has not emerged, although rising levels of political disaffection and outright dissent and opposition on a national scale are increasingly evident.

Assuming that economic crisis and social decay would force the revolutionary leadership to either abandon socialism or approve major structural reforms that would transform it was a mistake. A survival strategy of adaptation introduced in the early 1990s—combining major ideological reversals with limited macroeconomic changes and a partial opening for foreign capital—generated sufficient resources to maintain social stability and elite cohesion, one of the crucial determinants of the regime's survival.

Although downsized, the armed forces as an institution remain loyal to the revolution and its historic leaders, occupying a larger presence in Communist Party organs following the 1997 Party Congress. At the same time, high-ranking active and retired officers close to Second Secretary Raúl Castro expanded their economic presence, thereby creating a web of relationships with foreign capital that led to the emergence of a new class of entrepreneurs who are well-positioned to take advantage of economic opportunities.

There are, nonetheless, signs of political and economic change sprouting beneath the surface of a highly authoritarian one-party state. Democratic ideas are slowly reemerging. Political dissidence, for instance, is rapidly growing, and dozens of human rights organizations use what political space is available to call for free elections, democracy, and the rule of law. Elizardo Sánchez, Gustavo Arcos, and other prominent dissidents are well known abroad and receive support from influential Latin American and European governments. Finally, the long-silent hierarchy of the Catholic Church is publicly calling for change and reconciliation through a national dialogue between the regime and its opponents in Cuba as well as in the exile community. In a powerful pastoral letter in 1993 the Church points to "instances of uncertainty and hopelessness in the people" and speaks of a "deterioration in the moral climate that lead[s] to violent incidents in the cities and towns." In short, the Church is slowly taking sides against the regime. Its concerted moral and ethical appeal resonates among Catholics and nonbelievers alike and indicates that the Church is preparing for a post-Communist Cuba.

Some believe that a peaceful transition to a democratic system is possible—that, given reason and goodwill between the regime and its opponents, through negotiation and dialogue a social catastrophe can be avoided. Others maintain that a "hard" and resilient Communist dictatorship led by a messianic leader like Fidel Castro is unshakable, and therefore negotiations are unlikely to bring about a change in regime. The prospect of the Castros engineering their own departure from power seems remote because they have the specter of bloody reprisals against the old leadership in eastern Europe before them. Nor is it likely that they can survive by riding out the worst effects of the economic crisis.

Conclusion

Cuba's political development following its independence was characterized by clientelism, strongman rule, and military intervention in politics. The legitimacy of these early regimes seldom rested on popular consent. In the 1940s and 1950s democratic reformism failed to develop viable ruling institutions, and as a result, corrupt governments undermined public support for political democracy. Authoritarian regimes alienated the rising middle sectors and relied on coercion rather than consent, thus seldom ruling with popular support. Economic dependency made national development difficult and resulted in a social system that lacked cohesion.

Radical structural transformation uprooted capitalism and reordered the political system through mobilization and charismatic rule because the revolutionary elite believed that development could be achieved only through political and economic centralization. Egalitarianism, unity, and social militancy became the supreme values of the new Marxist order; pluralism, representative democracy, and a mixed economy were consciously rejected. Private education was abolished, and the state reshaped the entire educational system, expanding health services as well. State control of industry, commerce, telecommunications, agriculture, and even small-scale production created a large bureaucracy, which in turn led to a new technocracy composed of administrators, planners, managers, and "producers of culture and information." A new class with its own vested interests thus appeared.

The economic crisis has sped up the process of cultural decay and definitively demonstrated that revolutionary socialism will never produce prosperity or freedom. Neither an expanded tourist industry nor new developments in microbiology, liberalized rules for foreign investment, or the partial "dollarization" of the economy will reverse this economic debacle. In fact, these "concessions to capitalism" indicate just how desperate the regime is for any economic respite. Unanticipated social and psychological effects are already evident, as are confrontations between regime supporters and opponents.

Finally, the minimal satisfaction of some material needs is jeopardized by incompetence and corruption in the management of an economy that is spinning out of control. Its political impact is evident in increasing disaffection; the flight of thousands to the United States in perilous journeys; and the defection of hundreds of erstwhile regime supporters and members of the professional, military, cultural, technocratic, and sports elites. Losses of human capital aggravate the economic crisis and are a clear sign that millions of

Cubans have reached the end of the line and see no way out of a national calamity. And so it goes for the last Utopia.

Suggestions for Further Reading

Alfonso, Pablo. *Los Fieles de Castro.* Miami: Ediciones Cambio, 1991.

Azicri, Max. *Cuba: Politics, Economics, and Society.* London: Pinter, 1988.

Baloyra, Enrique, and James Morris, eds. *Conflict and Change in Cuba.* Albuquerque: University of New Mexico Press, 1993.

Brundenius, Claes. *Revolutionary Cuba: Economic Growth, Income Distribution, and Basic Needs.* Boulder, CO: Westview Press, 1983.

Del Aguila, Juan M. *Cuba: Dilemmas of a Revolution.* 3rd ed. Boulder, CO: Westview Press, 1994.

Díaz-Briquets, Sergio, ed. *Cuban Internationalism in Sub-Saharan Africa.* Pittsburgh, PA: Duquesne University Press, 1989.

Domínguez, Jorge I. *Cuba: Order and Revolution.* Cambridge, MA: Belknap Press of Harvard University Press, 1978.

Erisman, H. Michael, and John Kirk, eds. *Cuban Foreign Policy Confronts a New International Order.* Boulder, CO: Lynne Rienner, 1991.

Halebsky, Sandor, and John Kirk, eds. *Cuba in Transition.* Boulder, CO: Westview Press, 1992.

Horowitz, Irving L., ed. *Cuban Communism.* 7th ed. New Brunswick, NJ: Transaction Books, 1989.

Llovio Menéndez, José L. *Insider: My Hidden Life as a Revolutionary in Cuba.* New York: Bantam, 1988.

Mazarr, Michael J. *Semper Fidel: America and Cuba, 1776–1988.* Baltimore, MD: Nautical and Aviation Publishing Company of America, 1988.

Mesa-Lago, Carmelo. *The Economy of Socialist Cuba.* Albuquerque: University of New Mexico Press, 1981.

Oppenheimer, Andrés. *Castro's Final Hour.* New York: Simon & Schuster, 1992.

Pérez, Louis A. *Cuba: Between Reform and Revolution.* New York: Oxford University Press, 1988.

Rabkin, Rhoda P. *Cuban Politics.* New York: Praeger, 1991.

Smith, Wayne S. *The Closest of Enemies: A Personal and Diplomatic Account of U.S.-Cuban Relations Since 1957.* New York: W. W. Norton, 1987.

Stone, Elizabeth, ed. *Women and the Cuban Revolution.* New York: Pathfinder, 1981.

Notes

1. Carlos Moore, "Race Relations in Socialist Cuba," in *Socialist Cuba: Past Interpretations and Future Challenges,* ed. Sergio Roca (Boulder, CO: Westview Press, 1988), 175–206.

2. Franklin Knight, *The Caribbean* (New York: Oxford University Press, 1978), 32.

3. Ibid., 119.

4. Ramón Ruiz, *Cuba: The Making of a Revolution* (New York: W. W. Norton, 1968), 31.

5. Robert F. Smith, *The United States and Cuba* (New Haven, CT: College and University Press, 1960), 127.

6. Jaime Suchlicki, *Cuba: From Columbus to Castro,* 2nd ed., rev. (Washington, D.C.: Pergamon-Brassey's, 1986), 109.

7. Samuel Farber, *Revolution and Reaction in Cuba, 1933–1960* (Middletown, CT: Wesleyan University Press, 1976).

8. Suchlicki, *Cuba: From Columbus to Castro,* 125.

9. Ramón L. Bonachea and Marta San Martín, *The Cuban Insurrection, 1952–1959* (New Brunswick, NJ: Transaction Books, 1974).

10. All of the quotes appear in *Fidel y la Religión* (Santo Domingo: Editora Alfa y Omega, 1985).

11. Andrés Suárez, *Cuba: Castroism and Communism 1959–1966* (Cambridge, MA: MIT Press, 1967).

12. Nelson P. Valdés, "Radical Transformation of Cuban Education," in *Cuba in Revolution,* ed. Rolando E. Bonachea and Nelson P. Valdés (Garden City, NY: Anchor, 1972), 433.

13. Quoted from Donald C. Hodges, *The Legacy of Che Guevara: A Documentary Study* (London: Thames and Hudson), 96.

14. Carmelo Mesa-Lago, *The Economy of Socialist Cuba* (Albuquerque: University of New Mexico Press, 1981), 29.

15. On economic conditions see Eliana Cardoso and Ann Helwege, *Cuba After Communism* (Cambridge, MA: MIT Press, 1992); Carmelo Mesa-Lago, ed., *Cuba After the Cold War* (Pittsburgh, PA: University of Pittsburgh Press, 1993); and Andrew Zimbalist, "Teetering on the Brink: Cuba's Current Economic and Political Crisis," *Journal of Latin American Studies* 24, no. 2 (1992): 407–18. For a thoughtful analysis of the health system see Julie Feinsilver, *Healing the Masses* (Berkeley: University of California Press, 1993).

16. Archibald Ritter, "The Organs of People's Power and the Communist Party: The Patterns of Cuban Democracy," in *Cuba: Twenty-Five Years of Revolution, 1959–1984,* ed. Sandor Halebsky and John M. Kirk (New York: Praeger, 1985), 286.

17. Ibid., 289.

18. "Cuba: Fourth Congress of the Cuban Communist Party," *Foreign Broadcast Information Service—Latin America* (Washington, DC, October 1991).

18

Costa Rica

Mitchell A. Seligson

Virtually all the studies comparing Central American nations contain the phrase, "with the exception of Costa Rica." Travelogues—and even many academic studies—refer to Costa Rica as the "Switzerland of Central America." The propagation of the notion of Costa Rican exceptionalism has become so widespread that the first-time tourist is likely to be surprised to find a Central American nation, not an alpine one. Yet, as with most stereotypes there is more than a grain of truth in this one: Costa Rica is different from its neighbors in three very fundamental ways.

First, levels of social and economic development are far higher in Costa Rica than elsewhere in Central America.[1] Life expectancy at birth for Costa Ricans was seventy-nine years in 2007, exceeding by one year that of the United States and higher than any other country in Latin America. The under-five infant mortality, a universally used measure for comparing development, stood at eleven per one thousand live births in 2007, compared with thirty-five in Nicaragua and twenty-four in Honduras. In terms of the proportion of college-age students attending an institution of higher education, by 1989 Costa Rica surpassed even Switzerland, with 27 percent enrolled versus 26 percent in Switzerland. Costa Rica's rate also surpassed the United Kingdom (24 percent) and was nearly twice as high as that for El Salvador (17 percent), its closest competitor in Central America in the area of college enrollments.

Second, Costa Rica has the longest and deepest tradition of democratic governance of any nation in Central America. Indeed, for many years experts

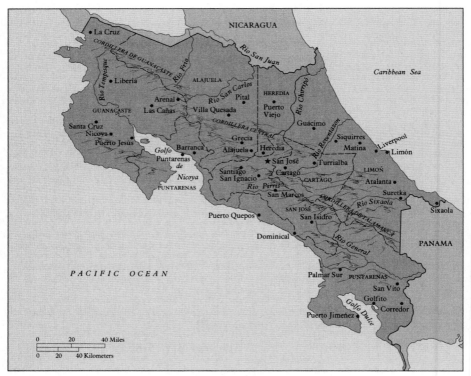

COSTA RICA

have rated Costa Rica as the most democratic country in all of Latin America.[2] Civil liberties, including freedom of press, speech, and assembly, are widely respected and protected. Free and open elections have become the hallmark of Costa Rica's style of politics, with observers throughout the world seeking to copy elements of an electoral system that faithfully guarantees against voting fraud and corruption. Human rights, so often brutally abused in other Central American nations, are carefully respected, and one rarely hears even of allegations of their violation.[3]

Third, Costa Rica is a peaceful island in a violent region. It abolished its army over forty years ago and is constitutionally prohibited from forming another one. Although there have been minor incursions and incidents over the years along Costa Rica's northern and southern borders, border guards and paramilitary units have been adequate to cope with these international conflicts. Costa Rica would be incapable of mounting a credible defense against a determined aggressor, but Costa Rica's friends in Latin America have often made it clear that they would use their military forces to deter thoughts of any such move. Strikes and protests are rarely violent, and negotiation is the most common mechanism for resolving disputes. Although Costa Rica has not been immune to terrorist attacks, their number and severity have been quite limited.

Costa Rica, then, stands out from its neighbors as being more advanced socially, economically, and politically and as more democratic and peaceful. There have been many attempts to determine why Costa Rica diverges from the regional pattern. Some studies have focused on historical accidents as an explanation, others on the mixture of resources (especially land and labor), and yet others on questions of ethnic homogeneity. To date, no comprehensive explanation has been established, yet partial explanations incorporating each of the mentioned features seem plausible. In this short introduction to Costa Rica these elements will be articulated as factors that seem to explain Costa Rican distinctiveness.

History and Political Culture

Costa Rica, the southernmost country in the group of five colonies that united into a loose federation shortly after gaining independence from Spain in the early 1820s, developed in isolation from its neighbors to the north. This isolation was partially a result of historical factors, since politics pivoted around Guatemala, the colonial seat of power. It was also partially the result of a geographic factor—namely, that the bulk of Costa Rica's population resided in San José, Cartago, and Heredia, towns located on the *meseta central* (central plateau), and thus was largely cut off from both the Pacific Ocean and the Caribbean Sea as well as from Nicaragua to the north and from Panama to the south.

Although Costa Rica can boast that it is more than twice the size of El Salvador, its 19,650 square miles (50,900 square kilometers) make it less than half the size of Guatemala and Honduras and only slightly more than one-third the size of Nicaragua. In U.S. terms, it is tiny—about the size of West Virginia. The usable territory is further reduced by the presence of a mountain chain that cuts through the center of the country, running from north to south. The mountain chain is studded with active volcanoes, and the most recent eruption in 1963 caused widespread damage to crops. The net effect of the mountains, volcanoes, and other natural formations is a reduction of arable land to an estimated 53 percent of the total land area.

Costa Rica was further weakened by the absence of large Indian populations widely found elsewhere in Central America. In Guatemala, for example, the conquering Spaniards were able to rely on a large supply of Indians to undertake heavy labor in the mines and in the fields. Although there is evidence that prior to the conquest there were perhaps as many as 400,000 Indians living in the territory that was to become Costa Rica, by the end of the sixteenth century there were fewer than 20,000, and according to some estimates as few as 4,500 by 1581.[4]

Isolation, mountains, volcanoes, and the absence of a sizable indigenous workforce do not seem to add up to a very promising basis for the impressive developments that Costa Rica was eventually to achieve. Paradoxically, however, what seemed like disadvantages turned out to be significant advantages. Isolation proved a blessing because it removed the country from the civil wars and violence that so rapidly came to characterize postindependence Central America. Later, the dictatorial rule and foreign invasions that plagued the rest of the region had little direct impact on Costa Rica. Hence, in contrast to its neighbors to both the north and the south (Nicaragua and Panama), Costa Rica has never experienced an invasion of U.S. marines. The mountains provided the altitude and the volcanoes the rich soil, both of which were required for what was to prove to be a highly successful coffee industry. Finally, the absence of a large indigenous population meant that the repressive labor systems (especially the *encomienda* system) that predominated in much of the rest of Latin America could not prosper in Costa Rica.

The colonial period in Costa Rica was one of widespread poverty. Early explorers found little of the gold and silver that so strongly stimulated Spanish migration to the New World. Had they discovered major mines, no doubt they would have found ways of importing a labor force to work them. But significant mines were never found, the labor was not imported, and the flood of colonizers who settled elsewhere proved to be only a trickle in Costa Rica. There are reports that as late as 1675 there were only five hundred to seven hundred Spanish settlers in Costa Rica, and by 1720 the number barely exceeded three thousand. It was not until the mid-1850s that the total population of the country had grown to more than one hundred thousand.

The small population, both indigenous and immigrant, together with the absence of major gold and silver mines, meant that agriculture became the principal source of economic activity throughout the colonial period. Although the soil was rich and a wide variety of crops grew well, farming was directed toward subsistence agriculture. As a result, Costa Rica had little to trade in exchange for needed goods that were not available locally. The initial poverty reinforced itself by placing beyond the reach of the settlers the farm tools and other implements needed for a more productive economy.

Throughout the colonial period efforts were made to add vitality to the fragile local economy. Attention was focused on export agriculture, especially cacao and tobacco. Both crops grew well and fetched high prices on the international market, but both eventually failed in Costa Rica. In the case of cacao, which was grown in the tropical lowlands bordering on the Caribbean Sea, marauding Indians from Nicaragua, in league with British pirates, systematically raided the plantations and stole the crop. Tobacco grew in the highlands and therefore was protected against such raids, but Spain declared a monopoly on tobacco exports and drove down profit margins for producers to the point where the cultivation of tobacco no longer proved worth the effort. By the end of the colonial period Costa Rica had not been able to find a way out of its poverty.

Independence was delivered as a gift to Costa Rica in 1821 when the isthmus, under the leadership of Guatemala, became independent from Spain. Although there was a brief period in which Costa Rica was joined with the other nations of Central America into a federation, shortly afterward independent political rule was established. Very early on in the postcolonial period the fledgling government took critical steps to help develop a stronger economic base for the country. One of these was the granting of land to all people who were willing to plant coffee on it. As a result, coffee cultivation increased dramatically in the first half of the nineteenth century, and by the 1840s direct exports of Costa Rican coffee to the markets in Europe had begun. The product was well received by the buyers and quickly achieved recognition for its high quality.

Coffee exports soon became the principal engine of economic growth for Costa Rica. The income from these exports made it possible for coffee producers to import new tools and building materials, and the government was also able to invest funds in critical infrastructure projects, especially roads and ports to facilitate the production and export of coffee. One major project that grew out of the effort to facilitate coffee exports was the construction of a railroad to the Caribbean port of Limón. Until the completion of this project, virtually all coffee exports had been shipped to Europe via the Pacific coast port of Puntarenas, around the tip of South America, and then to Europe. The high shipping costs of the lengthy voyage, however, reduced profits for the producers. The railroad to the Caribbean therefore served to cut those costs. Its construction was financed by a series of foreign loans, which Costa Rica found itself unable to repay even before the railroad was completed. As a result, the U.S.-owned firm that had contracted to build the railroad began to plant bananas to subsidize its construction. From this small start the United Fruit Company developed, and it became the major economic influence in the Caribbean tropical lowlands of Costa Rica up through the 1930s, after which time the company moved its operations to the Pacific coastal lowlands. Banana cultivation provided employment for the railroad workers who had migrated to Costa Rica from Jamaica and later for job seekers from Costa Rica's highlands. Jamaican blacks came to be the only demographically significant ethnic minority in the country, although today they account for less than 2 percent of the population.

Coffee and bananas proved to be the mainstays of the economy through the middle of the twentieth century. Over the years coffee fields were expanded to cover a wide area along the chain of mountains that runs through the country, an expansion caused by farmers in search of new land on which to grow coffee. As the territory suitable for coffee growing shrank, settlers moved to other areas where they planted basic grains, and in the higher mountain regions they grew vegetables or raised dairy cattle. In the province of Guanacaste the broad flatlands proved suitable for cattle raising, and a major export industry of fresh beef developed between Costa Rica and the United States. When the United Fruit Company left the Caribbean lowlands because of the onset of debilitating banana diseases there, those banana fields lay abandoned until the 1950s, when the discovery of new, resistant varieties allowed other companies to reinitiate the banana industry in that area. The economy of the 1980s, then, rested on the export of coffee, bananas, and beef. The recent introduction of nontraditional crops, such as pineapples, flowers, melons, tropical fruits, and vegetables, began to produce significant export earnings. The largest increase in income, however, has been from tourism, especially ecotourism, drawing on Costa Rica's natural beauty accompanied by a wise policy of establishing a large network of national parks. Tourists come from all over the world to visit Costa Rica's rain forests and enjoy its incomparable beaches. Today tourism earns more foreign exchange than bananas and coffee combined. The most recent expansion of the economy has been in the area of high technology, especially the manufacture of computer components for such giants as Intel as well as in the export of software.

Although agriculture has been the traditional base of the economy, when Costa Rica joined the Central American Common Market in the early 1960s it led to significant industrialization. By 1990 agriculture was producing only one-sixth of the gross domestic product and industry and manufacturing nearly one-half. The growth of industry has paralleled the growth of urbanization, and today over half of the population is urban. For many years Costa Rica's entry into the Central American Free Trade Agreement (CAFTA) with the United States was stalled by opposition in the legislature, but a national referendum held in 2007 gave a narrow edge to the pro-agreement side, and in late 2008 the final pieces of legislation were put in place for Costa Rica to join. This legislation paves the way for several market liberalization measures, including the introduction of competition into the telecommunications and insurance industries, which up until that point were closely held state monopolies.

Politics and Parties

Poverty and the absence of a wealthy ruling class that derived its power from a slave or Indian population proved to be factors that favored the development of democracy in Costa Rica.[5] Local government had its origins in colonial Costa Rica when local *cabildos* (city councils) were established in 1812. When independence was announced, a procedure was established that involved the popular election of delegates to a constitutional convention, and thus indirect, representative democracy was established in the first constitutional arrangements. A weak presidency was created, with the term of office limited to only three months, within a rotating directorate.

But all was not favorable for democratic rule. The system was weakened by regional rivalries between the two major population centers, San José and Cartago, and civil wars punctuated the first twenty years of independence—as did coups, assassinations, and invasions. In 1844 a new constitution was drafted and approved, dividing the government into three separate branches: legislative, executive, and judicial. Voting rights were established, but restrictions were many: To be eligible to vote, one had to be married, male, a property owner, and at least twenty-five years of age. Less than three percent of the population voted in the first elections under this new constitution. However, even this limited form of democracy was extinguished by a coup within two years.

Additional efforts at constitution-making, more coups, and countercoups occurred until 1890. In that year a period of political stability and democratic rule was initiated, and this one lasted, virtually unbroken, until 1948. Direct elections were instituted in 1913, and a new constitution drafted in 1917 granted numerous social guarantees to the working population. Although this document was to be replaced in 1919, in the years that followed, Costa Ricans made continual improvements in the election laws and procedures. In

1925 the secret ballot was instituted, and in 1927 the Civil Registry, a verifiable voter registration system, was established.

Political parties were first organized in the nineteenth century, but until 1940 they were little more than loose, personalist coalitions built around the leading economic interests. In that year the coffee oligarchy elected Rafael Angel Calderón Guardia to power and was surprised when he quickly moved in a populist direction. Calderón, a physician who had developed a large following among the urban poor, embarked on a major program to introduce social legislation. In 1942 he began a social security program and approved a minimum wage law. He also established an eight-hour workday and legalized unions. In 1943, after the Nazi invasion of the Soviet Union, he formed an electoral alliance with the Costa Rican Communist party, known as the Popular Vanguard party. This party, organized in 1929, had attempted to run candidates for local office in the 1932 elections, but after it was barred from doing so it became increasingly involved in labor protests that took place during the Great Depression, especially among banana workers.

The alliance between Calderón and the Communists caused great concern and division within Costa Rica, but in the 1944 elections the alliance forces won, supporting a candidate of Calderón's choosing. With World War II over and the Cold War beginning, the wartime alliance of convenience with the Communists became the target of increasingly strong protests within Costa Rica, and in 1948 a coalition of the traditional coffee oligarchy in league with young reformist social democrats defeated Calderón, who was once again running for the presidency. The legislature, however, had the responsibility of declaring the results of the election, and with Calderón's supporters in the majority, it annulled the election.

The reaction to the maneuver was swift and violent. An armed group led by José (Pepe) Figueres Ferrer organized in the mountains to the south of the capital and began a series of skirmishes with the government forces, aided by unionized banana workers. After a brief but bloody civil war, Figueres triumphed. He took over the government and ran it for a year and a half, during which time a new constitution was drafted and approved. Although it was a modern constitution, guaranteeing a wide range of rights, it outlawed parties that were perceived as threatening to democratic rule, such as the Communist party.

Four major consequences of the civil war of 1948 have served to shape Costa Rican politics ever since. First, the new constitution abolished the army and replaced it with a paramilitary force of civil guards. Without an army, it is far more difficult for dissenting forces to engineer a coup, and indeed, there have been no successful attempts to dislodge civilian rule since 1948. Second, Figueres did what no other successful leader of a coup in Latin America has ever done: He voluntarily turned the control of the government over to the victor of the annulled election. By doing so he firmly established a respect for elections that had been growing in Costa Rica since the turn of the century. Third, the civil war largely delegitimized the Communist party, and since that time, even after the elimination of the constitutional prohibition on Communist candidates running for office, the voting strength of the Communist party has not exceeded 3 percent of the total presidential vote. Fourth, Figueres ushered in with him a group of social reformers who, though in many ways they merely expanded on programs begun by Calderón, sought to spur economic development and social progress without resorting to outright socialist schemes.

Once Figueres relinquished power he began to build a new party, called the National Liberation party (PLN), to compete in the 1953 elections, which he won handily. From the moment of that election through 1998, the presidency oscillated between control by the PLN and control by a coalition of opposition forces.

Since 1998, however, party politics in Costa Rica have been shifting. New political parties, often forming coalitions with other minor parties, have entered the electoral arena in force. At the same time, electoral abstention has been increasing substantially. The result has been that the PLN has lost much of its firm grip on the presidency. In 2002, for the first time ever, elections went into a second round because of a strong run by a third party. In 2006 the election victory by Oscar Arias, allowed to run for office a second time as a result of a Supreme Court (Sala IV) decision, was by only a 1 percent margin. It was worrisome that abstention increased again—to almost 35 percent of registered voters. At the local level the *cantón* votes for third parties has become even stronger. Corruption scandals at the very top of the political system served to discredit the major opposition party, whose electoral alliance crumbled. There has also been a rapidly growing increase in the number of females in politics, first at the local level and more recently, after the approval of a quota law, at the level of the national legislature.

Governmental Structure

Since 1949 Costa Rica has operated under the constitution that grew out of the 1948 civil war. Power is shared among the president, a unicameral legislature, and the courts. Members of the legislature and the president are elected every four years. Candidates for the legislature, representing each of the seven provinces of the country, are selected by party conventions. The ability of a sitting president to implement programs has always depended on the strength of congressional support.

In order to implement the wide range of social and economic development programs envisioned by the leaders of the PLN, numerous autonomous and semiautonomous agencies have been created. Hence, one agency handles electric and telephone services, another water supply, and yet another automobile and home insurance. These agencies have been a positive force for development and have spawned many creative ideas. For example, the automobile and home insurance agency also runs the fire department, which guarantees that it is in the insurance agency's interest to have an efficient firefighting service. The autonomy of these agencies has helped to isolate them from partisan political pressure. Yet, along with their autonomy has come the problem of an excessive decentralization of control. As a result, central planning and budgetary control have become extremely difficult as agencies and their functions have proliferated over the years. The free trade agreements, however, have served to reduce the power of these agencies.

Policymaking

The modern state that Costa Rica has evolved into can be largely credited with the achievements that were noted at the beginning of this chapter. The high standard of living that has been attained, however, has been built on an economy that has limited industrial capacity. Most industrialization is of the assembly type, and as much as 90 cents of each dollar of output is comprised of imported materials. The continuously growing government and parastatal bureaucracies further increased costs without adding to production.

By the mid-1970s it was beginning to become clear that the growth model of the post–civil war period was running out of steam and that the economy could no longer support the expense of a widespread social welfare net and a bloated public sector. Yet little was done to correct the system under successive PLN presidents. Then, beginning in 1980, under the leadership of an opposition president, the system began to come apart. In order to shore up local production and consumption—and taking advantage of cheap loans being offered by foreign banks that were awash in petrodollars as a result of the dramatic rise in world petroleum prices—Costa Rica began to borrow wildly. Over a very short span of time the country's foreign debt grew to the point at which it exceeded the equivalent of the total annual national production, and by 1982 Costa Rica had one of the highest per capita foreign debts in the world. The local currency was devalued again and again, inflation and unemployment rose, and the system seemed headed for a crash.

By late 1981 the future seemed grim indeed. Yet, while similar circumstances have led to coups in other Latin American countries, Costa Ricans waited patiently for the elections of 1982 and once again voted in the PLN. A dramatic plan for recovery was put in place by the victorious president, and the plan proved successful in stabilizing the economic picture. Inflation dropped, employment rose, the currency was revalued, and an effort was made to rationalize the foreign debt. These actions restored confidence in the system, but they did not return to the citizens the benefits of the growth that had been lost during the 1980–1982 period. Belts had to be tightened, taxes were increased, and prices rose. Economic growth picked up a bit, but there was no dramatic recovery.

Throughout the 1980s Costa Rica followed a slow path to economic recovery. Under the competent leadership of the Central Bank's president, Eduardo Lizano, the PLN conducted a strenuous and ultimately successful effort to renegotiate important components of the foreign debt. The recovery would have been stronger if it had not been for the precipitous decline in coffee prices brought on by the collapse of the International Coffee Organization's system of quotas and prices. Throughout the period and on into the 1990s, when the opposition again took office as a result of the 1990 election, Costa Rica operated under a strict International Monetary Fund (IMF) mandate to cut public expenditures and hold down inflation. Although the IMF goals have not always been met, by 1993 the economy had essentially recovered to its pre-1980 levels, and it enjoyed modest growth in the 1990s and strong growth, often over 6 percent a year, in the new millennium. The global financial meltdown that began in 2008, however, threatened to greatly weaken the economic outlook for Costa Rica, driving down tourism and threatening exports.

The International Arena

In 1986 the PLN broke the pattern of electoral victory that had normally oscillated between the opposition party and itself by winning the election. It did so under the leadership of Oscar Arias Sánchez, and Arias took power in an increasingly threatening international environment brought on by crisis in Nicaragua.

When the Sandinista revolutionaries were fighting to overthrow the Somoza dictatorship in the late 1970s, they found extensive support in their neighbor to the south. Although Costa Rica remained officially neutral in that conflict, there was a longstanding antipathy for Somoza and the harsh dictatorial regime that he represented. Public support for a Sandinista victory was overwhelming, and there is much evidence that the government of Costa Rica did what it could to help.[6]

Once the Sandinistas took power, however, relations between Costa Rica and the new regime rapidly deteriorated. Costa Ricans perceived the revolution as having a Marxist-Leninist orientation, and as such, it presented two threats to Costa Rica. First, it was a threat because of the fear that Communist expansionism would mean Nicaragua would eventually attempt to take over Costa Rica. Second, it presented a threat to internal stability because it was feared that disgruntled Costa Ricans, especially among the university youth, would turn to revolutionary activity. In fact, in a small way the second expectation was realized. Terrorism, which had been almost unknown in Costa Rica, erupted with a number of ugly incidents in which lives were lost, and several clandestine "people's prisons" were discovered that were apparently designed to hide victims of political kidnappings. With the Reagan administration in the White House, yet a third fear gripped Costa Ricans. This was the fear that the United States would invade Nicaragua, possibly using Costa Rican territory as a base of operations. Such an event would have thrust Costa Rica into an international military conflict for which it was not prepared and that it did not want. Indeed, as the Iran-Contra hearings in the United States were later to demonstrate, a clandestine airstrip was built in Costa Rica to help ferry arms to the contra rebels, and a plan was developed for a so-called Southern strategy involving Costa Rican territory.

On top of all of these concerns was the growing problem of Nicaraguan refugees. As the contra war grew in ferocity and the Nicaraguan economy deteriorated, waves of refugees joined those already in Costa Rica who had fled the initial takeover of the Sandinistas. In short, Costa Ricans mortally feared being caught up in an impossible international conflict that could only result in deep harm being done to their country's national economy and society.

Upon assuming office Oscar Arias dedicated himself to bringing peace to the region. Doing so was not only appropriate for a country that had long been noted for its internal peace and lack of an army, but it was also urgently needed if Costa Rica hoped to avoid the problems noted above. Arias managed to draw together the leaders of all of the Central American countries and develop a peace plan that was not only to involve Nicaragua but would also serve to end the civil war in El Salvador and the guerrilla war in Guatemala. For his efforts Arias was awarded the Nobel Peace Prize.

Conclusions

In the 1990 elections the PLN lost the presidency to an opposition coalition led by the son of Calderón Guardia. Within a few months of this loss, the Sandinistas in Nicaragua were defeated in an upset election. These two elections saw the new decade emerging with new leadership in these two Central American neighbors. The dominant parties of the decade of the 1980s, the PLN in Costa Rica and the Sandinista National Liberation Front in Nicaragua, were being asked by the voters to take a backseat in order to allow fresh faces to try their hand at economic development, democratization, and peace. The dramatic changes in the Soviet Union and Eastern Europe did not go unnoticed in Central America, as capitalism and democracy rapidly began to replace socialism and dictatorship. New elections in 2002 brought the opposition Social Christian Party (PUSC) to power with the election of Abel Pacheco, a physician, who had participated in an attempt to overthrow Figueres in 1955. Elections in 2006 and 2010 returned the PLN to power.

In this context, peaceful, democratic Costa Rica faces new opportunities for regional leadership as the one country in Central America with a long tradition of democracy. On the domestic scene the ability of the economy to continue to grow remains a major challenge. Nontraditional exports, computer chip manufacture, and tourism are critical factors in continued success. Costa Rica's open, democratic style of governance has enabled the country to withstand crises that would cause others to wilt. If the past is any guide to the future, Costa Rica will rise to the test and overcome its problems.

New challenges face Costa Rica. Democratic rights were being expanded as a result of the creation of the "Sala IV," a constitutional court, which has been augmenting individual liberties at a rapid pace. Yet, many Costa Ricans wonder if this movement has gone too far, and there are signs of growing discontent. In the new century Costa Rica has had incidents of mass protest that it had not experienced before. As already noted, voting abstention, historically never very high, has increased markedly, a sign for some of growing disenchantment with the political system.[7] Political leaders have been sensitive to this shift in voter sentiment and have begun a new process of institutional reform that promises to maintain Costa Rican politics on an even keel, but many feel that the old parties are not capable of real democratization. Corruption scandals have become more widespread and have reached higher than ever before, implicating several former presidents. If the past is any guide to the future, however, Costa Ricans will find a way to retain their democratic and peaceful traditions.

Suggestions for Further Reading

Bell, John Patrick. *Crisis in Costa Rica.* Austin: University of Texas Press, 1971.

Biesanz, Richard, Karen Zubris Biesanz, and Mavis Hiltunen Biesanz. *The Costa Ricans.* Englewood Cliffs, NJ: Prentice Hall, 1982.

Booth, John A. *Costa Rica: Quest for Democracy.* Boulder, CO: Westview Press, 1999.

Booth, John A., and Mitchell A. Seligson. *The Legitimacy Puzzle in Latin America: Democracy and Political Support in Eight Nations.* Cambridge: Cambridge University Press, 2009.

Cruz, Consuelo. *Political Culture and Institutional Development in Costa Rica and Nicaragua: Worldmaking in the Tropics.* New York: Cambridge University Press, 2005.

Edelman, Marc, and Joanne Kenan, eds. *The Costa Rica Reader.* New York: Grove Weidenfeld, 1989.

Gudmundson, Lowell. *Costa Rica Before Coffee: Society and Economy on the Eve of the Export Boom.* Baton Rouge: Louisiana State University Press, 1986.

Hall, Carolyn. *Costa Rica: A Geographical Interpretation in Historical Perspective.* Boulder, CO: Westview Press, 1985.

Hall, Carolyn, and Héctor Pérez Brignoli. *Historical Atlas of Central America.* Norman: University of Oklahoma Press, 2003.

Lehoucq, Fabrice Edouard, and Iván Molina Jiménez. *Stuffing the Ballot Box: Fraud, Electoral Reform, and Democratization in Costa Rica, Cambridge Studies in Comparative Politics.* New York: Cambridge University Press, 2002.

Seligson, Mitchell A. *Peasants of Costa Rica and the Development of Agrarian Capitalism.* Madison: University of Wisconsin Press, 1980.

———. "Ordinary Elections in Extraordinary Times: The Political Economy of Voting in Costa Rica." In *Elections and Democracy in Central America,* ed. John A. Booth and Mitchell A. Seligson, 158–84. Chapel Hill: University of North Carolina Press, 1989.

Seligson, Mitchell A., and Edward N. Muller. "Democratic Stability and Economic Crisis: Costa Rica, 1978–1983." *International Studies Quarterly* 31 (September 1987): 301–26.

Vargas-Cullell, Jorge, Luis Rosero-Bixby, and Mitchell A. Seligson. *La Cultura política de la democracia en Costa Rica, 2004.* San José, Costa Rica: Centro Centroamericano de Población (CCP), 2005.

Wilson, Bruce M. *Costa Rica: Politics, Economics and Democracy.* Boulder, CO: Lynne Rienner, 1998.

Deborah J. Yashar, *Demanding Democracy: Reform and Reaction in Costa Rica and Guatemala, 1870s–1950s,* Stanford, CA: Stanford University Press, 1997.

Notes

1. The data in this paragraph are drawn from the World Bank online data.

2. See the various years of the Freedom House index.

3. The Latin American Studies Association reports that the National Reconciliation Commission, established as part of the Central American peace accord of 1987, found that "no one in Costa Rica claimed that there were systematic violations of human rights or denial of freedom of expression in the country" (Latin American Studies Association, "Final Report of the LASA Commission on Compliance with the Central America Peace Accord" [Pittsburgh, PA: LASA, March 15, 1988], 8).

4. Hall reports 17,166 in 1569 (ibid., 72), whereas another source reports the lower figure (Mitchell A. Seligson, *Peasants of Costa Rica and the Development of Agrarian Capitalism* [Madison: University of Wisconsin Press, 1980], 4).

5. This section draws on Mitchell A. Seligson, "Costa Rica and Jamaica," in *Competitive Elections in Developing Countries,* ed. Myron Weiner and Ergun Ozbudun (Durham, N.C.: Duke University Press, 1987).

6. See Mitchell A. Seligson and William Carroll, "The Costa Rican Role in the Sandinista Victory," in *Nicaragua in Revolution,* ed. Thomas W. Walker (New York: Praeger, 1982), 331–44.

7. Seligson, Mitchell A. "Trouble in Paradise: The Impact of the Erosion of System Support in Costa Rica, 1978–1999," *Latin America Research Review* 37, no. 1 (2002): 160–85.

19

Nicaragua

The Politics of Frustration

Richard L. Millett

Nicaragua, largest in area of the Central American Republics, has a history marked by unfulfilled promises, frustrated hopes, and violent internal conflicts and external interventions. The Sandinista revolution of 1979–1990 now seems to be yet another episode in this dreary history. Obsessed with the past and dominated by conflicting personal ambitions, Nicaragua's political system offers few solutions to the nation's overwhelming social and economic problems.

Despite—or perhaps because of—this history, Nicaragua has enjoyed disproportionate attention from U.S. scholars and political activists. Ruled briefly in the nineteenth century by an American filibuster, William Walker; occupied twice by the U.S. Marines in the first third of the twentieth century; and the scene of a nearly decade-long conflict between a Marxist regime and U.S.-sponsored counterrevolutionary insurgents in the 1980s, the nation has frequently been the subject of fierce policy debates within the United States. The United States and other nations have also been interested in Nicaragua's potential as an interoceanic canal route. In addition, the Sandinista revolution in 1979 seemed to present an opportunity to test both the potential for social revolution in Central America as well as the possibility of creating a less dogmatic socialist state. Such hopes, like Nicaragua's aspirations to be the site of a canal, would remain unfulfilled.

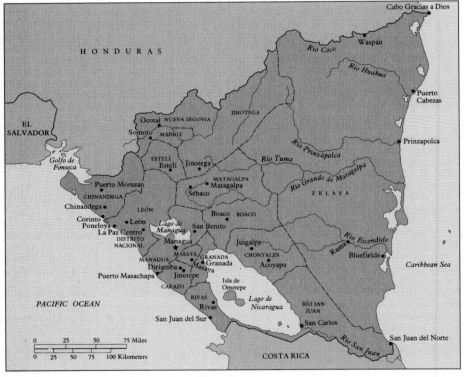

NICARAGUA

History

From the colonial period until the present Nicaragua has been the scene of international rivalries. Its indigenous population was decimated in part to provide labor for the mines of Peru. The British waged a prolonged conflict over the rule of the Caribbean Coast and competed with the United States for control over the potential transisthmian canal route. The nineteenth-century filibustering expedition of William Walker reflected both rivalries over control of the isthmian transit route as well as plans to annex lands for the expansion of slavery. It also was a product of the interminable civil conflicts between the Liberal and Conservative parties, both of which at times preferred foreign intervention to defeat at the hands of their domestic opponents. Ultimately, fear of reviving the slavery issue led the Pierce Administration to cut off supplies and reinforcements to Walker, thereby thwarting his ambition to rule Central America and underscoring the U.S. tendency to determine regional polices based on domestic political issues. Washington's decision to build a canal through Panama rather than Nicaragua damaged relations and led to the 1912 Marine intervention. Fearing that Nicaragua's Liberals might grant a canal concession to some other nation, the United States entered into a de facto alliance with the Conservatives, with the presence of a small Marine unit ensuring Conservative rule until the mid-1920s.

The United States then attempted to withdraw the Marines and promote honest elections and a professional military, but these efforts only contributed to another civil conflict and a much larger intervention in 1927. Washington imposed a peace settlement on Nicaragua's warring factions, providing for general disarmament, U.S. supervision of the next two presidential elections, and the creation of a U.S.-officered and -trained constabulary force to be known as the National Guard.

One Liberal general, Augusto César Sandino, rejected these terms and launched a guerrilla war against the Marines and the National Guard. Although never able to seriously threaten the government, Sandino's resistance endured until the last Marines departed at the start of 1933. Sandino then negotiated peace terms, but a year later he was murdered by the National Guard.

That force's commander, General Anastasio Somoza García, used the Guard to propel himself into the presidency in 1936, inaugurating over forty-two years of Somoza family rule. The Somozas used three basic instruments—control of the National Guard, manipulation of the Liberal Party, and the image of a close alliance with the United States—to perpetuate themselves in power. In the process they amassed vast personal wealth and established a network of corruption. The dynasty's founder was assassinated in 1956, but his sons Luís and Anastasio Somoza Debayle managed to hold onto power.

They provided the United States with the launching pad for the abortive 1961 Bay of Pigs invasion of Cuba, and in turn, Fidel Castro supported the creation of an anti-Somoza insurgency. When the Somozas used the devastating 1971 earthquake that leveled Managua to further enrich themselves and their cronies, popular discontent increased dramatically. A Marxist guerrilla movement, the Sandinista Liberation Front (FSLN), had been in existence since the early 1960s, but now it began to attract support from wider elements of society. When opposition newspaper editor and political leader Pedro Joaquín Chamorro was murdered in early 1978, popular discontent exploded. Political and economic pressures exerted by business leaders, with some support from the Carter administration, failed to oust President Anastasio Somoza Debayle, and national and international support increasingly coalesced around the Sandinistas. After a prolonged and bloody struggle, the Sandinistas forced Somoza into exile and occupied the capital in July 1979.

Sandinista leaders initially convinced non-FSLN politicians and business leaders to cooperate with the FSLN in forming a broad-based government. However, it soon became clear that real power lay with the nine-member Sandinista National Directorate, which was intent on creating a controlled economy, supporting other Central American insurgency movements, and establishing close ties with Cuba and the Soviet Union. Internal political conflict increased, and with the inauguration of the Reagan administration in 1981, the United States began to support armed resistance to Sandinista rule. Known as contras, these forces inflicted significant economic damage, but they were never able to seriously challenge Sandinista power. Elections were held in 1984 but, protesting conditions that they claimed made effective participation impossible, major elements of the internal political opposition boycotted the process. The FSLN used these elections to consolidate control, installing party leader Daniel Ortega as president and adopting a new constitution that incorporated the aims and principles of a Socialist revolution. However, a combination of the costs of the ongoing contra war, the impact of a U.S. economic boycott, and the FSLN's own economic mismanagement ultimately devastated the economy and undermined FSLN efforts to consolidate their control.

A combination of mediation by Central America's presidents and a decision by the first Bush administration to pursue negotiated solutions to Central America's conflicts led to internationally supervised elections in 1990. To the surprise of the FSLN, these were won decisively by a fourteen-party coalition headed by Violetta Barios de Chamorro, widow of Pedro Joaquín. The FSLN, however, remained the largest bloc in the legislature. To govern effectively, the Chamorro administration made working agreements with the FSLN, including leaving General Humberto Ortega, brother of ex-president

Daniel Ortega, in command of the military. This, however, broke up Chamorro's own coalition and created new problems with the U.S. Congress.

Under the Chamorro administration Nicaragua experienced six years of
political turmoil, economic crisis, and citizen insecurity. Determined to "govern from below," the FSLN promoted strikes, obstructed legislation, and resisted military reforms. Conservative elements ultimately gained control of
the legislature and engaged in a fierce battle with the administration over
constitutional amendments. Jobless and landless, former members of both the
contra and Sandinista forces again took up arms, returning some rural areas
to a virtual state of war. Despite all this, some progress was made. Annual inflation, which under FSLN rule had surpassed 30,000 percent, fell to under
20 percent. The strength of the military was greatly reduced, the police
brought under government control, and the draft ended. Most contras disarmed and some refugees returned. Humberto Ortega was eventually replaced as military commander, demonstrating a loss of FSLN control over
the armed forces.

After a bitter fight the constitution was amended to reduce executive powers, protect private property, depoliticize the military, and bar the reelection
of the president or of any close relative. Finally, the Chamorro administration
conducted reasonably fair—if far from perfect—elections in 1996 and peacefully transferred power to another party. The 1996 elections produced over
twenty candidates, but quickly became a race between Daniel Ortega of the
FSLN and an alliance of Nicaragua's fractionated Liberals, headed by Managua Mayor José Arnaldo Alemán. Alemán was elected president with 51
percent of the vote to 37.7 percent for Ortega. The Alemán administration
managed to improve relations with the United States, but the economy remained a disaster and charges of corruption threatened to engulf the regime.
In addition, the devastation of Hurricane Mitch in 1998 further undermined
efforts at economic recovery. By the end of his term Alemán was seeking means
to ensure his immunity from future prosecution. Constitutional amendments,
approved by the legislature at the start of 2000, reduced the role of smaller
parties, undercut the independence of the Comptroller General's office, and
made it more difficult to convict a president.

A combination of the changes in the electoral system and fears of a Sandinista return to power ensured the victory in the 2001 elections of Alemán's
hand-picked candidate, his Vice President Enrique Bolaños Geyer. Once in
office, however, President Bolaños turned on his predecessor, actively seeking
his prosecution for massive corruption. He succeeded in getting Alemán convicted and imprisoned, but it cost him the support of the Liberal Party, leaving him with only a small minority support in Congress and producing
efforts by the Liberals to form an alliance with the FSLN to force him from

office. Alemán continued to control the party even while under house arrest and, in alliance with the FSLN, gained control of the legislature and used it against Bolaños. Nicaragua entered into a prolonged period of political paralysis as various factions maneuvered to gain an advantage in the scheduled 2006 elections.

A deeply divided opposition opened the way for a return to power by Daniel Ortega and the FSLN in the 2006 elections. The Liberals split between pro- and anti-Alemán factions. A dissident group of Sandinistas formed their own party, the Sandinista Renewal Movement (MRS), and for a time appeared to be a major factor. Their candidate, however, Managua Mayor Herty Lewites, suffered a fatal heart attack a few months before the election. The Nicaraguan Constitution had been amended to give victory to anyone with a plurality in excess of 35 percent, and in the election Ortega and the FSLN won 38 percent to 28.3 percent for the anti-Alemán Liberals. The Alemán faction received 27.1percent and the MRS 6.3 percent. The FSLN also won thirty-eight of the ninety-two seats in the National Assembly.

Social Structure

At the beginning of the twenty-first century Nicaragua had a population of approximately 4.5 million, most of whom are *mestizos*. Some Indians along the Caribbean coast do remain ethnically distinct, and there is also a strong Afro-Caribbean influence on the Atlantic coast, where much of the population emigrated from the British Caribbean. Because of its ethnic makeup and its isolation from the rest of the nation, the Caribbean coast was granted a measure of political and cultural autonomy in 1987.

The majority of Nicaraguans are Roman Catholic, but Protestant groups have made major inroads, so the nation today is perhaps 15 percent Evangelical. In fact, an evangelical political party finished third in the 1996 elections.

Nicaragua is the largest Central American nation in area, and its economy is heavily dependent on agriculture. Nevertheless, it is also the region's most urbanized nation. Flows of refugees from conflict in the countryside exacerbated this situation in the 1980s and 1990s, and today the nation is over 60 percent urban. Unemployment and underemployment often run above 50 percent in urban areas. Nicaragua has the hemisphere's second-lowest GNP per capita and Central America's highest infant mortality rate.

Both business and labor are relatively well organized in Nicaragua. Many of the largest labor and peasant organizations are controlled by the FSLN. The major business group, the Superior Council of Private Enterprise (COSEP), was a center of anti-Sandinista opposition. Its former president, Enrique Bolaños, served as Nicaragua's president, succeeded by Daniel Ortega.

In contrast to most of the hemisphere, the military has never been a truly autonomous actor in Nicaraguan politics. It was first the tool of traditional parties, then the instrument of a foreign intervention, then the guardians of a prolonged family dynasty, and finally the bulwark of support for a revolutionary political project. Today, its ties to the FSLN have considerably weakened, and it is becoming more like a traditional Central American military. Several regular changes of command have taken place, any fears that it would intervene in the political process have largely evaporated, and its size has been greatly reduced. It even sent a contingent to Iraq in 2003. Today the greatest remaining issue is disposal of its aging surface-to-air missiles, which Washington fears might find their way into terrorist hands.

Nicaragua's mass media have always been highly politicized. Under the Somozas and then again under the Sandinistas the newspaper *La Prensa*, controlled by the Chamorro family, became a symbol of resistance to the regime in power. Over the last forty years radio has become even more important than print media in efforts to boost support for or mobilize opposition to a particular regime. Television, too, has steadily increased its influence. By the mid-1990s there were nearly a quarter of a million television sets. Television was largely government-controlled until the 1990s, but today both national channels and widely available foreign programming reflect a wide variety of views.

Political Institutions and Parties

Nicaragua is governed under the Sandinista-authored constitution of 1987, but this was significantly altered by a series of amendments adopted in 1995 and by others added in this century. In many ways the government structure follows traditional Central American patterns, with a unicameral legislature, a prohibition on immediate presidential reelection, an independent electoral authority, a Supreme Court, and numerous autonomous agencies. Local government consists of two levels—departmental and municipal. There are fifteen departments plus the two semi-autonomous regions along the Caribbean coast. Outside of these coastal regions, departments are generally dominated by the central government, but municipal governments have had a growing degree of autonomy.

Beginning in 1990 Nicaraguans elected municipal officials directly. The powers of municipal government were strengthened, and mayors became the most important local political figures. At least fifteen Nicaraguan cities have populations over fifty thousand, and metropolitan Managua's population is about two million.

Under the rule of the Somoza family the executive branch was totally dominant, and the legislature and courts generally rubber-stamped whatever the president wanted. The FSLN's 1987 constitution then strengthened executive authority even further. In both cases there was an extraconstitutional power that controlled the government. Under the Somozas this was the Somoza family and the National Guard. Under the Sandinistas it was the FSLN's nine-member national directorate. Today, political power is largely in the hands of elected officials. The president and vice president are elected for five-year terms and, along with close family members, are barred from immediate reelection. Presidential powers have been broad, including the right to propose a budget, appoint cabinet members and other high officials, and, prior to 1995, to rule by decree. These powers were significantly reduced by recent amendments, but the president still retains considerable independent authority, especially if a state of national emergency is declared.

Nicaragua's unicameral legislature has ninety-three members. Complex constitutional provisions provide that twenty seats be elected from national party lists and seventy be elected departmentally under a system of proportionate representation. In addition, defeated presidential candidates who win a bit over 1 percent of the vote are also given a seat. This encouraged a proliferation of parties, with eleven actually winning one or more seats in 1996. However, in 2001 only the Liberal Alliance, the FSLN and the Conservatives (who won just one seat) gained seats in the legislature. Electoral law reforms in 2000 had changed the system, curbing the proliferation of smaller parties but also concentrating power in the hands of the two dominant parties. The revised constitution gives the Legislative Assembly broad powers, including the ability to enact laws, override presidential vetoes with a simple majority vote, and amend the constitution with a 60 percent majority. Under present circumstances this is virtually impossible unless the Liberals and the FSLN agree.

As in much of Latin America, a weak judicial system presents a significant obstacle to efforts at democratic consolidation. Nicaragua has little tradition of an independent judiciary, and partisan efforts to manipulate the Supreme Court are constant. As a result, the Court at times is unable to function. Lower courts are poorly staffed and overwhelmed by the rising crime rate. Conviction rates in criminal cases have run under 5 percent. One result is that prisoners often spend prolonged periods of incarceration before coming to trial. Prisons are badly overcrowded and conditions fall well below minimal international standards.

A fourth power is the Supreme Electoral Council (CSE), which not only runs elections and certifies the results but also controls the Civil Register and issues citizens their identity cards (*cédulas*). In January 2000 an agreement between the Liberals and the FSLN reformed the electoral law, eliminating provisions requiring broad representation of political parties in the administration of local polling stations and giving the CSE virtual carte blanche in the appointment of these officials. The seven members of the CSE would be appointed by the Legislative Assembly and would need the approval of 60 percent of those voting. This ensured that the FSLN and the Liberals would have to agree on members and that smaller parties would have no effective voice in the process. To gain a place on the ballot any party that failed to win 3 percent of the vote in the previous general election must obtain the signatures of 3 percent of eligible voters. Only the Liberal Alliance, the FSLN, and the Nicaraguan Christian Way (CCN) qualified for exemption from this provision. Nicaragua's Conservative Party managed to gain a spot on the 2001 ballot, but its presidential candidate only garnered 1.4 percent of the vote. Municipal elections in 2004 gave control of most of Nicaragua's cities to the FSLN. Elections for president, vice president, and assembly members were again held in late 2006. Suffrage is universal for those sixteen and older. In presidential elections there will be a second round of voting between the two leading candidates if the leading candidate does not obtain 40 percent of the vote or 35 percent or more with a margin of 5 percent over the second-place candidate. The CSE will set the date for this election, but it must be within forty-five days of the general election.

Among the most important of the autonomous governmental institutions are the Central Bank and the Office of the Comptroller. The Central Bank controls the currency, disburses government funds, and exercises some control over private banks. The Comptroller oversees the disbursement of government funds and audits government accounts. Both have been the scene of bitter partisan fights.

Nicaragua has dozens of political parties, many of which exist only to promote individual ambitions and have no national structure. Only three currently have the right to a place on the ballot. The political scene is dominated by the two major Liberal factions and the FSLN. The Constitutional Liberal Party is dominated by former President Alemán and merges three elements of Nicaragua's traditional Liberal Party. Because this party was long the vehicle of the Somoza dynasty, it is frequently accused of having ties with elements of that regime. The party has support among Nicaragua's upper and middle classes. It is probusiness, generally supportive of the United States in international affairs, and has traditionally been strongly anti-Sandinista. Today it seems equally preoccupied with opposing the dissident Liberal faction, headed by Eduardo Montealegre, and has forged a pact with the FSLN to inhibit efforts of other parties and/or political alliances to gain legal status. Together they dominate the Electoral Tribunal that, in turn revoked the legal status of the MRS and of Nicaragua's traditional Conservative Party. The pact, however, shows signs of coming apart, first because of massive FSLN fraud in the 2008 municipal elections and second because of Ortega's effort to amend the Constitution to permit his reelection.

The FSLN has somewhat modified its Marxist rhetoric and now portrays itself as more of a social democratic party. It has strong support within the labor movement and in other mass popular organizations. It advocates increased government control over the economy, expanded social welfare policies, and an independent foreign policy. Its support has been damaged by a reputation for corruption derived from the massive looting of state resources at the end of its period in power; by deep internal divisions that resulted in the defection of some of the leadership before the 1996 elections; and by personal scandals revolving around the Party's leader, former President Daniel Ortega and his common-law wife, Rosario Murillo. Many of the Party's original leaders have defected, including former Vice President Sergio Ramírez, former culture minister Ernesto Cardenal, and former official newspaper editor Carlos Chamorro. Other parties account for less than one-tenth of the electorate.

Nicaragua's traditional Conservative Party is divided into several factions, and many of its supporters voted for Alemán in 1996 in order to ensure a Sandinista defeat. It gained a spot on the 2001 ballot, but won only 1.4 percent of the vote. In 2007 it joined the anti-Alemán Liberals, and since then it has lost its legal status. The MRS has strong intellectual leadership, but it lacks mass support and has also been deprived of its legal status. The Christian Democrats are smaller and even more divided, and their future is more problematic.

Public Policy

Nicaragua's public policies are a strange mixture of the revolutionary heritage of the Sandinistas and the personal ambition of Daniel Ortega. Efforts to keep inflation under control have been undermined by persistent budget deficits. In addition, the decline in coffee prices has badly hurt export earnings. The prevailing climate of corruption has jeopardized many international aid sources and held up agreements with the International Monetary Fund. Industry has lagged behind other sectors in the limited economic recovery that has occurred, thus further exacerbating the high rate of urban unemployment. Economic growth in 2004 was the best in many years, but rising petroleum prices and domestic political turmoil combined with global economic problems have largely undone this. Foreign investment in real estate grew under Bolaños, but it has largely stopped and in some cases even reversed under Ortega. This loss of foreign assistance has been somewhat compensated by aid from Venezuela, but falling petroleum prices may reduce this.

The Bolaños administration had made some efforts to deal with the crisis in social welfare, health, and education, but its lack of support in the Assembly crippled its efforts. Privatization efforts had begun, but the combined effects of a lack of investor confidence, continued concerns over Sandinista influence, and high-level corruption have produced disappointing results. Ortega has largely abandoned such efforts.

Nicaragua's external debt totals over US$6 billion. Prospects for debt forgiveness by foreign governments and international financial organizations seemed significantly enhanced, however, in the wake of Hurricane Mitch. Nicaragua was included in the World Bank's "Highly Indebted Poor Countries" program, thus making it eligible for the forgiveness of up to 80 percent of its debt, but this has been limited by the ongoing political crisis. The nation consistently runs a high deficit in its current accounts and depends on external aid to cover this. It even depends on foreign assistance for such basic programs as conducting elections.

Nicaragua has little in the way of a regular civil service. Most government positions, at both the national and local level, are seen as rewards for political support. The bureaucracy has been reduced from the massive levels it reached in the 1980s, but it is still inefficient and widely viewed as corrupt. Disputes over political patronage are a constant theme because apportioning positions is both a major motivation for and a constant source of tension in the formation and maintenance of political alliances.

Foreign Policy

Nicaragua's foreign policy revolves around four principal foci: relations with the United States; an alliance with other left-wing governments in Latin America, notably Venezuela; the constant search for foreign assistance and debt relief; and relations with other Central American nations, notably with Honduras and Costa Rica.

Initiatives in these areas are, at times, openly contradictory. The Bolaños administration was a strong supporter of free trade arrangements with the United States (CAFTA), but the Ortega administration has abandoned this track, instead joining the Venezuelan-sponsored ALBA group. Relations with Costa Rica have been complicated by disputes over rights along the San Juan River and by issues involving Nicaraguan immigrants to Costa Rica. The Honduran political crisis has further polarized regional politics, with Nicaragua taking the most extreme position in support of ousted President Zelaya. Foreign policy is further hampered by the tendency to make major appointments on the basis of domestic political considerations rather than competency, by the deteriorating international image of the Ortega regime, and by persistent property disputes dating back to the 1979 revolution.

Despite open U.S. efforts to topple the Sandinista regime, formal diplomatic relations were never broken off. The inauguration of President Chamorro ended these tensions, but other issues soon arose. Conservative circles in the

United States opposed the Chamorro administration's working arrangements with the FSLN and made a constant issue of property claims against the government advanced by Nicaraguans living in the United States. Aid and loans were delayed, contacts with the Nicaraguan military were blocked, and investment discouraged. Relations improved somewhat under the Alemán administration. Progress was made in resolving the property issue, and military-to-military contacts were established. The Bolaños administration attempted to improve relations with the United States, even sending troops to Iraq in 2003, but its efforts were handicapped by domestic political turmoil and by the emerging issue of disposal of the surface-to-air missiles. The U.S. openly opposed Ortega in the 2006 elections, but initially relations with the Ortega administration were not hostile. However, the fraud in the 2008 municipal elections, combined with evidence of massive corruption and increased efforts at political repression, has led to increasing conflict.

Nicaraguan governments over the past decade had generally good relations with Europe and with some of the international financial institutions. The Scandinavian nations were especially forthcoming with assistance. Spain and other members of the European Union also provided vital assistance. Hurricane Mitch did produce a new outpouring of assistance, but increased evidence of corruption, the failure of the government to undertake needed economic reforms, and constant political conflict caused nations such as Denmark and Sweden to end aid disbursements, and in 2008 the European Union likewise suspended its assistance. Nicaragua's decision to recognize the tiny Russian puppet states taken from Georgia then further damaged relations with Europe.

Relations with other Central American states were very tense during the Sandinista years. Nicaragua's support for regional revolutionary movements created constant problems with El Salvador. The contras' use of Honduras and Costa Rica as bases for actions against the Sandinistas led to a series of bitter clashes that, in the Honduran case, frequently spilled over the border. For a time fears of a regional war were quite real. Ultimately, however, a regional initiative, led by Costa Rican President Oscar Arias, helped resolve the tensions and end the contra war.

Relations under the Chamorro and Bolaños administrations were largely quiet. Many of the refugees returned home, and the emphasis was on rebuilding regional cooperation rather than preparing for armed conflict. Regional presidents met frequently, and fears of regional war vanished.

Under the Alemán administration a series of border disputes with both Costa Rica and Honduras, combined with Nicaraguan anger over Honduran recognition of Colombia's claim to disputed areas in the Caribbean, produced renewed tensions, which the Bolaños administration was unable to resolve. In addition, Nicaragua's continued economic crisis has provided a major obstacle to regional growth and development. Under Ortega, relations with Honduras and El Salvador improved as those nations moved more to the left, but the Honduran crisis over the ouster of President Zelaya has undone much of this.

An Uncertain Future

Nicaragua's future, at best, is uncertain. Although there seems little danger of a return to the open violence of previous decades, both common and organized criminal activity is at near-record levels, and the Ortega administration is increasingly inclined to use force against its opponents. Politics remain mired in bitter conflicts, reflecting both personal rivalries and past disputes. The population seems increasingly cynical about the entire process, as they see little hope offered by any party and believe corruption and extreme partisanship will continue to be the norm. The nation's reservoir of international sympathy and goodwill, generated by the events of the 1970s and 1980s and reinforced by the impact of Hurricane Mitch, seems exhausted, and both the United States and the European Union have suspended most assistance. Social conditions are terrible, poverty is endemic, much of the infrastructure is inadequate and worn out, and both human and financial capital tend to seek foreign prospects. The global economic recession of 2009 has also significantly reduced remittances—a vital element of the economy.

However, Nicaragua is not without important assets. Rural areas are generally not overpopulated, and the nation has some of the best soils in the hemisphere. Its geographic position offers several advantages, especially if a project to improve traffic to the Atlantic via the San Juan River reaches fruition. International contacts forged in the past two decades, along with the considerable resources of the Nicaraguan Diaspora, notably those in Miami, are significant potential assets.

The situation is far from hopeless, but the key will be in developing a credible, competent political leadership concerned more with national well-being than with personal aggrandizement. Unfortunately, the nation has little tradition of such leadership, and the most likely prospect seems to be continued suffering and turmoil for the bulk of the population.

Suggestions for Further Reading

Literature on Nicaragua is extensive, but much of that produced in recent decades is highly partisan and of limited value. There has also been a sharp drop-off in scholarly work on Nicaragua in the past decade. The following are recommended as starting points for a fuller understanding of Nicaragua's past and present.

Booth, John A. *The End and the Beginning: The Nicaraguan Revolution*. Boulder, CO: Westview Press, 1985.

Christian, Shirley. *Revolution in the Family*. New York: Vintage, 1986.

Close, David. *Nicaragua: The Chamorro Years*. Boulder, CO: Lynne Rienner, 1999.

Colburn, Forrest D. *Post-Revolutionary Nicaragua*. Berkeley and Los Angeles: University of California Press, 1986.

Gilbert, Dennis. *Sandinistas: The Party and the Revolution*. Malden, MA: Basil Blackwell, 1988.

Kirk, John M. *Politics and the Catholic Church in Nicaragua*. Gainesville: University Press of Florida, 1992.

Lean, Sharon, "The Presidential and Parliamentary Elections in Nicaragua, November, 2006," *Electoral Studies* 26 (December 2007): 828–32.

Macaulay, Neill. *The Sandino Affair*. Durham, NC: Duke University Press, 1985.

Merrill, Tim L., ed. *Nicaragua: A Country Study*. Washington, D.C.: Government Printing Office, 1994.

Millett, Richard. *Guardians of the Dynasty*. New York: Orbis, 1977.

Pastor, Robert. *Condemned to Repetition: The United States and Nicaragua*. Princeton, NJ: Princeton University Press, 1987.

Seligson, Mitchell, and John Booth, eds. *Elections and Democracy in Central America Revisited*. Pittsburgh, PA: University of Pittsburgh Press, 1995.

Spalding, Rose. *Capitalists and Revolution in Nicaragua: Opposition and Accommodation, 1979–1993*. Chapel Hill: University of North Carolina Press, 1995.

Walter, Knut. *The Regime of Anastasio Somoza, 1936–1956*. Chapel Hill: University of North Carolina Press, 1993.

El Salvador

Civil War to Uncivil Peace

Tommie Sue Montgomery and Christine J. Wade

> Today I am your president. But on June 1, you will be my president.
> —PRESIDENT ANTONIO SACA TO PRESIDENT-ELECT MAURICIO FUNES, MARCH 16, 2009

These deceptively simple words summarized the culmination of a long, tortuous journey toward democracy in a country that has endured, since Spaniards first arrived in 1522, the intentional violence of a political system whose leaders were more committed to maintaining themselves in power than to addressing the profound socioeconomic needs of the population. The decade of the 1990s into the new century, however, witnessed unprecedented efforts, following eleven years of civil war, to establish a competitive and honest electoral system, a functioning judiciary, an apolitical military, a civilian police force—in short, an open, democratic political system.

It was, however, an imperfect peace, characterized by excessive social violence, inequality, poverty, corruption, and political polarization. For twenty years—from 1989 to 2009—the Nationalist Republican Alliance (ARENA), a right-wing party founded in 1982, dominated Salvadoran politics, winning four successive presidential elections. Its main rival after the 1992 peace accords that ended the civil war was the former revolutionary organization–turned legal political party, the Farabundo Martí Front for National Liberation (FMLN).

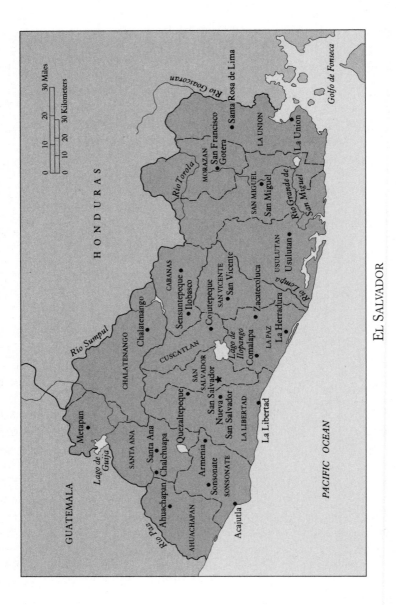

EL SALVADOR

The FMLN enjoyed electoral success at the local level and in National Assembly races, but it could not capture the big prize: the presidency—until 2009. The selection of Mauricio Funes, a well-known former television political talk-show host, appealed not only to the FMLN's base, but also to many Salvadorans tired of two decades of neoliberal economic policies, uncontrolled urban violence, and an inability to develop social policies aimed at helping the 48 percent of Salvadorans who remained mired in poverty.

Funes's election with a clear majority signaled a maturation of the Salvadoran political process and political culture. The next challenge, of course, would be to govern and to address the profound socio-economic problems confronting the country. In this dramatic transition, symbolized by the peaceful transfer of power from a right-wing to a left-wing government, El Salvador offers a model of how to move from war to peace, how to create (however imperfect) democratic processes, and how to change the political culture of a country.

Background

Geography

El Salvador is the only country in Central America without an "Atlantic coast"—or, more accurately, a Caribbean coast. About the size of Massachusetts (21,040 square kilometers) and lying east to west, it is bordered by Honduras on the north, Guatemala on the west, and the Gulf of Fonseca (on the other side of which lies Nicaragua) on the east. From the black volcanic sand of the flat Pacific coast, to the necklace of volcanoes that dot the landscape from west to east and the volcanic lakes in between, to the mountains in the north, El Salvador is a country of dramatic contrasts. Its tropical climate, only ten degrees north of the equator, means that it enjoys two seasons: wet (May–October) and dry (November–April). In the rainy season the country is a lush green, and the rest of the year it is brown and arid. These conditions have been exacerbated over the last half century by increasing deforestation, which has contributed to appalling erosion and a decline in arable land. From 1990 to 1995 El Salvador's deforestation rate was the highest in Central America at 3.3 percent.[1] From 2000 to 2005 El Salvador's natural forested area continued to decline. The impact was magnified by devastating earthquakes in January and February 2001, which resulted in landslides that wiped out entire neighborhoods. In 2005 only 26 percent of El Salvador's territory remained permanent pastures, 8 percent were permanent crops (mostly coffee and sugar cane), and 31 percent arable land.

History

Until the end of the twentieth century the history of El Salvador could be understood in terms of an interlocking and interacting series of phenomena that took shape during the three hundred years after the Spanish conquest in the 1520s and continued beyond independence in the early 1800s.[2] These phenomena may be summarized as follows:

1. an economic cycle of "booms" and depressions that replayed itself as variations on a theme several times between the sixteenth and nineteenth centuries;
2. dependence on a monocrop economy as the "key to wealth,"[3] leading to dependence on outside markets;
3. exploitation of the labor supply, first the Indians and later the peasants;
4. concentration of the land in the hands of an ever-decreasing number of proprietors;
5. extreme concentration of wealth in a few hands by the late nineteenth century, coupled with the utter deprivation of the overwhelming majority of the population;
6. a laissez-faire economic philosophy and an absolute belief in the sanctity of private property;
7. a classical liberal notion of the purpose of government—to maintain order; and,
8. periodic rebellion by exploited segments of the population against perceived injustices.

These phenomena produced two persistent patterns. First, the distribution of resources was unequal from the beginning and the effects were cumulative as population pressures exacerbated inequities in the extreme. Second, there was always conflict between communal lands and private property, with the latter regularly gaining at the expense of the former.

The earliest colonists in Cuzcatlán, like their countrymen elsewhere in Spanish America, were driven by a desire for instant wealth that could be sent back to Spain as a nest egg (after giving the crown its share) to await the master's return. However, because the land called *Cuzcatlán* by its indigenous inhabitants had few natural resources—unlike Bolivia and Mexico with their rich silver and gold mines—the search for a "key to wealth" began soon after the first Spanish settlement in Villa San Salvador. This search was the first step in a cycle that would repeat itself three times before 1900 and was characterized by

1. discovery of a new crop;
2. rapid development of the crop;
3. a period of great prosperity from the export of the crop;
4. dramatic decline or stagnation;
5. an economic depression during which a frantic search for a replacement crop ensued; and,
6. discovery of a new crop and the beginning of another cycle.

Cacao, which was being cultivated by the Indians when the Spanish arrived—and was usurped and converted into an export crop by the conquerors—was followed by indigo in the eighteenth century and coffee in the nineteenth. Not until the mid-twentieth century would there be any significant effort at crop diversification. As each cycle unfolded, more and more communal land—which was the indigenous pattern of land tenure throughout Latin America—was taken over by the Europeans and turned into private property. The development of a monocrop economy, in which the cycles of development and decline were similar and only the crop changed, had significant consequences for El Salvador's later history.

The decline of cacao in the late seventeenth century and the extended economic depression that followed created a need for the colonials to find a means of survival. This led to development of the *hacienda* system, which was not unlike plantations in the antebellum South in that they were largely self-sufficient. The development of *haciendas* led, in turn, to the creation of new relationships between landowners and indigenous folk or peasants that could be characterized, for the most part, as feudal. These new relationships were established primarily through debt peonage, a means of permanently binding the Indians to a hacienda, usually by tricking them into a debt they could not repay. Another dependent relationship was sharecropping, in which the peasants either gave part of the harvest from their small plots or worked several days a week for the *patrono*.

The expansion of haciendas in the eighteenth century, which grew in number with each succeeding depression, had the added effect of concentrating land in a decreasing number of hands, primarily through usurpation of communal lands without compensation to the former owners. Meanwhile, the *hacendados* (land owners) exercised increasingly firm control over the political life of the colony by the late eighteenth century, establishing a pattern of economic and political control that would continue for 150 years.

This pattern of land concentration and crop choice had other effects. The indigo and coffee cycles, which provided three months' employment, caused off-season migration of men looking for work. Women largely stayed put and birth rates outside marriage became the highest in the region—59 percent in El Salvador compared with 49 and 24 percent in Guatemala and Costa Rica, respectively, in the 1920s. Other social costs included extreme malnutrition and rampant alcoholism; in 1918 liquor consumption produced 25 percent of public revenue. The emphasis on a monocrop economy produced, from the 1500s onward, a need to import foodstuffs, including basic grains. Although the landowners and small middle class could afford to pay for the imported goods, the peasantry could not. As a result, sorghum, which was used as fodder in Guatemala, was a principal food grain in El Salvador. Finally, the usurpation of land led, during the colonial period, to periodic indigenous revolts that grew in size and number after independence. A major revolt occurred in 1832 in central El Salvador and lasted a year until its indigenous leader, Anastacio Aquino, was captured, shot, decapitated, and had his head publicly displayed as a warning to other would-be rebels. The unrest in the countryside required the creation of local and then state "security forces," which were, from the beginning, in the pay of the landowners and always at their beck and call.

The struggle for independence in El Salvador coincided with movements elsewhere in Central America during the second decade of the nineteenth century. Growing popular demonstrations in support of independence were joined by political leaders; in 1814 one demonstration was led by San Salvador's mayor, who organized and armed his people with what, by 1980, would be called "popular arms"—rocks, machetes, and the like. In the 1820s a newly independent Mexico, looking to assert its hegemony over the region, twice invaded El Salvador and twice was driven out. In July 1823 the Federal Republic of Central America was created by the five former Central American colonies, and a year later Manuel José Arce, a Salvadoran, was elected its first president. This experiment lasted for fifteen years, then broke apart in the wake of a liberal-conservative struggle[4] that was exacerbated by regional economic woes—the beginning of the end of the indigo cycle. The desire for some sort of Central American union, however, survived as part of the regional political culture and would reemerge in the late twentieth century in the forms of the Central American Common Market and the Central American Parliament.

Political Culture

The principles on which the republic was founded were those of classical liberalism—namely, that the role of the state was to maintain order, and economic policy was strictly laissez-faire with the sanctity of private property its guiding principle. There were differences in emphasis between those who stressed economic themes of the liberal creed and others who stressed political themes like free speech. All agreed, however, on the basic policies that would shape the Salvadoran nation: encouragement of coffee production (which replaced indigo), construction of railroads to the ports, elimination of communal lands, laws against vagrancy that permitted the state to force peasants to work for hacendados at low wages, and repression of rural unrest. From the latter part of the nineteenth century into the early twentieth century most Salvadoran presidents were both generals and major coffee growers; they shared this ideology and brooked no resistance to it.

The 1886 constitution guaranteed that the liberals' policies would be pursued without obstacle. It established a secular state, decentralized state authority by allowing for the popular election of municipal authorities, and confirmed the inviolability of private property. The notion that the state has some responsibility for the health, education, and general well-being of the people it governs was not a part of Salvadoran political culture. For example, the idea of collecting taxes to pay for roads, sewers, and schools was not on the radar screen of the Salvadoran elite—even into the late twentieth century. These notions, as we shall see, continue to struggle for legitimacy in the political discourse of the country.

The problem of dealing with irksome peasants who periodically rebelled against their patronos was solved by employing private armies for which the patronos paid. Elements of these armies would become the Rural Police and the Mounted Police, created by decrees in 1884 and 1889, respectively, in the western coffee growing departments. An 1895 decree extended these two forces over the entire country, and the Rural Police eventually became the National Police. In 1912 the National Guard was created and trained by officers from Spain. Designed for the countryside, it was intended to eliminate the hacendados' private armies and their excesses. Within a few years, however, the Guard gained a reputation for being the "most cruel, most barbaric" security force.[5] A third security force, the Treasury Police (*Policía de Hacienda*), was created in 1936.

A national army was created in the late 1850s because El Salvador was living in fear of invasion from Guatemala. The army's attention was directed to defense of the national territory, while the task of maintaining order was left to the three "security forces." Not until the last quarter of the twentieth century would the army be used to control the people—a role that only ended with the 1991 peace accords.

By the late 1920s coffee was central to the economic life of the country. Production of *el grano de oro* (the gold grain) expanded rapidly while other crops and industries stagnated. This, coupled with growing business acumen and sophistication, moved the national economy from depression to boom.

Coffee averaged between 75 and 80 percent of all exports between 1900 and 1922, then soared to 92 percent during the remainder of the 1920s. Similarly, land use increased dramatically. In 1919 70,000 hectares were planted in coffee; by 1932 the figure had increased 34 percent to 106,000 hectares.[6]

Meanwhile, the average Salvadoran's living conditions deteriorated further. In a biting commentary El Salvador's most eloquent social critic, Alberto Masferrer, declared:

> The coffee industry . . . has already occupied the high lands and is now descending to the valleys, displacing corn, rice, and beans. It is extended like the *conquistador*, spreading hunger and misery, reducing the former proprietors to the worst conditions. . . . Although it is possible to prove mathematically that these changes make the country richer, in fact they mean death. It is true that the costs of importing corn are small in relation to the benefits of the export of coffee, but do they give the imported grain to the poor? Or do they make them pay for it? Is the income of the *campesino* who has lost his land, adequate to provide corn, rice, beans, clothes, medicine, doctors, etc.? So, what good does it do to make money from the sale of coffee when it leaves so many people in misery?[7]

The hacendados were recalcitrant. In a letter to *Patria*, a newspaper that Masferrer edited, one wrote: "Why must one be bothered with planting corn . . . when one can plant coffee with little effort or risk? The idle lands around the volcanoes must be utilized. If the owners of these lands do not want to make use of them, they must sell them to those who would make them productive."[8] Many insisted that the peasants were being treated fairly—but Masferrer warned that "as long as justice is not the same for everyone, none of us is safe."[9] A more prescient observation came from James Hill, an immigrant hacendado: "The working people have meetings on Sundays and become excited. They say: 'We dig the holes for the trees, clean out the weeds, pick the trees, harvest the coffee. Who, then, earns the money? We earn it!' . . . Yes, there will be problems one of these days."[10]

Those "problems" erupted five years later—the result of the socioeconomic conditions described above; an increasingly militant labor union movement, which had begun as World War I ended; and a flirtation with authentic electoral democracy at the beginning of the 1930s that ended in a coup d'état, stolen local elections, a disastrous peasant uprising that left thirty thousand dead, and a political division of labor: the army assumed control of the state for the next sixty years while the oligarchy continued to control the economy.[11]

Ethnicity, Social and Class Structure, and Interest Groups

Ethnic Patterns

As land ownership became increasingly concentrated in fewer hands during the eighteenth and nineteenth centuries, the ethnic composition of the country also changed. At the beginning of the seventeenth century the country was about 85 percent indigenous, 10 percent *mestizo,* and 5 percent white. To this were added four to five thousand African slaves who were imported to work the cacao plantations as the indigenous population died out. That the country was well on its way to becoming a mestizo nation was evident by 1780, and that it had become one was clear thirty years later. By the twentieth century the slaves, who were freed in 1823, had been assimilated and officially ceased to exist as a separate racial group.[12] At the beginning of the twenty-first century El Salvador's six million inhabitants were 94 percent mestizo, 5 percent indigenous, and 1 percent white.

Social and Class Structure

El Salvador has produced great wealth since the conquest, yet 48 percent of its people live below the poverty line, with 19 percent of those surviving on US$1 per day. Poverty in rural areas is more acute, where close to 50 percent live below the poverty line. A "poor family" is defined by the Salvadoran Ministry of the Economy as one whose income is below the level that would finance the purchase of the "expanded food basket" (housing, food, education, health, and miscellaneous). The fifteen years following the peace accords saw a doubling of its cost along with a doubling of the minimum urban salary. Unfortunately, this meant an increased gap between the two. In 1992 the "basket" cost US$350 and the minimum salary was US$93—a difference of US$257. By 2000 the cost of the basket was US$519; the minimum salary was US$145. In 2007 the basket had risen to US$706 while the minimum salary rose to US$183—a difference of US$523.[13] Obviously, many Salvadorans had difficulty meeting their basic needs. Between January 2007 and January 2009 the cost of the food basket had increased about 20 percent.

With a per capita income in 2008 of US$3,916, El Salvador ranked second highest in Central America. Although El Salvador's human development indicators improved in recent years, much work remained. In 2005 for every one thousand live births, twenty-three infants died, and the death rate for children under five was twenty-seven children per thousand live births. In

2004 only 69 percent of students reached grade five and 53 percent were enrolled in secondary education. Fewer than 50 percent of the population completes six years of school, 33 percent complete the ninth grade, and 20 percent finish high school. The literacy rate, at 86 percent nationwide and 78 percent in the countryside, is one of the lowest in Latin America. Like poverty, inequality has persisted in El Salvador despite overall growth during the past decade. In 2002 the richest 10 percent of the population consumed 38.8 percent of national income, while the poorest 10 percent consumed a mere 0.7 percent.[14] El Salvador's Gini coefficient was 52.4.[15]

Remittances

The income information not reflected in these data are the remittances sent home by Salvadorans living and working abroad. In 2005 more than 1.5 million Salvadorans lived in the United States, and nearly 250,000 of them were under Temporary Protected Status (TPS), a special program that allowed individuals from specified countries to register to work legally in the U.S. In 1991 US$790 million was sent to families in El Salvador; by 2004 that figure had increased to US$2.5 billion, or 17 percent of El Salvador's GDP. In 2008 remittances totaled US$3.8 billion, nearly 20 percent of the GDP. Approximately one quarter of the Salvadoran population received remittances, which were commonly used for housing and consumer goods such as vehicles, televisions, and VCRs as well as food and clothing. Furthermore, they kept the lid on a social pressure cooker. The impact of remittances on inequality in El Salvador was striking. In 2005 the Gini coefficient for those who received remittances was .44, as opposed to .52 for nonrecipients. Without remittances, unhappiness with government inaction could have led to major social unrest. Remittances, then, not only increased the purchasing power of many Salvadorans, they also contributed to social stability during relatively low periods of growth.

The Churches and Social Change

The Second Vatican Council (1962) and the 1968 bishops' conference at Medellín, Colombia, precipitated profound changes in the Latin American Catholic Church. Vatican II defined the Church as a "community of equals" while Medellín called on the Church to denounce injustice, defend the oppressed, and establish a "preferential option for the poor"—providing what many viewed as the basis for liberation theology. The development of Christian Base Communities (*Comunidades Eclesiales de Base*, CEB) in the late 1960s and 1970s throughout the region was a reflection of and a means of teaching these tenets to people for whom the Church had been little more than a place for receiving the sacraments. In El Salvador the message of social justice offered through CEBs was labeled "Communist" and "subversive" by the right. Between 1972 and 1989 eighteen Catholic priests, one seminary student, one Lutheran minister, three nuns, and a lay worker from the United States were murdered or disappeared for their work in defense of the poor and human rights.

Although he was selected in 1977 by the Vatican for the post of Archbishop because he was thought to be conservative, San Salvador's new archbishop, Oscar Arnulfo Romero, soon became a champion of social justice and called for an end to the violence that was consuming the country. His assassination while delivering mass on March 24, 1980, served as a catalyst for many to join the guerrillas. The murder of three Maryknoll nuns and a lay worker in December reiterated the danger faced by religious workers. After Romero's death dozens more priests and nuns were driven into exile, while a handful continued their ministries in guerrilla-controlled areas. Despite the violence, the Catholic Church, along with the Anglicans and Lutherans, pushed for a negotiated end to the war throughout the 1980s. Ironically, it was this targeted violence against the Church that ultimately helped end the war. On November 16, 1989, the U.S.-trained Atlacatl Batallion entered the grounds of the Jesuit *Universidad Centroamericana "José Simeón Cañas"* and killed six Jesuit professors, including the rector, their housekeeper, and her daughter. The murders forced the United States to suspend military aid, and El Salvador's new president, Alfredo Cristiani, was forced to the negotiating table.

Many of the CEBs disbanded by the violence have not recovered, and a change in archbishops has hindered their regrowth. The 1994 appointment of Spanish-born Fernando Sáenz Lacalle, a member of Opus Dei, following the death of Romero's successor, Archbishop Arturo Rivera Damas, was seen as a blow to human rights and social justice. Sáenz LaCalle's contention that, like Marx, liberation theology was dead, signaled a return of the church to a pre-Vatican II sacramentalist role. In December 2008 José Luis Escobar Alas was appointed to replace Sáenz LaCalle as Archbishop. The appointment overlooked Msgr. Gregorio Rosa Chávez, the auxiliary bishop of San Salvador for twenty-five years, who was, perhaps, the most respected figure in the Church in El Salvador. Escobar Alas, however, shared many of Sáenz LaCalle's positions, including his outspoken positions against mining and gay marriage.

Evangelicals came to play an increasingly important role in politics. The evangelical movement, which gained momentum during the war, represented a conservative social counterpoint to the Catholic lay community. Powerful figures, such as Edgar López Bertrand ("Brother Toby") of the Baptist Biblical Tabernacle Friends of Israel, drew considerable crowds to their services. They also had increasing political clout. President Tony Saca, himself an evangelical protestant, invited Brother Toby to deliver the prayer at his inauguration.

Presidential candidates for the 2008 elections, both Catholic, aggressively courted evangelical congregations, which broke for ARENA in 2004. The general dissatisfaction with twenty years of ARENA policies persuaded some to vote for the FMLN, despite pleas from Brother Toby.[16]

Political Parties and Elections[17]

Political parties did not emerge in El Salvador until the 1920s. Until that time the presidency was passed around among members of the oligarchy. The first modern party was the Communist Party (*Partido Comunista de El Salvador*, PCS), which was founded during a period of political liberalization in the late 1920s by Augustín Farabundo Martí, the educated son of a mestizo landowner. The party focused its organizing in southwestern El Salvador and participated in the January 1932 municipal and Assembly elections. The government's unwillingness to recognize PCS gains at the local level contributed directly to the uprising later that month. Another left-leaning party, the Salvadoran Labor Party, had won the 1931 presidential election, but its candidate, Arturo Araujo, a progressive oligarch, was toppled in a coup d'état a month before the local elections. The coup and the uprising brought Araujo's vice president, General Maximiliano Hernández Martínez, to power. The PCS was banned after the uprising, and for the next thirteen years the *Pro-Patria* (Pro-Fatherland) National Party, a personalist party created by Martínez, became the official—and only—political party allowed. Martínez's excesses led to his overthrow in 1944, the first of five coups that would be attempted by dissident elements in the army over the next thirty-five years. The official party changed names several times, finally becoming the National Conciliation Party (*Partido de Conciliacion Nacional*, PCN) in 1961. Regardless of name, the official party dominated elections until 1982, ensuring that its candidate, always an army colonel or general, was elected president.

Meanwhile, a political opening in the early 1960s—promoted by the Alliance for Progress and an aggressive, strongly prodemocratic U.S. Ambassador, Murat Williams—led to the creation of several opposition parties, most notably the Christian Democrats (*Partido Demócrata Christiano*, PDC; a social democratic party, the Revolutionary National Movement (MNR); and the Nationalist Democratic Union (UDN), which was the PCS's legal front. The Christian Democrats won increasing numbers of seats in the Assembly during the 1960s followed by the mayoralty of the three largest cities, including San Salvador, in 1968. These gains, together with smaller gains by other opposition parties, presented a growing challenge to the PCN. However, as Stephen Webre observed in his study of the PDC, the logical flaw in this opening of political space was that it "encouraged an active opposition but, by definition, forbade that opposition to come to power."[18] This reality was borne out by the 1972 presidential elections, in which a civilian coalition comprised of the PDC, MNR, and UDN was denied electoral victory by the army.

This event led many Salvadorans to conclude that electoral politics would get them nowhere, and so they opted for a revolutionary alternative that included political (mass, grassroots organizing) and military (armed struggle) dimensions. During the 1970s five revolutionary organizations, which had their roots in peasant uprisings of the previous century, in labor organizations of the 1920s, and in the PCS, began working among urban laborers and peasants. Divided over ideology and strategy for a decade, the five came together in the Farabundo Martí National Liberation Front (*Frente Farabundo Martí para la Liberación Nacional*, FMLN) in October 1980. In January 1981 the FMLN initiated military operations that would plunge El Salvador into eleven years of civil war.

The last coup d'état of the twentieth century occurred in October 1979. Its goal was to remove military conservatives, derail the revolutionary movement, and institute long-overdue socioeconomic reforms. A number of prominent civilians who had been leaders of opposition parties and were forced into exile after 1972 returned to participate in the new government. It soon became clear, however, that a group of extremely conservative officers had displaced the progressive coup leaders, and two months after the coup most of the civilians resigned. The United States encouraged the Christian Democrats to join the military in a new government. This, however, split the party as some leaders—notably José Napoleón Duarte, the former mayor and exiled presidential candidate—accepted the military's offer while others left the party and created the Popular Social Christian Movement (MPSC), which allied itself with other center-left opposition parties, labor unions, and nongovernmental organizations (NGOs) to create the Democratic Revolutionary Front (FDR) in the spring of 1980. The FDR formed a political alliance with the FMLN and served as its international political voice for much of the next decade.

The United States, fearing another revolution in Central America, increased its involvement via a two-track policy. Politically, reforms and elections were emphasized; militarily, the Salvadoran armed forces were trained in counterinsurgency. Meanwhile, in May 1979 the generals informed their old allies in the oligarchy that they had to begin taking care of themselves.[19] This had two effects. One was the creation of paramilitary death squads, funded by wealthy members of the oligarchy in collaboration with sympathetic elements in the armed forces. The second was the creation in 1981 by some of these same oligarchs of their own political party, the Nationalist Republican Alliance (*Alianza Nacionalista Republicana*, ARENA).

Following Ronald Reagan's assumption of the presidency in 1981, elections were identified as the means of putting El Salvador on the road to democracy and robbing the revolutionary movement of any remaining raison d'être. Elections for a Constituent Assembly that would write a new constitution were held in 1982, and to everyone's shock, ARENA won a plurality of the seats and effective control of the Assembly. Only intervention by the U.S. Ambassador prevented ARENA from electing its founder, Roberto D'Aubuisson—a man closely tied to the death squads and identified ten years later by the United Nations' Truth Commission as the intellectual author of Archbishop Oscar Romero's assassination in March 1980—as interim president of the country. He had to settle for president of the Assembly.

In the 1984 presidential elections the man who had been denied in 1972, José Napoleón Duarte, defeated D'Aubuisson. This and subsequent elections in the next decade—for the Legislative Assembly in 1985, 1988, and 1991 and for president in 1989—provided a "democratic government" that rarely exhibited the conditions of a functioning democracy: freedom of speech, the media, and party organization; freedom for interest groups; the absence of state-sponsored terror; the absence of fear and coercion among the population; and subordination of the military to civilian rule. Indeed, the armed forces, formally removed from power, continued to wield effective political control of the country. Duarte, elected on a platform of economic reform and peace negotiations with the FMLN, delivered neither while presiding over one of the most corrupt governments in Salvadoran history. The PDC, rent by internal squabbles, split again in 1988, and they then lost the 1989 presidential election to a center-right ARENA candidate, Alfredo Cristiani, who successfully negotiated an end to the civil war.

The electoral process, nevertheless, had unintended and unanticipated consequences: It opened political space that had been closed by state repression in the early 1980s. New political parties emerged, split, and faded. Furthermore, NGOs and existing labor unions began to organize and demand better wages, working conditions, economic reforms, and peace. ARENA and the PDC tried to co-opt or organize parts of this movement, and those who resisted were labeled "FMLN fronts" and suffered renewed repression. MPSC and MNR leaders then returned from exile to begin testing the political waters. One of the earliest among these was Dr. Héctor Silva, who in 1997 and again in 2000 would be elected mayor of San Salvador in a coalition led by the FMLN.

At the presidential level El Salvador experienced two elections between the end of the war and the end of the century. The 1994 elections were hyperbolically dubbed the "elections of the century" because they were the first to occur after the war's end, because the FMLN was participating for the first time as a legal party, and because a president (who serves for five years), Assembly deputies, and mayors (who serve three year terms), were being elected. The results gave lie to the "common wisdom" of the previous decade that the

FMLN had no popular support. Its candidate, Rubén Zamora, forced a runoff with ARENA's candidate, Armando Calderón Sol, who ultimately won. Meanwhile the FMLN won twenty-one seats in the Legislative Assembly and thirteen mayoralties.

By the time of the next local elections in 1997 growing unhappiness across the country with ARENA's economic policies was reflected at the ballot box. The number of ARENA deputies dropped from 39 to 28 and the number of municipalities it controlled declined from 207 to 162. The FMLN, meanwhile, increased its Assembly seats to 27 and its mayoralties to 48. These results led the former rebels as well as many political pundits to predict that, with a strong candidate in 1999, the FMLN had a real chance of winning the presidency. It was not to be, however. The FMLN irretrievably damaged itself in a bitter internecine fight over who would be its presidential candidate. The August 1998 party nominating convention began in a spirit of unity, but it deteriorated into chaos as a relatively small group of radicals without credentials invaded the convention and drowned out the speech of the moderates' candidate, San Salvador mayor Héctor Silva. A month later the FMLN nominated a former guerrilla, Facundo Guardado, as its candidate. In March 1999 U.S.-educated Francisco Flores was elected president on the ARENA ticket in a landslide.

The widespread assumption following the 1999 election was that the FMLN was too deeply divided to put itself back together. That assessment, however, did not take into account the continuing and growing disenchantment with ARENA, which had been in power for a decade. To almost everyone's surprise, the FMLN came roaring back in the 2000 local elections, virtually matching ARENA's popular vote, winning for the first time more seats in the Assembly than its political nemesis (thirty-one to twenty-nine), and increasing by 30 the number of municipalities it would control for the next three years to 78. ARENA's hold on municipalities continued to decline, dropping to 124.[20] This pattern continued in the 2003 legislative and municipal elections, with the FMLN maintaining its 31 seats in the Assembly while ARENA lost two. The number of municipalities under ARENA governance fell to 113, and the FMLN experienced minimal losses, although it managed to retain the capital. Other parties benefited from ARENA's decline. The PCN gained two Assembly seats and increased its municipalities from 53 to 50 while the center-left *Centro Democrático Unido* (CDU) also enjoyed small gains.

Many believed that the FMLN was on its way to winning the 2004 presidential election. However, the FMLN was again unable to duplicate its electoral successes of the previous four years. Having broken with former San Salvador mayor Héctor Silva, the FMLN nominated former Communist Party leader Shafik Handal as its candidate for president after another turbulent nomination process. ARENA's Antonio (Tony) Elías Saca, a thirty-eight-year-old businessman and former sportscaster, purportedly represented the new face of ARENA. ARENA's campaign war chest dwarfed that of the other parties, as they outspent the FMLN by more than three to one. The campaign was fierce, as ARENA reverted to Cold War rhetoric, labeled Handal a Communist who would turn El Salvador into "another Cuba," and alleged that he supported terrorism. Worse, ARENA claimed, a Handal victory would severely damage relations with the United States and endanger the influx of remittances. The U.S. State Department intervened openly by sending the Assistant Secretary for Latin America to El Salvador to make it clear that his government preferred an ARENA victory, then allowing a White House aide to conduct a telephone interview with the Salvadoran press gathered for the occasion at ARENA's headquarters. It was, in essence, a campaign of fear. Saca soundly defeated Handal in the first round of voting.

After the election long-simmering internal tensions within the FMLN became full-blown arguments over the lessons of their second successive electoral debacle. Handal and his faction—called the "orthodox"—succeeded in maintaining control of the party apparatus at a November 2004 party congress despite widespread sentiment favoring their removal. By June 2005 some of the party's most prominent "reformers" left the FMLN and created a new party, whose name they took from their history: the *Frente Democrático Revolucionario* (Democratic Revolutionary Front, FDR).

The 2006 elections signaled something of a comeback for ARENA, whose electoral fortunes in municipal and legislative races had declined since 1994. The return of ARENA's traditional base to the ballot box in 2004, Saca's popularity, and divisions within the FMLN helped ARENA at the municipal level. ARENA increased its mayoralties from 113 to 147 while the FMLN declined from 74 to 59. The FMLN narrowly held onto San Salvador by a margin of about forty votes; the race was called only after protests erupted accusing the TSE of fraud. ARENA's gains came at the expense of its allies; the PCN won 39 municipalities, down from 52, and the PDC won 14, down from 19. While ARENA appeared to reverse its decline in the Legislative Assembly, winning 34 seats, so did the FMLN. Following defections in 2005, the FMLN held only 29 seats in the Assembly; in 2006 it won 32. Some speculated that the death of Shafik Handal shortly before the election may have given the party a small boost from nostalgia. The three smaller parties, the CD, PDC, and PCN all lost seats—a testament to the country's growing political polarization.

The 2009 elections were the first time since 1994 that elections for all offices would be held during the same year. However, the TSE implemented reforms that separated polling days for the legislative and municipal and presidential elections by more than a month. It was a contentious campaign, pitting ARENA's former PNC director Rodrigo Avila against popular television journalist Mauricio Funes for the FMLN. Twenty years of failed ARENA policies left it vulnerable to the FMLN's moderate candidate. As such, ARENA returned to the fear campaign of 2004, avowing that an FMLN victory would hand El Salvador over to the "Communists" and threaten the flow of remittances. Funes, who had not been a guerrilla in the FMLN, skillfully navigated El Salvador's highly polarized political terrain, eschewing traditional FMLN policies in favor of more centrist positions. Unlike Handal, Funes vowed not to reverse dollarization or withdraw from CAFTA. Although a few U.S. Congressmen proclaimed the necessity of preventing an FMLN victory, the new Obama administration vowed to work with the victorious party.

The January legislative and municipal elections promised to be a preview of the presidential elections. The FMLN won 35 seats, ARENA 32, PCN 11, PDC five, CD one, and FDR none. The FMLN also increased its share of mayoralties from 58 to 96 (75 on its own and 21 in coalitions), although it lost San Salvador. ARENA, which won San Salvador, suffered a number of losses, dropping from 148 to 122 municipalities. The PCN and PDC lost 14 and 6 municipalities respectively. On the center-left the CD won two municipalities in addition to those in coalition with the FMLN. Following the legislative and municipal elections, the PDC and PCN withdrew their presidential candidates and lent their support to ARENA. Most of the FDR, which failed to win any seats in the legislative assembly, supported the FMLN.[21]

Funes defeated Avila, 51 to 48 percent. On June 1, 2009, Tony Saca transferred power to Mauricio Funes, the first transfer of power from one party to another since the signing of the peace accords. During his first month in office Funes reestablished diplomatic ties with Cuba, announced an US$11.5 million plan to improve the national police, and established a commission to investigate incidences of corruption under past administrations. In the aftermath of the election former president Alfredo Cristiani, who initiated ARENA's dominance in 1989, returned to head the party—a clear sign that the party was regrouping.

Post-War Government and Public Policy

The FMLN's conversion from revolutionary organization to legal political party was the result of peace negotiations that occurred between 1989 and the end of 1991. Leading a country that was demonstrably fatigued by war, President Cristiani pledged in his June 1989 inaugural to pursue peace negotiations with the FMLN. The flaw was that ARENA and the U.S. government, now headed by President George H. W. Bush, who wanted to extract the United States from Central America as expeditiously as possible, assumed that the only thing to negotiate with the FMLN was its surrender. The government's failure to negotiate in good faith and several assassinations of leftist political leaders in the fall of 1989 convinced the FMLN that it had to demonstrate its power. The most significant offensive since 1981, launched on November 11, 1989, brought the war to San Salvador for the first time. It revealed both the FMLN's inability to provoke a general uprising and the army's incompetence. It also exposed the bankruptcy of U.S. policy: Despite nine years of training and over US$2 billion in U.S. military aid, the army could not rout the FMLN from the capital. The army's murder of the Jesuits had an impact at least as great as the offensive itself. Together they marked the beginning of the end of the war.

In early 1990 the United Nations, at the request of both the government and the FMLN, initiated several months of shuttle diplomacy that resulted, by April, in an agreement to negotiate an end to the war. In July the first significant agreement, on human rights, was reached. This would lead, exactly one year later, to the establishment of the United Nations Observation and Verification Mission (ONUSAL), which opened with a human rights observation team that operated throughout the country—six months before the end of the war. Government balking in late 1990 led to another, smaller FMLN offensive, and thereafter the negotiations proceeded to a successful conclusion on December 31, 1991.

The Chapultepec accords, so named for the castle in Mexico City where they were signed, sought to deal with the fundamental causes of the war by ending the armed conflict as quickly as possible by promoting democratization, guaranteeing absolute respect for human rights, and reunifying Salvadoran society. These objectives were unprecedented; no previous civil war had ended with an agreement not simply to stop shooting but to restructure society. The accords established a precise calendar for implementation during the cease-fire period that was to end October 15. They mandated demilitarization, including halving the size of the Armed Forces, eliminating the state security forces and the FMLN's guerrilla army; legalizing the FMLN as a political party; amending the constitution; reforming the electoral and judicial systems; settling the land distribution issue, one of the root causes of the war; and establishing independent commissions to identify those responsible for major human rights abuses and to purge the army of its most serious human rights violators.

To the credit of both sides the cease-fire was never broken. Despite difficulties, some of which threatened to derail the peace process at times, ONUSAL, with occasional help from several friendly embassies (Spain, Mexico, Venezuela, Colombia, and the United States), was able to keep the process moving forward. By 1993 a new police force, the National Civilian Police (*Policía Nacional Civil*, PNC) had replaced the old security forces; a new governmental institution, the National Council for Human Rights (*Procuraduría de Derechos Humanos*, PDH), was created where citizens could bring their complaints about governmental abuses; the army was reduced in size and in its barracks with all its special units disbanded and its officer corps purged; the virtually nonfunctioning judicial system was experiencing the first steps toward reform; the FMLN was a legal political party; and perhaps most significantly, there was a sea change in El Salvador's political culture: It was no longer acceptable to kill people for political reasons.

All these positive developments, however, took place in a context of effective political authoritarianism (albeit authoritarianism under continual assault by the peace accords themselves and the new actors on the political stage) and, during the Calderón Sol administration, weak presidential leadership. Calderón was a model of indecision, whose failure to follow through on policies he originally embraced caused frustration across the political spectrum. For example, Calderón promised to implement a system of property taxes, a much more progressive tax than the IVA (ad valorem)—which, at 13 percent on all purchases, hit the poor and working class much harder than the upper classes. Nothing happened. More significantly—because this was tied to compliance with the Peace Accords—he promised electoral reform, a dire need in view of the incompetence and partisanship that characterized the work of the Supreme Electoral Tribunal (TSE) in preparation for the 1994 elections. Calderón appointed a presidential commission that produced a series of recommendations that he publicly embraced and submitted to the Assembly. There they were buried by his own party.

The election of Francisco Flores brought hope of greater competence and flexibility in the presidential palace. At the end of his first six months in office, however, the Central American University's (*Universidad Centroamericana*, UCA) year-end analysis noted that Flores had

> promised to change the ways of doing politics and said he was the friend of dialogue and citizen participation. . . . But the new president was not everything he said he was. . . . [He] was hard and intransigent, even more than his predecessor. Far from infusing change between politics and society, he exacerbated lamentable and dangerous attitudes: negative toward dialogue with social sectors and civic participation, and lost to the value of *concertación* (collaboration and agreement) in policy making.[22]

Nowhere was this more apparent than Flores's response to a strike by the Social Security Institute Union (STISSS) in November 1999. Objecting to government plans to privatize the entire health system and the firing of 221 workers (in a grossly understaffed and inefficient system), physicians, technicians, and hospital workers shut down hospitals and clinics, literally occupying them in the style of traditional Latin American strikes. President Flores refused to negotiate and threatened to order the PNC to remove the strikers by force. The union refused to budge on its demands, San Salvador mayor Silva's effort to mediate failed, and the strike continued until thirty-six hours before the March 2000 elections, when a marathon session resulted in an agreement to return to work. The government had already changed its privatization plan to awarding concessions (contracts) for service, and the strikers agreed to let the Supreme Court of Justice decide the fate of the 221 dismissed workers. The eleventh-hour resolution was intended to reflect positively on the government and ARENA, and negatively on the FMLN, which had supported the workers' demands. As a strategy, it failed. A second major health care strike erupted in October 2002 over the privatization of services. The strike ended nine months later following government assurances that the health care system would not be privatized. Whether this is the end of the health care privatization battle remains to be seen.

Flores's commitment to the neoliberal model was unwavering, despite significant public opposition to the policies. In January 2001 Flores's Law of Monetary Integration, which dollarized the economy, was passed by the legislature. Several public opinion surveys indicated that a majority of Salvadorans opposed dollarization and believed it had a negative effect on their pocketbook. The policy has had a disproportionate impact on the standard of living of the poor, where "rounding up" prices from the conversion became a common practice among vendors in the informal sector.[23] Thus, inflation for the poor was higher than for the general population.

In addition to the increasing unrest in the public sector the Flores government was also confronted with growing public insecurity. In 1999 El Salvador's murder rate was 127 per 100,000—the highest in the hemisphere. Flores cited the influx of criminal street gangs from the United States, such as *Mara Salvatrucha* and MS–18, as the reason for El Salvador's insecurity. Flores's *mano dura* legislation targeted gang activity, but it did little to address the growing problem of social violence.

ARENA's fourth consecutive president, Antonio Elías Saca, promised to promote social and economic security. Shortly after taking office, Saca imposed *super mano dura* in a further effort to crack down on gang violence. Although *mano dura* and its successor have been very popular with the public, they had little effect on stemming the violence.[24] Indeed, the judicial system refused to cooperate with Saca's policy of arresting and jailing young men who sport the identifying tattoos of gang members, arguing that individuals must be arrested for doing something, not for how they look. By July 2005—more than a year after *super mano dura* went into effect—El Salvador's murder rate climbed to twelve per day, nearly double that of the previous year. The government continued to blame gangs for a majority of the homicides, but the level of impunity in the country made any statistics dubious. Saca also sought to control social protest through the 2006 Special Anti-Terrorism Law (*Ley Especial contra Actos de Terrorismo*). The law criminalized common means of protest, including demonstrations and marches. More than a dozen prominent social activists were arrested in the town of Suchitoto in July 2007 en route to the town to protest water privatization. Although the charges were ultimately dropped, the arrests revealed the government's intention to quash its opposition.

Saca inherited a deteriorating economy from Flores. His solution for the country's economic malaise relied heavily on El Salvador's relationship with the United States. Saca's first priority was to guarantee the renewal of TPS status for Salvadorans in the United States in order to ensure the continued flow of remittances. The renewal of TPS was, in part, secured by El Salvador's troop commitment to the U.S.-led war in Iraq.[25] Additionally, by El Salvador's commitment to the Central American Free Trade Agreement (CAFTA) he hoped to bolster El Salvador's growing *maquila* industry, which was fast becoming the centerpiece of the economy. In addition to this outward-oriented economic policy, Saca also announced the creation of a multipoint poverty reduction program. Part of the program, *Red Solidaria*, entailed a plan to reduce extreme poverty by one-half, targeting some of El Salvador's poorest communities by providing nutrition, education, and health care. The plan targeted twenty thousand families its first year, growing to one hundred thousand families within the following four years. Although the relative success of these programs is difficult to assess at the time of this writing, it was the first comprehensive antipoverty program launched by the government.

Women

Women's participation in public life grew from near zero in the 1970s to an increasing number of women in government a decade later. During the Cristiani administration, two of his most competent ministers, Planning and Education, were women. Two women were members of the FMLN's negotiating team at the peace talks. In 1999 the FMLN's vice presidential nominee was a woman, and in 2004 the vice presidential nominees of ARENA and the CDU-PDC coalition tickets were women. The ARENA victory in 2004 gave El Salvador its first female vice president. Neither ARENA nor the FMLN had women on their presidential or vice presidential tickets in 2009. After the 2003 elections, seventeen of 262 mayors were women, down from twenty-nine after 2000. All but six belonged to ARENA, four FMLN, and two PCN. In 2009, however, once again twenty-nine women were elected mayors. In the Legislative Assembly sixteen of eighty-four deputies were women, an increase of two from 2006 and ten from 2000.

In preparation for the 1994 elections a broad coalition of women's organizations hammered out an agenda called *Mujeres '94* (Women '94), which it asked every party to adopt as part of its platform. Only the FMLN agreed, thanks to the pressure of its women members. The FMLN also adopted a rule that one-third of all its candidates for office be women. This was a compromise; the women had pushed for 50 percent. By the mid-1990s women's organizations had formulated legislative bills to guarantee workers' rights in the *maquiladoras*; make rape a public crime; no longer require a witness (other than the victim) to the rape in order to press charges; require men to prove they are NOT the father of a child; and ensure inclusion of articles that protect women in the new penal code. None of these issues were on the national agenda five years earlier. A new education law guaranteed equal access for girls; barred discrimination based on gender, and proscribed sexist stereotypes in textbooks. Another issue absent from the national agenda at the end of the war was violence against women. Before the end of the decade the issue was receiving attention in the major newspapers—although too often it was accompanied by gratuitously exploitative photographs. The ban against abortion, which provides for no exceptions, is the most stringent in the region. Beyond simply banning the procedure, El Salvador's law criminalizes it, imposing harsh jail sentences for both the provider and woman. The ban has led to the rise of "back alley" abortions, mostly among poor women.[26]

Post-War Economic Policy

During the 1990s significant disagreement emerged among the economic elite over economic policy as well as between important parts of the elite and the government.[27] El Salvador's once monolithic oligarchy disappeared. A generation earlier the monolith had two parts: the traditional agricultural sector whose wealth was exclusively in the land—coffee, cotton, and/or sugar cane—and the landowners who had diversified into finance and industry. By the middle of the decade there were four clearly identifiable sectors: financial, commercial, industrial, and agricultural. Agriculture, which dominated the Salvadoran economy into the 1980s—contributing 43 percent of the GDP in 1978, for example—became relatively insignificant in economic terms, commanding only 11 percent of the GDP in 2003—far behind remittances. By 2004 once-dominant coffee was only 7 percent of export earnings. In each of the first three sectors there was a small subsector that controlled the overwhelming majority of the capital within that sector. The result was not only intersector conflicts but intrasectional disputes, as smaller players battled to stay in the game.

Making matters worse, the Calderón government substituted sloganeering about "modernization of the state" and "privatization" for a coherent economic plan that could generate confidence for industrial investors—El Salvador's only hope for a stable economic future. After floundering for two years, in January 1995 Treasury Minister Manuel Enrique Hinds produced a five-point scheme that brought down on the government the wrath of the commercial and industrial sectors. The plan's components were (1) reducing import taxes to zero; (2) establishing a fixed and convertible exchange rate; (3) "modernization" understood as (a) deregulation, (b) decentralization, (c) privatization of all goods and services administered by the state where possible and socially acceptable, and (d) administrative and financial restructuring; (4) increasing progressively public expenditures for social programs such as education and health up to 50 percent of the national budget in 1999; and (5) increasing the value added tax (IVA) from 10 to 14 percent. Eliminating import taxes meant El Salvador would be flooded with cheap imports against which local producers could not compete. Raising the IVA was viewed by parts of the private sector and the political opposition as having a profoundly negative—and regressive—impact on consumers.

The firestorm forced the government to back down for a time and completely scrap the first two points. Between 1995 and 1997, however, other parts of this plan were implemented piecemeal. Several of the bills requiring parliamentary approval were rammed through the Legislative Assembly by ARENA, often without following the Assembly's own procedures for hearings and debate. In practice, however, "decentralization" of power from the central government to the municipalities meant "deconcentration"—the opening of central government offices in selected municipalities. "Privatization" meant selling off national utilities at prices well below their real value. And the increase in the IVA—to 13 percent, a compromise—outraged voters. Indeed, support for this measure by ARENA and the Democratic Party (PD, a splinter of the FMLN) cost both parties votes in the March 1997 elections. The pieces, however, were less than the sum of their parts and did not a coherent economic policy make.

The sale of the state-owned telephone and electric companies did not bring the much-touted efficiencies and reduced cost. On the contrary, as the UCA's weekly news analysis, *Proceso*, noted at the end of 1999, "many of the irregularities that existed when the state administered the telephone and electricity services were repeated point by point in the private providers." Free of state regulation, *Proceso* commented, these companies arbitrarily fixed prices and treated customers dismissively. This view was supported by a September 1999 survey; 95 percent of the respondents said that privatization of the phone company had not translated into lower prices; 77 percent said the quality of service had not improved, and 80 percent complained about access to installation. Even higher levels of unhappiness were found in relation to the delivery of electricity.[28] Still, the Flores government remained committed to privatizing the public sector.

By 2000, after eleven years of neoliberal policies and World Bank and Inter-American Development Bank–mandated restructuring, El Salvador's economy was in deep trouble. From 1990 to 1995 GDP growth averaged 5 percent, but it slowed during the second half of the decade. By the turn of the century the economy showed no signs of recovery (GDP growth was 3.4 percent in 1999, 2.2 percent in 2002, and 1.8 percent in 2003). Equally significant, that growth was concentrated in very few hands—mostly in the financial sector—and "redistributive policies" was a dirty word in government circles. In its year-end review and analysis *Proceso* noted that neither the Calderón nor Flores governments had "developed policies to achieve an effective modernization of the economy, which implies diversification of production and agricultural exports, as well as a process of industrial reconversion that permits improvement in the competitiveness of that sector."[29] Indeed, industrialization after the war was largely confined to the creation of (mostly Asian-owned) maquiladoras, which, it might be argued, have become the latest "crop" in the economic cycles described earlier.[30]

Inflation complicated the picture for much of the 1990s. Running as high as 19.9 percent in 1992, by 1998 the cumulative inflation rate was 186 percent. By the turn of the century the government had inflation under control, although it continued to exceed growth. In 2003 the annual rate of inflation was 2.5 percent, with less than 2 percent growth. Inflation doubled in 2004 while growth lagged at a mere 1.5 percent. The damage was done. Between December 1991 and August 1999 minimum daily salaries declined from 28.18 to 27.37 Colones.[31] In another measure, the GDP per inhabitant grew dramatically over the decade: from US$1,002 in 1991 to US$2,258 in 2003. Most of that increase, however, was lost to inflation. Further, some price increases disproportionally affected the poor. In late 1996, for example, bus fares increased 50 centavos—about 11 cents. Not much—until one realizes that many people have to take two buses to get to work (no "transfers") and that the increase applied to children attending school as well as to their parents. That 11-cent increase could approach $1.00 per day for a family whose monthly income may be only US$200 to US$250.

Although the GDP increased 4.2 percent in 2006 and 4.7 percent in 2007, it was insufficient to keep pace with the rising cost of living. Despite minimum wage increases for industrial and agricultural workers in 2006, real wages were still lower than their 1996 levels—and before the war. A 20 percent increase in bus fares and 14 percent increase in electricity rates exacerbated the problem. Any economic growth was seemingly imperceptible for most Salvadorans. An IUDOP poll indicated that an overwhelming majority of respondents believed the economy was growing worse and poverty increasing.[32] The global economic recession of 2008–2009, particularly in the United States, had a negative impact on El Salvador. By early 2009, indications were that growth and remittances would stagnate—or worse—decline in the coming year.

Conclusion

In 1992 El Salvador experienced one of the region's most profound political and social transformations. Years of war and violent oppression gave way to peace and democracy in one of the United Nations' most successful peacekeeping endeavors. However, it was the political will of the actors in El Salvador that paved the road to peace. Philosophical changes in the ruling class and FMLN leadership, submission of the military to civilian rule, and respect for human rights were vital prerequisites for the transition to democracy. In 1994 El Salvador held the first truly democratic elections in its history, bringing the FMLN into the electoral fold. The 2000 and 2003 elections for mayors and members of the Legislative Assembly brought significant gains for the FMLN and losses for ARENA. The seventy-four FMLN-controlled municipalities—including seven of fourteen departmental (provincial) capitals—meant that at the local level the former rebels governed well over 50 percent of the Salvadoran population. Still, the FMLN was unable to woo voters in the 2004 presidential election, and ARENA continued to dominate Salvadoran presidential politics. Further, the FMLN's internal woes raised concerns about whether it would be able to hold onto its Assembly seats and town halls.

Despite the problems described above, El Salvador's prospects for stable democratic governance continued to be positive. However, the socioeconomic horizon was cloudy. Despite significant growth in the early 1990s, fifteen years later the gap between rich and poor was still vast and government rhetoric on the issue had not been matched by a coherent policy to address it. The government's neoliberal agenda caused increasing public dissatisfaction, and there appeared to be few alternative ideas on how to reactivate the slumping economy. The country's immense dependency on remittances was increasingly apparent, as people replaced coffee as El Salvador's most profitable export. Declining poverty and inequality were attributed to remittances rather than concerted economic and social policies. Social violence replaced political violence as the number one social problem, and in 2009 the PNC was still ill-equipped and insufficiently trained to control it. Corruption and impunity infiltrated government institutions charged with protecting the population. Growing dissatisfaction with ARENA's policies was increasingly reflected at the ballot box in local and Assembly elections. Then, the 2009 elections were a watershed moment for El Salvador. The FMLN's presidential victory was the first successful transfer of power during peace, and Mauricio Funes became the country's first leftist president. The expectations for the new government were immense, as were the challenges facing it.

Suggestions for Further Reading

Boyce, James K., ed. *Economic Policy for Building Peace: The Lesson of El Salvador.* Boulder, CO: Lynne Rienner, 1996.

Ladutke, Larry. *Freedom of Expression in El Salvador: The Struggle for Human Rights and Democracy.* Jefferson, NC: MacFarland, 2004.

Montgomery, Tommie Sue. *Revolution in El Salvador: Origins and Evolution.* Boulder, CO: Westview Press, 1995.

Popkin, Margaret. *Peace Without Justice: Obstacles to Building Rule of Law in El Salvador.* University Park: The Pennsylvania State University Press, 2000.

Stanley, William. *The Protection Racket State: Elite Politics, Military Extortion, and Civil War in El Salvador.* Philadelphia, PA: Temple University Press, 1996.

Wood, Elizabeth Jean. *Insurgent Collective Action and Civil War In El Salvador.* New York: Cambridge University Press, 2003.

Notes

1. "The January 13, 2001 Earthquake in El Salvador: Socioeconomic and Environmental Impact," ECLAC, accessed at www.bvsde.paho.org/bvsade/i/fulltext/earthquake/earthquake.pdf.

2. This section and the next on political culture is drawn from *Revolution in El Salvador: From Civil Strife to Civil Peace* (Boulder, CO: Westview Press, 1995), chap. 1, 25–28, 30–32.

3. Murdo J. MacLeod, *Spanish Central America: A Socioeconomic History 1520–1720* (Berkeley: University of California Press, 1973), 49. The concept of a repeating economic cycle, discussed below, is drawn from MacLeod.

4. Latin American conservatives and liberals bear little resemblance to liberals and conservatives in the Anglo-American political tradition. Conservatives were aristocrats and monarchists who wished to keep church and state tied closely together and who were dedicated to preserving the church's wealth and privileges. Liberals were anticlerical and often antireligious. They were inclined to support free trade while conservatives preferred to erect tariff barriers to protect local textile production. Within El Salvador the differences were less than in other countries because the church did not have much wealth that could be confiscated. The liberals succeeded in abolishing monastic orders, establishing civil marriage, and taking some initial steps toward removing education from control by the clergy and creating a state education system.

5. Robert Varney Elam, "Appeal to Arms: The Army and Politics in El Salvador 1931–1964" (Ph.D. dissertation, University of New Mexico, 1968), 9.

6. Max P. Brannon, *El Salvador: Esquema estadística de la vida nacional* [Statistical outline of national life] (San Salvador: n.p., 1936), 22–24. By 1950 there were 115,429 hectares, or 75 percent of the total land, under cultivation; in 1961, 139,000 hectares, or 87 percent of the total. Eduardo Colindres, *Fundamentos económicos de la burguesía salvadoreña* [Economic Fundamentals of the Salvadoran Bourgeoisie] (San Salvador: UCA Editores, 1978), 72.

7. "La crisis del maíz" [The corn crisis], *Patria*, January 18, 1929.

8. *Patria*, January 4, 1929.

9. "Como anda la justicia en esta San Salvador" [How justice operates in San Salvador], *Patria*, November 30, 1928.

10. Arthur Ruhl, *The Central Americans* (New York: C. Scribner, 1928), 206.

11. How did El Salvador escape becoming another "banana republic" like Guatemala and Honduras? According to Dr. David Reyes-Guerra, who as a young engineer employed by the United Fruit Company in Guatemala in the early 1950s read exchanges of letters from the 1930s between UFCo and Salvadoran president General Martínez, Martínez refused to give UFCo entrée. Said Dr. Reyes-Guerra, "That's why there are no bananas in El Salvador!" Conversation with David Reyes-Guerra, July 21, 2005, San Salvador.

12. Blacks were officially barred from living in El Salvador for many years, although this broke down in the 1980s as African American diplomats and military trainers were posted to the U.S. Embassy and U.S. Military Group, respectively. Other blacks came as journalists, human rights workers, and staff members of nongovernmental organizations and the United Nations. Still, racism is an ugly fact, particularly among the white (European) elite. In the early 1990s, for example, a very senior Salvadoran political official informed a senior official of the UN peacemaking mission (ONUSAL) that one of his aides, a Jamaican political officer (and a woman) was not welcome at their meetings.

The African heritage of many Salvadorans is, however, apparent in a stroll down any street, especially in the capital. There seems to be no societal discrimination because of this. Rather, discrimination stems more from class than ethnic background.

13. "Impacto diferenciado de los salaries y los precios en el costo de la canasta básica y del mercado." www.cdc.org.sv, March 2008.

14. United Nations Development Program, Human Development Report 2004, Table 14. Accessed at http://hdr.undp.org/reports/global/2004/pdf/.

15. The GINI Index measures inequality of income distribution on a scale of 1 (perfect equality) to 100 (perfect inequality).

16. "Evangelicals Key to Salvadoran Elections," *Christian Science Monitor*, March 13, 2009. Accessed at www.csmonitor.com/2009/0314/p07s01-woam.html.

17. Portions of this section are drawn from Tommie Sue Montgomery, "El Salvador," in *Political Parties of the Americas 1980s to 1990s*, ed. Charles Ameringer (Westport, CT: Greenwood Press, 1992), 281–301.

18. Stephen Webre, *José Napoleón Duarte and the Christian Democratic Party in Salvadoran Politics 1960–1972* (Baton Rouge: Louisiana State University Press, 1979), 181.

19. Laurie Becklund, "Death Squads: Deadly 'Other War,'" *Los Angeles Times*, December 18, 1983.

20. Throughout this period the Christian Democrats continued to fracture, becoming less of a viable party with each split. In 2000 the PDC won only five seats in the Assembly and eighteen municipalities.

21. Salvadoran election law requires that parties receive a minimum of 3 percent of the national vote to be officially registered. As such, the FDR will cease to exist in the aftermath of the 2009 elections.

22. "Balance Social," *Proceso*, no. 884, December 30, 1999. Accessed at www.uca.edu.sv/publica//proceso/proc884.html.

23. Marcia Towers and Silvia Borzutzky "The Socioeconomic Implications of Dollarization in El Salvador," *Latin American Politics and Society* 46, no. 3 (Autumn 2004): 29–54.

24. According to one University Public Opinion Institute poll, 88 percent agreed with *mano dura*. See "2003: The Supremacy of Politics," *Proceso*, no. 1079, December 24, 2003.

25. By 2005 El Salvador was the only Latin American country with troops still in Iraq.

26. "Pro-Life Nation," *New York Times*, April 9, 2006. Accessed at www.nytimes.com/2006/04/09/magazine/09abortion.html?pagewanted=1&_r=2.

27. This section is adapted from Tommie Sue Montgomery, "Constructing Democracy in El Salvador," *Current History*, February 1997, 62–63.

28. "Balance Social," *Proceso*, no. 884, December 30, 1999.

29. "Balance económico," *Proceso*, no. 884. December 30, 1999. Accessed at www.uca.edu.sv/publica//proceso/proc844.html.

30. Like coffee, the *maquilas* offer cheap labor (US$4 per day) and poor working conditions. Unlike coffee, however, the workforce is largely female and the *maquilas* are mostly foreign-owned.

31. Ibid. In the late 1990s the Colon was stable at 8.8 to the dollar.

32. IUDOP, "Los salvadoreños evalúan el cuarto año de gobierno de Antonio Saca."

21

Guatemala

Democracy by Default

Dwight Wilson

In the 2007 Guatemalan presidential race the social democratic candidate for president, Álvaro Colom Caballeros, won a runoff election to become the fifth democratically elected president since a transition to civilian government in 1986. During this time the presidential term of office was interrupted only when President Jorge Serrano Elías was forced to resign after attempting to overthrow his own government and assume dictatorial powers. More than twenty years of upholding the principle of the democratic election of government seems to give every indication that democratic procedure has become institutionalized and durable. Given this fact, we may presume further that a consolidated liberal democracy is in the making.

After more than two decades of watchful waiting, however, it has become apparent that things are not so straightforward in Guatemala. Transitions to democracy can go in different directions: consolidated liberal democracy or a democratically elected government without the same respect for the rule of law, individual rights, and limitations on government power normally associated with liberalism. Although the situation of Guatemala has improved markedly in the last several decades, lawlessness and insecurity are the norm in Guatemala and faith in democratic institutions to solve the country's problems is not widespread. Rather than the consolidation of liberal democracy

GUATEMALA

and its enthusiastic embrace by the Guatemalan citizenry, it appears more that democracy in Guatemala has been adopted by default.

History

The conquistador Pedro de Alvarado arrived in the western highlands of modern Guatemala in 1524 leading an expedition of a few hundred Spaniards and an auxiliary army of recently defeated Aztecs. Whereas the Aztecs in Mexico were united under Tenochtitlán, the Mayans lived in independent and squabbling city-states. Alvarado walked in on a war between the Quiché and Cakchiquel Indians that divided the cities into competing alliances. The conquest required separate attention for each of the decentralized cities; Indians in the northern forests of Petén beat back the invading Spanish until the 1690s. Eventually, Hispanization was proceeded by conversion to Catholicism, the priestly hierarchy and rituals of which mirrored indigenous religion. Uniquely in Central America, though, the majority Indian population stayed largely autonomous and unassimilated, a fact only beginning to change in recent generations.

The area eventually developed into the Kingdom of Guatemala, the seat of colonial government for all Central America, which stretched from Chiapas to Costa Rica. It was the spiritual, cultural, and economic heart of the isthmus as well, but next to Mexico and Peru, the colonial jewels in the royal crown, Guatemala was a backwater. The precious metals prized by Spain dried up early there, and the colony languished in relative obscurity, supplying the monarchy with mahogany, cacao, and dyes. Eighteenth-century revolutions in Europe, however—political and intellectual—could not escape notice even in the furthest corners of the empire.

Independence and Liberal Dictatorship

The independence movements agitating for separation from Spain in Mexico and South America were greeted in Central America with confusion and indecision, with many municipalities acting separately from the central government in Guatemala. Most Central Americans resolved in favor of separation from Spain, but the question remained whether to form a separate country or append to Mexico. In the end Mexico itself decided in favor of the second alternative, swallowing Guatemala as a part of the short-lived Empire of Augustín Iturbide. After he was deposed Central Americans went their own way, and Guatemala declared their sovereignty (minus Chiapas, which stuck with Mexico).

Initially the former kingdom stayed together, proclaiming itself the United Provinces of Central America in 1823. Under Liberal leadership the government set out to erase the Hispanic past in order to fashion the new nation according to Enlightenment ideals. Hopes ran high that its location and prospects for an interoceanic canal would propel the federation into the ranks of the wealthiest nations on earth. In fact, the factional strife between anticlerical Liberals and traditionalist Conservatives that burned across the continent doomed the arrangement from the outset. The federation was pulled apart by dissension, jealousies, and rebellions, and by 1837 it was a dead letter.

As the federation crumbled in civil war, a popular backlash against the Liberal assault on tradition filled the vacuum. In Guatemala a rustic and illiterate conservative *caudillo*, José Rafael Carrera, swept into power in 1840 at the head of a ragged army of devout Catholic Indians with the approval of the Church and landowning elite. Ruling until his death in 1865, Carrera dismantled the Liberal reforms, reinstituted the paternalistic fusion of church and state from the colonial regime, and oversaw the hegemony of Conservatism in Central America.

A Liberal counteroffensive across the isthmus closely followed Carrera's death. Another strongman came to rule Guatemala as an autocrat, this time in the name of democracy and constitutionalism rather than religion. Justo Rufino Barrios led the revolt that turned out the floundering Conservative regime, and he ruled with a stern hand beginning in 1873. He persistently denounced the tyranny of lifetime presidency while ruling until his death in 1885. Barrios believed firmly in order and progress and, following the ascendant Liberal program, did what he could to thrust Guatemala into the modern world of science and capitalism. He sponsored Liberal dictators in neighboring republics who nevertheless resisted his unilateral decree reuniting the federation. He was killed in action in El Salvador while attempting to enforce his decision.

Liberal presidents reigned supreme following the Barrios years. Many were elected, and most served their country until they died or were forcibly ejected. Executives enjoyed wide latitude, and constitutional niceties were easily amended to extend presidential terms and powers, making the presidency essentially an elective dictatorship. The Liberal reforms rotated the membership of the ruling class—the Catholic Church was the big loser—but did not drastically change living conditions for the multitudes of Guatemalans.

The orthodoxy of the Liberal era dictated that the government hand stay out of the free exchange of goods and services except to ensure an attractive environment for commerce and investment. Agricultural export (mainly coffee) was encouraged as the road to development, and Indian communal lands were put on the market to encourage production. Land-holding planters held unchallenged dominion over peasants. Landowners and the state frowned upon (and severely punished) labor organization, which was practically unknown. Continuing the *encomienda* tradition, labor laws ensured a continuing source of forced work for export agriculture.

The last of the long-term Liberal dictatorships was that of General Jorge Ubico y Castañeda. Taking power in 1931, he oversaw the modernization of national infrastructure, professionalized the military, encouraged commerce, and expanded the bureaucracy. In doing so he also let loose a new and implacable political force: a frustrated and politically minded middle class. During his third term in office Ubico managed to alienate much of the citizenry, whose condition had been made worse by the deplorable economic conditions of the Great Depression. Student protests in June of 1944 sparked a chain reaction of popular unrest that led to the general's resignation that same month and an uprising in October that ousted the military from the government altogether.

The Revolutionary Decade

The democratic revolution of 1944 lasted for ten years and came to be known as the Decade of Spring. The movement that installed the new regime was a modern one in which the mobilized middle classes cast out the outdated nineteenth century–style despotism. The budding popular sectors demanded an opening of the political sphere and participation in the affairs of state—a new development in Guatemala. Until now, the multitudes had been unorganized and pliant, requiring periodic, forceful correction. The revolution opened unprecedented avenues of communication and participation for the excluded classes. Pluralism and liberal democracy could not so painlessly penetrate traditional Guatemala, however. The revolutionary period polarized Guatemalan society over progressive reforms, and all the while the threat of violence, a familiar political tool, loomed darkly.

Juan José Arévalo, a "spiritual socialist" known as the philosopher of the revolution, headed the first administration from 1945 to 1951. His moderately progressive government created channels of participation for the previously disenfranchised—a kind of New Deal for Guatemala. A new constitution at last gave popular organizations freedom to organize and strike, ended forced labor in the countryside, encouraged the assimilation of the Indians into national life (which was fiercely resisted by some Indians), and instituted a social security system. The relatively mild changes upset the traditional balance of interests, but Arévalo carefully sidestepped any radical impulses, such as serious agrarian reform, that could have sent conservative forces over the edge. He failed, however, to establish a coherent party that would secure the future of the revolution after his tenure, and the following administration did not imitate his tact.

Jacobo Arbenz Guzmán, a colonel who took part in the revolution, was elected in 1950 after his chief opponent, another revolutionary leader, met an untimely end at the hands of assassins. The Arbenz regime sought to further level the playing field for Indian peasants and urban laborers, funneled state resources to education and health, and broached the taboo subject of redistributing the highly concentrated land. In this way Arbenz collected no few enemies among conservative forces in the military, business, and the Catholic Church.

The increasingly radical Arbenz regime also alarmed an Eisenhower administration on the lookout for communist infiltration in the West. Arbenz stepped up fiery nationalist rhetoric toward the United States, looked benignly on the participation of communists in the government and labor unions, expropriated land owned by the United Fruit Company (the largest landholder in the country), and imported weapons from Czechoslovakia—the arms merchant of the Soviet bloc—to arm peasant and labor groups. Convinced Arbenz was intent on bolting to the Soviets, Eisenhower could swallow no more and threw his lot in with the armed opposition. The CIA lent financial and material support to disaffected members of the military led by Colonel Carlos Castillo Armas that was plotting to overthrow Arbenz.

The coup came on June 18, 1954. After ten days of an ineffectual defense, Arbenz gave up the fight. The covert assistance of the CIA has been hailed as a smashing success against creeping international communism in some quarters, and in others it is remembered bitterly as the imperialist overthrow of a popularly elected reformer. Though the long civil war that would follow had its immediate catalyst in these events, social divisions and oppression had planted the seeds of discord long before the Cold War.

The Counterinsurgency State

The post-1954 military government was confronted with a disintegrating society. Officers viewed the military as the last bastion of order compelled to take extraordinary measures to defend against chaos and communism. So as to restore a semblance of order, the Armas and succeeding regimes set out to forcibly quell the activity of popular organizations let loose during the revolution. Economic indicators were upbeat in the 1960s and 1970s, contributing to middle- and upper-class satisfaction, but it also fed the restiveness of peasant and labor sectors anxious for the right to organize and share the wealth. Military governors allied with civilian technocrats who attempted to manage economic and social diversification while also guarding security as a revolutionary crisis gripped all of Central America.

A variety of leftist insurgents, including communists and Indian peasant groups, took up arms around the country beginning in the early 1960s. The fighting waxed and waned with the strength of the guerrillas, who were twice nearly crushed—in the late 1960s and again in the early 1980s—only to regroup later and continue their campaign of attrition. Four of the principal groups banded together in 1982 to form the Guatemalan National Revolutionary Unity (URNG). The state nearly ceded control of the use of violence as guerrillas staged kidnappings and sabotaged infrastructure while the military blinked at private militias assassinating suspected subversives. The country had descended into intense polarization and civil war.

The dirty war reached its low point in the early 1980s during the rule of General Efraín Ríos Montt, a Protestant evangelical with a penchant for messianic imagery. During Ríos Montt's eighteen-month dictatorship he implemented his vision for securing peace and development, a plan of *frijoles y fusiles* (beans and guns) that combined populist redistributive measures with a merciless counterinsurgency campaign. The toll of the internecine war fell most heavily on the Indian population, thus provoking charges of a systematic campaign of genocide that invited international attention and sparked political fires in the United States and Europe.

Transition to Democracy

An elongated process of democratic transition began with the promulgation of a new constitution in 1984. Elections in 1985 then ushered in the first civilian government since 1969. The government and URNG only signed peace accords in December of 1996, ending the shooting after thirty-six years and transforming the rebels into electoral campaigners. During the war the military fended off rebellion and social conflict with systematic repression. Now elected civilians try to maintain the integrity of the same fractious nation as disillusionment and discontent seethe. The frustrations of governing provoked President Serrano Elías to attempt a Fujimori-style *autogolpe* in 1993 by illegally suspending the constitution and dismissing the legislature and Supreme Court, a maneuver that cost him the presidency. The fragile democracy seems to lurch from one crisis to the next, but it has nevertheless lived to see successive elections and orderly administrative turnover.

Society and Political Culture

Around thirteen million Guatemalans live in a land of renowned natural splendor that has promised—and delivered—easy riches, but only to a select few colonists, adventurers, and investors. Sixty percent of the population is Indian, situated primarily in the western highlands, speaking twenty-four different languages, and many of whom are ignorant of Spanish. Most people (approximately 80 percent) live in poverty, and the majority of those are Indians. Nearly three million inhabitants crowd the only major urban center, Guatemala City. It is a young country; over 40 percent of its people are younger than fifteen.

The hierarchical system of exploitative labor familiar to most of Latin America characterizes centuries of Guatemalan political and social history. The Spanish adventurers of the sixteenth century coming to the new world on a civilizing and Christianizing crusade (one that might also prove quite profitable) formed the core of a feudal society of landowners and state authorities squeezing labor out of Indians and poor *ladinos* in the hinterland, thus entrenching a strict observance of race and class that persists even now. A corporatist pyramid sent orders down and services up, first to the monarch and later to a president. Participation by the masses, when it occurred at all, was usually limited to rubber-stamping preselected candidates in safely mediated elections.

The mixture of blood between Europeans and Indians did not create understanding through living together. Liberal, Conservative, and military regimes varied in their policy approaches toward Indians, but all shared a haughty disdain for the indigenous peoples. Conquerors crusaded to civilize the savage, which was usually limited to promising to Christianize their subjects while pressing them into semislavery. Europeanized ladino elites have also viewed Indians with contempt, but this is mixed with an enthusiasm for assimilation into Guatemalan national society. Curiously, this can be accomplished within a single generation; racial identity is supplied through language and dress rather than genetics. An Indian who picks up Spanish and moves to the city becomes a ladino. Mayan communities have nonetheless demonstrated remarkable resilience in maintaining distinctive cultural patterns, unlike in Mexico and her sister republics where Hispanic hegemony was more complete. Though their cultures are unavoidably modified through synthesis, Indians stayed outside the national structure, identifying with their parochial communities rather than an abstract Guatemala.

The culture of the conquest was particularly strong in the old colonial capital. Strong currents of personalism, patrimonialism, militarism, and traditional Catholicism ran deep here and radiated outward to the rest of Central America. Recently, though, currents have shifted, perhaps foreshadowing a striking shift in social and political relationships: Democratic procedure has operated since the 1980s; Indians have continued a trend from the war years of greater organization and participation in national politics; the military has receded from outright domination of the political process; and Catholicism has watched half the churchgoing population embrace Protestantism.

Try as they might to reinforce elite rule and subservience of the lower strata, traditionalists failed to hold the clock still in the twentieth century. As the country diversified and modernized and the economy and government expanded to serve new demands, new groups impatient for their rights were thrown into the political mix. The middle class, the engine of democratization, exploded during the Ubico era, and although the 1944 October Revolution changed the social and political terrain for good, it could not disenfranchise the old powers. Hierarchical, bossist patterns of behavior thus operate side by side with elements of participatory, constitutional democracy.

Political Parties and Interest Groups

Iberian organic corporatism (reinforced by group-centered Indian traditions) has sharply conditioned state-society relations in Guatemala. Accordingly, the Guatemalan state has always kept a watchful eye on social segments, maintaining special laws for the formation and oversight of political parties and interest groups. Independent political opposition and civil society are only solidifying themselves since the rather recent transition to civilian government.

Political parties, usually considered the driving force in political competition, are weakly institutionalized in Guatemala. Without the political space to breathe in an elite-directed despotism, ideological parties offering alternative platforms to voters were scarcely known. The Liberal and Conservative parties that battled for total political domination in the nineteenth century engaged in machine politics, dispensing patronage in return for loyalty. Family and social ties normally determined party membership, and the factions took turns ruthlessly punishing each other when in power. Modern parties, on the other hand, are fluid—a group of erratic coalitions and constantly shifting alliances, often fashioned to serve the personal ambitions of political bosses or military factions, only to fizzle with the death or irrelevance of their leaders.

In the closed political atmosphere of the post-1954 era, parties were subject to severe restrictions that allowed only officially tolerated parties to operate, while the military acted as the power behind the throne. Only candidates representing vying military factions contested the first elections following the coup. Reformist military leaders in 1963 opened the door to a structured multiparty system, thus allowing a carefully managed pluralism. Since the latest constitution took effect, a multitude of new parties and coalitions across the political spectrum has crowded the ballot—including the former armed guerrillas. Most of the main players in the old party system have reorganized or splintered into obscurity. In current elections voters choose from around fifteen parties, many of which will not survive until the next election.

The National Unity of Hope (UNE) has emerged in recent years as the leader among left-leaning parties, earning thirty-five legislative seats in the 2007 elections as well as the presidency. The Grand National Alliance

(GANA) is the largest of the center-right parties, having won the presidential election of 2003 and thirty-seven legislative seats in the 2007 elections. Former dictator Ríos Montt has fared rather well through his political party, the Guatemalan Republican Front (FRG), placing third in the presidential election of 2003.

Given the underdeveloped state of most parties, organized interest groups have offered the most energetic representation for social sectors. Established interest groups are older, better organized, and more stable than most parties. The term "interest group" can be extended to embrace a wide range of sectors, including the old feudalistic corporate bodies as well as newer power contenders such as business, urban labor, and human rights groups. Lobbying in the halls of government is frequent, but because politics was a closed affair among tightly knit elites for so long, many groups, particularly among the popular sectors, have been pushed into confrontational tactics. Rather than orderly, consensus-driven bargaining, competition often assumes a zero-sum character. Groups often resort to direct action over official channels, each threatening to use its own trump card—strikes, lockouts, demonstrations, or coups. Claimants to power might use whatever means at their disposal; the guerrillas, for instance, remade themselves from armed insurgents to a legal political party.

Among prominent interest groups, the Coordinating Committee of Agricultural, Commercial, Industrial, and Financial Associations (CACIF) gives voice to the economic elite that all governments hear; the National Coordination of Peasants' Organizations (CNOC) initiates seizures of uncultivated land; the General Coordination of Guatemalan Workers (CGTG) clashes with employers over pay and working conditions; and the Group for Mutual Support (GAM) publicizes human rights concerns internationally. Insular groups and low social trust contribute to intergroup hostility and the occasional outburst of violence. Pluralism is a brute fact of social life in Guatemala, but it is not a part of public culture.

The State and Government Institutions

Historically reliant on simple force, the state has suffered from low legitimacy, and a lack of resources contributes to low effectiveness. A modern, centralized state structure began to emerge in the Liberal reform period, but many of the significant powers of the state authorities remained outside the definitions provided in the constitution and laws. Strong presidents and military dictators found it easy to give legal sanction to this or that preferred policy option through parliamentary fig leaves, decrees, and constitutional amendments or suspensions. State power hardly projected itself outside the capital, however, so large planters and political bosses acted with impunity in their rural domains. The fact of power has thus traditionally beaten out the rule of law.

Guatemala's constitutions have separated powers as in the tripartite U.S. model, but in practice servile legislatures and judiciaries have respected the Hispanic tradition of strong executives. In addition to the three branches, modern constitutions have created an independent Supreme Electoral Tribunal (TSE) to monitor elections. The unicameral Congress consists of 158 members elected for four-year terms, one quarter of them chosen by proportional representation and the rest by district as is done in the United States. Parties that cannot muster 4 percent of the vote lose their registration and cannot compete in the next election. The president and vice president are also elected to four-year terms without the possibility of reelection.[1]

A Supreme Court of Justice sits at the top of the judicial branch, to which thirteen justices are elected by the Congress for five-year terms. The constitution guarantees the independence of the judiciary, and a special panel acting as a constitutional court exercises judicial review of legislative acts. The courts are weak, though, and are criticized for the appearance of openness to political manipulation and threats.

Few radical changes are evident in the new fundamental law, but there is evidence that democratic practices are becoming more fully institutionalized. Perhaps most dramatically, the military appears satisfied that it need no longer control the political system (the defense minister, a general, negotiated an end to the standoff during Serrano's autogolpe). It has thus accepted deep cuts in its budget and subordinated itself to civilian command. Positive signs, no doubt, but it bears remembering that legal prohibitions have always proved parchment barriers to political participation by the military, and a coup in neighboring Honduras in 2009 clearly showed that the era of military intervention in Central America was not only a phenomenon of the twentieth century.

International Relations and Globalization

As a colony, Guatemala was kept isolated from the world around it, lest exotic ideologies infect a safely Iberian colony. After independence its foreign relations were limited mainly to securing foreign investment and disputing boundaries with neighbors Mexico and Belize.[2] Just as the old feudal order crumbled away under the forces of economic and social modernization, Guatemala in the twenty-first century is ineluctably drawn further into a global web of trade, communication, and migration. Further, an international ethos celebrating democracy means that Guatemala must contend with constant scrutiny by foreign governments and international human rights organizations in addition to domestic civil and political groups.

Guatemala's primary international concerns are with regional economic integration and international crime. A glimmer of the old dream of a united Central America shines through in efforts to confront these issues through cooperative regional organizations like the Organization of Central American States (ODECA), the System of Central American Integration (SICA), and the Central American Parliament (PARLACEN). Concrete steps toward integration are modest, though, and skeptics see PARLACEN in particular as a costly talk-shop and harbor for corrupt ex-presidents fleeing justice.[3]

Guatemala has always been deeply sensitive to conditions in the United States, which has at least partly determined the fates of a number of political leaders besides Arbenz. The Guatemalan economy is heavily dependent on aid from the United States, primarily provided through USAID. Assistance is tied to achievement of political and economic reforms aimed at democratic institutionalization and transparent government. Remittances from migrant Guatemalan workers in the United States funnel perhaps US$3 billion yearly into Guatemalan homes (accurate figures are hard to come by)—a desperately needed lifeline in a nation of dire unemployment and poverty.

As have most Latin American governments, successive administrations have pursued economic liberalization and diversification. Free trade agreements govern commerce with the Central American states and Mexico, and Guatemala joined the WTO in 1995. Political and business leaders hope a new free trade agreement passed in 2006, the Dominican Republic-Central American Free Trade Agreement (CAFTA-DR), will reinforce commercial growth, while detractors fear that it will only compound already gross inequalities. The overall economic outlook of the country has improved dramatically in recent years, but the risks of economic integration have been on display during the worldwide financial crisis beginning in 2008. A smaller economy like Guatemala's is particularly vulnerable, as remittances from abroad drop and exports slow.

Improvements in transportation, underresourced authorities, and a central location combine to make Guatemala prime real estate for international drug smugglers on their way to the United States. The government has committed itself to cooperating with the United States to counter the burgeoning drug trade, but smuggling rings have worked themselves thoroughly into Guatemalan society. Just as is the case in neighboring countries, police and military officials tasked with fighting smuggling have themselves been discovered to be cooperating with criminal gangs.

Democracy and Discontent

Though there has been great improvement in the political situation since the worst of the civil war in the 1980s, in some ways there have been few changes for decades. Corruption and crime continue unabated, only adding to the tragically proportioned problems of much of the Guatemalan citizenry. The democratic election of governments has not, of course, been a panacea for problems, with sources so deeply embedded in the social terrain.

Government officials have always engaged in corruption at all levels as a matter of course, and perceptions of graft within the public sector have not been helped by government officials' continued misbehavior. In 2000, for example, President Alfonso Portillo Cabrera solemnly vowed to root out the massive corruption responsible for public contempt for officials. Four years later Portillo dodged corruption charges by absconding to Mexico, only to be returned in 2008 to face the charges in court.

Availability of guns and human desperation fuel an epidemic of violent street crime in both the cities and the country. Armed gangs target foreign tourists for highway holdups and kidnappings. Police have proven inadequate in dealing with the crisis and are often charged with complicity in organized crime. Meanwhile, the new social plague of *maras*—street gangs exported from Los Angeles to El Salvador to Guatemala—stretches the already-thin resources of law enforcement in Guatemala City. The government declared war on the gangs responsible for hundreds of grotesque murders—a war it is ill-equipped to wage. The court system has fecklessly watched the large majority of crimes go unpunished.

Attacks against political activists, assassinations of candidates for public office, and the remobilization of death squads offer sobering reminders that politically motivated violence does not vanish when the military retires from the presidential palace. Indeed, accusations of criminal conspiracy within the highest ranks of government continue even in the era of civilian government. In 2007 the murder of three Salvadoran legislators in Guatemala created a political storm throughout Central America. Suspicions of official involvement only grew, as a series of subsequent murders made even investigating the crime—much less solving it—impossible.

Perceptions of government officials forming an elitist clique are common in Guatemala, further damaging the credibility of the democratic process. Beyond simply lining their own and their friends' pockets, though, the powerful are at times accused of committing the worst sorts of crimes while placing themselves beyond the reach of the law. In 2009, for instance, President Colom came under intense pressure to resign after a video of a murdered lawyer surfaced in which the victim posthumously accused the president of complicity in his own murder. President Colom hotly denied this charge from beyond the grave and vowed to remain in office. Furthermore, Colom's primary competitor in the 2007 presidential election was himself linked in the press to the 1998 murder of a prominent human rights activist, Bishop Juan Gerardi.

The conduct of elections reveals that democratic consolidation does not come easily. Guatemalan elections are not a sham; citizens have a choice among manifold parties, and in large measure their votes are counted and the results respected. As essential as they are, though, elections alone are insufficient for robust, consolidated democracy. Electoral season in Guatemala is often attended by unruly protests, intimidation, and assassinations. The corrosive violence endemic to the nation supplied the principal campaign theme of the elections of 2007, and the elections themselves were marked by an unprecedented wave of bloodshed, with dozens of candidates and other public figures murdered.

Freedom House, an organization that measures civil rights and political freedoms around the world, rates Guatemala as "partly free," a designation that calls attention to the complex character of democracy. Even the freest and fairest elections do not guard against corruption, official impunity, crime, and destitution. All of these permeate Guatemalan society, demonstrating that the democratic political process is not sufficient for a peaceful and prosperous society. Since the transition to democracy we have witnessed two seemingly contradictory trends: the stabilization of electoral democracy and a continuing atmosphere of public crisis.

In spite of radical changes in the last century, and maybe unsurprisingly in this divided country with no history of limited government, liberal democracy has not met with immediate success. Some commitment to the rule of law manifested itself during Serrano's autogolpe, when massive civil condemnation and even military disapproval forced his resignation. Nevertheless, support for democracy as a regime among the public has dropped consistently since then, and in 2008 its support limped in at a dismal 34 percent, the lowest number in Latin America. Confidence in government institutions and political parties in Guatemala is in many cases worse.[4]

Conclusion

Since the end of the civil war an unquestionably more open and participatory political atmosphere has replaced the counterinsurgency state's blanket of oppression, and the military has (for now) surrendered its historical veto power. A transition to procedural democracy has taken place, but commitment to liberal democracy as valuable in itself—essential to democratic consolidation—remains tenuous. In the absence of an alternative that is better able to secure the public good, Guatemalans may simply be democratic by default. After more than two decades of democratic governance, we are confronted with the probability that Guatemala is not undergoing a process of liberal democratic consolidation. Rather than a semiconsolidated liberal democracy, Guatemala is perhaps better described as a consolidated semidemocracy.

Suggestions for Further Reading

Brett, Roderick. *Social Movements, Indigenous Politics, and Democratization in Guatemala, 1985–1996.* Boston: Brill, 2008.

Cullather, Nick. *Secret History: The CIA's Classified Account of its Operations in Guatemala, 1952–1954,* 2nd ed. Stanford, CA: Stanford University Press, 2006.

Garrard-Burnett, Virginia. *Protestantism in Guatemala: Living in the New Jerusalem.* Austin: University of Texas Press, 1998.

Grandin, Greg. *The Blood of Guatemala: A History of Race and Nation.* Durham, NC: Duke University Press, 2000.

Trudeau, Robert H. *Guatemalan Politics: The Popular Struggle for Democracy.* Boulder, CO: Lynne Rienner, 1993.

Woodward, Jr., Ralph Lee. *Central America: A Nation Divided,* 3rd ed. New York: Oxford University Press, 1999.

Yashar, Deborah. *Demanding Democracy: Reform and Reaction in Costa Rica and Guatemala.* Stanford, CA: Stanford University Press, 1997.

Notes

1. Amendments changed the original length of terms served by elected officials, in addition to other changes.

2. The British colony was considered a violation of Spanish and Guatemalan sovereignty. President Serrano surprised—and angered—many when he unilaterally recognized Belize in 1991.

3. Presidents Portillo of Guatemala, Arnoldo Alemán Lacayo of Nicaragua, Mireya Moscoso Rodríguez and Ernesto Pérez Balladares, both of Panama, have all served as deputies to PARLACEN and been subjects of corruption investigations.

4. Figures are from the Latinobarómetro 2008 public opinion survey. Available on the Web at www.latinobarometro.org.

22

Honduras

Democracy in Distress

J. Mark Ruhl

Honduras seems an unlikely candidate for democracy. It is one of the four poorest, least developed countries in the Americas. Throughout most of its history, it has been ruled either by dictatorial political bosses or military strongmen. In spite of the end of formal military rule in the early 1980s, this authoritarian tradition persisted. Behind a democratic facade, the armed forces continued to exercise political control in an anticommunist alliance with the United States. Nevertheless, post–Cold War U.S. policy turned against the military during the 1990s, and an emboldened civil society pressured elected Honduran politicians to challenge the armed forces. As the power of the military receded, Honduras moved in a democratic direction for more than a decade. However, democratic progress was abruptly interrupted in June 2009 when a constitutional crisis that set President Manuel Zelaya against most of the rest of the Honduran civilian political elite, sparked a military coup that removed him from power.

The consolidation of democracy requires that both political elites and the mass public accept the democratic process as legitimate and as "the only game in town." In recent years Honduran civilian and military elites had appeared, at last, to have learned to abide by democratic rules, but the 2009 coup and the illegal actions by President Zelaya that precipitated it proved otherwise.

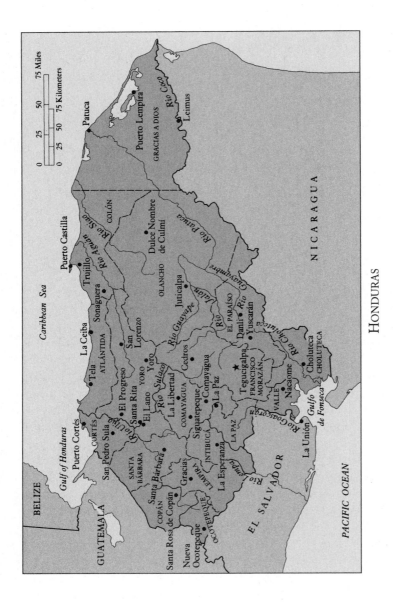

HONDURAS

Most ordinary Hondurans had, by this time, already found democratic governance to be a great disappointment. Neoliberal economic reforms required by international financial institutions have only modestly reduced poverty in a country where more than half of the population still lives below the poverty line. Moreover, widespread embezzlement and bribery have discredited one democratically chosen government after another. Elected leaders also have proven unable to stem the expansion of organized crime and gang violence that places all Hondurans at risk. Because of these failures, the Honduran democratic system has been unable to earn broad, unconditional mass support.

History and Political Culture

Honduras is a mountainous, Pennsylvania-sized country of over seven million people. Its capital Tegucigalpa is located high in the southern mountains, but its economic center is the commercial-industrial city of San Pedro Sula on the tropical north coast. The majority of Hondurans live in rural areas where illiteracy is common (24 percent of Honduran adults are illiterate). Nearly 90 percent of the population is *mestizo*, but there are significant African Honduran concentrations on the north coast and Bay Islands as well as some remaining indigenous communities. Most Hondurans are Roman Catholics, although evangelical Protestants have made important inroads. With a per capita GDP of US$4,400 at purchasing power parity, Honduras is one of Latin America's poorest countries. Its economy depends on remittances from over one million Hondurans working in the United States (US$2.5 billion in 2007) and on the export of bananas, coffee, and simple manufactured products assembled in *maquiladora* factories.

Honduras has been ruled by authoritarian governments for most of its history. However, Honduran rulers and political elites were less repressive of popular sector groups and more willing to institute moderate reforms than their more violent counterparts in neighboring El Salvador, Guatemala, or Nicaragua. One of the reasons for this less confrontational style of elite-mass relations may lie in the fact that no coffee oligarchy ever gained dominance in Honduras. While many powerful families in other Central American countries made their fortunes in coffee, Honduran elites of the late nineteenth and early twentieth centuries focused on small-scale cattle ranching, silver mining ventures, or small banana-export enterprises.[1] None of these activities posed a threat to the peasantry in an underpopulated country where agricultural land was widely available well into the 1930s. Later, when coffee did become important in Honduras, it was grown primarily on small and medium-sized farms. Although there was little friction between peasants and large landowners, constant battles for power among rival landed *caudillos* rendered the nation chronically unstable. These warring political bosses fought over the spoils of office rather than public policy. They promoted a clientelistic political tradition in which constitutional or electoral rules were regularly violated.

At the beginning of the twentieth century the United Fruit Company and other American banana enterprises established large plantations on the sparsely populated north coast. Hondurans who went to work for the banana giants eventually formed the strongest trade union movement in Central America. Although the banana companies exercised considerable leverage over Honduran governments, they could not always rely on public officials to repress striking workers. Stabilizing dictator Tiburcio Carías Andino (1932–1949) of the National Party was a loyal ally of United Fruit in this respect, but leaders of the weaker Liberal Party were closer to labor. Juan Manuel Gálvez (1949–1954), Carías's moderate National Party successor, also negotiated a reasonably equitable settlement to the pivotal banana workers' strike of 1954. In addition, a new, commercial-industrial elite with an important Arab-Honduran ("*Turco*") element that generally backed the banana workers formed on the north coast. [2] This cross-class, reformist coalition provided critical support to social democrat Ramón Villeda Morales, a physician who revitalized the Liberal Party in the 1950s.

The Honduran military also sometimes played a reformist role. Created with U.S. assistance in the 1940s, the armed forces soon became an important political actor independent of the feuding Liberal and National parties. The Honduran military first intervened in politics in 1956 to depose an unpopular provisional president. A military junta organized constituent assembly elections that produced a landslide victory for the long-repressed Liberal opposition. Before relinquishing control, however, the military demanded that the new 1957 constitution guarantee its political autonomy. Future civilian presidents lost the power to select or dismiss the chief of the armed forces or to give orders directly to the military.

Liberal president Villeda Morales (1957–1963) met popular sector demands by introducing an urban social security system, a progressive labor code, and a limited agrarian reform, but his actions upset new agricultural export elites (cotton, beef, and sugar) as well as traditional rural political bosses. Moreover, his creation of a Liberal-led Civil Guard to counterbalance the military incensed the armed forces leadership. When the Liberals' candidate to succeed Villeda threatened to end the military's autonomy, the armed forces formed an alliance with the National Party and staged a preemptive coup in 1963.

Armed forces commander General Oswaldo López Arellano ruled Honduras for almost the entire period from 1963 to 1975. During the López era, peasants organized to demand land reform in response to a land scarcity problem caused by rapid twentieth-century population growth and the post–World War II expansion of commercial agriculture. Although López initially repressed these groups, he later permitted some land invasions. He also evicted about eighty thousand Salvadoran peasants living in Honduras in order to make more land available. During the subsequent 1969 war with El Salvador, Honduran peasants, trade unionists, and the north coast business community rallied around the armed forces despite their previous differences with General López. Shortly thereafter, the air force general broke with the National Party to form a progressive political alliance with these groups. After briefly allowing a bipartisan civilian government to take office in 1971, López returned to power via military coup in late 1972. His new government was populist in orientation, redistributing land to about one-fifth of the landless and land-poor population.

López was compelled to resign the presidency in 1975 after having been accused of taking a bribe from United Brands (formerly United Fruit) in exchange for reducing the export tax on bananas. His more conservative successors, Colonel Juan Melgar Castro (1975–1978) and General Policarpo Paz García (1978–1982), re-allied with the National Party and large landowners. Nonetheless, some land distribution continued, and trade unions remained important political players. The Honduran military's more accommodative stance encouraged popular sector organizations to continue to press their demands within established political channels. While highly repressive, intransigent governments in El Salvador, Nicaragua, and Guatemala drifted into civil war with radicalized popular sector oppositions, Honduras remained stable.

Democratic Elections and Military Dominance in the 1980s

With strong encouragement from the United States, the Honduran armed forces allowed an elected civilian, Liberal Roberto Suazo Córdova, to assume the presidency in 1982. Nonetheless, the military remained the dominant political actor, with its autonomy reaffirmed in a new 1982 constitution. In spite of the democratic veneer, the armed forces grew larger and more powerful than ever as the United States raised military aid to unprecedented levels in return for permission to base anti-Sandinista Nicaraguan guerrillas in Honduras. President Suazo became the junior partner in an unsavory political alliance with right-wing armed forces chief General Gustavo Álvarez Martínez. General Alvarez conducted a small but brutal "dirty war" of torture and assassination against suspected revolutionaries, using the army and police to infiltrate unions, student organizations, and peasant groups. His violent antisubversive campaign was a sharp break with Honduran traditions. Alvarez's arrogance and drive for total control within the armed forces ultimately led to his ouster in an internal military coup in 1984. After his fall from power the military nonetheless continued to maintain its supremacy over civilian authorities throughout the rest of the 1980s. Corruption within the armed forces reached new extremes. Honduras had by then become an important transshipment point in the international narcotics trade; some senior officers became rich by protecting drug trafficking.

Civilian president Suazo (1982–1986) also proved to be a threat to democratization. Like most other Honduran politicians, the former country doctor had embarked on a political career not to pursue policy convictions but to acquire *chamba* (patronage) for his followers as well as wealth and power for himself. Not surprisingly, corruption was widespread in his administration, and short-term personal power calculations determined policy. As his term drew to a close, Suazo used a variety of illegal means in an unsuccessful attempt to stay in power beyond the single presidential term allowed by the constitution. Most of civil society mobilized against him, but the crisis was not resolved until it was mediated by the armed forces.

A Suazo opponent, Liberal José Azcona (1986–1990), emerged victorious from the 1985 presidential contest. Although the new president respected the constitutional limits of his office, his policy achievements were few. He lacked both a coherent plan of action and a secure base of support in the National Congress. Decisions about internal or external security policies remained mostly matters for negotiations between the United States embassy and the Honduran military. [3]

The Decline of the Military

The democratic electoral process Suazo had undermined was strengthened in 1990 when Liberal president Azcona passed the presidential sash to his freely-elected National Party successor Rafael Callejas. This ceremony marked the first democratic turnover of power between competing Honduran political parties in nearly sixty years. During the rest of the decade, the electoral process became institutionalized with regular presidential and legislative elections every four years. Yet, in spite of its free elections and expanded civil and political liberties, Honduras could not be considered a genuine democracy as long as the military continued to be the strongest political actor.

With the end of the Cold War and the Central American civil wars, the United States no longer needed the Honduran military as an ally against communism. [4] Instead, U.S. policymakers began to see the military as an unnecessary obstacle to democratization. By 1993 American military aid had been cut to almost nothing, and the U.S. embassy had become a strident critic of the armed forces. Encouraged by this dramatic reversal in U.S. policy, Honduran human rights organizations, student groups, unions, the Catholic Church, and even many business groups joined forces in an attack on the military's power and prerogatives. The unusual strength and breadth of this anti-military movement persuaded Honduran political party leaders to challenge the military on a range of issues. Mounting internal and external pressures forced conservative President Callejas (1990–1994) to take action. In 1992 he appointed the nation's first human rights commissioner, who issued a report implicating the armed forces in the disappearances of the 1980s' dirty war. Callejas also appointed an Ad Hoc Commission for Institutional Reform headed by Archbishop Oscar Andrés Rodríguez that recommended that the corrupt investigative arm of the military-controlled national police be replaced by a civilian unit. These developments as well as an avalanche of press revelations about military corruption and other criminal activity placed the once-unassailable armed forces on the defensive.

The political decline of the military accelerated under Liberals Carlos Roberto Reina (1994–1998) and Carlos Flores Facussé (1998–2002). Reina instituted the Ad Hoc Commission's recommendations and passed constitutional reforms that ended obligatory military service and stripped the armed forces entirely of control over the national police. He also trimmed the military budget and removed the Honduran telecommunications system and other sources of illicit funding from armed forces management. With no draft and only low wages to offer, the military shrank dramatically in size.

In early 1999 President Carlos Flores passed a constitutional reform that ended the military's formal political autonomy, thereby placing the armed forces under a civilian defense minister for the first time since 1957. The formerly independent post of armed forces chief and the Superior Council of the Armed Forces, the military's collegial decision-making body, were abolished. In mid-1999 the Liberal president demonstrated his new authority by dismissing an armed forces chief of staff with whom he disagreed and several other high-ranking officers. By the time National Party leader Ricardo Maduro (2002–2006) assumed the presidency, the political subordination of the armed forces to civilian control seemed to be an accomplished fact.

The 2009 Coup and the Breakdown of Democracy

The polarization of civilian elite politics during the term of Liberal President Manuel Zelaya (2006–2009) ushered the armed forces back onto the political scene. Although a centrist politician throughout his career, President Zelaya allied himself with radical populist President Hugo Chávez of Venezuela and brought Honduras into the Bolivarian Alternative for the Americas (ALBA). Zelaya's move to the left alienated most of the nation's civilian political class, including his own party, without winning him majority popular support. In 2008, when the Honduran chief executive began to campaign for a constituent assembly to revise the constitution, his opponents suspected that he intended to end the ban on presidential reelection and stay in power beyond the conclusion of his term in 2010 (or return to office in 2014). The National Congress, the Supreme Court, the Supreme Electoral Tribunal, and the Attorney General united in ruling his actions illegal and unconstitutional. President Zelaya, nevertheless, continued with preparations to hold a nonbinding referendum on adding the constituent assembly issue to the upcoming November 2009 ballot. When the president ordered the armed forces to assist with the referendum, the Chief of the Joint General Staff General Romeo Vásquez refused, citing the poll's illegality. President Zelaya immediately dismissed Vásquez and personally led a crowd of supporters onto an air force base to take possession of referendum materials stored there. The Supreme Court, which had quickly reinstated General Vásquez, ordered him to arrest the president. Military units deposed Zelaya on the day the referendum was to take place (June 28) and forced him to leave the country. National Congress President Liberal Roberto Micheletti became acting president with nearly unanimous congressional support as the international community clamored for Zelaya's reinstatement. By early 2010 new elections had been held and democracy restored.

Political Parties and Elections

Relatively few Hondurans go into politics to serve the public interest. The traditional Liberal (PLH) and National (PNH) parties are both nonprogrammatic, patrón-client political machines primarily organized to compete for state jobs and resources. Each party is divided into competing personalist factions. Both parties choose their presidential candidate in a national primary election that pits factional contenders against one another. The Nationals and the Liberals are centrist, multiclass parties that traditionally benefited from widespread, hereditary party affiliation. Today, however, about half of Hondurans are political independents. Three minor political parties, the centrist Innovation and National Unity Party (PINU), the center-left Christian Democrats (PDCH), and the socialist Democratic Unification Party (PUD), also participate in Honduran elections. In 2005 the three minor parties together won only 3.6 percent of the presidential vote and eleven congressional seats.

The Honduran president is elected by plurality to a single four-year term. The unicameral National Congress is selected at the same time by open-list proportional representation (PR). Honduran elections are supervised by a Supreme Electoral Tribunal (TSE) chosen by the National Congress. Since the 1980 constituent assembly elections restored electoral politics, Honduras has held seven consecutive general elections free of significant irregularities. The National Party won control of the presidency and the National Congress in the 1989 elections, while the Liberal Party won both in 1993 and 1997. In

2001 the Nationals again captured the presidency but took only a plurality of seats in the National Congress. In 2005 the Liberals were victorious in the presidential race, but they also failed to win an outright congressional majority.

The 2005 presidential election[5] pitted wealthy rancher Manuel "Mel" Zelaya of the Liberal Party against National Congress President Porfirio "Pepe" Lobo Sosa of the National Party. Underdog Zelaya won the election by a narrow margin (45 percent to 42 percent) by opposing the death penalty that his hard-line opponent advocated and by promising more convincingly to fight poverty and corruption. Zelaya's campaign also reportedly benefited from financial support from Venezuelan President Hugo Chávez. The Liberals won 62 of the 128 congressional seats contested, compared to the Nationals' 55 seats and, subsequently, formed a legislative coalition with the Nationals and the Christian Democrats (four seats). The other two minor parties divided the remaining legislative seats (five PUD, two PINU). The use of open-list PR for the first time resulted in the defeat of many long-serving deputies and in an increase in female representation (to 25 seats). In a context of worsening public disillusionment with the performance of the democratic political system, about 55 percent of eligible Hondurans turned out to vote in 2005. This level of voter turnout represented a steep decline from the over 80 percent turnout levels of the 1980s.

A new electoral cycle began with primary election campaigns in 2008 that involved five Liberal Party presidential candidates and four National Party candidates. The party primaries gave easy victories to the Elvinist Movement led by Vice-President Elvin Santos of the Liberal Party and to 2005 National Party presidential candidate Porfirio Lobo Sosa. In 2009, after the convoluted series of events recounted earlier, Lobo won the presidency.

Major Interest Groups

The military was the most powerful actor in Honduran politics from the 1960s until the middle 1990s, but its political significance declined markedly in succeeding years. However, the armed forces did regain political influence in 2009 when the clash between President Zelaya and his civilian opponents led both sides to try to enlist military support. Internal factional squabbling among *promociones* (military academy graduating classes) has divided the officer corps in the past, but the military was unified behind the 2009 coup. The armed forces also control the nation's only intelligence agency and play a key internal security role in assisting the police to patrol Honduras's crime-plagued cities.

The U.S. government's interest in Honduras declined dramatically after the end of the Central American civil wars. Nevertheless, the U.S. embassy has remained a major political actor. American Ambassador Hugo Llorens was a key player in negotiations to prevent the 2009 coup and to deal with its consequences. In addition, U.S. economic leverage has helped international financial institutions persuade Honduran presidents to sustain unpopular neoliberal economic programs.

The fragmented Honduran private business sector encompasses several competing investment groups that contribute to political campaigns and vie for influence over government economic decisions. The business community is also split by region (San Pedro Sula-based versus Tegucigalpa-based enterprises), ethnicity (Arab Honduran–owned companies versus others), and economic sector. The principal umbrella organization for the private sector is the Honduran Private Enterprise Council (COHEP). Foreign investors in the maquiladoras, the banana industry, and elsewhere also naturally seek to influence Honduran government policy. Most of the private sector and its mass media organs strongly opposed President Zelaya, but selected entrepreneurs friendly to his government profited from contracts to handle Venezuelan oil imports.

Honduras traditionally has had the strongest independent labor movement in Central America, but its unions have suffered from ideological divisions and internal leadership conflicts. Only about 8 percent of the workforce is unionized today. The moderate, AFL-CIO-linked Honduran Workers' Confederation (CTH), which includes most banana workers, is the country's most important labor federation. The other major national labor organizations are the Social-Christian General Confederation of Workers (CGT) and the smaller, leftist United Federation of Honduran Workers (FUTH). Some organizations within the fragmented peasant movement are affiliated with these three labor confederations, while others exist independently. Labor unions that organize public sector employees, particularly teachers and health care workers, have been very successful in using strikes to win economic concessions from the government despite external demands for fiscal austerity. Most trade unionists backed President Zelaya before and after the 2009 coup because of his enactment of generous minimum wage increases and other prolabor policies.

Honduran civil society has expanded in the last two decades as indigenous and environmental groups have joined existing human rights proponents such as the Committee for the Defense of Human Rights in Honduras (CODEH) and traditional actors like the Roman Catholic Church to pressure government officials on a range of issues. In addition, student groups and women's organizations as well as organized urban slum dwellers have become more active. Since the late 1990s unions, peasant organizations, and indigenous groups have increasingly resorted to direct action (road blockages, protest marches on the capital) to press their demands for governmental assistance.

Government Institutions and Public Policymaking

The Honduran governmental system is highly centralized with power traditionally concentrated in the presidency. The president directs the activities of executive branch agencies and usually introduces most legislation. If the president heads a majority coalition of party factions in the National Congress, his policy initiatives generally become law. However, public policymaking is often not the president's highest priority. The chief executive typically spends much of his time protecting his personal power base by distributing patronage and other material payoffs to supporters in his own and allied party factions and by countering the moves of his political enemies. The National Congress historically did not play a significant policymaking role; congressional seats traditionally have been viewed as rewards for factional loyalty rather than opportunities for public service. However, of late the National Congress has become much more important in policymaking and executive oversight. This has been true especially when the National Congress has been controlled by party factions not affiliated with the president or when the president of the National Congress has harbored ambitions to become chief executive. President Zelaya never enjoyed strong congressional support; he was always required to bargain with National Congress President Liberal Roberto Micheletti over legislation and appointments. When their relationship collapsed in 2009 over Zelaya's proposed referendum, Micheletti easily rallied the legislative body against the unpopular chief executive.

The National Congress appoints the fifteen justices of the Honduran Supreme Court from a list of forty-five candidates approved by a nominating committee composed of civil society representatives. The Supreme Court justices then appoint the judges of the lower courts. The current high court was selected in January 2009 and is composed of eight Liberals and seven Nationals. It played a decisive role in the ouster of President Zelaya in 2009. The Honduran judiciary is highly politicized, and judicial corruption and incompetence are widespread. Few high-ranking officials or major drug traffickers have been prosecuted successfully.

Effective policymaking is difficult in Honduras. Resources are scarce, the state bureaucracy is notoriously inefficient, and the political class is driven by spoils rather than policy goals. Some Honduran presidents, such as Liberal reformer Carlos Reina, come into office with clear policy objectives. However, the enactment of public policies to address national problems more often is driven by external pressure or by an acute internal crisis. The fundamental changes in Honduran economic policy that led to the adoption of neoliberalism in the 1990s, for example, were forced by an international credit boycott orchestrated by international financial institutions and the U.S. government.

President Rafael Callejas began the process of orthodox structural economic reform in 1990. He cut the size of the nation's chronically high fiscal deficit by shrinking the bureaucracy and by increasing taxes. He also liberalized trade, devalued the currency, and persuaded foreign investors to establish new maquiladora factories. These IMF-mandated policies initially reduced inflation and restored external financial support, although Callejas later lost control over public spending and inflation. His successor, Liberal Carlos Reina, more capably implemented the nation's neoliberal program. Although Reina made more concessions to organized labor than the IMF recommended, the Liberal government restored fiscal discipline and eventually met most IMF targets. Aided by rising coffee prices, booming maquiladora exports, and cheap oil imports, the Honduran economy was growing at about a 5 percent yearly rate when Reina left office in 1998. Hurricane Mitch, however, devastated the country later that year and disrupted President Carlos Flores's plans to deepen neoliberal reforms. The worst natural disaster to strike Honduras in the twentieth century forced a suspension of banana exports and destroyed most of the nation's roads and bridges. Total damage exceeded US$3 billion.

Flores personally supervised the rebuilding of the Honduran economy with international assistance. By 2000 GDP growth resumed a nearly 5 percent rate before falling coffee prices and a U.S. recession caused a slowdown the following year. President Ricardo Maduro, a Stanford-educated economist, maintained neoliberal policies while the country prospered from rising remittances from Hondurans who had emigrated to the United States since the 1980s. Maduro also signed the Central America Free Trade Agreement (CAFTA) with the United States. Beginning in 2005 international creditors rewarded Honduras with more than US$4 billion in debt relief for adhering to neoliberal policy guidelines. GDP growth then accelerated to over 6 percent in the last year of Maduro's term.

President Zelaya's alliance with Venezuelan populist leader Hugo Chávez helped the Honduran economy with low-interest loans, reduced oil-import costs, and development assistance, although it raised investors' suspicions. Zelaya granted hefty wage increases to public sector employees and generally demonstrated less financial discipline than Maduro. Inflation rose to over 11 percent. Nevertheless, basic neoliberal policies remained in place. The Honduran economy continued to grow at an over 6 percent rate in 2006 and 2007, but it slowed to 4 percent GDP growth in 2008 following the onset of the global recession and then began to contract in 2009. Remittances from the United States, exports, and investment all declined sharply. Tens of thousands of Hondurans were thrown out of work.

Although Honduran presidents have won praise from international financial institutions for their efforts to reform and expand the nation's economy, most ordinary Hondurans have seen only small improvements in their miserable living conditions. The poverty rate did decrease from 75 percent to 63 percent of the population between 1990 and 1998, but it has remained at about the same high level over the last decade. Reforms to combat tax evasion by the nation's well-to-do minority might have helped to better fund social programs to reduce deep inequalities, but few of those with influence in Honduran politics are interested in paying more taxes. A program of small income subsidies to poor families has been in place since 2000, but this is only because international assistance made it possible. Recent governments, including Zelaya's, also have not revived the agrarian reform program that came to a halt during the Callejas administration.

It is not difficult to understand why most Hondurans have been critical of the economic and social policies of their elected leaders. Hondurans have also been deeply disillusioned by the high level of government corruption. In 2008 Transparency International rated Honduras as one of the six most corrupt countries in Latin America.[6] But for many the greatest disappointment has been their democratic rulers' inability to control the crime wave that has enveloped the country since the mid-1990s. Bank robberies, homicides, car thefts, kidnappings, and muggings have exploded, and criminal organizations have proliferated. President Ricardo Maduro, whose own son was killed by kidnappers, made attacking crime his highest priority, but his zero-tolerance policies directed against Mara Salvatrucha, Calle 18, and other youth gangs had limited success. Estimates of youth gang membership still range up to seventy thousand. President Zelaya also adopted tough measures, only to admit later that he could not bring crime under control. Furthermore, drug trafficking continues to expand in Honduras. President Zelaya's security chief claimed that Mexican drug cartels have corrupted half of the nation's small, underfunded police force.

Few Hondurans base their opinions about government performance on foreign policy, although this is an area of major concern to Honduran presidents and the nation's political elite. Honduran foreign policy officials traditionally have devoted more attention to their relations with the United States than to their ties with all other nations combined. Their principal goal has been to secure economic resources, trade preferences, and favorable immigration policies by demonstrating loyalty to the United States. Honduras has been one of the strongest supporters of CAFTA and briefly contributed a military unit to the U.S.-led coalition in Iraq. President Zelaya then broke with this tradition by joining the anti-U.S. ALBA alliance headed by Venezuela's Hugo Chávez, regardless that the Honduran president hoped to retain U.S. economic assistance. Most other Honduran politicians criticized the Venezuelan connection, but Zelaya offered enough financial and political inducements needed in order to win congressional approval of ALBA. Future Honduran presidents can be expected to return to the American fold.

Future Prospects

Honduras made important democratic strides after civilian rule was restored in the 1980s. Four turnover elections (1989, 1993, 2001, 2005) appeared to demonstrate that the electoral system had become institutionalized. The long-dominant military also seemed to have returned to the barracks for good. However, the 2009 coup showed how fragile these achievements actually were. When President Zelaya violated basic democratic rules by moving ahead with an illegal referendum and appeared to pursue an unconstitutional second term, his opponents felt justified in using whatever means they could to stop him. They conspired with the military to oust the president, and not even opposition from the United States could dissuade them.

Long before the 2009 coup took place, the performance of elected democratic leaders had fallen far short of public expectations. Most public officials have concentrated on capturing the legal and illegal spoils of office for themselves and their political networks rather than on addressing the needs of one of the poorest populations in the Americas. Neoliberal economic reforms have yet to substantially improve the lives of the underprivileged majority; crime continues to rage out of control; and too many young Hondurans have come to believe that only immigration to the United States will solve their problems.

The mass public's unhappiness with the quality of democratic governance in Honduras was clearly indicated in the 2008 *Latinobarómetro* survey of Latin Americans, in which only 24 percent of Hondurans expressed satisfaction with the functioning of democracy in their country. Just 44 percent of Honduran respondents preferred democracy to any other political system; only Guatemalans and Mexicans were less supportive of democracy.[7] The 2008 Latin American Public Opinion Project (LAPOP) poll found Hondurans to be one of the three least politically tolerant populations in Latin America and the least supportive of democracy. If democracy is ever to consolidate in the future, the Honduran mass public must develop a much stronger sense of allegiance to democracy and its values. However, this can only occur if elected officials start to behave in a manner more worthy of public respect and begin to implement more governmental policies that tangibly improve the lives of ordinary people.

Suggestions for Further Reading

Coleman, Kenneth M., and José René Argueta. *Political Culture, Governance and Democracy in Honduras, 2008.* Nashville, TN: Latin American Public Opinion Project (LAPOP), Vanderbilt University, 2008.

Euraque, Darío A. *Reinterpreting the Banana Republic: Region and State in Honduras, 1870–1972.* Chapel Hill, NC: University of North Carolina Press, 1996.

Mahoney, James. *The Legacies of Liberalism: Path Dependence and Political Regimes in Central America.* Baltimore, MD: Johns Hopkins University Press, 2001.

Morris, James A. *Honduras: Caudillo Politics and Military Rulers.* Boulder, CO: Westview Press, 1984.

Schulz, Donald E., and Deborah S. Schulz. *The United States, Honduras, and the Crisis in Central America.* Boulder, CO: Westview Press, 1994.

Notes

1. The historical section of this chapter draws extensively on J. Mark Ruhl, "Honduras: Militarism and Democratization in Troubled Seas," in *Repression, Resistance, and Democratic Transition in Central America,* ed. Thomas Walker and Ariel Armony (Wilmington, DE: Scholarly Resources, 2000).

2. Darío A. Euraque, *Reinterpreting the Banana Republic: Region and State in Honduras, 1870–1972* (Chapel Hill: University of North Carolina Press, 1996), 96–97.

3. Mark B. Rosenberg, "Narcos and Políticos: The Politics of Drug Trafficking in Honduras," *Journal of Interamerican Studies and World Affairs* 30, no. 2–3 (1988): 152–53.

4. This analysis draws from J. Mark Ruhl, "Redefining Civil-Military Relations in Honduras," *Journal of Interamerican Studies and World Affairs* 38, no. 1 (1996): 41–53.

5. Michelle M. Taylor-Robinson, "Presidential and Congressional Elections in Honduras, November 2005," *Electoral Studies* 26 (2007): 515–18.

6. Transparency International Corruption Perceptions Index, 2008. Accessed at www.transparency .org.

7. "Democracy and the Downturn," *The Economist,* November 15, 2008, 46, 48.

23

Panama

New Politics for a New Millennium?

Steve C. Ropp

Panama's fifth president since the end of military authoritarian rule two decades earlier was sworn into office on July 1, 2009. President Ricardo Martinelli is a businessman who owns not only the largest supermarket chain in the country but also a host of associated enterprises. Educated in the United States at Staunton Military Academy and the University of Arkansas, he is thoroughly familiar with the country that used to control Panama's destiny as well as with the world of multinational business and banking. From all appearances he would seem the perfect person to lead his country during times of rapid economic change and uncertainty due to what some observers have called financial "deglobalization."[1]

Precisely because presidential leadership plays such an important role in a rapidly changing world, it is instructive to compare President Martinelli's background to that of his two most recent predecessors. Former President Mireya Moscoso (1999–2004) grew up poor as the daughter of a schoolteacher in rural Panama. At a very young age she joined the Panamenista Party (PP) that was founded and led by her future husband Dr. Arnulfo Arias. Dr. Arias, who was elected president in 1940, 1949, and 1968, espoused a brand of incendiary nationalist and racially exclusionary populism that won him no friends in either his country's racially mixed military or in the United States. Never allowed to complete a full term in office, his third

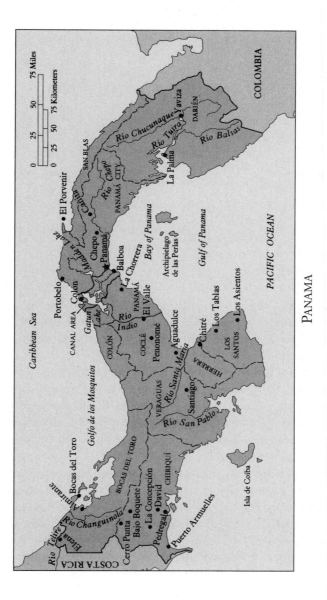

PANAMA

and final overthrow in 1968 led directly to two decades of military rule. Following the U.S. invasion of Panama in 1989 and the death of Dr. Arias, Mireya Moscoso became the standard bearer for his particular brand of nationalist politics.

President Martinelli's immediate predecessor represented a somewhat different but related branch of Panama nationalist political family. Former president Martin Torrijos (2004–2009) is the son of the late General Omar Torrijos, who was one of the main leaders of the military coup that had overthrown Dr. Arias in 1968 and founder of the Democratic Revolutionary Party (PP). Espousing his own brand of nationalist though more racially inclusive populism, he is best known for having successfully negotiated new Panama Canal Treaties with U.S. President Jimmy Carter in 1977. It was the passage of these treaties that eventually led to the transfer of the Canal to Panama in the year 2000 and hence to that country's attainment of integral state sovereignty. Just as Mireya Moscoso had represented the continuing twenty-first-century influence of the PP, so too did Martin Torrijos represent the influence of the PRD.

Although these two nationally based movements and their associated political parties differed in many respects, they both suggest the enduring presence during the decades prior to President Martinelli's election of the political phenomenon known as populism. Populism is simply the direct and unmediated personal relationship that a charismatic leader establishes with his or her "people." As a result of its long and tortured history of authoritarian populist politics, Panama's contemporary democratic political scene resembles nothing more than a landscape dominated by two extinct volcanoes. The first of these populist volcanoes erupted long ago in the 1930s, when the followers of Dr. Arias rebelled against a rising tide of uncontrolled immigration and against an elitist urban commercial class that was perceived as too closely aligned with the United States. The second erupted in the late 1960s when officers within Panama's emerging military institution rebelled against the inept antimilitary populism of Dr. Arias and the continued presence on Panamanian soil (in the Panama Canal Zone) of the United States. Although these two populist volcanoes have lain dormant since their main vents were capped following the U.S. military invasion of 1989, they sometimes still show a few signs of life in this supposedly postpopulist age of liberal representative democracy and market economy.

President Martinelli currently leads a country that has experienced more than twenty years of democratic governance, which followed closely on the heels of another twenty of uninterrupted authoritarian military rule.[2] Military rule came to an abrupt end in December 1989 when President George W. Bush sent U.S. troops into Panama to destroy the Panamanian Defense Forces (PDF) and to capture its commander, General Manuel Antonio Noriega.[3] During the ensuing years democratic government was reestablished and four general elections were successfully held (1994, 1999, 2004, and 2009). From the standpoint of assessing the current quality of Panama's new democracy, it is also important to note that the two largest political parties (the PP and PRD) have demonstrated a willingness to relinquish the reigns of power when defeated in free and fair elections.

However, any meaningful assessment of Panama's current political conditions and continuing prospects for democracy must rest on an understanding of the forces that lie just below the country's political surface. Most fundamentally, Panama's two extinct populist volcanoes rest upon rigid underlying social and economic "tectonic plates" that have historically kept Panama's rich very rich and poor very poor. Although the end of military government in 1989 and four successive democratic elections have created the impression that the country's political system has matured and that democracy has been consolidated, the underlying social and economic realities suggest that serious problems still remain. Can Panama's new political leaders and their parties successfully deal with the challenges presented by lingering class and racial differences in an age of rapid globalization? Will they prove willing and able to modernize the Panama Canal? And will they be able to shape a new role for their country in a changing twenty-first-century world? A closer look at Panama's history and political culture may allow us to make a few preliminary judgments regarding these questions.

History and Political Culture

The Republic of Panama is a small, narrow country that joins Central America to South America. Shaped like a giant S and some 420 miles (675 kilometers) long, it winds from the border of Costa Rica in the west to Colombia in the east. In total area Panama encompasses some 29,209 square miles (75,651 square kilometers), making it slightly larger than the state of West Virginia. The population of about three million is largely composed of *mestizos* and mulattos, together with black West Indians brought to Panama in the late nineteenth century to help construct the canal. Small numbers of native Indians occupy some of the interior provinces as well as the San Blas islands along the northern coast.

Panama is as much a location as it is a country. Its lack of significant size and its position between the Atlantic and Pacific oceans make Panama a vital strategic bridge. Although geography is not always destiny, the enduring legacy of the country's location has been to constantly reinforce a particular kind of laissez-faire economic thought and open economic practices.

Faith in the benefits of an open economy developed during colonial times when the isthmus served as a major transit point linking Spain to its most important colonial possessions along the west coast of South America. Legal trade with the Spanish colonies was supplemented by contraband trade in slaves and other "commodities." These illicit activities, particularly critical to the isthmian economy in hard times, served as a precursor to the more recent traffic under both military and civilian rule in merchandise such as arms and cocaine.

The result of Panama's early role as a strategic bridge was to concentrate economic resources in the hands of a small white urban commercial elite. The politicians who assumed leadership positions in Panama following independence in 1903 did not have ties to the traditional agricultural sector. Panama had never developed an *encomienda* system because of a lack of a large indigenous population, and unlike its Central American neighbors, Panama never experienced a nineteenth-century coffee boom.[4]

Throughout the twentieth century Panamanian politics was dominated by a struggle for power between the largely white urban commercial class and largely nonwhite (mestizo and black) groups who felt themselves excluded from the full benefits of nationhood. During the period of French and U.S. canal construction (1878–1914), large numbers of black workers were imported from Caribbean islands such as Jamaica and Barbados. These workers spoke English and were physically incorporated as an underclass into the U.S.-controlled Canal Zone. Although their wages were low compared to those for white workers from the United States, they constituted an urban labor elite when compared with Panama's mestizo and black Spanish-speaking population.

During the 1920s and 1930s the Panamanian economy deteriorated owing to the termination of canal construction activities and, later, the Great Depression. Resentment began to grow, particularly among mestizos from the interior provinces, against West Indian blacks and members of the urban commercial elite, who were viewed as natural allies of the United States. This resentment crystallized in 1923 with the formation of Community Action, a movement whose intent was to gain access for mestizo professionals and urban day laborers to the more lucrative jobs associated with the canal.

In the 1930s Dr. Arnulfo Arias emerged as the leader of this highly nationalistic popular movement. Elected president in 1940, he quickly promulgated a new constitution that contained discriminatory provisions against West Indians and Chinese. The political crisis precipitated by this constitutional change was resolved when the United States, upset with Arias's apparent sympathy with Italian Fascism, helped remove him from office. Although the political crisis associated with the rise of Community Action became more attenuated with the passage of time, Arnulfo Arias remained a major fixture in Panamanian politics until his death in 1988.

From the 1940s on, the struggle for political power between urban elites and populists such as Dr. Arias was increasingly influenced by the reemergence of the Panamanian military as a political force. The army was disbanded for the first time (the second time was in 1989) shortly after independence in 1903 because it was viewed as a threat to both the political hegemony of the commercial elite and to the United States. Through a slow evolutionary process, however, the army was reconstituted out of the small police force that had taken its place.[5] By the early 1950s the national police had been turned into a national guard and a colonel had been elected president with military backing.

After a turbulent period of civilian elitist democracy during the late 1950s and early 1960s, a military coup against Arnulfo Arias brought Omar Torrijos to power. Torrijos then built a populist political base among marginal groups in both Panama City and the countryside. Farm collectives were formed, labor unions organized, and the government expanded dramatically to accommodate popular needs. In this regard the Panamanian military government looked much like the one that emerged in Peru at the same time, and for much the same reasons.

When General Omar Torrijos and the military first seized power from President Arias in 1968, they did so as agents of social and economic change. Traditionally, Panama had been governed by an urban commercial elite who controlled the vast majority of the country's economic resources. Although some significant changes were made in this traditional structure of power during the earliest years of military rule, the military's social reform agenda slowly fell by the wayside as top officers became increasingly concerned with their own well-being. This in turn led them to become involved in a variety of illicit activities such as arms trafficking and drug smuggling.

The military's increasingly repressive and corrupt behavior following the 1968 overthrow of Dr. Arias finally created a significant domestic and international backlash in the mid-1980s. The precipitating event was the death of General Torrijos in 1981 and his eventual replacement by General Manuel Antonio Noriega. As head of the intelligence branch within the PDF, Noriega was in a position not only to spy on his fellow officers but also to control the most lucrative of the military's illicit activities. The rapidly growing Medellín drug cartel (headquartered in neighboring Colombia) found his services useful for the laundering of their cocaine profits, and by the mid-1980s the PDF had become a drug-trafficking mafia masquerading as a formal military institution.

Panama's crisis of military rule became so intense that it eventually drew the attention of the Reagan administration in the United States. For a variety of complex reasons having to do with General Noriega's stance on regional issues, his corruption, and increasing repression of domestic dissent, the Reagan Administration applied economic sanctions in 1988. At the same time, it supported the domestic political opposition that was now to be found not only within Arnulfo Arias's Panamenista Party but also among portions of the urban commercial class who had previously supported the military government.

Beneath its surface complexities we can thus see the workings of the underlying "tectonic plates" in Panamanian politics. Historically, they produced a consistent tension that pitted urban elites against poverty-stricken groups who were excluded from the full benefits of Panama's strategic location. The result was cycles of elitist democracy and authoritarian populism that occurred in slightly different form at various points in time, depending on the strength of various domestic political forces, the state of the global economy, and the level of involvement of the United States.

During the 1930s and 1940s Arias led a civilian popular movement aimed at increasing the political voice of rural mestizos and urban day laborers. In the 1970s the military then spearheaded attempts to include additional marginalized rural and urban groups. Both of these authoritarian populist movements were eventually challenged and displaced by traditional urban forces acting in collaboration with the United States. Thus, the successful effort to restore civilian democratic rule in Panama, which resulted from the U.S. military invasion in 1989, was not particularly unique but rather reflective of a longstanding cyclical historical process.

Political Parties and Interest Groups

Panama's pattern of elitist democracy followed by periods of populist authoritarian rule influenced the development of the country's party system. During periods of civilian elitist rule, political parties reflected divisions within the urban commercial class based on personality clashes between individual leaders. There was a general lack of real differences in the policy agendas of these parties, extreme fragmentation reflected in their relatively large numbers, and an absence of party structures that survived any given election.

Although Panama's political party system has historically been fragmented and elitist, the sporadic emergence of both civilian (Arias) and military (Torrijos) populist movements has on occasion led to efforts by populist leaders to create dominant parties through outright elimination or manipulation of the competition. The urban commercial elite's "power resources" have been primarily its private sector financial assets, whereas those of the populists have been their control of the government apparatus itself. Thus, when populist leaders such as Arnulfo Arias and Omar Torrijos came to power, they attempted to create dominant political parties largely based on their supporters in the various government bureaucracies.

During the period of elitist democracy that immediately preceded the military coup of 1968, approximately twenty small political parties vied for power. These parties were banned when General Torrijos assumed dictatorial control in the name of popular reform. However, deteriorating economic conditions in the mid-1970s led Torrijos to reassess the costs and benefits of direct military rule, and in 1978 he formed the Democratic Revolutionary Party (PRD) to incorporate various groups who supported his military regime.

Although the military, in response to internal and external pressures, allowed the holding of multiparty elections after 1976, the political system was clearly dominated by the PRD and its allies. Formation of the PRD suggested that the military wished to give permanent institutional form to its reformist ideals through the establishment of a new political party that would regularly win elections with military backing. When presidential elections were held in 1984 and 1989, the military had to resort to fraud in order to ensure a victory for the PRD candidate.

Following the U.S. military invasion the restoration of democracy led to a return of highly fragmented and personalistic party politics. The coalition of political parties that attempted to govern Panama in the wake of Noriega's removal quickly collapsed when leaders found that they had little in common beyond opposition to the military government. Although all of the elections that followed Panama's return to civilian rule have been generally democratic, they also took place within the context of a multiparty system that remained unstable and highly polarized. In sum, the historical tendency to find extreme party fragmentation associated with elitist and/or externally imposed democratic structures has persisted into the new millennium.

However, twenty years of military rule did lead to some important changes in the relative importance and strength of various Panamanian interest groups and social movements. General Torrijos encouraged the formation of new labor unions to strengthen his popular base, and labor was legally empowered through the passage of a new labor code in 1972. Other groups that experienced changes after 1968 were business organizations and the Catholic Church. The business sector diversified and expanded to the point that there was less direct correspondence between its interests and those of most traditional political parties. Similarly, the Catholic Church, an historically docile institution, became increasingly involved in politics.

Although Panamanian politics retains many of the features it exhibited prior to twenty years of military rule, there have been a number of significant changes. One of the most important of these has been the growing gap between the traditional parties and newly emerging sectors, social movements, and interest groups. The party leadership is aging and increasingly out of touch with the realities of a new generation of Panamanians, whose aspirations the party leaders have not been able fully to ascertain. Continued movement of rural dwellers to Panama City has created a new electorate that is largely detached from the patterns of self-interest and coercion that assured its vote for the traditional parties in the past. In an effort to deal with the growing gap between political parties and the electorate, both the PRD and the PP selected candidates in recent elections who would appeal to younger voters and to women. As we shall see below, this tendency to reach out to new groups of voters was also important in Martinelli's successful campaign for the presidency.

Formal Government Structures

Panama's formal government structures are delineated in the country's four constitutions, those of 1904, 1941, 1946, and 1972. All of these constitutions assigned a predominant role to the president within a centralized unitary form of government that included executive, legislative, and judicial branches. Thus, Panama's formal government structures have historically been very much within the Iberian tradition, with the executive branch intended to dominate the other two. The president appointed provincial governors, so his power extended directly down to the regional level, and although local municipalities theoretically possessed some autonomy, this idea was rarely honored in practice.

Although all four of these constitutions created governments in which the president was the dominant figure, Panama's populist governments assigned greater powers to the executive branch than did ones dominated by the urban commercial elite. The Constitution of 1941, promulgated during the presidency of Arnulfo Arias, and the 1972 Constitution, promulgated under military rule, are more expansive in terms of the president's prerogatives than those of 1904 or 1946.

When the Panamanian military seized power in 1968, it considerably altered traditional formal government structures. The National Assembly, which had come to be viewed by the military as an elite-dominated institution, was replaced with a much larger legislature, whose members were elected from the country's 505 municipal subdistricts. The traditional political parties were banned from electoral participation, and short legislative sessions ensured that there would be no time to mount meaningful challenges to military executive authority.

The 1972 Constitution, which created this new "popular legislature," also recognized the central role within the executive branch of General Torrijos and the defense forces. Although there was still a civilian president, real power was given to Torrijos as "maximum leader" of the Panamanian Revolution. The impotency of the president within this new constitutional structure was best expressed by the fact that he could neither appoint nor remove military personnel. The military legally became a fourth branch of government and the other three branches were constitutionally required to act in "harmonic collaboration" with the military.

As this military government gradually began to move toward the restoration of civilian democratic rule in the late 1970s, it allowed the 1972 Constitution to be amended in such a way as to restrict the powers of the executive branch and expand those of the legislature. However, none of these changes transformed the military's original authoritarian constitution into a fully democratic one. Provisions that allowed for full protection of human rights and freedom of expression were particularly lacking.

Panama's current constitutional situation is quite different from that which followed President Arnulfo Arias's period of populist rule in the 1940s. This is because his attempt to expand presidential powers through constitutional change in 1941 was reversed by urban commercial elites in 1946 through promulgation of a new constitution. When civilian democrats replaced populist authoritarians in 1989 following the U.S. invasion, however, they continued to govern according to the provisions of the military's partially amended authoritarian constitution. This has created a difficult situation in which the fact that democratically elected governments have ruled using the military's old constitution has undermined their political legitimacy. It has also complicated the country's legislative picture because restoration of the National Assembly did not lead to abolition of the military's "popular legislature."[6]

Under the terms of the 1972 Constitution political power continues to be concentrated in the executive branch and, more specifically, in the office of the president. President Ricardo Martinelli governs with the help of a Cabinet Council comprising the various ministers of state. The Legislative Assembly is limited in its general powers and has little control over the national budget. Although a Supreme Court does exist, it has historically demonstrated minimal independence from the executive branch, and various presidents have attempted to pack it with their followers. Perhaps the most significant change in formal government structures during the 1990s was a provision for the independent election of mayors. Because Panama City and Colon are major metropolitan areas, this change from appointment to election created important new centers of political power.

Government Policies

As in most countries, government policies in Panama have varied depending on the administration in power. The primary factor determining the general content of policy has been whether any particular administration fundamentally represented the interests of the urban commercial class or those of urban and rural middle- and lower-class groups.

When populist leaders have controlled the government, there has been a tendency to alter the constitution in such a way as to allow for a broader role of government in public policy formation and implementation. For example, Arnulfo Arias's 1941 Constitution mentioned the "social function" of private property for the first time, and the government was granted the right to intervene in conflicts between business and labor. New government agencies were also created to pursue expanded goals and objectives.

Then, during the 1950s and 1960s presidential administrations dominated by the urban commercial class pursued social and economic policies that relied somewhat less on the central government. Their policies were reformist within the context of the U.S.-sponsored Alliance for Progress. Economic growth strategies were aimed at simultaneously expanding the dynamic, outwardly oriented service sector and encouraging continued growth of the domestically oriented industrial sector.

The military coup of 1968 initiated another wave of populist policymaking. Observers of politics under military rule noted a curious blend of populist development policies mixed with more conventional ones. Populist policies that were intended to redistribute goods to the popular sectors were the natural result of the military's disdain for the urban commercial class. The simultaneous pursuit of more conventional developmental policies, emphasizing continued growth of the more dynamic areas of the private sector, reflected the permanent historical reality of Panama's open service economy.

Major components of the military's populist policies included the implementation of land reform, enactment of a progressive labor code, and efforts to gain national control of the Panama Canal. The military's broadest popular constituency consisted of those Panamanians who wished to see the canal brought under national control. General Torrijos worked hard during the early 1970s to create an international support group that would help speed negotiations with the United States for a new treaty. Through such international coalition-building as well as support for changes in the treaty arrangements on the part of several U.S. presidential administrations, Torrijos was able to achieve his goal. In 1978 a treaty was ratified that returned the Canal Zone to Panama and stipulated that Panama would gain full control of the canal in the year 2000.

When Panama's thoroughly corrupt but populist military regime was overthrown in 1989, government policy underwent a radical reorientation, which was partly due to the fact that the commercial elite once again exercised considerable influence with those who controlled the levers of state power. However, it also resulted from a sea change in global thinking concerning strategies of economic growth. In the post–Cold War world, a new economic model emerged that stressed reduction of the size of the public sector through privatization of state corporations and a shift from the traditional economic growth strategy of import-substitution-industrialization to one of export-oriented industrialization.

Since 1989 successive Panamanian governments have attempted to restore the country's credibility with international financial institutions, foreign governments, and private investors. President Guillermo Endara (1989–1994) made some progress in reorienting Panama toward an export-oriented growth strategy. Tariffs were reduced on industrial goods to make the industrial sector more internationally competitive, and tax legislation was passed to encourage more foreign investment in export-oriented activities. The most significant changes in this regard, however, came during the administration of Pérez Balladares (1994–1999). More strenuous efforts were made to attract foreign investment by selling off state-run companies and reverted properties in the former Canal Zone—thus curbing the power of organized labor—as well as seeking membership in important world trade organizations.

President Moscoso's economic policies were largely aimed at mitigating some of the negative side effects of these various neoliberal economic reforms, particularly as they impacted her core political constituencies within the agricultural sector and government bureaucracy. When Martin Torrijos succeeded her in 2004, however, he returned to policies that placed more emphasis on fiscal responsibility. As for the current president, it is still too early to tell whether Martinelli's campaign promises will be followed by concrete action. If they are, he will create new jobs building national infrastructure, attack rampant corruption, and clamp down on the criminal gangs who now operate with impunity in Panama's largest cities.

Panama in a Twenty-first Century World

During the twentieth century Panama's place in the world was largely defined by its relationship with a single Great Power: the United States. This key bilateral relationship long determined the overall nature of Panama's global involvement because U.S. diplomats made sure during World War II and the subsequent Cold War years that relationships with adversarial Great Powers either were not allowed to develop in the first place or were subsequently minimized.

Panama's international contacts, however, did multiply rapidly during the 1970s and 1980s due to a number of factors, including the progressive ideological stance of the country's military regime, its growing importance as a global service center, and the conflict in Central America. Despite these developments, Panama's pattern of global involvement during those decades can still largely be seen as resulting from the continued dominance of the United

States. Efforts to expand international contacts were a reaction to such dominance and part of a national strategy designed to gain diplomatic leverage in
the battle to negotiate new canal treaties.

During the Cold War years (1947–1989) the United States treated Panama
as a "constant" in a relatively simple global security equation. With troops on
the ground and planes in the air, the Panama Canal Zone could be used as a
platform from which known quantities of U.S. power could be projected in
order to deal with various global/regional security and humanitarian contingencies. Even during the years of the populist military rule (1968–1989),
the United States was able to treat Panama as a "constant" in dealing with the
civil wars then raging in Central America. When Panama itself became a
problem during the Noriega years, the same simple calculus applied.

Now all of that has changed. Following the departure of U.S. troops and
planes from the isthmus and transfer of the canal, Panama has become more
of an "unknown" in a vastly more complex global security equation. This
equation has become more complex in part because of the reemergence of a
multipolar international system following the end of the Cold War. For example, one does not have to be an alarmist to note that the influence of the
Asian Great Powers of Japan and China has grown significantly in Panama
during recent years. Asian shipping firms control three of the country's four
major ports and a significant proportion of foreign investment comes from
that region. The Panamanian case is not unique in this regard, reflecting the
broader pattern of Asian global and regional influence in the wake of economic globalization.[7]

Panama's future position in the world will also be affected by the political
and economic strains in neighboring South American countries. Most important, Colombia remains engaged in a seemingly endless civil war that pits
several guerrilla groups against the central government. This civil war has
been spilling over into Panama in the form of heightened tensions in the border area associated with illicit flows of drugs, arms, people, and money. In addition, Colombians from all economic classes are playing an increasingly
important role in Panama's development following the transfer of the canal.[8]

Also directly impacting Panama is the presence of President Hugo Chávez
in neighboring Venezuela. Chávez, a former army colonel who attempted to
stage a coup in 1992, came to power in 1998 through democratic elections as
a result of the frustration of ordinary Venezuelans with the corrupt nature of
their country's political class. As President he moved quickly to render impo-
tent Venezuela's formal democratic institutions and formed alliances with other
leftist leaders in Latin America who fed on popular frustrations with the effects of globalization and neoliberal economic reforms. Although no official
statistics exist to prove it, there is considerable evidence to suggest that many

Venezuelans have sought refuge in Panama due to the deteriorating political and economic situation at home.[9]

Finally, Panama's future role in the world will continue to be shaped by the presence on its territory of one of the most important transportation arteries in the world—the Panama Canal. Run by an autonomous government agency (The Panama Canal Authority) for the past decade, plans are now in place to add a third set of locks that will allow the waterway to accommodate a whole new generation of ships that are currently too large to use it. If sufficient financing can be obtained, these plans call for the expansion project to be completed by 2014. President Martinelli, who served as Minister of Canal Affairs during the Moscoso administration, intends to use the expansion project and upgrading of urban transportation infrastructure as the twin pillars of his public works plan for dealing with growing unemployment.

Conclusions

President Martinelli's election to the Presidency reflects many of the elements of both change and continuity in Panamanian politics that were mentioned earlier in our discussion of political parties and interest groups. With regard to change, his electoral success reflected the growing disenchantment within newly emerging groups in Panamanian society with the actions and activities of the country's traditional political parties. In the past Martinelli might have chosen to run for the presidency as the candidate of an assemblage of these parties. Rather than going that route, however, he founded his own party and used his own substantial economic resources to "market himself" to the public.

As for continuity, Martinelli's election would not have been possible without considerable support from one of the two largest traditional political parties, the PP. Furthermore, the new Democratic Change party (CD) that he founded in 1998 was populist in a manner very much like that of the PP of Dr. Arias and the PRD of General Torrijos. Just as was the case with his predecessors, Martinelli established a direct and unmediated relationship with his followers that resulted in his electoral success. Although a member of the white business elite, he was able to position himself as a "man of the people," willing to stand with them against members of the corrupt and self-enriching political class.[10]

In sum, Panama does seem to be gradually moving toward a new type of politics more suited to the new millennium and its global economic challenges. However, it is a style of politics that remains grounded in and influenced by the populist practices of the past. Although Martinelli's election to the presidency, as the result of his formation of a new political party, has broken a two-decade-old pattern of PP/PRD alternation in power, the type of party that he created and his own personal political style suggest that Panamanian political practice remains populist to the core. Furthermore, given the fact that the gap between rich and poor remains one of the largest in the world, it is not altogether clear that populism will ever lose its appeal among marginalized groups in the country. As long as this remains the case we may hear new rumblings from new volcanoes in the not-too-distant future.

Suggestions for Further Reading

Greene, Julie. *The Canal Builders: Making America's Empire at the Panama Canal.* New York: Penguin Press, 2009.

McCullough, David. *The Path Between the Seas: The Creation of the Panama Canal, 1870–1914.* New York: Simon and Schuster, 1977.

Pearcy, Thomas L. *We Answer Only to God: Politics and the Military in Panama, 1903–1947.* Albuquerque: University of New Mexico Press, 1998.

Perez, Orlando J., ed. *Post-Invasion Panama: The Challenges of Democratization in the New World Order.* Lanham, MD: Lexington Books, 2000.

Phillipps Collazos, Sharon. *Labor and Politics in Panama: The Torrijos Years.* Boulder, CO: Westview Press, 1991.

Sanchez, Peter M. *Panama Lost? U.S. Hegemony, Democracy, and the Canal.* Gainesville: University of Florida Press, 2007.

Ward, Christopher. *Imperial Panama: Commerce and Conflict in Isthmian America, 1550–1800.* Albuquerque: University of New Mexico Press, 1993.

Notes

1. John Pender, "Homeward Bound: Deglobalization," *Financial Times*, April 30, 2009, 7.

2. This was one of the longest periods of military rule in the modern-day history of Latin America. See Steve C. Ropp, "Explaining the Long-Term Maintenance of a Military Regime: Panama before the U.S. Invasion," *World Politics* 44, no. 2 (January 1992): 210–34.

3. General Noriega was subsequently tried in the United States and sentenced to forty years in prison. His sentence was later reduced to thirty years.

4. For an overview of Panama's early economic development and its implications for the distribution of political power, see Andrew Zimbalist and John Weeks, *Panama at the Crossroads: Economic Development and Political Change in the Twentieth Century* (Berkeley: University of California Press 1991), 1–19.

5. Thomas L. Pearcy, *We Answer Only to God: Politics and the Military in Panama 1903–1937* (Albuquerque: University of New Mexico Press, 1998).

6. Indeed throughout Central America, there are many constitutional remnants of authoritarian and corporate practice that have endured during this new post–Cold War "age of democracy." For a description of the various corporatist aspects of present-day Central American constitutions, see Steve C. Ropp, "What About Corporatism in Central America?" in *Authoritarianism and Corporatism in Latin America Revisited,* ed. Howard J. Wiarda (Gainesville: University Press of Florida, 2004).

7. Growing Asian influence in Central America and, more broadly, throughout the region has been noted for some time and by many observers. For example, trade between China and Latin America increased five-fold between 1999 and 2004. Richard Lapper, "Run for Investment Bulls as China Shops," *Financial Times*, April 13, 2005.

8. Steve C. Ropp, "Beyond U.S. Hegemony: Colombia's Persistent Role in the Shaping and Reshaping of Panama," *The Journal of Caribbean History* 39, no.2 (2005).

9. From interviews conducted in Panama during April 2009 as well as various newspaper accounts. See for example "El respeto de los extranjeros," *La Estrella*, January 14, 2009.

10. Some of Martinelli's campaign practices were traditionally populist, reminding one even of those used some fifty years ago by figures such as Juan Perón in Argentina. For example, he used a foundation headed by his wife to distribute thousands of small scholarships to primary- and secondary-school students throughout the country.

24

The

Dominican Republic

A Winding Road to Democracy and Development

Esther Skelley Jordan

The story of the Dominican Republic is one of resilience. It is a little country of about ten million people and forty-nine thousand square miles on the island of Hispaniola. It has suffered multiple dictatorships, foreign invasions, and economic crises, and yet it has emerged triumphant. Dominicans are proceeding along a winding road to democracy and development. The road is paved with patronage and great inequality, but it is headed in the right direction. The country has integrated into the globalized world, experienced multiple spans of record economic growth, and become a key trading partner with the United States. It recovered strongly from the domestic economic crisis of 2003 and is expected to do the same in response to the current international economic crisis.

The Dominican Republic has experienced tremendous change over the last several decades. It long followed Latin American tradition with a triumvirate of power (oligarchy, church, and military). That is no longer so. After two

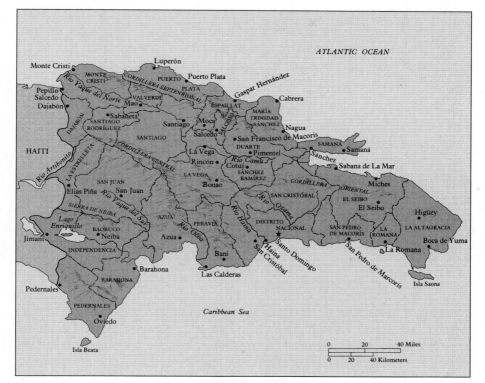

THE DOMINICAN REPUBLIC

U.S. interventions and many decades of dictatorship and authoritarian "democracy," the Dominican Republic is maturing into a unique democratic state. Economic diversification has diminished the once-dominant agricultural sector to less than 12 percent of the national gross domestic product.[1] The land-holding oligarchs have gone into business and maintained a position at the top of society—albeit a somewhat diminished one. Meanwhile, the church and military have declined in power, but they continue to act as arbiter and counterbalance to the state, respectively.

Although much has changed, Dominicans continue to live in a society characterized by family connections, patronage, and strict class divisions based on race and socioeconomic status. Despite great leaps in economic growth, a severe income gap remains, as a very large segment of the population still does not have access to even the most basic necessities of life. Although the country at this time appears on an upward trajectory of democratic development in many regards, corruption remains rampant. After all, patronage is the grease that oils the institutions of the Dominican Republic. It remains to be seen whether a society that has long preferred public handouts to public service is ready for drastic change in this regard.

Background

Hispaniola was discovered by Columbus in 1492. The Spanish soon established Santo Domingo (now the Dominican capital) as their first capital in the New World. As agriculture and mining took off, Spain built churches, schools, and hospitals. Through disease as well as arms the Spanish quickly eliminated most natives on the island and then imported slaves from Africa. Over the next fifty years the colony received an influx of Spaniards and built a racially based, two-class authoritarian system.

The early years of a state-run extraction economy quickly depleted the colony's mineral supply. The next two hundred years were marked by economic decline and social and political disarray as the Spanish, French, British, and pirates from the Netherlands competed for control of the island. The Spanish ceded the western third of the island to the French in 1697.

At the outset of the nineteenth century Santo Domingo's economy lagged far behind that of its western neighbor, Saint-Dominique (now Haiti), then the largest sugar producer in the world. The French colony's large slave population began to revolt in 1793. Soon thereafter former slaves from Saint-Dominique invaded Santo Domingo. In response Spain sent forces in 1809 to occupy Santo Domingo and prevent a slave revolt there. After several years of weak Spanish rule the colony declared independence in 1821. No sooner did the Dominican Republic break free than the newly independent Haiti invaded and seized control. The Haitians began to modernize the sugar industry and freed the slaves. They also redistributed the land and drove out the Spanish elites. These moves greatly upset the Catholic Church, which owned most of the former colony's land, and led Santo Domingo to declare independence from Haiti in 1844.

The first two decades of Dominican independence were marked by repeated coups and Haitian invasions. Then in 1861 the Spanish reannexed their former colony. The Dominican Republic declared independence again in 1865, and power shifted between parties until Ulises Heureaux's dictatorship in 1882 provided stability and modernization. This modernization, however, also put the country into great debt.

After Heureaux's assassination in 1899 the United States feared a European intervention aimed at collecting debts. Consequently, the United States took control of Dominican customs receipts in 1905 and began economic restructuring in 1915. One year later U.S. Marines invaded to quell increasing political instability and depose the anti-American faction in power. Until their 1924 departure the marines built infrastructure, trained a Dominican army, and established the procedures for democratic government. The U.S. troops brought great advances in many areas, from health and sanitation to roads and education. They left behind a nation obsessed with baseball, one that in time produced major league greats such as Pedro Martínez, Manny Ramírez, and Sammy Sosa. They also left behind a fledgling electoral democracy and a well-trained army under General Rafael Trujillo.

In 1930, soon after the United States withdrew, Trujillo wrested power from the weak democratic government of President Horacio Vásquez. Trujillo immediately established a semifascist, totalitarian dictatorship that is widely regarded as the most repressive in Latin American history. He wielded a heavy and often brutal hand in all aspects of Dominican society for thirty years. He controlled the food supply and was responsible for sordid crimes ranging from forced prostitution to murder. In 1937 he ordered the massacre of thousands of Haitians along the Dominican border. This massacre marked the beginning of an anti-African and anti-animist nationalist ideology, which the leading intellectuals of the day, Joaquín Balaguer and Manuel Arturo Peña Battle, contended was essential for the maintenance of independence and protection of the Haitian border. These same intellectuals helped Trujillo construct a corporatist system in which the government created state-sponsored, -regulated, and -controlled business, labor, and other groups to help regiment the citizenry.

The 1959 Castro Revolution in Cuba sparked fear in the United States that rising opposition against Trujillo would culminate in another socialist revolution in the Dominican Republic. With U.S. support, a group of assassins killed Trujillo in 1961. However, there was no contingency plan in place and the political system spun into crisis.

Trujillo's puppet president, Joaquín Balaguer, assumed control of the state following the dictator's assassination, but was replaced by elected leftist Juan Bosch in 1962. A military coup removed Bosch from power, which quickly led to civil war. The United States' fear that a socialist government would emerge victorious prompted another U.S. invasion of the Dominican Republic in 1965. Leading scholars contend that this fear was unfounded given that the rebels heading the revolt supported both democracy and the United States.[2] After a year of fighting, the U.S. peacekeepers and the Dominican factions reached an agreement that called for elections. This imposed reconciliation between Dominicans and led to U.S. withdrawal.

Balaguer, a conservative, was elected in a 1966 violence-ridden election. He did, however, bring stability to the country. The United States contributed millions of dollars to his administration while turning a blind eye to his practices of clientelism and political repression. The 1978 election then replaced Balaguer's corrupt government with the candidate favored by the Carter Administration, Antonio Guzmán. Four years later Jorge Blanco won on an anticorruption message, but he did not follow through. He also failed to make good on his promise to never accept an IMF package. In 1984 he reached an agreement with the IMF that brought on mass riots and subsequent police brutality.

Balaguer was consequently returned to power in the 1986 election. He then won the next two elections amid accusations of electoral fraud. This time his still-authoritarian regime governed with less violence. He closed the economy despite the trend of liberalization spreading throughout Latin America. He invested in infrastructure and espoused an anti-Haitian nationalist ideology characterized by consistent police harassment of Haitian workers. Despite his authoritarian rule and election fraud, Balaguer was considered by many to be a strong leader and father figure. Not only did he establish stability and promote modernization, he was known to garner support in the countryside by handing out money to passersby. In the end the 1994 election irregularities aroused so much domestic and international opposition that a constitutional amendment was passed to prevent the president from seeking reelection. Nonagenarian Balaguer was also forced to serve only two years of his term.

The 1996 election that followed brought Leonel Fernández to power. Already on the upward path, the Dominican economy took off under the Fernández administration through diversification. The undeveloped and traditional sugar-dependent economy gave way to a sustained average growth rate of over 7 percent. It even surpassed the growth rates of the newly industrialized countries of East Asia. The constitution, however, prevented Fernández from seeking reelection for a second term in 2000. Despite the candidacy of an aging Balaguer, power was yielded to the opposition party of

Hipólito Mejía. Growth was sustained for two years under the new administration, although at a lower rate of 3 to 4 percent.

By 2007 the economic and political outlook was very promising. With the national gross domestic product up to US$36.7 billion (more than triple that of the early 1980s), literacy up to 89 percent, and a rural population of less than one-third, the Dominican Republic was well on its way to modernization.[3] To top it all off, a peaceful exchange of power through three elections (1996, 2000, and 2004) placed Dominicans in the company of maturing democracies.

However, a devastating banking crisis brought this positive trend to a halt in 2003. It was discovered that the country's largest banks were engaged in rampant fraudulent activity that involved government officials and members of competing political parties alike. The Mejía administration's failure to prosecute those involved evoked widespread public protest. A government bailout of the banks that diverted a huge share of the national budget began a sharp economic decline. Inflation soared, business confidence dropped, and capital flight began. The cost of living increased exponentially as salaries decreased. Public unrest ensued. In response Mejía took control of several media outlets. He also doubled the size of the military, reinstated and increased the pensions of retired officers, and issued large numbers of motorcycles, helicopters, and cars to the military.

Despite Mejía's apparent attempts to buy off the armed forces and limit negative press as he campaigned for reelection, he conceded defeat in the 2004 election and transferred power peacefully. Leonel Fernández was elected to a second, nonconsecutive term on promises to increase government transparency and restore the prosperity of the 1990s.

Although President Fernández succeeded in this regard by returning the country to significant growth—10.7 percent GDP growth in 2006 and 8.5 percent GDP growth in 2007—this positive trend has reversed amidst the international financial crisis of 2008 and 2009. With its strong dependence on the U.S. economy for remittances and foreign direct investment, the Dominican Republic has suffered greatly at the hand of the U.S. recession. Further, the Dominican agriculture sector was devastated, and eighty thousand Dominicans were displaced by tropical storms Noel and Olga in 2007. President Fernández increased food subsidies to alleviate suffering from the subsequent food crisis and continues to supply natural gas subsidies for cooking. All of this spending, however, has placed great strains on a government budget already stretched thin with decreased revenues.

President Fernández was reelected to a third (second consecutive) term in 2008. However, the financial crisis and recent allegations of corruption within his government, although not against him directly, have somewhat bruised his image. That said, at printing, headlines have emerged that the Dominican economy is stabilizing and growth is predicted for 2010, although at much lower levels than previous years. In addition, indicators of democratic development continue to rise, despite the stress that natural disasters and financial crises have placed on the political system.[4]

Here we have a case of a country that, since independence in 1844, has experienced weak institutions, great instability, and only about ten years of relatively effective government. If we consider Trujillo's assassination in 1961 and the subsequent political opening as the beginning of the Dominican Republic's transition to democracy, then that transition has been a very long one—forty-five years so far—and it is still incomplete and nonconsolidated. The Dominican Republic case shows that transitions to democracy in countries based on clan rivalries, patronage politics, and weak civil society and institutions can be very long indeed.

State-Society Relations

State-society relations in the Dominican Republic are characterized by class divisions, personality politics, and clientelism. The primary interest groups include extended family groups, the military, the Catholic Church, economic elites, the middle class, students, and organized labor. In addition to these domestic groups the United States has tremendous influence on public policy.[5]

Class relations are based not only on socioeconomic status but also on race. The upper class is comprised primarily of Dominicans of white or European descent. Mulattos form the middle class, and the lowest class includes black Dominicans descended from African slaves as well as Haitian immigrants. Those of European descent have historically dominated society, politics, and the economy. However, some black Dominicans have been able to work their way up, primarily through the military.

While the lowest 20 percent of the population earns only 4 percent of the nation's income, the highest 20 percent earns 57 percent.[6] This income gap translates into a deep divide between the political interests of the upper class and those of the lower classes. The interests of the upper class include trade, relations with the United States, the tourism industry, and social connections. In stark contrast and despite the significant improvements of the 1990s, the lower class is interested primarily in basic quality of life improvements. Although the urban poor are more likely to participate in the political process, it is the rural poor who are much worse off, with significantly lower literacy rates, life expectancies, and income.

It is important to also note the emerging middle class, which has grown to nearly 40 percent of the population since the economic boom of the 1990s. This group is politically divided. The upper-middle class is comprised of businessmen and high-ranking military officers who tend to be politically conservative. The mid-middle class includes professionals, military officers, university students, and government midlevel managers, who also tend to be conservative, albeit less so. The lower-middle class is comprised of workers whose political leanings fluctuate between conservative and reformist politics, depending on the economic climate of the day.

Another defining characteristic of state-society relations is the centrality of extended family groups in politics and economics. Old family rivalries and clientelistic exchanges of favors shape even the most far-reaching national policies. This is facilitated by the reality that those in power are usually inter-related on one level or another. From political parties to civil-military relations, family ties play an even greater role than policy issues and political ideology.

The oligarch-church-military triumvirate no longer holds the reins of power as it did in times past. The power of the Dominican military has de-creased drastically in recent decades. It does, however, continue to ensure that its interests are served by the civilians in power. Given the Dominican history of military occupation, those civilians are always conscious of the mil-itary's ability to take the reins of power by force. Contrary to that of Western armed forces, the role of the Dominican military is not one of national de-fense. Instead, it serves as a political apparatus for its own self-preservation, self-enrichment, and the maintenance of social order. Once active in the foreground, its political machinations now take place primarily in the back-ground. As recently as 2002 President Mejía provided financial incentives and resources to the military in an effort to secure its support. Further, the military's support of democracy is highly dependent on their satisfaction with salaries and perks. To this day rumors of impending coups are common, and officers are known to facilitate drug trafficking through the Haitian bor-der. In 2009 the Fernández administration forced more than five hundred military officers to retire as a consequence for aiding drug trafficking and/or perpetrating acts of domestic violence. These are steps in the right direction for democratic consolidation, but much remains to be done to clean up mili-tary corruption.

The Dominican Catholic Church has also traditionally been a power bro-ker in Dominican politics. For many years the Church supported the brutal Trujillo regime and told parishioners how to vote. However, a lack of resources and personnel has diminished the Church's current influence on voting and public policy. Although the Church's strength has declined significantly in re-cent decades, the Dominican Republic is still a Catholic country and the Church still plays a significant role in education and society. Successful Church mediation of election irregularities and political disputes are but two examples.

Just as the military and Church have declined in power, so too has the oli-garchic pillar of the power triumvirate. The small landed oligarchy who once governed the Dominican Republic does so no more. The oligarchs did, however, go into business and, consequently, continue to have significant influence on the affairs of state. It was the business groups they formed that played a central role in the 1963 overthrow of Bosch's democratic government. Their influence has only grown since then, as they have organized into a chamber of commerce and various business associations. Not only are they well connected and wealthy, but the well-being of the Dominican economy depends on their success.

Organized labor seeks to influence public policy, but it is far less influential than it was in days past. The labor movement was long kept at bay under the authoritarian dictatorship of Trujillo. Following his assassination, however, it became an important player in Dominican politics. Another period of suppression followed the revolution, but the booming economy of the 1990s reestablished the opportunity for organized labor to become a significant political player. The effectiveness of the eight confederations that comprise the labor movement is now diminished, not from external forces but rather through internal division and competition.

The once-prominent political role played by students has likewise lessened in recent years. After contributing significantly to the political transformation of the 1960s and the establishment of a more competitive democracy in the late 1970s, students have become decreasingly involved in politics and more oriented toward moving up the social and economic ladder. The major universities still serve as a platform for debate, and students still participate in political protests on occasion. However, students are now far more focused on economic advancement than they were in the long-gone 1970s, when they incited political violence in protest against the repressive Balaguer regime.

As the political influence of the above groups has decreased over time, that of civil society has risen. Despite a conflict-ridden lead-up to the 1998 and 2000 elections as well as the economic crisis that preceded the 2004 election and the tropical storms that wreaked havoc before the 2008 election, all recent elections went off without major incident. This victory for free and fair elections is due in part to the legitimizing effects of a large international observation presence. However, it is also the result of a civil society that has recently begun to thrive. In recent decades Dominican nongovernmental organizations have secured the attention and responsiveness of the country's leadership, and they have done so in a very creative way. Although the Dominican Republic is progressing toward democratic maturity, it still runs largely on patronage and clientelism. Consequently, Dominican civil society stimulates grassroots activism, then when either local or national institutions serve as impediments to change, it employs the old patronage practices to secure its aims. Although this may be criticized as only partial democracy, it works. New social groups now have more of a say because they have found the way to secure the ear of the leadership first through mobilization and then through patronage.[7]

Finally, the United States plays a major role in domestic Dominican policymaking. Although some anti-American sentiment followed the long military occupations, many Dominicans view the United States as a protector and benefactor. The Dominican Republic is one of the few countries where the Washington Consensus has proven a successful approach to development. The who's who of Dominican society frequent American embassy parties, and the U.S. ambassador has tremendous access to and influence over Dominican policymakers. It must also be noted, however, that the Dominican Republic has likewise learned how to secure its interests from the United States. This small Caribbean state is a large market for U.S. products, with US$6.5 billion in imports from the United States in 2008.[8] There are also hundreds of thousands of Dominican citizens who live in the United States and send a total of over US$2 billion in remittances home each year. In addition, a large American citizen population resides in the Dominican Republic and is active in banking, business, religious groups, and educational institutions. These three factors significantly empower the Dominican lobby in Washington, D.C.

In sum, power still rests in the hands of the few. The economic elites, the military, well-connected civil society groups, and the United States have the greatest influence. The church, university students, and organized labor play a significant, albeit lesser, role. Unfortunately, the impoverished masses are still excluded from the equation. Perhaps the emerging civil society will take on the plight of and make a difference for the least fortunate bottom rung of Dominican society. In fact, a couple of organizations have attempted to do so in recent years in the education and health care arenas. However, secondary school enrollment remains just above 50 percent, and infant mortality rates average approximately twenty-six deaths per one thousand births (as compared to deaths in the low single digits in Western Europe and North America).[9] There is still much to be done.

Political Parties, Elections, and the Consolidating Democracy

The political parties of the Dominican Republic contrast sharply with those of the developed nations. Many have arisen over the years, but three main parties have withstood the test of time. Each was formed in the *caudillo* tradition around the personality of one dynamic individual as opposed to a particular political ideology. Despite the recent passing of all three founding fathers, election campaigns continue to extol the legacies of their deceased leaders and pay minimal attention to policy platforms. Social democrat Juan

Bosch established the Dominican Revolutionary Party (PRD) in exile in the 1930s in support of social justice for the poor. However, it was not until Trujillo's 1961 assassination that the PRD became a significant player in Dominican politics, with close ties to the left wing of the U.S. Democratic Party and socialist parties in Europe and Latin America. Bosch was elected president in 1962, but he was thrown out of office by a military coup after only seven months in office. Following the U.S. intervention in 1965 he lost the 1966 election to Balaguer.

The party suffered repression under the Balaguer administration and boycotted the elections of 1970 and 1974. Soon thereafter Bosch left the PRD to form the Party of Dominican Liberation. The party he left behind successfully united under Antonio Guzmán to become a formidable contender in the elections of 1978, 1982, and 2000. Guzmán won the 1978 election and another PRD candidate, Salvador Jorge Blanco, won the 1982 election. Both administrations were rife with corruption but allowed far more freedom than did earlier repressive regimes. PRD candidate Hipólito Mejía won the election in 2000. He then amended the constitution to allow his own reelection to an immediate second term, but his 2004 reelection campaign struggled to a defeat that resulted in yet another party split. The PRD was thus unable to win a congressional majority in 2006. It lost again to Leonel Fernández in the 2008 race, with Miguel Vargas as the presidential nominee. The party remains divided, with newspaper headlines labeling it a party in crisis as controversy surrounds the procedures through which members vie for leadership posts—most notably pitting party leaders Mejía and Vargas against each other.[10]

The Party of Dominican Liberation (PLD) was formed by Juan Bosch following his split from the PRD in 1973. He contended that both U.S. policy and democratization had failed. On this basis he sought a "dictatorship with popular support" in the likeness of the then populist revolutionary regime in Peru. The PLD, however, did not win popularity until discontent mounted with Balaguer's corrupt regime in the late 1980s. Bosch then lost the fraudulent election of 1990 and lost again in 1994, with young and charismatic running mate Leonel Fernández. Upon Bosch's retirement Fernández redirected the party to advocate for economic liberalization and foreign investment, á la the Washington Consensus. This move appealed to the middle class and business interests, while his dynamic personality appealed to young voters. His victory in the 1996 election drew an end to the Balaguer era. Following Balaguer's steps toward modernization Fernández oversaw a period of record economic growth. Despite his success, the constitution forbade him from seeking a second term. Further, corruption charges led to waning support for the party and a loss in the 2000 election. It was not until the economic crisis of 2003 that the PLD regained its footing. The charismatic Fernández returned to the presidency in 2004, with promises to restore economic stability and progress, which he fulfilled. He was then reelected in 2008 after securing public approval through grocery and cooking gas subsidies in the wake of two severe tropical storms and a subsequent food crisis.

The center-right Reformist Party (PR) was established by Balaguer upon his return to the Dominican Republic in 1965. From 1966 through 1978 the PR served as his personal political apparatus. It mobilized voters, doled out favors, secured support, and repressed his opposition. Always savvy to an evolving political climate, Balaguer was quick to recognize that the PR in that form would no longer be acceptable to an increasingly democratic society. He therefore merged his party with the Social Christian Party to form the Social Christian Reform Party (PRSC), which still exists today. This was a smart move, as the PRSC won all three elections from 1986 through 1994, albeit amidst allegations of electoral fraud in 1990 and 1994. After the constitutional amendment was passed to prohibit Balaguer from seeking reelection, PRSC support declined. It garnered only 15 percent of the vote in 1996. Balaguer was allowed to run again in 2000, but he lost to the PRD. In a surprising move he waived his right to participate in a second round of voting against Mejía. The 2004 PRSC ticket was led by Eduardo Estrella in an attempt to honor the legacy of Balaguer. However, Estrella did not fare well in 2004, and the party went on to win a mere 4 percent of the vote in the 2008 presidential elections—forcing many among the party leadership to resign.

Dominican elections have been rife with allegations of electoral fraud. As recently as 2000 the federal election board (*Junta Central Electoral*) was accused of political bias, as thousands of voters were disenfranchised by inaccurate voter registration lists. Charged with ensuring a free, fair, and smooth election process, this politically appointed board went to great lengths in the 2004 election to shed its controversial past. More than ever before, domestic civil society groups such as *Participación Ciudadana* (PC) kept careful watch over 2004 and 2008 election preparation activities. These groups monitored everything from the preparation of voter registration lists, *cedulas*, to ballot box delivery. In addition, large contingents of international election observation teams were sent by groups such as the Organization of American States. A welcome presence, these election observers once again provided a legitimizing scrutiny of the electoral results in the 2004 elections and 2008 presidential elections.

Despite irregularities the last four elections were widely considered fair, honest, and open. None was contested by a major candidate. This indicates that the Dominican Republic has officially institutionalized the democratic process. At the same time it would be foolish to ignore the political corruption, patronage practices, and restricted media coverage that accompanied the 2004 election. Also worrisome in 2004 was the continued threat of the use of violence as a campaign tactic. Not only did the incumbent double the size and increase the pay of the military prior to the 2004 election, but other candidates implied that they would send their supporters out into the streets if the balloting produced the "wrong" results. The 2008 election was much cleaner, with open media coverage and very little violence. Even so, in the 2008 race the Fernández administration was accused of—and forced to cease—paying supporters with public funds to do campaign work.[11]

It can therefore be concluded that the Dominican transition toward democracy is not yet complete. However, it is well on its way. Its political institutions have thus far withstood the 2003 domestic economic crisis, devastation from the 2007 tropical storms and food crisis, and the 2008–2009 international economic crisis. All the while civil society has become increasingly engaged not only in elections but also in the fight against corruption, poverty, drug trafficking, and human trafficking. Democracy is taking a uniquely Dominican form (more centralized, executive-centered, patronage-as well as program-oriented), and although there have been many bumps in the road, it is maturing nonetheless.

Government Institutions

Dominican government institutions were built in the three-branch likeness of the U.S. system. However, the executive, legislative, and judiciary branches have yet to function together as the system of checks and balances they were intended to be. The first two decades following the second (1965) U.S. intervention were characterized by a very weak and patronage-based legislature, judicial system, and bureaucracy that was dominated by the authoritarian Balaguer regime. This was then briefly interrupted by the Guzmán and Blanco administrations of the late 1970s and early 1980s, both of which were significantly less authoritarian. Their regimes allowed a significant degree of conflict and debate between parties as well as branches. But this small step toward greater independence of the other branches of government as well as greater accountability was reversed with the return of the Balaguer regime. From 1986 to 1996 Balaguer resumed authoritarian rule that bypassed the legislature and judiciary. He also used the government purse to pay for allegiance and secure favors. The 1996 election of Leonel Fernández ushered in a new era, as he formed coalitions with competing factions and negotiated with the legislature. Nonetheless, congress successfully impeded much of Fernández's legislation proposals during his first administration, especially those related to privatization and administrative reform.

The judiciary also has more power now than in earlier years, but it is plagued with corruption. The Mejía administration did little to prosecute those in the government and private sector who held responsibility for the banking scandal. Despite advocacy by groups such as the Foundation of Institutionality and Justice (*Fundación Institucionalidad y Justicia*) as well as efforts by the second Fernández administration to implement reforms that increase judicial independence, the system is still deeply flawed. Its inability to decrease police violence (especially toward Haitians and the poorest Dominicans) is but one example.

The military has also played a central role in the affairs of the state. However, its role has decreased over time as democracy has advanced and military repression has become less the norm. Military force has not been used against political opponents or social protestors for quite a few years. Current military targets include the poor and drug traffickers along the Haitian border.

Finally, family ties and clientelist governance are so entrenched in the Dominican system that they combine to form an institution of their own. Every administration has worked this institution to its advantage. So too has much of the Dominican public. Unfortunately, patronage politics is responsible, at least in part, for the mismanagement of public funds and has consequently done little to alleviate the plight of the poor. Although there is continual discussion of the need to reduce corruption and decrease patronage practices in order to secure international confidence, real change in this area is highly unlikely. Institutional patronage is practically synonymous with the very essence of Dominican politics. As noted earlier, even civil society groups have figured out how to work within this framework in order to achieve their goals. The continuance of corrupt practices by all sectors is confirmed by the World Bank's governance indicators, which assigned the Dominican Republic a 31.9 percent on the 2008 corruption index, in contrast to better performers in the region such as Chile at 85 percent and Costa Rica at 70 percent.[12]

Main Public Policy Issue Areas

The top of the current Dominican public policy agenda continues to be occupied by the pursuit of economic growth and stability. Record growth of 7 to 8 percent GDP in the 1990s declined to 3 to 4 percent in 2001 to 2002 and gave way to economic crisis in 2003. The Fernández administration restored economic confidence from 2004 until 2008 by bringing rampant inflation under control, increasing transparency to some extent, liberalizing trade, and restoring the economy to a sustained period of strong growth. Foreign direct investment was also on the rise until the international economic crisis began in 2008. Although the economy has contracted and public debt has reached 42.7 percent of the GDP since the crisis began, international economists predict that the Dominican economy will return to slow growth by 2010. This expected recovery is remarkable given gross mismanagement in the energy sector and the extent to which Dominican institutions are wrought with patronage practices and a bloated civil service.

The electricity sector was near collapse when Fernández assumed the presidency for the second time in 2004. Despite rhetoric espousing change, the Dominican Corporation of State-Owned Electrical Enterprises (CDEEE) remains bloated with one hundred times the staff it needs, while nearly a third of all electricity is consistently stolen. The result has been rolling blackouts that disrupt industry and leave consumers in the dark. In response to the energy crisis the government has subsidized nearly 90 percent of consumers' power supply and has taken measures to improve the financial administration of the electricity sector (by improving bill collection, reducing operating costs, etc.). However, many blame the president for not holding his friends who run the company accountable for their mismanagement.

Although the legislative branch has historically failed to serve as an effective check-and-balance to the executive, this trend was reversed as the 2004 Fernández administration faced an opposition Congress. This reversal was indicative of progress toward democratic consolidation, but it proved a challenge to good faith efforts by the executive to restore economic stability and investor confidence. However, the president's PLD party assumed a legislative majority following the 2006 election, and they succeeded in pushing through their economic reform agenda. At the same time, there was a return to business as usual with minimal legislative check on the executive. In addition, public administration is still highly centralized, with few institutions in place to increase expenditure transparency. As a consequence, the public continues to expect and prefer favors above services. Although several initiatives by the Fernández administration have been aimed at decreasing the patronage culture of government, its record in this regard remains mixed, as political survival still depends on the practice of clientelism.

Despite these stumbling blocks, great strides have been taken toward current policy goals. IMF loans and the reforms they require have strengthened the banking system and decreased public expenditures. The Dominican Republic-Central America-United States Free Trade Agreement (CAFTA-DR) was passed, thus giving the Dominican Republic unrestricted access to U.S. markets as of 2007.

Also on the public policy agenda are social issues such as drug trafficking, human trafficking, organized crime, and immigration across the Haitian border. In addition, the country suffers from high levels of youth unemployment and a deficient education system. This has only been exacerbated by the numerous schools that were destroyed or damaged by tropical storms Olga and Noel in 2007. As a result of persistent challenges in all of these areas, crime rates are on the rise and race-based human rights violations continue.

Globalization

The Dominican Republic is an active participant in the world system, albeit a primarily dependent one. The evolution from an agricultural export economy to a diversified economy has decreased Dominican dependence on some levels. However, the export of goods and services still accounts for more than a third of the country's gross domestic product.[13] Reliance on IMF loans, financing assurances from the Paris Club of rich countries, and foreign direct investment make dependence a continuing state of affairs. There is even a large international presence to monitor domestic elections. The electoral process continues to be overseen at the invitation of the Dominican government by multiple observation groups, such as those sent by the Carter Center and the Organization of American States.

The Dominican Republic has much at stake in its relations with the United States. To that end, Dominicans continually seek American favor. Recent examples of engagement with the United States include the Mejía Administration's contribution of troops to Operation Iraqi Freedom (although Mejía was forced by domestic political outrage to withdraw all troops when injuries mounted). As is evidenced by his frequent trips to the United States and ardent support for CAFTA-DR, President Fernández is especially focused on relations with the giant to the north. His presence in policy conferences and his support for U.S.-policy priorities are unprecedented. This is partly due to his upbringing in Queens, New York, but it is also due to a deep understanding of all the Dominican Republic can gain from the maintenance of good relations with the United States.

Finally, the forces of globalization are apparent in many aspects of Dominican life, albeit with great discrepancies between classes. Cable television, the Internet, and SUVs are common only among the upper classes. From the tourist industry that recovered from the negative effects of September 11, 2001, and the tropical storms of 2007, to fast food and shopping malls, affluent Dominicans have kept step with the globalization trend, while the poor lag far behind. Perhaps the greatest evidence of the impact of globalization is the sustained period of economic growth that quickly turned to contraction amidst the international economic crisis of 2008 and 2009. The subsequent drop in remittances from abroad, foreign direct investment, and tourist traffic has had a direct negative effect on all Dominican's lives—rich and poor alike.

Conclusion

Dominican politics and development have taken many twists and turns, but this small Caribbean nation appears to be slowly progressing toward democratic consolidation, economic development, modernization, and global integration. Despite two American interventions, the brutal thirty-year Trujillo dictatorship, frequent election irregularities, and multiple administrations under an authoritarian Balaguer, the Dominicans have built a democracy that is well on its way toward maturity. Following the modernization efforts of Balaguer and the diversification of its economy, the unprecedented economic growth of the 1990s and the mid-2000s ushered in a new era for the Dominican people. Full consolidation of democracy, however, is still a distant goal.

A severe income gap remains, and a majority of the population is still stuck in the lower class, isolated from many benefits of globalization but nonetheless suffering from the effects of the international economic crisis. In addition to this recent crisis, the banking fiasco of 2003 and a continuing energy crisis have dealt severe blows to the economy. However, with international support and the leadership of Leonel Fernández, both the Dominican economy and democracy are emerging triumphant. At printing, all indicators point to a return to economic growth by 2010. Corruption and patronage still characterize the Dominican political system, but civil society is emerging as a force to be reckoned with. Despite media restrictions and threats of violence in the 2004 presidential election, all elections since have been remarkably free and fair. Additionally, the government appears to be taking steps toward greater transparency and accountability. These changes are likely to proceed in a characteristically inconsistent—sometimes chaotic—and particularly Dominican way. Nevertheless, the Dominican Republic has weathered the storm of economic crises and natural disasters. At present the political and economic future of the Dominican Republic looms brightly on the horizon despite the great challenges it continues to face.

Suggestions for Further Reading

Atkins, G. Pope, and Larman C. Wilson. *The Dominican Republic and the United States: From Imperialism to Transnationalism*. Athens: The University of Georgia Press, 1998.

Betances, Emilio. *The Catholic Church and Power Politics In Latin America: The Dominican Case in Comparative Perspective*. Plymouth, UK: Rowman and Littlefield, 2007.

Choup, Anne Marie. "Limits to Democratic Development in Civil Society and the State: The Case of Santo Domingo." *Development and Change* 34, no. 1 (2003): 25–44.

Hartlyn, Jonathan. *The Struggle for Democratic Politics in the Dominican Republic*. Chapel Hill: University of North Carolina Press, 1998.

Kryzanek, Michael J. *U.S.-Latin American Relations*. Westport, CT: Praeger, 1996.

Moya Pons, Frank. *The Dominican Republic: A National History*. New Rochelle, NY: Hispaniola Books, 1995.

Oostindie, Gert, ed. *Ethnicity in the Caribbean*. London: Macmillan Caribbean, 1996.

Pomeroy, Carlton, and Steve Jacob. "From Mangos to Manufacturing: Uneven Development and its Impact on Social Well-Being in the Dominican Republic." *Social Indicators Research* 65 (2004): 73–107.

Soderland, Walter C. *Mass Media and Foreign Policy: Post–Cold War Crises in the Caribbean.* Westport, CT: Praeger, 2003.

Vargas-Lundius, Rosemary. *Peasants in Distress: Poverty and Unemployment in the Dominican Republic.* Boulder, CO: Westview Press, 1991.

Vega, Bernardo. *Dominican Cultures: The Making of a Caribbean Society.* Princeton, NJ: Markus Wiener Publishers, 2007.

Wiarda, Howard J., and Michael J. Kryzanek. *The Dominican Republic: A Caribbean Crucible*, 2nd ed. Boulder, CO: Westview Press, 1992.

Wiarda, Howard J., and Esther Skelley. *The 2004 Dominican Republic Elections: Post-Election Report.* Washington, D.C.: Center for Strategic and International Studies, 2004.

Notes

1. The World Bank, *World Development Indicators 2007* (Washington: The World Bank Group, 2007).

2. See Michael J. Kryzanek, *U.S.-Latin American Relations* (Westport, CT: Praeger, 1996).

3. The World Bank, *World Development Indicators 2007*.

4. The Economist Intelligence Unit, "Country Forecast: Dominican Republic," www.economist.com/countries/dominicanrepublic/profile.cfm?folder=Profile-Forecast, accessed June 2009.

5. See Howard J. Wiarda and Michael J. Kryzanek. *The Dominican Republic: A Caribbean Crucible*, 2nd ed. (Boulder, CO: Westview Press, 1992).

6. The United Nations, Human Development Report 2007/2008, http://hdrstats.undp.org/en/countries/data_sheets/cty_ds_DOM.html, accessed June 2009.

7. See Anne Marie Choup, "Limits to Democratic Development in Civil Society and the State: The Case of Santo Domingo," *Development and Change* 34, no.1 (2003): 25–44.

8. U.S. Trade Representative, "Dominican Republic," www.ustr.gov/countries-regions/americas/dominican-republic, accessed June 2009.

9. The United Nations, Human Development Report 2007/2008.

10. Dominican Today, "Crisis Rocks Dominican Opposition Party," www.dominicantoday.com/dr/local/2009/6/9/32240/Crisis-rocks-Dominican-Republic-opposition-party, June 9, 2009, accessed June 2009.

11. See Howard J. Wiarda and Esther Skelley, *The 2004 Dominican Republic Elections: Post-Election Report* (Washington, D.C.: Center for Strategic and International Studies, 2004). See also Organization of American States, "Informe de la Misión de Observación Electoral de la Oeaen la República Dominicana" (Santo Domingo: Consejo Permanente, 2008).

12. The World Bank, Governance Matters 2009: Worldwide Governance Indicators 2007/2008, http://info.worldbank.org/governance/wgi/mc_chart.asp, accessed June 2009.

13. The United Nations, Human Development Report 2007/2008, http://hdrstats.undp.org/en/countries/data_sheets/cty_ds_DOM.html, accessed June 2009.

Haiti

The Search for Democratic Governance

Georges A. Fauriol

Haiti, discovered by Columbus in 1492 during his first voyage to the Americas and the second-oldest independent nation in the Western Hemisphere, celebrated its bicentennial in 2004. Throughout much of its history the country has experienced all shades of development—except that of effective political and economic management. This dysfunctional character of Haitian political dynamics, an absence of coherent economic policymaking, and decayed social institutions have triggered an unhappy and at times tragic record of interaction with the external world. Most recently this has played itself out in several episodes, first as a result of the collapse of the Duvalier dynasty in 1986, then in the context of U.S. military intervention to return President Jean-Bertrand Aristide to power in 1994, and again in 2004 to manage a messy transition in the wake of an abrupt conclusion to Aristide's second presidential term. What's more, in a total game-changer, in January 2010 an earthquake destroyed much of the nation's capital.

Born out of the economic excesses of slavery and the political violence of the French Revolution, Haiti emerged in 1804 as an independent nation. Its economy in ruins and its population exhausted, it began its career as a modern nation without any foreign friends. Haiti's early status as an outcast

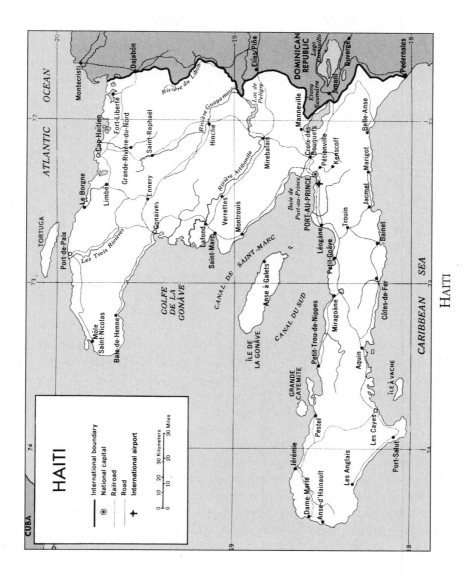

HAITI

among the community of nations further increased its vulnerability to both internal and external threats. At the beginning of the twentieth century this overlap of threats ultimately generated direct U.S. political and military administration (1915–1934). Since 1986 Haiti's political crises have ensured enduring engagement from the international community, notably the Organization of American States, the United Nations, key governments (the United States, France, and Canada), and an extensive NGO and humanitarian community. In fact, the UN peacekeeping force introduced after the 2004 political transition has become a permanent feature of the Haitian landscape.

Despite these misfortunes, Haiti has not lost the basic features of its national character. Its roots lie in a hybrid of African ethnicity and culture, French eighteenth-century colonialism, a marginal brand of Catholicism, and the aftereffects of the United States' strategic sweep in the Caribbean region. The African cultural and spiritual features have remained almost unaltered for a majority of the population since they were first imported in the seventeenth century. The vitality of this primarily rural environment has survived in the face of economic adversity and the extraordinary failures of political leadership in advancing national development.

Roughly the size of the state of Maryland, Haiti occupies the western third of the island of Hispaniola, which it shares with the Dominican Republic. It lies at a crossroads of trading passages and strategic interests: Cuba lies to the immediate west across the Windward Passage, the open waters of the Atlantic Ocean bound Haiti on the north, and the Caribbean Sea lies to the south. Haiti nonetheless remains ethnically and culturally distinct, being 95 percent black and the only independent French-speaking nation in the Caribbean region.

With an estimated average per capita gross national product (GNP) income of about US$570, Haiti is the poorest country in the Western Hemisphere. On a global basis Haiti ranks 146 of 177 countries in the UN Human Development Index. A mountainous topography coupled with failing agriculture and land-management neglect have not only concentrated the country's estimated over nine million people into the negligibly fertile 28 percent of the country, but it also in recent years has accentuated the flows of emigration. Revenues from a few odd agricultural and mineral exports and collapsed offshore manufacturing and tourism sectors have limited economic impact, leaving much of the workforce on the margins of economic life. Haiti's surplus talent keeps leaving for other shores, including the United States, where the current population of Haitian origin is estimated to be about 1.5 million. Finally, an indeterminate portion of the economy is dependent on drug trafficking.

The most charitable characterization of Haiti's public administration is that the government has been at its relative best when pursuing a policy of benign neglect—leaving most of Haiti's peasants to their own autonomous devices. A very small and generally urbanized political and economic elite has for the most part focused on maintaining its own fragile status quo and in sustaining a limited enclave of export-oriented commercial activity. Some have described the environment as "kleptocracy," a "predatory state," and as the "politics of squalor." Some allude to the "colonial" or "self-colonized" character of the Haitian society. Others borrow from development literature and assess Haiti in the context of a "transitional society." More recent characterizations draw attention to Haiti's status as a "failed state."[1]

The arrival on the political scene in the late 1980s of Jean-Bertrand Aristide, a Roman Catholic priest espousing liberation theology and populist politics, gave currency to new notions of governance. "Deliberative" democracy suggested a more direct form of interaction between citizen and leadership, a process inclined to override institutional intermediaries found in mainstream western democracies, such as parliaments and political parties.[2] The theory and promises of this approach have not been borne out by Haiti's political experience since the late 1980s, and hopes for a consolidation of democracy have not been met.

The Decay of the State

Haiti entered the historical record of the European world in 1492, and three hundred years later fought its way to independence from France in 1804. In between there flourished a plantation colony characterized by extraordinary wealth and deep social and racial divisions. Few factors have had a more dramatic impact on today's Haitian and Caribbean polities than their transformation some three hundred years ago from small colonies of settlement into economic dependencies of European powers.

The environment of slaves and sugar came crashing down in the late eighteenth century. Saint-Domingue, as Haiti was then known, was the crown jewel of France's overseas empire, fueled by the importation of over eight hundred thousand African slaves. This untenable socioeconomic mix triggered open racial conflict with the violent explosions of the French Revolution after 1789. What followed was Haiti's own revolution and War of Independence (1789–1804), which ravaged the country to the core. In the bloody confusion, blacks, lighter-skinned mulattoes, and whites built shifting alliances and were helped along by the intervention of British, Spanish, and, naturally, French forces.

After independence in 1804 the early Haitian leaders faced the traditional patterns of nineteenth-century power politics. As a smaller state Haiti was treated as an object of policy—if dealt with at all. A spiritual heir to the French

Revolution, it also provided a serious challenge as the first non-European postcolonial state in the modern world. According to diplomatic historian Rayford Logan's characterization, Haiti started out as a "power and enigma," turned into an "anomaly," became a "threat," and ultimately was an "outcast" among the nations of the earth.[3]

Lacking any viable institutions, Haiti initially evolved a remarkable collection of powerful personalities who shaped the nation's style of governance—authoritarian figures anchored to coercive power: Jean-Jacques Dessalines (1804–1806), Haiti's first emperor and efficient exterminator of the whites in Haiti; Henri Christophe (1807–1820), Haiti's first crowned king; Alexandre Pétion (1807–1818), Haiti's first president for life; and Jean-Pierre Boyer (1818–1843), who ruled over an increasingly crippled nation.

At midcentury another extraordinary figure appeared—Faustin Soulouque (1847–1859), later Emperor Faustin I. He ordered a general massacre of the mulattoes, led the country in several abortive campaigns into the neighboring Dominican Republic, and further precipitated Haiti's deterioration. Of the twenty-two presidents who served between 1843 and 1915, one finished his term in office, three died a natural death while in office, one was blown up with the presidential palace, another one was probably poisoned, one was hacked to pieces, and one resigned. The fourteen others were overthrown.

The effects of nineteenth-century economic globalization did not mix well with Haiti's instability. France had underwritten all external loans between 1825 and 1896 and owned the National Bank. The Germans held the trading sector. Most imports came from the United States, and after 1900 U.S. influence expanded into banking.

Ultimately, the sorry state of Haitian finances was also perceived by Washington as a Trojan horse for European interference in the Caribbean. In 1915 U.S. Marines landed in Haiti following political violence in the capitol, Port-au-Prince. The purported object of the U.S. action was not to expose Haiti to U.S. exploitation but instead to promote Haitian political stability, financial rehabilitation, and economic development.

Yet Haiti remains one of the United States' least successful interventions. True, a minimum of financial order was established, debt was reduced, and the administration infrastructure was improved. However, U.S. presence did not lead to the emergence of democratic political virtues or national development coherency. Then, violent anti-U.S. feelings triggered a review of U.S. policy in 1930. Faced with similar problems in Nicaragua, President Herbert Hoover and his successor, Franklin D. Roosevelt, were determined that the United States would exit from Haiti's tropical imbroglio as quickly as possible. Following the 1915–1934 U.S. period were twenty years during which Haitian governance slowly decayed under the weight of presidential excesses. This period came to an uninspired end with the 1957 elections that brought

François Duvalier to power. What ensued was a harsh family rule that was to last until his son's downfall in 1986.

This was followed by a succession of failed attempts to establish and consolidate democratic governance, during a roughly twenty-year period that might be termed the Aristide Presidencies. This begins with Jean-Bertrand Aristide's election in late 1990, rapidly followed by his ouster in September 1991. The ensuing military regime gave rise to international isolation (1991–1994) and a UN-mandated and U.S.-led military intervention (September 1994) that returned Aristide to office in October 1994. With high hopes for a democratic resurgence, elections designated a successor (René Préval) in late 1995, but those hopes were dashed with subsequent political paralysis (1997–2000). A turbulent election cycle led to Aristide's reelection in late 2000, and this was followed by three years of continuous crises and his forced resignation in late February 2004. An interim regime operating under a UN mandate oversaw new elections that were delayed to February/April 2006 and then the return of former President Préval for a five-year term (2006–2011).

The Character of Society

Formal ideology is not a particularly useful tool in explaining the course of the Haitian polity. Its broadest context underscores the isolated and traditional character of the country's society. A close-up analysis reveals four salient factors: religion, the nation's rural-urban bifurcation, cultural values, and the Haitian society's interaction with world.

Religious institutions are numerically and culturally important in the Caribbean, but in Haiti established churches have been to a degree displaced or absorbed by indigenous cults and practices derived from tradition and folklore. Although marginal in much of the region (the Rastafarians in Jamaica, for example), Voodoo in Haiti has been enriched by both Christianity and ancestral African rites for over three centuries so as to provide Haitians with a great emotional outlet.

Basic to Voodoo is the ancestral past and its impact on the present. There is fatalism in its cosmos that does not leave much room for shaping the present or the future. This defensive character of Haitian religious culture has thus intermixed with the country's unique historical experience.

The product of slavery and of harsh colonial conditions, the very origins of modern Haiti were fixed in a rejection of the white race—if not entirely of the culture that it represented. Although French and modernizing sociopolitical influences engaged the minute portion of the nation represented by the elite, the vast majority of the population remained tied psychologically to the experience of slavery. Even today, more African and Creole than French, more illiterate than not, and historically and politically more isolated than any other country in the Caribbean, Haitian societal experience has to a degree generated an enduring demoralized character.

This societal experience has been shaped by the arguably exploitative character of Haiti's dual elites: the mulatto (lighter-skinned) minority, historically associated in more recent decades with the country's commercial activity, and the black elite, representing a politically governing class. This duality has been exacerbated by an ensuing geographical separation of the elite from the masses and of the urban population from the rural one, with significant political and social implications. Accounting for perhaps 80 percent of the population, the peasantry has been excluded from national decision-making. The fact that national debates take place partly in French, a language that the vast majority of the population does not speak or read, underlines the fissures in Haitian political dynamics.

The emotional heart of Haiti is its inner country—rural, poor, and dedicated to basic agricultural production. Long periods of isolation have made this part of Haiti a conservator of African traditions, and the traditional milieu is still the dominant environment of Haiti today. Much of the rural peasantry speak Creole and no French, are essentially illiterate, and live in socioeconomic conditions reminiscent of past centuries. Traditional spiritual influences remain strong despite the presence of Catholic as well as increasingly Protestant and evangelical churches.

What probably made life bearable for the average Haitian was the fact that government had historically not intruded too much into their lives. After 1957 the Duvalier regimes modernized notions of "government" by introducing a more formal and occasionally brutal local security presence. Disbanded in the late 1980s, neither modern law enforcement nor much of an effective local administrative structure had emerged. The growth of a corrupting drug trafficking economy since the mid-1990s has further undermined the capacity of local government in some parts of Haiti to address economic, social, and security needs.

Sharply contrasted with Haiti's rural environment is the capital, Port-au-Prince, and a few secondary towns that are not only urban but also coastal in character. This is shaped by an urbanized and somewhat cosmopolitan elite dedicated to trading as opposed to developing a national economy. This community includes the mulatto economic elite in an uneasy association with the black political classes.

Institutional Patterns

The weakness of Haitian institutions has for the most part made it very difficult for the process of change to be channeled toward productive ends. In turn, the absence of a viable development pattern has stunted the growth of socioeconomic and political interest groups normally found in a modernizing society, thus further weakening key political institutions.

Government administration has constituted a center of influence, if for no other reason than that it has represented the source of jobs, money, gifts, and public favors—if not outright access to the national treasury. At its most senior echelon, the public sector includes the lucky few who have access to government patronage emanating from the presidential palace. It is through this inefficient as much as corrupt machinery that Haiti's international development assistance is managed—or, some argue, wasted. This economic infrastructure has supported the semblance of a lower middle class, docile and at the mercy of the vagaries of Haitian politics. Unionization, paralyzed under the Duvaliers, has not been a factor despite the limited rebirth of a trade union movement in recent years.

The Catholic Church's influence has at times rivaled that of the government. After the 1860s the church fulfilled an important educational mission and provided isolated communities with the rudiments of continuity and linkage to the outside world. As elsewhere in the region in recent decades, the clergy is split between conservative and liberal contingents.

Additionally, the Catholic Church played a decisive role in the 1986 ouster of Jean-Claude Duvalier. Under pressure from the Vatican, the church pulled back from a formal political role, but its engagement continued to be the conduit through which human rights and sociopolitical concerns were exposed. The grassroots or "Ti Legliz" movement in the 1980s that was the basis for Aristide's arrival to power in 1990 highlighted splits within the church hierarchy and more generally within Haitian society. More recently the expanding grassroots involvement of evangelical protestant denominations has translated into political movements with national presence.

Born out of revolutionary violence, Haiti never succeeded in establishing the structures of a civilian society capable of minimizing the rule of force. As a result, consolidation of political power in the hands of strongmen made the armed forces the institutional pillar of society. Part of Haiti's history is the story of competing mercenary bands (*cacos*) and peasant groups (*piquets*) fighting a ragtag government military. Admittedly, the trend was partially reversed during the U.S. occupation after 1915. Ironically, the most visible product of this period turned out to be the U.S. Marines–trained Garde d'Haiti—later transformed into Haiti's armed forces. They remained by default the only organization with a national political reach and a semblance of institutional cohesion.

With the Duvalier regime's collapse in 1986 the military inherited political control and promptly failed the test. The army was ultimately disbanded by Aristide in late 1994, and in a return to the past, replaced by a national police. The rapid politicization of the police in the late 1990s began to fuel the return of intimidation and corruption. Worse yet, the intersection of a politicized police and the impact of drug trafficking created new pressures of their own. This came back to haunt the second Aristide presidency (2001–2004), whose credibility was undermined by the expanding role of renegade police and former military along with the infiltration of these into the higher echelons of Haiti's government leadership.

Haiti's low level of political participation has generated few alternative institutions. Not only has the overall poverty of the nation centralized national authority into a minute urban constituency, but the cumulative ravages of crises since the 1980s have also undermined the reservoir of political leadership. The political party structure, anchored more by personalities than viable agendas, remains weak. In order to appeal to a wider public, national leadership has been tempted by populist solutions that often lack any practical policy deliverables. In contrast, more traditional political parties have oscillated between legalistic political platforms and well-intentioned technocratic proposals—often appropriate solutions for Haiti's challenges but devoid of any contextual meaning for the average citizen.

Likewise, modern social or political pressure groups typical of democratic environments (for example, human rights organizations, local community interests, women's groups, students, labor unions, and the media) have found limited space to prosper. The small modern business community remains cautious or is sometimes co-opted by changing political winds. Yet in the growing vacuum created by two decades of crisis and paralysis, civil society in general and portions of the private sector in particular have increased their political profile. A source of controversy, a politicized civil society and business community played a salient role in the collapse of the Aristide presidency in 2004. Another pressure group is Haiti's large and notably U.S.-based exile community. Vibrant in its Haitian-American context, it is the source of a significant flow of remittances (an estimated US$1.65 billion annually prior to 2008) and is potentially the source of political experience helpful to energizing democracy in Haiti.

From Duvalier to Aristide

The Duvalier era began in 1957 (François Duvalier, or "Papa Doc," became president for life in 1964) during a period of political confusion that included the collapse of the previous government (Paul Magloire), violence, and fraudulent elections. Duvalier was the product of a movement toward a return to black culture and of a political resurgence that took hold during the U.S. occupation (1915–1934). In the 1920s a Haitian intellectual class emerged subscribing to a political racialism derived from a reevaluation of the country's

African tradition. This racialism initially evolved into a conception associated with the French-African Negritude movement, which entailed a belief in the distinctive character of an African environmental heritage and a rejection of the superiority of European culture. As a form of "cultural decolonization," it was later elaborated by Haitians into a rationale for black political power and framed Duvalier's quasi-philosophical government control in the 1950s through the early 1970s.

Who was François Duvalier? The person who held such a spell over Haitian affairs after 1957 was a soft-spoken physician and part-time ethnologist. A black, or *noir,* by Haitian standards, Duvalier had four children, including one son, Jean-Claude (later to be known as "Baby Doc"). Unlike many of his colleagues in Haitian history, François Duvalier was never a military man, and as a result of his writings he was perceived as something of an intellectual. These characteristics confounded most observers and political opponents, and they initially misled the United States.

In practice, the Duvalier years were characterized by brutal political control, corruption, income inequalities, illiteracy, and environmental degradation, which was all compounded by brain drain. A shrewd autocrat, he ruthlessly suppressed opponents who were or appeared to challenge his authority. The influence of the mulatto elite was eroded, the political power of the Roman Catholic church was reduced by allowing the government to have a say in the nomination of the Haitian church's leadership (which until then had been essentially French), and the army was purged and brought into line. A powerful paramilitary organization (*Volontaires de la Securité Nationale,* VSN)—the famed *Tonton Macoutes* (TTMs)—was established to protect the regime and enforce its directives.

Confounding most predictions, Jean-Claude Duvalier (Baby Doc) did initially show some durability after taking over in April 1971 following his father's death. An unknown quantity when he assumed office at age nineteen, his contact with the outside was limited by a closed environment of presidential advisers, family members, security guards, and, most notably, his dynamic and controversial wife, Michèle Bennett, daughter of a mulatto business family. What was ultimately termed an "economic revolution" operationally implied greater solicitation of economic assistance from major donor countries (United States, France, and Canada) and a consortium of international and private lending agencies. Yet, the authoritarian and often aimless nature of Haitian governance ultimately led to Duvalier's downfall in 1986.

Jean-Claude Duvalier faced Catholic Church militancy and declining support from Washington. The ensuing mobilization of the population was formalized during a visit by Pope John Paul II in 1983. The Pope's references to "injustices" and the need for a more equitable society were seen as an indication of the Church's intent to champion change and take on an active political role. Furthermore, U.S. policy also shifted gradually, beginning with the Carter administration's emphasis on human rights followed by a broader global theme of freedom and democracy under the Ronald Reagan presidency. Likewise, Haiti became a matter of interest in the halls of the U.S. Congress. This was driven by public awareness resulting from the drama of Haitian refugee flows in the early 1980s as well as the political mobilization of segments of the African American political community on behalf of Haiti's struggles.

The collapse of the Duvalier regime began in November 1985 with a series of spontaneous riots in Gonaives that turned into a major antigovernment protest. The regime's ineptitude coupled with the army's reluctance to confront these street demonstrations with deadly force led to the government's collapse and Duvalier's departure on board a U.S. military transport plane for exile in France on February 6, 1986. What followed was not, however, what either the Haitians or the international community had hoped for.

Governmental authority passed to the military-led Council of National Government for a transition period of unspecified length, led initially by General Henri Namphy. The ensuing near-anarchy subdued temporarily when it appeared that the interim regime was planning for elections. U.S. foreign aid flows then increased, as did support from other donors. Some progress was even achieved in stabilizing the economy. However, the foundations upon which this stability was constructed were flawed. International policy designs were tied to notions of democratic consolidation, when the reality on the ground visibly lacked the political consensus to achieve that objective.

The first casualty was the bloody elections of November 1987, halted in the first hour of balloting by armed thugs linked to the army and Duvalierist allies. A truncated election was scheduled in January 1988, in which exiled academic-turned-politician, Leslie Manigat, won the presidency. This unstable situation received little international support, and Manigat was overthrown by the military in June. The political situation then unraveled further as Namphy returned as head of the government, but in September he himself was pushed aside by General Prosper Avril. Avril governed from a position of declining authority and faced a nearly successful intramilitary coup in April 1989. Soon, the patience of the international donor community began to wear thin. Avril's reluctance to move toward elections led to the regime's collapse in March 1990, giving way to an interim consensus government that in turn led to elections in December 1990.

By an overwhelming majority, Haitians chose a charismatic ordained priest, Jean-Bertrand Aristide, as president in what was regarded by most observers as the nation's first modern election. The 1990 elections presaged a period of intermittent euphoria as well as a succession of spectacular failures that has so far lasted twenty years in what might now be termed the Aristide Presidencies.

The Aristide Presidencies and Global Politics

During an approximately fifteen-year period (1990–2004) Aristide was the principal political variable in Haiti. He has since then remained a significant shadow. Born in the south and brought up in Catholic schools, his capacity to speak the social and political language of Haiti's overwhelmingly poor population and appear to convey a message of hope has been a powerful attribute. In tandem are the demands for societal transformation directed most sharply at the elites. This is encapsulated most vividly by Aristide's signature concept, "Lavalas," the cleansing flood that will lead Haiti's masses "from misery to poverty with dignity."

Aristide is a survivor, having escaped death several times since the late 1980s. A very complex personality, he displays an almost mystical vision of his country. What began as a liberation theology–based political movement anchored in Port-au-Prince's slums was catapulted into national prominence in the late 1980s at a time when the nation's military leadership was providing neither stability nor hope. Often accused of holding a questionable commitment to the Western-based notions of representative democracy, Aristide sprung into the 1990 elections late in the game.

The 1990–2004 period includes three presidential elections, two won by Aristide (1990 and 2000) and another won by a close ally (René Préval in 1995). The period also is composed of two constitutional interruptions (late 1990 and early 2004), both involving Aristide. This underscores the uncertain verdict of Haiti's steps toward democratic governance, let alone coherent management of national policy issues. It also suggests the deep chasm that continues to frame Haitian political dynamics and the unique role played by Aristide in this regard.

In 1990 Aristide was chosen by the Haitian electorate to achieve justice, address the concerns of Haiti's poor, and provide a clear break with the recent Duvalier era. Within eight months he was ousted in a coup whose causes continue to be debated. Whether it was the army's paranoia, Aristide's inflammatory rhetoric, or the reaction to violence directed at Aristide's political opposition, the crisis endured through interim military regimes and the international crusade that returned Aristide to power in October 1994.

Aristide was succeeded in 1995 by his protégé, René Préval, whose only achievement was to complete his five-year mandate. His term (1996–2001) was highlighted by increasing zero-sum political dynamics. The distrust between Aristide's Lavalas movement and the rest of the political community not only deepened but in turn brought about conflict within Lavalas. This generated break-away groups and ultimately formed the basis of an enlarged if disjointed political opposition. By the late 1990s some of Aristide's early allies had become his opponents. A major impediment was the inability of the government and the national assembly to work together to pass laws, approve budgets, and sign off on appointments (notably for prime minister), all of which led to political paralysis and a festering crisis.

Aristide returned to office in early 2001 following local and national elections the previous year whose credibility was questioned by the international community. What was a serious but manageable technical dispute regarding the May 2000 parliamentary races instead triggered a deepening mistrust among Haitian political actors as well as with the international community. Diplomatic mediation by the OAS failed, and by 2003 the political atmosphere between the Aristide government and multiple opponents had deteriorated close to the point of no return. Pockets of violence erupted, generated by loose coalitions of Aristide's tactical allies turning against him along with an assortment of gangs, former military, and renegade police. Increasingly large segments of Haiti's urban civil society also began to mobilize against Aristide.

The ensuing stand-off in early 2004 was broken under pressure from Paris and Washington. Facing a violent rebellion, Aristide left the country (some argue was forced out), headed ultimately for exile in South Africa. An interim government led by Gérard Latortue, an international civil servant with no political experience, oversaw a transition that brought Préval back to office in 2006. Somewhat akin to his tenure in the 1990s, he again governed weakly.

A noteworthy backdrop to these domestic dynamics has been the continuous intervention of external actors. This frustrating record is highlighted by 1) a messy four-year post-Duvalier transition (1986–1990); 2) a disjointed and drawn-out response following the September 1990 coup against Aristide; this period was anchored by an increasingly tough diplomatic and economic embargo against the "de facto" military led regime, concluding with a U.S.-led and ultimately UN-mandated military intervention in September 1994; 3) the costly and inconclusive postintervention period (1994–1997); 4) unresolved electoral disputes in the 2000 cycle of elections, triggering lethargic OAS-led diplomatic negotiations (2001–2003); 5) military intervention in the wake of the rebellion against Aristide's second presidency (2004); and 6) a postintervention period with delayed elections (2006) that brought Préval back to office.

Remarkably, the international community has midwifed every political transition since the 1980s without really consolidating democracy or improving the socioeconomic well-being of most Haitians. Approximately two decades after Aristide's first election, a quasi-permanent international peace-keeping presence, led by Latin American countries, highlights the international community's continued commitment to Haiti's political development process.

Continuing Challenges

It is fair to conclude that much of Haiti's contemporary experience has been built on shaky domestic political foundations and exaggerated expectations among international community actors. The record is one of economic activity and little growth, extensive misuse of foreign assistance, and intervals of political upheaval with bouts of bloody violence, refugee crises, and natural disasters. The devastating January 2010 earthquake will further deepen the quasi-permanent internationalization of Haiti's challenges.

The extensive international financial commitments (over US$1 billion) promised upon Aristide's return in 1994 were either wasted or went unused. While major donors were a bit more cautious following the 2004 intervention, another US$1 billion followed. In contrast, political uncertainties have limited significant private-sector, job-creating investments. The assembly sector went from one hundred thousand jobs in 1986 to about twenty thousand jobs twenty years later in 2006—and it has yet to recover. Corruption and narcotics trafficking have also had significant corroding effects. However one defines "globalization," Haiti has felt its effects through various forms of international interventions without measurably absorbing its possible benefits.

A nation with no clear productive base and no track record of purposeful governance faces limited choices. Haiti has a reservoir of individual skills and political acumen, but the challenge lies in the pooling of these human resources and the development of relevant economic and political organizations. There may be egalitarian and cooperative features in the nation's peasant environment, yet Haiti's traditional political culture and linguistic bifurcation are profound obstacles to the development of a modern democratic government. The dubious interest of portions of the elite in collaborating in the economic, political, and cultural integration of the nation also renders near-term national development problematic at best.

This represents a fragile basis upon which Haiti's future is to be built. So far in this new century political culture and decayed institutions have not overcome the nation's endemic frustrations. With the nation's catastrophic social and ecological collapse—worsened by almost-yearly hurricanes—any Haitian government therefore faces a daunting task. This has now been heightened even further by the 2010 earthquake. Fears of political crisis will continue to attract external interest, exacerbated by concerns with their humanitarian implications. This is particularly true for Washington, whose vision of regional strategic interest is amplified by a concern that any crisis in

Haiti will affect the United States directly. The tensions among competing elements of Haitian political leadership, Haiti's fragile civil society, and the international community are likely to continue. This will define the search for what has so far been an elusive national consensus toward generating socially measurable economic development and politically responsible governance in Haiti.

Suggestions for Further Reading

Abbot, Elizabeth. *Haiti: The Duvaliers and Their Legacy.* New York: McGraw-Hill, 1988.

Bell, Madison Smartt. *All Souls' Rising.* New York: Penguin Books, 1995.

Dandicat, Edwidge. *The Farming of the Bones.* New York: Soho Press, 1998. (Also the author of *Krik? Krak!*)

Deibert, Michael. *Notes from the Last Testament: The Struggle for Haiti.* New York: Seven Stories Press, 2005.

Diederick, Bernard, and Al Burt. *Papa Doc: The Truth About Haiti Today.* New York: McGraw-Hill, 1969.

Dubois, Laurent. *Avengers of the New World: The Story of the Haitian Revolution.* Cambridge, MA: Belknap Press of Harvard University Press, 2004.

Dupuy, Alex. *The Prophet and Power: Jean-Bertrand Aristide, The International Community, and Haiti.* Lanham, MD: Rowan & Littlefield, 2007.

Fatton, Robert. *The Roots of Haitian Despotism.* Boulder, CO: Lynne Rienner, 2007.

Fauriol, Georges A. *Foreign Policy Behavior of Caribbean States: Guyana, Haiti, and Jamaica.* Lanham, MD: University Press of America, 1984.

Fauriol, Georges A., ed. *Haitian Frustrations: Dilemmas for U.S. Policy.* Washington, D.C.: Center for Strategic and International Studies, 1995.

Gibbons, Elizabeth D. *Sanctions in Haiti: Human Rights and Democracy under Assault.* Westport, CT: Praeger/CSIS Wash Papers-#177, 1999.

Girard, Philippe R. *Clinton in Haiti: The 1994 U.S. Invasion of Haiti.* New York: Palgrave Macmillan, 2004.

Greene, Graham. *The Comedians.* New York: Penguin Books, 1965.

Healy, David. *Gunboat Diplomacy in the Wilson Era: The U.S. Navy in Haiti, 1915–1917.* Madison: University of Wisconsin Press, 1976.

Heinl, Gordon Debs Jr., Nancy Gordon Heinl, and Michael Heinl. *Written in Blood: The Story of the Haitian People 1492–1995.* Revised and expanded. Lanham, MD: University Press of America, 1996.

Herskovitz, Melville J. *Life in a Haitian Valley.* Garden City, NY: Doubleday, 1971.

Langley, Lester D. *The Americas in the Age of Revolution 1750–1850.* New Haven, CT: Yale University Press, 1996.

Leyburn, James G. *The Haitian People.* 2nd ed. New Haven, CT: Yale University Press, 1966.

Logan, Rayford W. *The Diplomatic Relations of the United States with Haiti, 1776–1891.* Chapel Hill: University of North Carolina Press, 1941.

Lundhal, Mats. *Politics or Markets? Essays on Haitian Underdevelopment.* London: Routledge, 1992.

Malone, David. *Decision-making in the UN Security Council: The Case of Haiti, 1990–1997.* Oxford: Oxford University Press, 1998.

Nicholls, David. *From Dessalines to Duvalier: Race, Colour, and National Independence in Haiti.* Cambridge: Cambridge University Press, 1979.

Pezzullo, Ralph. *Plunging into Haiti: Clinton, Aristide and the Defeat of Diplomacy.* Jackson: University Press of Mississippi, 2006.

Renda, Mary A. *Taking Haiti: Military Occupation and the Culture of U.S. Imperialism, 1915–1940.* Chapel Hill: University of North Carolina Press, 2001.

Rotberg, Robert I. *Haiti: The Politics of Squalor.* Boston: Houghton Mifflin, 1971.

Schmidt, Hans. *The United States Occupation of Haiti, 1915–1934.* New Brunswick, NJ: Rutgers University Press, 1971.

Smith, Matthew J. *Red & Black in Haiti: Radicalism, Conflict, and Political Change, 1934–1957.* Chapel Hill: University of North Carolina Press, 2009.

Stotzky, Irwin P. *Silencing the Guns in Haiti: The Promise of Deliberative Democracy.* Chicago: University of Chicago Press, 1997.

Trouillot, Michel-Rolph. *Haiti, State against Nation: The Origins and Legacy of Duvalierism.* New York: Monthly Review Press, 1990.

United Nations. *Les Nations Unies et Haiti 1990–1996.* New York: United Nations Blue Book Series, 1996.

Wilentz, Amy. *The Rainy Season.* New York: Simon and Schuster, 1989.

Notes

1. Compare among others, David Nicholls, *From Dessalines to Duvalier: Race, Colour, and National Independence in Haiti* (Cambridge: Cambridge University Press, 1979); Robert I. Rotberg, *Haiti: The Politics of Squalor* (Boston: Houghton Mifflin, 1971); and Robert Fatton, *The Roots of Haitian Despotism* (Boulder, CO: Lynne Rienner, 2007).

2. The most articulate exposé of this approach is Irwin P. Stotzky, *Silencing the Guns of Haiti: The Promise of Deliberative Democracy* (Chicago: University of Chicago Press, 1997).

3. Rayford W. Logan, *The Diplomatic Relations of the United States with Haiti, 1776–1891* (Chapel Hill: University of North Carolina Press, 1971).

PART IV

Conclusion

Howard J. Wiarda
Harvey F. Kline

26

Latin America and the Future

A Living Laboratory

Latin America has long been one of the world's most exciting "living laboratories" of economic, social, and political change. Historically it has been a hotbed of conflict between democracy and authoritarianism; mercantilism, capitalism, and socialism; First- and Third-World perceptions; change and continuity; the traditional and the modern. These conflicts have often torn Latin America apart and hindered its progress.

By now some of these earlier conflicts have faded, although they have not disappeared. By the early 1990s and continuing into the new millennium a new consensus seemed to have emerged between the United States and Latin America on the desirability of (1) democracy in the political sphere, (2) open markets and liberalization mixed with state regulation in the economic sphere, and (3) an international order focused on free trade. Under this rubric a large number of changes have occurred in Latin America, and much of the area is freer and more democratic than it was a decade or two ago. However, the various chapters of this book also make clear how limited, incomplete, and perhaps even reversible these changes are. History has not yet "ended" in Latin America.

Both the common trends and the differences among the countries make Latin America a fertile laboratory for studying comparative economic, social, and political change. Few areas of the world offer such rich conditions for

study and research on the processes of comparative change and modernization. Here we have countries with a common historical background, colonial
experience, law, language, religion, sociology, and politics. All were cast five
hundred years ago in a common feudal and medieval setting and relationship
to the mother countries of Spain and Portugal. Yet because of geography, topography, resources, ethnic mix, and history, each country has developed differently and now has its own system of values, sociology, politics, and national
identity. Moreover, the countries of the area, although retaining many common traits, are becoming more and more unlike rather than alike. As President Ronald Reagan once told the reporters who accompanied him on a trip
to Latin America (and knew no more about the area than he did): "There
really are different countries down there."

These common background features, combined with increasingly diverging
trends among the countries of the area, are what make Latin America such an
interesting "laboratory" for study. Here we have countries with similar backgrounds and yet very different developmental patterns. How do we explain
why some countries have become democratic, others remain authoritarian, still
others a mixture of authoritarianism and democracy, and Cuba pursues a
Marxist-Leninist course? How can we account for why some countries have
developed economically while others remain mired in poverty? In answering
these questions, once again the living laboratory metaphor comes into play.
Latin America is like a laboratory in which we can hold some variables constant (law, language, religion, colonial experience), while we examine other
variables, such as resources, social structure, or political institutions, in order to
help account for why and how some countries succeed and develop economically and politically while others do not. There is probably no other area in the
world that offers so many individual country cases combined with such a clear
delineation of converging and diverging variables as does Latin America.

Looking at Latin America comparatively, it is clear that almost all the
countries conform more or less closely to the general model set forth in the in-
troductory chapters of this book. There were colonial experiences and institutions common to most of the countries, similar patterns (as well as differences)
in the interrelations of the races, and common problems of organization and
underdevelopment to overcome. All the countries remained locked in a medieval and semifeudal colonial experience for three centuries, and all had
common problems of instability, rigid class structure, lack of viable political
institutions, and economic underdevelopment in the nineteenth century.
However, the strength of the Spanish model was stronger in some places
(Mexico and Peru) than in others (Costa Rica, Chile, Uruguay), and accordingly their developmental patterns were different.

In the twentieth century all the countries experienced accelerated economic development, greater social change, industrialization, and more rapid

political change. Yet even in colonial times the differences (geographic, re-source-wise, ethnic makeup, value to the monarchy) among the several colonies were apparent—differences that were accentuated in the nineteenth and twentieth centuries. It is in this context of similarities and widening differences that we can begin to explain national variations, developmental success or the relative lack thereof, and why some countries became democratic and others did not. Hence the imperative in studying Latin America is that we know and understand the general pattern of the region as a whole while also comprehending the individual country variations. That is what this book, with the substantive general introduction followed by detailed treatment of all the countries, seeks to provide.

Change and Continuity

Although the main structures and institutions of Latin American society and politics remained remarkably stable through three centuries of colonial rule and even on into the postindependence nineteenth and early twentieth centuries (the "twilight of the middle ages"), in recent decades the process of change has been greatly accelerated. In the introduction we identified six broad areas of change and asked the authors of our individual country chapters to assess these as well: changes in the political culture and values, changes in the economy, changes in social and class structure, changes in political groups and organizations, changes in public policy, and changes in the international environment. Now it is time to assess and pull all these themes together, to link the general propositions set forth in the introduction to the concrete cases provided in the individual chapters, and to see what general trends and conclusions apply.

The country chapters make clear the degree to which Latin American political culture is undergoing transformation. New values and ideologies—democracy, participation, liberalism, capitalism, and socialism—have challenged the traditional belief system of fatalism, elitism, hierarchy, and resignation. New communications and transportation networks are increasingly breaking down traditional beliefs and isolation. The hold of the traditional Catholic Church and religion on Latin America is also decreasing, as Protestantism, secularism, a changed Catholic Church, and other belief systems make serious inroads. Although varying from country to country, the older authoritarian assumptions are being questioned, and the older bases of legitimacy are being undermined. Latin American political culture is changing rapidly.

However, many of the old beliefs linger on, particularly in the backward rural areas and in the more traditional and poorer countries, but by no means exclusively there. For example, although Latin America prefers democratic rule, it tends to define that as "strong government." It wants regular democratic elections but often wants spoils, patronage, and government favors in return for the vote. It believes in separation of powers, but it still vests strong authority in an all-powerful executive. Hence, although formal democracy has been established throughout the region (except in Cuba), a genuinely egalitarian and participatory democracy is still weak in most countries. Most of the countries lack a well-developed "civil society," which is a network of independent interest groups that mediate between the citizen and the government.

The economic structure has also been dramatically changed in recent decades even while many problems remain. These are no longer sleepy, traditional, backward "banana republics"; rather, the Latin American economies have become much more dynamic and diversified. The older subsistence agriculture and one-crop economies are increasingly giving way to industry, manufacturing, commerce, business, tourism, and services. Latin America is now far more integrated into the world economy; feudalism and semifeudalism have given way to capitalism, neoliberalism, and in some cases social democracy and socialism. All these changes have put more money into the economies of the area; provided new jobs, including jobs for women; quickened the way of life; and increased general prosperity.

Yet these changes are very uneven. Much of Latin America remains poor, backward, and Third World. Some countries and some people are "making it" in the developed world, but others lag behind. Moreover, even with the new wealth, Latin America has the worst distribution of income of any area in the world. In addition, although some markets have been freed up, the temptation to return to the older mercantilism and statism is still powerful. So although there has been economic progress, many problems remain.

One of the most serious is the continuing social dualism that exists with a few very wealthy people and a large number of abjectly poor ones. This led to Brazil sometimes being referred to as "Belindia": one part modern and wealthy like Belgium and another part traditional and poor like India. This dualism exists in all Latin American countries, with the possible exception of Cuba, and in some countries—Peru, Bolivia, and Guatemala, most notably—the dualism is accentuated by the fact that the traditional, poor sector also contains Indians who do not even speak Spanish. Hugo Chávez in Venezuela claims to speak and govern for the marginalized sectors of the population.

Economic development has given rise to widespread social changes in all the countries. Latin America has gone from 70 percent rural to 70 percent urban, and from 70 percent illiterate to 70 percent literate; life expectancy is up from sixty to seventy years; and per capita income has significantly increased. In addition, the once feudal, two-class societies of Latin America now have business, industrial, commercial, banking, and other elites along with the traditional landholding oligarchy. All the societies now have sizable middle classes ranging from 20 to 50 percent of the population. Trade union movements, peasants, women, indigenous elements, and the urban poor are all being organized for the first time. There are new community groups, social movements, and NGOs. These social changes have made Latin America far more pluralistic than in the past and have thus provided a more solid base for democracy.

However, these gross figures are often deceiving. Poverty, malnutrition, illiteracy, and disease are still often endemic in Latin America in both the rural and urban areas. Most of the wealth has remained in the hands of the elites and middle classes; little has trickled down to the poor. In most countries these same elites still rule; despite elections, power is still mainly in the hands of the social, economic, and political elites. The social system is still unbalanced: As compared with the elites, the trade unions, peasant leagues, women's groups, indigenous movements, and other mass organizations tend to be weak, divided, and with limited power. As pointed out in Chapter 3, traditionally interest groups could exist only if given permission by the elite. Today there seems to be a change in this, as new groups and civil society can survive even if the government does not grant them recognition. Yet it is unclear to what extent the change from a system of government or "corporatist" sanction of groups to a new one of de facto liberal, pluralist legitimacy has been made. In addition, although Latin America is undoubtedly more pluralist than before, the mass of the population is still excluded from effective participation in decisions that affect them most closely. Nor does Latin America, despite the greater pluralism, have the kind of counterbalancing interest group competition and lobbying characteristics of U.S. democracy.

Many of the same problems are characteristic of political institutions. Nineteen of the twenty Latin American countries hold elections regularly and are at least formally democratic—and that is encouraging. Similarly, the human rights situation is significantly better in most countries than it was thirty years ago. However, the cultural and institutional bases of many of these new democracies are still fragile. Polls indicate that democracy's popularity is actually declining in some countries of Latin America, that the public doesn't think democracy has delivered on its promise. Cronyism and patrimonialism are still widely practiced rather than egalitarianism and advancement based on merit. Corruption, violence, and crime are increasing. At the same time political parties, local government, and political institutions in general are not held in high esteem by the public. Latin America seems to practice democracy at election time, but in the intervening years presidents rule almost as constitutional dictators.

If we look at public policy, many of the same disclaimers apply. Economic growth is occurring, but the gap between rich and poor in many countries is widening. Liberalization, privatization, and economic reform are going forward, but ever so slowly. Agrarian reform is all but dead as an issue, and where there is urban reform, the problems seem to mount up faster than the solutions. There are new social reforms, but they seldom seem to reach those most in need. In the areas of education, housing, health care, and employment, important steps have been taken, but the difficulties seem often to outstrip government's capacity to cope with them.

The final area of major change in Latin America is in the international realm. It is clear that Latin America no longer lives in isolation. Globalization has come to the area. Global television and movies bring in new styles of taste and comportment: blue jeans, dating, McDonald's, Coca-Cola, freedom, consumerism. Globalization also brings with it the requirements of democracy and human rights, and if these are abused, international sanctions on the country involved are likely to follow. Globalization also means economic competition, thus requiring that Latin America lower its protective tariffs and be prepared to compete with the world's most efficient economies. Competition has major political implications as well, requiring state downsizing, privatization, lessened patronage, and the likely going out of business of thousands of small, inefficient, "mom-and-pop" stores and businesses.

So the balance sheet on Latin American politics and development is still a mixed one: lots of progress on economic growth, social change, and democratization, but all of these with major weaknesses and problems as well. The gross figures sound wonderful—nineteen of twenty countries democratic—but the deeper we probe into the individual countries, the more problems we see.

What overall conclusions emerge from these considerations? First, most of Latin America is now in a transitional stage: It is in the process of breaking the back of the past, but is not yet fully modern or developed. Second, we need to recognize that sustained development, whether in Africa, Russia, or Latin America, requires several generations, not just a few years. Third, modernization is uneven: Urban areas are affected more rapidly than rural ones. Fourth, the benefits of development are also uneven: Some groups benefit more than others, and there is always a tradeoff between growth and equity. Fifth, it is clear that those countries that have ample resources, strong institutions, and good public policy—Brazil, Chile, Colombia, Costa Rica, Mexico, and Uruguay—are doing better than those that lack these features.

Latin America today represents a dynamic, ever-changing mix of traditional and modern. Abject poverty exists alongside gleaming skyscrapers and the most modern, high-tech industry. Widespread corruption and patronage coexist with efficient firms and new public policy agencies. Latin America has embraced democracy, but it is sufficiently concerned about instability, chaos, and ungovernability to retain authoritarian features. The countries, their businesses, their governments, and their unions all recognize the need to streamline and eliminate waste, but that is hard to do if it is job, business, agency, or family that will be hurt in the process. Given these conditions it is probably no accident that we get such leaders as Chávez in Venezuela, Morales in Bolivia, Fujimori in Peru, the Kirchners in Argentina, or the Revolutionary Institutional Party (PRI) in Mexico—leaders who combine democratic with authoritarian and populist tendencies. It is in the bridging of these gaps between traditional and modern, authoritarian and democratic, statism or mercantilism and liberalism that the genius of Latin American politics and politicians often shines through.

The future now looks brighter in Latin America than it has previously. On both the political (democracy) and economic (development) fronts, even with all the problems here enumerated, Latin America seems to be doing better than at any time in its history. Although there may be reversions to authoritarianism in some of the poorer, weakly institutionalized countries, the possibility of a continent-wide reversion to authoritarianism as occurred in the 1960s and 1970s seems unlikely. Over time the social, economic, and political base for authoritarianism is being eroded by greater literacy, affluence, middle-classness, and democracy. However, the attractiveness of authoritarianism has not yet entirely disappeared in some countries.

Among the most important questions remaining to be answered are which Latin American countries can succeed in consolidating and institutionalizing their still-fragile political systems; whether they can adapt rapidly enough to globalization; whether they can combine economic growth with equity and social justice; and whether they can reconcile their recently renewed democratic precepts with their own past historical traditions that are often authoritarian, corporatist, and patrimonialist. On the answers to these and other important questions hang not only the possibilities for Latin America's future success but also why Latin America remains such a fascinating area.

Common Currents and Distinctive Situations

Although the Latin American countries have become increasingly diverse over time, the common currents that emerge from this book remain equally interesting. These include the continued decline of the traditional semifeudal order in all countries; the emergence throughout the region of greater social and political pluralism; the continued weakness of modern institutions, including those necessary for democracy; and the ongoing power of elite groups. The balance of power within Latin American politics is changing as the Roman Catholic Church, the armed forces, and the landed oligarchy lose power relative to the expanded influence of commercial, banking, manufacturing, and political elites and middle classes. Similar changes are occurring at the international level, with the United States being less interested in the domestic politics of Latin America but more interested in trade and commercial relations.

Although Latin America as a whole is undoubtedly more democratic than it was three or four decades ago, democracy is often limited, partial, and blended with authoritarian and corporatist features. Similarly, in the economic sphere greater liberalization has occurred but with persistent mercantilist and statist features. If we were to rank order the twenty Latin American countries in terms of the strength of democracy, the list at the end of the first decade of the new millennium would be as follows:

1. Most democratic: Chile, Costa Rica, and Uruguay
2. Democratic but not fully consolidated: Argentina, Brazil, Dominican Republic, Mexico, and Panama
3. Democratic in the past but now threatened: Colombia and Venezuela
4. Formally democratic but with weak institutions: Bolivia, Ecuador, El Salvador, Guatemala, Honduras, Nicaragua, Paraguay, and Peru
5. Having some fragile democratic institutions but lacking a democratic base: Haiti
6. Marxist-Leninist, undemocratic: Cuba

Note that very few of the countries are fully consolidated democracies. Instead, most are in transition where democracy is still weak and may still be precarious. Remember the injunctions of the introduction: Elections are a good start on the route to democracy, but many other criteria—human rights, civil liberties, genuine pluralism, freedom and equality, civic consciousness and participation, civilian supremacy over the military, separation of powers, social justice—must also be met before a country can be considered fully democratic.

Most of Latin America made an impressive transition to electoral democracy during the 1980s when the region's economies were in severe recession and plagued by foreign debt. In the 1990s most of the economies of the area began to recover, to show positive growth, and to begin a process of economic reform to go with the earlier political reforms. Economic reform helped to free up what had been overly statist and inefficient economic systems just as democratization had challenged the older authoritarianism. Increasingly, liberalism and a mixed public-private partnership in the economic sphere were seen as related to democracy in the political sphere. More recently globalization has laid down the imperative that Latin America must continue with both political and economic reform if it wishes to be competitive and a significant player in the world of the twenty-first century.

Latin America has made great strides in recent decades, but many problems and uncertainties remain. Both the progress and the problems provide good reason for students of the area to remain fascinated by it. We hope that some of our enthusiasm for the area has rubbed off on you!

About the Editors and Contributors

Co-Editors

HOWARD J. WIARDA is the Dean Rusk Professor of International Relations and Founding Head of the Department of International Affairs at the University of Georgia. He is also a Senior Scholar at the Center for Strategic and International Studies (CSIS) and a Public Policy Scholar at the Woodrow Wilson Center in Washington, D.C. He is co-author with Harvey Kline of *A Concise Introduction to Latin American Politics and Development* (Westview Press, 2007) and author of *Civil Society: The American Model and Third World Development* (Westview Press, 2003).

HARVEY F. KLINE is Professor Emeritus at the University of Alabama. He has studied Colombia for forty-five years, during which time he received three Fulbright fellowships to research and teach there. He has written seven books on Colombian politics, including *Colombia: Democracy Under Assault* (Westview Press, 1995), *State-Building and Conflict Resolution in Colombia* (University of Alabama Press, 1999, Choice Outstanding Academic Book for 1999), *Chronicle of a Failure Foretold* (University of Alabama Press, 2007), and *Showing Teeth to the Dragons* (University of Alabama Press, 2009).

Contributors

Linda Chen is Professor of Political Science at Indiana University, South Bend, where she teaches courses on Latin American politics, politics of the developing world, and women and global politics. She has published on democratic transition in Argentina and currently works on issues related to gender and politics. She currently directs the Master of Public Affairs program.

Catherine M. Conaghan is Professor of Political Studies at Queen's University in Kingston, Ontario. She writes on politics in the Andean region. She is the author of *Fujimori's Peru: Deception in the Public Sphere* (University of Pittsburgh Press, 2005).

Juan M. del Aguila is Associate Professor of Political Science at Emory University. He is author of *Cuba: Dilemmas of a Revolution, Third Edition* (Westview Press, 1994).

Georges A. Fauriol is Vice President of Programs-Planning, Grants Management, Compliance, and Evaluation at the National Endowment for Democracy and Senior Associate at the Center for Strategic and International Studies. He is editor of *Haitian Frustrations* and co-author with Scott MacDonald of *Fast Forward: Latin America on the Edge of the 21st Century* (Transaction Publishers, 1997).

Judith A. Gentleman is Professor in the Department of International Security Studies of the Air War College and is adjunct instructor in the USAF Special Operations School at Hurlburt. She is author of *The Regional Security Crisis in the Andes: Patterns of State Response* (Strategic Studies Institute, U.S. Army War College, 2001).

Vanessa Joan Gray is Assistant Professor of Political Science at the University of Massachusetts at Lowell. Dr. Gray specializes in resource and conflict issues in Colombia. She is currently writing a book on Colombian communities that have avoided displacement and dispossession by practicing nonviolence and sustainability with support from transnational activist groups.

Esther Skelley Jordan is a doctoral candidate at the School of Public and International Affairs at the University of Georgia. She teaches international relations and empirical research methods at the Georgia Institute of Technology and holds a master's degree in political science from the University of Georgia. She has contributed chapters to or co-authored numerous publications, including: *The Window of Favor: Public Opinion and the Urgency of Reformation in Transitioning Democracies* (IRI, 2009); *Globalization: Universal Trends, Regional Implications* (The University Press of New England, 2008); *The 2004 Dominican Republic Elections: Post Election Report* (CSIS, 2004); and "Communism in Latin America" (Charles Scribner and Sons, 2004).

Fabrice Lehoucq is Associate Professor of Political Science at the University of North Carolina, Greensboro. He is the author of several books, including *Stuffing the Ballot Box: Fraud, Democratization, and Electoral Reform in Costa Rica* (Cambridge University Press, 2002), and articles in *Comparative Political Studies*, *Comparative Politics*, and the *Journal of Democracy*.

Ronald H. McDonald is Professor Emeritus of Political Science in the Maxwell School, Syracuse University, and is former chair of the department. He is the author of *Party Systems and Elections in Latin America* (Markham, 1971) and co-author with J. Mark Ruhl of *Party Politics and Elections in Latin America* (Westview Press, 1989).

Richard L. Millett is adjunct professor at the Defense Institute of Security Assistance Management and is a Senior Advisor for Political Risk to the PRS Group. He is co-editor with Jennifer S. Holmes and Orlando J. Pérez of *Latin American Democracy: Emerging Reality or Endangered Species?* (Routledge, 2009).

Tommie Sue Montgomery was a Fulbright Professor at the Universidad Centroamericana "José Simeón Cañas" in 2004 and a visiting professor in the Political Studies department at Trent University. She is editor of *Peacemaking and Democratization in the Western Hemisphere* (North-South Center Press, University of Miami, 2000). In retirement she often lectures on Holland-America cruises to Latin America.

David J. Myers is Associate Professor of Political Science at Penn State University. His primary research interests are in comparative politics with special attention to Latin America (emphasis on the Andean South America and Brazil), political parties, elections, and comparative urbanism. He has published more than fifty articles and book chapters, some of which have appeared in *Comparative Politics, Comparative Political Studies*, the *Latin American Research Review*, and *Latin American Politics and Society*. He has authored, edited, or co-edited eight books, most recently (with Jennifer McCoy) *The Unraveling of Representative Democracy in Venezuela* (Johns Hopkins University Press, 2005).

David Scott Palmer is Professor of International Relations and Political Science and Director of Latin American Studies at Boston University. He previously served as Chair of Latin American and Caribbean Studies and Associate Dean at the U.S. State Department's Foreign Service Institute, where he continues to lecture on U.S.-Latin American relations and Latin American politics. He was a Peace Corps Volunteer Leader in Ayacucho, Peru, and a Fulbright Senior Lecturer in Peru. He has written widely on Peruvian topics, including Shining Path, local politics, U.S.-Peruvian relations, and the Peru-Ecuador border dispute and its resolution. His most recent book is *U.S.-Latin American Relations during the Clinton Years* (University Press of Florida, 2006).

Steve C. Ropp is Professor of Political Science at the University of Wyoming. During his academic career he has written a number of books and articles dealing with Panama, Central America, militarism, populism, and human rights. Professor Ropp was a Senior Fulbright Scholar at the University of Panama during the late 1990s and continues to maintain an interest in various aspects of Panamanian politics.

J. Mark Ruhl is Glenn and Mary Todd Professor of Political Science at Dickinson College. He is co-author with Ronald H. McDonald of *Party Politics and Elections in Latin America* (Westview Press, 1989).

Mitchell A. Seligson is the Centennial Professor of Political Science and Professor of Sociology at Vanderbilt University. He founded and directs the Latin American Public Opinion Project (LAPOP). He is co-author with John Booth of *The Legitimacy Puzzle in Latin America: Democracy and Political Support in Eight Nations* (Cambridge University Press, 2009) and co-editor with John Passé-Smith of *Development and*

Underdevelopment, the Political Economy of Global Inequality, Fourth Edition (Lynne Rienner Publishers, 2008).

Paul E. Sigmund is Professor Emeritus of Politics at Princeton University, specializing in political theory and Latin American politics. He has published many books, including *The Overthrow of Allende and the Politics of Chile, 1964–1976* (University of Pittsburgh Press, 1977), *The United States and Democracy in Chile* (Johns Hopkins University Press, 1993), and *Chile 1973–1998: The Coup and Its Consequences* (Program in Latin American Studies, Princeton University, 1999) as well as over one hundred articles and chapters in books on Chilean politics. He has also lectured and taught courses at Chilean universities and has observed every major election since the 1960s.

Paul C. Sondrol is Associate Professor of Political Science at the University of Colorado at Colorado Springs. He specializes in comparative politics, Latin American politics and semi-authoritarianism, militarism, and political violence in Latin America. He is the author of *Power Play in Paraguay: The Rise and Fall of General Stroessner* (Institute for the Study of Diplomacy, School of Foreign Service, Georgetown University, 1996).

Christine J. Wade is Associate Professor of Political Science and International Studies at Washington College. She is co-author with John A. Booth and Thomas W. Walker of *Understanding Central America: Global Forces, Rebellion, and Change* (Westview Press, 2006).

Martin Weinstein is Professor of Political Science at William Paterson University. During his almost four-decade career he has authored two books, *Uruguay: The Politics of Failure* (Greenwood Press, 1975) and *Uruguay: Democracy at the Crossroads* (Westview Press, 1988), as well as dozens of book chapters, encyclopedia entries, and articles on that country's political, economic, and social development.

Iêda Siqueira Wiarda is Luso-Brazilian Specialist at the Library of Congress and International Relations and Comparative Government Professor at the University of Georgia. She is a consultant to various governmental and nongovernmental institutions such as the State Department, and on the Board of Directors of various organizations such as the International Women's Health Coalition. She has authored and co-authored many books, articles, and papers and is a lecturer in the United States, Latin America, Europe, and Asia.

Dwight Wilson is a doctoral candidate at the University of Georgia specializing in Latin American politics and political theory. His current research focuses on the role of culture in conditioning democratic performance in Latin America.

Index